organizational
behaviour

THIRD EDITION

an introductory text

David Buchanan and **Andrzej Huczynski**

Prentice Hall

London ■ New York ■ Toronto ■ Sydney ■ Tokyo ■ Singapore
Madrid ■ Mexico City ■ Munich ■ Paris

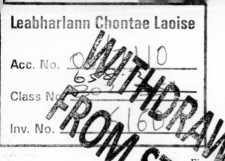
First edition published 1985 and
second edition published 1991 by
Prentice Hall International (UK) Ltd
This third edition published by
Prentice Hall
A Pearson Education company
Edinburgh Gate
Harlow
Essex CM202JE, England

Typeset in Baskerville 10.5/12pt
by Mathematical Composition Setters Ltd, Salisbury, Wiltshire

Printed and bound in ITALY by
Rotolito Lombarda, Milan

Library of Congress Cataloging-in-Publication Data

Available from the publisher

British Library Cataloguing in Publication Data

A catalogue record for this book is available from
the British Library

ISBN: 0-13-207259-9

---

4 5   01 00 99

From Dave
to Lesley, Andrew and Mairi

From Andrzej
to Janet, Sophie and Gregory

contents

guide to the book

This book has three objectives:

1 To provide an introduction to the study of human behaviour in organizations for students with little or no previous social science education. This book is designed to serve both as a comprehensive introduction to the field and as a starting point for further and more advanced study. We seek to stimulate wider interest in the subject of organizational behaviour and an enthusiasm for more knowledge.

2 To make the subject matter of social science applied to the study of organizations intelligible to students from a range of different educational and disciplinary backgrounds.

3 To overcome the prejudice that some natural science, computer science, engineering and related student groups hold with respect to the value and significance of social science ideas and methods.

This book is written for readers new to the social sciences in general, and to the study of organizational behaviour in particular. This subject is now taught at various levels and on courses where the main subjects are not social sciences. Accountants, lawyers, doctors, nurses, engineers, teachers, architects, computer scientists, personnel managers, bankers, hoteliers and surveyors, for example, often have no background in the social sciences, but find themselves nevertheless studying organizational behaviour as part of their respective professional examination schemes.

Many organizational behaviour texts are written from the perspective of a single culture. The American texts which have tended to dominate this field are particularly open to that criticism. Social science theories can be culture-bound in ways that natural science cannot be, as laws, norms and traditions vary from country to country, sub-culture to sub-culture. It is thus important to stimulate awareness of the range of social and cultural factors that influence behaviour in organizations. While admitting a British bias in the authorship of this text, we – along with many colleagues – find ourselves typically working with multicultural student groups, and the text incorporates where possible appropriate material from other cultural settings. It will be increasingly important as we move into the twenty-first century for students and organizational members alike to understand and work effectively with cultural differences.

One way of bringing into relief the ways in which we behave in organizations is to compare our practice with that of others. Comparative studies have a long tradition in the social sciences. Each year, most of the readers of this book engage in some comparative study, in airlines, railways, buses, hotels, restaurants and hospitals simply through exposure to different settings when on holiday. Throughout the text, research summaries and STOP exercises provide opportunities for comparative issues to be explored.

This text is written from a multidisciplinary social science perspective. Our understanding of organizations derives from a number of disciplines. Many texts in this field adopt a managerial, a psychological or a sociological perspective. However, our readers are not all going to be managers, psychologists or sociologists, and many readers beyond those occupations require and can benefit from an understanding of organizational behaviour. If one is going to work for, work with, subvert or actively resist organizations, then one needs to know something of how and why they exist and function as they do.

We use a more structured format and style than is commonly found in applied social science texts. Each chapter is introduced by a list of the key concepts to be covered and the learning objectives to be achieved. Each chapter ends with a brief assessment of the subject matter, and with a list of sources for further study, if required. The aim of these features is to encourage an active and questioning approach to the subject. We have tried to make the book interesting by using novel, varied and unusual material where relevant. Examples, cartoons, illustrations, exercises and cases are used to vary the pace, rhythm and appearance of the text; to make it more digestible.

We want to challenge readers by inviting them to confront real, practical and theoretical problems and issues for themselves. Readers are invited to stop reading at regular intervals, to consider controversial points, individually or in group discussion. We want to alert readers to the significance of organizational behaviour in everyday life. The study of organizational behaviour should not be confined to the lecture theatre and library. Eating a pizza in a restaurant, joining a queue at a supermarket, returning a faulty product to a store, arguing with a colleague at work, considering the leadership style of a fictional starship captain in a movie – all are experiences that can be related to some of the material in this book.

The style and content of this book reflect the participative teaching and learning strategies now commonly used across the business and management studies curriculum. This implies a limited use of conventional lecturing input and extensive use of a range of individual and group case and exercise work. To this end, the text is now complemented by:

▶ A *Student Workbook*, with a complete set of materials for use in lecture and tutorial settings and for individual study and revision.

▶ An *Instructor's Manual*, which reproduces the workbook materials, but also provides session running guides, model answers to case, exercise and test questions, and full debriefing materials for classroom activities.

▶ A book of *Integrated Readings*, offering a platform for further study of classic and contemporary contributions to the field, and presented in an innovative self-study format.

Most instructors will, therefore, not teach *to* this text, but teach *from* it, using it to introduce key ideas and theories as a platform for discussion, exercise, casework and further advanced study.

Each chapter is self-contained, introducing and defining new terms clearly. The understanding of one chapter does not rely on a prior reading of the preceding chapters, although in practice these topics are interrelated. Ideas and theories build systematically throughout the text, from individual psychology, through group and social psychology, to organizational sociology, politics and management topics. Each chapter introduces practical applications as well as theoretical background. Many of the issues covered are controversial, and the text aims to present contrasting perspectives rather than to resolve debates. The book can be used in a flexible way, appropriate for a two-semester programme or a traditional three-term course. The material does not have to be covered in the sequence in which it is presented here, leaving individual instructors the choice of which material to cover, in which sequence and with which additional learning support.

David Buchanan and **Andrzej Huczynski**
Leicester and Glasgow, 1997

acknowledgements

The third edition of this book has benefited, as have previous editions, from the comments, criticisms and advice of a number of students who have used the text, and from several colleagues who have contributed many insights from their own experience of using this as a teaching text. We must thank in particular Claire Maitland for reviewing the draft chapters and suggesting valuable improvements, Dr James M. Wilson for reviewing the chapter on Scientific Management, Tim Claydon for reviewing the chapter on Motivation, and David Webster for reviewing the chapter on Organization Development. All have provided us with invaluable suggestions for improving the text.

Their advice and feedback have been of enormous benefit to us in the development of this text. The errors and flaws in the text remain, however, fully our responsibility.

In addition we wish to express our thanks for the permission to include the following material: to Harley L. Schwadron for permission to use his cartoon on p.12, and to Alex Mann Ltd for permission to use the Alex cartoons on pp. 115, 134, 166, 332, 524 and 528.

For the portrait photographs our thanks go to the following people or their estates for permission to reproduce their photographs: Victor H. Vroom, Edward E. Lawler III, Frederick Herzberg, Albert Bandura, Fred Luthans, Hans Jürgen Eysenck, David C. McClelland, Henry Mintzberg, Charles Perrow, Warren Bennis, Terrence Deal, Edgar H. Schein, Geert Hofstede, Eric Miller, Fred E. Fiedler, Robert J. House, Paul Hersey, Kenneth Blanchard, Kenneth Thomas, Jeffrey Pfeffer, to Mrs F.M. Asch for the photograph of Soloman E. Asch, and to Mrs J. Evans for the photograph of Albert Kenneth Rice.

Acknowledgement is made to the Harvard Business School for permission to reproduce the photographs of Fritz L. Roethlisberger, George Elton Mayo, George Casper Homans, Robert Freed Bales, Paul Lawrence, Jay Lorsch, Rosabeth Moss Kanter, and to the University of Oklahoma for the photograph of Muzafer Sherif, to the University of Michigan for Rensis Likert and Ronald O. Lippitt, to Belbin Associates for Meredith Belbin, to Yale University for Irving L. Janis, to the MIT Museum for Douglas McGregor, to the Stevens Institute of Technology for Frederick Winslow Taylor and Henry Laurence Gantt, to the Bettman Archive for Lillian Evelyn Gilbreth and Frank Bunker Gilbreth, to the Ford Motor Company Limited for Henry Ford, to Hewlett-Packard Limited for the photographs of David Packard and Bill Hewlett and David Packard, to The Tavistock Institute for Eric Trist, to the Ohio State University for Ralf M. Stogdill, to Vauxhall Motors for Alfred Pritchard Sloan, to Camera Press for Walter Lippmann, to the University of Pennsylvania Archives for James D. Thompson, The Sunday Times Photo

Library for Joan Woodward, Brandeis University for Abraham Maslow, the Bentley Historical Library for Charles Horton Cooley, and the Carl Rogers Memorial Library for Carl Ransom Rogers.

Every effort has been made to locate all copyright holders for all items reproduced in this text but in the event of there being any query or omission please contact the publisher.

the ORBIT series

We hope that you enjoy using this book, and that it lives up to your expectations. However, we would welcome your suggestions on how it could be improved. We would like to invite you to send us criticisms, suggestions, ideas and general comments about this book, or indeed about any of the four books in the ORBIT series: core text, readings, student workbook, instructor's manual. We would like to learn about features which you liked, as well as about features which you think could be changed, dropped or improved. Your advice will be used to improve these books, and all suggestions will be fully acknowledged. The simplest way to do this is through email, and here are our addresses. We look forward to hearing from you.

David Buchanan   d.buchanan@dmu.ac.uk
for chapters 1–6, 16, 17, 19, 20 and 23

Andrzej Huczynski   a.a.huczynski@mgt.gla.ac.uk
for chapters 7–15, 18, 21 and 22

introduction

"R.J.'s never been very good with people . . ."

concepts and learning objectives
the study of organizations
the organizational dilemma
sources

concepts and learning objectives

This chapter offers a definition of organizational behaviour, a field of study which draws on a number of disciplines, but which is now recognized for teaching and research purposes as a distinct subject domain in its own right. We explore the problems of defining the term 'organization', suggesting that this is not a simple task, and offering contrasting perspectives on the matter. The ways in which organizations are designed and function affect several factors, from health and well-being, through organizational effectiveness, to wider social and economic conditions. This chapter introduces the central dilemma of organizational design, in the potential conflict between personal and corporate needs and interests.

key concepts
▸ organizational behaviour
▸ organization

▸ controlled performance
▸ the organizational dilemma

learning objectives
When you have read this chapter, you should be able to define those key concepts in your own words, and you should also be able to:
1 Explain the significance of an understanding of organizational behaviour.
2 Explain and illustrate the central dilemma of organizational design.

the study of organizations

Groups can achieve much more than individuals acting alone. The quality and standard of life that we enjoy can be improved by tackling human needs and problems collectively. We, like many other creatures on this planet, are social animals. We enjoy the company of others; we achieve psychological satisfaction and material gain from organized activity.

Our society is dependent on collective organized activity. Organizations have a strong claim to the position of dominant institution in contemporary industrial and post-industrial society. The world's largest multinational corporations have annual revenues that dwarf the gross national product of most countries. For example, Mitsubishi and General Motors had sales of $176 billion and $155 billion, respectively, in 1994. Measured in gross domestic product, the world's twentieth largest economy in 1994 was Taiwan (GDP $176 billion), and the twenty-first largest was Austria (GDP $158 billion). Some organizations are larger than many countries, and are thus potentially more influential – economically and politically.

The ultimate limitation on human aspirations lies neither in intelligence nor in technology, but in our ability to work together effectively in our organizations. The causes of most publicized disasters and accidents (Bhopal, Chernobyl, the *Challenger* shuttle crash) can be traced to organizational factors, as well as (if not contributing to) technical problems. If we eventually destroy this planet, the cause will not lie directly with our technology or our weaponry. We will have destroyed it with ineffective forms of organization. The study of human behaviour in organizations is thus recognized as a significant field of investigation in its own right.

---

definition

*The study of **organizational behaviour** is: 'the study of the structure, functioning and performance of organizations, and the behaviour of groups and individuals within them' (Pugh, 1971, p. 9).*

Fritz Jules Roethlisberger

Derek Pugh

Organizational behaviour is a relatively young subject. Jack Wood (1995) claims that the term was first used by Fritz Roethlisberger (see Chapter 7) in the late 1950s, as it suggested a wider scope than the then fashionable, but contentious, term 'human relations'. Organizational behaviour became a recognized subject area at Harvard Business School in 1962, with Roethlisberger as the first area head. The first British appointments to chairs in organizational behaviour went to Professor Derek Pugh (whose definition of the subject appears in our *definition*) at London Business School in England in 1970, and to Professor David Weir at Glasgow University Business School in Scotland in 1974.

Organizations, of course, do not 'behave'; only people can be said to behave. The term 'organizational behaviour' is a verbal shorthand, which refers to the activities and interactions of people in organizational settings such as hospitals, workshops, banks and police stations. Organizations pervade our social, cultural, political, economic and physical environment, offering jobs, providing goods and services, presenting us with substantial portions of our built environment, and in some cases contributing to the existence and fabric of whole communities. However, we tend to take organizations for granted precisely because they affect everything we do. Such familiarity can lead to an underestimation of their impact.

The study of organizations is multidisciplinary, drawing principally from psychology, social psychology, sociology, economics and political science, and to a lesser extent from history, geography and anthropology. The study of organizational behaviour has become a distinct discipline, with its own research traditions, academic journals and international networks, but this is an area in which the contributions of the respective social and behavioural sciences can be integrated. The extent of that integration, however, is still weak. 'Multidisciplinary' means drawing from a number of different subjects. 'Interdisciplinary' implies that the different contributing subjects collaborate. Full interdisciplinary collaboration is rare.

---

organizational behaviour – a coherent subject area?

Management textbooks frequently state as fact that organizational behaviour is an inter-disciplinary field. It is not. It is in no way inter-disciplinary; multi-disciplinary perhaps, but not inter-disciplinary. OB is not a coherent field. It is a general area that encompasses thinking and research from numerous disciplines. It draws its material from psychology, sociology, anthropology, economics, the arts and humanities, law and medicine. Organizational behaviour is in reality a hodgepodge of various subjects; a collection of loosely related or even unrelated streams of scholarly and not-so-scholarly research. It is neither a discipline, nor is it a business function. And that makes it an anomalous area of management study.

from Jack Wood, 1995, 'Mastering management: Organizational behaviour', *Financial Times* supplement, 3 November, p. 3.

Some extraordinary changes have taken place over the past two decades, shaping our expectations of the ways in which organizations and their members should function. These expectations have generally been raised and these pressures look set to prevail into the twenty-first century. If the early years of the next century are going to reflect the late 1990s, then at least three major factors will remain significant: globalization, the development of the 'lean and mean' organization, and demographic trends.

globalization

Most sectors, including education, will face increasing international competition in the twenty-first century. The motor cars on sale in the showrooms of Europe now come from Mexico, Korea and America as well as from other European countries (and, of course, Japan). Want to change your credit card? New suppliers of 'affinity cards' from the motor and entertainment sectors are now competing with traditional banks (the American MBNA Corporation will give you a 'Rolling Stones' card with a 'Jumping Jack Cash' facility). A private American healthcare organization built a prestige hospital, subsequently sold to a Kuwaiti organization, at Clydebank in Scotland to sell hospital treatment to affluent patients in the Middle East. Developments in the technology and methods of distance learning allow universities to sell their courses anywhere in the world, increasingly supported by electronic mail and video conferencing to bring instructors and students into regular close contact. You can now study for a university degree over the internet. The traditional or 'paradigm' university is no longer limited by local geography in student recruitment. An international exchange in organizational thinking and practice has also developed. Organization managers working internationally may be expected to understand the working of Korean *chaebols* (integrated organizational conglomerates), Japanese *kaizen* (the continuous improvement of methods), Chinese *guangxi* (informal business networks) and Chinese *feng shui* (the art of effective office design), and the relevance of these approaches to their own sector.

The European Union, expanding to include Scandinavian and former Soviet bloc countries, is generating pressure for pan-European legislation affecting employment and working practices. The European labour market, which opened significantly in the 1990s, can potentially penalize organizations and countries that do not meet what come to be regarded as standard conditions of work, by making recruitment and retention of staff more difficult. Cultural differences have a significant influence on organizational behaviour, and knowledge of global trends and developments is likely to become increasingly important with respect to our individual job prospects and careers, and to organizational effectiveness (Hickson and Pugh, 1995).

lean and mean

The world economic climate became increasingly volatile and unpredictable during the 1990s, for several reasons. Most commercial organizations faced even stronger competitive winds, and the public sector in most of the industrialized world experienced a combination of budget cuts, efficiency drives, government scrutiny of various kinds and attempts to privatize or commercialize public services. One beneficiary of these pressures has been 'Heathrow Organization Theory' (HOT) – that is, books on sale in the airport departure lounge that claim to tell you in the course of a single international flight just how to run your organization more effectively, more productively, more competitively.

HOT books have been remarkably consistent in their message. They have advocated approaches such as total quality management, continuous improvement, business process re-engineering, delayering, downsizing, high-performance work systems, cellular manufacturing and customer orientation.

if we eventually destroy this planet

On 24 March 1989, the tanker *Exxon Valdez* hit a reef in Prince William Sound, spilling 11 million gallons of crude oil into the sea off Alaska. This was the worst environmental disaster in American history. The owners and crew of the vessel attracted global condemnation. The vessel later created another 18 mile-long oil slick off San Diego whilst being towed for repairs. First reports of the disaster blamed the captain, Joseph Hazelwood; the headline in the *New York Times* read, SKIPPER WAS DRUNK. He was harassed by journalists, received several death threats, was fired by Exxon and was charged with criminal damage. Richard Behar, a reporter for *Time* magazine, argued that the evidence revealed a 'wider web of accountability', including organizational factors (which also contributed to the slow pace of the clean-up operation):

1 There was no clear evidence to confirm that Hazelwood was drunk when the ship ran aground. Although he had a history of alcohol abuse, which the media publicized, crewmates said he was sober.

2 Although Exxon officially banned alcohol from its ships, it supplied low alcohol beer to tanker crewmen. Hazelwood claimed to have drunk two bottles before 9.00 pm on the eve of the accident which took place while he was asleep at 12.10 am.

3 After the accident, Hazelwood adjusted the engines to keep the vessel stable against the reef, avoiding further spill and maybe saving lives; the coastguard praised his action.

4 Exxon had cut the *Valdez* crew sharply, arguing that new technology made this possible, leaving fewer sailors working longer hours; fatigue may have contributed to the disaster.

5 The Second Mate, who should have been piloting the vessel, was exhausted and asleep. The 'pilotage endorsement' of the Third Mate, in charge of the vessel in the Sound, was disputed.

6 The acting Helmsman had been promoted to Able Seaman one year earlier, from his job as Room Steward and waiter in the galley.

7 The coastguards failed to monitor the *Valdez* after it veered to avoid ice. They blamed this lapse on weather conditions, poor equipment and the 'change of shift preoccupations of a watchman'. The coastguards also argued that they were not required to track ships as far as the reef which the *Valdez* struck; seamen said they depended on coastguard monitoring in the Sound.

The case was resolved in 1991 when Exxon and the pipeline service company paid over $1 billion to the State of Alaska. Hazelwood said in an interview: 'I feel terrible about the effects of the spill, but I'm just an ordinary fellow caught up in an extraordinary situation – a situation which I had little control over.'

based on Richard Behar, 'Joe's bad trip', *Time*, 24 July 1989, pp. 54–9.

The climate in which this advice has flourished is one characterized by rapid and radical change, in customer needs and expectations and in economic conditions. Organizations that are able to combine a competitive product (quality and price) with a skilled and committed workforce and a flexible, rapid response to change are thus more likely to survive, on these assumptions, than those too rigid to adapt. During the second half of the 1990s, there were many well-publicized redundancy programmes, leading many commentators to predict 'the end of the career' and 'the end of the job' – or at least the end of secure jobs and traditional career paths.

In manufacturing during the 1990s, 'lean production' became the conventional approach. This involved the standardization and continuous refinement of work methods, the elimination of waste and non-productive activities, reduced inventory, continuing cost reduction, no defects or errors, and the use of teams or 'quality circles' to involve workers in achieving these goals. Lean methods create problems. As the number of people employed falls, those who remain can experience increased stress through work intensification. Lean production can, therefore, be 'mean' too (Womack, Jones and Roos, 1990; Wickens, 1995).

A lot of HOT books told organizations how to introduce change more effectively, how to provide more quality goods and services with fewer people, and how to beat the competition by being more flexible and responsive. Were 'the new work order' and the 'high performance workplace' overstated? By the middle of the 1990s, there was some recognition that a preoccupation with becoming lean – the *anorexic organization* – had a cost in terms of lack of dynamism and loss of employee satisfaction and commitment (*The Economist*, 1994).

demographics

Declining birthrates, one established consequence of rising affluence and education levels, can generate labour shortages. Increasing life expectancy is shifting the balance of the population. In Britain, the number of people over 65 is expected to double by the year 2035. In response to these trends, some organizations have introduced schemes to recruit employees from minority ethnic groups, and to recruit older people and married women. These groups are generally considered to be more conscientious and reliable employees, but are more likely to require help with language, with flexible working hours, with retraining, and with crèche facilities for children. Many countries have sex and race discrimination legislation. Discrimination against people over 40 is also known to be widespread, although this is not yet the subject of legal control. You may find it instructive to scan job advertisements for professional and managerial positions, noting how many explicitly mention the age of potential candidates. The effective management of a diverse workforce became a significant organizational theme in the 1990s and beyond.'

The combination of an ageing population with a declining birthrate means an increasing number of elderly people for each member of the labour force – that is, for each taxpayer. Facing the same problem with respect to supporting the future costs of healthcare and pensions, many governments in industrialized economies have adopted policies designed to reduce public expenditure and to pass costs back to individuals and private companies. This has led to the creation of a number of newly privatized industries (in telecommunications, utilities and transport), and to cost and efficiency pressures on the remaining public infrastructure (such as healthcare, education and local government).

These trends – demographic, organizational, global – have made the task of running an organization more complex. The number of different and related issues that demand attention has increased dramatically. The range of priorities has grown. The 'management of diversity', given the varied backgrounds represented in a typical organization, has become a critical skill. Public expectations concerning the behaviour of organizations and their members have grown substantially. Training and development programmes have grown up around the notions of ethical leadership (for middle and senior managers) and total quality management (for everybody, including shop and office floor workers).

Another pervasive trend through the 1990s has concerned the emphasis on 'customer care'. Staff at all levels are encouraged to regard everyone as a customer for the service or product, or part of the service or product, for which they are individually responsible. This customer orientation applies to relationships inside the organization as well as to the 'end users' of the organization's output. The concept is particularly relevant for those in direct contact with external customers – typically, those in comparatively junior organizational positions, such as receptionists, telephonists, sales staff, secretaries, and so on. Staff in those positions are usually responsible for the first encounter that an external customer has with an organization and are therefore in a unique position to maintain – or to damage – the organization's reputation through their attitudes and behaviours.

These trends are reinforced by wider political and cultural forces. The ecology movement has heightened concern for 'green' issues and has encouraged (some would say forced) many companies to reconsider what they will do with waste materials, who will manufacture their products and where, and how they design and test products in the first place. Recognition of the pervasive role of power in human affairs, and of the disproportionate power of the state and of organizations, has strengthened the position of minority and pressure groups. In his book *Culture of Complaint* (1993) Robert Hughes argues that, in America, minority groups now demand a hearing precisely because of their isolated and disadvantaged status. The related development of 'political correctness' in the use of language has introduced fresh considerations, and limitations, to everyday conversation. One of the authors of this text was challenged in 1993, by separate management groups in Australia, when using the terms 'subordinate' and 'discipline', as these words were felt to be derogatory and therefore unacceptable in an organizational context. (You may wish to consider acceptable alternatives to these terms.)

The British Institute of Personnel and Development (previously the Institute of Personnel Management) issued a 'position paper' in 1995, summarizing some of the pressures identified here, as well as others. The paper identified the 'driving forces' behind change, typical organizational responses and the implications for organizations, employees and managers. The summary figure from this position paper is reproduced on p. 8. Many of the themes raised by the Institute will be encountered in this text.

These are some of the main reasons why an understanding of organizational behaviour is important, particularly in the developing global and European social and economic climate of the twenty-first century.

At various points in this book, we shall confront the issue of how terms are to be defined. This problem arises in a variety of contexts concerning, for

COMPETITION - THE DRIVING FORCES AND CRITICAL SUCCESS FACTORS

The driving forces

- customers demanding products and services increasingly customised to their needs

- customer satisfaction standards which are increasingly established by global competition

- reductions in international trade barriers

- industrialisation of Pacific rim countries

- slow growth in the mature economies

- new overseas competitors in mature production and service sectors

- technology which is rapidly changing and easily transferable

- public sector financial constraints, political pressures for higher value for money and privatisation or market testing

- communities becoming more concerned about the effects of economic development on the environment and social well being

How organisations are responding

- highly differentiated goods and services

- customer-led organisations

- 'step' change and continuous improvement of products, processes and services

- quicker response times

- lower costs and sustainable profits

- flexibility from people and technology

- investing in and developing the core competences of people

How this is affecting the way people are organised and managed

- decentralisation and devolvement of decision-making

- slimmer and flatter management structures

- total quality and lean organisational initiatives

- fewer specialists directly employed

- developing a flexible workforce

- more project based and cross functional initiatives and team working

- empowered rather than command structures

- partnership approach to supplier links

What this means for employees

- customer-orientation to meet the needs of both internal and external customers

- greater self-management and responsibility for individuals and teams

- contributing to the continuous improvement of processes, products and services

- commitment to personal training, development and adaptability

What this means for managers?

- facilitating, co-ordinating roles

- greater interpersonal, team leadership and motivational skills

- integrated management and communication systems

- openness, fairness and a partnership in employment relations

- managing constructively the interests of groups of employees and their collective and individual representation

- ensuring part-time and temporary employees and those contracted to supply services are fully integrated

from *People Make the Difference: An IPD Position Paper*. Institute of Personnel and Development, London, 1995, p. 2.

example, what we mean by apparently straightforward terms like 'personality' or 'group' or 'conflict'. We must also address the problem of what we mean by the term 'organization'.

STOP!

Why should the term 'organization' be difficult to define? Before you read on, consider the following list. Decide which of these you would call an organization and which not, identifying the reasons for your decision in each case:

▸ a chemicals processing company   ▸ the local squash club
▸ the Jamieson family, who live next door   ▸ a babysitting circle
▸ the University of Dhaka   ▸ a mountaineering club
▸ Leicester General Hospital   ▸ a famine relief charity
▸ a local streetcorner gang of boys   ▸ the Azande tribe
▸ Clan Buchanan   ▸ a primary school

What makes organizations different? Why should you feel uncomfortable about calling some of the items on this list an 'organization'? Perhaps you considered size as a key factor? Or the provision of goods and services for sale? Or the existence of paid employment? If we define the term too widely, it can become meaningless. However, it seems difficult to pin it down.

Consider the following definition:

---

definition

Organizations *are social arrangements for achieving controlled performance in pursuit of collective goals.*

This definition should help to explain why you may have found it awkward to describe a streetcorner gang as an organization, but not a hospital, a company or a club. What about families, tribes, clans and babysitting circles? Let us examine the definition more closely.

social arrangements

To note that organizations are social arrangements is simply to observe that they are collections of people who interact with each other in a particular way as a consequence of their membership. However, all the items on our list are social arrangements from this point of view, from the company to the club to the gang to the tribe. This, therefore, is neither a unique nor a distinguishing feature.

collective goals

Common membership of an organization implies shared objectives, collective goals. Organizations are more likely to exist where individuals acting alone cannot achieve goals that are considered worth pursuing. Once again, all the items on our list are social arrangements for the pursuit of collective goals, including families, clans, clubs and charities, so this is not a distinctive feature either.

controlled performance

---
definition

Controlled performance *means setting performance standards, measuring actual performance, comparing actual with standard, and taking corrective action if necessary.*

Organizations are concerned with performance in the pursuit of goals. The performance of an organization as a whole determines its survival. The performance of a department determines its survival within the organization and the amounts of resources allocated to it. The performance of individuals determines pay and promotion prospects.

Not any level of performance will do, however. We live in a world in which the resources available to us are not sufficient to meet all our conceivable needs. We have to make the most efficient use of those scarce resources. Levels of performance, of individuals, departments and organizations are, therefore, tied to standards which determine what counts as inadequate, satisfactory or good.

It is necessary to control performance, to ensure either that it is good enough or that something is being done to improve it. Control involves setting standards, measuring performance against standards, taking decisions about the extent to which performance is satisfactory and taking appropriate action to correct deviations from standards. The characteristics of organizational control mechanisms are explored in Chapter 23.

An organization's members thus have to perform these control functions as well as the operating tasks required to fulfil the collective purpose of the organization. The need for controlled performance leads to a deliberate and ordered allocation of functions, or division of labour, between organizational members. The activities and interactions of members are also intentionally programmed and structured.

Admission to membership of organizations is controlled, usually with reference to expected standards of performance and behaviour (i.e. will the person be able to do the job?). The price of failure to perform to standard is usually loss of membership. The need for controlled performance leads to the establishment of authority relationships. The controls only work where members comply with the orders of those responsible for performing the control functions.

To what extent are the Jamieson family, the Azande tribe or the street gang preoccupied with determining and monitoring and correcting deviations from performance standards? To what extent does their continued existence depend on their ability to meet predetermined norms? To what extent do they allocate control functions to their members, order and programme their activities, and control their relationships and interactions with other members? The way in which you answer these questions may explain your respective readiness and reluctance to label items in the STOP! list as organizations.

The *preoccupation with performance* and the *need for control* thus distinguish organizations from other forms of social arrangements.

> **STOP!**
> ▶ In what ways could the Jamieson family be assumed to be concerned with performance and control?
> ▶ How is membership of a street gang determined? What do you have to do to become a member? What behaviours lead to exclusion from gang membership?
> ▶ Are organizations different from other forms of social arrangement in degree only, and not different in kind? Are *all* social groupings not concerned with setting, monitoring, and correcting standards of behaviour and performance (defined in different ways)?

The way in which one defines a phenomenon determines ways of looking at and studying it. The study of organizational behaviour is characterized in part by the view that organizations should be approached and studied from a range of different perspectives. In other words, it is pointless to dispute which is the 'correct' way to define and view an organization. The American management guru, Peter Drucker, presents another angle of view on the organization, arguing that it can be compared with a symphony orchestra. Information technology, he argues, reduces the need for traditional manual and clerical skills, and increases demand for 'knowledge workers' who are less likely to respond positively to dictatorial management. Like musicians, Drucker sees such employees exploring outlets for their creative abilities, seeking interesting challenges, enjoying the stimulation of working with other specialists. There are clear implications in this perspective for individual careers, organization structures, and management styles (Golzen, 1989).

One author who has popularized the 'multiple perspectives' view of organizations is the Canadian academic Gareth Morgan. In his book *Images of Organizations* (1986), he offers eight metaphors which invite us to see organizations through a series of different lenses:

▶ machines   ▶ political systems
▶ biological organisms   ▶ psychic prisons
▶ human brains   ▶ systems of change and transformation
▶ cultures, or sub-cultures   ▶ instruments of domination

Morgan presents these contrasting metaphors as ways of thinking about organizations, as approaches to what he describes as the 'diagnostic reading' and 'critical evaluation' of organizational phenomena. The organization as machine metaphor suggests an analysis of its component elements and their interaction. The psychic prison metaphor, in contrast, implies an analysis of how the organization constrains and shapes the thinking and intellectual growth of its members. He suggests how, 'By using different metaphors to understand the complex and paradoxical character of organizational life, we are able to manage and design organizations in ways that we may not have thought possible before' (Morgan, 1986, p. 13).

It is necessary, therefore, to view critically our simple definition of the concept of organization. There is value in adopting other perspectives and ways of seeing.

the organizational dilemma

"We're all team players here, Furgis. Miss Parmenter will break you in"

Organizations, in their recruitment and other publicity materials, usually like you to think that they are 'one big happy family' of colleagues working towards the same ends. Everyone is a team player, shooting towards the same goals. Organizations, of course, do not have goals. Only people can have goals. Collectively, the members of an organization may be making biscuits, curing patients, educating students – but individual members pursue a variety of goals of their own. Senior managers may decide on objectives and attempt to get others to agree with them by calling them an 'organizational mission' or 'corporate strategy'; but they are still the goals of the people who determined them in the first place.

Organizations are efficient ways to produce the goods and services that we consider useful and essential to our way of life. But organizations mean different things to those who use them and who work in them. Organizations are significant personal and social sources of:

- money and physical resource
- meaning, relevance, purpose
- order and stability
- security, support and protection
- status, prestige, self-esteem and self-confidence
- power, authority and control

The goals pursued by individual members of an organization can be quite different from the collective purpose of their organized activity. This creates a central practical and theoretical problem in the design and study of organizations.

definition

The **organizational dilemma** *concerns the question of how to reconcile the potential inconsistency between individual needs and aspirations on the one hand, and the collective purpose of the organization on the other.*

The need for control over the use of resources creates opportunities for some people to control others. Organizations are social arrangements in which people strive to achieve control over resources in order to produce goods and services efficiently. Some individuals inevitably hold positions from

---

forces of light, forces of darkness

From the beginning, the forces of light and the forces of darkness have polarized the field of organizational analysis, and the struggle has been protracted and inconclusive. The forces of darkness have been represented by the mechanical school of organizational theory – those who treat the organization as machine. This school characterizes organizations in terms of such things as: centralized authority, clear lines of authority, specialization and expertise, marked division of labour, rules and regulations, and clear separation of staff and line.

The forces of light, which by mid-20th century came to be characterized as the human relations school, emphasizes people rather than machines, accommodations rather than machine-like precision, and draws its inspiration from biological systems rather than engineering systems. It has emphasized such things as: delegation of authority, employee autonomy, trust and openness, concerns with the 'whole person', and interpersonal dynamics.

from Charles Perrow, 1973, 'The short and glorious history of organizational theory', *Organizational Dynamics*, summer.

---

which they control and coordinate the activities of others in the interests of the organization as a whole. However, as Morgan (1986) and others remind us, organizations are also political systems in which individuals strive to achieve control over each other, to gain wealth, status, and power.

Power to define the collective purposes or goals of organizations is not evenly distributed among their membership. One of the main mechanisms of organizational control is hierarchy of authority. It is widely accepted (if, sometimes, with reluctance) that managers have the right to make the decisions and lower-level employees are obliged to follow instructions. Organizational members who have little or no influence on decision-making typically must comply with directives, or leave. Organizations are thus open to criticism for their undemocratic procedures, and for excessive interference with individual liberty.

A concern with performance leads to work that is simple and monotonous, and to strict rules and procedures which employees are expected to follow. These features of work design may be efficient because they simplify the tasks of planning, organizing, co-ordinating and controlling the efforts of large numbers of people. This efficiency drive, however, conflicts with the human desire for freedom of expression, autonomy, creativity and self-development. It is difficult to design organizations that are efficient both in using resources and in developing human potential. Many of the 'human' problems of organizations can be identified as conflicts between individual human needs and the constraints imposed in the interests of collective purpose. Attempts to control and co-ordinate human behaviour are thus often self-defeating.

That is a pessimistic view. Organizations are social arrangements, constructed by people who can also change them. Organizations can be repressive and stifling, but they can also be designed to provide opportunities for self-fulfilment and individual expression. The point is that the human consequences depend on how organizations are designed and run.

---

happy cows give more milk

In his book *Dairy Cattle and Milk Production* (Macmillan, New York, 1956, pp. 332–3), Clarence H. Eckles identifies a number of methods for maximizing milk production:

1 Cows become accustomed to a regular routine; disturbing this routine disturbs them and causes a decrease in milk production.
2 Attendants should come into close contact with the cows, and it is important that the best of relations exist between the cows and keepers.
3 The cows should not be afraid of the attendants.
4 Cows should never be hurried.
5 Chasing cows with dogs or driving them on the run should never be allowed.
6 In the barn, attendants must work quietly; loud shouting or quick movements upset cows and cause them to restrict production.

cited in Jerry L. Gray and Frederick A. Starke, 1984, *Organizational Behavior: Concepts and Applications*, Merrill Publishing, Columbus, third edition, p. 14.

> **STOP!**
>
> ▶ Suppose the attendants are managers, and the cows are an organization's employees. Here we have a way of addressing the organizational dilemma.
> ▶ To what extent can such methods be applied to students on courses, or workers in factories, hospitals, schools, shops and offices?
> ▶ To what extent is the organizational dilemma sharpened or resolved by such attempts to treat organizational members in an apparently 'humane' way?

sources

The Economist, 1994, 'When slimming is not enough', 3 September, pp. 67–8.

Golzen, G., 1989, 'Maestro, learn the company score', *The Sunday Times*, 25 June, Appointments section.

Gray, J.L. and Starke, F.A., 1984, *Organizational Behavior: Concepts and Applications*, Merrill Publishing, Columbus, OH, third edition.

Hickson, D.J. and Pugh, D.S., 1995, *Management Worldwide: The Impact of Societal Culture on Organizations around the Globe*, Penguin Books, Harmondsworth.

Hughes, R., 1993, *Culture of Complaint: The Fraying of America*, The New York Public Library/Oxford University Press, New York/Oxford.

Morgan, G., 1986, *Images of Organizations*, Sage Publications, Beverly Hills, CA.

Perrow, C., 1973, 'The short and glorious history of organizational theory', *Organizational Dynamics*, summer.

Pugh, D.S. (ed.), 1971, *Organization Theory: Selected Readings*, Penguin Books, Harmondsworth.

Wickens, P.D., 1995, *The Ascendant Organization: Combining Commitment and Control for Long-term, Sustainable Business Success*, Macmillan, Basingstoke.

Womack, J.P., Jones, D.T. and Roos, D., 1990, *The Machine that Changed the World*, Rawson Associates, New York.

Wood, J., 1995, 'Mastering management: Organizational behaviour', *Financial Times*, supplement (part 2 of 20).

chapter 2 natural and social science

Calvin and Hobbes

concepts and learning objectives
are the social sciences different?
organizational research methods and designs
sources

concepts and learning objectives

This chapter explores the ways in which organizational researchers study their subject and introduces some of the main problems that such study faces.

key concepts

operational definition	phenomenology
behaviourism	research method
positivism	research design
behaviour	internal validity
action	external validity
cognitive psychology	social construction of reality

This chapter offers an introduction to the social sciences as 'science', summarizing the debate surrounding the equivalence of natural and social science, and indicating the main differences which, for some commentators, give social science a distinctive status as a field of enquiry. There are two competing views on this issue. The naturalistic or *positivist* view claims that, as part of the natural world, human behaviour should be studied using methods comparable with those used to study the natural world. In this view, biology is more a natural science, because it does not study human social behaviour or the ways in which we understand and interact with each other. The interpretive or *phenomenological* view claims that, as we are self-interpreting beings, humans cannot be studied using techniques that apply only to natural objects and events. Chemical substances and rare metals, for example, do not give interviews or fill in questionnaires. This straightforward division into two competing camps obscures the fact that there are a number of different shades of positivism and a variety of interpretive postures; however, an examination of this diversity is beyond the scope of our discussion (see, for example, Burrell and Morgan, 1979). We shall, however, define the terms positivism and phenomenology more precisely later in the chapter.

Our aim is to offer readers new to this field an overview of the main sources of research data and theory presented throughout the book. We do not aim to equip you with practical research skills, but with an understanding of methodological issues which will allow you to assess published research work from this perspective. This material can be skipped without affecting understanding of later chapters.

learning objectives

When you have read this chapter, you should be able to define those key concepts in your own words, and you should also be able to:
1 **Identify the features that differentiate the natural and social sciences.**
2 **Understand the research implications of the fact that people attach meanings and purposes to what they do.**
3 **Describe the various research methods and designs used in organizational research.**
4 **Explain the criteria on which the findings of organizational research can be evaluated.**

are the social sciences different?

Are the social sciences really 'sciences'? Can we study human behaviour in the same way that we study chemicals and metals? The study of organizational behaviour draws from a range of social and behavioural science disciplines. But is it possible to submit people to any study that can be called scientific? One major stumbling block seems to be that, when we know that we are being studied, and why, we are likely to react by altering our behaviour – to appear more competent, more enthusiastic, more diligent, or just to help the researcher. As a result of these 'reactive effects', what the researcher observes and measures can be artificial, or unreal, a false reflection of our 'true' selves and our behaviour. Avoiding these reactive effects can be a methodological headache for the researcher. Studying people without their knowledge could be one solution, but this raises ethical problems. It seems that the standards of investigation used in natural science cannot easily be transferred to the study of people. For these reasons, some social scientists deny that they are scientists in the sense that biologists, physicists and astronomers are scientists. What we know about organizational behaviour is based on social science research. We should be clear about the nature of that research before we begin.

STOP!

Here are some typical criticisms of social science, taken from a questionnaire given to a group of Scottish managers, mainly accountants and engineers, studying organizational behaviour. Do you agree with these statements? Give reasons for your answers.

social science is not science because . . .

there are problems with observation and measurement:

- Social science deals with the intangible. You cannot see motives or perceptions, so you cannot measure them.
- There are just too many variables.
- Natural science problems are easy to express clearly and unambiguously in terms of fixed laws and precise definitions.
- Social and human problems cannot be quantified, expressed in numbers.
- Social science is forced to rely on the judgement of the researcher rather than on measuring instruments. It is based on intuition and guesswork.

there are problems establishing cause and effect:

- You cannot observe cause and effect.
- People cannot be studied like chemicals and metals. They do not behave in consistent ways.
- People change, so you cannot repeat experiments under the same conditions.
- You cannot conduct controlled experiments on individuals and groups of people, so you cannot test hypotheses.
- The presence of the researcher influences the activity studied.

there are problems with generalizing findings and making predictions:

- People have attitudes, ideologies, philosophies and perspectives that change over time, and differ from culture to culture, so we cannot make generalizations.
- Nature is well ordered, but people act irrationally and are subject to group pressures.

therefore:

- The social sciences have no practical, material, tangible, economic benefit.

The contribution of social and behavioural sciences to human knowledge is often regarded with scepticism and suspicion. It is a relatively simple matter to demonstrate the practical value of natural scientific endeavour. We can put people on the moon, deliver newspapers and films to your personal computer down a telephone line, genetically engineer fast-growing, disease-resistant crops, perform surgery using minimally invasive or 'keyhole' techniques, and so on. Textbooks in electrical engineering, naval architecture, quantum mechanics and vascular surgery tell the reader how the world works, how to make things and how to fix things. Students from disciplines such as these can find psychology and sociology texts disappointing because they do not offer such direct practical guidance. Social science texts often raise more questions than they seek to answer, and draw attention to debates, conflicts, ambiguities and paradoxes which are left unresolved. Put simply, science gives us material technology, but social science has not given us a convincing social engineering.

Are we, and our organizations, really beyond the reach of scientific study? Surely not. One aim of this chapter is to encourage you to assess this issue for yourself. However, we would like to address the prejudice that can lead to a dismissal of anything that 'soft' social science may try to offer. We would like to encourage instead a critical approach to the social science enterprise in general, and to organizational research in particular, and to base that critical stance on an understanding of the issues that face all students of human behaviour.

The natural sciences – physics, astronomy, chemistry, biology, genetics – seem to rely on:

- direct observation
- consistent causal relationships between variables through time and space
- experimental methods to test hypotheses
- mathematical reasoning

The goals of science include description, explanation, prediction and control of events. These four goals represent increasing levels of sophistication in scientific endeavour. Some natural and social science work is content with description. Prediction and control can be considerably more difficult achievements. If we take the criticisms of our Scottish managers seriously, the problems for social science *seem* to be as follows:

goals of science	practical implications	social science problems
description	measurement	invisible and ambiguous variables people change over time
explanation	identify the time order of events establish causal links between variables	timing of events is not always clear cannot always see interactions
prediction	generalizing from one setting to another	uniqueness, complexity and lack of comparability between social settings
control	manipulation	ethical and legal constraints

These 'problems' become serious only if we really expect social science to conform to natural science practice. However, if the study of people is a different kind of enterprise, then we need different procedures to advance our understanding, and different criteria will apply in evaluating our success. Social science can thus be viewed as a different kind of science from the natural sciences. Social scientists are themselves divided on this issue.

Some social scientists argue that there is 'unity of method' in the study of natural and human phenomena. The theoretical basis of this argument lies in the claim that human behaviour must be governed by universal laws of the same kind that govern the behaviour of natural phenomena. These laws may just be particularly complex and difficult to discern, and our social sciences may be relatively young.

One implication of the 'unity of method' perspective is concern with refining social science methodology. Great care is taken to define terms precisely, to measure and quantify, to conduct rigorously controlled experiments, and to avoid or at least minimize the reactive effects generated by a researcher's presence and activities. Social scientists and organizational researchers may have to work harder on these issues.

A second implication of the 'unity of method' perspective is a concern with producing a social technology that can be used to predict and control human social behaviour as effectively as we use material technologies to manipulate the natural order. The concepts of social technology and social engineering clearly suggest manipulation, and this perspective triggers a series of ethical or moral concerns, as well as technical or methodological ones.

Other social scientists argue that social and natural sciences are fundamentally different, and that the study of people cannot become more scientific simply by following more closely the procedures of quantum physicists and laboratory chemists. This distinction can be explored with respect to the four goals of description, explanation, prediction and control.

description

There are three methods by which social scientists produce descriptions of the phenomena they study. These are observation, asking questions, and studying

---

jury science: a step towards social engineering?

To win a court case in America, litigants may soon need good behavioural scientists as well as good lawyers. Some companies are using them to help their lawyers distinguish friendly from unfriendly jurors, and to assess how arguments in court are being received by the jury. University professors who are already boosting their earnings by providing such help occasionally must now reckon with Litigation Sciences, a firm based in California with 90 psychologists, sociologists, psychometrists and other professionals.

Its chairman, Dr Donald Vinson, holds a doctorate in marketing and sociology from the University of Colorado. He first got into the litigation business when, as an academic at the University of Southern California, his brains were picked by IBM in a $100 million anti-trust suit brought against it by California Computer Products. He recruited surrogate jurors who were as similar as possible to the real ones. Without disclosing which side had hired them, he asked his shadow jury to sit in court each day and quizzed them on their reaction to the arguments they had heard. His findings were passed on each night to IBM's lawyers to help them refine their strategy. IBM won the case.

from *The Economist*, 8 July 1993, p. 86.

documents. These methods can be applied in various different ways. The people studied may or may not know that they are research subjects. Questions can be asked in person by the researcher, or through a self-report questionnaire. Documents of interest can include diaries, letters, company reports, committee minutes, or published work. Physicists and chemists, for example, use only observation, albeit under specially designed and controlled conditions. Metals and chemicals, for example, do not respond to interrogation and do not publish autobiographies in the style that has become popular among senior organization executives.

Some of the interesting variables in social and organizational research, like workforce motives, male managers' perceptions of women, and the learning process, cannot be observed directly. Observation is often possible and helpful. The organizational researcher can listen to and watch informal discussion in a cafeteria, join a selection interview or promotions board, or follow participants through a skills training programme. However, in settings like these, it is often not possible to produce reliable measurements of terms that can be defined without ambiguity. Suppose you want to measure aggression – a social phenomenon – at student dances through observation. How are you going to do this? A few moments' thought should suggest that it is going to be difficult to decide *what counts* as 'aggressive' behaviour. Can you count as 'aggressive' the joking and friendly physical contact between people who know each other reasonably well? For research purposes, we must use terms like this precisely, and consistently, but clearly this is not a straightforward matter.

The approach that we use to decide what counts in a setting like this is known as an *operational definition* of the term in which we are interested.

---

definition

An **operational definition** *of a term or variable is the method that we are going to use to measure the incidence of that variable in practice.*

Your operational definition of aggression could include raised and angry voices, physical contact, inflicting pain and damage to property. You could count each event that you observe where at least one factor is evident. You could use this operational definition to construct a simple 'aggressiveness scale', with events where all four factors are evident rated as 'more aggressive'. Compare this with an operational definition of 'job satisfaction'. In practice, this can be measured by asking our target population a single question ('How satisfied are you with your job?') and seeking answers on a five-point rating scale from very satisfied, through neutral, to very dissatisfied. However, we may feel that job satisfaction is affected by a range of factors such as management style, financial rewards, development opportunities, promotion chances, flexible working hours, and so on. Our operational definition could thus include a series of questions relating to each of these factors and could generate a large questionnaire.

We can overcome our inability to observe interesting factors. Consider the process of learning (explored further in Chapter 5). As you read through this book, we would like to think that you are indeed learning something about

for research purposes, we must use terms precisely and consistently

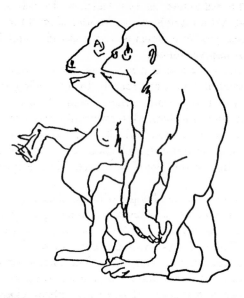

'. . . and then he raises the issue of, "how many angels can dance on the head of a pin?", and I say, you haven't operationalized the question sufficiently – are you talking about classical ballet, jazz, the two-step, country swing . . .'
Anon.

organizational behaviour. However, if we could open your head as you read, we would have difficulty finding anything that could be meaningfully described as 'the learning process'. This is a convenient label for an invisible (or at least, invisible to a social scientist) activity, whose existence we can assume or infer.

Some changes must take place inside your head if learning is to occur. Neurophysiology can help to track down the precise physical and biochemical events involved, but these specialized techniques are of little use in the lecture theatre or training suite. It is also not clear how an improved understanding of the biochemistry of learning would help us to design better learning and training programmes. Our inability directly to observe the learning process has not stopped psychologists from using the concept of learning, and we now have a reasonably good understanding of the process, and of ways to make it more effective.

The procedures for studying learning by inference are relatively straightforward. We can, for instance, examine your knowledge of organizational behaviour before you read this book and repeat the examination afterwards. We would expect, of course, that the second set of results would be significantly better than the first. So we can confidently infer that some learning has taken place. Your ability to perform a particular task has changed, and we can use that change to help us identify the factors that caused it. We can proceed in this manner to study the effects of varying inputs to the learning process, with respect to characteristics of the teachers, learners, abilities, and the time and resources devoted to the process. We can study variations in the teaching process itself, in terms of delivery methods and materials. We can study the outputs from the process with respect to changes in the behaviour of our learners. In this way the relationships between the variables involved can be identified. Our understanding of the learning process can thus develop systematically, and from this knowledge we can suggest improvements.

Observation as a research method has obvious limitations. What can we say about someone's motives merely by observing their behaviour? We could follow somebody – our target – around for a day or two, and make guesses about their motives. But eventually we would probably want to engage them in conversation and ask some probing questions. The answers that we get are now our research data. The validity of those data, as an accurate reflection of the 'truth' of the situation, is questionable for at least three reasons.

First, our targets may lie. People who are planning a bank robbery, or who resent the intrusion of a researcher, may give deliberately misleading responses. There are ways in which we can check the accuracy of what people tell us, but this is not always possible or convenient.

Second, our targets may not know. The mental processes related to our motives typically operate without our conscious effort. Few of us make the effort to dig these processes out from our subconscious and examine them critically. Most of us struggle through life without the self-critical reflection that leads to answers to questions like, 'Why am I here?' and 'What am I doing?' The researcher gets the answers of which the person is consciously aware, or which seem to be appropriate, rational or 'correct' in the circumstances. The answers we get to some of our questions could be convenient inventions of the moment.

Third, our targets may tell us what they think we want to hear. People rarely lie openly to researchers. Instead, they create difficulties by being helpful. Easier to give someone a simple answer than to spend time relating a complex history of intrigue, heartbreak and family strife. The socially acceptable answer is preferable to no answer at all, particularly when the person feels that they should have an answer. People may tell researchers about their favourable or dismissive attitudes to, say, a controversial item of government legislation although they have never studied the details or implications. This third point is more significant than the other two. A research interview is a peculiar form of social interaction. The participants in this interaction are usually total strangers who engage in a one-way exchange of (sometimes sensitive) information within a short time after the start of the conversation. The interview thus typically unfolds according to what the participants believe to be the unwritten social rules that guide such peculiar interactions. The researcher is expected to be curious, in control of the conversation, objective, friendly, non-threatening, treating responses in confidence. The interviewee is expected to be informed, open, honest and co-operative, and is allowed in many settings to be mildly curious about the researcher and the aims of the study. Both parties to this exchange thus want to appear competent and ethical, criteria which can be shown to influence both the questioning strategies that researchers use and the answers that respondents or informants provide. This does *not* mean that the answers we get are false; rather, we need to be aware of the social context in which our information was collected.

explanation

It is often possible to infer that one event has caused or has led to another even when the variables or phenomena are not observable. If your organizational behaviour test score is higher after reading this book than before, and if you have not been studying other relevant material at the same time, then we can confidently infer that reading this book has caused you to improve your examination performance. The relative timing of events is not always so easy to establish. Causes must happen before the effects they are said to explain. You are going to have an argument with someone who believes that, because you are female, you have a higher tolerance for repetitive work than men. Try arguing that the causal arrow points in the opposite direction. Women learn, in some sectors of society, to expect that the work available to them (in some secretarial, clerical, retail, hotel, catering and manufacturing activities) will be boring and repetitive. In other words, the existence and perpetuation of the idea of 'women's work' pre-dates, and explains or causes, the development of female 'acceptance' of it.

The rules or laws that govern human behaviour seem to be different from those that govern the behaviour of natural phenomena. The way in which we understand causality in human affairs thus has to be different.

Consider, for instance, the meteorological law that states 'clouds mean rain'. This law holds invariably around our planet, particularly in Scotland. Now, a cloud cannot break that law deliberately or by accident. The cloud's behaviour is determined by natural forces. The cloud does not have to be told, either as a youngster or when it approaches hills and mountains, about the business of raining. It has no choice in the matter. These are obvious comments, but compare this situation with the social law that states 'red means stop'. A society could choose to change this law to one that says that blue means stop, because some people are red–green colour blind (and thus cause hideous accidents). The human driver can get it wrong in two distinct ways – by deliberately jumping the red light (in the quiet early hours of a Sunday morning with no police in sight), or through lack of concentration and going through the red light accidentally. Note that clouds cannot vote to change the laws governing their behaviour; neither can they mischievously break these laws or get them wrong on some occasions.

People learn the rules of their society from the actions of others. We can choose to disobey those rules, and unfortunately we make mistakes and get them wrong some times. This has some profound implications for social scientific research and understanding. The social scientist clearly cannot expect to discover rules that govern human behaviour consistently across time and place. Behaviour towards people over 40 years of age as potential employees changed markedly in the late 1990s, compared with what has come to be known as an 'ageist' attitude common in the 1980s and early 1990s (to judge from the wording of job advertisements and the job-seeking experiences of those over 40). The employment of children is illegal in most of the northern hemisphere, but is still commonplace – and acceptable for social and economic reasons – in some developing countries.

Our cloud came into existence with a built-in set of instructions on how to behave. We are not born with such a convenient behavioural guide. We have to learn the rules that apply in our society. The rules differ from society to society, from culture to culture, and also differ within a single society and through time. There are strikingly different cultural rules concerning relatively trivial matters, such as how close people should stand in relation to each other in different kinds of social setting. We have (mostly unwritten) rules about how and when to shake hands, about the styles of dress and address appropriate to different social occasions, about relationships between superior and subordinate, between men and women, between elderly and young. Even across the comparatively homogeneous countries of Europe (in contrast with, say, countries on the Pacific Rim), there are striking cultural differences in social rules, both between and within countries.

We humans are self-interpreting. We attach purpose and meaning to what we do. We are able to offer explanations and justifications for our behaviour. We can ask motor car factory workers why they strike; we cannot ask a motor car body why it rusts. Physicists and chemists and engineers and biologists and geneticists have to stop at discovering how things happen. The social scientist has to go much further to understand why.

Social scientists concerned with explaining social or organizational behaviour thus have to start with the self-interpretations of their subjects. People behave in accordance with their own theories and understanding of how the world works. These theories are not rigorously formulated or systematically tested. However, we share this understanding with other members of our society, and we are able to act competently without being objective and scientific about what we do. We know what behaviour is appropriate in particular settings, and what is not acceptable. We take our theories of how the world works for granted. We take our knowledge of how society and its organizations function as common sense.

In addition, we live in a social and organizational world in which 'reality' means different things to different people. We live, therefore, in a world of multiple realities. The natural scientist does not have to confront this complication. Our individual views of reality depend on our unique social positions and are influenced in particular by our organizational positions. As customers who have done nothing obviously wrong, we have probably all met the unhelpful bus driver, the disgruntled waiter or the angry store manager – whose emotional response to us seems to have been triggered at least in part by a recent work experience.

Social science uses common words in unusual and special ways. This is not a unique stance. The medical profession also uses jargon. Your indigestion is dyspepsia to the doctor. This way of using language helps to ensure rigour and consistency in our thinking. The problem is that the 'technical' terms are often words that we use regularly in everyday conversation. This can lead to confusion if we are not careful. A critical reading of the scientific literature is necessary – natural and social – to identify and overcome these jargon problems.

It will be helpful, for the purposes of our argument, to define some relatively common words in a more precise manner:

---

definition

Behaviour *is the term given to the things that people do that can be directly observed by others.*

We see you walk, hear you talk, smell your perfume or aftershave, touch your hair and taste your cooking. In other words, we can directly observe much of your behaviour. There is a school of psychology called *behaviourism* which argues that psychological study should be confined to human phenomena that can be directly observed in this manner, and which thus rejects the study of internal mental states which can only be the subject of speculation.

---

definition

Behaviourism *is a school of psychology which focuses on the study of observable behaviour, arguing that it is pointless to explain behaviour in terms of unobservable factors, such as needs, drives, thought processes, attitudes or motives.*

The behaviourist stance seems to have much in common with the *positivist* approach to social scientific study mentioned earlier in the chapter. We cannot address in this text the range of perspectives and philosophical positions to which this broad term can now be applied. However, a brief definition will be helpful.

---

definition

Positivism *is a broad social scientific perspective which assumes that the social world and its properties can be studied using objective methods, and not through the use of subjective inference; the organization in this perspective possesses an objective reality or truth, which exists independently of anyone's attitudes towards or interpretations of it.*

The behaviourist and positivist perspectives strike many commentators as incomplete and restrictive. In particular, behaviourism does not seem to fit comfortably with our self-understanding. (We do have motives and attitudes, do we not?) We do seem to have thought processes and internally stored images of the world around us. These processes and images are certainly part of our daily, personal, conscious experience. As they appear to influence our behaviour, do they not deserve to be recognized as valuable objects of study, with the same research status as observable behaviour?

Various schools of thought have developed in response to the criticisms and limitations of behaviourism and positivism, both in psychology and across the social sciences. In psychology and sociology, a research tradition has been established around the notion that, as people are self-interpreting beings, it makes sense to subject those self-interpretations to investigation, through the study of what is often now called *action* rather than just behaviour.

---

definition

Action *is the term given to the things that people do and the reasons that they have for doing them; action is thus also defined as meaningful behaviour, prompting us to ask the question 'why?' as well as 'what?' and 'how?'*

In psychology, the school that has developed in response to behaviourism is generally known as *cognitive psychology*.

---

definition

Cognitive psychology *is a school which accepts as legitimate the study of internal mental states and processes, and which seeks to develop explanations of human behaviour based on the study of these factors, even though they are not directly observable.*

The cognitive psychology perspective also seems to have much in common with the· *phenomenological* approach to social scientific study, mentioned earlier in the chapter. Once again, we cannot address the range of perspectives and philosophical positions to which this broad term now applies (including, for example, hermeneutics, ethnomethodology, symbolic interactionism, semiotics, interpretive sociology), but a brief definition will be helpful.

---

definition

Phenomenology *is a broad social scientific perspective which claims that the social world has no external, objective, observable truth, but instead that our reality is socially constructed; the social science task is not to gather facts and measurements, but to study patterns of meanings and interpretations, to discover how experience is understood.*

The claim that 'reality is socially constructed' is not necessarily a straightforward one to grasp on first reading. However, a straightforward illustration might help. Earlier in the chapter, we asked you to think through the problems of how you would measure the incidence of aggression at student functions, by devising an operational definition of the term. If we now argue that 'the reality of aggression at student functions is socially constructed', what do we mean? Suppose you observe one male student shout at and punch another male student on the upper arm, and the second student responds by shouting back and pushing the first student away, putting both hands on his chest to achieve this; a table is moved, a glass is broken. This seems to have all the trademarks of an aggressive encounter – raised voices, physical contact, possibly inflicting pain, the violent move-ment of someone against their will, damaged property. However, on speaking to the parties involved, you find that they describe their behaviour in terms of friendship, fun and play. The other members of their group agree with this definition of the situation which they too have observed. The socially defined version of events, for actors and for observers, does not concern aggression at all, but confirms – and perhaps strengthens – an existing relationship. The researcher who only observes could be in danger of making inaccurate measurements, and thus of reaching wholly inaccurate conclusions. From this perspective, your operational definition is somewhat arbitrary. What counts is how those directly involved in this social setting understand their own and each others' actions.

---

definition

*The **social construction of reality** is a perspective which, like phenomenology, argues that our social and organizational surroundings possess no ultimate truth or reality, but are determined instead by the way in which we experience and understand those worlds which we construct and reconstruct for ourselves in interaction with others.*

Positivism and phenomenology are now represented by many varying shades of opinion within and between these two extreme and oversimplified views. The main point which we want to establish here is that there are two broad standpoints from which people and organizations can be studied. There are, therefore, two approaches to producing explanations of human behaviour in social and organizational settings. While phenomenology and related perspectives seem to have become more influential in the second half of the 1990s, much published organizational research is evidently rooted in a positivist tradition. Even the relationship between these perspectives is controversial. Some commentators argue that these views are irreconcilable, while some researchers claim to draw from both perspectives in their work.

STOP!

We would like you to consider further the implications of this distinction between positivism and phenomenology.

Working alone, or in collaboration with a colleague:

- Identify the rules that govern the way in which you dress for lectures.
- Identify the implications of breaking that unwritten 'dress code'.
- Identify the rules that govern conversation topics at lunchtime.
- And again identify the implications of breaking those conversation rules.

A positivist approach, relying on observation, could quickly identify those rules. But could observation establish why you 'obey' those rules and why they are so rarely broken? How can you explain why most students, most of the time, obey the rules? What is the significance of keeping to the rules? What does this observance *mean* to those concerned?

---

prediction

Social science predictions are often probabilistic rather than determinate. We may be able to predict the rate of suicide in a given society, the incidence of stress-related disorders in a particular occupational group, or the likelihood of strike action in particular types and sizes of factory. We can rarely predict whether or not specific individuals will try to kill themselves, or suffer sleep and eating disorders, or forecast when a factory is going to experience industrial action. This limitation in our predictive ability is not necessarily a serious one. We are often more interested in the behaviour of groups of people than in individuals. We are often more interested in probabilities and tendencies than in individual predictions.

There is a more fundamental problem. Organizational researchers communicate their findings to other people, and sometimes to those they have studied. Suppose you have never given much thought to the ultimate reality of human nature. One day, you read a chapter about an American psychologist, Abraham Maslow, who claims that we have a fundamental need to develop our capabilities to their full potential. He talks about the need for self-actualization and about peak experiences when the need is met. If this sounds like a good idea to you, and you think you believe this too and act accordingly, then what he has said has indeed become true, in your case. His prediction has fulfilled itself. This may be because he has given you a new perspective on human existence, or because he has given you a label to explain some aspect of your existing intellectual makeup.

Some social science predictions can be self-fulfilling. The act of saying something is going to happen can either make that happen, or increase the likelihood of its happening. Equally, some social science predictions are self-defeating, and intentionally so. Many of the disastrous predictions from economists about exchange and interest rate movements, for example, are designed precisely to trigger action to prevent the worst of their prophecies from coming true. In an organizational setting, one could predict that a particular management style will lead to the resignation of a number of valuable employees in the hope that this prediction will lead instead to a change in management style.

We can change the social arrangements that we construct. Organizational research can point to the options, and can demonstrate how those options can be evaluated. The organizational researcher is often in a position to tell, say, a manager that if a payment and appraisal system is designed and operated in a particular way, the employee response is likely to be undesirable and that an alternative approach would lead to different (more desirable) responses. The prediction is thus made in the expectation that other options will be explored. The kinds of prediction that natural scientists make cannot have such an effect on the phenomena they study.

We can discover regularities and patterns in human behaviour and action, and these patterns enable us to make predictions about what people are likely to do in given circumstances. But it is important to remember that it cannot be assumed that these regularities represent fixed and universal laws of human nature. We can also see these patterns as social products based on individuals' own interpretations of their circumstances, which are generally shared with and influenced by others in their society.

control

Social science findings induce social change; organizational research findings similarly induce organizational change. The natural scientist does not study the natural order of things in order to be critical of that order, or to encourage that order to change and improve itself. It does not make much sense to argue about whether nature could be better organized. It is hardly appropriate to evaluate, as good or bad, the observation that a gas expands when heated, or the number of components in a strand of DNA. Social scientists, on the other hand, are generally motivated by a desire to change society, or aspects of it, and its organizations. An understanding of how things work, and the strengths and weaknesses of current arrangements, is essential for that purpose. Such understanding, therefore, is not necessarily a useful end in itself. Social science can be deliberately critical of the social and organizational order that it uncovers, because that order is only one of many that we are capable of constructing.

An agenda directed at inducing social and organizational change is not the same as controlling or manipulating human behaviour, which many people would regard as unethical. As already indicated, we do not have a social technology, comparable to a 'hard' or material technology, that enables us to manipulate other people. And perhaps we should be grateful for this.

It is important to recognize that our judgements and our recommendations are based on our evidence, as well as on our values. Social science has indeed been criticized as ideology in disguise. However, if one studies organizations in order to change and improve them, then that criticism is accurate and inescapable. Suppose we study repetitive clerical work in an insurance company, or unskilled packing work at the end of a biscuit-making process. The people doing these jobs may be bored and unhappy, and research identifies a number of work redesign options. Management may claim that their work system is a cost-effective way of producing the goods and services their customers, who have no complaints, want. The tension between these two positions cannot be resolved easily with reference only to empirical evidence.

What one says about a social or organizational arrangement depends at least in part on one's values. Textbooks in this field sometimes confuse students from other disciplines by admitting an attachment to value-judgements which are given the same importance as facts.

We have presented two broad perspectives from which human behaviour in general and organizational behaviour in particular can be studied. Here is a brief summary of these contrasting views:

	perspective	
	behaviourist or positivist	cognitive or phenomenological
description	studies observable behaviour	studies internal mental states, meanings and interpretations
explanation	seeks fixed universal laws governing behaviour	focuses on individuals' understanding and interpretation of the world to explain behaviour
prediction	based on knowledge of consistent relationships between variables	based on shared understanding and awareness of multiple social and organizational realities
control	aims to shape behaviour by manipulating external variables	aims at social and organizational change through stimulating critical awareness

In this section we have introduced the view that social science is a different kind of enterprise from natural science. The organizational researcher adopting this position cannot, therefore, rely on the observational and experimental methods of the physicist or chemist. Many of the issues raised here continue to generate controversy and are far from resolution. We hope that you will debate these issues with colleagues and instructors whose positions will undoubtedly be different from, and perhaps more elaborated than, the outline offered here. It is our intention to present the main lines of this debate in an accessible manner, which will stimulate you to think them through for yourself, rather than simply to agree with the arguments presented.

organizational research methods and designs

One can appreciate and assess the findings of organizational research more effectively if one knows how those findings have been produced. Researchers have a range of techniques at their disposal, each with its own strengths and limitations.

definition
A **research method** *is a technique for collecting information or data.*

As mentioned earlier, organizational research uses three main research methods:
- observation
- analyzing documents
- asking questions

observation

This simply means watching and listening to what is going on in a given organizational setting and paying attention to what one can smell, touch and occasionally taste if these factors are also relevant to the study. Observation can be carried out in three principal ways.

First, through the use of *unobtrusive measures*, the researcher can identify patterns of behaviour without actually coming into direct contact with those being studied. Examples of unobtrusive measures might include:
- wear on floor coverings which identifies popular and unpopular routes through office blocks
- video recording of shoppers' movements through a mall using surveillance cameras
- seasonal variations in coffee and cigarette sales, which could reflect fluctuations in levels of stress due to cyclical variations in workload

Unobtrusive measures have the apparent advantage that the subjects do not necessarily know that they are the object of research and will not alter their behaviour accordingly. Some researchers would argue, however, that this 'advantage' is gained at an ethical price. Such measures can, undoubtedly, produce valuable insights, but they are not widely used by organizational researchers.

Second, using *non-participant observation*, the researcher is physically present, but only as a spectator who does not become directly involved in the activities of those being studied. The researcher's presence typically allows a wide range of observations to be made. The researcher may take notes or record interactions on audio or video tape for subsequent analysis. People sometimes behave abnormally in the presence of an outside observer, particularly if some form of permanent (or semi-permanent) recording technology is being used, and this has to be taken into account when interpreting data gathered in this way.

Third, with *participant observation*, the researcher takes part in the activities under investigation. In organizational research, this typically means that the researcher becomes, say, an assistant storekeeper in a factory, or joins a group of trainee nurses, or works as a delivery driver for a local store. By becoming a member of the group to be studied, the researcher can achieve a depth of understanding of their behaviour, feelings, values and beliefs. People studied in this way are more likely to behave naturally, particularly when they have become accustomed to the presence of the researcher. Non-participant observers, on the other hand, can clearly be identified as 'outsiders'. Participant observation is, obviously, limited to the roles which the researcher can credibly perform, so not all organizational settings are readily open to this approach. Participant observation is sometimes used without the knowledge of the subjects of the research, and this raises ethical issues.

STOP!

» Do you think that it is ethically justifiable, in the interests of developing our organizational knowledge, to study people at work without telling them that they are the subjects of research?
» What, in your view, are the benefits and disadvantages in such secrecy as far as the researcher is concerned?
» What, in your view, are the benefits and disadvantages in such secrecy as far as the research subjects are concerned?

analyzing documents

Organizations are typically rich sources of documentary materials. These can include:

» committee minutes
» letters
» diaries
» productivity analyses
» management consulting reports
» mission and vision statements
» company accounts and reports
» memoranda
» equipment operating manuals
» project reports
» customer or client records
» personnel records

There are various ways in which documents can be analyzed and used. Statistical techniques may be applied to quantitative records. Qualitative or textual data are usually analyzed using a procedure known as content analysis, in which the data are classified into mutually exclusive and comprehensive themes and sub-themes. Documentary evidence can sometimes be useful in confirming the involvement of key actors in organizational events and processes, and in confirming the time order of important events.

asking questions

This is undoubtedly the most popular organizational research method, and is used in two main ways.

First, respondents can be interviewed in person. In a structured interview, respondents are taken through a predetermined sequence of questions. In an unstructured approach, respondents are asked to talk about general themes with no scheduled sequence of questions.

Second, respondents can be asked to complete a self-report questionnaire. Questionnaires can be sent to people whom the researcher cannot contact personally, and can be completed by large numbers of people in a short time. Every respondent answers the same questions in the same sequence. Answers are in a uniform format, which may be more suitable for computer analysis than the 'conversational' data produced by interviews. However, if a question is ambiguous and is misinterpreted, the researcher may not be available to correct the error.

The choice of research methods depends on the kind of data required, and on the researcher's time and resources. Interviews produce rich information about people's experience, values and feelings, but are extremely time-consuming to conduct and analyze. Questionnaires can generate systematic information from a large number of people quickly, but the data are usually superficial and shallow.

STOP!

You have been asked to evaluate the opinions of your colleagues concerning your organizational behaviour course.

What are the advantages and disadvantages, in your educational setting, of using interviews or questionnaires to do this?

---

definition

A **research design** *is a strategy, or overall approach, for tackling a research question or problem.*

There are three broad types of research design used in organizational research:

- experiments
- case studies
- surveys

experiments

Social science uses experimental research to study social phenomena in much the same way as natural science. The advantages of *laboratory experiments* lie with the control that the researcher has over the variables to be studied. The real world tends to vary in ways which make it difficult to establish precise cause and effect relationships. The disadvantage of laboratory experiments lies in their artificiality. People may not behave normally in a scientific laboratory setting.

Experiments are used to measure the effects of one variable on another. Suppose we want to study the effect of Scotch whisky consumption on student examination performance. Whisky consumption is called our *independent variable*. Examination performance is called the *dependent variable* because we believe that it will depend on how much whisky students have drunk. If we were studying alcoholism among the student population, we would want to explain why students consumed alcohol, and whisky consumption would become the dependent variable in such a study. You might like to consider what the independent variables could be in such research.

The laboratory setting allows us to measure these variables very accurately. We control how much each student is given to drink and assess how well they perform in our examination. Everybody works under the same examination conditions, and the only factor that could cause variations in behaviour is the quantity of whisky consumed.

Organizational researchers are sometimes able to manipulate events in the real world and conduct *field experiments*. The work methods of one group in an organization can be changed in some way, and the effects on their job satisfaction and performance compared with another group whose work methods have not changed. This is less rigorous than a laboratory setting because there are many factors which the researcher cannot control, but which can affect the outcomes. Other organizational changes, affecting employee performance, could take place independently of the field experiment. Factors in the domestic lives of the participants in this study could affect performance too. The main advantage, however, is that the experiment is conducted in a real setting. The main difficulty, of course, is that organizations rarely permit social scientists to experiment with their members.

The *naturally occurring experiment* is an answer to that last problem. Organizations often change slowly, a section or department at a time. This can create opportunities for researchers to simulate field experiments.

case studies

Case studies are detailed investigations of individuals, groups, or departments in an organization, or a whole organization. No attempt is made at experimental control, although it is important to identify accurately the time sequence of events recorded. Case study data can be extremely rich and varied and detailed. The sequence of events can help to establish cause and effect relationships. Case study data can also be collected over an extended time-series to produce *longitudinal studies*.

Case study work has traditionally been used to study new fields and to generate insights for further systematic investigation. However, from a phenomenological perspective, case studies can produce interesting and valuable findings in their own right. Case studies have been widely used in organizational research, particularly with organizations that have introduced valuable innovations (in technology, organization design, human resource policies, and so on) from which other organizations could potentially learn.

surveys

Surveys are perhaps the most popular social science research method, and tend to be equated in the public mind with social research. Surveys can be based on interview, questionnaire, observation or document collection and analysis methods. Surveys are *cross-sectional* as they study a range, or variety, or cross-section of people, occupations or organizations. This approach enables the researcher to establish a form of control over independent variables at the analysis stage. For example, in a study of voting behaviour, the age and sex of all respondents can be recorded, and results for each sex and age range can then be computed separately. This allows the detection of systematic differences in behaviour across those categories. However, this is not a true experimental approach, but is useful if the coverage of the survey is wide, and the setting is real rather than artificial.

Within any one research study, methods and designs can be varied and mixed according to the requirements and constraints of the topic and the setting being considered. The research design does not always dictate the methods that have to be used, and vice versa. A combination of methods and designs can be used to approach the same issue, from different angles.

STOP!

You have to design a research project to test the effectiveness of different types of study techniques for passing organizational behaviour examinations.
  Which research design or designs would you use to tackle this problem?
  Justify your choice.

Research findings can be assessed on two principal criteria: *internal validity* and *external validity*.

---

definition

Internal validity *is the degree of confidence with which it can be claimed that the independent variable really did cause the observed changes in the dependent variable, and not some other factor or factors.*

Internal validity is assessed by considering factors other than the independent variable that could have caused the changes in the dependent variable. In our whisky-drinking students, we may have to consider the amount of sleep, exercise and food and perhaps the number of other alcoholic drinks each student may have had before taking part in our experiment.

---

definition

External validity *is the degree of confidence with which the findings from one particular research setting can be said to apply in another setting. This is also known as the* **generalizability** *of the findings.*

This again is a matter of judgement. Our results may only apply to Scottish students (who may be more accustomed to whisky consumption) and not to students of other nationalities. The results may only apply to students of a particular age (younger students may prefer beer), or to those of a particular body weight (your tolerance of alcohol increases with size).

Research designs that are strong on internal validity tend to have poor external validity. The reverse also applies. The ability to control variables in experiments helps internal validity, but the artificiality can limit the external validity of the findings. The reality of case study work strengthens external validity, but the lack of control over key variables weakens the internal validity of the findings. The position of surveys is more complex and depends on the nature of the research subjects and the type of analysis to which the data are subjected. Although surveys might appear to lie in some middle ground between the respective strengths and weaknesses of other designs, they are not necessarily best.

The concerns with internal and external validity are positivist concerns. A phenomenological or interpretive perspective considers other criteria significant. Remember our discussion about the social construction of reality. Here the key validity questions concern the extent to which the subjects agree with, recognize, accept, and otherwise consider accurate and appropriate the findings of research that has involved them. A positivist would rarely consider asking the respondents in a research investigation to check the validity of their findings. To a phenomenologist, the findings may not be considered valid unless respondents have checked and agreed with them. In other words, *respondent validation* is what counts from a phenomenological perspective, more than internal or external validity.

sources

Berger, P. and Luckmann, T., 1966, *The Social Construction of Reality*, Penguin Books, Harmondsworth.

Bryman, A. (ed.), 1988, *Doing Research in Organizations*, Routledge, London.

Bryman, A., 1989, *Research Methods and Organization Studies*, Routledge, London.

Burrell, G. and Morgan, G., 1979, *Sociological Paradigms and Organizational Analysis*, Heinemann, London.

Denzin, N.K. and Lincoln, Y.S. (eds.), 1994, *Handbook of Qualitative Research*, Sage, Thousand Oaks, CA.

The Economist, 1993, 'Jury science', 8 July, p. 86.

Harrison, M.I., 1994, *Diagnosing Organizations: Methods, Models, and Processes*, Sage, Thousand Oaks, CA.

Silverman, D., 1985, *Qualitative Methodology and Sociology: Describing the Social World*, Gower, Aldershot.

Smith, M., Thorpe, R. and Lowe, A., 1991, *Management Research: An Introduction*, Sage, London.

Yin, R.K., 1994, *Case Study Research: Design and Methods*, Sage, Thousand Oaks, CA.

part 1 the individual in the organization

chapter 3 communication and perception

Peanuts

© 1993 United Feature Syndicate, Inc.

concepts and learning objectives

This chapter offers an introduction to the related topics of interpersonal communications and the psychology of perception. This is a useful starting point for a study of organizational behaviour for a number of reasons. Communication processes are central to the conduct of organizational life and to our own personal effectiveness. The complaint, 'communications around here need to be dramatically improved', is all too common in most organizations. Our communications depend to a large extent on how we perceive those round about us, their motives and intentions, and how we perceive or interpret the communications we receive from them. Human behaviour is a function of the way in which we perceive the world around us, and other people and events in that world.

We often find ourselves unable to understand other people's behaviour. People can say and do surprising things in settings where it is obvious to us

39

that some other behaviour would be more appropriate. The problem is that we each perceive the world in different ways. If we are to understand why you behaved in that way in that context, we first need to discover how you perceive that context and your place in it. When we are able to 'see it the way you see it', to put ourselves in your position, then what initially took us by surprise is likely to become readily understandable behaviour. To understand each other's behaviour, and to improve our interpersonal communications, we need to be able to understand each other's perceptions. We need to be able to understand why we perceive things differently in the first place.

---

key concepts

the communication process	coding and decoding
non-verbal behaviour, or body language	impression management
perception	habituation
selective attention	perceptual organization
perceptual set or perceptual expectation	perceptual world
halo effect	stereotyping
	attribution

---

learning objectives

When you have read this chapter, you should be able to define those key concepts in your own words, and you should also be able to:

1 Explain the main components of the interpersonal communication process.
2 Identify the main sources of error in interpersonal communication.
3 Explain the significance of non-verbal behaviour and impression management.
4 Identify the main features of the process of perception.
5 Give examples of how behaviour is influenced by our perceptions.
6 Explain and illustrate the main processes and problems in person perception.

Of all the topics covered in this text, perception is perhaps the one which most directly sets social science apart from natural science. We humans seem to attach meanings, interpretations, values and aims to our actions. What we do in the world depends on how we understand our place in it, how we perceive ourselves and our social and physical environment, and how we perceive our circumstances. We explain behaviour with terms like 'reason', 'motive', 'intention', 'purpose', 'desire', and so on. Physicists, chemists and engineers do not face this complication in coming to grips with their subject matter.

We do not passively register sense impressions picked up from the world around us. The incoming raw data are processed and interpreted in the light of our past experiences, in terms of our current needs and interests, in terms of our knowledge, expectations, beliefs and motives. From a psychological point of view, the processes of sensation on the one hand, and perception on the other, work together. However, what is sometimes described as the 'bottom-up processing' of sensory data is different from 'top-down processing' which is conceptually based and allows us to order, interpret and make sense of the world. This distinction between sensation and perception can be illustrated in our ability to make sense of incomplete, or even incorrect, sensory information. The missing letter or comma and incorrectly spelled term that stops the computer does not normally interfere with the comprehension of the human reader. We are able to fill in the gaps and correct the mistakes and make sense of 'imperfect' incoming data.

We each have a similar nervous system and share more or less common sensory equipment. But we have different social and physical backgrounds which potentially give us different expectations, and therefore different perceptions. We do not behave in, and in response to, the world 'as it really is'. This chapter demonstrates that this idea of 'the real world' is arbitrary, and argues that this concept is not a useful starting point for developing an understanding of human behaviour in general, or organizational behaviour in particular.

We behave in, and in response to, the world as we *perceive* it. We each live in our own *perceptual world*. Successful interpersonal communication depends on some overlap between our perceptual worlds, on some common perceptions, or we would never be able to understand each other. Our perceptual worlds, however, are in a detailed analysis unique – which makes life interesting, but also gives us problems.

The central role of perception in explaining behaviour can be seen clearly through the study of interpersonal communications. It is helpful, therefore, to explore these two related topics together. We do not simply 'receive' messages from other people in any passive sense of the term 'receive'. The perceptual process goes to work on those incoming messages, to interpret or decode them. To the extent that we perceive and interpret the communications from others in the manner they intended, and they in turn interpret our communications with a similar level of accuracy, then maybe we can claim that our communications are effective. However, as we shall see, interpersonal communication is an error-prone process. We shall also demonstrate how we can get people to respond to the perception or image or impression of ourselves that we want to display, and that we want them to have. In other words, we can *manage* through the interpersonal communications process the perceptions that others have of us, and use this to our advantage. Sounds like unethical manipulation ? Well, we are all doing this most of the time, more or less unconsciously, anyway.

interpersonal communication: coding and decoding

definition
Conversation: *a competitive sport in which the first person to draw breath is declared the listener.*

We ask you the time. You tell us the time. Information has been transmitted. Interpersonal communication has been effectively achieved. However, communication is both more subtle, and more interesting, than this simple illustration suggests.

---

definition

The interpersonal **communication process** *involves the transmission of information, and the exchange of meaning.*

We shall concentrate on interpersonal communications in this chapter, because of their significance in understanding organizational behaviour. A detailed study of communications, on the other hand, would recognize the significance of other aspects of communications, including the use of different media, mass communications, and communications technologies. The principles that we shall explore, however, have wide application.

For the moment, let us focus on 'one-on-one' communication, between two people, and let us examine more carefully our definition of the *communication process*.

This definition suggests that communication involves more than the transmission of information between two (or more) people. Pay close attention to the next person who asks you what time it is. You will almost always be able to tell, by the way in which the question is asked, something about how they are feeling at the time, and about why they need to know. You will be able to tell, perhaps, if they are in a hurry, or if they are anxious or nervous, or if they are bored with waiting for something or someone. In other words, their question has a purpose or a meaning, and although it is not always stated directly, we can usually work out what that purpose or meaning might be from the context.

The same considerations apply to your response. Your willingness to reply suggests a willingness, at least, to be helpful, may imply friendship and may also indicate that you share the same concern as the person asking the question (we are going to be late; when will this film start?). Your reply can also indicate frustration and annoyance: 'Five minutes since you last asked!' Communication, therefore, involves more than the transmission of information. Interpersonal communication is a process that involves the *exchange of meaning*.

"Must I actually smile when I say hello to you? Isn't it enough that I acknowledge your existence?"

This process of exchange is illustrated more fully in the following figure or model.

exchanging meaning: a model of the communication process

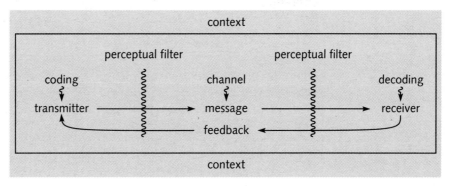

At the heart of this model, we have a transmitter sending a message to a receiver. We shall assume that the channel is face to face, 'one-on-one' rather than over a telephone, or through a letter or memo, or a video conference, or electronic mail. It is useful to think of the way in which the transmitter phrases and expresses the message as a *coding* process; the transmitter chooses words, and chooses also how the message will be expressed (loudly and with exasperation, or quietly and in a relaxed and friendly manner, for example). We can say that communication has been successful if the message is accurately *decoded* by the receiver; did they understand the language used, and appreciate the exasperation or friendship?

---

definitions

Coding *refers to the manner in which a transmitter chooses to word and express a message;* **decoding** *concerns the way in which the receiver interprets the message.*

This is a particularly useful way of examining the communication process because it identifies many of the problems that can arise and also points to solutions. There are many ways in which the coding and decoding aspects of the process can go wrong. Some fairly common terms and expressions, for example, can be particularly awkward. The dictionary definition of the word 'decimate', for example, says that it means to cut back by 10 per cent, or to kill every tenth person. However, this term is commonly used to imply widespread devastation. The branch manager who receives from head office an instruction to decimate his or her salesforce would thus be advised to check the original coding of the message before taking any action. The word 'exotic' is commonly used to imply colourful, novel, exciting, out of the ordinary. The 'correct' definition is simply 'from another country'. So, motor cars made by, for example, Daewoo, Hyundai, Skoda and Lada are 'exotic' cars in Britain. To be successful, therefore, both the transmitters and receivers in the communication process need to share a common 'codebook', and also need to use that 'codebook' consistently.

> **STOP!**
>
> From your experience, what other terms and expressions create coding and decoding problems? Identify specific examples (which can sometimes be humorous).

The communication process is further complicated by the 'perceptual filters' which affect what we want and are willing to say, and which in turn affect what we hear and how we hear it. The processes involved in perception are explored in more depth later in this chapter, but we need to mention here how perceptual filters affect communications. The transmitter of a message has motives, objectives, personality traits, values, biases and prejudices – all of which colour or influence the content and expression of communications. We decide the information we wish to reveal, and we decide which information we wish to withhold or conceal from others. We do not always perform this filtering consciously. Similarly, at the receiving end, perceptual filtering can affect what is heard, what is decoded, what is not decoded, and the way in which the message is understood. When you asked what time it was, did you 'hear' the exasperation or frustration or friendship in the response? Or did you simply focus on the time issue, because that was more important to you?

There is a further complicating factor: the context or setting. The casual remark by a colleague across a restaurant table may be dismissed. The casual remark by a work colleague across an office desk can become a source of considerable alarm and concern. Our physical and social settings influence a number of factors, which in turn influence our communications. Relationships in organizations can be collaborative, but they can also be hierarchical and competitive. Status differentials colour our communications. We do not reveal to the boss what we reveal to colleagues. The style and content of conversation depends often on our organizational relationships with others. The style and content can change in a striking manner when organizational relationships are 'suspended' for any reason – such as the Christmas office party.

Electronics engineers use the term 'noise' to refer to anything which interferes with a communications process. Interpersonal communication suffers from 'noise', which covers more than the sound of machinery, telephones, and other people talking in the background. Noise can be defined as anything that gets in the way. This includes coding and decoding problems, the perceptual filters, anything that interferes with the integrity of our chosen channel, and issues arising from our relationships with other people in the organization. Our motives and feelings can thus also constitute noise. The effectiveness of our coding and decoding can deteriorate with anxiety, pressure, stress, or with enthusiasm and excitement.

Noise constitutes a barrier to effective communication. Our past experiences condition the way in which we see things today and lead us to filter what we transmit and what we receive. Communications stumble when transmitter and receiver have different frames of reference, and do not share experience and understanding, even where they share a common language. We make judgements about the honesty, integrity, trustworthiness and credibility of others, and decode their messages and act on them (or not) accordingly. People in an organizational setting may have time to reflect, or they may be under considerable time pressure which will affect the care and attention devoted to communication. Some of us, from time to time, suffer from communications overload (or information overload), and our effectiveness can deteriorate for this reason also.

There is a final aspect of our communications model which we have still to consider: feedback. When we communicate face to face, we can usually tell if the other person likes us, or if they agree with us, or if they are interested in what we have to say. We can usually tell if they don't understand what we are saying, if they disagree with us, or if they are simply bored and don't want to listen any longer. How do we know this? Well, they may simply say, 'that's interesting', or 'I'm going to catch my bus now' – or we can tell from the tone of their replies, the expression on their face or the posture of their body. We shall explore the coding and decoding of *non-verbal behaviour* or body language later in the chapter.

When we communicate face to face, we get instant feedback on what others say, and on how they say it. Our ability to exchange meaning effectively is greatly assisted by this rich feedback loop. Our communications can be awkward where feedback is delayed or absent. Feedback allows us to check constantly the accuracy of the coding and decoding processes. We ask a question, see the other person look annoyed or puzzled, realise that we have not worded our question appropriately, and 'recode' the message. Face to face, if we are paying attention, this can work well and smoothly. We can do this to some extent over the telephone, decoding the tone of the other person's voice. With other more formal and more distant forms of communication, feedback can be slow or non-existent, and we need to take considerably more care over our coding, particularly with important messages.

However, we can be careless coders and lazy listeners. What might at first appear to be a simple process can in practice be highly error-prone. Both sides of the exchange – coding and decoding – are subject to error. We cannot confidently assume that our receivers will always decode our messages in a manner that leaves them with the sense of meaning that we wanted to transmit. It is perhaps obvious to claim that communication processes are

from *Personnel Management*, November 1994.

central to organizational effectiveness, and to the quality of working life, but this claim has major practical implications. We assume that organizations will function better if communication is open, if relationships are based on mutual understanding and trust, if relationships are co-operative rather than competitive, if people work together in teams, and if decisions are reached in a participative way. These features, however, are not widespread.

What guidelines can we derive from this analysis, to improve our communications? The following general advice applies in many specific contexts, such as counselling.

face to face	When we are able to speak with someone directly, we can use the feedback constantly to check the coding and decoding processes, and to correct mistakes and misunderstanding.
reality checks	We should not assume that others will necessarily decode our messages in the way we intended, and we should instead check the way in which our messages have been interpreted.
time and place	The right message delivered in the wrong place or at the wrong time is more likely to be decoded incorrectly, or even ignored, so choose the time and place with sensitivity and care.
the 'you' attitude	Put yourself in the other person's position, try to see things the way they see things, try to decode the message the way they might decode it, listen attentively to their feedback – adopt what Maureen Guirdham (1995) calls the 'you' attitude.

There is a further interesting side of interpersonal communications still to explore. This concerns the ways in which we code and decode messages using what is commonly known as body language, for which the 'correct' technical term is *non-verbal behaviour*. To put these phenomena in context, however, we shall first explore a key aspect of human perception.

selectivity and organization in perception

definition
Perception *is the dynamic psychological process responsible for attending to, organizing and interpreting sensory data.*

Our perceptual processing is normally carried out without much conscious deliberation or effort. In fact, we often have no effective control over the process, and fortunately such control is not always necessary. We can, however, control some aspects of the process simply by being consciously aware of what is happening. There are many settings where such control is desirable and can avoid dangerous and expensive errors. Understanding the characteristics of perception can be useful in a variety of organizational settings, for example, with the design of aircraft instrumentation and displays for pilots, and in the conduct of selection interviews for new employees.

Perception is defined here as a dynamic process because it involves ordering and attaching meaning to 'raw' sensory data. Our sensory apparatus is bombarded with vast amounts of information. Some of this information comes from inside the body, such as sensations of hunger, lust, pain and fatigue. Some of this information comes from people, objects and events in the world around us. We are not 'passive recorders' of this sensory data. We are constantly sifting and sorting this stream of information, making sense out of it and interpreting it. Perception, therefore, seems to be an information-processing activity. This information-processing is fairly well understood, and concerns the phenomena of *selective attention* and *perceptual organization*.

---

definition

Selective attention *is the ability (often exercised unconsciously) to choose from the stream of sensory data, to concentrate on particular elements, and to ignore others.*

Our senses – sight, hearing, touch, taste, smell – each consist of specialist nerves that respond to specific forms of energy, such as light, sound, pressure and so on. There are some forms of energy that our senses cannot detect such as radio waves, sounds of very low and very high pitch, and infrared radiation. Owls have much better eyesight than us, and bats, dogs and dolphins have better hearing. Our sensory apparatus has built-in limitations that we cannot overcome without the aid of special equipment.

The constraints imposed by our sensory apparatus can be modified in certain ways by experience. The boundary, or threshold, between what we can and cannot detect can be readily established by experiment. It is also a straightforward matter to explore individual differences in these thresholds across the various senses. These thresholds may be altered by experience, in the following manner. If there is a clock ticking in the room where you study, you will almost certainly not be aware of the sound – until somebody mentions it, or the clock stops. Next time you use the library, close your eyes for a few seconds and listen carefully. Pay attention to the 'background' noise that you do not usually 'hear'. But surely you must have heard it, as you must have heard the clock ticking, if your ears are working properly? Our sensory apparatus responds, not simply to energy, but rather to changes in energy levels. Having detected a stimulus, such as a clock, the nerves concerned seem to become tired of transmitting the same information indefinitely and give up, until the stimulus changes. This explains our surprise, on some occasions, at the silence which follows when machinery stops suddenly. Once stimuli become familiar, they stop being sensed. This phenomenon, in which the perceptual threshold is raised, is known as *habituation*.

---

definition

Habituation *concerns the decrease in response to familiar stimuli.*

Our sensory apparatus has design limitations which filter or screen out some information, such as X-rays and dog whistles. Perception involves other filtering processes, as the phenomenon of habituation suggests. In particular, information that is familiar, non-threatening and unnecessary to the task in hand is 'screened out' of our conscious awareness. Just how this screening operates, and what happens to the unwanted information, is still the subject of controversy and research, but the implications are fairly clear.

Stand on the pavement of a busy street for a few minutes and pay attention to as much of the available information as you can; the noise and speed of the traffic and the makes and colours and condition of passing vehicles, the smell of rubber tyres and exhaust fumes, the pressure of the pavement on the soles of your feet, the breeze across your face, the smell of the perfume of a passing woman, the clothes of the man across the street and the type of dog he is walking . . . and so on. When you think you are taking it all in, start to cross the road. If you get across safely, you will find that your heightened awareness has lapsed dramatically. You would be mown down fairly quickly if this were not the case. Selective attention allows us to concentrate on the important and significant, and to ignore the insignificant and trivial.

There is simply too much information available at any one time for us to pay adequate attention to all of it. The image of the world that we carry around inside our heads can only ever be a partial representation of what is 'really out there'. This observation leads to the conclusion that our behavioural choices are determined not by reality as such, but by what we perceive that reality to be.

The internal and external factors which affect selective attention are illustrated in the following figure.

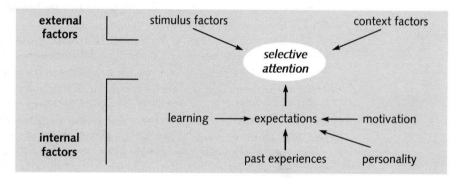

The external factors affecting selective attention concern stimulus factors and context factors. With respect to the stimulus factors, our attention is drawn more readily to stimuli that are large rather than small, bright rather than dull, loud rather than quiet, moving rather than stationary, and so on. Stimuli which are unfamiliar and which stand out from their surroundings are more likely to receive attention than familiar stimuli that blend into the background. Note, however, that we do not merely respond to single features, as this list might imply; we respond to the *pattern* of stimuli available to us.

Our attention is also influenced by context factors. The naval commander on the ship's bridge and the cook in the kitchen may both have occasion to shout 'fire', but these identical utterances will mean quite different things to those within earshot, and will lead to radically different forms of behaviour

STOP!

Identify examples of the ways in which advertisements creatively use stimulus factors to attract our attention, in newspapers and magazines, and on billboards and television.

---

the endless landscape of awareness

All the time we are aware of millions of things around us – these changing shapes, these burning hills, the sound of the engine, the feel of the throttle, each rock and weed and fence post and piece of debris beside the road – aware of these things but not really conscious of them unless there is something unusual or unless they reflect something we are disposed to see. We could not possibly be conscious of these things and remember all of them because our mind would be so full of useless details we would be unable to think. From all this awareness we must select, and what we select and call consciousness is never the same as the awareness because the process of selection mutates it. We take a handful of sand from the endless landscape of awareness around us and call that handful of sand the world.

from Robert M. Pirsig, 1974, *Zen and the Art of Motorcycle Maintenance: An Inquiry Into Values*, Corgi Books, London, p. 75.

(perhaps involving the taking and the saving of lives, respectively). We do not need any assistance to make this crucial distinction beyond our knowledge of the context.

The internal factors affecting perception include motivation, learning and personality. These topics are covered in later chapters. The most powerful influences on perception seem to be personality, learning, and past experience.

Much of perception can be described as classification or categorization. We categorize people as male or female, lazy or energetic, extravert or shy. In fact, our classification schemes are usually more sophisticated than that. We classify objects as cars, buildings, furniture, crockery, and so on, and we refine our classification schemes further under these headings. However, we are not born with a neat classification scheme 'wired in' with the brain. These categories are learned. They are social constructs. What we learn is often culture-bound or culture-specific. An Indonesian visitor to one of our institutions once remarked, 'In your country, you feed the pigeons. In my country, the pigeons feed us'. Our revulsion at the thought of eating dog (classified as pet, not food), the Hindu revulsion at the thought of eating beef (classified as sacred) and the Islamic aversion to alcohol (classified as proscribed by the Koran) are all culturally transmitted emotions, based on learned values.

Problems arise when we act as if our culture had a monopoly on 'right thinking' on such issues. Different does not necessarily imply wrong. Different people within the same culture have different experiences and develop different expectations. The internal factors – our past experience and what we have learned, our personalities, our motivations – contribute to the development of our expectations of the world around us, what we want from it, what will happen in it, and what should happen. We tend to select information that fits our expectations, and pay less attention to information that does not.

Our categorization processes, and the constant search for meaning, for pattern and for order in the world around us, are key characteristics of human perception. This perceptual work is captured by the concept of *perceptual organization*.

---

definition

Perceptual organization *is the process through which incoming stimuli are organized or patterned in systematic and meaningful ways.*

*Max Wertheimer
(1880–1943)*

Photo source:
Archives of the History of American Psychology, The University of Akron, Ohio, USA.

The principles by which the process of perceptual organization operates were first identified by Max Wertheimer in 1923. The 'proximity principle' notes that we tend to group together or to classify stimuli that are physically close to each other and which thus appear to 'belong' together. Note how you 'see' three sets of pairs rather than six blobs here:

●●   ●●   ●●

The 'similarity principle' notes that we classify or group together stimuli that resemble each other in appearance in some respect. Note how you 'see' four pairs here, not eight objects:

■ ■ ● ● ■ ■ ● ●

The fact that we are able to make use of incomplete and ambiguous information, by 'filling in the gaps' from our own knowledge and past experience, is known as the 'principle of closure'. These principles of perceptual organization apply to simple visual stimuli. Of more interest here, however, is the way in which these principles apply to person perception. How often do we assume that people are similar just because they live in the same neighbourhood, or work in the same section of the factory or office building (proximity principle), or just because they wear the same clothes or have similar ethnic origins (similarity principle)? How often do we take incomplete information about someone (he's Scottish) and draw inferences from this (closure principle)? This can cause the spread of false rumours in organizations through what is sometimes called 'the grapevine'.

the significance of non-verbal communication

There is one aspect of behaviour, mentioned earlier in the chapter, which selective attention seems frequently to filter out of our conscious awareness.

When we interact with others, we are not only constantly sending and receiving messages through spoken and written language, but also when interacting face to face through the signs, expressions, gestures, postures and vocal mannerisms that we seem to adopt unconsciously. Messages coded using language can be called verbal communication; everything else just mentioned is defined as *non-verbal communication*. (Note: Verbal simply means 'in words', which can be either written, or spoken. Unqualified expressions like 'verbal agreement', therefore, are ambiguous and are prone to incorrect decoding.) As a general rule, we code and transmit factual information primarily through verbal behaviours. We code and transmit our feelings and emotions, and the strength of our feelings, through our non-verbal communication.

---

definition

Non-verbal communication *is the process of coding meaning through behaviours that do not involve the use of words.*

The term 'body language' has come into use in recent years, as our knowledge of this fascinating side of behaviour has developed. We use the more cumbersome technical term here for two principal reasons. First, non-verbal behaviour is extremely rich and varied, and the term 'body' language is either partial or inaccurate if it is taken to imply a concern only with bodily movements and postures. Second, the term body language seems to suggest, and in the hands of some commentators does tend to imply, that particular gestures have particular meanings; in other words, we can produce a 'dictionary' of body language. That, as we shall demonstrate, is rarely the case. The longer technical term has the advantage of including a range of behaviours, including bodily movements and postures. It also signals our concern with the way these behaviours are embedded in the communications process.

Alan Pease (1985), a popular writer and speaker on the subject of non-verbal communication (which he calls body language), implies in the sub-title of one of his books that one can 'read' or decode somebody else's feelings, attitudes and emotions from this source. Does a knowledge of this aspect of human behaviour really give us the ability to read minds? Well, to some extent, maybe, if we are careful, sometimes. This 'mind reading' claim

Calvin and Hobbes

deserves some cautious support. We are able to exchange meaning with non-verbal codes.

Non-verbal behaviour is rich and varied. Maureen Guirdham (1995, p. 165) lists 136 non-verbal behaviours, in nine categories. These include what we do with our mouths, eyebrows, eyelids and eyes, gaze, facial expressions, head movements, hands and arms, and our lower limbs and trunk movements. The sub-heading 'mouth region' lists 40 behaviours, such as tongue out, open grin, yawn, wry smile, sneer, tight lips, lower lip tremble, and so on. The sub-heading 'hands and arms' lists a further 40 behaviours, such as scratch, sit on hands, hand flutter, digit suck, palms up, caress, hand on neck – and so on. The study of what we do with our eyes is known as 'occulesics'; the study of limb movements is known as 'kinesics'.

HERMAN

"He's not very sociable."

There are other aspects of non-verbal behaviour. One of these is 'paralanguage', and concerns the rate of speech, and pitch and loudness of our voice, regardless of the words we are using. Another concerns the way in which we use distance in interpersonal behaviour, and this is sometimes called 'proxemics'. British and European culture requires a 'social distance' of about half a metre or more between people in normal conversation. If you step into someone's 'personal space' they will usually move backwards to retain the distance; a failure to 'retreat' implies intimacy. The comfortable distance in Arab and Latin American cultures is much smaller, and you in turn are likely to be regarded as arrogant and distant by trying to maintain your personal space when interacting with members of those cultures.

Non-verbal behaviour can also be extremely powerful. Consider the simple statement: 'That was a really great lecture'. Think of the many ways in which you can say this, the differences in gaze and posture as you say it, and the differences in the tone and pitch of your voice. For some of these forms of expression, listeners will hear you say that you really did enjoy the lecture. However, there are a number of ways in which you can 'code' this statement such that listeners will be left in no doubt that you thought the lecture poor – even though the wording remains as it is written here. When the verbal message (great lecture) is inconsistent with the non-verbal message (lousy lecture), the non-verbal message is the part that is believed, and listeners discount the verbal component of the statement. When we are lying, we may unconsciously send non-verbal 'deceit cues': rapid shifts in gaze, fidgeting in our seats, long pauses and frequent corrections in our speech. To lie effectively, it is important to control the deceit cues and ensure that our verbal and non-verbal messages are consistent. Similarly, when we want to emphasize the sincerity or strength of our feelings, it is important that the non-verbal signals we send are consistent with our verbal messages.

What has all this to do with reading someone's mind? Guirdham (1995) calls non-verbal behaviour a 'relationship language'. This is how we communicate trust, boredom, submission, dislike and friendship without having to indicate these feelings openly or directly. When decoding non-verbal behaviour, it is important to pay attention both to the context of the behaviour and to the pattern or cluster of verbal and non-verbal behaviours on display. For example, when someone wishes to indicate liking or friendship, they are likely to turn their body towards you, look you straight in the face, establish regular eye contact and look away infrequently, and to nod and smile a lot, keeping their hands and arms by their sides or in front of them. This cluster conveys openness or positive non-verbal behaviour.

We can, therefore, decode openness, liking, agreement and friendship with the help of this non-verbal cluster. Similarly, we can often identify disagreement or dislike by negative non-verbal behaviour. This cluster includes a 'closed posture' which often involves turning the body away, folding the arms tightly and crossing the legs in such a manner that they point away from the other person. Negative non-verbal behaviours also include loss of eye contact, wandering gaze, looking at someone else or at the door (suggesting a desire to leave) and a lack of nods and smiles. Sometimes, when someone starts to disagree with you, you can detect this from their non-verbal behaviour cluster even before they state their disagreement in words. An awareness of the context is critical to this decoding or 'mind reading'. People also engage in these negative non-verbal behaviours when they are unwell, or when they are anxious about something, perhaps unrelated to your conversation and relationship. People 'close up' and fold their arms when they are cold, as well as when they disagree.

Our eye behaviour has attracted much research. The dilation and contraction of our pupils is largely outside our direct control, unlike, say, the movements of our hands, but this can convey significant non-verbal information. Our pupils dilate (expand) in low light, but also when we see something or someone in which we have interest, and this also conveys honesty, openness and sexual interest. (The 'deep, dark, limpid pools' of the romantic novelist have a basis in non-verbal behavioural response.) However, our pupils dilate when we are relaxed, and following the consumption of alcohol and other drugs. Once again, a knowledge of context is critical to an accurate decoding. Pupils that are contracted can signify bright lighting conditions, lack of interest, distrust, hatred, hostility, fatigue, stress and sorrow. Once again, our pupils contract following the consumption of some drugs, and when we are hung over.

Someone who is anxious usually indulges in non-verbal behaviour known as 'self-manipulation'. This includes playing with an ear lobe, stroking lips or chin, or playing with hair or a moustache. Anxiety can also be signalled by shifting the direction of gaze. Friendship is conveyed, as we have indicated, by an open non-verbal behaviour cluster. There are a number of other friendship signals, and these can sometimes be amusing to use and to identify. When we meet someone to whom we are attracted, we typically use unconscious 'preening gestures': straightening our clothes, stroking our hair, straightening our posture. Observe a group of friends together and you will often see them standing, sitting and even holding cups or glasses in an almost identical manner. This is known as 'posture mirroring'. Sometimes you can identify the 'outsider' as the one not adopting the similar posture. Friendship groups also copy each other's gestures; this is known as 'gesture mirroring'.

We usually send and receive non-verbal messages unconsciously. However, it is possible both to control most of the non-verbal signals we send, and consciously to be aware of and read the cues that others are giving us. This level of conscious attention and control may be difficult for most of us to sustain, but it can be significant in organizational settings. This is an important aspect of the way in which we present ourselves to others.

---

definition

Impression management *is the process whereby people seek to control the image others have of them.*

The concept of *impression management* has its foundations in the work of Erving Goffman (1959). It is now recognized as a significant aspect of organizational behaviour. Our definition is taken from the more recent work of Paul Rosenfeld, Robert Giacalone and Catherine Riordan (1995, p. 4) and they add:

> We impression manage in many different ways: what we do, how we do it, what we say, how we say it, the furnishings and arrangement of our offices, and our physical appearance – from the clothes and make-up we wear to non-verbal behaviours such as facial expressions or postures.

> All these behaviours in some way can help define who and what we are.

Effective impression management means being consciously aware of and in control of the cues that we send to others through verbal and non-verbal channels. This suggests that we consciously seek to manipulate the impression or perceptions that others have of us.

STOP!

Is impression management simply a form of deceit? What in your view are the *ethical problems* raised by the advice that we consciously seek to manipulate the impression that others have of us through a range of verbal and non-verbal behaviours? What are the practical problems? How long can you keep this up?

---

perceptual sets and perceptual worlds

We have shown how the perceptual process selects incoming stimuli and organizes them into meaningful patterns. We have also argued that this processing is influenced by learning, motivation and by personality – factors which give rise to expectations, which in turn make us more ready to respond to certain stimuli in certain ways and less ready to respond to others. This readiness to respond is called the individual's *perceptual set*.

Garfield

The drawing on p. 56 was published by an international accounting firm in 1995. In fact, some readers will recognize this as a variant on a drawing published in 1915 by the cartoonist W.H. Hill. What do you see here? An old woman, or a young woman? Your answer may be influenced by what you are predisposed to see at the time you are reading this. The reactions of different individuals will not be consistent, and it does not make sense to argue over which perception is 'correct'. We must accept that two people can observe the 'same' thing, but perceive it in quite different ways. Failure to appreciate this feature of the perceptual process creates many organizational problems, and particularly communication problems. Hospital consultants, for instance, may perceive that junior doctors are overreacting to trivial issues and may dismiss their complaints lightly. The junior doctors, on the other hand, may perceive that their grievances are genuine, and that the consultants are simply not taking them seriously. It is not difficult to predict some of the outcomes in a situation like this. It makes little sense to ask whose perceptions are correct. The starting point for resolving issues such as these must lie with the recognition that different people hold different, but equally legitimate, views of the same set of circumstances.

We distinguished in Chapter 2 between two views of the study of human behaviour. The 'positivist' perspective sets out to discover 'the world out there, as it really is'. The 'phenomenological' perspective, on the other hand, sets out to discover how our world is socially constructed, and how we experience and interpret that world. The argument in the last paragraph seems to suggest that 'the world out there as it really is' is not such a good starting point for developing an understanding of human behaviour, or perhaps for resolving organizational communications problems. We each have a unique version of what is 'out there' and of our own place in it. In other words, we each live in our own *perceptual world*.

We each have a perceptual world that is selective and partial, and which concentrates on features of particular interest and importance to us. Through the processes of learning, motivation and personality development, we each have different expectations and different degrees of readiness to respond to objects, people and events in different ways. We impose meaning on received patterns of information; the meanings that we attach to objects, people and events are not intrinsic to these things, but are learned through social experience and are coloured by our current needs and objectives.

This illustration appeared in a Price Waterhouse advertisement in The Sunday Times *on 26 February, 1995, p. 5, city section; and is reproduced with permission. Artwork supplied by* The Broadbent Partnership, *London.*

To understand an individual's behaviour, therefore, we need to know something of the elements in their perceptual world, and the pattern of influences that have shaped that world. Developing an understanding of one's own perceptual world can be awkward because there are so many influences of which we are not fully aware. Information about the perceptual worlds of others can also be elusive and, although this is by no means impossible, this does create a barrier to mutual understanding and to effective interpersonal communications. Unfortunately, we tend to forget that our own perceptual world is not the only possible or correct one.

Fortunately, we as individuals are not as isolated from each other as the argument so far seems to suggest. We do not live in a social and organizational world of constant misunderstanding and failed communication. A high proportion of our interactions are effective, or tolerably so. Why? We are, of course, not unique, and our personal perceptual worlds overlap to a great extent. We share the same, or similar, sensory apparatus. We share the same basic needs. We share much of the same background social environment. Within the same society, although there are vast differences in experience, we share some of the same problems and environmental features. All this common ground makes the tasks of mutual understanding and interpersonal communication possible.

perceptual set and assumptions about human behaviour

The concept of perceptual set, or perceptual expectation, applies to the ways in which we see other people. An understanding of the psychology of perception is therefore useful in our understanding of human behaviour in general, and of behaviour in organizations in particular. To understand the nature of perception is to understand, at least in part, the sources and nature of many organizational problems. There are two related and prominent features of the process of people perception: the *halo effect* and *stereotyping*.

definition

A **halo effect** *is a **judgement** of someone based on a striking characteristic, such as an aspect of their dress, speech or posture. Haloes can be positive or negative.*

Edward Lee Thorndyke (1874–1949)

Photo source:

Archives of the History of American Psychology, The University of Akron, Ohio, USA.

The term *halo effect* was first used by the psychologist Edward Thorndyke in 1920. Remember the concept of *selective attention*. This phenomenon applies to our perception of people. It is a natural human response, on meeting a stranger, to 'size them up', to make judgements about the kind of person they are and whether we will like them or not. We do this to others on a first encounter; they do this to us. It seems as if first impressions really do count after all (and we don't get a second chance to make a first impression). However, faced with so much new information about someone – the physical and social setting, their appearance, what they say, how they say it, their posture, their non-verbal behaviour, how they respond to us – we are forced to be selective with respect to the information to which we pay attention. Our judgements can thus rely on a single striking characteristic: the sound of their voice or a familiar accent, a perfume, their dress or tie, the car they drive or their hairstyle. If this judgement is favourable, we give the other person a *positive halo*, regardless of other information that, if we gave it due attention, might lead us to a different, more balanced, evaluation. If our judgement, on the other hand, is not favourable, we give the other person a *negative halo*. The *halo effect* can work in both directions.

The halo effect can thus act as an early screen, which filters out later information which is not consistent with our earlier judgement. The problem, of course, is that what we notice first about another person is often not relevant to the judgement that we want to make. A confounding factor is that we tend to give more favourable judgements to people who have characteristics in common with us. But since when did somebody's voice, hairstyle,

---

the halo effect and the job applicant

> There are people who will not hire short men.
> There are people who rely more on star signs than on the conduct of an interview.
> Some people will not recruit those they think are ugly.
> Some people are prejudiced against men who have beards.
> Some managers will not hire people who live alone, no matter what their marital status, because they have no 'sheet anchor' or 'sounding board'.
> There are dog lovers who dislike cat lovers – and vice versa.
> Men with 'feminine' hobbies and women with 'masculine' hobbies may be suspect.
> Fat people and anorexics are often assumed to have personality problems.
> People who habitually wear suede shoes attract negative judgements.
> Some recruiters dislike certain types of moustache, monocles, mean mouths, eyes that are too close together, 'Scargill' haircuts (baldness hidden by hair trained over from one side), scruffy dress, particular accents, dirty shoes, odd spectacles or bow ties.

based on Milton D. Hakel and Allen J. Schuh, 1971, 'Job applicant attributes judged important across seven diverse occupations', *Personnel Psychology*, vol. 24, pp. 45–52.

aftershave or clothes enable us to predict, say, their ability to design bridges or manage a department in a hotel? Some people feel that they can make such predictions from such limited evidence, based presumably on their own past experiences.

---

definition

A **stereotype** *is a category, or personality type, to which we consign people on the basis of their membership of some known group.*

Walter Lippmann (1889–1974)

Remember the concept of *perceptual organization*. This phenomenon too applies to person perception. The term *stereotyping* was first used by typographers to made-up blocks of type, and was used to describe bias in person perception by Walter Lippmann in 1922. The concept refers simply to the way in which we group together people who seem to us to share similar characteristics. So when we meet, say, an accountant, a nurse, an engineer, a poet or a mechanical engineering student, we attribute certain personality traits to them because they are accountants, or students, or whatever. Everybody knows, for example, that Scots are mean, and that blondes have more fun.

STOP!

Explore your own stereotypes by completing each of the following sentences with three terms that you think describe most or all members of the category concerned:
- University lecturers are
- Artists are
- Electrical engineers are
- Trainee nurses are
- Airline pilots are

You may find it interesting to share your stereotypes with those of colleagues, particularly if some of them have friends or close relatives who are pilots, nurses, electrical engineers . . .

If we know, or assume, somebody's apparent group membership in this way, our instant categorization allows us to attribute a range of qualities to them. Stereotypes are overgeneralizations and are bound to be radically inaccurate on occasion. But they can be convenient. By adopting a stereotyped point of view, we may be able to shortcut our evaluation process, and make quicker and more reliable predictions of behaviour. We can have problems, on the other hand, with those who fall into more than one category with conflicting stereotypes: the mechanical engineer who writes poetry, for instance.

sex, appearance, attractiveness and discrimination

We emphasized earlier in the chapter that the perceptual process is concerned with making sense of and explaining the world around us, and the people and events in it. Our need for explanation and understanding is reflected in the way in which we search for the causes of people's actions. Our perceptions of causality are known as *attributions*.

---

definition

Attribution *is the process by which we make sense of our environment through our perceptions of causality. An* attribution, *therefore, is a* belief *about the cause or causes of an event or an action.*

Attribution theory was developed during the 1950s and 1960s by Fritz Heider and Howard Kelley. Heider and Kelley argued that our understanding of our social world is based on our continual attempts at causal analysis based on how we interpret our experience. This understanding potentially allows us both to predict and to control certain future social events.

Why is that person so successful? Why did that project fail? Why are those people still arguing? If we understand the causes of success, failure and conflict, we may be able to adjust our behaviour and other factors accordingly. Attribution is simply the process of attaching or attributing causes or reasons to the actions and events we see. We tend to look for causes either in people's abilities and personalities, or in aspects of the setting or circumstances in which they find themselves. This distinction is usually described in terms of internal causality and external causality. We may explain a particular individual's success or promotion with reference to their superior skills and knowledge (internal causality) on the one hand, or with reference to luck, 'friends in high places' and coincidence on the other hand (external causality).

Research has revealed patterns in our attributions. For example, we tend to attribute our own behaviour to factors in our situation, and to attribute the behaviour of others, particularly if it is unusual, to features of their personality. However, research has also revealed how, when we are explaining our personal achievements, we point to our own capabilities, but when we are explaining our lack of success, we blame our circumstances. This is termed 'projection': we project blame onto factors outside our control or, in other words, to external causality.

Attribution theory may help to explain aspects of discrimination in organizational settings.

It has been demonstrated that sex and appearance influence the way in which we are perceived, paid and promoted. Two American researchers, Susan Averett and Sanders Korenman (1993), found that the hourly wage of overweight women, aged 23–31, was 20 per cent lower on average than that of women of average weight. They even found that underweight women also received underweight pay packets. However, the husbands of thin women earned on average 45 per cent more than those of fat ones. (You might like to consider why this should be the case.) Almost the reverse was found to be true for American men. Those who were underweight had the lowest earnings, with slightly overweight men earning as much as 26 per cent more than their lightweight colleagues. Daniel Hamermesh and Jeff Biddle (1993) found that attractive men and women earn about 5 per cent more than those with average appearance (based on interviewers' ratings of attractiveness). Plain women in their study were found to be earning 5 per cent less than those rated average, and plain men earned 10 per cent less.

---

watch your language

Deborah Tannen argues that boys and girls acquire different linguistic styles in childhood, and that these differences affect the different career prospects of men and women at work. A linguistic style is a characteristic speaking pattern. This pattern includes factors such as tone of voice, speed of speech, loudness, directness or indirectness, pacing and pausing, choice of words, and the extent to which we use jokes, stories, figures of speech, questions, and apologies. Tannen (1995, p. 140) claims that:

. . . girls learn conversational rituals that focus on the rapport dimension of relationships whereas boys tend to learn rituals that focus on the status dimension.

Boys as they grow up play in large groups, emphasize status and leadership, display their knowledge and abilities, challenge others, take 'centre stage' by telling jokes and stories, and try to acquire status in their group by giving orders to others. Girls, on the other hand, focus on a small group of friends, sharing secrets with their best friend, emphasizing similarities and playing down ways in which someone could be better than others. Girls tend to be more modest, appear less self-assured and ostracize those who claim superiority.

These childhood differences affect adult behaviour in organizational settings. Men tend to think more in hierarchical terms, and are concerned with being 'one up'. Men are thus more concerned with losing status, with not being 'one down', than are women. Men strive to retain 'one up' by driving and by interrupting conversation sequences.

Men are more likely to jockey for position by putting others down, to appear competent by acting confidently and to appear knowledgeable by asking fewer questions. Men tend to give negative feedback quickly, and to look for opportunities to criticize, rather than pay others compliments. Women, on the other hand, are more likely to avoid putting others down and to act in ways that are face-saving for others. Women can appear to lack self-confidence by playing down their certainty and by expressing doubt more openly. Women also appear less self-assured and knowledgeable by asking more questions, tend to soften criticism by offering positive feedback first, and pay others compliments more often than men do.

These linguistic differences are particularly important when speaking of achievements. Men tend to be more direct and use 'I' more often. Women tend to speak indirectly and speak of 'we' when talking about accomplishments. In summary, men tend to adopt linguistic styles and to behave in ways that are more likely to get them recognized, and that are more likely to earn them attributions of effectiveness and competence. Women adopting a more 'masculine' linguistic style can be seen as too aggressive. Tannen advises us all to be more aware of these differences in linguistic styles, and to pay attention to the dynamics of our conversations.

based on Deborah Tannen, 1995, 'The power of talk: Who gets heard and why', *Harvard Business Review*, September–October, pp. 138–48.

Why should appearance have such an effect on career progression? Our attributions are related to the phenomenon of stereotyping. We seem to attribute explanations of, or causes for, people's behaviour to aspects of their appearance. Discrimination against particular groups and individuals, on the basis of sex, sexual orientation, age or ethnic background, is now widely recognized. Legislation seeks to address (with mixed results) sexual and racial discrimination, and social attitudes towards homosexuals and the elderly in organizational settings do seem, slowly, to be changing. However, attribution research suggests that discrimination, based on our perceptions of causal links between sex, appearance and job performance, are more subtle than this, and considerably less public.

Leslie Martel and Henry Biller (1987) have demonstrated how the problems of sexism, ageism and racism apply also to 'heightism'. Their research showed how both men and women thought that short men, from 5 feet 2 inches to 5 feet 5 inches were less mature, less positive, less successful, less capable, less confident, less outgoing, more inhibited, more timid and more passive. In other words, short men are judged negatively, as their behaviour – and competence – is attributed to size and related personality characteristics. A summary of research in this field by *The Economist* argued that the Western 'ideal' height for men is now 6 feet 2 inches, and rising. This summary argued that discrimination on grounds of height, or heightism, is now well established. In all but three American presidential elections this century, the taller man won. In 1980, over half the chief executives in America's largest 500 companies were 6 feet tall or more, and only 3 per cent were 5 feet 7 inches or less. A recent British study suggested that for each 4 inches of height in adolescence earnings rose by 2 per cent in early adulthood.

With respect to attractiveness, sex, height and weight, we are dealing with factors which cannot have any meaningful impact on performance for most jobs or occupations. The tall, attractive female computer programmer of average weight *may* be more effective in her job than the short, overweight male programmer with the unremarkable features. A moment's consideration, however, would probably lead us to reject height, weight and attractiveness as causal factors in this equation, and lead us to look for differences in ability

© Bryan Reading

and education and experience instead. The problem seems to be, however, that we make attribution errors by jumping too quickly and unconsciously to judgements of this kind, particularly when we have little information about the other person on which to base a more careful assessment.

We can regard any aspect of our appearance as a form of *non-verbal communication*. We cannot control our age or height, for example, but these factors, however combined with behaviour that is under our control, send signals that others decode in the light of their experiences (age is related to reliability), expectations (tall and handsome means self-confident and knowledgeable) and prejudices (short and overweight women will deter customers). There is one further aspect of our non-verbal communication that we have not discussed: clothing, or styles of dress. This is an aspect which is, of course, within our control. Dress style can be a significant indicator of organizational culture, and can contribute significantly to the individual's *impression management*. The way in which we dress can tell others how we want to be seen (as formal, relaxed, creative, businesslike) rather than what we are really like. However, we may not always be aware how others 'decode' our attempts to manage our impression through dress style.

STOP!

Let us consider the styles of dress adopted by the instructors in your current educational establishment, across all the subjects you may be studying at the moment. (Let us not pick on organizational behaviour instructors in particular.) How does their style of dress influence your perceptions of their:

▸ approachability?
▸ subject knowledge?
▸ professionalism?
▸ understanding of the world beyond the academic 'ivory tower'?

How would you advise individual instructors to change their style of dress to improve the ways in which they manage their impression on those criteria?

Is there a 'dress code' in your institution – a code to which you adhere? What are you personally saying by sticking to this dress code? What messages would you send by deliberately breaking or ignoring this dress code?

---

person perception: errors and avoidance

The main sources of errors in person perception seem to include:

1 Not collecting enough information about other people.
2 Basing our judgements on information that is irrelevant or insignificant.
3 Seeing what we expect to see and what we want to see, and not investigating further.
4 Allowing early information about someone to affect our judgement, despite later and contradictory information.
5 Allowing our own characteristics to affect what we see in others and how we judge them.
6 Accepting stereotypes uncritically.

7 Attempting to decode non-verbal behaviour outside the context in which it appears.
8 Basing attributions on flimsy and potentially irrelevant evidence.

The remedies, therefore, include:

1 Taking more time and avoiding instant or 'snap' judgements about others.
2 Collecting and consciously using more information about other people.
3 Developing self-awareness and an understanding of how our personal biases and preferences affect our perceptions and judgements of other people.
4 Checking our attributions – the assumptions we make about the causes of behaviour, particularly the links we make between aspects of personality and appearance on the one hand and behaviour on the other.

If we are to improve our understanding of others, we must first have a well-developed knowledge of ourselves – our strengths, our preferences, our flaws and our biases. The development of self-knowledge can be an uncomfortable process. In organizational settings, we are often constrained in the expression of our feelings (positive and negative) about other people, due to social or cultural norms, and to the communication barriers erected by status and power differentials. This may in part explain the enduring appeal of training courses in social and interpersonal skills, self-awareness and personal growth designed to help us overcome these problems, to 'get in touch' with other people, and to 'get in touch with ourselves'. Training in interpersonal communication skills typically emphasizes openness and honesty in relationships, active listening skills, sensitivity to non-verbal behaviour, and how to give and receive both critical and non-evaluative feedback.

assessment

Interpersonal communication is critical to personal and organizational effectiveness. The communication processes and skills involved are relatively straightforward, but in practice our communications can be particularly error-prone. The modern, computer-assisted communications technologies such as video-conferencing, cellular phones and electronic mail, open up communication channels and possibilities on the one hand, but potentially increase the frequency with which we communicate with others 'at a distance', down a wire, over a fibre-optic network. Errors are more likely to occur in communications where feedback is either absent or delayed, and where the information-rich texture of face-to-face conversation is replaced with simple written messages. The way in which we decode or perceive a brief electronic mail message may be quite different from the perception we would gain if the sender were sitting in our room and explaining the message in person.

Perception is critical to our understanding of each other's behaviour, in organizational and social settings. This is one argument for placing this chapter at the beginning of the text. Another reason for using this issue as a starting point concerns the observation that we humans are self-interpreting, a feature which potentially makes the social science enterprise distinctive. However, we have only touched the surface of this topic, particularly from a psychological perspective. A more detailed discussion of the debates surrounding, for example, the development and use of language skills, or the nature of selective attention processes, would be beyond the scope of this text. Our concern has been to explain the fundamental characteristics of communication and perception processes, in relation to our understanding of organizational behaviour.

sources

Arkin, A., 1995, 'Tailoring clothes to suit the image', *People Management*, 24 August, pp. 18–23.

Averett, S. and Korenman, S., 1993, 'The economic reality of the beauty myth', *NBER Working Paper*, no. 4521.

The Economist, 1995, 'Heightism: Short guys finish last', 23 December, pp. 21–6.

Goffman, E., 1959, *The Presentation of Self in Everyday Life*, Doubleday Anchor, New York.

Goss, B. and O'Hair, D., 1988, *Communicating in Interpersonal Relationships*, Macmillan, New York.

Guirdham, M., 1995, *Interpersonal Skills at Work*, Prentice Hall, Hemel Hempstead, 2nd edition.

Hamermesh, D. and Biddle, J., 1993, 'Beauty and the labour market', *NBER Working Paper*, no. 4518.

Martel, L. and Biller, H., 1987, *Stature and Stigma*, D.C. Heath, New York.

Pease, A., 1985, *Body Language: How to Read Others' Thoughts by Their Gestures*, Camel Publishing, Avalon Beach, Australia.

Rosenfeld, P., Giacalone, R.A. and Riordan, C.A., 1995, *Impression Management in Organizations: Theory, Measurement, Practice*, Routledge, London.

Tannen, D., 1990, *You Just Don't Understand: Women and Men in Conversation*, William Morrow, New York.

Tannen, D., 1995, 'The power of talk: Who gets heard and why', *Harvard Business Review*, September–October, pp. 138–48.

Torrington, D., 1991, *Management Face-to-Face*, Prentice Hall, Hemel Hempstead.

Zalkind, S.S. and Costello, T.W., 1962, 'Perception: Some recent research and implications for administration', *Administrative Science Quarterly*, vol. 7, pp. 218–35.

chapter 4 motivation

Latin: *movere*, to move

concepts and learning objectives
motives as goals of human behaviour
motives as individual decision-making processes
the social process of motivating others
empowerment, high performance systems and the new generation
assessment
sources

concepts and learning objectives

Have authoritarian foremen passed into history, or can a similar style be found in organizations today? There was a lot of commentary during the 1990s about 'the new leadership' in organizations, about the need for sensitivity to the 'soft' issues like communication and motivation as well as the 'hard' issues of control and finance. However, Buchanan and Preston (1992, p. 69) quote from their research a typical foreman in an engineering plant in England:

> 'People only come to work for money. You're not telling me that if you just left them they wouldn't go and have a chat or sit down and read the newspaper. If you're telling me that wouldn't happen, then one of us is kidding and it isn't me.'

---

the driving method of supervision

In the American factory at the turn of the century, the foreman had primary responsibility for implementing management's goals: he was the 'undisputed ruler of his department, gang, crew, or ship'.

When in 1912 a congressional committee investigated the United States Steel Corporation, they attempted to understand just how the foremen functioned. They learned that foremen throughout American industry practised something known as 'the driving method', an approach to supervision that combined authoritarian combativeness with physical intimidation in order to extract the maximum effort from the worker.

The driving method was well suited to work that depended upon the consistent exertion of the human body. The foreman's profanity, threats, and punishments were complemented by the workers' methods for limiting output.

from Shoshana Zuboff, 1988, *In the Age of the Smart Machine: The Future of Work and Power*, Heinemann Professional Publishing, Oxford, p. 35.

This engineering company had planned to change the role of the foremen, from traditional 'policemen' to facilitators and coaches. The study revealed that this had not happened and that the foremen retained their directive, policing approach. In the manufacturing cell where the research was conducted, the machinists had pinned up a notice which read: *The floggings will stop when morale improves*. The foremen kept taking this down, but the machinists just pinned it up again. The 'driving method', it seems, is still with us.

Motivation is a perennial organizational problem. The *context* in which this problem arises, however, changes with economic conditions and social values. The organizational context of employee motivation changed dramatically during the 1990s, with increasing job insecurity, with rapid developments in new technology affecting job skills, with the pressures of constant change and unpredictability, and with the work intensification that followed the introduction of new organizational approaches such as 'lean manufacturing' and 'downsizing'. A contemporary expression for 'the driving method' is 'kick ass and take names'. This chapter considers other approaches to motivation.

key concepts

- drives
- subjective probability
- motivation (as an energizing process)
- motivation (as a decision-making process)
- empowerment
- self-actualization
- job enrichment
- high performance work systems
- expectancy theory
- motive
- valence
- motivating potential score

When you have read this chapter, you should be able to define those key concepts in your own words, and you should also be able to:

1 Understand different ways in which the term motivation is used.
2 Understand the nature of motives and motivation processes as influences on behaviour.
3 Use expectancy theory and job enrichment to diagnose organizational problems and to recommend solutions.
4 Explain the renewed interest in this field in the 1990s, with respect to the evolving link between organization strategy and high performance work systems.

motives as goals of human behaviour

What motivates us to act and perform in particular ways? The organizational concern with controlled performance puts a premium on correct answers to this question. Our ability consistently and predictably to design organizations that motivate their members to adequate and superlative levels of performance still seems to be poor. Significant developments have been made in this field over the past 20 years, but the successful application of known methods is patchy as we move into the twenty-first century. One explanation for this may lie with the proliferation of techniques intended to improve employee motivation: facilitative supervision, suggestions schemes, quality circles, job enrichment, employee of the month awards, self-managing teams, performance-related pay and incentives, quality management, corporate entertainment programmes, and so on. Organizations which keep introducing new schemes and techniques, in repeated attempts to improve motivation, may suffer from what has come to be known as the 'BOHICA syndrome'. This acronym stands for Bend Over, Here It Comes Again. In this setting, innovation and change invite cynicism, and are easily dismissed.

We know that fear and money are not necessarily the best ways to motivate people at work. We certainly know that there are many other effective approaches. However, the technique of 'kick ass and take names' seems still to be widely appreciated, practised and experienced. How can we even call this a 'motivational technique'? Consider the following definition.

definition

Motivation *is the internal psychological process of initiating, energizing, directing and maintaining goal-directed behaviour.*

This internal process can be self-initiated, and is also influenced by the actions of others. Intimidation is one way to get somebody to do what you want them to do or, in other words, to energize and direct their behaviour in a particular direction for a specific purpose. Defined in this way, motivation is a broad concept which covers individual preferences (self-defined or defined by others) for particular forms of action, strength of response (half-hearted or enthusiastic), and persistence (in the face of, for example, fatigue or barriers).

We attach reasons to the things that we do. Our behaviour is directed towards particular goals. In other words, our behaviour is purposive. We signal this sense of purpose through our use of language in explaining behaviour. We use terms such as:

- purpose
- aim
- intent

- need
- desire
- plan

- want
- drive
- demand

- plan
- objective
- resolve

We behave as we do because we choose, usually, to do so. We do not simply react passively to factors in our physical and social environment. We process sensory information, impose meaning and order on that information, and make decisions about what we are going to do next and why. We are typically *proactive* rather than reactive. A lot of our day-to-day decision-making is habitual and unconscious, but we have access to our decision-making processes through our ability consciously to reflect on and examine them.

Our needs, purposes and motives are part of our experience. We naturally think of our behaviour as related in meaningful ways to our motives. The need to make sense of behaviour is a particularly strong human motive in its own right. To make sense of the behaviour of others, we attribute motives to them (see definition of *attribution*, and the explanation of attribution theory, in Chapter 3). To claim that someone's behaviour is senseless, thoughtless, mindless or without reasons, is to admit our own ignorance of their motives. We discussed in Chapter 2 the *self-interpreting* nature of human beings. Our motives are a central component of that self-understanding.

The terms 'motive' and 'motivation' are used in everyday conversation in at least three distinct ways. They are used to refer to:

1 The *goals* that people have, or the outcomes they want to reach. Achievement, status, power, friends and money are commonly regarded as important human motives. These ends constitute reasons for acting in particular ways, reasons that lead to behaviours directed towards the achievement of those goals. These are some of the more important outcomes of particular actions in an organizational setting.

2 The *cognitive processes*, or decision-making processes, that lead people to pursue particular outcomes or goals in the first place. We have, or we develop, desires for, say, achievement and friendship, and we develop expectations about the links between our actions and these outcomes. In other words, we acquire an understanding of what we have to do to achieve those goals. These cognitive processes involve the individual in taking *decisions*, or making choices, about what to aim for and how to go about it.

3 The *social processes* through which some individuals try to change the behaviour of others. Managers are usually trying to find ways to get employees to work harder, or to be more co-operative, or to act with more initiative and creativity, and so on. Western industrialized cultures still tend to emphasize the value of wealth and status acquired through hard work and monogamous family life. Most of us learn about, and direct, our desires for money, achievement and sex in these more or less conventional ways. These social processes, therefore, involve attempts to *influence* what other people do.

When we discuss motives and motivation, we must be clear about the sense in which we use the terms: goal-directed behaviour in pursuit of particular outcomes, cognitive processes that concern decision making, or social processes that involve influence attempts. These contrasting perspectives have different implications.

Are the goals that we pursue part of our genetic inheritance, or are they acquired in the processes of our upbringing and wider social experience? This is still a controversial question, and the resolution has profound practical implications. If our motives are innate, then we may be able to do little to change them. We may simply have to tolerate those motives, in ourselves and in others, which we do not like. There is, for example, a long-running debate concerning whether or not humans are innately aggressive. If aggression is given and fixed, then we need to find mechanisms to control the implications of this. However, if we take the view that motives are acquired through social processes, then we need to find social causes and implement social solutions to energize and direct our actions in the pursuit of non-aggressive goals.

Our behaviour is clearly influenced by the biological and physiological equipment with which we are born. We have a strong need for survival which appears to be innate. When deprived of essentials, our needs for oxygen, water, food, shelter, safety, warmth and sex can be overpowering. However, some religious orders impose celibacy on willing members.

Altruism can overcome personal safety needs in extraordinary circumstances, such as war and disaster. The best we can claim is that biological forces are basic determinants of the behaviour of most of us, most of the time. These biological forces, our physiological needs, are known as *drives*, and they come into play when we are deprived, say, of food or water.

---

definition

Drives *are innate, biological determinants of human behaviour activated by deprivation.*

Drives come with the body. We cannot easily will them away. We do not have to learn to be cold, or thirsty or hungry. These drives energize our behaviour when we lack warmth, water or food. It is important to note, however, that there are circumstances in which other goals can displace these drives. We can override the physical needs of the body when our priority is to satisfy intellectual and emotional needs. In other words, cognitive and social motives can override biological drives in certain circumstances.

Drives do not necessarily influence behaviour in direct and predictable ways. The concept of drive is related to that of instinct; when birds build nests, and when squirrels collect nuts, they do so instinctively and in quite specific and repeated ways. An instinct is simply a pre-programmed tendency, an inherited predisposition, to act in a particular manner in pursuit of a specific goal. At one time, psychologists thought that human behaviour could be explained in terms of instincts. However, the number of instincts that have to be postulated runs to thousands, and the variation in behaviour patterns between individuals indicated that this was not a fruitful line of enquiry. The idea that our behaviour is instinctive, pre-programmed and aimed at drive-reduction turns out to be too mechanical and simplistic. We may claim 'I reacted instinctively', and believe that we did. In response to danger, this response is probably accurate. In other circumstances, it is useful to consider the extent to which our responses are at least in part based on learned habits, which have been socially acquired.

Animal behaviour patterns are typically triggered by events in the environment and are dictated by instinct as a computer's functioning is programmed. Birds and squirrels cannot override their programming and remain locked into their niche in nature. The ways in which we, on the other hand, seek to satisfy our biological drives are innumerable and vary from culture to culture. This argument can be illustrated by the differences in eating preferences and habits around the world, and by the vast range of things that people do to satisfy their sex drives. Our behaviour patterns are flexible, or *plastic*.

---

definition

Motives *are learned needs, which influence our behaviour by leading us to pursue particular goals because they are socially valued.*

Much of what we do is clearly influenced by the ways of thinking and behaving typical of the society into which we have been born. Our culture, and in some cases sub-culture, shapes our motives through the values, ideals, standards and modes of behaviour of other people. We seek status because that is the appropriate and accepted thing to do in our society. We seek gainful employment for the same reason. Those behaviours that are typical and conventional tend to become socially necessary, as those who choose not to conform are shunned, ridiculed and are sometimes even imprisoned. In other words, most societies have more or less subtle ways of making life awkward for those who do not comply with social norms. Polygamy is a crime in most Western cultures, but a social norm and a sign of male achievement, wealth and status in parts of the Arab world. In some Muslim countries, the consumption of alcohol carries severe punishment, but a gift of alcohol may be considered a social requirement when invited to dinner in Britain.

There is another feature which distinguishes drives from motives. If we have just eaten, hunger ceases to motivate our behaviour. Our pursuit of food is energized, naturally, by food deprivation. However, if we have made friends and money, or learned something new and interesting, for example, we do not necessarily regard ourselves as having had enough for the time being. We typically strive for more (friends, belongingness, money, status, interesting new knowledge). This distinction between drives and motives can be summarized as follows:

drives	**motives**
are innate	are learned
have a physiological basis	have a social basis
are activated by deprivation	are activated by environment
are aimed at satiation	are aimed at stimulation

However, we noted earlier that human beings tend to be proactive. We are active sensation-seekers as well as passive responders in our environment, an observation that is often overlooked, but which has significant implications in an organizational setting. This proactivity has led some psychologists to claim that we have innate cognitive drives concerning:

sense-making	the need to impose meaning and order on the world around us
effectance, or competency	the need to understand the world around us, to control it, to exert mastery
self-understanding	the need to know better who and what we are
curiosity	the need to explore, to uncover the new, to play, to learn more
order and meaning	the need for certainty, equity, consistency, and predictability in our environment

We must now point out that the distinction between innate biological drives on the one hand, and socially acquired motives on the other, is not as clear-cut as we have suggested. It is difficult to sustain a firm division between biological drives (for food, drink, safety), cognitive drives (competency, self-understanding) and social drives (belongingness). We seek to satisfy our innate drives in ways that are acceptable to our society. If we regard cognitive and social drives as innate, it is clear that in their expression they are socially mediated. The socially accepted ways in which we behave satisfy what may be innate sensation and affiliation and information-seeking motives. We get pleasure from eating, drinking and breathing, but that is not enough. We also get satisfaction from exploring, learning about and influencing the world around us. It has been suggested that these knowledge-seeking motives are the driving force behind scientific enquiry, natural and social. It can also be argued that stimulation and information-seeking have survival value in physical terms. The more we know about the world around us, through any means, the more able we become to survive in it by adapting to it, or by manipulating it to make it more amenable.

The motivation theory of Abraham Maslow integrates the points made so far in this chapter and helps to resolve some of the potential confusion. Maslow argues, in an early article (1943), and two later books (1954; 1971) that we have eight innate needs. The needs which Maslow identified are:

*Abraham Maslow
(1908–70)*

- *biological* needs, for sunlight, sexual expression, food, water, rest and oxygen – in other words, needs basic to our individual and collective survival
- *safety* needs, for security, comfort, tranquillity, freedom from fear, threat from the environment, for shelter, order, predictability, for an organized world
- *affiliation* needs, for attachment, belongingness, affection, giving and receiving love, relationships
- *esteem* needs, for strength, confidence, achievement, self-esteem, adequacy, independence, and also for reputation, prestige, recognition, attention, importance and appreciation – in other words, the need for a stable and high self-evaluation, based on capability and the respect of others
- the need to *know and to understand*, to gain and to systematize knowledge, the need for curiosity, learning, philosophizing, experimenting and exploring
- *aesthetic* needs, for order and beauty

▶ *self-actualization* needs, for the development of our capabilities and potential to their fullest

▶ the need for *transcendence*, a spiritual need, for 'cosmic identification', or 'to be at one with the universe'

(Most texts mention only five, usually omitting aesthetic and transcendence needs which may appear less relevant in an organizational setting.)

---

definition

Abraham Maslow defined **self-actualization** in his 1943 article (p. 382), 'A theory of human motivation', in this way:

> A musician must make music, an artist must paint, a poet must write, if he is to be ultimately happy. What a man can be, he must be. This need we may call self-actualization . . . it refers to the desire for self-fulfilment, namely, to the tendency for him to become actualized in what he is potentially . . . the desire to become more and more what one is, to become everything that one is capable of becoming.

The biological and safety needs are essential to human existence. If they are not satisfied, we die. Love and esteem needs involve our relationships with others. If these needs are satisfied, we feel self-confident, capable and adequate. We feel useful and wanted in the world. If these needs are not satisfied, we feel inferior, helpless and discouraged, and these emotional responses can in turn lead to mental disorder.

Self-actualization and 'transcendence', Maslow argued, are ultimate human goals. He also argued, however, that fully satisfied and self-actualized people were rare. He felt that establishing the conditions appropriate for enabling people to develop their capabilities to this extent was a challenging social and organizational problem. In the organizational behaviour literature, the spiritual, metaphysical concept of transcendence has been largely ignored. Establishing the preconditions for self-actualization seems challenging enough.

Abraham Maslow's need hierarchy

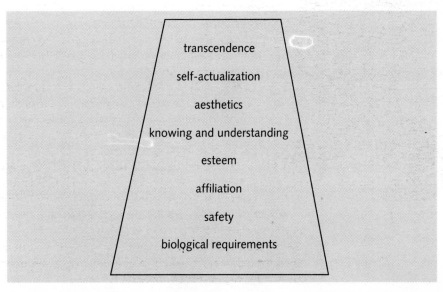

Just to complicate matters further, Maslow postulated a ninth need, the need for *freedom of enquiry and expression*, arguing that this was an essential *prerequisite* for the satisfaction of the other needs. As a 'prerequisite', this need is also often missing from textbook accounts of his theory. However, this need can be significant, both in a wider cultural context (there are wide variations between countries with respect to such freedoms) and in an organizational setting (where free enquiry and expression is frequently constrained by organizational procedure, rules, and social norms).

Maslow argued that these needs may be organized in a loose hierarchy, with basic biological and safety needs at the bottom, and self-actualization and transcendence needs at the top.

This hierarchy, he further argued, has a number of interesting properties.

1 A need is not an effective motivator until those lower in the hierarchy are more or less satisfied. You are less likely to be concerned by the sharks (safety need), if you are drowning (lack of oxygen, a biological requirement), and even less likely in such circumstances to be concerned about striking a good first impression with a new friend.

2 A satisfied need is not likely to be a particularly strong motivator. If you are well fed and safe, you cease to be preoccupied with food and shelter and turn your thoughts elsewhere. We would presumably find it difficult in these circumstances to energize and direct your behaviour significantly with offers of more food and shelter. Once deprived, absolutely or relatively, of these comforts, they become energizing inducements once again.

3 Dissatisfaction of these needs affects our mental health. This is a controversial argument. Consider the frustration, anxiety and depression that can arise from lack of self-esteem and low self-confidence, loss of the respect of others, an inability to form and to sustain loving relationships and an inability to develop one's capabilities. Frustration, anxiety and depression can in turn lead to a range of behaviours, some healthy (positively to deal with the problem) and some less so (leading possibly to mental ill health). Maslow's mental health argument is intuitively appealing, but be aware of the controversy, as an exploration of the rich but inconclusive evidence is beyond the scope of this text.

4 We have an innate desire to 'work our way up' the hierarchy of needs, pursuing the satisfaction of our 'higher order' needs once our basic or 'lower order' needs are more or less satisfied.

5 The experience of self-actualization stimulates the desire for more. Once we have eaten, we stop thinking about food for a while. Not so, argued Maslow, with respect to self-actualization. He claimed that self-actualizers have what he termed 'peak experiences'. When you have had one of these,

STOP!

» Can you recognize the needs in Maslow's hierarchy in your own actions?
» Can you identify the things that you do to satisfy each of those eight needs?
» At what points in the hierarchy are you currently concentrating?
» From your experience, perhaps in your current position and/or educational institution, what have you observed about the ways in which organizations help and block their members in meeting needs for esteem, knowing and understanding, aesthetics, self-actualization, and freedom of enquiry?

you want more. The need for self-actualization, therefore, cannot be satisfied in the same way as the other needs in the hierarchy.

Maslow's theory can easily be translated into a set of prescriptions for meeting needs in an organizational setting. This can be seen in the following list to which you may, from your experience, be able to add, so there are a couple of blanks.

these needs:	can be met by:
transcendence	… ? …
self-actualization	▶ challenging new job assignments ▶ discretion over core work activities ▶ scope to develop and introduce new ideas ▶ promotion opportunities … ? …
aesthetics	▶ encouraging and rewarding creativity ▶ well-designed organizational buildings ▶ well-designed working environments … ? …
knowing and understanding	▶ opportunities and encouragement for learning ▶ open communications, across hierarchy ▶ access to information, at all levels ▶ regular constructive feedback on performance … ? …
esteem	▶ regular positive feedback ▶ prestige job title ▶ your photograph in the in-house magazine ▶ promotion … ? …
affiliation	▶ sports and social clubs and events ▶ office parties, barbecues, outings ▶ encouraging open communication ▶ developing collaborative teamwork … ? …
safety	▶ safe working conditions ▶ 'no redundancy' policy ▶ attractive pension provisions ▶ private health insurance cover … ? …
biological requirements	▶ good working conditions (warm, dry, well-lit) ▶ attractive wage or salary ▶ subsidized (or free) catering … ? …

> **STOP!**
>
> To what extent is it realistic to expect an organization to address all of these needs, systematically? Can it be argued that the satisfaction of any of these needs is not an organizational responsibility?

Maslow did not intend this hierarchy to be regarded as a rigid description of the development of human motivation. He offered this as a typical picture of what might happen under ideal (and, therefore, rarely attained) social or organizational conditions. As different individuals, we regard the needs in this list or hierarchy in different ways. A lot depends on your past successes and failures in trying to satisfy them. Some of us seek self-actualization at the expense of our love needs. Some of us put affiliation needs before almost everything else. Some of us even pursue creativity at the cost of personal safety and survival. Traumatic and depressing experiences can potentially affect an individual such that they become 'blocked' at one level in the hierarchy. Lengthy deprivation of a particular need may lead the individual to

Cartoon by S. Gross

overemphasize that need, to concentrate on its satisfaction so they are not deprived again – but at the expense of not satisfying other needs. The emphasis we place on each need may change with time, with age and with our accumulated experience. Most of us pursue several needs, to greater or lesser degrees, at the same time.

There seem to be two main problems with Maslow's theory of motivation.

First, it is difficult to see how it can predict behaviour. The amount of satisfaction that has to be achieved before one may progress from one step to the next in the hierarchy is difficult to define and measure. If we could take measurements, the extent to which different people emphasize different needs would make our predictions shaky. The theory is vague.

Second, this psychological theory is more like a social philosophy. We can produce evidence to show that some, if not many, people pursue these needs. Some of us perhaps pursue them in the order that Maslow suggested. It is still

---

Maslow and American middle-class values

The Islamic model of the individual identifies three sets of basic needs (Nusair, 1985). *Spiritual* needs concern love, belongingness, trust, security, faith, loyalty and recognition. *Intellectual* needs concern knowledge, thinking, observation, perception, experiment and speculation. *Physiological* needs concern food, water, shelter, health and money. Compare this expression of fundamental needs with that of Maslow.

Islam considers the human psyche as a three-part hierarchy:

mutmainna: self-fulfilment, complete satisfaction and full security

lawama: self-reproach, conscience, resistance, repentance and self-consciousness

ammara: evil-prone, impulsive, headstrong and passionate

Culture and economic conditions also have a profound influence on motivation. Peter Blunt (1983, p. 61) concludes that, 'in developing countries, where political and socio-economic systems may be regarded as less stable and more problematic, managers report much higher levels of need dissatisfaction than managers in relatively developed countries'. In particular, research suggests that:

- Liberian managers report high dissatisfaction with security needs.
- Kenyan (Kikuyu) managers attach high importance to security needs.
- Indian culture encourages managers to prioritize security needs.
- Middle Eastern executives in contrast attach little importance to security needs.

The Igbo in Nigeria are more economically successful and occupy a disproportionately high number of senior management positions in contrast to the Hausa of northern Nigeria. The Igbo show more initiative and readiness to explore new places and ideas; this can be potentially explained as a response to acute land shortage.

Blunt (1983, p. 74) further concludes that, in Africa, while there are cultural differences, the emphasis on security needs is predominant:

. . . mainly because more basic needs have yet to be satisfied. A lower-level Yoruba or Luo or Xhosa worker is unlikely to care very much about self-actualization or his growth needs if he has difficulty feeding, clothing and housing himself and his family on the money that he earns.

unclear, however, whether the 'higher order' needs (beyond biology and safety) are innate or learned. This is a 'good' theory, to the extent that it has 'face validity': it feels right. Would the world not be a much better place if what Maslow proposed were true? Maslow may have been reflecting, at least in part, American middle-class values and the pursuit of the good life, and it is tempting to see reflected in his hierarchy of needs some of the deprivations of the Second World War and its aftermath – during which time Maslow was writing about this. This may not, therefore, be a statement of fundamental truths about human psychology.

However, criticism aside, Maslow's work has been extremely influential and has stimulated a lot of further thinking and research on the issue of motivation. It has also led a number of organizations to change their practices for motivating employees in ways that most of us would consider beneficial. It is a pleasant theory, and if it is a prescriptive social philosophy, we can at least evaluate it and consider how far we are from the ideal that it specifies, and what we might have to do to get there should we wish to do so.

More important, Maslow is clearly right to draw attention to the fact that our actions are influenced by a range of motives. He also demonstrated that people behave in ways that they believe to be intrinsically valuable and independent of material reward. It is significant for the study of organizational behaviour to examine the motivating potential of money in this context.

motives as individual decision-making processes

We do not seem to come into the world with a mental package neatly labelled 'motives', containing the goals that we are predestined to pursue. Different people are motivated by different outcomes. Different cultures encourage different patterns of motivation in their members. We thus appear to have some choice of motives, and the means of achieving them, although social conditions may push us in some directions and inhibit others.

Maslow's theory is called a *content* theory because it adopts a package approach to human motivation, specifying the contents of the package. It is possible to suggest other sets of contents for this package, and other commentators have indeed done so. Content theories are all open to the criticism, however, that they tend not to recognize either individual choice or social influence. Maslow's theory is also called a *universalist* theory because he argued that it applied to everyone. Universal theories of human behaviour attract similar criticisms. They cannot easily explain differences between individuals and between cultures.

---

definition

Motivation *can also be defined as the cognitive, decision-making process through which the individual chooses desired outcomes, and sets in motion the actions appropriate to their achievement.*

A motive is an outcome that has become desirable for a given individual. The process through which outcomes become desirable and are pursued is explained by the *expectancy theory* of motivation. This is a *process* theory, because it does not assume that we come complete with a package of ready-defined motives to pursue.

Motivation theories are divided into two broad and opposing groups, each dominated by a different philosophical perspective on human nature (see the discussion in Chapter 1). Behaviourist, or 'stimulus–response', theories consider behaviour to be reflexive and instinctive, driven by inherited and unconscious drives and instincts. Cognitive theories assume that we are aware of our goals and our behaviours, and consider us to be purposive and rational in our actions.

Edward Chace Tolman (1886–1961)
Photo source:
Archives of the History of American Psychology, The University of Akron, Ohio, USA.

Expectancy theory is a cognitive theory. It was developed by the American psychologist Edward C. Tolman in the 1930s as a challenge to the behaviourist perspectives of his contemporaries. Tolman argued that behaviour is directed by the conscious *expectations* that we have about our behaviour leading to the achievement of desired outcomes. That is why it is called expectancy theory.

Expectancy theory is a general theory of motivation, which has been applied to work settings by a number of organizational psychologists. The theory was initially used by Georgopoulos, Mahoney and Jones in 1957 in a study of the work performance of over 600 employees in a household appliance company. They called their theory a 'path–goal approach to productivity' because they assumed that motivation to work productively depended on the individual's needs (goals), and the expectation of fulfilling those needs through productive behaviour (paths).

In other words, productivity has to be seen as a path to valued outcomes. Behaviour depends on the outcomes that an individual values, and the expectation that a particular type of behaviour will lead to those outcomes. If an individual needs more money and expects to be given more money for working hard, then we can predict that the individual will probably decide to work hard. If the same individual expects that hard work will win pleasant smiles from the boss and will not bring in more cash, then we can predict that the individual will decide not to work hard (unless the boss's smile is indeed a valued outcome). In expectancy theory, we are assumed to behave in ways that are *instrumental* to the achievement of our valued goals.

Georgopoulos, Mahoney and Jones found that workers who expected high productivity to lead to valued goals tended to produce at a higher level than workers who felt that low production led to valued goals. Suppose the individual values the friendship of colleagues at work and expects that outstanding work performance will anger those friends, by forcing them, perhaps, to work at a more intensified rate too. We can explain and predict the individual's low production in terms of particular valued goals and expectations of achieving or frustrating those goals. (Chapter 9 explores more fully the mechanisms by which group norms influence individual motivation and behaviour at work.) Returning to the household appliance assemblers, the researchers established that their most important goals were:

▶ Making more money in the long run.
▶ Getting along well with the work group.
▶ Promotion to a higher wage rate.

Victor H. Vroom

Another American psychologist, Victor H. Vroom, produced in 1964 the first systematic formulation of an expectancy theory of work motivation. His approach offers a way of measuring human motivation, using the two key concepts of *valence* and *subjective probability*.

---

definition

Valence *is the degree of preference that an individual has for a particular outcome.*

As one may either seek, or seek to avoid, certain outcomes, or be ambivalent about them, valence can be positive, negative or neutral. Valence can thus, potentially, be measured.

---

definition

Subjective probability *is the individual's expectation that particular behaviour will lead to particular outcomes.*

We differ in our expectations or estimations of the relationships between behaviour and outcomes, so these estimations are *subjective*. Expressed in terms of probability, this expectation may vary from 0 to 1, from no chance at all to certainty. The strength of our motivation to behave in a particular way thus depends both on the valence of the outcome and on our subjective probability of achieving it.

---

definition

Expectancy theory *is a theory of motivation which argues that the strength or 'force' of an individual's motivation to act in a particular way can be expressed as:*

$$M = E \times V$$

where M = motivation to behave,
E = the subjective probability or expectation that the behaviour will lead to a particular outcome,
V = the valence, or strength of preference, for the outcome.

This is also known as the **expectancy equation**.

In most circumstances, however, a number of different outcomes will result from particular ways of behaving. Working hard can affect one's financial reward, friendships at work, status, levels of fitness or fatigue, and social life beyond the organizational setting, and so on. The expectancy equation thus has to be summed across all of these possible outcomes. The full *expectancy equation*, therefore, is:

$$M = \Sigma (E \times V)$$

The sign Σ is the Greek letter sigma, which here means 'add up all the values of the calculation in the brackets'.

Expectancy and valence are multiplied, not added together, because when either E or V is zero, then the motivation force will also be zero, and this is what we would expect. If we add expectancy and valence, we get unrealistic results. If you believe that a particular behaviour will certainly lead to a particular outcome, but place no value on that outcome, then you will not be motivated to behave in that way. On the other hand, if you place a high value on a goal, but expect that the probability of attaining it is zero, your motivation will again be zero. Only when both the terms in the expectancy equation are positive will the motivating force be positive.

The full calculation thus has to take into account all the values – positive, neutral and negative – that the individual places on the range of outcomes. The individual may expect that hard work will lead to more money, smiles from the boss and loss of friends. Money may be valued highly, smiles from the boss may count for nothing and friendships lost may cause some discomfort. Someone else in the same circumstances may place different valences on these outcomes and, as a consequence, behave differently. The calculation also has to take into account the different probabilities or levels of expectation that the individual has of achieving these outcomes. You may expect that hard work will certainly not lead to more money, will definitely lead to more smiles from the boss and will almost certainly cost you some friendships.

We can do this simple calculation for the individual's motivation to work hard, and then do the same calculation for the motivation to take it easy and relax at work. The higher M value should tell us which behaviour the individual will adopt. The absolute value of the M number itself tells us very little. It is useful when compared with the results of calculations for other behaviours that the individual may choose to adopt, and for comparison with similar calculations for others.

This process theory of motivation, expectancy theory, is more complex and more difficult to understand than the straightforward content theory of Maslow. We have introduced a lot of new and unusual terms in a short space. Let us sum up what we have covered so far:

- Expectancy theory states that behaviour results from a conscious decision-making process based on the individual's *subjective probability* – the *perceptions* that the individual has about the different results of alternative behaviours.
- Expectancy theory, because it is based on individual perceptions, helps to explain *individual differences* in motivation and behaviour, unlike Maslow's universal content theory of motivation.
- Expectancy theory attempts to *measure* the strength of the individual's motivation to behave in particular ways.
- Expectancy theory is based on the assumption that behaviour is to some degree rational, and that we are consciously aware of our goals or motives. As we take into account the probable outcomes of our behaviour, and place values on these outcomes, expectancy theory attempts to *predict* individual behaviour.

Expectancy theory is complex. Do we really carry out the analysis implied by the theory before we choose to behave in a particular way? Are we indeed capable of carrying out such a calculation? Edward Lawler emphasizes that, although we may be rational, our rationality is limited. Our behaviour is based on perceptions that are simplified by taking into account only a limited

STOP!

Behaviour depends on the outcomes that an individual values, and the expectation that a particular type of behaviour will lead to those outcomes.

Will you work hard for your organizational behaviour course?

We can use expectancy theory to predict the answer to this question.

first	List the outcomes that you expect will result from working hard for your organizational behaviour course, such as: 1 high assignment and exam marks 2 bare pass 3 sleepless nights 4 no social life 5 poor grades in other subjects 6 ? 7 ?
second	Rate the value that you place on each of those outcomes, giving those you like a score of up to $+10$, those you dislike a score down to -10, and a zero for those for which you are neutral (the choice of value range is arbitrary, and you could score your valences from $+100$ to -100 if you thought that would be appropriate).
third	Estimate the probability of attaining each of those outcomes, giving those which are certain the value 1, those which are most unlikely the value 0, and those for which there is an even chance the value 0.5. Estimate other probabilities as you perceive or judge them at other values between 0 and 1; these are your E values.
fourth	Now put your E and V values into the expectancy equation: $$M = \Sigma(E \times V)$$ and add up the result.
fifth	Compare your *M* score with the scores of colleagues on your course. We predict that: ▸ those with higher scores are the course 'swots'; ▸ those with higher scores will get higher assignment and exam grades.
finally	1 Are we really as rational, in making behavioural choices like this, as expectancy theory implies? 2 Is this a realistic attempt to measure and quantify the strength of your motivation? 3 How can work experience influence someone's subjective probabilities, the outcomes that they value, and the strength of those preferences?

Edward E. Lawler III

number of factors and options. Our behaviour is 'satisficing' rather than 'maximizing', and Lawler argues that expectancy theory is suitable for analyzing and illustrating this.

Expectancy theory suggests how some goals, through experience, may come to be desirable for the individual. This does not mean that we have to drop Maslow's approach altogether. Many of the outcomes that we are likely to want to pursue are in Maslow's hierarchy. Whether we are born with these, or whether we adopt them as the current values and circumstances of our society, we can still feed them into the expectancy equation as potentially valued outcomes. The process and content theories of motivation are not necessarily mutually exclusive approaches to the explanation and understanding of motivation. They each have something distinctive to contribute to our knowledge of why people act the way they do.

Expectancy theory has been influential in stimulating research, and in providing a tool for diagnosing and helping to resolve organizational problems. Our experience in an organization constitutes a significant influence on our perceptions, that is, on how we work out the expectancy equation in relation to our behaviour. We learn from experience and observation the rewards that are available and the outcomes that are not open to us. We come to recognize what actions are rewarded in a particular organizational setting, and we come to recognize behaviours that are ignored, overlooked or perhaps sanctioned. We emulate the former; we avoid the latter. It is, therefore, possible to identify features of organizational life that influence people's expectations and valences. If these features lead to dissatisfaction and poor performance, then it should be possible to identify and change them. One of the main ways in which expectancy theory has contributed to organizational practice is through the technique of job enrichment, explored in the following section.

the social process of motivating others

We have looked at motivation from two of the three perspectives outlined at the beginning of the chapter. First, we considered motivation in terms of the *goals* or outcomes towards which behaviour is directed. Second, we considered motivation as the *cognitive decision process* through which those goals are selected and pursued. Our third perspective explores motivation as a *social process* which involves influencing the behaviour of others.

Motivation in an organizational setting is a social process in which some members try to influence others, to work harder, work smarter, work more effectively. Organizations as social arrangements are dependent on being able to motivate people to join up in the first place, to stay with the organization, and to perform at acceptable levels. Organization managers are thus very interested in theories of motivation in the hope that they will discover techniques for encouraging employees, and indeed other managers, to work competently and generally act in a loyal, committed, flexible and innovative manner when appropriate.

A significant proportion of manual jobs on factory shop floors, and clerical jobs in offices, have been designed throughout this century using a method advocated by an American engineer called Frederick Taylor. His influential

diagnosing and resolving an organizational problem using expectancy theory

One of the answers to the organizational dilemma defined in Chapter 1 is to involve employees in management decisions affecting the organization and their jobs in it. This is called 'participative management'. Linda Neider studied whether or not participative management increases employee performance. Neider studied attempts to increase the sales of 110 clerks in four retail shops. The chain that owned the shops had a history of employee dissatisfaction with pay and company policies. Managers were not participative.

One store set up discussion groups to examine and to resolve grievances about work methods and conditions. A second store set up a 'cafeteria' incentive scheme, where employees could choose from a range of rewards, as well as basic pay, for good sales records. These rewards included cinema tickets, days off with pay, and being assistant manager for a week. A third store had both the discussion groups and the incentive scheme. A fourth store was not changed in any way, and had neither.

- The store with the discussion groups and the cafeteria incentive scheme had the sharpest rise in sales.
- The fourth store then went through the full treatment, with similarly impressive results.
- The participation and incentive schemes, on their own and in the other two stores, had no significant effects on sales.

Using expectancy theory, Neider argues that people only work well when:

- They expect their efforts to lead to good performance.
- They expect rewards for good performance.
- They value these rewards.

The cafeteria incentive scheme gave employees a choice of rewards and covered the third of these conditions. Employees who are not sure what to do to perform well, and who perhaps do not know what level of performance is considered to be 'good', need participative managers to tell them. In other words, management behaviour influences the expectations of employees about the consequences of their efforts.

based on Linda Neider, 1980, 'An experimental field investigation utilizing an expectancy theory view of participation', *Organizational Behaviour and Human Performance*, vol. 26, no. 3, pp. 425–42.

work is examined in detail in Chapter 12. Taylor's 'scientific management' technique for designing jobs was as follows:

1. Decide on the optimum degree of *task fragmentation*. This means breaking down a complex job into its simple component parts. The job of assembling a table lamp, for example, can be fragmented into the elements of fixing the base to the stem, fitting the bulb holder, mounting the shade, fixing the flex, wiring the plug, and inserting the bulb.
2. Decide the *one best way* to perform each part of the work efficiently. Studies should be carried out to find the most effective method for doing each of the fragmented tasks that have been identified, and for designing the layout of the workplace and the design of any tools that are to be used.

3   *Train* employees to carry out these simple and fragmented tasks precisely in the one best way that has been identified.

STOP!

Imagine that you are employed on a job in which you repeat precisely the same simple task every thirty seconds, perhaps wiring plugs for lamps, 9.00 am until 5.30 pm, every day (with a lunch break), five or perhaps six days a week. Maybe you have done work like this before?

Describe your likely emotional responses to work of this kind.

Do you think that it is *inevitable* that some jobs just have to be like this, given the nature of work and technology, and the need to keep quality high and costs low?

The advantages of task fragmentation include:
- Employees do not need expensive and time-consuming training.
- Specialization in one small task makes employees very proficient through repetition.
- Lower pay can be given for such unskilled work.
- Some of the problems of achieving controlled performance are simplified.

The disadvantages, however, include:
- The work can be extremely repetitive and boring.
- The individual's contribution to the organization is meaningless and insignificant.
- Monotony leads to apathy, dissatisfaction and carelessness.
- The employee develops no skills that might lead to promotion.

Taylor's approach to job design appears to create efficient ways of working. However, it creates fragmented jobs that are dissatisfying and that do not stimulate motivation. So, there are economic and social reasons for rejecting Taylor's methods. One popular technique derived from work motivation theory, largely as an antidote to Taylorism, is *job enrichment*.

---

definition

Job enrichment *is a technique for broadening the experience of work to enhance employee need satisfaction and to improve work motivation and performance.*

Expectancy theory can be used to aid understanding of a range of human behaviours. Edward Lawler and his colleagues have been concerned mainly with its relevance to questions of work motivation and performance. The experience of work can affect the individual's perceptions of the terms of the expectancy equation. By changing the design of a job, and thus changing the experience of those performing that work, it is possible to change individuals' perceptions and to create a different expectancy calculation. The organizational aim, typically, is to create an expectancy calculation which increases need satisfaction and improves performance.

The design of an individual's job determines both the kinds of rewards available and what the individual has to do to get those rewards. Intrinsic rewards are valued outcomes within the control of the individual, such as feelings of satisfaction and accomplishment. For some of us, and for some actions, 'the outcome is its own reward', an intrinsic reward. Mountaineers, poets, athletes, painters and musicians are usually familiar with the concept of intrinsic reward (very few people ever get paid for climbing hills, and there are very few rich poets on this planet, for example). Extrinsic rewards are valued outcomes that are controlled by others, such as recognition, promotion, and salary increases. The relationships between performance and intrinsic reward are usually more immediate and direct than those between performance and extrinsic reward. Lawler thus argues that intrinsic rewards are more important influences on our motivation to work.

---

eat what you kill: do incentive schemes improve motivation and performance?

Performance-related payment schemes flourished in the 1990s as organizations tried to find new ways to motivate employees. These schemes link financial rewards to the achievement of performance targets. Alfie Kohn argues that these 'eat what you kill' incentive schemes are based on a false psychological assumption. People do not perform better when paid more, and may even perform worse. His argument is based on six observations:

1 Money helps us to meet many of our needs, but research reveals that money is not an overriding concern for most people.

2 Pay that is dependent on performance ('If they have to bribe me to do this . . .') is manipulative and heightens the perception of being controlled.

3 Competition for rewards can disrupt relationships between individuals whose collective performance would be improved by co-operation, but is damaged by rivalry.

4 Dependence on financial incentives to improve productivity diverts attention from attempts to understand and solve the underlying problems facing an organization.

5 Incentive schemes discourage risk-taking, experiment and creative exploration, by sending and reinforcing the signal, 'do exactly what you are told'.

6 Rewards that are contingent on particular levels of performance undermine interest in the job itself, but intrinsic motivation is usually the real basis of exceptional work.

Kohn concludes that performance-related pay schemes are based on a misunderstanding of the nature of extrinsic and intrinsic motivation. These two aspects of motivation cannot be 'added', and it is not simply a case of 'targeting' the behaviours that will attract additional bonuses. Extrinsic rewards buy compliance, and do not encourage long-term commitment:

> The more we experience being controlled, the more we will tend to lose interest in what we are doing. If we go to work thinking about the possibility of getting a bonus, we come to feel that our work is not self-directed. Rather it is the reward that drives our behaviour. . . . anything presented as a prerequisite for something else – that is, as a means toward another end – comes to be seen as less desirable. (p. 62)

based on Alfie Kohn, 1993, 'Why incentive plans cannot work', *Harvard Business Review*, vol. 71, no. 5, pp. 54–63, and *The Economist*, 'Just deserts', January 1994, p. 77.

Job design can affect the outcomes that the individual values. The individual discovers through experience in different jobs and organizations what kinds of outcomes to expect. It is thus possible that changes in work experience can change our perceptions of what is available, thus shaping the outcomes valued by a particular individual. In other words, our current subjective probabilities are a function of past experience.

The design of jobs can thus have a significant impact on the terms of the expectancy equation. The *job characteristics model* shown below is the basis of the job enrichment strategy of the expectancy theorists.

The job characteristics model sets out the links between the features of jobs, the individual's experience of those features and the results in terms of motivation, satisfaction and performance. This model also takes into account individual differences in the desire for personal growth and development. The theory labels this 'growth need strength', and this is broadly what Maslow described as the need for self-actualization. Your growth need strength is an indicator of your readiness to respond positively to an enriched job. The validity of the causal chain, from job design, through individual experience, to performance outcomes, is determined by growth need strength. Enriched

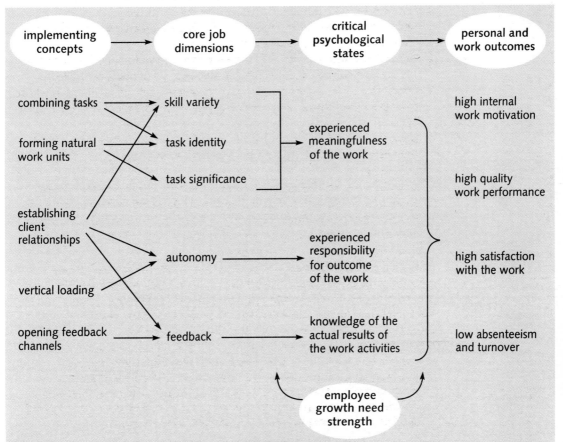

adapted from J.R. Hackman, G. Oldham, R. Janson and K. Purdy, 1975, *California Management Review*, vol. 17, no. 4, p. 62. Reprinted by permission of the Regents of the University of California.

jobs will *not*, according to the theory, lead to the performance outcomes with employees whose growth need strength is low. This is a contingent model, not a universalist one.

At the heart of this model is the proposition that jobs can be analyzed in terms of five *core dimensions* which are defined as follows:

1 *Skill variety* is the extent to which a job makes use of different skills and abilities.
2 *Task identity* is the extent to which a job involves a 'whole' and meaningful piece of work.
3 *Task significance* is the extent to which a job affects the work of other organization members, or other people in society.
4 *Autonomy* is the extent to which a job gives the individual freedom, independence, and discretion in carrying it out.
5 *Feedback* is the extent to which information about the level of performance attained is related back to the individual.

The content of a job can be assessed on these five core dimensions. Hackman and Oldham (1974) produced a Job Diagnostic Survey for this purpose. This questionnaire asks employees to respond to questions about aspects of their work, and of their reactions to it. For example, skill variety and autonomy are measured by the questions:

▶ How much *variety* is there in your job ? That is, to what extent does the job require you to do many different things at work, using a variety of your skills and talents?

▶ How much *autonomy* is there in your job ? That is, to what extent does your job permit you to decide *on your own* how to go about doing the work?

For each question, a seven-point scale runs from 'very little', through 'moderate' variety or autonomy, to 'very much'. One section of the Job Diagnostic Survey asks respondents how much they '*would like*' the presence of certain (i.e. growth-related) conditions in their work. The following section asks respondents to express their relative preference for pairs of hypothetical jobs, such as a job where one is required to make important decisions, versus a job with lots of pleasant people to work with. Through these two kinds of questions, dealing with work preferences, the individual's growth need strength is measured.

In terms of our discussion of research methods in Chapter 2, the Job Diagnostic Survey provides *operational definitions* of the variables in the job characteristics model. The core job dimensions are the independent variables in the theory, and the critical psychological states and performance outcomes are the dependent variables. The variable 'employee growth need strength', which is also operationalized in the Job Diagnostic Survey, is known as a *mediating variable* in this causal chain. Discussing the use of this questionnaire, Hackman and Oldham point out that respondents 'must be moderately literate', that 'the instrument is readily fakeable', and that it 'is not recommended for use in diagnosing the jobs of single individuals'.

The Job Diagnostic Survey can thus be used to establish how motivating a job is, by permitting the calculation of a *motivating potential score*, from answers across groups of employees on the same job, on those seven-point scales.

---

definition

The **motivating potential score** *for a particular job is the result of the following equation, where the values of each of the variables have been measured using the Job Diagnostic Questionnaire:*

$$MPS = \frac{skill\ variety + task\ identity + task\ significance}{3} \times autonomy \times feedback$$

Autonomy and feedback are considered, according to the theory, as more important in their motivating influence than the other three core job dimensions. The equation is designed to reflect this, by treating them as separate components, and by treating as one component the mean of the ratings for skill variety, task identity and task significance. If one of the three main components in this equation is low, then the motivating potential score will be low. A near-zero rating on either autonomy or feedback would pull the score down disproportionately (remember that $5 + 0 = 5$, but $5 \times 0 = 0$). Note, however, that a near-zero rating on either variety, identity or significance would not have such a significant effect on the overall score.

The five core dimensions stimulate the three psychological states critical to high work motivation, job satisfaction and performance. These states are defined as follows:

1 *Experienced meaningfulness* is the extent to which the individual considers the work to be meaningful, valuable and worthwhile.
2 *Experienced responsibility* is the extent to which the individual feels accountable for the work output.
3 *Knowledge of results* is the extent to which individuals know and understand how well they are performing.

Jobs that have high motivating potential scores are more likely to lead their incumbents to the experience of those critical psychological states than jobs that have low scores. Expectancy theorists argue that all three critical psychological states must be experienced if the personal and work outcomes on the right-hand side of the model are to be fully achieved. One or two of the three is not good enough. It is important to recall that individuals who put a low value on personal growth and development – whose growth need strength is low – will not respond in the way suggested by the model. No point, then, in offering them enriched jobs, unless one believes that experience of personal development can in itself stimulate growth need.

The model also shows how the motivating potential of jobs can be improved by applying five *implementing concepts*. These are:

1 *Combining tasks*: Give employees more than one part of the work to do. This increases the variety of the job and increases the contribution that the individual makes to the product or service. For example, all typists could handle short memos, letters and major reports instead of having separate groups of typists each specializing in one of these kinds of task.
2 *Forming natural work units*: Give employees a meaningful sequence of work to perform, rather than a fragmented part of what is required. This increases the contribution that the individual makes to the work, and increases the

significance of the job. For example, groups of motor car assemblers could be assigned to cover all the tasks concerned with a particular stage of the process, such as fitting the engine, or fitting the interior trim or electrics, rather than each performing a single repetitive element on the assembly track.

3 *Establishing client relationships*: Give employees responsibility for making personal contact with others within and outside the organization for whom and with whom they work. This increases variety, gives the person freedom in performing the work and also increases the opportunities for receiving feedback. For example, members of staff working in a hospital pharmacy could each be allocated to one or more specific wards in the hospital, and deal directly with the doctors, nurses and patients on 'their' wards, rather than making anonymous contact, with all task allocations by the pharmacy manager, on a 'first come first served by whoever is free at the time' basis.

4 *Vertical loading*: Give employees responsibilities normally allocated to supervisors. Such additional responsibilities include granting discretion for:

▶ work scheduling	▶ work methods	▶ problem-solving
▶ quality checks	▶ training others	▶ cost control
▶ work times and breaks	▶ deciding priorities	▶ recruitment decisions

This gives individuals increased autonomy in their work and can be achieved by removing the supervisory role altogether, or by redesigning it to involve activities other than direct supervision, such as training, coaching and liaising with other departments. During the 1990s vertical loading and other similar approaches to increasing employee discretion, have come to be called *empowerment*. The multinational electronics company Hewlett Packard uses the acronym LTPMTD, which stands for 'Let The People Make The Decisions'.

5 *Opening feedback channels*: Give employees direct relationships with 'clients' (see factor 3) and also to direct performance summaries. This is aimed at improving opportunities for feedback of the results of work activity. University lecturers are now often provided with performance evaluation data collected from students, during and towards the end of each module that they teach. Performance feedback, in any setting, lets people know how well they are doing, and provides a basis for performance improvement. We shall examine in Chapter 5 how timely and appropriate feedback is critical to the learning process.

The technique of job enrichment and the concept of vertical loading were first 'invented' by the American psychologist Frederick Herzberg in the 1950s. To find out what characteristics of work influenced job satisfaction and dissatisfaction, 203 Pittsburgh engineers and accountants were interviewed and asked 'critical incident' questions. They were asked to recall events which had made them feel good about their work and events which had made them feel bad about it.

Content analysis of these critical incidents suggested that the factors which led to satisfaction were different from those which led to dissatisfaction at work. Herzberg called this a 'two factor theory of motivation'.

Frederick Herzberg (b. 1923)

·The events which led to satisfaction were called 'motivators' or 'content factors' and were:

- achievement
- recognition
- responsibility
- advancement
- growth
- the work itself

The events which led to dissatisfaction were called 'hygiene' or 'context factors' and were:

- salary
- company policy
- supervision
- status
- security
- working conditions

Improvement in the hygiene factors, Herzberg concluded, might remove dissatisfaction, but would not increase satisfaction and motivation. The redesign of jobs to increase motivation and performance should thus focus on the motivators. Herzberg suggested the application of seven *vertical job loading factors* to achieve job enrichment. Herzberg's loading factors are:

- Remove controls.
- Introduce new tasks.
- Increase accountability.
- Allocate special assignments.
- Create natural work units.
- Grant additional authority.
- Provide direct feedback.

STOP!

Compare the theories of Maslow, Hackman and Oldham, and Herzberg with respect to their implications for job design and job enrichment. What are the main similarities and differences?

Apply Herzberg's critical incident questioning technique to your own work experience. Recall a time when you felt particularly satisfied. Why – and what were the circumstances? Recall a time when you felt particularly dissatisfied. Why – and what were the circumstances? Compare your replies with those of colleagues. To what extent do your answers support Herzberg's conclusions about content and context factors?

What issues would you consider in assessing the internal and external validity of Herzberg's research design and method?

Herzberg's approach to job enrichment has probably been written about more often than it has been applied in practice. However, a number of successful applications were reported during the 1960s and 1970s. The popularity of job enrichment apparently waned during the 1980s, as the industrialized economies of Europe and America became more preoccupied with the problems of unemployment. However, work enrichment and empowerment methods enjoyed a renewed popularity in the 1990s.

In America, the best publicized applications of job enrichment were at American Telephone and Telegraph which conducted nineteen job enrichment projects between 1965 and 1969 affecting over 1000 blue- and white-collar employees (Ford, 1969). The company was concerned mainly with the rising costs of employee dissatisfaction and labour turnover, which were attributed to monotonous, meaningless jobs. In Britain, the best publicized applications of job enrichment were at ICI, a chemicals company. Paul and Robertson (1970) reported eight applications between 1967 and 1968, mainly with white-collar groups, including sales representatives, design engineers, foremen and draughtsmen.

Geoff White (1983) reported a work redesign experiment at a continuous process plant where managers wanted to enrich jobs, reduce labour turnover and improve product quality. New equipment had reduced work variety and increased speed. Management introduced job rotation and breaks which were arranged by the plant operators themselves. Operators were given increased control and variety in their work, and developed better understanding of the process. Direct links were created with other departments and with senior management, to improve the systematic communication of information about output and quality – information which had previously spread by grapevine.

John Bailey (1980) reported the reorganization of work at Watney Mann (West) brewery where management wanted to improve employee participation in decision-making, improve job satisfaction and thus improve customer service, efficiency and profitability. The distribution department was split into four depots, with job rotation, teamwork and with small units focusing on essential tasks. This improved cost-savings and customer service, job satisfaction, flexibility, industrial relations and team problem-solving. With clearer goals, workers reported an improved sense of accomplishment.

Asplund (1981) described how job enrichment was used at the British Driver and Vehicle Licensing Centre in Swansea, when staff complained that they were unable to handle the volume of public enquiries. The staff helped to decide how their work would be enriched, by making each individual responsible for all the case work arising from an enquiry, and dealing with problems personally, with limited management backup.

---

is Herzberg's theory 'culture-bound'?

We noted earlier in this chapter that Maslow's 'universalist' theory of motivation may not apply beyond Western, capitalist, industrialized economies and cultures. Herzberg, however, makes a strong claim for the broad applicability of his theory, writing that:

> This is not a theory for American workers alone. Recent research by myself and others reveals that these principles hold up in diverse cultures. In other words, there *are* some common characteristics among workers throughout the world.

Herzberg's two-factor theory of motivation states that while dissatisfaction is caused by context or 'hygiene' factors, satisfaction is improved with context or 'motivator' factors.

This pattern was revealed initially in American studies. Herzberg claims that similar patterns have been identified in Finland, Hungary, Italy, Israel, Japan and Zambia. Studies in South Africa, on the other hand, produced different results. While managers and skilled workers – black and white – produced the expected results, unskilled workers' satisfaction appears to be dependent on hygiene factors. Herzberg claims that 'the impoverished nature of the unskilled workers' jobs has not afforded these workers with motivators – thus the abnormal profile'.

Herzberg cites a comparable study of unskilled Indian workers who were 'operating on a dependent hygiene continuum that leads to addiction to hygiene, or strikes and revolution'.

based on Frederick Herzberg, 1987, 'Workers' needs the same around the world', *Industry Week*, 21 September, pp. 29–30, 32.

empowerment, high performance systems and the new generation

Throughout the 1960s, the American Telephone and Telegraph company suffered high labour turnover. One of the top managers made the following comment when shown the figures:

> We are going to have to make some changes in our thinking about the attitudes of young people today.
>
> We are told our potential employees are not motivated by fear of job security, for instance. We are going to have to appeal to them through having a reputation for providing jobs that allow a young person to make meaningful contributions in challenging work. Something is wrong, and we are going to have to look closely at our work, our measurements, our style of supervision . . .

from Robert N. Ford, 1969, *Motivation Through the Work Itself*, American Management Association, New York, p. 15.

Meaningful contribution? Challenging task? These were identified as key expectations of young adults in the 1960s. Have these expectations changed? During the 1990s, many organizations, in Britain, Europe, Scandinavia, Australia and America, have reconsidered job enrichment and other ways of *empowering* employees, for some of the same reasons that triggered the American Telephone and Telegraph applications thirty years previously.

definition

Empowerment *is the term given to organizational arrangements that allow employees more autonomy, discretion and unsupervised decision-making responsibility.*

Rapid economic and technological change, and increasing global competition, further encouraged this trend. It became commonplace in the 1990s to argue that an organization with a loyal, committed, skilled and motivated workforce would be more effective, more able to deal with change and better able to fight off the competition. Job enrichment and related methods became popular again under the heading of empowerment. Contribution and challenge are just as likely to be motivating in the late 1990s as they were in the late 1960s. If there is a direct link between employee motivation and an organization's ability to develop, cope with change and survive, then these job characteristics assume greater significance.

Michael Maccoby (1988) argues that advanced technology creates jobs that require information-processing, diagnostic abilities and problem-solving skills. This, he claims, requires higher levels of education and a change in the relationship between management and shop or office floor employees. He is critical of the theories examined so far in this chapter because they are partial and because they 'do not explain how to motivate people to become more involved in the management of the business and to work interdependently' (p. 29).

---

unsupervised teams: the only way forward?

There is ample evidence that American economic performance will increasingly depend on quality, service, constant innovation/improvement, and enhanced flexibility/responsiveness. Committed, flexible, multi-skilled, constantly retrained people, joined together in self-managing teams, are the only possible implementers of this strategy. . . . if you do not drastically widen the span of control, and shift the supervisor's job content, the self-managing team concept will not work – period.

from Tom Peters, 1987, *Thriving on Chaos: Handbook for a Management Revolution*, Macmillan, London, pp. 300, 302–3.

Automation and intense competition require employees to work co-operatively, sharing information to solve problems, caring for customers and colleagues. Maccoby describes how motivation in this changed environment 'requires attention to psychological concepts totally lacking in partial-man theory: trust, caring, meaning, self-knowledge, dignity' (p. 35).

Maslow's approach is thus misleading, he argues, because the bureaucratic industrial structure and the values that it encouraged have changed. Maccoby claims that 'the new generation of self-developers will not be motivated by praise from fathers but by opportunities for self-expression and career development, combined with a fair share of the profits' (p. 34).

Maccoby's research has been based on the concept of *social character types*, which can best be described as clusters of values which in turn influence what different individuals will find motivating. In identifying contemporary social characters, he is describing 'ideal types' or 'exaggerations based on dominant values'. An individual is likely to have values that fall into more than one of these 'ideal types'.

Through a combination of survey and interview research, Maccoby identified five 'new social character types' (see the discussion in Chapter 6 of personality types). These are:

type	dominant values
expert	mastery, control, autonomy, excellence in making
helper	relatedness, caring for people, survival, sociability
defender	protection, dignity, power, self-esteem
innovator	creating, experimenting, glory, competition
self-developer	balancing mastery and play, knowledge and fun

This is a 'type–environment fit' theory. Where work environments and social values are consistent, people respond to opportunities for personal development and are more successful in work. However, if working conditions are not consistent with social character type, the outcome is a feeling of frustration, resentment, defensiveness and lack of appreciation.

The organizational message in this analysis is that the different social character types must be motivated differently in terms of their key drives. In the language of expectancy theory, the outcomes valued by the Expert are likely to be different from the outcomes valued by the Defender. To motivate Experts, work has to be organized to provide autonomy, control and an expanded sense of expertise. The problems with Experts include encouraging them to learn from others and to share what they know with colleagues (who may not be Experts). On the other hand, to motivate Helpers, work must be organized to provide opportunities for meaningful relationships. The problems with Helpers lie in encouraging them to think also in terms of costs and profitability. Helpers are willing to learn new skills and behaviours, if this will make them more helpful. Catering for this varied range of motivational demands could represent a formidable management challenge.

Maccoby's research suggests that a higher proportion of those under 40 years old are Self-developers. This group he identifies as 'the new generation' whose needs from work are:

- clear management commitments on responsibilities and rewards
- opportunities for expression, challenge and development
- increased business understanding and involvement
- teamwork combined with individual growth
- fair and meaningful rewards
- reasons, information, to be included, to know why

Self-developers in the late twentieth century's highly competitive, rapidly changing, extensively automated office or factory have to be motivated in ways quite different from their counterparts in the traditional, stable, 'low-tech' organizations of the 1960s or 1970s. Maccoby claims:

> motivation does not require promotion up the hierarchy. Responsibilities can be expanded, for example, to deal with more customers, make loans, cut deals, teach other employees, and solve problems that bureaucracies usually hand to experts. There is less need for management, since individuals and teams learn to manage themselves and share management functions. This may be frustrating for the expert, who measures success by promotion and status, but not necessarily for the new generation, more interested in the challenge of a bigger job and learning from experiences, with the possibility of future ventures in other companies. (Maccoby, 1988, p. 80)

The evidence suggests that Maccoby's 'new generation' and their Self-developer social character type have been around for some time. However, other evidence reinforces his argument about the demands arising from technological advance on skills and competences in rapidly changing organizations. Many organizations seem to have been attempting to change their management style, reward systems and organizational designs in the directions indicated by Maccoby's argument, to improve employee motivation and performance at work.

The most popular organizational techniques for improving employee motivation and performance during the 1990s have involved some form of teamwork. Empowered teams are the basis of what have come to be known as *high-performance work systems*.

---

definition

A **high-performance work system** *is a form of organization that operates at levels of excellence far beyond those of comparable systems.*

The features of *high-performance work systems* were first explored by Peter Vaill (1982, p. 25). For Vaill, organizations or teams qualify for the title 'high-performing system' if they:

1 Perform excellently against a known external standard.
2 Perform beyond what is assumed to be their potential best.
3 Perform excellently in relation to what they did before.
4 Are judged by informed observers to be substantially better than comparable groups.
5 Are achieving levels of performance with fewer resources than are assumed necessary.
6 Are seen to be exemplars, as a source of ideas and inspiration.
7 Are seen to achieve the ideals of the culture.
8 Are the only organizations that have been able to do what they do at all, even though it might seem that what they do is not that difficult or mysterious a thing.

Many organizations have developed high-performance systems through empowering teams of workers, usually at the lowest level of the organization. Some of the better known examples include the Digital Equipment Corporation plants at Enfield in America (Perry, 1984) and Ayr in Scotland (Buchanan and McCalman, 1989). In Britain, empowered self-managing teams can also be found in The Body Shop, Unipart, Frizzell Financial Services, Ciba UK and in the Harvester Restaurant in Dulwich (Pickard, 1993). Perhaps contrary to the popular image, garment manufacturers in Hong Kong are now adopting autonomous teamworking methods (Li, 1992). Many American companies have publicized their teamworking methods, including Shenandoah Life Insurance, Harley-Davidson, Compaq, Cummins Engine Company, Procter and Gamble, and General Motors (Hoerr *et al.*, 1986; Hoerr, 1989; Peters, 1987). In most of these examples, the role of the traditional first line supervisor has been radically

---

team empowerment: a new means of organizing

Individual responsibility offers a much lower level of service than team responsibility. Individuals may argue about who exactly is responsible for what, whereas a team is responsible for the result. How any problem arising is best resolved then becomes an internal matter.

Team empowerment offers a new means of organizing work at a local level. The focus now shifts from the tasks to the output that is needed. It is up to the team to produce the results, which means that the members of the team have to divide the work in the most appropriate way between themselves. Team empowerment only works if the team is given the resources by management. Resources mean money, machines and people. How the three are best combined is up to the team.

It is difficult for team empowerment to work unless management relinquishes insistence on control over the process. That is why team empowerment fits so uncomfortably in a system of traditional hierarchy.

from Meredith Belbin, 1996, *The Coming Shape of Organization*, Butterworth-Heinemann, London, p. 51.

changed. In some organizations, this position has been removed completely, and teams appoint their own, often rotating, leaders (Dumaine, 1990).

Tom Peters (1987) argues that the traditional 'kick ass and take names' style of supervision has to change, and that the supervisory role, if it still exists in relation to an empowered team, should have the following features:

- a span-of-control of 50 to 75
- act as a coach, sounding board, co-ordinator, facilitator, trainer
- do a lot of wandering around rather than watching people work
- work across the organization, with other functions, to solve problems
- help the team to develop and implement ideas to improve performance

This change in the supervisory role has been described as a transition from 'policeman to coach' (Buchanan and Preston, 1992). Some traditional supervisors, and some managers, find this transition difficult because it implies a loss of direct control over the activities of 'lower-level' employees. The available evidence shows, however, that the typical employee response is positive, and that the approach usually results in improved performance.

---

high-performance teams at Digital Equipment in Scotland

Digital Equipment Corporation (DEC) started to develop high-performance work systems around empowered teams at its manufacturing plant in Ayr, on the west coast of Scotland in the early 1980s. These teams were responsible for the manufacture of the company's range of small business computers, and had the following features:

- Autonomous teams of 6–12 employees were self-managing and self-organizing, functioning without first-line supervision.
- Each team had full 'front to back' responsibility for a whole section of the manufacturing process, such as assembling a complete printed circuitboard.
- Teams negotiated their production targets with their product manager, based on available staff, materials and equipment.
- Team members were expected to share their skills with each other, to become multi-skilled, and had no job titles.
- Team members were paid according to their skill level and not according to the particular job on which they were working at any one time.
- Team members were involved in the performance appraisal of colleagues and in the selection procedure for new recruits.
- The physical layout on the factory floor was open to facilitate communications; technical support staff had their 'offices' and desks on the shop floor too.

This approach to work design improved productivity, reduced the time required to introduce new products, and led to more effective problem solving and decision making. Shop floor personnel developed a range of analytic, problem-solving, interpersonal, process design and group management skills through this approach, leading in many instances to significant career opportunities and development.

based on David Buchanan and James McCalman, 1989, *High Performance Work Systems: The Digital Experience*, Routledge, London.

Approaches to empowerment have thus come to involve more than teamwork. This approach implies radical changes to the role of management, particularly first line supervisory management. Edward Lawler argues that, in what he calls 'new design plants', 'almost no aspect of the organization is left untouched'. New design plants are characterized by:

- common entrance and car parking, with no reserved top management slots
- common eating and restaurant areas, with no executive dining room
- salaried status for all staff, no 'hourly paid' employees
- self-managing teams performing 'whole' work processes with elected leaders
- flat management hierarchy – no foremen
- team responsibility for goals, task allocation, quality control and absenteeism
- team responsibility for selecting and training new members
- some support functions performed within teams
- other support staff becoming consultants and trainers

High-performance work systems based on empowered, autonomous teamwork in new design plants potentially represent a new organizational philosophy. In other words, organizational practice has apparently evolved beyond the application of a job enrichment method. Edward Lawler claims that, 'Because so many features are altered, in aggregate they amount to a new kind of organization' (Lawler, 1986; 1995). This is a grand claim to make on behalf of techniques aimed initially at relieving the monotony and boredom of jobs designed according to the task fragmentation principles of scientific management.

assessment

Maccoby has highlighted a trend already noted by several other authors. Approaches to employee motivation through empowerment, in a variety of forms, are likely to remain popular. Several commentators in the late 1970s argued that the scope of work reorganization should be widened to involve more significant organizational design and culture changes, if such approaches were to have a real impact on organizational effectiveness (Wild, 1975; Weir, 1976; Buchanan, 1979). But those arguments were advanced at a time when their implications were seen as inappropriate or unacceptable by many managers. As long as the organizational problems to be resolved were limited in scope, the degree of acceptable change was limited. More fundamental changes to organizational design, and to the role of management, were not considered appropriate responses to the issues surrounding the vague concept of social responsibility and the annoying costs of labour turnover and absenteeism.

Those arguments have been set in a new context by developments in product markets, trading conditions and manufacturing technology. Robert Reich (1983) argued that rapid changes in the technology of products and production required the development of 'flexible production systems' to sustain competitive advantage. Global market segmentation, better informed consumers, increasingly complex products and the rapid changes in tastes and fashions, Reich argued, mean that speed and flexibility of response are essential organizational characteristics. Charles Perrow (1984) highlighted the dangers in the potentially lethal combination of sophisticated technology and unskilled employees. Richard Schonberger (1986) argued that 'world class manufacturing' status is not achieved merely through buying the latest equipment, and the roles and skills of operators, in equipment set-up, maintenance and quality control, need to be recombined. Walton and Susman (1987, p. 98) argued that advanced manufacturing technology makes human skills and workers' commitment more important than ever.

Are the claims for empowered teamwork and high-performance work systems justified? While the basic work and organization redesign methods have remained the same, and the underlying theories of motivation have seen little development since the 1970s, what is relatively clear is that the organizational context to which these theories and techniques are applied has changed dramatically. The main distinctions between the quality of working life (QWL) approach of the 1960s and 1970s, and the empowered high-performing team approach of the 1990s and beyond, seem to include the following:

QWL in the 1970s	empowered teams in the 1990s
aimed to reduce costs of absenteeism and labour turnover and increase productivity	aims to improve organizational flexibility and product quality for competitive advantage
based on argument that increased autonomy improves quality of work experience and job satisfaction	based on argument that increased autonomy improves skill, decision making, adaptability and use of new technology
had little impact on management functions	involves redefinition of management function, particularly for supervision
'quick fix' applied to problematic groups	can take significant time to change organizational culture, attitudes and behaviour
personnel administration technique	human resource management strategy

The argument of this chapter can be summarized by setting out, in simplified form, the line of argument that has been followed. The argument begins with the needs and expectations of 'the new generation', with the motives or goals that we pursue and expect to satisfy through work. These needs now seek fulfilment in an organizational setting that faces multiple socio-economic pressures. The approach advocated for addressing these needs and pressures involves empowered and self-managing teams whose members are better able to satisfy their individual needs, and whose collective performance is both high and flexible.

The human needs for challenge, meaningful work and self-actualization, combined with the pressures of rapid change, new technologies and increased expectations of work, have encouraged the use of a range of techniques for empowering employees. Empowerment is a broad concept, involving work enrichment through autonomous teams, the development of a redefined coaching role for first-line supervision and other changes to organization structures, reward systems and working condition in 'new design' organizations. The outcomes from this approach are twofold. First, there is an

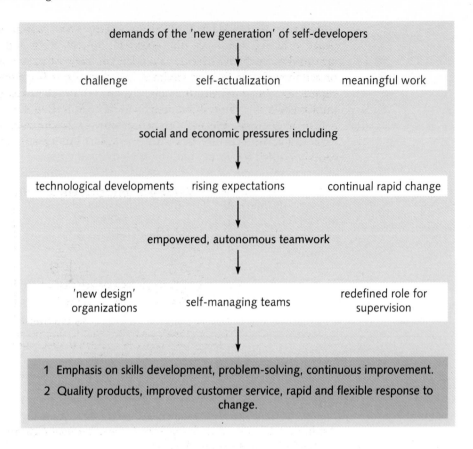

expectation that empowerment develops employee skills, job satisfaction and motivation, and leads to improved decision-making and problem-solving and to the development of a climate of continuous improvement. Second, skilled and motivated employees are expected to produce quality products, to provide customers with high levels of service and to respond in a rapid and flexible way to change.

Teamwork, empowerment, new design organizations and high-performance systems have been advanced as panaceas – as widely applicable answers to the questions of employee motivation and organizational effectiveness. Despite current claims, autonomous teamworking is *not* a new approach. Herbst (1962, pp. 7–8) summarized the circumstances in which this approach would be appropriate, in terms of task, territory, controls and culture. Summarizing what was known at that time, Herbst argues that autonomous teamworking is appropriate:

▶ when the work task itself is independent, complete and autonomous
▶ when the work can be completed within a defined physical boundary or territory
▶ when the controls on team performance can be specified with respect to quantity and quality of output (i.e. in terms of results, not the details of how the results are actually achieved)
▶ when members are able and willing to accept these responsibilities as a team

Clearly these conditions are unlikely to apply in all work settings. The caution expressed by some of the originators of the self-managed team concept is not evident in much contemporary organization theory and practice in this area. Are the organizations adopting and developing these approaches in the late 1990s at the leading edge of innovative work practice, or are they simply fashion victims? The evidence is fragmented and is mainly supportive, but typically the 'success stories' are the ones more likely to be published, whilst the failures remain hidden. It is, therefore, difficult to reach a firm judgement. We will revisit the issue of autonomous teamwork in our exploration of the effects of technological innovation on jobs and work redesign in Chapter 14.

'Ruston, you've handled that boring thankless job so well I've decided to give you another one.'

sources

Asplund, C., 1981, *Redesigning Jobs: Western European Experience*, European Trade Union Institute, Brussels.

Bailey, J., 1980, 'Employee involvement in the brewery industry', *Industrial and Commercial Training*, September, pp. 360–5.

Belbin, M., 1996, *The Coming Shape of Organization*, Butterworth Heinemann, London.

Blunt, P., 1983, *Organizational Theory and Behaviour: An African Perspective*, Longman, London.

Buchanan, D.A., 1979, *The Development of Job Design Theories and Techniques*, Saxon House, Aldershot.

Buchanan, D.A., 1987, 'Job enrichment is dead: long live high performance work design', *Personnel Management*, May, pp. 40–3.

Buchanan, D.A., 1994, 'Principles and practice in work design', in Keith Sisson (ed.), *Personnel Management: A Comprehensive Guide to Theory and Practice in Britain*, Blackwell, Oxford, second edition, pp. 85–116.

Buchanan, D.A. and McCalman, J., 1989, *High Performance Work Systems: The Digital Experience*, Routledge, London.

Buchanan, D. and Preston, D., 1992, 'Life in the cell: Supervision and teamwork in a "manufacturing systems engineering" environment', *Human Resource Management Journal*, vol. 2, no. 4, pp. 55–80.

Dumaine, B., 1990, 'Who needs a boss?', *Fortune*, 7 May, pp. 10 and 40–7.

The Economist, 1992, 'Unipartners', 11 April, p. 89.

The Economist, 1994, 'Just deserts', January, p. 77.

Ford, R.N., 1969, *Motivation through the Work Itself*, American Management Association, New York.

Georgopoulos, B.S., Mahoney, G.M. and Jones, N.W., 1957, 'A path-goal approach to productivity', *Journal of Applied Psychology*, vol. 41, no. 6, pp. 345–53.

Hackman, J.R. and Oldham, G.R., 1974, 'The job diagnostic survey: An instrument for the diagnosis of jobs and the evaluation of job redesign projects', Technical Report no. 4, Department of Administrative Sciences, Yale University.

Hackman, J.R., Oldham, G., Janson, R. and Purdy, K., 1975, 'A new strategy for job enrichment', *California Management Review*, vol. 17, no. 4, pp. 57–71.

Herbst, P.G., 1962, *Autonomous Group Functioning: An Exploration in Behaviour Theory and Measurement*, Tavistock Publications, London.

Herzberg, F., 1966, *Work and the Nature of Man*, Staples Press, New York.

Herzberg, F., 1968, 'One more time: how do you motivate employees?', *Harvard Business Review*, vol. 46, no. 1, pp. 53–62.

Herzberg, F., 1987, 'Workers' needs the same around the world', *Industry Week*, 21 September, pp. 29–30 and 32.

Hoerr, J., 1989, 'The payoff from teamwork', *Business Week*, 10 July, pp. 56–62.

Hoerr, J., Pollock, M.A. and Whiteside, D.E., 1986, 'Management discovers the human side of automation', *Business Week*, 29 September, pp. 60–5.

Kohn, A., 1993, 'Why incentive plans cannot work', *Harvard Business Review*, vol. 71, no. 5, pp. 54–63.

Lawler, E.E., 1973, *Motivation in Work Organizations*, Brooks-Cole Publishing, New York.

Lawler, E.E., 1986, *High Involvement Management: Participative Strategies for Improving Organizational Performance*, Jossey-Bass, San Francisco.

Lawler, E.E., 1995, *The Ultimate Advantage: Creating the High Involvement Organization*, Macmillan, New York.

Li, A.Y.L., 1992, 'Team concept in apparel manufacturing: Hong Kong experience', *The Hong Kong Manager*, November–December, pp. 18–21.

Maccoby, M., 1988, *Why Work: Motivating and Leading the New Generation*, Simon & Schuster, New York.

Maslow, A., 1943, 'A theory of human motivation', *Psychological Review*, vol. 50, no. 4, pp. 370–96.

Maslow, A., 1954, *Motivation and Personality*, Harper & Row, New York.

Maslow, A., 1971, *The Farther Reaches of Human Nature*, Penguin Books, Harmondsworth.

Neider, L., 1980, 'An experimental field investigation utilizing an expectancy theory view of participation', *Organizational Behaviour and Human Performance*, vol. 26, no. 3, pp. 425–42.

Nusair, N., 1985, 'Human nature and motivation in Islam', *The Islamic Quarterly*, vol. 24, no. 3, pp. 148–64.

Paul, W.J. and Robertson, K.B., 1970, *Job Enrichment and Employee Motivation*, Gower, Aldershot.

Perrow, C., 1984, 'The organizational context of human factors engineering', *Administrative Science Quarterly*, vol. 24, no. 8, pp. 521–41.

Perry, B., 1984, *Enfield: A High-Performance System*, Digital Equipment Corporation, Educational Services Development and Publishing, Bedford, MA.

Peters, T., 1987, *Thriving on Chaos: Handbook for a Management Revolution*, Macmillan, London.

Pickard, J., 1993, 'The real meaning of empowerment', *Personnel Management*, November, pp. 28–33.

Reich, R.B., 1983, *The Next American Frontier*, Times Books, New York.

Schonberger, R.J., 1986, *World-Class Manufacturing: The Lessons of Simplicity Applied*, Free Press, Chicago.

Vaill, P.B., 1982, 'The purposing of high-performing systems', *Organizational Dynamics*, Autumn, pp. 23–39.

Vroom, V.H., 1964, *Work and Motivation*, John Wiley, New York.

Walton, R.E. and Susman, G.I., 1987, 'People policies for the new machine', *Harvard Business Review*, March–April, no. 2, pp. 98–106.

Weir, M., 1976, 'Redesigning jobs in Scotland', *Work Research Unit Occasional Paper*, no. 18, March.

Wellins, R.S., Byham, W.C. and Wilson, J.M., 1991, *Empowered Teams: Creating Self-Directed Work Groups That Improve Quality, Productivity and Participation*, Jossey-Bass, San Francisco.

White, G., 1983, 'Redesign of work organization – its impact on supervisors', *Work Research Unit Report*, August.

Wild, R., 1975, *Work Organization: A Study of Manual Work and Mass Production*, John Wiley, New York.

Zuboff, S., 1988, *In The Age of the Smart Machine: The Future of Work and Power*, Heinemann Professional Publishing, Oxford.

chapter 5 learning

concepts and learning objectives
the learning process
the behaviourist approach to learning
the cognitive approach to learning
behaviour modification techniques in practice
socialization and feedback
assessment
sources

concepts and learning objectives

This chapter introduces one of the most fundamental, and still one of the most controversial, topics in individual psychology. The two extremes of this controversy are presented, in the form of behaviourist and cognitive theories of learning. Practical applications of these perspectives are then described.

Using behaviourist learning theory, American organizations in particular have experimented with techniques of 'behaviour modification'. These techniques attempt to change employee behaviour in a way that contrasts sharply with the approaches described in the preceding chapter on motivation. Learning theory also highlights the important role of feedback in sustaining and improving human performance at work, and the implications of this view for supervisory and managerial practice are also explored.

It is our intention to set out these contrasting views, and not necessarily to present one of them as correct and the other wrong. Beyond the logical reasoning and empirical evidence which supports each of these perspectives lie value-judgements concerning the relative importance of different aspects of the human experience. The position that psychologists and others take in this controversy depends ultimately as much on values as on evidence and argument.

key concepts

- learning
- Pavlovian (classical or respondent) conditioning
- intermittent reinforcement
- behaviour modification
- cognitive or information processing psychology
- intrinsic and extrinsic feedback

- behaviourist or stimulus–response psychology
- Skinnerian (instrumental or operant) conditioning
- shaping
- the cybernetic analogy
- socialization
- concurrent and delayed feedback

learning objectives

When you have read this chapter, you should be able to define those key concepts in your own words, and you should also be able to:

1 Explain the main components of the behaviourist and cognitive approaches to learning.
2 Identify the main arguments for and against each of these approaches.
3 Illustrate how theories of learning can be applied to training, performance appraisal, the induction of new employees and to behavioural change in organizations.
4 Explain the technique of behaviour modification and assess its advantages and limitations.
5 Explain the socialization process in an organization and assess the practical relevance of this concept.

the learning process

How do we learn? How do we come to know what we know, and to do the things that we are able to do? These questions have puzzled philosophers and teachers for centuries, and continue to generate controversy. These problems lie at the heart of human psychology and our knowledge of them is in a constant state of development. It is therefore not surprising that the student of learning is confronted with a variety of different approaches to the topic. This variety helps to maintain controversy, excitement and interest in the subject, which in turn help to generate new ideas, new theories and new methods.

This chapter explains two approaches to learning which are current and influential, based on *behaviourist psychology* and *cognitive psychology*. These perspectives are in many respects contradictory, but they may also be viewed as complementary.

Psychology is associated by many people with the study of rats in mazes. Rats and other animals have indeed contributed much to our understanding of human behaviour, and have been widely used by psychologists concerned with the development of theories of learning. Rat biochemistry is in fact similar to ours. We have to face the fact that we humans are animals in many (if not all) respects, and that we can learn something of ourselves through studying the behaviour of the other creatures on this planet.

The ability to learn is not unique to human beings. Animals can and do learn, as dog owners and circus fans are well aware. A feature that seems to distinguish us from animals is our ability to learn about, adapt to and manipulate our environment for purposes that we ourselves define. Animals can adapt to changes in their circumstances, but their ability to manipulate their environment is restricted and they appear to have no choice over their goals. So although animals can learn, they have developed no manipulative science, technology or engineering comparable with our own.

The study of rats and pigeons has given us insights into human abilities and so has the attempt to give machines 'intelligence', or what we might recognize as intelligence. When students of 'artificial' intelligence try to build a smart machine that can do something that humans do easily, naturally and effortlessly, they quickly discover how complex human skills are. The development of computer-based 'expert systems' has also proved difficult with success limited so far to some fairly well-defined and narrow domains.

The ability of humans to learn is important to organizations preoccupied with controlled performance. The members of an organization have to know what they are to do, how they are to do it, how well they are expected to do it and the consequences of achieving poor, adequate and superior levels of performance. New employees may need to be trained in job-specific and organization-specific knowledge and skills if they are to perform adequately. Learning theories have thus influenced a range of organizational practices, concerning:

 ▶ the induction of new recruits
 ▶ the design and delivery of job training
 ▶ the design of payment systems
 ▶ how supervisors evaluate and provide feedback on employee performance

The theories explained in this chapter thus have far-reaching practical implications for skills training and staff development in organizations, and for indoctrination in the values and practices of particular occupations and professions.

The terms skill and training are used here in a sense broader than that normally implied in common usage. Skill to a psychologist covers a wide range of human behaviours, from the specially acquired ability to play tennis, to the routine ability to walk down the street. When the latter skill is analyzed in detail, it turns out to be a complex and sophisticated performance, and quite an achievement for the individual doing it. It therefore earns the label skill. Training in organizations covers not just the acquisition of manual skills, but also the learning of the 'correct' attitudes, values, beliefs and expectations.

We hope that when you have finished reading this book you will be able to say that you have learned something. The test of this hope concerns whether or not you will be able to do things that you could not do before you read the book. You should, for example, know what the study of organizational behaviour is concerned with and you should be able to tell others what you know and think about it. You should be able to write essays and answer examination questions that previously you could not tackle. However, if you can do none of these new things, then we will have to admit that you have learned little or nothing.

We are concerned here with two related aspects of learning:
1 How we come to know things at all, through the process of learning.
2 The organization in our minds of our ideas, thoughts and knowledge, which constitutes the content of memory.

We refer to the process as learning, and to the result as knowledge.

---

definition

Learning *is the process of acquiring knowledge through experience which leads to an enduring change in behaviour.*

Learning is defined here in terms of *enduring changes in behaviour through experience*. It is important to note these limitations on what counts as learning. Behaviour can be changed temporarily by many other factors, and in ways which we would not wish to call learning. These other factors include growing up or maturation (in children), ageing (in adults), drugs, alcohol and fatigue (in the case of some academic staff, for example).

We cannot see what goes on inside your head as you learn. We can only infer that learning has taken place by examining changes in behaviour. If we assume that human behaviour does not alter spontaneously for no reason, then we can look for experiences that may be causes of behaviour change. These experiences may be derived from inside the body, or they may be sensory, arising from outside. The task of inferring whether or not learning has taken place may be an obvious one, but observable behaviour may not always reveal learning. It is helpful to distinguish between two types of learning. Procedural learning, or 'knowing how', concerns your ability to carry out particular skilled actions, such as riding a horse or painting a picture. Declarative learning, or 'knowing that', concerns your store of factual knowledge, such as an understanding of the history of our use of the horse, or of the contribution of the Futurist movement to modern art. Special testing procedures may thus be required to explore that inner knowledge or covert learning.

Changes in behaviour, particularly those at work, can be quantified using a 'learning curve'. This graph could represent the learning curve for a trainee word processor operator:

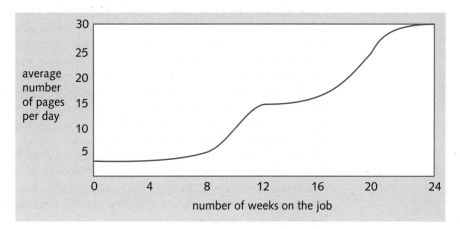

The learning curve can be plotted for an individual or for a group of trainees. This (fictitious) learning curve shows that:

1 It takes about 6 months for operators to become proficient, and for performance to 'level out' or peak at its maximum.
2 Top output is around 30 pages a day.
3 The trainee's ability develops slowly at first, rises sharply during the third month and hits a 'plateau' during the fourth month of training.

Most learning curves for manual skills suggest that trainees experience this plateau, although not always in the position illustrated here. The shape of a learning curve depends, as one would expect, on the characteristics of the task being learned and the individual learner. It is, however, often possible to measure or to quantify learning in this way, to compare individuals with each other, and thus to establish what constitutes good performance. If we know what form a learning curve takes, and if we understand the factors influencing the shape of the curve, we may be able to develop fresh approaches to make learning more effective and rapid.

STOP!

▸ How could your learning of this subject, organizational behaviour, be measured throughout your course of study?
▸ What is the shape of your learning curve for this course? Draw it.
▸ Why is it that shape? Write down the factors that you feel determine its form.
▸ Should it be that shape – and what would be your ideal?
▸ What could you do to change the shape of your learning curve?

The experiences that lead to changes in human behaviour have a number of important features.

First, the human mind is not a passive recorder of information picked up through the senses. (This argument was explored in Chapter 3 where we examined the psychology of perception.) We can usually recount the plot of a novel that we have read, for example, but remember very few of the author's actual words, beyond those that refer to key actors and events. We can usually remember none of the author's sentences, apart from those that we have deliberately committed to memory. These observations suggest that we do not record our experiences in any simple, straightforward way.

Second, we are usually able to recall events in which we have participated as if we were in fact some other actor in the drama. We are able to see ourselves 'from outside', as objects in our own experience. Now, at the time when we experienced those events, those cannot have been the sense impressions that we picked up. This feature of our thought processes is the product of reflection which takes place after the events concerned.

Third, new experiences do not inevitably lead to changes in behaviour. Our declarative learning, for example, may not be evident until we are asked the right questions (perhaps in an examination). Our experiences must be processed in some way to become influential in determining future behaviours.

Fourth, the way in which we express our innate drives depends partly on our experiences. We raised the question of whether motives are innate or learned in Chapter 4. This distinction, as we saw, is too simple and artificial. Humans do have innate drives, but these are expressed in behaviour in many different ways. How they are expressed depends on many factors, including past experiences. This is also true for animal learning. Our innate makeup biases our behaviour in certain directions, but these biases can be overridden or modified by variations in experience.

We shall explore in this chapter two contrasting perspectives on the psychology of learning.

---

definition

Behaviourist *or* **stimulus–response psychology** *argues that what we learn are chains of muscle movements. As brain or mental processes are not directly observable, they are not considered valid issues for study.*

---

definition

Cognitive *or* **information-processing psychology** *argues that what we learn are mental structures, and that mental processes are both important and amenable to study.*

These two different approaches are based on the same empirical data, but their interpretations of those data are radically different. This debate has more than theoretical significance. The stance that one adopts has implications for practice, in both educational and work contexts. These approaches are summarized in the following table for convenience and reference.

behaviourist, stimulus–response	cognitive, information processing
studies only observable behaviour	also studies mental processes
behaviour is determined by learned sequences of muscle movements	behaviour is determined by memory, mental processes and expectations
we learn habits	we learn cognitive structures and alternative ways to achieve our goals
problem-solving occurs by trial and error	problem-solving also involves insight and understanding
dull, boring, but amenable to research?	rich, interesting, but complex, vague and unresearchable?

We should not, of course, refer only to difficulty and complexity as criteria for accepting or rejecting a particular perspective. Note how the cognitive position contradicts the behaviourist position on some counts, but adds to it on others. We suggested earlier that these approaches may be considered complementary in some respects; surely a comprehensive study of learning must explore behaviour and thinking, habits and cognitive structures, and different approaches to problem-solving.

the behaviourist approach to learning

The oldest theory of learning states that ideas that are experienced together tend to be associated with each other. Today, behaviourist psychologists speak of the association between stimulus and response.

Learning is a result of experience. We use the knowledge of the results of past behaviour to change, modify and improve our behaviour in future. You learn to write better assignments and get higher examination grades by finding out how well or how badly you did last time and why. We cannot learn without appropriate *feedback*. Behaviourists and cognitive psychologists agree that experience affects behaviour, but disagree over how this happens.

Feedback may be either rewarding or punishing. Common sense suggests that if a particular behaviour is rewarded, then it is more likely to be repeated; if it is punished, it is more likely to be avoided in future. Rats are thus trained to run through mazes at the whim of the psychologist using judicious applications of electric shocks and food pellets. Behaviourist psychology makes a more subtle distinction between:

▶ positive reinforcement, or reward for particular responses, which encourages the preceding behaviour

▶ negative reinforcement, or the removal of undesirable consequences, which also encourages the preceding behaviour

▶ punishment, or the administration of sanctions including pain, which discourages the preceding behaviour

The American psychologist John B. Watson (1878–1958) introduced the term *behaviourism* in 1913. He was critical of the technique of *introspection*, a popular psychological research method at that time, which was used to find out what went on inside people's minds. Subjects were simply asked to talk about their sensory experiences and thought processes as clearly as possible. They were asked to look inside their own minds, to introspect, and to tell the psychologist what they found there.

Watson wanted objective, 'scientific' handles on human behaviour, its causes and its consequences. He could see no way in which introspection could ever produce this. This took him, and many other psychologists, away from the intangible and invisible contents of the mind to the study of the relationships between *visible stimuli* and *visible responses*. That is why behaviourist psychology is sometimes referred to as 'stimulus–response psychology'.

The behaviourist perspective assumes that what lies between the stimulus and the response is a mechanism that will be revealed as our knowledge of the biochemistry and neurophysiology of the brain improves. This mechanism must relate stimuli to responses in a way that governs behaviour. We can therefore continue to study how stimuli and responses are related without a detailed understanding

*John Broadus Watson
(1878–1958)*
Photo source:
Archives of the History of American
Psychology, The University of Akron,
Ohio, USA.

---

to punish or reward: the basis of behaviour modification

One well-established principle of behaviourist psychology is that reward is more effective than punishment in changing behaviour. This principle has been derived from extensive work with rodents and has also influenced practice with humans. The problem with punishment is that it creates fear, resentment and hostility in the punished person. Rewards for good behaviour are thus more likely to ensure compliance, now and in the future.

Charles O'Reilly and Barton Weitz studied how 141 supervisors in an American retail chain store used punishments to control the behaviour of their subordinates. Four sanctions were in use:

- informal spoken warnings
- loss of pay
- suspension from work
- dismissal

Supervisors used these sanctions to discourage 'incorrect' behaviours such as:

- slack timekeeping
- low sales records
- sloppy appearance at work
- discourtesy to customers

Supervisors dealt with these incorrect behaviours in different ways. Some supervisors preferred to confront problems directly and quickly, gave subordinates frequent warnings and were quite prepared to fire those who did not behave correctly. One supervisor described his readiness to sack subordinates as 'an acquired taste'.

Other supervisors had difficulty in dealing with these problems, tried to avoid them, and got depressed when they had to fire someone. They described their dealings with poor performers as 'traumatic'. These 'employee-oriented' supervisors were more sensitive to subordinates' needs and liked to give them time to put problems right.

The research showed that the departments run by the employee-oriented supervisors had poorer performance ratings than the departments run by the hard-line supervisors.

Does this contradict the behaviourist position that punishment is not an effective way to influence or to modify behaviour?

We learn from others the behaviours and attitudes that are appropriate in particular circumstances. The employee who comes late to work regularly, or who does not work as hard as colleagues, violates *socially* established and accepted standards. The punishments used by supervisors can thus be effective where:

- They are perceived as maintaining the accepted social order.
- They are perceived as legitimate by the 'victim'.

based on Charles O'Reilly and Barton A. Weitz, 1980, 'Managing marginal employees: the use of warnings and dismissals', *Administrative Science Quarterly*, vol. 25, no. 3, pp. 467–84.

---

of the nature of the mechanism. In other words, behaviourists argue that nothing of psychological importance lies between the stimulus and the response.

Learning is thus the development of associations between stimuli and responses through experience. This happens in two different ways, known as *Pavlovian conditioning* and *Skinnerian conditioning*.

*Ivan Petrovich Pavlov
(1849–1936)*
Photo source:
Archives of the History of American
Psychology, The University of Akron,
Ohio, USA.

Pavlovian conditioning

This is also known as *classical* and as *respondent* conditioning. The concept and related conditioning techniques were developed by the Russian physiologist, Ivan Petrovich Pavlov (1849–1936).

---
definition

Pavlovian conditioning, *also known as* **classical** *and as* **respondent conditioning**, *is a technique for associating an established response (a dog salivating at the sight of food, for example) with a new stimulus (say, the sound of a bell).*

Pavlov's conditioning work with dogs is well known and his name is a household word. Dog owners who attend classes in how to train their pets are still trained today in the use of classical conditioning techniques. If you show meat to a dog, the dog will produce saliva. The meat is the stimulus, the saliva is the response. The meat is an *unconditioned stimulus*, because the dog will salivate naturally. Similarly, the saliva is an *unconditioned response*. The dog will produce saliva without any intervention or manipulation by a psychologist.

Unconditioned responses are also called *reflexes*. Your lower leg jerks when you are struck just below the kneecap; your pupils contract when light is shone into your eyes. These are typical human reflexes. Humans also salivate naturally – another unconditioned response – at the sight and smell of food.

Suppose we now ring a bell when we show the meat to the dog. Do this often enough, and the dog will associate the bell with the meat. Eventually the dog will start to salivate at the sound of the bell, without food being present. The bell is a *conditioned stimulus*, and the saliva is now a *conditioned response*. The dog has now learned, from that experience, to salivate at the sound of a bell as well as at the sight of food. It does not, of course, have to be a bell. All kinds of stimuli can be conditioned in this way. Pavlov in fact discovered this form of conditioning by accident. His research was initially concerned with salivation, but he observed that his dogs salivated at the sight and sound of his laboratory assistants, before they received their meat. He found this more interesting and switched the focus of the research accordingly.

Suppose we now stop giving the meat to the dog after the bell. The dog will continue to salivate at the sound of the bell alone. But if we continue to do this, the amount of saliva produced falls and the association between the conditioned stimulus and conditioned response eventually suffers *extinction*.

The conditioned response may also be invoked by stimuli similar to the original conditioned stimulus, such as a bell with a different pitch. This phenomenon is called *stimulus generalization*. A complementary phenomenon, *stimulus discrimination*, can also be demonstrated by conditioning the dog to salivate at a bell of one pitch, but not at another.

The conditioned response in animals is an observable and reliable phenomenon. Pavlov studied it in great detail, and with other animals, changing the stimulus, altering the timing of the conditioned and uncondi-

"It's most interesting. By pushing this lever twenty times you can get him to walk across here with a banana."

tioned stimuli, and measuring the quantities of saliva produced by his dogs under varying conditions. From this perspective, the basic unit of learning is the conditioned response. Changes in human behaviour must, therefore, be the result of further conditioning.

Skinnerian conditioning

Burrhus Frederic Skinner (1904–90)
Photo source:
Archives of the History of American Psychology, The University of Akron, Ohio, USA.

This is also commonly known as instrumental and as operant conditioning. It is the discovery of the American psychologist Burrhus Frederic Skinner (1904–90). Instrumental conditioning demonstrates how new behaviours or responses become established through association with particular stimuli.

> **definition**
> **Skinnerian conditioning,** *also known as* **instrumental** *and as* **operant conditioning***, is a technique for associating a response or a behaviour (a rat in a box nudges a lever) with its consequence (when the lever is nudged, food is delivered). If the consequence is desirable, the frequency of the behaviour is likely to increase.*

Given a particular context, any behaviour that is rewarded or reinforced in some way will tend to be repeated in that context. Skinner put a rat into a specially designed box (which has come to be known as a 'Skinner box') with a lever inside which, when pressed, gave the animal food. The rat was not taught in any systematic way to press the lever for its meals. However, in the process of wandering around the box at random, the rat eventually nudged the lever. It may sit on it, knock it with its head or push it with a paw. That random behaviour is rewarded with food, the behaviour is reinforced and it is likely to happen again.

Classical conditioning has that name because it is the older of the two conditioning phenomena described here. Skinnerian conditioning is also called instrumental conditioning because it is related to behaviours that are instrumental in getting some material reward, in this example food. Skinner's rat has thus to be under the influence of some drive before it can be conditioned in this way. His rats were, of course, hungry when they went into his box and their behaviour led to an appropriate reward.

Where do the terms *respondent* and *operant* conditioning come from? Watson's stimulus–response psychology stated that there was no behaviour, or no response, without a stimulus to set it in motion. One could, therefore, condition a known response to a given stimulus. In other words, one could attach that response to another stimulus. Such responses are called *respondents*. Knee jerks, pupil contractions and salivation are well known and clearly identified responses that are amenable to conditioning.

Skinner argued that this was too simple and inconsistent with known facts. Animals and humans do behave in the absence of specific stimuli. In fact, he argued, most human behaviour is of this kind. Behaviours that are emitted in the absence of identifiable stimuli are called *operants*. Operant conditioning explains how new behaviours and new patterns of behaviour can become established. Respondent conditioning does not alter the animal's behaviour, only the timing of that behaviour.

Skinner also introduced the concept of *shaping* behaviour by selectively reinforcing desired pieces of behaviour. In this way he was able to get pigeons to play ping pong and to walk in figures of eight – a famous demonstration of how random, aimless or spontaneous behaviour can be shaped by operant conditioning. The desired behaviours and movements are rewarded; unwanted or irrelevant behaviours attract no reward.

---

definition

Shaping *concerns the selective reinforcement of desired behaviours in a manner that progressively established a desired behaviour or pattern of behaviours.*

Apart from this distinction between respondent and operant conditioning, Pavlov's other concepts apply to operant conditioning also, including extinction, generalization and discrimination.

Like Pavlov, Skinner studied numerous variations on the operant conditioning theme. One important variation is not to reward the required behaviour every time, by varying the intervals between responses or by varying the proportion of correct responses that are rewarded. Why do gamblers keep playing when they lose so often? Why do anglers continue to fish when they are catching nothing? Life is full of examples that demonstrate the power of what Skinner called *intermittent reinforcement*.

---

definition

Intermittent reinforcement *is the procedure whereby a reward is provided for only a proportion of correct responses, and not for every correct response.*

> **STOP!**
> ▶ In what ways is your behaviour conditioned by intermittent reinforcement?
> ▶ How important is operant conditioning as a determinant of your behaviour?

Skinner claimed to be able to explain the development of complex patterns of human behaviour with the theory of operant conditioning. This shows how our behaviour is shaped by our environment, by our experiences in that environment, and by the selective rewards and punishments that we receive. Thinking, problem-solving and the acquisition of language, he argued, are dependent on these simple conditioning processes. Skinner rejected the use of 'mentalistic' concepts and 'inner psychic forces' in explanations of human behaviour because these were not observable, were not researchable and were therefore not necessary to the science of human psychology. Why use complicated and unobservable concepts when simple and observable phenomena seem to provide adequate explanations?

Skinner's objective was to predict and to control human behaviour. Mental, invisible, intangible constructs are not useful because they do not tell us which variables to manipulate to control that behaviour. If behaviour is determined by environment and experience, we need to be able to identify the factors in that environment that affect behaviour, and to discover the laws that relate behaviour to these variables.

Skinner's ambitious project and its output have been enormously influential. His experimental work has been extended to animals and humans of all types and ages. It has led to the widespread use of programmed learning, a technique of instruction designed to reinforce correct responses in the learner and to let people learn at their own pace. The *behaviour modification* techniques described later in this chapter are based on Skinner's ideas. And as the behaviour of a conditioned animal is consistent and predictable, this knowledge can be used to test for the effects of drugs for eventual human use.

STOP!

In this Alex cartoon, is young Oliver's problem the result of respondent conditioning or of operant conditioning?

Behaviourist learning and behaviour modification principles can be applied in domestic as well as organizational settings. It is generally accepted that rewarding and reinforcing desired behaviour is more effective than punishing undesirable behaviour. However, such reinforcement may not be rapid, and in some instances may not be possible, leaving punishment as the main option. C.C. Walters and J.E. Grusek (1977), summarizing research in this field, suggest that punishment can be effective if it meets the following conditions:

▶ The punishment should be quick and short.
▶ It should be administered immediately after the undesirable behaviour.
▶ It should be limited in its intensity.
▶ It should be specifically related to behaviour and not to character traits.
▶ It should be restricted to the context in which the undesirable behaviour occurs.
▶ It should not send any 'mixed messages' to the recipient about what is and what is not acceptable.
▶ Penalties should take the form of withdrawal of access to rewards and not physical pain.

Look back over the punishment episodes in your own experience and consider the extent to which these conditions were or were not met, and the effectiveness of the punishment received.

the cognitive approach to learning

It is possible to study the internal workings of the mind in indirect ways, by inference. Why should we look only at observable stimuli and responses in the study of human psychology? Behaviourism seems to be unnecessarily restrictive. It also seems to exclude those aspects that make us interesting, different and, above all, human.

How do we select from all the stimuli that bombard our senses those to which we are going to respond? Why are some outcomes seen as rewarding and others as punishments? This may appear obvious where the reward is survival or food and the punishment is pain or death. However, with intrinsic or symbolic rewards this is not clear.

Norbert Wiener
(1894–1964)

To answer these questions we have to consider states of mind concerning perception and motivation. Cognitive psychology admits that things happen inside the mind that we should and can study.

The rewards and punishments that behaviourists call reinforcement work in more complex ways than conditioning theories seem to suggest. Reinforcement is always knowledge about the results of past behaviour. It is *feedback* on how successful our behaviour has been. That knowledge or feedback is *information* that can be used to modify or maintain previous behaviours. This information, of course, has to be perceived, interpreted, given meaning and used in making decisions about future behaviours. The knowledge of results, the feedback, the information, has to be processed. Cognitive theories of learning are thus also called *information-processing* theories.

This approach draws concepts from the field of *cybernetics*, which was established by the American mathematician Norbert Wiener. He defined cybernetics in 1947 as 'the science of communication in the animal and in the machine'. One central idea of cybernetics is the notion of control of system performance through feedback. Information processing theories of learning are based on what is called the *cybernetic analogy*.

definition

The **cybernetic analogy** *explains the learning process with reference to the components and operation of a feedback control system.*

The elements of a cybernetic feedback control system are:

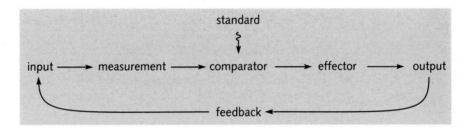

Consider a domestic heating control system. The temperature standard is set on a thermostat adjusted by the householder. When the system is switched on, a heater (effector) starts to warm up the room. The output of the system is heated air. Changes in temperature are detected (measured) by a thermometer in the thermostat. The temperature of the room is continually compared with the standard. When the room reaches the required temperature, the effector is switched off. When the room cools, the effector is switched on again.

The cybernetic analogy claims that this feedback control loop is a model of what goes on inside the mind. For standard, read motive, purpose, intent, goal. The output is behaviour. The senses are our measuring devices. The comparator is the perceptual process which organizes and imposes meaning on sensory data which controls behaviour in pursuit of given objectives, and which learns from experience.

We have in our minds some kind of 'internal representation' or 'schema' of ourselves and the environment in which we function. This internal representation is used in a purposive way to determine our behaviour. This internal representation is also called the *image* – what in Chapter 3 we called the individual's *perceptual world*.

How does this image influence behaviour? Our behaviour is purposive. We formulate plans for achieving our purposes. The plan is a set of mental instructions for guiding and controlling the required behaviour. Within the master plan (get an educational qualification) there are likely to be a number of sub-plans (submit essay on time; pass the organizational behaviour examination; develop new friendships). The organization of our behaviour is hierarchical – a concept which can be illustrated by comparison with a computer program in which instructional routines and subroutines are typically 'nested' within each other.

However, unlike most computer programs, we can use information on how we are doing – feedback – to update our internal representation and to refine and adapt our plans.

---
definition

Feedback *is information concerning the outcomes of our behaviour.*

The *feedback* that we get comes in different forms.

---
definitions

Intrinsic feedback *is information which comes from within our bodies, from the muscles, joints, skin, and other internal mechanisms such as that concerned with maintaining balance when walking (and is also called 'proprioception').*

Extrinsic feedback *is information which comes from our environment, such as the visual and aural information needed to drive a car.*

Concurrent feedback *is information which arrives during the act and can be used to control it as it proceeds. This is of course also necessary in driving.*

Delayed feedback *comes after the task is completed, and can be used to influence future performances. Feedback on student essay and examination performance is usually delayed rather than concurrent.*

It is difficult, and often impossible, for us to behave at all without appropriate feedback. Consider walking down the street blindfold. It is also difficult to learn without appropriate feedback. Consider the student who consistently fails examinations but is never told why. The saying, 'practice makes perfect' should read 'practice with appropriate feedback . . .'.

The plans that we choose to pursue depend on our needs, motives, values and beliefs about ourselves and the world in which we live. The conduct of these plans depends on our ability to draw on acquired knowledge, skills, procedures, and on our ability to learn from the successes and failures of previous plans. Feedback is therefore vital to learning. Information on how things went in the past is required to control future actions. We learn to adapt to changes in our circumstances, and we learn to improve the effectiveness of our behaviour, by switching plans and subplans.

Cognitive psychology is therefore not concerned with the relationships between stimuli and responses, but with the plans that people choose and the means they adopt for pursuing them, and with how these plans and sub-plans are modified and improved by experience.

Feedback, rewards and punishments, and knowledge of results, can all have a *motivating* effect on behaviour, rather than simply a reinforcing effect. Several writers on motivation have argued that opportunities to learn new skills and knowledge, to understand more, to develop more effective ways of living and coping with our environment, are intrinsically motivating (see the discussion in Chapter 4). The theories of psychological growth of Abraham Maslow and Frederick Herzberg, for example, claim that we have innate needs to know more, and to be creative. Another American psychologist, Robert W. White (1959), has suggested that we have a need to develop 'competence' in dealing with our environment and that this gives us satisfaction. Abraham Maslow also examined the motivating role of curiosity, learning and experimenting. One of the most optimistic advocates of this argument is Gardner Murphy (1958, p. 19) who wrote:

> This urge towards discovery, this living curiosity, beginning with a sort of 'freeing of intelligence' from cultural clamps and moving forward in a positive way activated by thirst for contact with the world and for understanding and making sense of it, will begin to develop a society in which the will to understand is the dominant new component.

behaviour modification techniques in practice

The behaviourist approach to learning has led to the development of a range of techniques generally described as *behaviour modification*. They were developed initially for the treatment of mental disorders, learning disorders, phobias, and for psychiatric rehabilitation and accident and trauma recovery. Applications have since been effectively extended to educational and other organizational settings.

definition
Behaviour modification *is a technique for encouraging desired behaviours and discouraging unwanted behaviours using operant conditioning.*

Behaviour modification, as a means of changing employee behaviour, can appear particularly attractive to managers who are typically in ideal positions from which to manipulate reinforcement of different employee behaviours. Managers also tend to find this approach attractive because it argues that what has to be changed is *behaviour*, and that to achieve this one needs to know little about the internal workings of the people concerned. The approach is based on the behaviourists' 'law of effect'. This law simply states that we learn to repeat behaviours that have favourable consequences or rewards for us, and to avoid behaviours that lead to punishment or to other unfavourable or neutral consequences.

Desirable workplace behaviours could include, for example, working at weekends to meet deadlines, following training courses to develop new skills, and being helpful to colleagues. Undesirable behaviours could include consistent lateness, the production of inferior quality items, and being rude to customers. Behaviour modification uses the principles of positive and negative reinforcement, and shaping, to eliminate the undesirable behaviours and to increase the frequency of desired work behaviour.

Suppose a manager wants more work assignments completed on time, and less submitted beyond the required deadline. The behaviour modification options look like this:

procedure	operationalization	behavioural effect
positive reinforcement	manager compliments employee when work is completed on time	increases desired behaviour
negative reinforcement	manager offers to reduce or eliminate unpaid overtime or evening shifts when work is completed on time	increases desired behaviour
punishment	manager increases employee workload each time work is handed in late	decreases undesired behaviour
extinction	manager ignores the employee when work is handed in late	decreases undesired behaviour

Some typical illustrations of behaviour modification in practice demonstrate the procedures involved, and the benefits and problems.

Robert Smither (1988) cites an American factory in Mexico which suffered a serious timekeeping problem; 15 per cent of their workforce arrived late for work on a regular basis. Management decided to reward good timekeeping by paying workers two pesos (16 cents in 1982) a day extra if they started work early. Lateness fell from 15 to 2 per cent, at minimal additional cost to the company.

E. J. Feeney (1972) described how a performance audit at Emery Freight showed that employees were responding to only 30 per cent of customer enquiries within 90 minutes. They had thought they were responding to 90 per cent within this time. Packages were being combined for delivery in 45 per cent of cases, not the 90 per cent that management thought – and which would have reduced delivery costs significantly. A behaviour modification programme was introduced to improve speed of response to customer enquiries and to use containers with consolidated loads for shipment wherever possible. Managers were trained in the use of positive reinforcement and the importance of feedback. A management workbook identified 150 different recognitions and rewards to give employees, from a smile and a nod, to highly specific praise for a job well done. Employees were also required to keep a record of what they had accomplished each day and to compare their performance with the desired standard. Money was not used as reinforcement in any way; praise and recognition were felt to be sufficient on their own. The company saved $3 million over three years – considerably more than the cost of the programme which was extended to other operating areas.

Marsha Brown and colleagues (Parsons *et al.*, 1987) describe how behaviour modification was used to improve teaching methods for handicapped students in 21 classrooms in four American schools, faced with the criticism that some of the educational methods used were not appropriate for profoundly mentally retarded people. Learning to put pegs into a board, to dress dolls and to work with toy button boards were felt to be activities less useful than putting on a real overcoat or buttoning the individual's own shirt. Teaching staff were trained in the use of a 'functional curriculum', and the school principals encouraged their staff to increase their use of functional materials and activities in their classrooms. Staff were also asked to work on new ideas. At a follow-up meeting, principals gave either approving or critical feedback on new proposals, and target dates were agreed for incorporating new activities into the classroom work.

Principals also visited classrooms unannounced with varying frequency (average once a week), to ask staff questions about their use of functional activities and materials. These 'prompting interactions' were also used to give feedback to staff. Observation before the behaviour modification programme showed students working on functional activities on average 36 per cent of the time. Following the programme, this had risen to 92 per cent. The teaching staff were satisfied with the programme, with over 75 per cent reporting that 'the management approach was more acceptable to them than pre-existing approaches and no staff member reported that the management strategy was less acceptable'.

E. Scott Geller (1983) reports how the Radford Army Ammunition Plant in Virginia used behaviour modification to encourage the wearing of seat-belts among employees. The 'treatment' followed twelve days of unobtrusive observation at the three main entrances to the munitions complex to establish a 'baseline' of seat-belt wearing. 'Incentive fliers' were then distributed, encouraging seat-belt use, and offering opportunities to win prizes to those who did. The prizes included gift certificates and dinners at local restaurants, worth from $2 to $15. Only those wearing belts got a 'prize-winning' flier with a special symbol; those without belts got one which read, 'Next time wear your seat-belt and receive a chance to win a valuable prize'. This 'incentive condition' lasted for a month.

Seat-belt use increased from an average of 20 per cent and 17 per cent in the mornings and afternoons respectively to 31 per cent and 55 per cent. After the programme was discontinued, seat-belt use returned to baseline levels. Subsequent observation revealed that 'those individuals who showed the greatest response maintenance also evidenced the highest baseline rate of seat-belt usage' (which implies that those who continued to use their belts were those who used them before anyway). Only nine prizes were claimed at a cost of $126; four prizes had been donated by other local businesses covering 40 per cent of the expense.

These examples illustrate the main features of the practical application of behaviour modification in organizational settings – similar to the advice of Walters and Grusec (1977, p. 120) on the effective use of punishment discussed earlier in this chapter:

- The technique applies to clearly identifiable and observable behaviours, such as timekeeping, response rates, the use of particular work methods or the wearing of seat-belts.
- Rewards are clearly and unambiguously contingent on the performance of the desirable behaviours.

> Positive reinforcement can take a number of forms, from the praise of a superior to cash prizes.
> Behaviour change and performance improvements can be dramatic.
> The desired modification in behaviour may only be sustained if positive reinforcement is continued (although this may be intermittent).

socialization and feedback

When people join an organization of any kind they give up some personal freedom of action. That is part of the price of membership. The individual member thus agrees that the organization may make demands on their time and effort, as long as these demands are seen to be legitimate. The problem for other members of the organization is to teach new recruits what is expected of them, what is customary, what is accepted. The process through which new recruits are 'shown the ropes' is known as *socialization*. Cognitive psychologists regard behaviour modification as narrow and simplistic, and turn to more complex social explanations, and methods, for behaviour change in organizational settings.

---

definition

Socialization *is the process through which an individual's pattern of behaviour, and their values, attitudes and motives, are shaped to conform with those seen as desirable in a particular organization, society or sub-culture.*

This perspective draws on social learning theory which is based on assumptions about human psychology quite different from those behind behaviour modification techniques.

One of the most influential advocates of social learning theory has been Albert Bandura (1977; 1986). Bandura demonstrated that we learn new behaviours through observing and copying the behaviour of others, in the absence of any rewards or punishments. In this perspective, our capabilities for self-reflection, self-determination and self-regulation are central. We construct, through observation and experience, internal models of our environment and plan courses of action accordingly. The many ways in which we 'model' ourselves on the behaviours of others is most apparent perhaps in the behaviours of children. However, our propensity to model, copy, or imitate others continues into adulthood. In Part 2, we shall explore in more detail how those around us in an organization can influence our perceptions, motivations, and levels of performance.

The argument that we learn through social experience, through observation and modelling, does not deny the importance of reinforcement, which remains a factor in Bandura's social learning theory. Suppose, for example, that we choose to base some of our behaviours (how to handle a job interview, how to make new friends at parties) on a chosen model, presumably someone that appears particularly successful in those domains. Suppose that our new approach does not lead to the desired results (didn't get the job,

Albert Bandura
(b. 1925)

failed to establish new relationships). We are likely to abandon our new behaviours in the absence of reinforcement.

How does social learning theory apply in an organizational setting? Organizations tend to encourage different standards concerning, for example:

- what counts as adequate and good work performance
- familiarity in everyday social interactions at work
- the appropriate amount of deference to show to superiors
- timekeeping
- dress and appearance
- social activities off the job
- attitudes to work, colleagues, managers, unions, customers

The newcomer has to learn these standards, and the ways of behaving and related attitudes that they involve, to be a successful and accepted member of the organization. It is not enough just to learn the knowledge and skills required to perform work duties and responsibilities. The individual does not have to believe that the organization's standards are appropriate. What matters is that individuals behave as if they believed in them. Individuals arrive in a new organization with values, attitudes, beliefs and expectations that they have acquired elsewhere. These may have to change or be pushed aside for a time.

The socialization process is often an informal one, rather than a planned programme of instruction. The newcomers learn the ropes simply by watching their new colleagues. Some organizations do have 'induction programmes' for new recruits, but these are typically short and superficial, and concentrate on relatively mundane matters like the organization's structures and policies, and health and safety regulations, for example. Beyond formal programmes, we learn about an organization by just being there, in other words through observation and participation. Socialization is thus achieved without planned intervention, by giving rewards such as praise, encouragement, privilege and promotion for 'correct' behaviour. It is achieved by negative reinforcements and punishments, like being ignored, ridiculed or fined for behaviour that is 'out of line'. We quickly learn what attitudes to take, what style of language to use, what 'dress code' to obey, where to take lunch and with whom, and so on, if we are to 'fit in' and make friends with other members of the organization.

STOP!

Most organizations plan the punishments and material rewards that members will get, but leave symbolic rewards to chance. From your knowledge of motivation and learning theory, what would you predict to be the consequences of such a policy?

Note that some of the 'rewards for good behaviour' offered by organizations are material rewards, in the form of money and desirable working conditions (the bigger office and desk, the subsidized meals, access to free sports and leisure facilities, a space in the car park). Some of the available rewards, on the other hand, are 'symbolic rewards' such as prestige, status, recognition and public praise. It is the symbolic rewards that address our 'higher order' needs, according to Maslow.

---

socialization – an alternative to behaviour modification

Social learning theory argues that we learn correct behaviours through experience and through the examples or 'role models' that other people provide.

Bruna Nota argues that this process now requires specific and proactive management attention and should not be left to chance, if the levels of commitment and competence required to compete in the 1990s and beyond are to be achieved. He describes a typical socialization programme based on experience in a number of 'new design plants'.

New recruits are first invited to a meeting where plant philosophy, operations, products and management style are explained and they are invited to withdraw their job applications if they feel uncomfortable with this. Subsequent selection interviews are designed to find out whether applicants are 'team players', able to cope with uncertainty, take initiative, and if they are willing and able to learn new skills. They are also interviewed by a team supervisor who probes their technical ability and 'overall fit' within the team. They are then interviewed by potential colleagues to ensure 'person fit'. Finally, they are interviewed by a senior manager who looks 'for overall fit and appropriateness and ensures that the candidate is aware of the plant norms, mores, working and salary conditions, and so forth'.

People are hired in groups of 5–10 at a time, and go through the same induction programme, after which they are placed in different departments. For their first week they each wear a badge which says 'I am just starting', and they are met by department representatives who act as 'godfathers'. The induction programme begins with the usual briefing on conditions, operations, safety, customer and quality issues, and the organization's philosophy.

The godfathers are colleagues with good technical, social and administrative knowledge who act as counsellors, guides and role models for the new recruits, helping them to learn the tasks assigned to them, and also to become familiar with the culture of the plant. As recruits acquire this and take their full place in their teams, the role of the mentor is gradually phased out.

Once a month, families are invited to the plant to familiarize themselves with the activities and concerns of their spouse.

Nota admits that this is a complex process. However, turnover in one plant using these techniques had been under 6 per cent for its first three years of operation. Those hired are proud to have been selected in such a thorough process. Existing staff have a personal interest in those they are responsible for hiring and support them through difficulties, 'instead of automatically cursing the personnel office for "always sending us bums"'.

based on Bruna Nota, 1988, 'The socialization process at high-commitment organizations', *Personnel*, vol. 65, no. 8, pp. 20–3.

In contrast to induction procedures which are usually brief and informal, the process through which individuals learn the skills and knowledge required to carry out specific jobs is typically formal and more systematically organized.

Behaviourists emphasize the reinforcing functions of feedback in strengthening or weakening the probability of our choosing a particular behaviour. Cognitive learning theory emphasizes the informative and motivational functions of feedback, and offers advice for ensuring that job training is more effective.

1 **The trainee must be motivated to learn.**
   The trainer should establish what these motives are, and point out advantages of training that the trainees may not have considered. These motives may include money, a prestigious job title, future career opportunities, and the acquisition of a valued skill.

2 **The task to be learned should be divided into meaningful segments for which performance standards can be established.**
   The more meaningful the task, the stronger the motivation to learn. It may be possible to break the whole task down into a hierarchy of goals and subgoals, with specific objectives for each. If the trainee is asked to learn too little at a time, learning will be too easy and meaningless. If, on the other hand, trainees are confronted with too much at a time, they may become frustrated and lose confidence; learning is less effective.

3 **Trainees should be given clear, frequent and appropriate feedback on their performance and progress.**
   Intrinsic feedback is usually inadequate in learning job skills and the trainer has to provide the relevant extrinsic feedback. Recognition and praise for good work are more effective than hostile criticism. The reasons for poor performance should be explained and the trainee shown the correct procedures.

4 **Focus on rewarding appropriate behaviour, because punishment does not tell trainees what they are doing wrong or what they have to do to improve.**
   Punishment for poor work is more likely to instil dislike, distrust and hostility in trainees and remove their motivation for learning. The effects of punishment are thus likely to be less predictable than those of reward. Encouragement and recognition create feelings of confidence, competence, development and progress that enhance the motivation to learn.

5 **Concurrent feedback is more effective than delayed feedback.**
   Research into employee performance appraisal systems shows that this is often done annually and casually – in other words, too little is done too late to be of any use in developing job knowledge, skills and performance. Supervisors need to give frequent feedback in a helpful and considerate manner. Most of us prefer critical feedback to no feedback, and we tend to react positively to helpful, encouraging and motivating criticism.

assessment

Is behaviour modification a generally applicable approach to encouraging employee learning and to the development of appropriate behaviours in organizations? The evidence seems to suggest that the answer to this question must be a heavily qualified 'yes'. There are two major qualifications.

First, behaviour modification clearly needs careful planning to identify specific behavioural goals and specific procedures for reinforcing the behaviours that will achieve those goals. Where behaviour and appropriate

---

we need appropriate feedback at work . . .

Appropriate feedback on work performance is necessary to ensure the learning and development of job skills. But do supervisors always tell their subordinates the truth? Daniel Ilgen and William Knowlton designed an experiment to answer this question.

The researchers asked forty students each to supervise a group of three workers doing a routine clerical job for 2 hours. The supervisors were first shown the results of a test which was supposed to measure the abilities of their workers for such a task.

But each group had one worker, a confederate of the researchers, who performed much better or much worse than the others, working either enthusiastically or apathetically. The supervisors were led to believe that the level of performance of this exceptional group member was due to either high or low ability, or to their motivation.

After the work session, the supervisors rated the ability and motivation of all their subordinates on scales ranging from 'unsatisfactory' to 'outstanding'. They then completed a separate 'feedback report form', believing that they would have to discuss it with the exceptional (weak or strong) worker in person.

For the feedback, supervisors were asked to choose one of twelve statements which best described their evaluation of each worker, such as:

▶ 'You have done very well. I believe I would try to do even better next time if I were you.'
▶ 'Your performance is not good at all. You really need to put much more into it.'

The supervisors also had to recommend further action for the subordinate, to change either ability or motivation, such as:

▶ Attend a special training session.
▶ Concentrate more on the task.
▶ Try harder.

The supervisors were then told about the deception. There was no feedback session. The researchers wanted to find out how truthful the supervisors would have been with their feedback. As expected, ratings of ability and motivation were higher when supervisors believed that they would have to tell their subordinates this in person. Where low performance was attributed to low motivation, the feedback reflected this accurately. But where low performance was blamed on poor ability, supervisors recommended an inappropriate mix of feedback, directed at effort and skill.

The researchers conclude that supervisors systematically distort their assessments of subordinates and thus inhibit their learning.

based on Daniel R. Ilgen and William A. Knowlton, 1980, 'Performance attributional effects on feedback from superiors', *Organizational Behaviour and Human Performance*, vol. 25, no. 3, pp. 441–56.

---

reinforcement can be clearly identified and linked (if you wear your seatbelt, we'll give you a prize), the technique can be effective. Where this relationship is less clear (if you demonstrate commitment to the organization, we'll consider you for promotion), the applicability of the technique is less certain.

Second, the 'rewards for good behaviour' technique appears broadly consistent with American cultural values and aspirations. The transfer of this approach to other countries and cultures with different values is questionable. The most often cited practical examples, as those in this chapter, are American.

Behaviour modification is overtly manipulative, potentially ignores internal needs and intrinsic rewards, and can be seen as a threat to individual dignity and autonomy. Outside North America, it may be viewed as a simplistic and transparent attempt at manipulation, invoking only cynicism as a 'new' behaviour. The technique is clearly limited in its application, and there are severe practical difficulties in connecting specific reinforcements to correct behaviours.

In defence of behaviour modification, it involves the simple and clear communication of goals and expectations to employees in unambiguous terms. Many would argue that such clarity and communication are highly desirable.

Fred Luthans and R. Kreitner (1988) summarize the problems with behaviour modification:

1 Appropriate reinforcers may not always be available (in limited and boring work settings, for example).
2 We do not all respond the same way to the same reinforcers; what one person finds rewarding may be of little consequence to someone else.
3 Once begun, a behaviour modification programme has to be sustained over time.
4 There may not be enough extrinsic motivators (such as money and luncheon vouchers, for example) available.

They also argue, however, that the technique has made four significant contributions:

1 Behaviour modification techniques put the focus on observable employee behaviour and not on hypothetical internal states.
2 The approach recognizes that performance is influenced by contingent consequences.
3 It supports the view that positive reinforcement, or reward, is more effective than punishment in changing employee behaviour.
4 There are demonstrable causal effects on employee performance – a feature that is sometimes difficult to establish unequivocally with other behaviour change methods, such as job enrichment, for example.

Fred Luthans

Socialization has the advantage of flexibility. Social learning is dependent on the cultural context, and as a process rather than a specific technique, the approach in general terms cannot be limited to a single culture. American induction and socialization procedures may be quite different from Swedish, Belgian, Nigerian, Malaysian or French methods.

Socialization is a process that takes place anyway, whether management plan and organize it or not. The issue concerns *appropriate* socialization, with respect to existing organization culture and its planned goals and behavioural preferences. Because it is a 'natural' social process, and because there is no clear financial or other material benefit from investing in its operation, it may be difficult to persuade management to give the socialization process the degree of attention, support and resource that some commentators advocate.

The same comments apply to supervisory feedback. It can be argued that this is a 'taken for granted' responsibility of any supervisory role and that special attention is, therefore, not necessary. The evidence suggests that the delivery of effective feedback is a valuable skill that has to be learned and developed. Many managers and supervisors feel uncomfortable with this aspect of their work unless they have had appropriate training.

---

beyond supervisory appraisal: 360-degree feedback

Traditionally, it has been your immediate boss who conducts regular (usually annual) performance appraisals and gives you feedback on how well you are doing, and perhaps about what you need to do to improve. The limitations of this approach encouraged a number of organizations in the mid- to late 1990s to experiment with multi-source feedback for employees, at all levels including management. The technique that became popular is known as '360-degree appraisal'. In 360-degree appraisal, you are appraised by, and given feedback from, your immediate boss – and your colleagues, and your subordinates, and perhaps other senior organizational members, and you may be invited to conduct a self-appraisal as well.

This also means that you, in turn, get to appraise your manager, in a procedure known as 'upward appraisal'.

Assuming that the feedback is honest and constructive, the individual receives a much wider set of comments, which can be used to change behaviour and to improve performance. However, as most formal appraisal schemes involve the completion of an appraisal form, so that a record can be kept, 360-degree appraisal can increase the volume of paperwork and the administrative effort in circulating and filing forms.

> ### STOP!
> What other advantages and disadvantages of 360-degree appraisal can you identify?

based on Mike Thatcher, 1996, 'Allowing everyone to have their say', *People Management*, 21 March, pp. 28–30.

The personnel or human resource management function in medium to large organizations usually allocates responsibility for training and development to a specialist group. Training has traditionally concentrated on obviously relevant job skills and competencies, from the shop or office floor to senior management. However, competitive pressures in many organizations in the twenty-first century will continue to be translated into demands for employees who demonstrate higher levels of flexibility, commitment, initiative

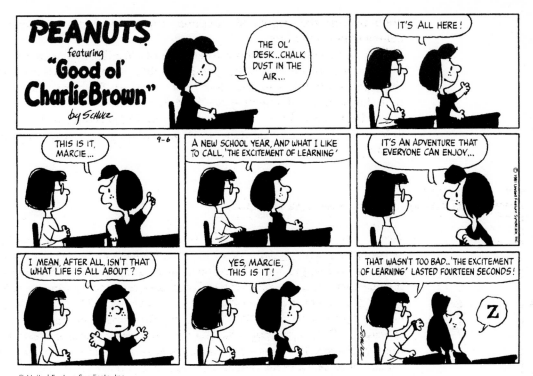

© United Feature Syndicate, Inc.

and creativity. This argument was explained in Chapter 4 on motivation. In this context, human resource management strategies that involve *qualitative* changes in performance at work may become more significant, and bring fresh attention to behaviour modification techniques and socialization processes to achieve these ends.

sources

Bandura, A., 1977, *Social Learning Theory*, Prentice Hall, Englewood Cliffs, NJ.

Bandura, A., 1986, *Social Foundations of Thought and Action: A Social Cognitive Theory*, Prentice Hall, Englewood Cliffs, NJ.

Bower, G.H. and Hilgard, E.R., 1981, *Theories of Learning*, Prentice Hall, Englewood Cliffs, NJ, 5th edition.

Davey, G. and Cullen, C. (eds.), 1988, *Human Operant Conditioning and Behaviour Modification*, John Wiley, Chichester.

Feeney, E.J., 1972, 'Performance audit, feedback and positive reinforcement', *Training and Development Journal*, vol. 26, no. 11, pp. 8–13.

Geller, E. S., 1983, 'Rewarding safety belt usage at an industrial setting: tests of treatment generality and response maintenance', *Journal of Applied Behavior Analysis*, vol. 16, no. 2, summer, pp. 189–202.

Ilgen, D. R. and Knowlton, W. A., 1980, 'Performance attributional effects on feedback from superiors', *Organizational Behaviour and Human Performance*, vol. 25, no. 3, pp. 441–56.

Leavitt, H.J. and Bahrami, H., 1988, *Managerial Psychology: Managing Behavior in Organizations*, The University of Chicago Press, Chicago and London.

Luthans, F. and Kreitner, R., 1988, *Organizational Behaviour Modification*, Scott, Foresman, New York, 2nd edition.

Martin, G.L. and Pear, J., 1978, *Behavior Modification: What it is and How to do it*, Prentice Hall, Englewood Cliffs, NJ.

Miller, G.A., Galanter, E. and Pribram, K.H., 1960, *Plans nd the Structure of Behavior*, Henry Holt, New York.

Murphy, G., 1958, *Human Potentialities*, George Allen & Unwin, London.

Nota, B., 1988, 'The socialization process at high-commitment organizations', *Personnel*, vol. 65, no. 8, pp. 20–3.

Parsons, M.B., Schepis, M.M., Reid, D.H., McCarn, J.E. and Green, C.W., 1987, 'Expanding the impact of behavioural staff management: A large-scale, long-term application in schools serving the severely handicapped', *Journal of Applied Behaviour Analysis*, vol. 20, no. 2, summer, pp. 139–50.

Smither, R.D., 1988, *The Psychology of Work and Human Performance*, Harper & Row, New York.

Thatcher, M., 1996, 'Allowing everyone to have their say', *People Management*, 21 March, pp. 28–30.

Walters, C.C. and Grusec, J.E., 1977, *Punishment*, Freeman, San Francisco.

White, R.W., 1959, 'Motivation reconsidered: the concept of competence', *Psychological Review*, vol. 66, pp. 297–333.

Wiener, N., 1954, *The Human Use of Human Beings: Cybernetics and Society*, Avon Books, New York.

chapter 6 personality

funny **Business**

EXECUTIVE SEARCH

— by MORRIS —

"What we are looking for is someone without an earstud"

concepts and learning objectives

useful Latin terms
per sonare to speak through *persona* an actor's mask; a character in a play *persona grata* an acceptable person *persona non grata* an unacceptable person

Organizational applications of personality assessment have grown in popularity through the 1980s and 1990s, and this trend appears to be well established. Most personnel and human resource managers believe that personality is related in some way to job performance and to career success. College and university graduates facing the selection procedures of large organizations in particular, whether in manufacturing, services, local government, civil service or healthcare, can expect to complete at least one of the more common personality inventories. It is now usual for job applicants to find themselves completing the same assessment questionnaire for a number of prospective employers. What are the foundations of these assessments, and of what value are they to organizations and to their members?

The term *psychometrics* is now used to refer to the broad range of different types of tests and measurements of aptitude, intelligence and also of personality characteristics.

---

definition
___
Psychometrics *is an area of psychology concerned with the systematic testing, measurement and assessment, of intelligence, aptitudes, and personality.*

The history of intelligence testing reaches back to the beginning of the twentieth century. There are numerous tests available for specific aptitudes related to particular occupations, such as the Computer Programmer Aptitude Battery. Similar tests are used to measure, for example, typing ability and arithmetic competence. There are also a large number of instruments and techniques for the assessment of personality factors. When measuring aspects of aptitude or intelligence, it is perhaps relevant to use the term 'test', because a high score, in most circumstances, is better than a low score. When measuring aspects of personality, on the other hand, it is more appropriate to use the term 'assessment'. A 'high' score on a personality factor (extraversion, for example), cannot be said to be 'better' or 'worse' than a 'low' score. There are no right or wrong answers in a personality assessment questionnaire; there are no correct or incorrect personality traits or types.

Ivan Robertson (1994) identifies a paradox here. The evidence reveals that tests of general mental ability are good predictors of performance across a number of occupations. However, the links between personality factors and job success are much more difficult to establish, for reasons explored later in this chapter. Despite the evidence, personality assessment procedures are more commonly used in organizational selection than intelligence testing, which remains controversial as some population sub-groups achieve relatively poor scores.

Psychometric assessment has a range of potential applications in, for example:
- shortlisting and selecting candidates for jobs
- assessment of suitability for promotion
- assessment for redeployment purposes
- evaluation of training potential
- career counselling and development
- graduate recruitment, where applicants have limited work experience
- vocational guidance
- redundancy counselling

In settings like these, psychometric assessments are now commonly used to complement less formal and more subjective methods, to help the organization reach more informed and objective judgements about people as employees or as potential employees.

In this chapter, we shall concentrate on personality assessment. The testing of intelligence and of specific aptitudes are separate and specialized topics beyond the scope of this text. Two broad approaches to personality are explained, with the rather awkward labels *nomothetic* and *idiographic*. Nomothetic approaches form the basis for most contemporary organizational psychometrics. These are usually based on self-report questionnaires or personality inventories, which are easier to administer, score and interpret than idiographic methods. The latter use open-ended questioning strategies to capture the unique modes of expression of the individual. Nomothetic techniques also appear to offer a level of objectivity in assessment, which idiographic methods do not seem to possess. However, idiographic techniques rely on assumptions about human psychology which are different from those underpinning nomothetic methods. It is on the validity of these assumptions that our judgements of different methods should be based, and not simply on matters of convenience.

key concepts

- psychometrics
- nomothetic
- type
- self-concept
- thematic apperception test
- neuroticism
- openness
- conscientiousness
- Type A personality
- need for achievement

- personality
- idiographic
- trait
- generalized other
- projective test
- emotionality
- agreeableness
- the big five
- Type B personality
- assessment centres

learning objectives

When you have read this chapter, you should be able to define those key concepts in your own words, and you should also be able to:

1 Assess realistically the main characteristics of your own personality.
2 Distinguish between type, trait and self-theories of personality.
3 Identify the strengths and limitations of both formal and informal approaches to personality assessment.
4 Explain the uses and limitations of objective questionnaires and projective tests as measures of personality.
5 Explain the relationship between personality and stress, and identify appropriate individual and organizational stress management strategies.
6 Evaluate the benefits and problems of psychometric assessment as a tool to assist management decision-making, particularly in selection.

> ## STOP!
>
> Opposite you will find a list of the 'core skills' which one British retail chain store now looks for when assessing graduates as potential employees. Compare this list with your own strengths and weaknesses.
>
> Do you think that, on this evidence, this company would hire you? Consider characteristics like:
>
> | | |
> |---|---|
> | ▶ Speaks with ease. | ▶ Has natural authority over others. |
> | ▶ Shows energy. | ▶ Is self-confident. |
> | ▶ Can present persuasive arguments. | ▶ Responds to situations quickly. |
>
> Are you born with these characteristics, or are these behaviours that you can learn and that you can improve and demonstrate more effectively with practice?
>
> Now, put yourself in the position of the person responsible for making the hiring decisions, based on whether or not, and the extent to which, potential recruits possess the following characteristics. How are you going to measure, assess or otherwise reach a judgement on each of these characteristics for each candidate?

the definition problem

We are unique individuals who deal with the world in our unique ways. What makes us different from each other? How can we identify and describe these differences and compare individuals with each other? Psychologists have tried to answer these questions using the concept of *personality*. It is useful, first, to distinguish between the popular uses of this concept, and the way in which psychology defines and uses the term.

---

definition

Personality *refers to the psychological qualities that influence an individual's characteristic behaviour patterns in a broadly distinctive and consistent manner, across different situations and through time.*

The term *personality* is often used to describe striking and habitual features of someone's behaviour. These characteristics, or properties, concern the individual's way of coping and dealing with life. Most of us know somebody,

W.H. Smith assess graduate recruits on nine 'core skills'

written communication

Communicates easily on paper with speed and clarity. Presents ideas concisely and in a structured way. Uses appropriate language and style. Grammar and spelling are accurate.

oral communication

Speaks to others with ease and clarity. Expresses ideas well and presents arguments in a logical fashion. Gives information and explanations which are clear and easily understood. Listens actively to others.

leadership

Shows skill in directing group activities. Has natural authority and gains respect of others. Capable of building an effective team. Involves all team members, gives advice and help when required.

team membership

Fits in well as a peer and as a subordinate. Understands own role and the role of others within the team. Shares information and seeks help and advice when necessary. Offers suggestions and listens to the ideas of others.

planning and organizing skills

Can make forward plans and forecasts. Can define objectives and allocate resources to meet them. Sets realistic targets and decides priorities. Devises systems and monitors progress. Makes good use of his/her time.

decision-making

Evaluates alternative lines of action and makes appropriate decisions. Identifies degrees of urgency for decisions. Responds to situations quickly and demonstrates flexibility.

motivation

Shows energy and enthusiasm. Works hard and is ambitious. Able to work on own initiative with little detailed supervision. Sets own targets and is determined to achieve them.

personal strength

Is self-confident and understands own strengths and weaknesses. Is realistic and willing to learn from past failures and successes. Is reliable, honest and conscientious. Can cope with pressure and control emotions.

analytical reasoning skills

Can quickly and accurately comprehend verbal and numerical information. Able to analyze arguments objectively and to reach logical conclusions. Can present well-reasoned and persuasive arguments.

based on Robin Jacobs, 1989a, 'Getting the measure of management competence', *Personnel Management*, June, pp. 32–7.

for example, who is usually late for meetings, or who typically responds aggressively to mild criticism, or who normally exhibits high levels of anxiety when about to meet someone for the first time. Once we have spotted these relatively stable patterns and coping mechanisms, we can begin to predict with reasonable accuracy some aspects of behaviour, and perhaps even adjust our own behaviour accordingly.

Personality is a broad, integrating concept, but we are not interested in all properties of an individual. Most of us get nervous in selection interviews, become anxious and sometimes aggressive when criticized, dislike pain and worry about tests and examinations. Such properties are not remarkable and do not set us apart from others. We become more interested, or concerned, when someone is speechless with nerves in an interview, when someone responds with violence to minor challenge, when someone sails with supreme confidence through every examination without a sign of anxiety. Our definition of personality, therefore, is restricted to those properties which set us apart, and which are both *stable* and *distinctive*.

stable

We are interested in behaviour patterns that appear consistently in different contexts, and that endure through time. We are not interested in properties that are occasional, random and transient, caused by temporary circumstances. People who are not punctual tend to be late for most or all occasions. People who are persistent, cheerful and optimistic tend usually to behave in that manner.

distinctive

We are interested in the pattern of dispositions and behaviours unique to the individual. We are not concerned with those properties that all or most other people possess. You may be aggressive towards waiters, friendly with

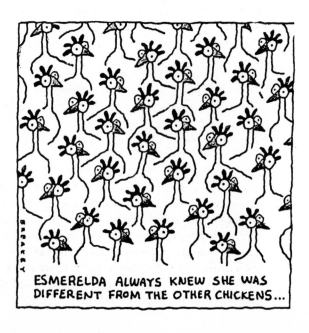

ESMERELDA ALWAYS KNEW SHE WAS
DIFFERENT FROM THE OTHER CHICKENS...

librarians, deferential to professors and terrified of mice. You may share some of these dispositions with a friend who breeds mice for a hobby.

Some personality dispositions may be strong and appear frequently. Other dispositions may be weak and aroused infrequently, or appear only in specific circumstances (like allergies, for instance). There can therefore be endless variations in personality differences.

If the concept of personality is to be useful in understanding behaviour, we have to accept two propositions.

First, we have to accept that our behaviour does have stable and enduring features and does not change, say, from year to year. Most of us can recognize consistency in our thought patterns, our emotional responses to particular events and our behaviours. We do seem to have our own established and routine ways of relating to others, of meeting our needs, of solving our problems, of coping with stress and frustration. Our behaviour patterns are not random and inconsistent. The regularities can be observed and studied.

Second, we have to accept that the distinctive properties of an individual's personality can be measured in some way, and compared with the properties of others. Measurement does not necessarily imply quantification, but nomothetic methods do rely on some sophisticated statistical analysis. Psychometrics relies on the assumption that personality can be measured.

The term *personality* is used in everyday conversation in two restricted senses.

The first of these concerns the use of *singular characteristics* to describe somebody's personality. We refer to people as having 'aggressive personalities', 'shy personalities', and so on. While it may be acceptable to describe others' personalities in terms of only one prominent feature for the purposes of everyday conversation, this approach is likely to be inadequate from a psychological perspective and for most organizational purposes.

The second views personality in terms of *quantity*. We refer to someone as having lots of personality, to somebody else as having little or no personality. The characteristics usually captured by this usage concern physical attractiveness and social success – as with 'television personalities'. Once again, this use of the term lacks precision.

These are not 'incorrect' uses of the concept of personality. They are adequate and cause no misunderstanding in the contexts in which they are normally applied. The psychologist, however, regards these uses as oversimplified and as inadequate for the purpose of understanding behaviour in a scientific sense. So, we shall avoid these approaches.

The issue, however, is that we are all *informal personality theorists*. We continually assess the personalities of those we meet and with whom we interact. We normally do this without conscious thought, and we usually only share and discuss our judgements in particular social contexts (when the object of the discussion is absent, for example, but when others who know them are present). As discussed in Chapter 3, where we explored aspects of person perception, we categorize or *stereotype* others on the basis of some of their main attributes; Scots have a reputation for being mean; blondes have more fun, we are told; women, it is claimed (by men) are too emotional and indecisive to be effective managers.

As informal personality assessments, stereotypes serve useful purposes. They give us simple explanations for behaviour, explanations that we can check against our observations. They help us to make predictions about the likely responses of others in particular settings. They give us a basis for determining our own behaviour in relating to others. Stereotypes are a useful starting point or benchmark – as long as we are willing to monitor their accuracy and to change our views if our observations suggest we are wrong.

Stereotypes, therefore, are *implicit personality theories*. Implicit, because they are not formally articulated, or precisely defined, and they are not supported by systematically collected empirical evidence. Theories, because we use them to help us explain and predict the behaviour of others, and to guide our own conduct in relation to others. Implicit personality theories do not conform to psychology's rigorous standards, but they have a value in the context in which they are popularly applied.

Our ability to assess the personalities of others rapidly and accurately is one key aspect of coping with our social world. We are not always consciously aware of this achievement, and we do not have to be aware to do it effectively. We interact competently with members of our families, with people at work, with friends, with restaurant staff, and so on. We ask them questions, tell them things, give them instructions, and each time know precisely how they will respond. If we were not able to make such accurate judgements, decisions and predictions about others, we would lead extremely difficult and embarrassing social lives.

However, research shows that we are poor judges of each other's personalities. Those stereotypes must be wrong. There may be a small, thin, dark-haired, mean Scotsman somewhere on the planet, but very few people have met him. There are many successful female managers. Women are typically excluded from managerial positions by the 'glass ceiling' erected by male discrimination and not by personality or ability problems. When we make informal personality assessments, we tend to rely on inadequate information, make rapid decisions, oversimplify – and therefore make mistakes.

We have another paradox here. How can we claim to display such competence in our interactions with others if we are such awful judges of personality? We must be able to assess others accurately enough to be able to interact successfully with them. We do this well, and effortlessly, because we interact with most other individuals in contexts in which only a limited range of behaviour is possible and relevant.

We usually interact with other people in specific roles. Roles are social positions defined by the sets of expectations which the role holder must fulfil. Our behaviour and the contents of our conversations are conditioned by our shared expectations of how people in particular roles should behave. Many of our social interactions – with strangers and close family members alike – have the characteristics of rituals. They begin and unfold each time in similar ways, and they close in similar ways too. Only in extraordinary circumstances will either or both parties break the rules and move out of their respective roles into the limitless field of other acts and utterances that they are quite capable of performing.

> **STOP!**
> Think of a common, everyday interaction in which you are often involved. Identify the role expectations, or the 'unwritten rules', that govern this interaction.
> Consider the consequences of breaking these expectations, of breaking the rules.
> Try breaking some of the rules next time, and note the consequences.

The point of this argument is as follows. There is no inconsistency in the twin claims that we are socially competent while being poor judges of personality. It is relatively easy to appear competent in social interactions, even with complete strangers, as long as everybody knows the rules and is prepared to play by them. We rarely interact in socially 'rule-free' settings, and we rarely interact with 'the whole person'. When we deal with others, we are typically confronted with only a small number of facets of their personality, which makes the assessment task a restricted and fairly straightforward one. This does, however, seem to give us a false confidence in our informal personality assessment capabilities.

Returning to our definition problem, there is no single, grand, unified and widely accepted theory of personality. The definition and understanding of the concept remains controversial. Psychology has developed a number of different approaches to the study of personality, and two broad perspectives will be explored here, echoing to some extent the discussion of different approaches to the psychology of learning in Chapter 5.

Some psychologists argue that our personality is inherited. This implies that our thoughts, feelings and behaviours are determined by a genetic inheritance from our parents and by the biochemistry of our brains. There is evidence to suggest that, because measures of individual job satisfaction are fairly stable through time and across different jobs, a predisposition to be content with or frustrated at work may have a genetic, inherited component. This relationship is, of course, 'one-way'. Your genetic endowment determines your personality, and the reverse cannot happen. In this perspective, your personality is fixed at birth, if not before, and life's experiences do little or nothing to alter it.

Other psychologists argue that personality is determined by environmental, cultural and social factors. This implies that our feelings and behaviour patterns are learned and shaped through our experience of living and interacting with other people in society. Motivation theory, explored in Chapter 4, suggests how individual job satisfaction can be influenced by manipulating aspects of work design and other aspects of the organizational environment, such as supervisory style. Social learning theory, explored in Chapter 5, suggests how we learn new behaviours through observing and imitating others.

Every culture has distinctive ways of doing things. We cannot possibly be born with this detailed local knowledge. We have to learn how to become *persona grata* in our society, or in any society in which we find ourselves. This relationship is two-way. Others influence us, and we in turn affect them. In this perspective, your personality is flexible and can change with experience.

It may also be the case that psychological well-being depends in part on your ability to adapt to changing circumstances by altering facets of your personality.

The controversy over the relative influences of heredity and environment on personality and intelligence is known as the 'nature–nurture' debate. The previous paragraphs have set out the extreme positions which very few, if indeed any, psychologists hold. It is clear that both genetic and situational factors influence our behaviour patterns. Theorists disagree over the emphases to be given to these different factors – how they should be measured and how they interact. This theoretical debate has profound consequences for organizational behaviour, with respect to the methods used to select organizational members, and with respect to the methods used to shape attitudes and motivations to work, and improve work performance.

personality types and traits

Attempts to describe the components and structure of personality have focused on the concepts of *type* and *trait*. One of the most straightforward ways of describing and analyzing personality concerns the categorization of people into personality *types*.

---

definition

A **type** is a broad, descriptive label for a distinct pattern of personality characteristics. Examples of personality types include extravert, neurotic, conscientious and agreeable.

One of the first personality theorists was Hippocrates, the Greek known as 'The father of medicine' who lived around 400 BC. He claimed that differences in temperament were caused by predominant body humours. His theory suggested the following relationships:

body humour	temperament	behaviours
blood	sanguine	confident, cheerful, optimistic, hopeful, active
phlegm	phlegmatic	sluggish, apathetic
black bile	melancholic	depressed, sad, brooding, prone to ill-founded fears
yellow bile	choleric	aggressive, excitable, irritable

These temperament labels are still in use today and have the same meanings. Hippocrates' theory, however, is unsound for two reasons. First, what we know about the relationships between body chemistry and behaviour fails to confirm the theory. Second, our personal experience should tell us that there are more than four types of people in the world.

typing Miss Piggy: a case study in personality creation

Irving Rein, Philip Kotler and Martin Stoller argue that career success depends more on a person's 'visibility' than their ability. This explains the growth of a 'celebrity industry', which helps people to acquire the personalities they desire for success in a chosen field.

The aspirant's need to adopt a type, or live out an archetype, is found in many sectors of society. Consider the politician who is challenging an incumbent. The challenger can adopt one of several archetypes: the 'white knight', 'underdog', 'dark horse', 'thinking man', 'angry man', 'idealist', or 'statesman'. The challenger will need to think through which type has the greatest vote potential and whether he or she has the stretch and adaptability to reach it. . . .

An excellent example of developing character in a celebrity is Miss Piggy, the inanimate creation of author Frank Oz and puppeteer Jim Henson. Miss Piggy's typing is well set; clearly she is a heroine who gets what she wants through competitive, sometimes unorthodox, strategies. Miss Piggy, labelled by her own creators as 'a femme fatale gowned in satin and blessed with a pulverizing left hook' fits [the] 'love queen' type. It is not incidental to her typing that Miss Piggy is a popular pin-up who is seen in all manner of porcine pin-up poses.

More important, the character of Miss Piggy demonstrates that different traits are important in communicating character. Although she is a complete fabrication, Miss Piggy has most of the characteristics and reactions of a person: unlike many puppets, Miss Piggy is a multidimensional pig. Besides her girth she has many of the traits that define *roundness*. Although Miss Piggy finds herself drawn to the security of family life with 'Kermie', her beloved frog, she also likes the glamour and fame of her position. In her personal life, she struggles with all the insecurities and self-doubts that mark most of our lives.

Miss Piggy also demonstrates *autonomy* through her notorious unpredictability. Like many humans, she displays a wide range of reactions to situations. *People* magazine observed of Miss Piggy:

One instant [she is] playing the Arrogant Superstar snarling at her beefy litter bearers as she finishes her big Cleopatra scene: 'Awright meat! Let's move it!' The next she is Daddy's little darling, giggling and cooing: 'I'll only be an eeeeetsy-teensy minute! Kissy, Kissy!' Then without warning she drops a karate chop on a luckless reporter who has enquired about her weight problem.

In the area of *character development*, Miss Piggy continues to grow and change. She was, after all, the first pig to move into a writing career. Finding a need to grow beyond her television and film career, Miss Piggy moved into diet and exercise guides. It would not be unexpected to see Miss Piggy, finding celebrity a chore, to move to Switzerland or take up with a European count.

from Irving J. Rein, Philip Kotler and Martin R. Stoller, 1987, *High Visibility*, Heinemann, London, pp. 205 and 206–7.

A more recent personality type theory came in the 1940s, from the work of William Sheldon (1898–1970), who argued that temperament was related to physique or build, or to what he called *somatotype*. In other words, your personality depends on your size and shape. In Sheldon's theory, the *endomorph*, who is fat, soft and round, is also sociable, relaxed and enjoys food. The *mesomorph* is muscular, strong and rectangular, and is energetic, physical, courageous and assertive. Finally, the *endomorph*, who is thin and fragile, is also introverted, artistic and intellectual. This typology may have some intuitive appeal, but it has been shown not to be an effective model for predicting behaviour. Think of someone with the build of an endomorph, who is also introverted and intellectual. Are you friendly with a mesomorph who is a relaxed gourmet, or with an ectomorph who is sociable and assertive?

Type approaches attempt to fit people into predetermined categories possessing common broad patterns of behaviour. A personality *trait*, on the other hand, is any enduring or habitual behaviour pattern that occurs in a variety of circumstances. Traits are also sometimes defined in terms of predispositions to behave in a particular way.

---

definition

A personality **trait** *is a relatively stable quality or attribute of the individual, influencing behaviour in a particular direction. Examples of traits include shyness, excitability, reliability, moodiness.*

The study of *traits* in personality research and assessment, and of how traits cluster to form personality *types*, is associated with the *nomothetic* approach in psychology.

---

definition

The **nomothetic** *approach to the study of personality emphasizes the identification of universal personality traits and looks for systematic relation-ships between different aspects of personality.*

Nomothetic means 'law-setting' or 'law-giving'. Psychologists who adopt this approach are thus looking for regularities or for universal laws that govern human behaviour. The nomothetic approach adopts the following procedures and assumptions.

First, the main dimensions – traits – on which human personality can vary are identified. Traits describe aspects of temperament and character, and reflect the individual's predisposition to behave in particular ways. This approach assumes that our otherwise unique personalities can be measured and compared on the same dimensions.

Second, the personalities of groups of people are assessed, typically through some form of self-report questionnaire or inventory. Popular magazines occasionally use short and 'fun' versions of these questionnaires. The questions usually ask individuals to choose between a fixed number of answers. Responses may be confined, for example, to 'true' or 'false', to 'yes'

The four basic personality types

or 'no', or to a rating scale that runs from 'strongly agree' to 'strongly disagree'. Because responses are constrained in this way, these are called 'forced choice' questions. The way in which individuals answer the questions determines their scores on each of the dimensions measured. This procedure also assumes that the answers reflect actual behaviour.

Third, an individual's personality profile is constructed across all the dimensions measured. Individual scores on each dimension are compared with the average score and distribution of scores for the group as a whole. This enables the assessor to identify individuals around the norm and those with pronounced characteristics that deviate from the norm. An individual's score in such an assessment carries relatively little interest and meaning outside the context of the scores of the population to which that individual belongs. You cannot have a 'high' score; you can only have a score that is high in comparison.

Fourth, the group may be split into sub-groups, say by age, sex or occupation. This produces other reference points or averages against which individual scores can be compared, and permits comparisons between sub-group scores. Patterns of similarities and differences among and between groups enable general laws about human personality and behaviour to be formulated. One may find, for example, that successful Scottish male managers tend to be introverted, or that women under the age of 25 employed in purchasing have abnormally low scores on shyness. This approach is rather impersonal, and it is difficult to use the results to predict the behaviour of individuals, even those with 'extreme' scores. However, it may be possible to make probabilistic predictions about the behaviour of groups of people in terms of behaviour tendencies.

The nomothetic approach relies on the assumption that personality is primarily inherited and that environmental factors and experience have little or limited effect. We are stuck with the personality with which we were born. If personality was influenced by environmental factors and was thereby unstable, the identification of universal laws of personality and behaviour would not be possible.

However, note how nomothetic assumptions determine the way in which the approach proceeds and the nature of the results that are obtained. The assumptions, the methods and the findings come as an integrated 'package', not just as separate stages of argument and evidence.

Personality is whatever makes you, the individual, different from other people. It may appear odd that one major approach to the study of personality relies on investigations that cover large groups of people at a time. But in assessing the personalities of groups of people, one discovers what is 'normal' or average for those groups and compares individuals with that. Note that the terms norm and average are used in this context in the *statistical* sense. Individuals who 'deviate from the norm' are not to be branded as abnormal social outcasts or criminals. Assessments based on this method are, however, often used as a guide to the personality profile of individuals, typically in personnel selection contexts.

STOP!

There are in the English language around 17,000 to 18,000 adjectives which describe behaviour (an observation first made by the American psychologist Gordon Allport). Examples include reserved, outgoing, emotional, stable, trusting, suspicious, conservative, experimenting, relaxed and tense, and so on. How many others can you identify, and can you identify contrasting pairs like those in the examples which we have just given?

How would you design a personality assessment around these adjectives?

*Hans Jürgen Eysenck
(b. 1916)*

Trait approaches assume that there is a common set of traits on which we can all be compared. The adjectives that you have listed are trait labels. Individuals can have different traits and have different strengths of the same traits. This does appear to do more justice to the uniqueness and complexity of the individual personality than type approaches. Another way to look at this distinction is to consider that traits belong to individuals, but that individuals belong to type categories. You *have* a trait, you *fit* a type.

One of the most powerful and influential theories of personality developed this century is that of Hans Jürgen Eysenck who was born in Germany in 1916, and who now lives and works in Britain. His research has identified two major dimensions on which personality can vary: the extraversion–introversion or '*E*' dimension, and the neuroticism–stability or '*N*' dimension.

Eysenck's approach is nomothetic. His sympathies lie with the behaviourist psychologists who seek a scientific, experimental, mathematical psychology. His explanations of personality, however, are based on genetics. Behaviourists claim that behaviour is shaped by environmental influences. As usual, the differences between these approaches can be traced to different underlying assumptions.

Eysenck's model is particularly interesting because it offers a way of linking types, traits and behaviour. Eysenck argues that personality structure is hierarchical. Each individual possesses more or less of a number of identifiable traits – trait 1, trait 2, trait 3, and so on. Individuals who have a particular trait, say trait 1, are more likely to possess another, say trait 3, than people who do not have trait 1 or who have it weakly. In other words, traits tend to 'cluster' in systematic patterns. These clusters identify a 'higher order' of personality description, in terms of what Eysenck calls personality types, as this simple diagram shows:

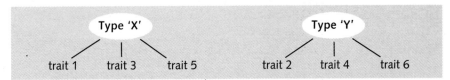

This does not mean that every individual who has trait 1 has a Type 'X' personality. It means that questionnaire analysis has shown that individuals with high scores on trait 1 are more likely to have high scores on traits 3 and 5 also, putting them into the Type 'X' category.

Eysenck argues that there is statistical evidence from personality assessments to support the existence of personality traits, trait clusters and types. Individuals vary in a continuous distribution on trait scores and this model takes into account the oversimplification problem of type theories.

The *E* dimension divides the human world into two broad categories of people – extraverts and introverts. These terms have passed into popular use and were first coined by a Swiss psychologist, Carl Gustav Jung (1875–1961). The American popular use of these terms tends to refer to sociability and unsociability. European use emphasizes spontaneity and inhibition. Eysenck's account combines these notions.

Extraverts are tough-minded individuals, who need strong and varied external stimulation. They are sociable, like parties, are good at telling stories, enjoy practical jokes, have many friends, need people to talk to, do not enjoy studying and reading on their own, crave excitement, take risks, act impulsively, prefer change, are optimistic, carefree, active, aggressive, quick-tempered, display their emotions and are unreliable.

Eysenck argues that seven personality traits cluster to generate the personality type extraversion. These traits are:

Carl Gustav Jung (1875–1961)
Photo source:
Archives of the History of American Psychology, The University of Akron, Ohio, USA.

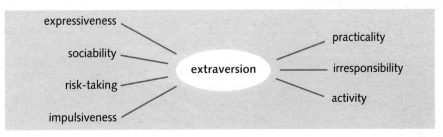

Introverts are tender-minded people who experience strong emotions and who do not need the extravert's intensity of external stimuli. They are quiet, introspective, retiring, prefer books to people, are withdrawn, reserved, plan ahead, distrust impulse, appreciate order, lead careful sober lives, have little excitement, suppress emotions, are pessimistic, worry about moral standards and are reliable.

The seven traits that cluster to form this personality type are:

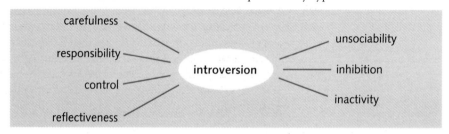

Most of us fall somewhere between these extremes. These are not exclusive categories; rather they lie on a continuum from one extreme to the other, with most people around the centre and a few at the extremes.

The *N* dimension assesses personality on a continuum between neuroticism and stability. Neurotics are also labelled emotional, unstable and anxious. Stable people can be described as adjusted. Neurotics tend to have a low opinion of themselves and feel that they are unattractive failures. Neurotics tend to be disappointed with life, pessimistic and depressed. They worry unnecessarily about things that may never happen and are easily upset when things go wrong. They are also obsessive, conscientious, finicky people, who are highly disciplined, staid and get annoyed by untidiness and disorder.

Neurotics are not self-reliant and tend to submit to institutional power without question. They feel controlled by events, by others and by fate. They often imagine that they are ill and demand sympathy. They blame themselves excessively and are troubled by conscience.

The seven traits that cluster to form emotional instability are:

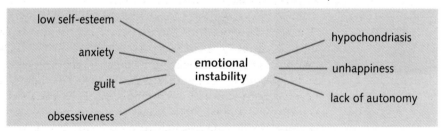

Stable individuals are self-confident, optimistic, resist irrational fears, are easy-going, realistic, solve their own problems, have few health worries and have few regrets about their past. The seven traits that form the emotionally stable type are:

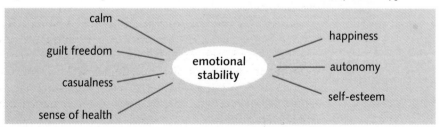

The questionnaire that Eysenck normally uses to measure the E and N dimensions of personality has 96 questions, 40 for each dimension, and 16 'lie detector' questions to assess the subjects' honesty. The questions are mainly in the 'yes/no' format. The E and N dimensions are not themselves correlated. So if you are extraverted, you could be either stable or neurotic. The individual's score on one of these dimensions does not appear to influence the score on the other.

The questionnaires are constructed in the following way.

First, questions are worded in ways that appear, on face value, to measure the trait under consideration. The question 'Are you inclined to be moody?' appears to concern emotional instability. The question 'Are you inclined to be quick and sure in your actions?' seems to be a measure of extraversion. Several questions are chosen to measure the same trait.

Second, a 'pilot' or trial questionnaire is constructed and given to a number of subjects to complete. The subjects may be chosen at random, they may be representative of a particular group or they may be chosen for their already known personality biases.

Third, the pilot results are used:

▶ To screen out questions which do not discriminate between those who have a trait and those who do not.
▶ To identify questions on which responses cluster, to provide an internal check confirming that different questions do measure the same thing.
▶ To label the answer clusters in terms of what they appear on face value to be assessing or measuring.
▶ To compare the results with those of other tests on the same people, and with the results of the same test on other people with known traits, to provide a check on the questions, confirming that the measure does identify the trait under consideration.
▶ To construct the main questionnaire.

It has been difficult to show that one personality type is more successful or desirable than another. The extravert may be considered desirable for the sociable, friendly, good company, cheerful, active, lively characteristics. But extraverts are also unreliable, fickle in friendships, easily bored and are poor at uninteresting or time-consuming tasks. So there are both positive and negative aspects of the extravert personality. Assessment is used in a clinical context to identify individuals with extreme scores which may (but not necessarily) indicate psychological problems. People with extreme scores have what Eysenck calls an 'ambiguous gift'. This may cause problems. However, if we are aware of such features, we may be able to act in ways to control and exploit them to our advantage. More problems arise when one does not have this awareness.

Surely a stable personality is more desirable than a neurotic one? Probably not. An open display of emotion is desirable in some settings and embarrassing in others. Emotions are a major source of motivation and an inability to display or share feelings can be a serious drawback. Sharing feelings of frustration and anger can be as important in an organizational setting as showing positive feelings of, for example, praise, satisfaction and friendship.

---

get a feel for the process: assess your own personality

Complete this short personality assessment – a short example of the type of questionnaire developed by Eysenck.

tick – yes or no:	Yes	No
1 Do you sometimes feel happy, sometimes depressed, without any apparent reason?		
2 Do you have frequent ups and downs in mood either with or without apparent cause?		
3 Are you inclined to be moody?		
4 Does your mind often wander while you are trying to concentrate?		
5 Are you frequently 'lost in thought' even when supposed to be taking part in a conversation?		
6 Are you sometimes bubbling over with energy and sometimes very sluggish?		
7 Do you prefer action to planning for action?		
8 Are you happiest when you get involved in some project that calls for rapid action?		
9 Do you usually take the initiative in making new friends?		
10 Are you inclined to be quick and sure in your actions?		
11 Would you rate yourself as a lively individual?		
12 Would you be very unhappy if you were prevented from making numerous social contacts?		

Now for the scoring. A 'Yes' answer in any of the first six questions scores one point towards emotionality, while a 'No' answer does not score at all. Similarly, a 'Yes' answer to any of the last six items scores one point towards extraversion. You can therefore end up with two scores, either of which may run from 0 (very stable, very introverted) to 6 (very unstable emotionally, very extraverted). The majority of people will have scores of 2, 3 or 4, indicating moderate degrees of emotionality or extraversion.

from H.J. Eysenck and G. Wilson, 1975, *Know Your Own Personality*, Maurice Temple Smith, London.

It is more important for us to be aware of our own personalities and to be aware of the characteristics that might be seen by others as our strengths and our weaknesses. To understand other people, one must begin with an understanding of one's own personality and of the effect that one has on other people. Self-assessments, like this one, can help us to look more objectively at the dimensions of our own personalities.

Eysenck's theory of personality has a physiological basis. Neuroticism, for example, appears to be associated with aspects of the human nervous system that control heartbeat, body temperature, sweating and digestion. Extraverts have a brain neurophysiology that is different from introverts. They need higher levels of stimulation to attract and maintain their interest. This

extraverts need higher levels of stimulation

Some students always sit in the busiest and noisiest sections of the library, seem to spend their time socializing instead of studying and disappoint the swots by passing their exams anyway. John Campbell and Charles Hawley produced evidence which shows how some people actually need these distractions to study effectively.

According to Hans Eysenck, extraverts need and enjoy the presence of others, but introverts prefer the peace and quiet of solitude.

Campbell and Hawley interviewed 102 students in the library at Colgate University in New York and gave them Eysenck's questionnaire. The first and third floors in the library contained individual desks separated by 8-foot high bookshelves. The second floor was an open area with soft chairs and large tables.

The researchers expected to find the introverts on the first and third floors and the extraverts on the second. The results confirmed their predictions.

The researchers argued that the extravert students were probably working as hard as their introverted classmates. Eysenck's personality theory is based on knowledge of the biochemistry of the brain. Extraverts need higher levels of stimulation to get their grey matter going and need frequent changes in stimulation to maintain their interest. Introverts need less stimulation to arouse them and can sustain their concentration without interruption.

So the crowded areas of the library give extravert students more opportunities for short study breaks which prevent them from getting bored. Introverts should clearly try to find areas of the library where they will not be interrupted by extraverts.

based on John W. Campbell and Charles W. Hawley, 1982, 'Study habits and Eysenck's theory of extraversion–introversion', *Journal of Research in Personality*, vol. 16, no. 2, pp. 139–46.

supports the argument that personality is inherited, that it is determined largely by genetic and biological factors rather than by environment and culture.

The search for trait clusters following Eysenck's hierarchical model, and Allport's earlier work on trait terms found in natural language, has culminated in the early 1990s in what have come to be termed *the big five*. The most influential advocates of this formulation have been Paul Costa and Robert McRae (McRae, 1992). This can be regarded as a significant development of Eysenck's approach.

definition

The big five *are broad personality types, or trait clusters, which appear in research studies consistently to capture the traits that we use to describe ourselves and other people.* **The big five** *can also, therefore, be defined as a comprehensive descriptive system, which captures in plain English most personality traits.*

In summary, *the big five*, which include Eysenck's dimensions, can be defined as follows:

definitions			
extraversion	gregarious, warm, positive	versus	quiet, reserved, shy
agreeableness	straightforward, compliant, sympathetic	versus	quarrelsome, oppositional, unfeeling
conscientiousness	achievement-oriented, dutiful, self-disciplined	versus	frivolous, irresponsible, disorganized
neuroticism	anxious, depressed, self-conscious	versus	calm, contented, self-assured
openness	creative, open-minded, intellectual	versus	unimaginative, disinterested, narrow-minded

While this approach has attracted criticism, it has also achieved relatively wide acceptance as a common descriptive system. Research seems to have reproduced these dimensions, in many different settings, with different populations, with different forms of data collection and in different languages. The labelling and interpretation of each remain controversial.

The interesting question for those who work in organizations is, what personality types and traits are needed to make one a successful manager, banker, machine tool operator, typist, lecturer, pilot, policeman or nurse? This is an awkward question. Personality is only one influence on an individual's role in life. Ability, opportunity and luck all have a significant impact on job performance. Most jobs are multifaceted. A trait that enhances your competence in one task may not improve your overall performance. The quality of your work depends on many factors, including motivation, the organization of the work, training, the payment system, physical facilities, supervisory style, company policy, and so on. Sex, age and general intelligence are also important.

It has, therefore, proved to be no simple matter to correlate personality assessments with job or career success. It is hazardous to make predictions about someone's performance on a job on the basis of personality assessment. However, the recent developments in *psychometrics*, defined earlier, are improving the predictive power of such selection and appraisal methods. We shall explore this later in the chapter.

There is another potential problem with the use of personality assessments in organizational settings. In clinical and research settings, most people co-operate willingly with doctors and researchers and give honest and accurate responses to questions. Most of us are interested enough in ourselves to be curious about our scores and their interpretation. Personality assessments, however, are fairly easy to falsify. They may not be considered reliable for job selection and promotion purposes where the individual's career may be at stake. The 'lie detecting' questions are fairly easy to detect and to answer in the 'correct' way. And some of us feel that this kind of assessment does not tap the depth, complexity and richness of individual thought processes; the forced choice questions are designed to inhibit freedom of expression.

Some of us have fixed or set reactions to completing questionnaires of this kind, complaining that we want to say 'maybe' instead of having to say yes or no, or always giving the middle, or most neutral response possible, or trying helpfully to give what we believe to be the desirable or expected response. These are called 'response sets', because they describe how the individual is set to respond to questions in a predetermined way. Response sets can thus bias systematically the results of personality assessment, but they can also help you to score 'well', as William H. Whyte (1956) once argued.

---

which response set should you adopt?

William H. Whyte offers the following advice on how to cheat on personality assessments:

> You should try to answer as if you were like everyone else is supposed to be. This is not always too easy to figure out, of course, and this is one of the reasons why I will go into some detail.

Whyte suggests that, to find the best answers, keep repeating these six statements to yourself as you fill in the questionnaire:

(a) I loved my father and my mother, but my father a little bit more.
(b) I like things pretty well the way they are.
(c) I never worry much about anything.
(d) I don't care for books or music much.
(e) I love my wife and children.
(f) I don't let them get in the way of company work.

from William H. Whyte, 1956, *The Organization Man*, Simon & Schuster, New York, p. 373.

---

personality Types A and B and the propensity to suffer stress

Personality and individual health appear to be linked in a manner that is of particular relevance to organizational behaviour. Meyer Friedman and Ray Rosenman (1974) claimed to have identified two extreme personality patterns or behaviour syndromes which helped to explain differences in stress levels. In other words, they claim to have identified a 'stress-prone' personality. Much subsequent research has focused on what Friedman and Rosenman called the Type A behaviour syndrome and its opposite, Type B.

---

definition

*A **Type A personality** or behaviour syndrome concerns a combination of emotions and behaviours characterized by ambition, hostility, impatience and a sense of constant time-pressure. People with Type A personalities are more likely to suffer stress-related disorders, including coronary diseases.*

---
definition

A **Type B personality** *or behaviour syndrome concerns a combination of emotions and behaviours characterized by relaxation, calm, lack of preoccupation with achievement, and an ability to take time to enjoy leisure. People with Type B personalities are less likely to suffer stress-related disorders and coronary diseases.*

In summary, the two personality types look like this:

Type A personality characteristics	Type B personality characteristics
competitive	able to take time out to enjoy leisure
high need for achievement	not preoccupied with achievement
aggressive	easygoing
works fast	works at a steady pace
impatient	seldom impatient
restless	not easily frustrated
extremely alert	relaxed
tense facial muscles	moves and speaks slowly
constant feeling of time pressure	seldom lacks enough time

Friedman and Rosenman found that Type A personalities were three times more likely to suffer heart disease than Type B personalities. The typical Type A thrives on long hours, large amounts of work and tight deadlines. These are, to some extent, socially and organizationally desirable characteristics, as are competitiveness and a high need for achievement. However, a Type A is seldom able to relax enough to stand back from a complex organizational problem to make an effective and comprehensive analysis. They tend to lack the patience and relaxed style required of many management positions. A further problem lies in the fact that their impatience and hostility can increase the stress levels in those who have to work with them.

In other words, although a Type A personality might appear to have many admirable and valued facets, this can be a dysfunctional style for the individual and for others.

STOP!

Look at the list of Type A and Type B personality characteristics.

To which category do you belong?

To help you confirm that you are Type A, do you suffer often from any of these: alcohol abuse, excessive smoking, dizziness, upset stomachs, headaches, fatigue, sweating, bad breath? If your answer here is 'yes', these are probably stress responses to your behaviour pattern. Expect your first coronary attack before the age of 45 (guesstimate). What are you going to do about it?

Friedman and Rosenman argued that a Type A can change into a Type B with awareness and the right training. They suggested a number of 're-engineering strategies' to this end:

- keep reminding yourself that life is always full of unfinished business.
- you only 'finish' when you die.
- learn how to delegate responsibility to others.
- limit your weekly working hours.
- schedule time for leisure and exercise.
- take a course in time management skills.

The problem, of course, is that the extreme Type A personality – the person most at risk – can never find enough time to implement these strategies effectively. Another potential problem lies with the question of whether you can 're-engineer' your personality this easily.

stress management: individual and organizational strategies

The work of Friedman and Rosenman is important in demonstrating a link between personality and health. It is widely accepted that negative emotional states such as depression, hostility and anxiety can result in heart diseases, respiratory disorders such as asthma, and headaches and ulcers. The health risks are greater where the negative states are chronic, as they can be if they are an aspect of personality. There are a number of other potential causes of stress at work that arise from individual characteristics; difficulty in coping with change, lack of confidence and assertiveness in interpersonal relationships, poor time management, and poor stress management skills (Clarke, 1989).

It is also important to recognize, however, that stress has many other causes beyond personality or behaviour syndromes, and has other significant implications for organizational behaviour. Stress is an unavoidable feature of life. The pace of life, work and change in contemporary society simply makes this worse by increasing the range and intensity of the demands on our time. A *stressor* is any condition that requires some kind of adaptive response from the individual. Typical stressors that are likely to arise in an organizational context include:

- *inadequate physical working environment*: noise, bad lighting, inadequate ventilation, lack of privacy, extremes of heat and cold, old and unsuitable and unreliable equipment.
- *inappropriate job design*: not enough people for the work, poor co-ordination, inadequate training, inadequate information, rigid procedures, no challenge, insufficient use of skills, no responsibility or participation in decision-making, role ambiguity.
- *poor management style*: inconsistent, competitive, crisis management, autocratic management, excessive time pressures placed on employees.
- *poor relationships*: with superiors, with colleagues, with particular individuals, lack of feedback, little social contact, racial and sexual harassment.
- *uncertain future*: job insecurity, fear of unemployment or redeployment, few promotion opportunities, low-status job.
- *divided loyalties*: conflicts between own aspirations and organization's requirements, conflict with family and social responsibilities.

Stress can, of course, be challenging, arousing and exciting, and can in some circumstances enhance our sense of satisfaction and accomplishment and improve our performance. The term *eustress* is sometimes used to describe this positive aspect of stress (the prefix 'eu' is Greek for 'good'). This is typically contrasted with *distress*, which for most of us means the unpleasant, debilitating and unhealthy side of stress.

Stress can be *episodic*, when dealing with life's many problems, we often get anxious, cope with the problem, and then relax again. Some 'life changes' can be very stressful indeed, such as the death of a close relative or friend, or a term in prison. Other 'life changes' can also be stressful, but can trigger a less extreme response, such as getting lower grades than expected in an exam, missing a tutorial, being fined for speeding or having an argument with a parent. Each of these episodes on its own is unlikely to cause lasting damage; most of us overcome these problems relatively quickly. However, when several of these episodes occur around the same time, in a manner outside our control, the potential health risk is increased.

Stress can also be *chronic*, this happens when we face constant stress, with no escape, and this can lead to exhaustion and 'burn out'. This may be due to an unfortunate coincidence of a number of unrelated stressful episodes. However, chronic stress also arises from the enduring features of our personal, social and organizational circumstances. If we are always under pressure, always facing multiple and unrealistic demands, always having difficulties with our work, our colleagues, and relationships with management, then the health risk from stress is likely to increase.

Stress can be a personal response to life's challenges. What you brush aside may be a debilitating problem for someone else. There seem to be three main factors moderating the impact of a stressor on an individual. The first of these is *condition*. You are better able to cope with stress if you are in good health and full of energy to begin with. The second is *cognitive appraisal*. If you believe that you are not going to be able to cope with a particular event, then this belief can become a 'self-fulfilling prophecy' (of course, the opposite can also be true). A third moderator is your degree of *hardiness*. Hardiness is an outlook on life characterized by a welcoming approach to change, a commitment to purposeful activity and a sense of being in control of one's life. This combination of challenge, commitment and control appears to increase resilience to stressful events in some people.

Stress has many symptoms. Many of the symptoms do not, on their own, appear significant and are not particularly threatening to us if they are transient. An occasional headache is seldom cause for concern. Many symptoms have other causes. So these symptoms are often overlooked, and stress passes unrecognized and untreated. Typical symptoms can include:

excess alcohol intake	heavy cigarette smoking	dependence on
tiredness	low energy	tranquillizers
headaches	stomach upsets and ulcers	dizziness
high blood pressure	sleep problems	bad breath
temper tantrums	irritability	hyperventilation
loss of concentration	aggression	moodiness
excess worrying	anxiety	overeating
pounding heart	feelings of inadequacy	inability to relax
		memory loss

Stress can thus have a number of emotional consequences for the individual – anxiety, fatigue, depression, frustration, nervousness, low self-esteem, and so on. At the (rare) extreme, stress can even contribute to mental breakdown and suicide. Stress also influences behaviour in many ways, from the so-called 'comfort tricks' involving alcohol and other drugs and excessive eating, to accident-proneness and emotional outbursts. Stress affects our thinking ability, interfering with concentration, decision-making, attention span and reaction to criticism. There are a number of accompanying physiological responses too, such as increased heart rate and blood pressure, sweating, and 'hot and cold flushes'.

The organizational consequences of stress can, therefore, be highly damaging. The work performance of stressed employees is likely to suffer. This can sometimes be revealed in higher than normal levels of absenteeism, staff turnover, accidents and wilful sabotage. Stress can cause relationships to deteriorate (although poor relationships may cause stress in the first place), and commitment to the work and to the organization are also likely to fall.

There are two broad strategies for reducing stress: *problem-focused strategies* and *emotion-focused strategies*. Emotion-focused strategies aim to improve individual resilience and coping skills, but do not necessarily change the stressors. These individual solutions include:

▷ consciousness-raising to improve self-awareness
▷ exercise and fitness programmes

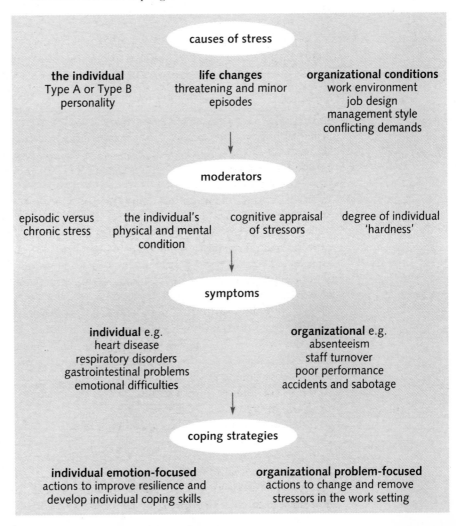

- self-help training, in biofeedback, meditation, relaxation, coping strategies
- time management training
- development of other social and job interests

Problem-focused strategies aim to deal with the stressors, by direct action to solve the problem. These organizational solutions include:

- improved selection and training mechanisms
- staff counselling programmes
- improved organizational communications
- job redesign and enrichment strategies
- development of team-working systems

It is therefore not always appropriate to 'blame' the individual for their experience of and response to stress, despite the known link to personality. Stress today is also likely to be caused by a number of organizational factors. While much can be done to develop individual resilience, the need for organizational, or problem-focused, solutions is inescapable.

The figure on p. 155 summarizes the argument of this section, with respect to the causes of stress, factors that moderate the experience of stress, stress symptoms, and coping strategies.

the development of the self

The nomothetic approach to the study of personality has been criticized by those who advocate an *idiographic* approach.

---

definition

The **idiographic** approach to the study of personality emphasizes the uniqueness of the individual, challenging the assumption that we can all be measured and compared on the same dimensions.

Idiographic means 'writing about individuals'. Psychologists who adopt this perspective begin with a detailed picture of one person. This approach aims to capture the uniqueness, richness and complexity of the individual. It is a valuable way of deepening our understanding, but does not readily lead to the generation of universal laws of human behaviour which is the aim of the nomothetic approach.

The idiographic approach makes the following assumptions.

First, each individual has unique traits, which are not directly comparable with the traits of others. My sensitivity and aggression are not comparable with your sensitivity and aggression. Idiographic research produces in-depth studies of normal and abnormal individuals, with information from interviews, letters, diaries and biographies. The data include what people say and write about themselves.

Second, we are not just biological machines driven by heredity. This is only part of our nature. We are also socially self-conscious. Our behaviour patterns are influenced by experience and conscious reflection and reasoning, not just by instinct, habit and heredity.

Third, we behave in accordance with the image that we each have of ourselves – our *self*, or *self-concept*. We derive this concept or image from the ways in which other people treat us. We learn about ourselves through our interactions with others. We take the attitudes and behaviours of others towards us and use them to adjust our self-concept and behaviour.

---

definition

Our **self-concept** *is our individual understanding of the unique coherence and stability of our own identity and personality.*

Fourth, as the development of the self-concept is a social process, it follows that personality is open to change through new social interactions and experiences. The development of the individual's personality is, therefore, not the inevitable result of biological and genetic inheritance. It is only through interaction with other people that we as individuals can learn to see and to understand ourselves as individuals. We cannot develop our self-understanding without the (tacit) help of others. There is no such thing as 'human nature'. We derive our nature through social interactions and relationships.

It is thus our self-understanding that determines our behaviour. For example, confidence in one's ability to do something is related to the successful demonstration of that ability. Ability combined with lack of confidence usually leads to failure or poor performance.

The mind's ability to reflect on its own functions is an interesting and important feature. We experience a world 'out there' and we are capable also of experiencing ourselves in that outer world, as objects that live and behave in it. We can observe, evaluate and criticize ourselves in the same conscious, objective and impersonal way that we observe, evaluate and criticize other people and objects, and we experience shame, anxiety or pride at our own behaviour. Our capacity for reflective (if not wholly objective) thought enables us to evaluate past and alternative future actions and their consequences.

Charles Horton Cooley (1864–1929)

The American psychologist Charles Horton Cooley introduced the idea of the 'looking glass self'. Our mirror is the other people with whom we interact. If others respond warmly and favourably towards us, we develop a 'positive' self-concept. If others respond with criticism, ridicule and aggression, we tend to develop a 'negative' self-image.

The personality of the individual is thus the result of a process in which individuals learn to be the person they are. Most of us learn, accept and use most of the attitudes, values, beliefs and expectations of the society or part of society in which we are brought up. This is the 'social learning theory' argument from Chapter 5. In other words, we learn the stock of knowledge available in and peculiar to our society. Red means stop. Cars drive on the left-hand side of the road. An extended hand is a symbol of respect and friendship, not of hostility or aggression. Considered singly, these examples sound trivial. Taken together, they comprise a critical, but 'taken for granted' knowledge of how our society works. Phenomenologists sometimes refer to this as 'recipe knowledge'. The 'rules' that govern our behaviour are created, recreated and reinforced through our continuing interactions with others based on these shared definitions of our reality. We interact with each other competently because we share this broad understanding.

How could we develop such a shared understanding on our own in isolation from society? What we inherit from our parents cannot possibly tell us how to behave in a specific culture. We have to learn how to become *persona grata* through our social interactions.

Rules such as 'red means stop' are not laws of human behaviour of the same type as the physical law that says 'clouds mean rain'. We can change these human laws, and we can break them. Change may be difficult and infringement may carry penalties, but we have this option. Clouds cannot alter or repeal the laws that apply to them.

If we all share the same ideas and behaviours, we have a recipe for a society of conformists. This is, of course, not consistent with the available evidence, and the theory does not imply this. George Herbert Mead argued that the self has two components:

I   The unique, individual, conscious and impulsive aspects of the individual; and

Me   The norms and values of society that the individual learns and accepts, or 'internalizes'.

Mead used the term *generalized other* to refer to the set of expectations one believes others have of one. 'Me' is the aspect of self where these generalized attitudes are organized. The 'Me' cannot be physically located. It refers rather to the mental process that enables us to reflect on our own conduct. The 'Me' is the self as an object to itself.

George Herbert Mead (1863–1931)

---

definition

*The **generalized other** is what we understand other people expect of us, in terms of attitudes, values, beliefs and behaviour.*

The 'I' is the active, impulsive component of the self. Other people encourage us to conform to current values and beliefs. But reflective individuals also adjust their part in the social process. We can initiate change by introducing new social values. Patterns of socially acceptable conduct are specified in broad and general ways. There is plenty of scope for flexibility, modification, originality, creativity, individuality, variety and significant change.

---

this sounds like a recipe for conformity

We can reform the order of things; we can insist on making the community standards better standards. We are not simply bound by the community. We are engaged in a conversation in which what we say is listened to by the community and its response is one which is affected by what we have to say ... We are continually changing our social system in some respects and we are able to do that intelligently because we can think.

from George Herbert Mead, 1934, *Mind, Self and Society*, University of Chicago Press, Chicago, p. 168.

Carl Rogers (1902–87) illustrated this two-sided self in the following way:

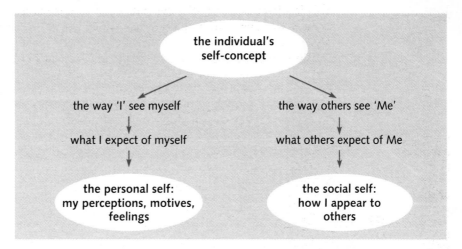

Our self-concept gives us a sense of meaning and consistency. But as our perceptions and motives change through new experiences and learning, our self-concept and our behaviour change. Personality, therefore, is not stable, as the self-concept can be reorganized.

We have perceptions of our qualities, abilities, attitudes, impulses, and so on. If these perceptions are accurate, conscious, organized and accepted, then we can regard our self-concept as successful in that it will lead to feelings of comfort, freedom from tension and of psychological adjustment. Well-adjusted individuals thus have flexible images of themselves, which are open to change through new experiences.

Personality disorders can be caused by a failure to bring together experiences, motives and feelings into a consistent self-concept. We usually behave in ways consistent with our self-images. When we have new experiences or feelings that are inconsistent we either:

- Recognize the inconsistency and try to integrate the two sets of understanding – the healthy response; or
- Deny or distort one of the experiences, perhaps by putting the blame on someone or something else – an unhealthy defence mechanism.

'Maladjusted' individuals are those who perceive as threatening those experiences and feelings that are not consistent with their self-concept. They deny and distort their experiences in such a way that their self-image does not match their real feelings or the nature of their experience. This leads to a build-up of psychological tension as more defence mechanisms are required to keep the truth at a distance.

Rogers also argued (with Maslow) that the core of human personality is the desire to realize fully one's potential. To achieve this, however, the right social environment is required. Rogers argued that this is an environment in which one is treated with 'unconditional positive regard'. This means a social setting in which one is accepted for whatever one is; in which one is valued, trusted, accepted and respected, even in the face of characteristics which others dislike. In this kind of environment, the individual is likely to become trusting, spontaneous and flexible, leading a rich and meaningful life with a harmonious self-concept.

*Carl Ransom Rogers
(1902–87)*

However, this is far from the type of social environment typical of most organizations in our society today. Most people at work, at all levels, face highly conditional positive regard in which only a narrow range of thoughts and behaviours is approved and accepted. Compared with nomothetic techniques, the idiographic approach appears to be a rather complex, untidy view of personality and its development. It has been influential in phenomenological research, but is conspicuous by its absence in contemporary psychometrics.

How can an individual's self-understanding be studied? Eysenck's questionnaires are not appropriate as the questions and answers are determined by a researcher. An individual can reject that wording as inappropriate to his or her self-concept. Standard questionnaires are too rigid and impersonal.

We therefore need a route into the mind that is independent of the understanding and biases of the researcher. We can ask people to write about themselves and record them speaking about themselves. These and other techniques of the clinical psychologist are in common use, including free association, interpretation of dreams and the analysis of fantasies. Here the individual has complete freedom of expression, and responses are not tied to predetermined categories. The researcher's job is to identify the themes in this material that reveal the individual's preoccupations and interests – and personality.

These techniques appear to be unstructured, and perhaps unscientific. One successful technique for getting access to the content of someone's mind is the *thematic apperception test*, or TAT.

---

definition

A **thematic apperception test** *is a type of 'projective' assessment in which the individual is shown ambiguous pictures and invited to create stories or accounts of what may be happening in these pictures, projecting their own interests and preoccupations into these accounts.*

Here, we must break our rule about not describing personality assessments as 'tests'. It is helpful to be consistent with the wider literature of this topic. You are unlikely to encounter discussion of a 'thematic apperception assessment'. This is how the TAT works.

First, you are told that you are about to take a test of your creative writing. Then you are shown photographs, typically including people, and asked to write an imaginative story about each of them, suggested by what you see. The images do not suggest any particular story.

These imaginative stories are then assessed in various ways. One of these concerns the assessment of *need for achievement*. This is not a test of your creative or imaginative writing at all. Need for achievement is a concept similar to that of self-actualization.

---

definition

The **need for achievement** *is a general concern with meeting standards of excellence, the desire to be successful in competition, and the motivation to excel in an activity significant to the individual.*

Henry Alexander Murray (1893–1988)

Photo source: Archives of the History of American Psychology, The University of Akron, Ohio, USA

The assessment procedure first involves determining whether any of the characters in your story have an *achievement goal*. In other words, does somebody in your story want to perform better? This could involve doing something better than someone else, meeting or exceeding some self-imposed standard of excellence, doing something unique or being involved in doing something well or successfully. Points are scored for the presence of these features in the story. The more *achievement imagery*, the higher the score, determined using a detailed and complex scoring manual.

The thematic apperception test was invented in 1938 by Henry Murray (1893–1988) and has since been developed by David C. McClelland as a means of measuring the strength of need for achievement. The TAT is also used to measure the needs for power and affiliation, using a similar scoring procedure, but looking for different imagery. In a full assessment, you would be asked to write stories about between 4 and 20 pictures. The minimum duration of the test is therefore 20 minutes.

What can short, creative stories about ambiguous pictures tell us about your distinctive and stable personality characteristics?

The thematic apperception test is a *projective* assessment.

---

definition

A **projective test** or assessment is one based on abstract or ambiguous images, which the person being assessed is asked to interpret, in a manner which reveals their feelings, preoccupations and motives, as these are 'projected' into their interpretations of the images presented.

David C. McClelland (b. 1917)

The label 'projective' is used because subjects are given the opportunity to project their personalities into the stories they write. The Rorschach inkblot test is another form of projective assessment where subjects are asked to describe the abstract images they see in random inkblots. The interpretations that you offer thus draw on the channels of thought predominant in your thinking. McClelland argues that it is reasonable to assume that the person with a strong concern with achievement is likely to write imaginative stories with lots of achievement imagery and themes, and the research evidence seems to support this view.

Why has this technique not found applications in modern organizational psychometrics? The output of the assessment is hard for the untrained eye to see as 'objective data' about someone's personality. The scoring procedure involves subjective interpretation. Expensive training is required in the full technical procedure to produce judges who can reach reliable assessments. On the other hand, anyone with a scoring key can calculate the same results on an objective test like one of Eysenck's (although the problem of interpretation remains).

Need for achievement is important from an organizational perspective. People with low need for achievement are concerned more with security and status than with personal fulfilment, are preoccupied with their own ideas and feelings, worry more about their self-presentation than their performance, and prefer bright Scottish tartans. (The Buchanan tartan is bright red and yellow and the author does not wear it.)

People with a high need for achievement tend to have the following characteristics:

- They prefer tasks in which they have to achieve a standard of excellence rather than simply carrying out routine activities.
- They prefer jobs in which they get frequent and clear feedback on how well they are doing to help them to perform better.
- They prefer activities that involve moderate risks of failure – high-risk activities lead to failure, low-risk activities do not offer challenge or an opportunity to demonstrate ability.
- They have a good memory for unfinished tasks and do not like to leave things incomplete.
- They can be unfriendly and unsociable when they do not want others to get in the way of their performance.
- They have a sense of urgency, appear to be in a hurry, to be working against time and have an inability to relax.
- They prefer sombre Scottish tartans with lots of blues and greens and dislike bright tartans with reds and yellows – the unobtrusive background allows them to stand out better.

How is the achievement need acquired? A classic study by Marian Winterbottom (1958) suggested that this depends on the process of early socialization. She asked 29 American boys aged 8 to 9 years to tell her stories in response to spoken instructions (not pictures) and scored their answers for achievement imagery and themes. She then interviewed their mothers and asked them questions about how they raised their sons. She found that the mothers of the high-scoring sons had treated them in the following ways:

- They had expected their sons to become independent and to do things on their own at an earlier age than the mothers of the lower-scoring boys.
- They rewarded independence with affectionate hugging and kissing.
- They imposed fewer restrictions on the behaviour of their children and relaxed any restrictions at an early age.
- Their total home atmosphere emphasized competitiveness, self-reliance, independence, accomplishment and aspiration.

The mothers of the low scorers believed more in the value of restrictions on their children and kept restrictions in force for longer. Domineering and authoritarian parents thus tend not to have children with high needs for achievement.

Can the thematic apperception test be used to identify people whose early socialization has given them a high need for achievement and who may therefore be good at a particular job or occupation? Organizations typically want to employ people with drive, ambition, self-motivation and so on. The TAT looks like a promising organizational selection test. It is however not used in this way.

It is probably not such a good test for this purpose. Once you know what the test is all about, it is fairly easy to fake a good score. The general definition of achievement imagery is close to popular understanding of the term, although the detailed scoring may not be obvious to the untrained. If the test ever became widely used, the scoring procedure would become widely understood. So we are left with the same conclusion here as with Eysenck's questionnaires. Personality assessments are not very good predictors of job performance.

McClelland has argued that individuals' achievement needs can be increased by teaching them the scoring system and helping them to write high-scoring stories. This may increase the need for achievement by encouraging the individual to see and understand daily life more vividly in achievement terms. This retraining in mental habits may thus be translated more readily into action.

nomothetic versus idiographic?

We have presented two approaches to the study of human personality. Here they are in summary form:

the nomothetic approach	the idiographic approach
has a positivist bias.	has a phenomenological bias.
is generalizing; emphasizes the discovery of laws of human behaviour.	is individualizing; emphasizes the richness and complexity of the unique individual.
is based on a statistical study of groups of people.	is based on intensive study of individuals.
uses objective questionnaires.	uses projective tests and other written and spoken materials.
describes personality in terms of the individual's possession of traits, and trait clusters or personality types.	describes personality in terms of the individual's own understanding and interpretation of their identity.
views personality as composed of discrete and identifiable elements.	believes that personality has to be understood and studied as an indivisible, intelligible whole.
believes that personality is primarily determined by heredity, biology, genetics.	believes that personality is primarily determined by social and cultural processes.
believes that personality is given at birth and cannot be altered.	believes that personality is adaptable, open to change through experience.

How should we choose between these competing perspectives? We might resort to academic criteria and examine the logic of the arguments, consider how adequately the evidence relates to and supports the theory, and consider how comprehensive the explanations are. We might resort to practical considerations and assess the techniques used to treat personality disorders, and to analyze and predict behaviour.

However, this stance misses the point that these two approaches are based on deeply divided and conflicting views of human nature. The evidence is such as to leave us debating for a considerable time without any satisfactory resolution. We thus have to resort to criteria that are in some respects unsatisfactory, such as:

▶ Which theory is more aesthetically pleasing?
▶ Which approach 'feels' right?
▶ How does each approach fit with my world view?

Another way to resolve this, however, is to regard these approaches as *complementary* They offer two broad research strategies, each of which is capable of telling us about different aspects of human psychology. What each alone reveals is interesting, but partial. So perhaps we should use both approaches and not concentrate on one alone.

psychometrics in action

Choosing the right candidate for a job, or selecting the right person for promotion, is a critical organizational decision for a number of reasons. Incorrect decisions can lead to frustrated employees and poor performance levels for the organization. Selection and appraisal procedures can be costly and time-consuming, and it is frustrating to have to repeat them to recover from previous errors.

A selection or a promotion decision is a *prediction* about the ability of the person chosen to perform well in their new position. Predictions are based on the understanding of the position to be filled, and on information about potential candidates. Traditionally, the information about the candidate has come from an application form, from the testimony of referees and from a face-to-face interview. The application form provides essential background details, but it is impersonal. Referees notoriously reveal only pleasant things about candidates. And research has revealed that interviews can be very unreliable guides to future job performance too.

Demographic trends present another set of selection problems for organizations. As the birth rate in industrialized countries has fallen, and with increasing life expectancy, the pool of available labour contains lower proportions of younger people, including graduates, and higher proportions of elderly people and minority groups currently under-represented in the working population. Selecting the right people, many of whom have limited previous work experience or no experience of the work for which they have applied, becomes more difficult.

Psychometric methods offer organizations a way to improve the quality of selection and promotion decisions by systematically collecting information about candidates in a way that improves on the predictive power of traditional sources of selection information.

Intelligence testing has been developing for most of this century. Applications of psychometrics have developed particularly rapidly during the 1980s and 1990s, and look set to develop further. In contrast with the personality assessments described in this chapter so far, the available evidence suggests that psychometric techniques are significantly superior in predictive ability to traditional methods. There are now over 5000 such tests in use.

The British consultancy firm Saville and Holdsworth have developed a widely used Occupational Personality Questionnaire (available in nine levels of complexity for different uses). The OPQ is based on 30 personality

great personnel disasters

My first job as factory personnel officer was in a plant which had not previously had the benefit of such an appointment. I soon decided that staff selection methods needed a complete overhaul. So far as I could establish, the system under the previous, elderly factory manager had consisted of one short interview at which the key question was: 'If you were offered this job, do you think you could do it?' Any applicant answering 'no' obviously lacked confidence and was failed. Anyone answering 'yes' was considered too cocky and was also failed. I inherited a lot of vacancies.

With the support of a new, young, keen factory manager I designed a suite of selection processes which I felt to be comprehensive and wholly objective. Final selection would be based on the gross score for a range of tests and interviews. Line managers would not make the final decision; that was left to the expert who calculated the score – me.

The first vacancy to be filled by the new method was for the factory storekeeper. Ten somewhat bewildered applicants spent a whole day being put through the selection mill. They had an interview with the factory manager; they were subjected to tests of numeracy and clerical aptitude; they completed a personality questionnaire and a motivational analysis; they performed a group task under observation; they wrote a mock letter to a recalcitrant supplier and they gave a three-minute talk on stock control. Finally, nearing exhaustion, they had an interview with me.

I took all the documentation home and spent five hours marking and analysing. One applicant emerged as the obvious winner, and around midnight I entered the starting details on the relevant application form, yawned, and, with a warm inner glow for a long day's work well done, went to bed.

The next morning, still feeling very satisfied with the result, I passed all the papers over to my secretary. She had to send out the rejection letters to the unsuccessful applicants, and an appointment letter to the winner.

Being as keen on thorough induction as on scientific selection, I used to meet all new employees on their first morning. On the day in question there was just one starter – the new storekeeper. My secretary brought him in from the waiting room. But something was wrong. This was not the successful applicant but one of the nine who had not made the grade. I returned him hastily to the waiting room and examined the file. Two things quickly became evident. First, the man in the waiting room was the next to worst applicant so far as all my scores were concerned. Second, I had written the starting details on the back of the wrong application form. My winner had consequently had a rejection letter and the job had gone to the failure in the waiting room.

What to do? Tell him that a mistake had been made and offer a month's pay in lieu of notice? Quick, positive action was called for. I made an instant and positive decision to do nothing. Not even my secretary was to be told. Time would have to tell. So in blissful ignorance of his good fortune, the wrong man started work. He turned out to be the best storekeeper the company ever had.

from Alan Fowler, 1987, 'Light and bitter', *Personnel Management*, May, p. 73.

'dimensions' or traits, and the scoring norms were derived from the 4000 British managers who took part in the development trials. The 30 personality scales are listed below. You may like to consider rating yourself on these dimensions, identifying your potential strengths and weaknesses.

A personality assessment across these 30 characteristics, when compared with established norms for the management population as a whole, could be considered a comprehensive profile. This information is helpful in screening marginal candidates, is useful where it can be compared and checked against other information about a candidate – say, from actual job experience – and can give an interviewer helpful guidance on what issues and aspects to probe during an interview.

However, the predictive power of tests of this kind is doubtful. The only effective way to check this is to assess a large applicant group, hire them all, wait for an appropriate period (say, five years), assess their performance, and see if those with 'good' profiles showed 'good' performance or not. If so, you have a useful test. The predictive power of such tests should therefore not be overestimated, and ultimately they cannot replace the need for human judgement. This is an extremely useful adjunct to aptitude and intelligence testing and interviewing, but it was not designed to function in isolation from these other sources of information about candidates who have to 'fit in' with other people in the organization as well as be able to carry out their assigned duties.

Nicky Willmore (1988) surveyed 35 leading 'headhunting' (professional selection) firms in Britain about their use of the OPQ; 16 said that they did not use psychometric assessment, and 17 said that they only did so at a client's request. One used testing to resolve awkward choices between comparable candidates, and only one company said that they used the technique as a standard procedure, claiming that the assessment reduced chances of making mistakes and reduced the guesswork involved in drawing up a shortlist. Used in this way, the consultant first constructs a profile of the candidate in discussion with the client organization. This covers the 30 OPQ dimensions and establishes the qualities required to 'fit' the culture of the organization. The result is an OPQ graph against which candidates can be matched.

The OPQ result should *never* be used as the sole basis of a selection decision, only in conjunction with other sources of information. The assessment is highly reliable, where reliability is measured in terms of satisfied client companies who give repeat business to the 'headhunting' firm.

Here are the 30 scales, with brief descriptors, used in the Saville and Holdsworth Occupational Personality Questionnaire:

1 **persuasive** negotiates, enjoys selling, convincing with arguments.
2 **controlling** takes charge, directs, manages, organizes.
3 **socially confident** puts people at ease, good with words.
4 **competitive** plays to win, determined to beat others, poor loser.
5 **achieving** ambitious, sets sights high, career-centred.
6 **active** has energy, moves quickly, enjoys physical exercise.
7 **decisive** quick at conclusions, may be hasty, takes risks.

  8 **democratic** encourages others to contribute, consults, listens.

  9 **caring** considerate to others, sympathetic, tolerant.

10 **modest** reserved about achievements, accepts others.

11 **introspective** analyzes thoughts and behaviour of self and others.

12 **outgoing** fun-loving, humorous, sociable, vibrant, talkative.

13 **affiliative** enjoys being in groups, likes companionship.

14 **artistic** appreciates culture, shows artistic flair.

15 **conceptual** theoretical, intellectually curious.

16 **innovative** generates ideas, shows ingenuity, thinks up solutions.

17 **traditional** prefers proven orthodox methods, conventional.

18 **change-oriented** enjoys new things, seeks variety, accepts changes.

19 **forward planning** prepares well in advance, enjoys target-setting.

20 **data rational** good with data, operates on facts.

21 **conscientious** sticks to deadlines, completes job.

22 **independent** has strong views on things, difficult to manage.

23 **detail conscious** methodical, keeps things neat and tidy, precise.

24 **practical** down-to-earth, likes repairing and mending things.

25 **relaxed** calm, relaxed, cool under pressure, free of anxiety.

26 **worrying** worries when things go wrong, anxious to do well.

27 **phlegmatic** difficult to hurt or upset, can brush off insults.

28 **emotional control** doesn't show emotions, keeps feelings back.

29 **optimistic** cheerful, happy, keeps spirits up despite setbacks.

30 **critical** good at probing facts, sees disadvantages, challenges.

---

the Barnum Effect

Why, then, are people so enthusiastic about personality tests? One view is that the tests are used to help the interviewer structure the interview, and that they are not used in a predictive sense at all. This may be all very well, but one wonders what candidates would make of the idea that they are being interviewed on the basis of information that has no demonstrated relevance to their likely job performance.

More sinister is a trick used by salesmen to peddle inferior testing to the unwary and unsophisticated. It goes like this. Would-be clients are invited to take the test, free of charge, and the salesman offers an interpretation. Clients are intended to be impressed by the uncanny accuracy with which the interpretation reveals aspects of their character.

This is a confidence trick. It was revealed as such 40 years ago, in a rather delicious experiment, when it was shown that most people considered that a fixed personality profile fitted them rather well. The phenomenon came to be known as the Fallacy of Personal Validation, or at least that's what it's called when it's taught to first-year psychology undergraduates. More widely, it's known in the trade as the Barnum Effect – because it shows there's a sucker born every minute.

If you spend 20 minutes or so answering a whole host of questions about yourself, you ought to recognize yourself in the way your answers are read back to you.

from Steve Blinkhorn, 1988, 'The hazards of occupational testing', *The Listener*, 14 January, p. 9.

David Nelson and Alexander Wedderburn (1988) produced a 'league table' of selection techniques based on data and research. Their table indicates how much one can improve on choosing people at random by using each of the following techniques on its own:

selection method	per cent better than chance
graphology or handwriting analysis	0
personality assessments	2.5
interviews	2–5
references	3–7
biodata	6–14
tests of general mental ability	6–20
supervisory evaluation	18
work sampling	14–29
assessment centre using multiple methods	17–18

This research reveals a group of techniques that are, used on their own, less than 10 per cent better than random selection. Graphology in particular has yet to demonstrate any effectiveness in this area at all. It is interesting in the context of the discussion so far in this chapter to note the position of interviews, references and personality tests in this table.

Biodata are basic facts about the individual's background and past experience collected on a standardized application form and scored by weighting particular responses on the basis of their relationship with demonstrated success by others in the type of work involved. Because such weightings can only be valid and reliable if based on significant sample sizes, only large intake occupations can use this method.

Tests of general mental ability are still in use and have proved to be relatively good at predicting success in training and job performance, particularly where there is a significant intellectual component to the work. Tests of general intelligence assess verbal, numerical, perceptual and reasoning skills.

The work sample is the most effective single method. This involves designing a short task which simulates elements of critical job skills. University lecturers are often asked to give a lecture presentation as part of their selection procedure. This technique can be useful in other settings with older candidates and minority groups whose abilities are typically underestimated from standard written materials.

A contemporary variation on the work sample approach is the technique of *situational interviewing*. Candidates are presented with a series of hypothetical situations based on what they have to do in the job, and asked how they would respond. Questions and situations are based on job analysis which focuses on critical skills. So, for example, Michael Syrett (1988) explains how applicants for a sales position in an insurance company are invited to consider this situation:

You have called on a broker to keep an appointment arranged by telephone to discuss the progress of a sales campaign. His secretary tells you he is out of the office all day. As you are leaving, you bump into the broker, together with a representative of another insurance company, coming out of another room. What would you do?

Effective candidates faced with this problem are those who say they would greet the person in a warm and friendly way, remain dignified and make another appointment. The ineffective response is to 'point out to the broker that you expect appointments to be kept', say 'that if the same thing occurs you would start wondering whether taking on a broker was worthwhile', or challenge the broker with the secretary's false information. This is a straightforward example; others are more complex and subtle. A number of companies, including National Westminster Bank, British Airways, ICI and Crusader Insurance claim to use this technique. One user manager is reported to have said:

It allows the interview to sound more professional, something which is increasingly important, as candidates today are getting fed up with enduring shoddy recruiting techniques. (Syrett, 1988)

Godfrey Golzen (1988) describes how The Burton Group used a similar approach, first examining the characteristics of their high performers in a particular job, then asking questions in interviews to discover candidates who match that profile. This is also supported by an OPQ assessment, to find out if applicants can handle the company's culture of quick response to change and individual accountability. The highest scoring candidates are invited to an assessment centre.

Given the Nelson and Wedderburn league table of effectiveness (or ineffectiveness), should organizations stop interviewing and testing? No. The answer is to *combine* these techniques to improve the overall predictive power of the selection process.

The most appropriate combination of techniques for managerial and professional assessment is through what is known as the *assessment centre*. Assessment centres have roots in military practice during the Second World War as an approach to the selection of officers, run by the War Office Selection Boards. The technique spread to the Civil Service, and is now common in industry. Groups of around 6–10 candidates are brought together for 1–3 days of intensive assessment. They are presented, individually and as a group, with a variety of exercises, tests of ability, personality assessments, interviews, work samples, team problem-solving and written tasks. Their activities are observed by a number of assessors who separately score candidates' performances and reach a consensus grading. This approach can be used for selection, and also for staff development, talent-spotting, and for career guidance and counselling. The evidence seems to suggest that this combination of selection methods, typical of an assessment centre approach, can significantly improve the probability of selecting appropriate candidates.

Advocates of the assessment centre technique argue that the information collected about candidates is comprehensive and comparable, and the techniques used give candidates the opportunity to demonstrate capabilities unlikely to appear in an interview alone. The self-knowledge gained from this type of assessment can be valuable to the candidate. Assessors develop useful skills, such as objectivity and fairness in assessment, accuracy in the presentation of personnel data and experience in work-related behaviours.

Critics of assessment centre methods point to the significant investment in time and money, both to set up and to run an assessment centre. There is a need for well-qualified assessors, and sometimes a lack of senior management commitment to the process can give both assessors and candidates inappropriate signals. The indiscriminate use of selection methods cannot meet the needs of individual organizations, and the focus on observable and measurable aspects of behaviour may overlook less apparent and less easily assessed skills.

assessment

The most effective approach to staff assessment for selection or promotion or counselling is one that uses a combination of approaches. The assessment centre does this, but it is time-consuming and expensive. What does seem clear from the available evidence and experience is that personality assessment alone is helpful but inadequate for making effective decisions in employee selection, placement, development, career guidance and promotion.

With situational interviewing, based on known characteristics of 'top performers' in a given occupation, it is very difficult for candidates to cheat or to practise their responses, not knowing in detail what specific behaviours and replies are being sought by assessors and interviewers. Correct answers to questions about job knowledge alone simply reveal that the applicant has done some homework. In this approach, the interviewer asks a series of structured questions about specific issues, instead of the conventional (and much less useful) 'Tell me why you want this job'. Companies using these methods report a high success rate.

One of the users of situational interviewing mentioned earlier was Tetley, part of Allied Brewers (Lunn, 1988). They used this approach long enough to allow them to compare the performance of their 'new' managers chosen in this way with their 'old' managers selected in a conventional manner:

	new group (%)	old group (%)
sales up on last year	12	2
controllable expenses down	14	5
controllable profits up	25	5
house net profit up	17	8

This company went on to use situational interviewing in the selection of its executives, salesmen and administrative staff, and the technique has been adapted for use in Mars Confectionery, Rover, Standard Life and for selecting nurses.

Does personality assessment, which remains popular, have a significant future role in employee selection procedures? As a way of assessing this issue,

Ivan Robertson (1994) offers this model of the relationships between personality constructs and overall job performance:

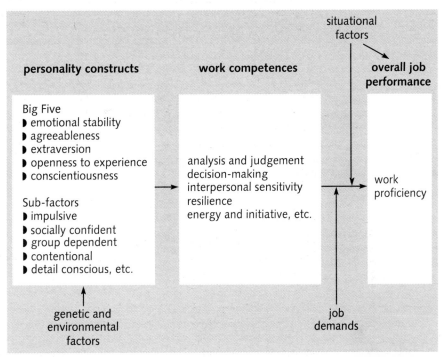

from Robertson, I.T., 1994, 'Personality and personnel selection', in C.L. Cooper and D.M. Rousseau (eds), *Trends in Organizational Behaviour*, John Wiley, London.

Robertson supports the view that the link between personality on the one hand, and job performance and career success on the other, must be weak. There are too many other factors in play to allow us to make realistic claims and predictions. The model identifies in particular the demands of the job, and factors in the organizational situation or context that can influence behaviour at work independently of (or in interaction with) personality. However, Robertson does argue that it is possible to relate personality measure to particular work competences, some of which are mentioned for illustrative purposes in the model; judgement, resilience, sensitivity, energy. This argument has strong intuitive appeal. Robertson claims that research evidence tends to support this view, and that this is where the future research agenda lies. He concludes that: 'When the personality constructs involved are clear and thought is given to the expected link between these constructs and work behaviour, it is likely that worthwhile information may be derived from personality measurement' (Robertson, 1994, p. 85).

As we are all expert implicit personality theorists, it is likely that personality constructs will continue to be a significant influence in employment and promotion decisions. Intuition tells us that personality is important, and research evidence, in general terms, supports this view. An understanding of the nature of personality, and the problems involved in its measurement or assessment should, however, make us more cautious about the weight we give to personality issues when reaching such critical organizational decisions.

sources

Allport, G.W., 1937, *Personality*, Holt, New York.

Bawtree, S. and Hogg, C., 1989, 'Assessment centres', *Personnel Management*, Factsheet 22, October.

Blinkhorn, S., 1988, 'The hazards of occupational testing', *The Listener*, 1988, 14 January, p. 9.

Campbell, J.W. and Hawley, C.W., 1982, 'Study habits and Eysenck's theory of extraversion–introversion', *Journal of Research in Personality*, vol. 16, no. 2, pp. 139–46.

Clarke, D., 1989, *Stress Management*, National Extension College, Cambridge.

Eysenck, H.J. and Wilson, G., 1975, *Know Your Own Personality*, Maurice Temple Smith, London.

Fowler, A., 1987, 'Light and bitter', *Personnel Management*, May, p. 73.

Friedman, M. and Rosenman, R.F., 1974, *Type A Behaviour and Your Heart*, Knopf, New York.

Golzen, G., 1988, 'Tailormade way to recruit the right stuff', *The Sunday Times*, 19 June, p. E19.

Jacobs, R., 1989a, 'Getting the measure of management competence', *Personnel Management*, June, pp. 32–7.

Jacobs, R., 1989b, 'Cadbury's dictionary of competence', *Personnel Management*, July, pp. 44–8.

Lunn, T., 1988, 'How to pick the winners', *The Sunday Times*, 1 May, p. E1.

McClelland, D.C., 1961, *The Achieving Society*, The Free Press, New York.

McRae, R.R. (ed.), 1992, 'The five-factor model: Issues and applications', *Journal of Personality*, vol. 60, no. 2 (special issue).

Mead, G.H., 1934, *Mind, Self and Society*, University of Chicago Press, Chicago.

Nelson, D. and Wedderburn, A., 1988, 'Staffing: new and surer methods', *Scotland on Sunday*, September 25, p. 13.

Rein, I.J., Kotler, P. and Stoller, M.R., 1987, *High Visibility*, Heinemann, London.

Robertson, I. T., 1994, 'Personality and personnel selection', in C.L. Cooper and D.M. Rousseau (eds.), *Trends in Organizational Behaviour*, John Wiley, London.

Rogers, C.R., 1947, 'Some observations on the organization of personality', *American Psychologist*, vol. 2, pp. 358–68.

Syrett, M., 1988, 'Giving job interviews a situational bite', *The Sunday Times*, 7 February, p. E1.

Whyte, W.H., 1956, *The Organization Man*, Simon & Schuster, New York.

Willmore, N., 1988, 'Interviews are not enough', *Personnel Today*, 30 August, p. 23.

Winterbottom, M. R., 1958, 'The relation of need for achievement to learning experiences in independence and mastery', in John W. Atkinson (ed.), *Motives in Fantasy, Action, and Society: A Method of Assessment and Study*, D. Van Nostrand Company Inc., Princeton, NJ, 1958, pp. 453–78.

Zimbardo, P., McDermott, M., Jansz, J. and Metaal, N., 1995, *Psychology: A European Text*, HarperCollins, London.

part 2 # groups in the organization

group formation

concepts and learning objectives
group-level analysis of organizational behaviour
historical background to the study of groups in organizations
concept of a group
formal and informal groups
Homans' theory of group formation
stages of group development
assessment
sources

concepts and learning objectives

A distinguishing feature of organizational work is that it is usually performed in groups or teams. It does not matter whether the work concerned is learning to read at school, checking insurance claims forms in an office or developing a mission statement for an organization or department. The lone artist in her garret or the window cleaner going from house to house tends to be the exception rather than the rule. Working alongside others is so important that companies explicitly select staff for their ability to be 'team players'.

Groups play an important and pervasive role in our lives. The average person belongs to five or six different groups. About 92 per cent of group members are in groups of five people or less. Such groups may include the lunchtime card school, the quality control section, the college debating club, the local women's group, the church group and the sports club. Our colleagues, friends, bosses and customers form the groups which are the fabric of our society. Whether at school, in the home or at work, we participate in and interact with members of groups. It has even been argued that one can view large organizations as a collection of small groups.

This chapter will begin by describing the history of the study of groups within organizations. It will then introduce key concepts, theories and research which have contributed to establishing group functioning as a central concern of organizational behaviour. It will conclude by indicating the current concerns in the study of group behaviour within the organizational context.

key concepts

interpersonal relations	psychological group
group relations	aggregate
Hawthorne effect	formal group
human relations approach	informal group

learning objectives

When you have read this chapter, you should be able to define those key concepts in your own words, and you should also be able to:

1 Place current thinking and research about group behaviour into a historical context.
2 Identify some of the different purposes which groups serve.
3 List the key characteristics of a psychological group.
4 Distinguish between a formal and an informal group.
5 Outline George Homans' theory of group formation.
6 Enumerate five stages of Tuckman and Jensen's model of group development.

group-level analysis of organizational behaviour

We shall begin by emphasizing the way in which individuals and groups are related in the context of the organization. Irrespective of their environmental context, groups are of interest because they represent mini-societies in which interaction takes place and in which the behaviour of individuals can be studied. A distinction will be made between the interpersonal level and the group level of analysis. The interpersonal level is concerned with the ways in which one person interacts with another person. Often such interaction is ordered and becomes predictable. This predictability in turn leads to people playing specific roles.

definition

Interpersonal relations *are the simplest social bonds which occur when two people stand in some relation to each other, such as husband and wife, or leader and follower. The term means 'between persons' and does not imply that the relationship must be a 'personal' one. It can be an impersonal or an intimate one.*

The group level is the next level. The inter-person behaviour builds up into group behaviour, which in turn sustains and structures future interpersonal relations. Groups develop particular characteristics, and relate to other groups in specific ways.

definition

Group relations *focus on the interaction within and between groups and the stable arrangements that result from such interactions.*

historical background to the study of groups in organizations

Industrial Fatigue Research Board studies

The earliest British interest in group behaviour in organizations dates back to 1917 when the Department of Scientific and Industrial Research and the

---

STOP!

two contrasting views of organization

view no. 1

In his chapter entitled 'The principle of supportive relationships', Rensis Likert attempted to derive a theory of organizational design with the group as the basic building block. He argued that:

1 Work groups are important sources of individuals' need satisfaction.
2 Groups in organizations that fulfil this psychological function are also more productive.
3 Management's task is therefore to create effective work groups by developing 'supportive relationships'.
4 An effective organizational structure consists of democratic/participative work groups, each linked to the organization as a whole through overlapping memberships.
5 Co-ordination is achieved by individuals who carry out 'linking functions'.

from Rensis Likert, 1961, *New Patterns of Management*, McGraw-Hill, New York, Chapter 8, pp. 97–118.

view no. 2

In his book, William H. Whyte offers a radical alternative to the view put forward by Likert. Whyte describes the horrors of:

> an environment in which everyone is tightly knit into a belongingness with one another; one in which there is no restless wandering but rather the deep emotional security that comes from total integration with the group.

from William H. Whyte, 1955, *The Organization Man*, Penguin Books, Harmondsworth.

Can you reconcile Likert's view with Whyte's?

Medical Research Council were asked to appoint a board to investigate industrial conditions. The purpose of this board was to continue the work that the Health of Munitions Workers Committee had done during the First World War.

The Industrial Fatigue Research Board (IFRB), as it was named, had as its terms of reference, 'to consider and investigate the relation of the hours of labour and other conditions of employment, including methods of work to the production of fatigue, having regard to both industrial efficiency and the preservation of health amongst workers.' In 1929, the IFRB became affiliated solely to the Medical Research Council and widened its scope of enquiries to become the Industrial Health Research Board.

In 1924 the Board launched a series of studies into the problem of monotony and the workcycle. One of these studies was conducted by Wyatt, Fraser and Stock (1928) on women wrapping soap, folding handkerchiefs, making bicycle chains, weighing and wrapping tobacco, making cigarettes and assembling rifle cartridges. It was published in 1928 as Report No. 52 of the Medical Research Council Industrial Fatigue Research Board. Among its findings was one which stated, 'the social conditions of work were found to have significant (but not emphasised) consequences, boredom being less likely to arise when operatives worked in groups rather than alone'.

Whilst great emphasis is placed on the early work of the American industrial psychologists such as Elton Mayo, Fritz J. Roethlisberger and William J. Dickson, it is worth remembering that the research which was carried out at the Western Electric Company in Chicago from the late 1920s, by staff of the Harvard Business School led to the creation of

> a school of management thought based on the rediscovery of two subsidiary findings of the earlier British industrial psychologists: that workers improve their performance when someone (a researcher or a supervisor) takes an interest in what they are doing (Vernon, Wyatt and Ogden, 1924, p. 15), and that the opportunity to interact freely with other workers boosts morale. The researchers emphasised the distinction between 'formal' and 'informal' worker groups and the relationships between informal organization and performance. The resultant 'human relations' school of management stressed the importance of the work group. Taylor's workers required only money, the human relations school's worker required group membership. The immediate impact of the Hawthorne studies concerned the role of the supervisor in handing work groups, and this became a major area of research for American industrial psychologists, inspired also by the work of Kurt Lewin and his associates. (Buchanan, 1979, p. 19)

the Hawthorne studies (1924–33)

In the early decades of the twentieth century, factories had used natural daylight or candles to illuminate the workspace of their workers. In an attempt to promote the sales of light bulbs in the early 1920s, the General Electric Company paid for a series of experiments to demonstrate a positive correlation between the amount of light in a workplace and the productivity of workers. Proven to GE's satisfaction, it proceeded to advertise the results. Then, to counter some questions about the objectivity of such experiments conducted by a light bulb manufacturer, a series of more independent studies was initiated. It is for this reason that the original team of researchers operated under the aegis of the National Academy of Sciences' National Research Council, which included the Council on Industrial Lighting. They hoped to show that artificial lighting in a factory would reduce accidents, save the workers' sight and raise productivity by as much as 25 per cent. The original experiments therefore examined the effect of physical changes, originally illumination and later room temperature and humidity, on worker productivity (Gillespie, 1991).

The experiments were conducted at the Hawthorne plant of the Western Electric Company, the manufacturing subsidiary of the American Telephone and Telegraph Company (AT&T), which supplied telephones to the entire Bell System. The factory was located in Cicero, a suburb of Chicago. In November 1924, the initial experiments began examining productivity improvements from a scientific management perspective assessing the

**the Hawthorne
plant of the
Western Electric
Company, 1929**

from Urwick and Brech
(1965)

*The main assembly plant is at the bottom centre of the photograph with its
distinctive tower at the corner of Cicero Avenue and Cermak Road. A railway
line intersects the 200-acre site which has a cable factory (shown far left) and a
timber yard (centre left). Workers' houses extend along two sides of the factory.*

physical factors. By 1927, the initial results were so confusing that the
company was preparing to abandon the work. Then, George Pennock,
Hawthorne's technical branch superintendent responsible for production
methods, heard Professor George Elton Mayo speak at a meeting, and invited
him to bring a team to the plant. In addition to Mayo, its main
members were Fritz J. Roethlisberger and William J. Dickson, and
they were supported by George Homans, Thomas North Whitehead and Lloyd Warner.

The Hawthorne studies are most often associated with an
Australian academic, George Elton Mayo, who was born in
Australia in 1880 and died in a nursing home in Guildford, Surrey,
nearly 69 years later. Initially a philosopher with psychoanalytical
training, Mayo came to the United States in 1922, and became a
professor of industrial research at the Harvard Business School two
years later. The studies, which are linked with his name, were
amongst the most extensive social science research ever conducted.

The Hawthorne studies revolutionized social science thinking.
They were intended to have direct financial benefits for the
company. That is, to appear as profits in company accounts rather
than as papers in academic journals. Their investigation results
demonstrated the overriding influence of social factors on

*George Elton Mayo
(1880–1949)*

**the chronology
of the
Hawthorne
experiments**

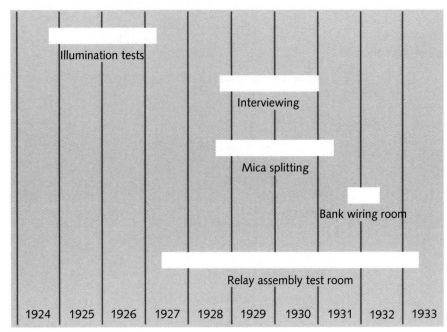

based on Gillespie, R., 1991, *Manufacturing Knowledge: A History of the Hawthorne Experiments*, Cambridge University Press, Cambridge.

workplace behaviour. Although there were many different studies conducted, four in particular stand out. These were the illumination experiments; the Relay Assembly Test Room experiment; the interviewing programme; and the Bank Wiring Observation Room experiment.

illumination experiments (1924–7)

The illumination studies lasted two and a half years. Their aim was 'to study the relationship of quality and quantity of illumination to efficiency in industry'. Three major illumination experiments were conducted. The illumination intensity was varied with the use of 3, 6, 14, 23 and 46 foot candles. The workers were divided into an experimental and control group, but the results obtained by the researchers were confusing. They discovered that in no case was the production output obtained in proportion to the lighting provided. Production even increased when the candle-power declined.

> The illumination at the bench in this room was cut down from the original amount of light to which the girls had been accustomed to 0.06 of a foot candle, an amount of light approximately equal to that of ordinary moonlight. Even with this very low intensity of light, the girls maintained their efficiency. (Roethlisberger and Dickson, 1939, p. 17)

The researchers reached two conclusions. First, as far as employee production output was concerned, lighting was only one factor (and an apparently minor one) among many others which affected it. Second, that a study of such a large group prevented the identification and control of the effect of any single variable on output. A different form of research study, utilizing a different research design and methods would be needed. The illumination experiments were abandoned.

Relay Assembly Test Room experiments (1927–33)

The new research format involved a small group of female workers drawn from the regular workforce of the Relay Assembly Department. Relays are electromagnetic switches that are activated by a weak signal and then sent out by a new, stronger signal. Each consisted of about 35 parts, and had to be assembled by hand. Six women assemblers were chosen for being average workers, neither inexperienced nor expert. They were placed in a separate room which gives its name to this phase of the research. The women worked a 48-hour week, including Saturdays, with no teabreaks. The general physical environment and conditions of the room were similar to those of the large assembly area.

Being separated in this way, they could be carefully and systematically studied by a researcher as they went about their task of putting together small telephone relays. The rate of output was then 5 relays in 6 minutes (approximately 500 a day). This allowed even small changes in productivity to be noted. The researcher was in the room with them. He kept a note of everything that happened and maintained a friendly atmosphere in the room by listening to their complaints and by telling them what was going on.

This phase of the research sought to answer six main questions. Did employees actually get tired out? Were rest pauses desirable? Was a shorter working day desirable? What were the effects of equipment changes? What were the women's attitudes to their work and the company? Why did production decline in the afternoon? A total of thirteen periods were studied during which changes were made to rest pauses, hours of work and breaks for refreshment. As the figure overleaf shows, there was a nearly continuous increase in output. This increase began when employee benefits such as rest periods and early finishes were added, but were maintained and even continued even when these benefits were withdrawn and the women returned to a 48-hour week.

**Relay Assembly
Test Room**

from Urwick and Brech
(1965)

original members of the Relay Assembly Test Room (1929)

selected results from the Relay Assembly Test Room experiments

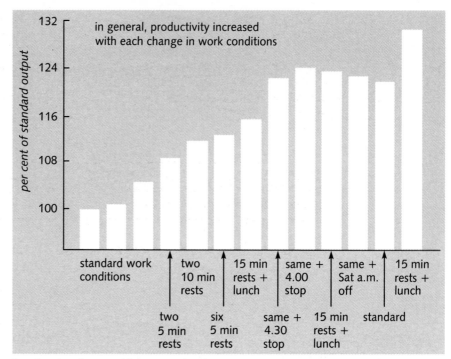

based on data from Roethlisberger and Dickson, 1939, in R.A. Baron and J. Greenberg, 1990, *Behavior in Organizations*, Allyn and Bacon, Chicago, third edition, p. 12. adapted by permission of Prentice-Hall, Inc., Upper Saddle River, N.J.

STOP!

Imagine you are a manager at the Hawthorne plant and the researchers have just passed you the research results shown above. You are used to analyzing a job and breaking it down into little tasks, giving those tasks to employees to do and motivating them with money. In your view, this is the best way of increasing productivity.

Review with a colleague or fellow student, the Relay Assembly Test Room results from the Hawthorne studies. Make a list of hypotheses that might explain these findings.

A great deal of controversy surrounds the results of the Hawthorne studies despite the attempts of the researchers to control the variables. Among the explanations put forward for the increases in output were that by being placed in a separate room, the women felt special and responded to their increased status; by being consulted about changes they gained a sense of employee participation; the researcher-observer was nice to them and thus raised their morale; a new supervisory relationship developed allowing the women to work freely without anxiety; and by selecting their co-workers, they had better interpersonal relationships and thus worked more as a team.

One of these explanations has even established itself as a concept in social science research. This says that the changed behaviour of the women was the result of being observed by the researchers, and that the manipulation of the variables played no part. This is now referred to as the Hawthorne Effect.

Whatever the true reasons were, the researchers were convinced that the women were motivated not solely by money or by improvements in their working conditions. Their attitudes towards and achievement of increased output seemed to be affected by the group to which they belonged. The results of the Relay Assembly Test Room experiment led management to decide that there was a need for more research into employee attitudes and the factors which influenced these. An interviewing programme was therefore established.

---

definition

The **Hawthorne Effect** *refers to the tendency of people being observed as part of a research effort, to behave differently than they would otherwise.*

---

interviewing programme (1928–30)

Management wanted to find out more about how employees felt about their supervisors and working conditions, and how these related to morale. The interviewing programme thus had the practical aim of improving supervision and ultimately of raising productivity. In total some 20,000 interviews were conducted, which makes it one of the most extensive research efforts in the history of social science.

At the start, the interviewers asked employees highly structured questions about how they felt about their work. Later, this form of questioning gave way to non-directive, open-ended questions on non-work topics which the interviewees considered to be important. The sympathetic and non-judgemental approach of the interviewers led them to discover the true feelings and attitudes of the workforce. The information that was obtained went beyond issues of work conditions and supervision, but extended to family and social issues. The interviewees also allowed employees to have their grievances heard and to get things 'off their chests'. The interview programme led to a more sophisticated view being taken by the researchers of the factors that led to employee satisfaction. This is shown in the figure below.

These interviews also revealed the existence of informal, gang-like groups within the primary working groups, with bosses and sidekicks who built an elaborate structure of sanctions to ensure production was controlled. The

scheme for interpreting complaints involving interrelationships of employees

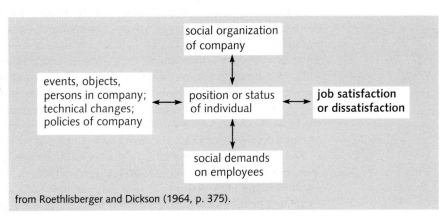

from Roethlisberger and Dickson (1964, p. 375).

discovery of this 'informal' organization with its own rules and hierarchy of positions was one of the findings of this phase of the research. It was to understand how this worked in more detail that the Bank Wiring Observation Room experiment was established.

Bank Wiring Observation Room experiments (1931–2)

The interviewing programme revealed that social groups in different shop departments of the company could exercise a great deal of control over the behaviour of their members. To test this and other hypotheses, a group of men were observed in another part of the company.

The Bank Wiring Observation Room consisted of 14 men who were formally organized into 3 sub-groups, each of which contained 3 wirers and 1 supervisor. In addition, 2 inspectors moved between the 3 groups. Detailed observation of interactions between all the 14 men involved revealed the existence of two informal groups or 'cliques' whose membership transgressed the formal group boundaries. These two informal groups are shown in the figure on p. 186.

Bank Wiring Observation Room: bank wirers at work

The two cliques were located at the front and the back of the room, and the workmen in them referred to as 'the group in front' (Clique A) and the 'group in back' (Clique B). The figure highlights the fact that W_2 and W_6 were not strongly integrated into these two cliques, and that W_5, S_2 and I_3 were not members of either. These two informal groups each produced informal leaders who were not designated by management, but who emerged from within each clique.

A second major finding of this phase of the research was that these cliques developed informal rules of behaviour or 'norms'. Not only did the workmen control the work that they physically produced, but individual members were found to be giving incorrect reports to management on the output achieved. The total figure for the week would tally with the total week's output, but the daily reports showed a steady, level output regardless of actual daily production.

the informal as opposed to the formal organization of the groups in the Bank Wiring Observation Room

Figure 1 shows the formal group structure as devised by the company's management. Three quartets of three bank wirers (W) and one solderer (S) were supervised by two inspectors (I). The lines in figure 2 reports the researchers' observations as to which individuals participated in whose work-time games. Notice that W_4 participated in games played by the group shown on the left, while W_6 was involved in the games of the group on the right.

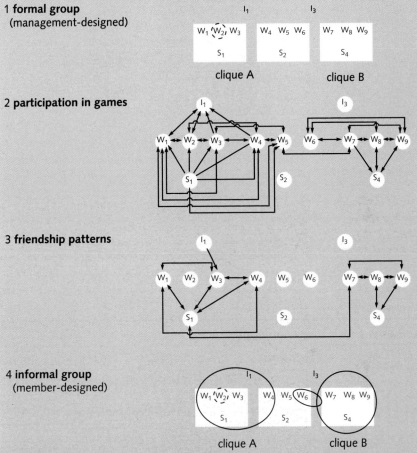

The lines in figure 3 reveal the friendship relations that existed between the people in the room. Individuals I_1 and W_3 are friendly, and note also the individuals who are not linked by any lines. Finally, on the basis of the researchers' analysis of who interacts with and likes whom, the researchers concluded that two informal groups or cliques could be identified in the Bank Wiring Observation Room. As figure 4 shows, clique A consisted of four workers, one solderer and an inspector; while clique B consisted of four different workers and a solderer. Three individuals did not appear to be members of either clique.

based on F. J. Roethlisberger and W. J. Dickson, 1939, *Management and the Worker*, Harvard University Press, Cambridge, MA, pp. 501, 507 and 509. Reprinted with permission.

definition

Human relations approach *in management is one that emphasizes people and their feelings and attitudes.*

The researchers determined that the group was operating well below its capacity and individual members were not earning as much as they could. The norms under which the group was operating were found to be the following:

1 You should not turn out too much work. If you do, you are a *rate-buster*.
2 You should not turn out too little work. If you do, you are a *chiseller*.
3 You should not tell a supervisor anything that will react to the detriment of an associate. If you do, you are a *squealer*.
4 You should not attempt to maintain social distance or act officious. If you are an inspector, for example, you should not act like one.

from Roethlisberger and Dickson (1939, p. 522).

The researchers discovered that members of the Bank Wiring Observation Room were afraid that if they significantly increased their output, the unit incentive rate would be cut and the daily output expected by management would increase. Lay-offs might occur and men could be reprimanded. To forestall such consequences, the group members agreed between themselves what was a fair day's output (neither too high nor too low).

Having established such a output norm, they enforced it through a system of negative sanctions or punishments. These included the practice of 'bingeing' in which a norm-violator was tapped on the upper arm; the use of ridicule as when a group member was referred to as The Slave or Speed King; and total rejection or exclusion. Roethlisberger and Dickson concluded that, 'The social organization of the bankwiremen performed a twofold function (1) to protect the group from internal indiscretions and (2) to protect it from outside interference . . . nearly all the activities of this group can be looked upon as methods of controlling the behaviour of its members' (pp. 523–4).

---

conclusions from the Hawthorne studies

1 People at work are motivated by more than pay and conditions alone.
2 Work is a group activity, and individuals should be seen as group members and not in isolation.
3 The need for recognition, security and a sense of belonging is more important in determining workers' morale and productivity than the physical conditions under which they work.
4 Through their unofficial norms and sanctions, informal groups exercise strong controls over the work habits and attitudes of individual group members. Hence, the ability of the informal group or clique to motivate an individual at work should not be underestimated.
5 Supervisors need to be aware of both individuals' social needs and the power of the informal group, in order to align these to achieve the formal (official) objectives.

These findings showed that the worker was more responsive to the social forces of his or her peer group than to the controls and incentives of management. Companies concluded that the employee's receptivity to management's goals depended on the extent to which the boss could meet employees' social needs, such as that for acceptance. In this sense, the human relations approach to management was born.

The first-line supervisor came to be seen as the single most important factor in determining the morale and productivity of the work group. For this reason, large numbers of supervisors were sent on human relations training courses to make them more sensitive to the social needs of the work group that they supervised, and to develop their interpersonal skills. Not all of these courses were successful!

from *Works Management*, August 1989, p. 17.

concept of a group

Given the importance of face-to-face interaction, social psychologists have studied the behaviour of groups. The idea of a group is well known to most people who work, live and play in groups. Very often we may refer to persons standing at a bus stop or in a queue as a group.

STOP!

Consider the following list and decide which of the following would in your view constitute a group.

1 people riding on a bus
2 blonde women between 20 and 30 years of age
3 members of a football team
4 audience in a theatre
5 people sheltering in a shop doorway from the rain

It is important to maintain a distinction between mere aggregates of individuals and what are called psychological groups. The latter are so called because they exist not only through the (often visible) interactions of members, but also in the (not observable) perceptions of their members. The term *psychological group* is thus reserved for people who consider themselves to be part of an identifiable unit, who relate to each other in a meaningful fashion, and who share dispositions through their shared sense of collective identity. In the STOP list above, only the football team would fulfil our criteria for a group.

---

definitions

A **psychological group** is any number of people who (a) interact with each other, (b) are psychologically aware of each other, and (c) perceive themselves to be a group.

An **aggregate** is a collection of unrelated people who happen to be in close physical proximity for a short period of time.

The use of this definition enables us to exclude aggregates of people who are simply individuals who happen to be gathered together at any particular time. Like the bus passengers, theatre audience or rain shelterers, they do not relate to one another in any meaningful fashion, nor consider themselves a part of any identifiable unit, despite their temporary physical proximity. By the same token, the definition allows one to exclude classes of people who may be defined by physical attributes, geographical location, economic status or age. Even though a trade union in an organization may like to believe it is a group, it will fail to meet our definition if all its members do not interact with each other, and if they are not aware of each other. This need for all members to interact has led to the suggestion that, in practice, a psychological group is unlikely to exceed twelve or so persons. Beyond that number, the opportunity for frequent interaction between members, and hence group awareness, is considerably reduced.

It is possible for small aggregates of people to be transformed into a psychological group through outside circumstances. In fact, a whole series of 'disaster movies' in the cinema have been made in which people fight for their lives on sinking ships, in hijacked aeroplanes and in burning skyscrapers. The story involves aggregates of people setting out at the start of the film. The danger causes them to interact with one another, and this increases their awareness of one another and leads them to see themselves as having common problems. By the end of the film, the survivors demonstrate all the characteristics of the psychological group as defined here. The disaster movie example helps us to understand some of the characteristics of a psychological group:

1 *A minimum membership of two people:* while it is clear that one cannot be a group on one's own, the more members a group has, the greater the number of possible relationships that can exist between them, the greater the level of communication that is required and the more complex the structure needed to operate the group.

2 *A shared communication network:* each member of a psychological group must be capable of communicating with every other member. In this communication process, the aims and purposes of the group are exchanged. The mere process of communication interaction satisfies some of our social needs, and it is used to set and enforce standards of group behaviour.

3 *A shared sense of collective identity:* each group member must identify with the other members of the group and not see himself as an individual acting independently. He must believe that he is both a member of, and a participant in, the group, which itself is distinctive from other groups.

4 *Shared goals:* the goal concerned is therefore shared and only achievable by the members working together and not as individuals. The goal may be the production of something (e.g. student group project, company marketing plan) or enjoying oneself (e.g. playing in a football team). While the individual may want to attain some particular objective, he must perceive that the other members of the group share this same disposition. He must feel obliged to contribute to the attainment of the shared goal.

5 *Group structure:* individuals in the group will have different roles, e.g. initiator/ideas man, suggestion-provider, compromiser. These roles, which tend to become fixed, indicate what members expect of each other. Norms or rules exist which indicate which behaviours are acceptable in the group and which are not (e.g. smoking, swearing, latecoming).

One can summarize this section by emphasizing the need to distinguish between aggregates of people and a psychological group. Not all groups will possess all the features listed above.

Groups will differ in the degree to which they possess such characteristics. To the extent that they do have them, it will make the group more easily recognizable by others as a group, and this will give it more power with which to influence its members. The topic of influence and control in groups is dealt with in a later chapter. What will be said in the remainder of this chapter and this part of the book will refer to psychological groups only. For this reason we shall use the shorthand label of group to refer to a psychological group.

Groups serve both an organizational and an individual function. The problem is that the task objective of a group, that is, the job it has to do (for example, speedily processing insurance claims forms), may conflict with its social objective, which may involve members deriving pleasure from interacting with other group members. Where there is such a conflict, either the organization or the individual group members will lose out. Another difficulty arises when different individual members seek to satisfy different needs through membership of the same group. One person may seek to fulfil her need for power and try to direct the behaviour of others in a group. These members may have a primary need for friendship.

Group membership gives the individual new experiences, which in turn may induce new desires. Thus once a group has formed, it may develop 'accessory goals', i.e. goals which were not there initially. If members are satisfied with their group, they are likely to find some aim to pursue in order to maintain the group's existence after its main objective has been achieved or become outdated. Thus the 'Build a Zebra Crossing in Byres Road' pressure group may turn itself into a permanent residents' association once the crossing has been built. Our group membership also influences the view we have of ourselves. This is what psychologists call our self-image. Ask a person at a party who he or she is, and it is very likely that they will answer your question by telling you the groups to which they belong. This is encapsulated in the phrase, 'Who I am is who we are'. Thus we use groups to define our social identity, and this in turn has an effect on our own behaviour and that of the individuals with whom we come into contact.

> ## STOP!
> Make a list of the groups of which you are a member. Against each, indicate whether their purpose is primarily work-related (W) or social (S).

formal and informal groups

In the chapter on motivation, we learned that people had a variety of different needs, amongst which were included those for love, esteem and safety. Love needs are concerned with belongingness and relationships; esteem needs focus on recognition, attention and appreciation; whilst safety needs concern security of employment. The failure to satisfy these needs may result in our inability to feel confident, capable, necessary or useful members of society. These needs concern our relationships with others, and whilst we may spend time outside work with our wives, husbands, girlfriends, boyfriends, children or social club members, the time that we do spend at work remains considerable. In our relationships with work colleagues, therefore, we frequently seek to satisfy these needs.

The difficulty is that the organizations in which we work are not primarily designed to allow individuals to meet such needs at work. The collective purpose of an organization may be to make washing machines, provide a repair service, earn £200,000 profit a year or achieve a 5 per cent return on investment. To achieve such collective purposes, the organization is structured in such a way as to use the limited resources it has at its disposal as efficiently and effectively as possible. It does this by creating what is called a formal organization. The overall collective purpose or aim is broken down into sub-goals or sub-tasks. These are assigned to different sub-units in the organization. The tasks may be grouped together and departments thus formed. Job requirements in terms of job descriptions may be written. The subdivision continues to take place until a small group of people are given one such sub-goal and divide it between themselves. When this occurs, there exists the basis for forming the group along functional lines. This process of identifying the purpose, dividing up tasks, and so on, is referred to as the creation of the formal organization. The groups which are formed as a result of this process are therefore known as formal groups.

It is through the division of labour that formal groups are created. A motor car company divides itself into departments responsible for sales, production, quality control, finance, personnel, training, and so on. Within each such department one finds further sub-groupings of individuals. It is the organization itself which gives the impetus for the formation of various smaller functional task groups within itself.

definition

Formal groups *are those groups in an organization which have been consciously created to accomplish the organization's collective purpose. These formal groups perform formal functions, such as getting work done, generating ideas, liaising, and so on. The formal group functions are the tasks which are assigned to it, and for which it is officially held responsible.*

Managers make choices represented as decisions, as to how technology and organization will be combined to create task-oriented (formal) groups. The purpose of the sub-groups in the production department may be to manufacture 100 cars a day, while that of the group in the design department may be to draw up a set of construction plans. Whatever type of formal group we are interested in, they all have certain common characteristics:

- They have a formal structure.
- They are task-oriented.
- They tend to be permanent.
- Their activities contribute directly to the organization's collective purpose.
- They are consciously organized by somebody for a reason.
- Two different types of formal group in organizations can be identified. They are distinguished by the duration of their existence. Examples of permanent formal groups would include a permanent committee (e.g.

union–management consultative board), a management team or a staff group providing specialist services (e.g. computer unit, training section). There are also likely to be temporary formal groups. For example, a task group which is formally designed to work on a specific project where its interaction and structures are pre-specified to accomplish the task. Such a task force might be formed when, for an unknown reason, a major delay or serious defect occurs in some area of manufacture. The aim of the task force would be to identify the causes and suggest remedies. This group would be disbanded once this objective had been achieved. What makes a formal group permanent or temporary is not the actual time it exists, but how it is defined by the company. Some temporary groups may last for years. What is important is whether the group's members feel that they are part of the group which might be disbanded at any time.

Alongside these formal groups, and consisting of the same employees, albeit arranged differently, will be a number of informal groups. These emerge in an organization and are neither anticipated, nor intended, by those who created the formal organization. They emerge from the informal interaction of the members of the formal organization. These unplanned groups share many of the characteristics of the small social leisure groups. They function alongside the formal groups. The informal structure of a group develops during the spontaneous interaction of persons in the group as they talk, joke and associate with one another.

---

definition

An **informal group** *is a collection of individuals who become a group when members develop interdependencies, influence one another's behaviour and contribute to mutual need satisfaction.*

Why do informal groups exist and what purpose do they serve? It was noted earlier that a formal organization is designed on rational principles and is aimed at achieving the collective purpose of the organization. To do this, staff are hired to perform clearly specified tasks and play clearly defined roles. The company only requires the worker to perform a limited range of behaviours, irrespective of whether they want or can do more. This limitation of behaviour is related to the organization's need to be able to control and predict the behaviour of its members.

Nevertheless, the worker comes to the job as a whole individual. While the organization may wish to hire a 'pair of hands', it gets the rest of the body and the brain thrown in! The individual brings his or her hopes, needs, desires and personal goals to the job. Whilst the company may not be interested in these, the employee will, nevertheless, attempt to achieve personal ambitions while at work. Many of these needs are in the area of love and esteem. Organizations are rarely designed to be able to fulfil these, or even feel that they have any responsibility to do so. This being the case, the employee will set about the job by developing relationships with other workers which will allow such need satisfaction to occur.

Individual employees will try to manipulate their surroundings or situation in such a way so as to allow them to meet their motivational needs. Most other staff will generally be seeking to do the same, so it will not be difficult to

Bull Dogs and Red Devils: a study of group formation

In 1949, Muzafer Sherif studied how a collection of individuals who had had no previous ties with each other formed themselves into a group. Sherif and his team of researchers used a field experiment research design to study the behaviour of 12-year-old boys who attended a summer camp in northern Connecticut in the summer of 1949. Unbeknown to the boys, all the camp staff – counsellors, leaders and handymen – were Sherif's collaborators. They created special test situations, and observed and noted what occurred.

Muzafer Sherif

camp grounds

Twenty-four boys were carefully selected and matched to be as similar as possible, so as to eliminate other possible bases for group formation (e.g. background, education, ethnicity, religion, friendship). Having arrived in camp, they were separated into two groups and directed to choose a bunkhouse, and then depart immediately on a hike. From then on, for five days, the two sets of boys were on separate schedules, sleeping in different bunkhouses and eating at different times.

Red Devils carrying a table to their hideout

Bull Dogs at the swimming pool which they appropriated and improved

Sherif considered that a common group goal was essential for group formation to occur, and predicted that, as members interacted to achieve this, the boys would produce a group organization with hierarchical status and role relationships, and develop common, unwritten rules (norms) of behaviour which would serve as the basis for individual members' attitudes. Hence, whilst the boys were allowed to choose their own activities, cooking, hiking, camping, all of these demanded co-operative behaviour. For example, food was supplied in bulk, and the boys had to cut it up, build a fire, and so on. Achieving the goals required discussion, planning and execution.

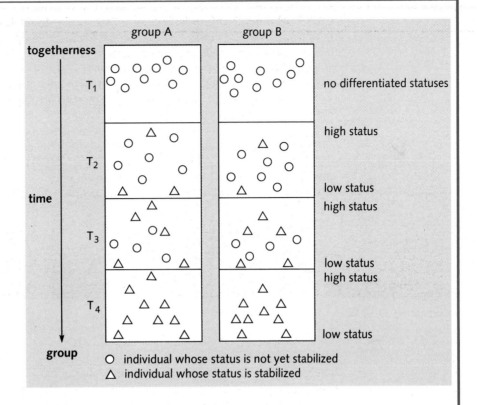

	group A	group B	
togetherness			
T_1			no differentiated statuses
T_2			high status
			low status
			high status
T_3			
			low status
			high status
T_4			
			low status

time →

group

○ individual whose status is not yet stabilized
△ individual whose status is stabilized

formation of status structure in two groups over a period of time

The figure shows the development of the two groups over time. The circles represent individual boys whose status within the group had not yet stabilized, while the triangles highlight those whose had. At the start (T_1), Sherif's researchers observed no consistent patterning of behaviour from one situation to the next. During swimming, one boy took the lead; when cooking, another took over, and so on. After a few days' interaction however, (T_2), it was the top and bottom status positions which stabilized first. The lower positions established as it became obvious that some of the boys were not contributing to the task, were playing around, or lacked interest or skill. Still later, at T_3, most positions, except those in the middle levels of each group, had stabilized, as those boys jockeyed for positions. By T_4, the status structure of each of the two had fully stabilized.

The early development of leadership showed that one person had begun to co-ordinate and initiate plans in a variety of different situations. Observational data revealed that certain boys were more popular than others, and gained undisputed authority over others. As the structure formed within each group, their members' attitudes to their group became positive, and norms were established.

One of these was the naming of the groups – 'Red Devils' and 'Bull Dogs'. Another was the conferment of nicknames on group members, 'Baby Face' and 'Lemon Head'. Each group came to prefer certain songs, developed its own jargon, special jokes, secrets and preferred places. Each group also had its special ways of performing tasks such as braiding lanyards and preparing meals, which was consistently followed by group members. Methods of praise and punishments (sanctions) were standardized in each group.   *continued overleaf*

Wayward members who failed to do the 'right' things or who did not contribute to the common effort found themselves receiving reprimands, ridicule, 'silent treatment' or even threats. In the Bull Dogs, the leader assigned any deviant to remove stones from the swimming pond.

The researchers concluded that when individuals who have no established relationships are brought together to interact in activities with common goals, they produce a group structure with hierarchical positions and roles within it. The process of interaction produces common goals, which constitute the basis of individual members' attitudes in matters important to the group.

based on M. Sherif and C.W. Sherif, 1953, *Groups in Harmony and Tension*, Harper and Brothers, New York.

© Solo

© Solo

set up a series of satisfying relationships. These relationships in turn will lead to the formation of informal groups. Because of people's social nature, there is a strong tendency for people to form informal groups. The task-oriented, formal groups rarely consider the social needs of their members. Indeed, these are frequently considered to be dispensable and counterproductive to the achievement of the formal purpose of the organization.

The fulfilment of the needs for love and esteem has been attempted by a number of companies such as the Disney Corporation, McDonald's and others, which possess a strong and distinctive corporate culture of their own. Through their processes of staff selection, training and socialization, they attempt to engender in their staff a feeling of loyalty, identification and commitment. These organizations are discussed in greater depth in Chapter 18, but tend to represent the exception rather than the rule.

STOP!

Consider the ways in which the college/institution in which you are studying this course has consciously organized the meeting of your social needs. Suggest any specific things it could do to meet these to a greater extent.

It is not just the social and esteem needs that are met by the informal group. The safety needs of group members regarding employment formed the basis of the actions of the wiremen in the Bank Wiring Room at the Hawthorne works. The informal group there sought to defend itself from outside interference. Many years later, Dalton (1959) described how all major parts of a work organization were threatened by invasion from other sections. These departments aggressively maintained their boundaries flexibly in the face of these offensive threats. They did it by creating a spy network to identify what other sections were planning to do and prepared defences against them. One of the strategies used was to create an informal, parallel organization whose purpose was to anticipate changes and institute their own which were within the departmental tradition. This allowed the defending department to maintain its control over its boundaries against any excessive demands which might be made by other sections. Thus the strategy used by the cliques in the Bank Wiring Room was similar to the one used by these line managers.

In any company, there will be numerous formal groups which interlink with each other, and also many informal groups which form a network. To distinguish these two different collectivities, they are referred to respectively as the *formal organization* and the *informal organization*. The formal and informal organizations are not totally separate. The composition, structure and operation of the different informal groups, which make up the company's informal organization, will be determined by the formal arrangements that exist in the company. These provide the context within which social relationships are established and within which social interaction can take place. Such formal constraints can include plant layout, work shifts, numbers of staff employed and the type of technology used.

It is important to understand that informal groups arise out of a combination of formal factors and human needs. The nature of the formal organization is based on the choices made by senior company managers. Both the formal organization, and the ensuing informal counterpart that it generates, can be changed when different choices are made.

Organizations only meet a small range of the individual's needs. The informal organization emerges to fulfil those needs neglected or ignored by the formal system. It differs from the formal system by being more casual in terms of its member composition and nature of interaction. To identify different informal groups, one does not look at the work flow or the organization chart, but needs to note who interacts with whom, and what friendship relations exist between individuals. The technique of sociometry, developed by Jacob Moreno, and discussed in the next chapter, is particularly relevant here. To summarize, therefore, one can say that formal groups exist to meet organizational objectives and fulfil the individual workers' lower level needs, as identified on Maslow's hierarchy. The informal group can meet some of their higher level needs.

'growing' informal groups

Elton Mayo was very aware of the importance of informal groups, and tried to organize them. He used the term *natural group* to refer to groups of 3–6 workers who, through the normal interaction of the members, developed high

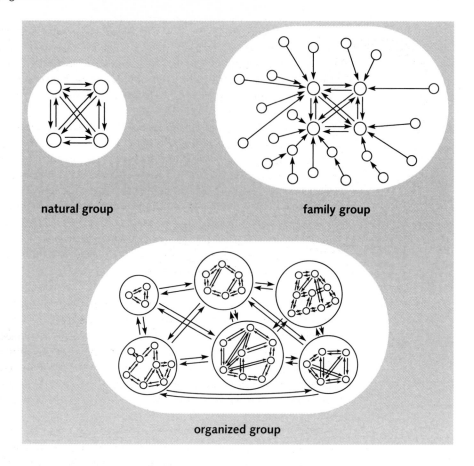

levels of intimacy and cohesiveness. Unless such natural groups were nourished and supported, the normal processes of interaction would be interfered with, and the group would not develop. A natural group, with a core of members who are held in high esteem by other workers, could be 'grown' into what Mayo called a *family group* of between 8 and 30 members.

This process would naturally take between 6 and 12 months of continuous association and lead finally to the development of one, large *organized group*, consisting of a plant-wide network of family groups, each with its natural groups. Mayo's vision was of a community organization, in which all or most employees were members of well-knit, natural groups, which were linked together in common purpose. These were not the formal groups discussed earlier. Mayo invited managers to act somewhat like gardeners rather than engineers, and use their skills, intelligence and experience deliberately to create group integrity of association.

Homans' theory of group formation

The research into the behaviour of groups in organizations has focused on three main questions: How do groups form? What keeps a group together? What makes it effective? The second and third of these questions will be dealt with in the chapters that follow under the headings of group cohesiveness and group effectiveness. The search for the answer to the first question has produced a great deal of research data, but few accepted theories. Of the theories that have been put forward to explain the formation of groups, perhaps the most often cited is that of the sociologist George Homans. Homans had been a member of Elton Mayo's Department of Industrial Research at the Harvard Business School.

George Caspar Homans

During his time there, he had been influenced by Mayo's thinking about group behaviour. Homans presented his ideas in his book, *The Human Group* (1951). He argued that any social system, such as a group, exists within a three-part environment. This includes a physical environment (terrain, climate, layout), a cultural environment (norms, values and goals) and a technological environment (state of knowledge). The environment imposes certain activities and interactions on the people involved in the system. These activities and interactions in turn arouse emotions and attitudes (sentiments) amongst the people towards each other and towards the environment.

This combination of activities, interactions and sentiments is primarily determined by the environment, Homans called this the 'external system'. It is so called because it was imposed on the people from outside, and was not of their own choosing. The activities, interactions and sentiments are mutually dependent on one another. For example, the more two people interact with each other, the more positive their sentiments towards each other are likely to be. The reverse is also true; that is, the more positive the sentiments, the higher the rate of interaction.

However, Homans noted that this external system did not exist alone. With increased interactions, people developed sentiments which were not specified by the external environment. That is, along with the new norms and shared frames of reference, new activities were generated which were not specified by the external environment. Workers were found to develop games, interaction patterns and sentiments not suggested and not sanctioned by the environment. Homans refers to this new pattern, which arose (or emerged) from the external system, as the 'internal system'. This corresponds to what other theorists have called the informal organization. Homans argued that the internal (informal) and external (formal) system developed norms about how working life should be organized (as some of the Hawthorne study groups did). This would often change the way in which work was performed, how much of it was done and what its quality would be.

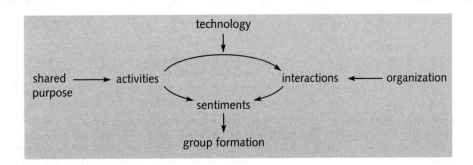

Finally, Homans stressed that the two systems and the environment were interdependent. Changes in the environment would produce changes in the formal and informal work organization. The activities and the norms of the internal system would eventually alter the physical, cultural and technological environment. The workers' informal method of solving problems might generate ideas for technological innovation, the redesign of work layout or the development of new norms about the nature of the relationship between workers and management. New microcomputer developments in the area of production control could mean that it might be possible for shopfloor-level staff to monitor product output and quality themselves. This was a task previously carried out by first-line management and would represent a change in the relationships between the two groups. The most valuable aspect of Homans' conceptual scheme is its explicit recognition of the various dependencies.

In his theory, Homans distinguished between required behaviour and emergent behaviour. The concept is considered from the viewpoint of

the Homans model of work group behaviour

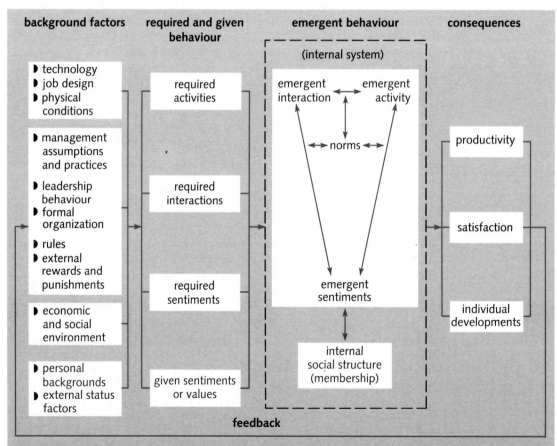

Source: Arthur N. Turner, 'A conceptual scheme for describing work group behavior', case no. 461-001. Boston: Harvard Business School, 1961. Copyright © 1961 by the President and Fellows of Harvard College. In Paul R. Lawrence and John A. Seiler, *Organizational Behavior and Administration: Cases, Concepts, and Research Findings, Revised edition*, Burr Ridge, IL: Richard D. Irwing, Inc, 1965. Reprinted by permission of the Harvard Business School.

management. In performing a job, there are certain activities that need to be done, certain interactions have to be performed and certain sentiments demonstrated, if the task is to be accomplished successfully (required behaviour). Consider the process of buying a personal computer by mail order from a major manufacturer. The freephone number connects you with a member of the company's telesales team. To accomplish the sales task successfully, the salesperson has to establish contact with the caller and have the product information to hand (required task); they then have to question the caller concerning the product's specifications and prices (required interactions); and acknowledge the customer's concerns and anxieties concerning purchasing an unseen good, costing £1000 to £2000, from a company at the other end of a telephone hundreds of miles away (requirement sentiments).

In the process of performing their job, the sales personnel are likely to engage in other activities, interactions and sentiments. For example, they may compile their shopping list when there are no customer calls; they make jokes with one another to relieve the boredom or stress of the work, and they may feel frustration about the stupidity or rudeness of the callers. These examples of activities, interactions and sentiments are not required for their task to be successfully performed. However, these emerge as a result of the existing background factors and the required and given behaviours (emergent behaviour).

STOP!

Consider the work of the checkout assistant at your local supermarket.
What are the required activities, interactions and sentiments for their job?
Can you spot any emergent activities, interactions or sentiments being manifested?

---

stages of group development

Since we have been using the terms formal group and informal group, it is important to relate these to our organizational definition of the psychological group. Whilst an informal group is always also a psychological group, a formal group may not necessarily be a psychological group. Consider for a moment the staff in a company finance office. As a task-oriented formal group they have the responsibility for the control of the company finances, costing and control. Of the twenty individuals who compose it, half may have been there for over twenty years, whilst others will have joined the company when it merged. Consider also the definition of the psychological group. There is no reason why these staff should all necessarily interact with each other or perceive themselves to be a single group. The finance department as a formally established unit may consist of different informal groups. The question then arises as to how a collection of individuals becomes a psychological group.

Groups of whatever type do not come into existence fully formed. Tuckman and Jensen suggested that groups pass through five clearly defined stages of development, which they labelled forming, storming, norming,

stages of group development

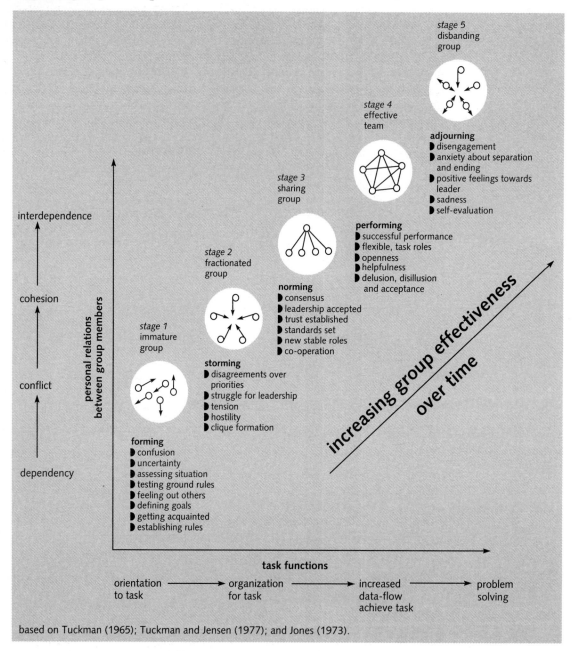

stage 5
disbanding
group

stage 4
effective
team

adjourning
▷ disengagement
▷ anxiety about separation
  and ending
▷ positive feelings towards
  leader
▷ sadness
▷ self-evaluation

stage 3
sharing
group

performing
▷ successful performance
▷ flexible, task roles
▷ openness
▷ helpfulness
▷ delusion, disillusion
  and acceptance

stage 2
fractionated
group

norming
▷ consensus
▷ leadership accepted
▷ trust established
▷ standards set
▷ new stable roles
▷ co-operation

increasing group effectiveness over time

interdependence

stage 1
immature
group

cohesion

storming
▷ disagreements over
  priorities
▷ struggle for leadership
▷ tension
▷ hostility
▷ clique formation

conflict

personal relations
between group members

forming
▷ confusion
▷ uncertainty
▷ assessing situation
▷ testing ground rules
▷ feeling out others
▷ defining goals
▷ getting acquainted
▷ establishing rules

dependency

task functions

orientation ———→ organization ———→ increased ———→ problem
to task   for task   data-flow   solving
                                        achieve task

based on Tuckman (1965); Tuckman and Jensen (1977); and Jones (1973).

performing and adjourning (Tuckman, 1965; Tuckman and Jensen, 1977). Of course, not all groups develop through all the stages; some get stuck in the middle and remain inefficient and ineffective. Progress through the stages may be slow, but appears to be necessary and inescapable. Complementing this original framework, Jones (1973) described the personal relations issues that affect group members, and the task functions that are addressed at each stage.

forming

This is the orientation phase, at which the set of individuals has not yet gelled. Everyone is busy finding out about each others' attitudes and backgrounds and establishing ground rules. Members are also keen to fix their personal identities in the group and make a personal impression on the others. In the personal relations area, members are *dependent* on some leader to provide them with structure in the form of ground rules and an agenda for action. Task-wise, they seek *orientation* as to what they are being asked to do, what the issues are and whether everyone understands the objective.

storming

This is a conflict stage in the group's life and can be an uncomfortable period. Members bargain with each other as they try to sort out what each of them individually, and as a group, want out of the group process. Individuals reveal their personal goals and it is likely that interpersonal hostility is generated when differences in these goals are revealed. Members may resist the control of other group members and may show hostility. The early relationships established in the forming stage may be disrupted. The key personal relations issue in this stage is the management of *conflict*, whilst the task function question is *organization* – how best to organize to achieve the group objective.

norming

In this cohesion stage, the members of the group develop ways of working to develop closer relationships and camaraderie. The question of who will do what and how it will be done is addressed. Working rules are established in terms of norms of behaviour (do not smoke) and role allocation (Jill will be the spokes-person). A structure is, therefore, created in which each group member can relate to the others and the questions of agreeing expectations and dealing with a failure to meet members' expectations are addressed. The personal relations within the group stress *cohesion*. Members feel that they have overcome conflict, have 'gelled' and experience a sense of groupiness. On the task side, there is an *increase in data-flow* as members become more prepared to be more open about their goals.

performing

By this stage, the group has developed an effective structure, and it is concerned with actually getting on with the job in hand and accomplishing objectives. The fully mature group has now been created which can get on with its work. Not all groups develop to this stage but may become bogged down in an earlier and less productive stage. In personal relations, *interdependence* becomes a feature. Members are equally happy working alone, in sub-groupings or as a single unit. Collaboration and functional competition occur between them. On the task side, there is a high commitment to the objective, jobs are well defined, and *problem-solving* activity ensues.

adjourning

In this final stage the group may disband, either because the task has been achieved or because the members have left. Before they do so, they may reflect on their time together and prepare themselves to go their own ways.

This model has been verified by research and can help us to explain some of the problems of group working. A group may be operating at half power because it may have failed to work through some of the issues at the earlier stages. For example, the efficiency of a project team may be impaired because it had not resolved the issue of leadership. Alternatively, people may be pulling in different directions because the purpose of the group has not been clarified, nor its objectives agreed. Members might be using the group to achieve their personal and unstated aims (so-called hidden agendas). For all these reasons, effective group functioning may be hindered.

---

diagnosing a given group's stage of development

Any existing group or team can assess which stage of its development it has reached in the Tuckman and Jensen model by using a self-administered questionnaire. Although these vary, typically group members evaluate their group under two headings. The first of these is how well they feel that their group is getting on in achieving the *task* in hand. The dimensions of task considered are the level of understanding of what the group's goals are; whether members are organized to achieve them; how willingly they exchange information with each other; and how well they solve problems. The second heading is *process* and relates to the social and emotional relations between group members. The dimensions judged here are the levels of dependence, interdependence, conflict and cohesion present in the team. A typical group assessment questionnaire will contain between 30 and 50 statements to which each team member is asked to agree or disagree on a scale of perhaps 1 to 6. The statements are used to measure each of the aforementioned dimensions grouped under the two headings. Examples of typical questionnaire statements are:

1 Our formal or informal leader directs much of what the group does.
2 It is unclear how the group is seeking to achieve its goals.
3 Hardly any group members are seeking to pursue their personal interests.
4 The group is learning how to overcome obstacles to achieving its goal.
5 Group members resist being led.
6 Group members get on well with each other.

The scores obtained from all the team members are collated, and the stage of the group's development is established according to Tuckman and Jensen's or a similar model.

A group can be considered as a society in miniature. A college department or company sales team will have a hierarchy, with leaders and followers. It will have rules, norms and traditions as well as goals to strive for and values to uphold. It will change and develop, and will also adapt to and create changes in the environment and its members. Like a society it may experience a period of difficulty and decline. It is in such mini-societies as the family and the workgroup that an individual learns about and is socialized into the wider society. It has been argued that small groups will reflect the social changes in the wider society. It is likely that the individual will most directly experience these through the small group. For example, as there are changes about the value and organization of work, these may be reflected in changes in job design and workgroup organization.

issues facing any work group

issue	questions
1 atmosphere and relationships	What kinds of relationships should there be among members? How close and friendly, formal or informal?
2 member participation	How much participation should be required of members? Some more than others? All equally? Are some members more needed than others?
3 goal understanding and acceptance	How much do members need to *understand* group goals? How much do they need to *accept* to be *committed* to the goals? Everyone equally? Some more than others?
4 listening and information sharing	How is information to be shared? Who needs to know what? Who should listen most to whom?
5 handling disagreements and conflict	How should disagreements or conflicts be handled? To what extent should they be resolved? Brushed aside? Handled by dictate?
6 decision-making	How should decisions be made? Consensus? Voting? One-person rule? Secret ballot?
7 evaluation of member performance	How is evaluation to be managed? Everyone appraises everyone else? A few take the responsibility? Is it to be avoided?
8 expressing feelings	How should feelings be expressed? Only about the task? Openly and directly?
9 division of labour	How are task assignments to be made? Voluntarily? By discussion? By leaders?
10 leadership	Who should lead? How should leadership *functions* be exercised? Shared? Elected? Appointed from outside?
11 attention to process	How should the group monitor and improve its own process? Ongoing feedback from members? Formal procedures? Avoiding direct discussion?

from Allan R. Cohen, Stephen L. Fink, Herman Gadon and Robin D. Willits, 1995, *Effective Behavior in Organizations*, Irwin, Burr Ridge, IL, 6th edition, p. 142.

Groups influence the behaviour, beliefs and attitudes of their members. Whilst we may all like to believe that we are free agents and would resent being told that we are influenced by others or conform to others' views, research shows that this is in fact the case. In varying degrees and under certain circumstances, we are all influenced by others when we are in a group. If it is any consolation, we can remember that we in turn play an important role ourselves in influencing and controlling other group members. This is the topic of a later chapter in this part of the book.

assessment

The Hawthorne studies are both a landmark in social science research and the source of a great deal of controversy. They are a landmark because of their influence in developing a social science perspective in management theory. One part of the controversy surrounds the adequacy of the research design and methods used in the study and the validity of the research findings. The second controversial legacy of the Hawthorne studies, and one that is currently most topical, is their contribution to the debate as to whether it is better to design organizations around individuals or around groups. As mentioned earlier, Rensis Likert (1961, p. 38) was very pro-group and argued that 'Group forces are important not only in influencing the behaviour of individual work groups with regard to productivity, waste, absence and the like, they also affect the behaviour of entire organizations.'

Likert proposed that the structure of an organization should be formed around effective work groups rather than around individuals. Likert is remembered for proposing the concept of the overlapping group membership structure. This involved a linking pin process in which the superior member of one group was a subordinate member of the group above as shown in the figure below. Likert argued that the benefits of such an organizational design include improved communications, increased co-operation, more team commitment and faster decision-making.

Rensis Likert's linking pin model

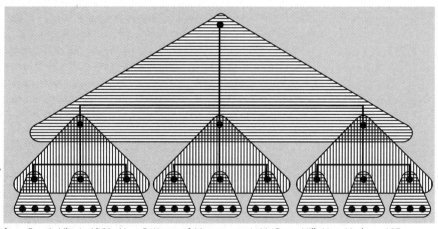

from Rensis Likert, 1961, *New Patterns of Management*, McGraw-Hill, New York, p. 105. Reproduced with permission of the McGraw-Hill Companies.

The idea of building an organization around groups rather than around individuals has received regular recommendations from various management writers every decade or so. Following Likert's writings in the 1960s, there was the work of Leavitt in the 1970s. Leavitt (1975) asked what 'might happen if we really took small groups seriously; if, that is, we really used groups rather than individuals, as the basic building blocks for an organization?' (p. 67). He went on to elaborate his argument, repeating in his conclusion that, 'Management should consider building organizations using a material now understood very well and with properties that look very promising, the small group' (p. 77). In the 1980s, Tom Peters (1987) said

the Japanese work group

Concepts of self and attitudes towards interdependence play a vital role in the Japanese work group. The work group is the basic building block of Japanese organizations. Owing to the central importance of group efforts in their thinking, the Japanese are extremely sensitive to and concerned about group interactions and relationships. They regard group phenomena primarily in terms of morals and emotion rather than role and function. Their view of groups is most closely analogous to that towards marital relationships in the West – and, interestingly, the Japanese recognize the kinds of problems and concerns in work relations that we focus on in marriage concerning trust, sharing and commitment. Like a Western marriage, the Japanese work group imposes task roles which are not always clearly delineated, tend to need revision, and require a constant investment of emotional capital.

The prime qualification of a Japanese leader is his acceptance by the group, and only part of that acceptance is founded on his professional merits. The group's harmony and spirit are the main concern. Whereas in the West work group leaders tend to emphasize task and often neglect group maintenance activities, in Japan maintenance of a satisfied work group goes hand in hand with the role. Group members expect a lot from their leaders, for grave problems can arrive if group maintenance is neglected (which is true of American groups, too, of course). The Japanese realize that they are creating a potentially troublesome force when they establish a group. They know how easily group process can become dysfunctional. They are keenly aware of group maintenance demands. As a result, they manage groups with great care – care of a kind an American manager might invest in meeting his end-of-year profit goals. While a great many American firms have adopted 'team approaches' in recent years, success has been mixed. The reason, we believe, is that American managers don't quite realize that what they are creating requires a lot of energy and attention from them to sustain.

To the Japanese, the birth of a group entails many of the concerns and worries attending the birth of a child. Groups require stroking and nurture and attention. Group participation increases the burdens of the manager as well as the participants by requiring that extra time be put in at meetings, at thinking about issues, at making arguments skilfully, at attending to rituals, ceremonies and relationships. Unless this investment is rewarded by improved options and increased power over outcomes, the result will be disillusionment and demoralization. The leader must balance carefully his use of arbitrary authority one moment with a readiness to be highly responsive in the next. Finally, the Japanese know that groups, as they increase in size beyond eight to ten people, have increasing difficulty in preserving personal and emotional connectedness. It is small wonder, in light of these considerations, that the Japanese invest as much as they do in groups, and that many Americans who dabble carelessly with groups do so with very mixed results indeed.

from Richard Tanner Pascale and Anthony G. Athos, 1982, *The Art of Japanese Management*, Penguin Books, Harmondsworth, pp. 125–7. Reproduced by permission of Penguin Books Ltd.

*Rensis Likert
(1903–81)*

that, 'The modest-sized, task-oriented, semi-autonomous, mainly self-managing team should be the basic organization building block' (p. 296).

These recommendations will no doubt be repeated in the 1990s. So far, however, the advice of Likert, Leavitt, Peters and others has only been paid lip-service in Western industrial companies. Such organizations tend to espouse a form of individualism and personal responsibility which are incompatible with a group ethos. Such individualism has become translated into concepts such as individual piece-rate bonuses and individual staff appraisal. The team bonus or group appraisal is rare if not unknown in European organizations. It is the Japanese who have applied the principles of group-based organization most extensively.

STOP!

To what extent do you feel that Western organizations, including schools, are pro-individual and anti-group in their approach to organizational design and management? Cite evidence to support your view.

Are there any cultural differences which might explain the pro-group or anti-group orientation of certain cultures and countries?

---

sources

de Board, R., 1978, *The Psychoanalysis of Organisations*, Tavistock, London.

Buchanan, D.A., 1979, *The Development of Job Design Theories and Techniques*, Saxon House, Farnborough.

Cohen, A.R., Fink, S.L., Gadon, H. and Willits, R.D., 1988, *Effective Behavior in Organizations*, Irwin, Homewood, IL, 4th edition.

Dalton, M., 1959, *Men Who Manage*, John Wiley, New York.

Drucker, P.F., 1989, *The New Realities*, Heinemann, London.

Gillespie, R., 1991, *Manufacturing Knowledge: A History of the Hawthorne Experiments*, Cambridge University Press, Cambridge.

Gray, J.L. and Starke, A., 1984, *Organizational Behavior: Concepts and Applications*, Charles E. Merrill, Columbus, OH, 3rd edition.

Homans, G.C., 1951, *The Human Group*, Routledge & Kegan Paul, London.

Jones, J.E., 1973, 'Model of group development', *The 1973 Annual Handbook for Group Facilitators*, University Associates, La Jolla, CA, pp. 127–9.

Katzenbach, J.R. and Smith, D.K., 1993, *The Wisdom of Teams: Creating the High Performance Organization*, Harvard Business School Press, Boston, MA.

Leavitt, H.J., 1975, 'Suppose we took groups seriously . . .', in E.L. Cass and F.G. Zimmer (eds.), *Man and Work in Society*, Van Nostrand Reinhold, London.

Likert, R., 1961, *New Patterns of Management*, McGraw-Hill, New York.

Likert, R., 1967, *The Human Organization*, McGraw-Hill, New York.

McGrath, J.E., 1964, *Social Psychology*, Holt, Rinehart and Winston, New York.

Miller, E.J. and Rice, A.K., 1967, *Systems of Organization*, Tavistock, London.

Organ, D.W., 1986, Review: *Management and the Worker*, by F.J. Roethlisberger and W.J. Dickson, Wiley, Science Editions, New York, 1964, in *Academy of Management Review*, vol. 11, no. 2, pp. 459–64.

Pascale, R.T. and Athos, A.G., 1982, *The Art of Japanese Management*, Penguin Books, Harmondsworth.

Peters, T., 1987, *Thriving on Chaos*, Heinemann, London.

Roethlisberger, F.J. and Dickson, W.J., 1964, *Management and the Worker*, Harvard University Press, Cambridge, MA.

Sherif, M. and Sherif, C.W., 1953, *Groups in Harmony and Tension*, Harper and Brothers, New York.

Sonnenfeld, J.A., 1985, 'Shedding light on the Hawthorne studies', *Journal of Occupational Behaviour*, vol. 6, pp. 111–30.

Tajfel, H. and Fraser, C., 1990, *Introducing Social Psychology*, Penguin Books, Harmondsworth.

Tuckman, B., 1965, 'Development sequences in small groups', *Psychological Bulletin*, vol. 63, pp. 384–99.

Tuckman, B. and Jensen, N., 1977, 'Stages of small group development revisited', *Group and Organizational Studies*, vol. 2, pp. 419–27.

Urwick, L. and Brech, E.F.L., 1965, *The Making of Scientific Management, vol. III; The Hawthorne Investigations*, Sir Isaac Pitman, London.

Vernon, H.M., Wyatt, S. and Ogden, A.D., 1924, *On the Extent and Effects of Variety in Repetitive Work*, Medical Research Council Industrial Fatigue Research Board, Report no. 26, HMSO, London.

Whitehead, T.N., 1938, *The Industrial Worker*, Harvard University Press, Cambridge, MA.

Whyte, W.H., 1955, *The Organization Man*, Penguin Books, Harmondsworth.

Wren, D.S., 1979, *The Evolution of Management Thought*, John Wiley, New York.

Wyatt, S., Fraser J.A. and Stock, F.G.L., 1928, *The Comparative Effects of Variety and Uniformity in Work*, Medical Research Council Industrial Fatigue Research Board, Report no. 52, HMSO, London.

chapter 8 group structure and process

concepts and learning objectives

Within organizations, a great deal of work is done by individuals working with others in groups and teams. Because it is so important, both social scientists and management consultants have sought to analyze how groups work in order to pinpoint any problems and suggest solutions that can lead to improved team effectiveness. The two key concepts that they have employed are group structure and group process. This chapter, therefore, considers both in depth. It begins by defining group structure and illustrating the different forms that it takes. It then introduces the concept of group process, and shows how it affects and is affected by group structure.

key concepts

- group structure
- formal status
- social status
- social power
- sociometry

- social role
- group process
- team role
- leadership in a group

learning objectives

When you have read this chapter, you should be able to define those key concepts in your own words, and you should also be able to:

1 Understand the concept of group structure.
2 Understand group interaction represented symbolically.
3 Distinguish between two common uses of the concept of status.
4 Distinguish between group process and group structure and explain the relation between them.
5 Give examples of task roles and maintenance roles in a group.

group structure

A central idea in helping us to examine the nature and functioning of groups is that of group structure. Structure refers to the way in which members of a group relate to one another. The formation of group structure is one of the basic aspects of group development. When people come together and interact, differences between individuals begin to appear. Some talk, whilst others listen. These differences between group members serve as the basis for the establishment of group structure. As differentiation occurs, relations are established between members. Group structure is the label given to this patterning of relationships.

---

definition

Group structure *is the relatively stable pattern of relationships among the differentiated elements in a group.*

Group structure carries with it the connotation of something fixed and unchanging. Perhaps the picture of scaffolding is brought to mind. Whilst there is an element of permanency in terms of the relationships between members, these do continue to change and modify. Group members continually interact with each other, and in consequence their relationships are tested and transformed. As we describe the structure of any group, it is perhaps useful to view it as a snapshot photograph, correct at the time the shutter was pressed, but acknowledging that things were different the moment before and after the photo was taken. Differences between the members of a group begin to occur as soon as it is formed. This differentiation within a group occurs along not one, but several dimensions. The most important of these are:

status status structure of a group
power power structure a group
liking liking structure of a group
role role structure of a group
leadership leadership structure of a group
communication communication flow between group members

There are as many structures in a group as there are dimensions along which a group can be differentiated. Although in common usage we talk about the 'structure of a group', in reality, a group will differentiate simultaneously along a number of dimensions. Group members will be accorded different amounts of status and hence a group will have a status hierarchy. They will be able to exert differing amounts of power and thus a power structure will emerge. In examining group functioning, social scientists have found it useful to consider differences among group members in terms of their liking for each other, status, power, role and leadership. Whilst it is possible to examine each structural dimension of the group in turn, we need to remember that all are closely related and operate simultaneously in a group setting. Cartwright and Zander (1968) suggest that a group's structure is determined by:

1 the requirements for efficient group performance
2 the abilities and motivations of group members
3 the psychological and social environment of the group

Why does a group have a structure?

Why does a patterning of relationships between individuals in a group occur and what purpose does it serve? Robert Bales (1950a: 15–16) argued that,

> The actions of other individuals are always relevant to the problem of tension reduction of any given individual . . . It is to the advantage of every individual in a group to stabilize the potential activity of others towards him, favourably if possible, but in any case in such a way that he can predict it . . . All of them, even those who may wish to exploit the others, have interest in bringing about stability. The basic assumption here is that what we call the 'social structure' of groups can be understood primarily as a system of solutions to the fundamental problems of interaction which becomes institutionalized in order to reduce the tensions growing out of uncertainty and unpredictability in the actions of others.

the Nortons: the internal structure of the group

During the 1930s, William F. Whyte studied a slum area of Boston which housed a large number of immigrant and American-born Italians. He wanted to study informally organized groups. Whyte used participant observation for his research method, an approach which had been developed in anthropology. He moved into the neighbourhood and became acquainted with a group of young men, most of whom were out of work and were looked down on even in their lowly neighbourhood as 'little guys'. The Nortons displayed characteristics similar to those found in earlier studies of groups. They engaged in patterned activities, and shared a body of norms and values which regulated their behaviour. Moreover, despite the casual nature of their interactions while 'hanging around', Whyte discovered that their relationships were organized and tied together in a structure of interrelated roles, even though the men themselves were not always aware of the fact.

Whyte observed who associated with whom, how often and with what effect. He noticed who made suggestions and to whom the communication flowed. He found that the Nortons were a differentiated group in which individuals of different capacities and statuses were bound together in a common unity. Members formed a well-understood and fairly status-stable hierarchy, from the peripheral members on the bottom to 'Doc' at the top, who was chosen for his toughness. This hierarchy he depicted on the chart shown opposite. On the basis of this, he produced a chart showing the hierarchical structure of statuses among the Nortons. The group members are arranged in terms of their power in the group, and the lines between them show the channels through which influence flowed from the leader (Doc) downwards (see figure).

The activities in which the group engaged reflected this group structure. Not only did the group usually do the things the leader suggested, but each member's behaviour tended to be a function of his position in the group. Whyte describes how the members' bowling scores reflected not only their innate skill but also their social standing. When one skilled but low-ranking member challenged a high-ranking member to a bowling match, other members exerted enough group pressure (through razzing and other more subtle means) to make the challenger come out a low scorer for the evening. More broadly, Whyte was interested in

> **STOP!**
>
> Explain the saying: 'Better the devil you know than the devil you don't.'

It is this basic need for predictability which causes structure to develop within a group. Members are differentiated along several dimensions (e.g. status, role, power). One person will therefore simultaneously have high status and power since each person stands at the intersection of several dimensions. All the differentiated parts associated with an individual group member are referred to as his position in the group structure.

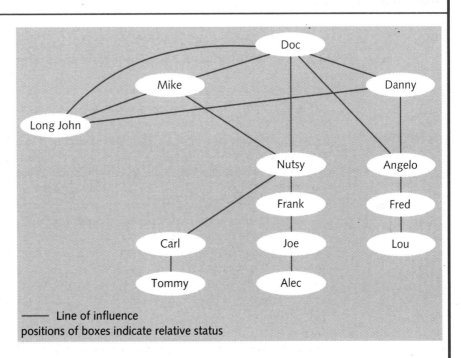

—— Line of influence
positions of boxes indicate relative status

how the group arrived at its decisions, that is, in the patterns of influence which characterized the group. Beneath the casual and seemingly random surface activity, Whyte detected a fairly consistent pattern of communication: remarks travelled 'up' the hierarchy during the planning of activities and, when a decision had been reached at the top, flowed 'down' to the lower ranks. It was not just a case of leaders telling followers what to do, but of a far more complex give-and-take in which each 'rank' tended to interact with the rank adjacent to it. The result was a pattern which, though informal, resembled the chain-of-command communication flow in a bureaucracy.

based on William F. Whyte, 1937, *Street Corner Society*, University of Chicago Press, Chicago.

---

position and status on Animal Farm

George Orwell's *Animal Farm* is a short, allegorical novel whose characters and events correspond to the Russian revolution and its aftermath. In the story, the pigs, particularly Napoleon and Snowball, secure the highest status for themselves. This is reflected in the modification of one of the farm's seven commandments from 'All animals are equal' to 'Some animals are more equal than others'. The farm's status structure is summarized below:

Napoleon/Snowball	HIGH STATUS
other pigs	MEDIUM STATUS
all other animals	LOW STATUS

Orwell's novel not only provides us with a vivid description of the interrelatedness of the power, status, liking, role and leadership structures that exist within a group, but also shows how these change over time. In the diagram the group structure is depicted as a static snapshot, but should more accurately be considered as a moving film.

based on George Orwell, 1946, *Animal Farm*, Harcourt, Brace, New York.

There is some confusion between the key concepts of group structure and of position within the group. Position is used to refer to an individual's locus in a communication network. In order to characterize adequately any group member's relations to others in the group over a period of time and in different social settings, it is necessary to locate them along a number of dimensions, that is, in a number of different positions. Consider a typical group of work colleagues or fellow students. Usually, the number will be about seven. After seven, inter-member communication becomes a problem. Each member of the group will occupy some position in it. It is the pattern of the relationships between the positions which constitutes the structure of the group. It is the lines which join the positions together.

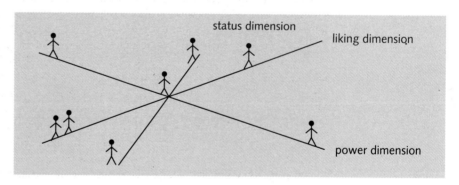

status structure

Status is a prestige ranking within a group. Studies of humankind's groupings have revealed the existence of Chiefs and Indians, lords and peasants, haves and have-nots. Even the smallest grouping will develop roles, rights and rituals to differentiate its members from one another. Status is important because it motivates people and has consequences for their behaviour. This is particularly the case when individuals perceive a disparity between their own perception of themselves and how others perceive them to be.

Each position in a group has a value placed upon it. Within the organization, a value is ascribed to a position by the formal organization (e.g. Chief Controller, Vice-President, Supervisor) and can be labelled formal status. Formal status is best thought of as being synonymous with rank, as in the police or the armed forces, and reflects a person's position on the organizational ladder.

definition

Formal status *refers to a collection of rights and obligations associated with a position, as distinct from the person who may occupy that position.*

A second way in which value is placed on a position is the social honour or prestige that is accorded an individual in a group by the other group members. In this second sense, the word status is prefixed by the word social and is a measure of informally established value and its comparison with other positions as perceived by the informal group or organization. Whilst one can view social status as a sort of badge of honour awarded for meritorious group conduct, it can also be viewed as a set of unwritten rules about the kind of conduct that people are expected to show one another. It can indicate the degree of respect, familiarity or reserve that is appropriate in a given situation.

definition

Social status *is the relative ranking that a person holds and the value of that person as measured by a group.*

One of the powers possessed by an informal group is its ability to confer status on those of its members who meet the expectations of the group. These members are looked up to by their peers, not because of any formal position they may hold in the organization, but because of their position in the social group. Since many people actively seek status in order to fulfil their need for self-esteem, the granting of it by the group provides them with personal satisfaction. Similarly, the withholding of status can act as a group control mechanism to bring a deviant group member into line. The status accorded by the group to a member is immediate in terms of face-to-face feedback. The recognition and esteem given to group members reinforces the individual's identification with the group and his dependence upon it.

An individual's formal status is based on hierarchical position and task ability. The organization is made up of a number of defined positions arranged in order of their increasing authority. The formal status hierarchy reflects the potential ability of the holder of the position to contribute to the overall goals of the organization. It differentiates the amount of respect deserved and it ranks individuals on a status scale. The outward symbols associated with formal status (e.g. size of office, quality of carpet) are there to inform other members in the organization of where exactly that person stands on the ladder. This topic leads ultimately to a consideration of organization structure, which is the subject of a later chapter.

Interaction with others perceived as lower in status can be threatening because of the potential identification of the person with the group or individual being associated with. Status is abstract and ascribed through the perceptions of others. One's status is therefore always tenuous. It may be withdrawn or downgraded at any time. The reference group with which one identifies and whose values and behaviour one adopts, plays an important part in establishing and maintaining one's status. To preserve that status, one cannot leave the reference group for a lower status reference group.

STOP!

Individually, think about the college/university at which you are studying OR the organization in which you work. Make a note of:
1 things that raise your status in it
2 things that lower your status in it
3 things that do not matter one way or the other
Compare and discuss this list with a colleague. Why should these things affect your status?

---

power structure

A second dimension on which differentiation occurs in a group is power – the control over persons. Individuals within the group are able to control the behaviour of others and may have to if the group is to achieve its goals. For this reason, it becomes necessary for the group to have established control relations between members. By having a power structure, the group avoids continued power struggles which can disrupt its functioning. It can also can link goal achievement activities to a system of authority which is seen as legitimate.

---

definition

Social power *is the potential influence that one person exerts over another. Influence is defined as a change in the cognition, behaviour or emotion of that second person which can be attributed to the first.*

John French and Bertram Raven (1958) defined power in terms of influence. Power is a feature in group relations, leadership relations and political issues. We shall therefore revisit the work of these authors several times in the book. French and Raven distinguished several different bases of power. A power base is the relationship between two people which is the source of that power. In a group the relationship between individuals will involve not one, but several, power bases. These are shown opposite. French and Raven conclude that the broader the basis of power the individual has, the greater the power which he will exert. Referent power had the broadest range of coverage.

Hells Angels' rank-and-file group structure

The Hells Angels were first organized in San Bernadeno, California in 1948 by World War II veterans. They received national attention in the movies when Marlon Brando played an angst-ridden gang leader in the 1953 film, *The Wild One*. At the same time as cultivating their rebel image, they became more businesslike. They have 1000 members world-wide organized into 70 local clubs called 'chapters'. There is a tight management structure, a communications system and paramilitary discipline. Each chapter has its own strict hierarchical status structure.

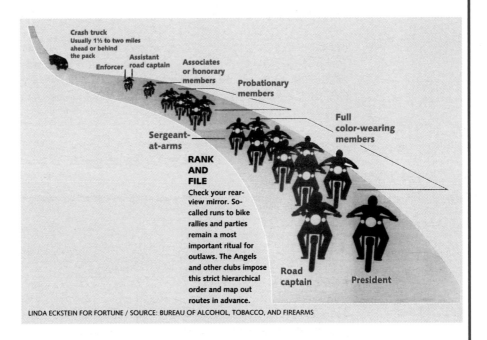

Crash truck
Usually 1½ to two miles ahead or behind the pack

Enforcer

Assistant road captain

Associates or honorary members

Probationary members

Sergeant-at-arms

Full color-wearing members

RANK AND FILE
Check your rear-view mirror. So-called runs to bike rallies and parties remain a most important ritual for outlaws. The Angels and other clubs impose this strict hierarchical order and map out routes in advance.

Road captain

President

LINDA ECKSTEIN FOR FORTUNE / SOURCE: BUREAU OF ALCOHOL, TOBACCO, AND FIREARMS

based on Andrew E. Sewer, 1992, 'The Hellish Angels' devilish business', *Fortune*, 30 November, pp. 84–90. © 1992 Time Inc. All rights reserved.

reward power where one person perceives that another is able to offer him a reward, for example, mother and child.

coercive power where one person perceives that another can punish him, for example, traditional father and child concept.

referent power where one person identifies with the other, that is, he feels at one with him, or desires to identify with him, for example, a pop fan adopting the dress style of his idol.

legitimate power where one person perceives that another has a legitimate right to order him to do something, for example, person accepting a judge's ruling despite his own views.

expert power where one person perceives the second to have some expert knowledge, for example, certain types of teacher–pupil relationships.

liking structure

The liking or affective structure in the group refers to the way in which members differentiate themselves in terms of whom they do and do not like. To identify the affective structure of a group, one uses a technique called sociometry. A sociometric test reveals the feelings which individuals have towards each other as members of a group.

Sociometry was invented by Jacob Moreno and his colleague when they worked in the New York Training School for Girls in the 1930s. His original application was the systematic sociometric mapping of friendship choices among children in classrooms and girls in reformatory cottages. Moreno asked individuals to complete the test shown below.

definition

Sociometry *is the technique of displaying patterns of human relationships that exist within groups. These relationships depend upon personal choice (i.e. selection and rejection) and can be represented diagrammatically using relatively few conventional symbols.*

SOCIOMETRIC TEST

On this sheet there are 8 boxes. In the box marked, Work With–Yes, put the names of 2 girls in the class you prefer to work with. In the box marked, Work With–No, put the names of the 2 girls you prefer not to work with. Proceed to do the other boxes in exactly the same fashion.

The information given in this sheet will be considered private and confidential.

WORK WITH	
YES	NO

STUDY WITH	
YES	NO

PLAY WITH	
YES	NO

LIVE WITH	
YES	NO

Members are asked, 'With whom would you like to work?' or 'With whom would you like to study?' Each person is asked to make two preference choices with respect to a specific situation. After analyzing the answers, Moreno calculated how many times an individual had been chosen as a comrade by the other members of the group for the activity in question. This feeling, the sociometric term for which is *tele*, may be one of attraction (positive *tele*) or repulsion (negative *tele*); alternatively there may merely be indifference.

Group members' choices are depicted on a sociogram. This visually reveals those individuals who receive a large number of votes. These people are designated *stars*. Some people vote for one another and are known as *mutual pairs* or *trios*. Finally, some receive only a few or no votes at all. They are called *isolates*. The sociogram quickly reveals the existence of any sub-groupings within the main team or group.

---

sociograms showing two groups' liking structures

The sociograms shown below are taken from Sherif's research study of boys at a summer camp which was summarized in the previous chapter. Individuals are represented by letters inside of circles, and their choices by lines drawn between the circles indicating the direction of the choice. Solid lines indicate reciprocated choices, while dotted lines show one-way choices.

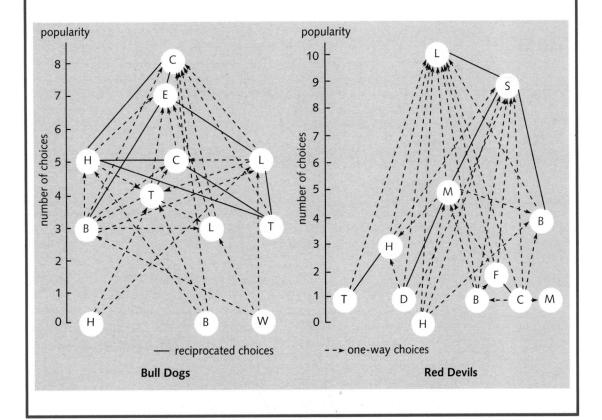

STOP!

Examine the two sociograms in the figure on page 217. Can you identify any:
1 stars
2 mutual pairs
3 mutual trios?
4 isolates?

How can sociograms be used? Not all group relations can be detected by observation alone. The use of sociograms in schools can reveal the existence of unhappy isolates who have not adjusted to the class group. In a factory, it can assist a supervisor to help an isolate worker adjust to the work team. More generally, sociograms of productive and unproductive teams can highlight situations where group structure may require modification. They have also been used in the selection and training of group leaders; to increase co-operation, productivity and morale amongst women workers in a steam laundry; and in the selection of flying partners in the airforce (Zeleny, 1947).

STOP!

Identify a small group and ask its members to respond to one of the two questions below. Use the answers you obtain to draw a sociogram.

With whom do you want to do a joint class project? With whom would you want to spend your leisure time? Give three preferences in each case.

A comprehensive sociogram represents a pattern of choice (selection, rejection, repulsion, indifference) at a given point in time and in relation to a specific aspect of the group's functioning (specified in the question asked). The pattern, and hence the liking structure of the group, will change over time. Thus several sociograms would be needed to display changes over a period of time.

role structure

The occupant of every position in the group is expected to carry out certain functions when the members of the group interact with one another. The expected behaviours associated with a position within the group constitute the social role of the occupant of that position. This is the concept which relates the individual to the prescriptive dictates of the group. People's behaviour within the organization is structured and patterned in various ways, and an understanding of role helps us to see and explain how this happens.

definition

Social role *is the set of behaviours that are expected of the occupant of a position by other members of the group.*

Social scientists differ in the way in which they use the term role. The definition above emphasizes the expectations of other people. The term has also been used to refer to the behaviours which the occupant of the position himself believes are appropriate for him to enact (called perceived role) and also to the behaviours in which the person actually engages in (called enacted role). It is sufficient to note the existence of these different uses of the concept and remind readers that it will be examined in another context when organizational structure is discussed. For the present, it is enough to know that the role be thought of rather like a script which actors have. The same actor changes his roles and can act out different parts in front of different audiences. Our concern here is with the different roles that exist within the group.

Robert Freed Bales

When we observe a group in action what we see are people behaving in certain ways and doing certain things. If we want to study how they behave in a group, it is necessary to have a precise and reliable way of describing what is happening within it. Social psychologists have developed precise techniques with which to describe and analyze the interactions of group members. In the late 1940s, Robert Bales and his colleagues at the Harvard University's Laboratory of Social Relations were amongst the first social scientists systematically to observe and describe the behaviour of individuals in groups in a systematic way (Bales, 1950a, 1950b). He focused on the who-to-whom-and-what interactions, and developed a comprehensive system of categorizing behaviour called Interaction Process Analysis (IPA).

Bales specified twelve categories which he used to classify or 'code' behaviours. For example (category 1) 'shows solidarity, raises other's status, gives help, reward' and (category 12) 'shows antagonism, deflates other's status, defends or asserts self'. Bales felt that with his twelve categories one could classify all the behaviours that were likely to occur in a group. In his original experiments, these categories were used by his observers who watched a group through a one-way mirror.

Bales used his behaviour classification system to gather data with which to propose a theory of group functioning. He argued that group behaviour could be explained by showing how groups dealt with certain problems such as orientation, evaluation, control, and so on. His scheme focuses on how people choose to express themselves in a problem-solving situation. It neglects the content of what is said, its quality or any accompanying non-verbal communication. It also claims that every act plays some part in the problem-solving process. While in reality a single comment can have several purposes, in IPA it is recorded in a single category and it is assumed that the observer can accurately judge what the group member intended by it.

These criticisms notwithstanding, Bales' observational technique is the most refined and exhaustive (empirically usable) method yet developed which can be used to study small group processes. It has been extensively tested, and an acceptably high agreement between observer-raters has been obtained. It has also provided the basis for other behaviour categorization schemes.

Bales' interaction studies

Robert Bales used an interaction recorder to obtain a record of categorized observations occurring in a time sequence. His original experiments and equipment are shown below.

experimental discussion situation observed through a one-way mirror

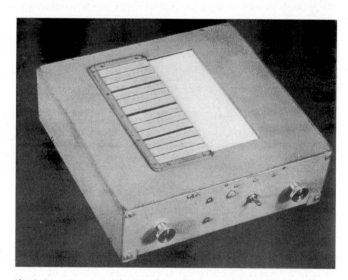

the interaction recorder used by observers. Observations were recorded using Bales' 12 categories on the moving paper. Time intervals were marked automatically.
Source of photographs: Robert F. Bales.

Bales' research, conducted in the 1950s, provided the first rounded picture of what happens in face-to-face groups. When facing an actual task that required a concerted attack, such groups encountered problems of communication and organization, which evoked a variety of individual member behaviours. These behaviours could be classified into four general categories. Over a period of time, with these behaviours occurring, the group could move from a phase of orientation, to a phase of evaluation, and on to a phase of control. Finally, within each group, members took on specific roles. Bales' original work has been developed by other writers and continues to provide the foundation for small group study and team development through to the present day. It is instructive to contrast so-called modern theory, research and training on groups and teams with Bales' original work in order to assess just how far we have progressed in this field.

problems faced by all groups

Bales concluded that all face-to-face groups, be they a child's play group, a project team or a management committee, faced similar problems which had to be dealt with effectively if the group was to achieve its task. These problems could be classed under these two headings – intra-group communication and group organization and maintenance.

intra-group communication

Individuals in the group must communicate with each other if there is to be a joint decision or joint action, but face three problems. The first communication problem is *orientation*. Each member of the group begins with a feeling of uncertainty and confusion as to what the situation is all about, but nevertheless has relevant facts to offer and relevant observations to make. Through communication, the group members have to establish a workable, common way of viewing a situation.

The second communication problem is *evaluation*. This relates to the difficulty of individuals reaching a common judgement about the value of whatever the group may be contemplating doing. Questions such as how important the problem is, and what its consequences are likely to be, have to be dealt with through communication.

The third communication problem concerns *control*. If the group is to exert action as a single collectivity, the behaviour of its individual members has to be controlled. Some members will have to suppress their individual preferences and may experience frustration. Through communication, some members will influence others in order to establish a common agreement.

group organization and maintenance

The second class of difficulties faced by every group whose members are in face-to-face interaction is that of establishing some kind of structure and avoiding disintegration. In every group there will be some shuffling around until the problems of leadership are resolved, and until some decision is made as to what roles group members will play. Each group also establishes its own prestige or ranking system. Until these problems are resolved, they create tensions within the group, and have to be managed, if the group is not to fall apart. As will be shown shortly, these two problems, first identified by Bales, of group communication and group organization and maintenance, later came to be considered in terms of task and socio-emotive needs of a group, and the appropriate type of leadership for each.

phases of group development

Building on his theory of communication problems in a group, Bales argued that all groups could potentially pass through three predictable phases. First, they had to deal with the problem of orientation, deciding 'what's it all about?'; then to the evaluation phase, where the focus was on 'how do we feel about it?'; before ending up at the control phase, when the problem of 'what do we do about it?' was addressed. A group could become stuck in a phase and be unable to move to the next. In each phase, the problems of organization and maintenance reappeared as disagreements and anxieties created uncertainties and antagonisms, and generated negative and perhaps aggressive reactions. In the previous chapter, Tuckman and Jensen's (1977) model of group development was introduced and elaborated. It can now be seen that it had its source in the pioneering work of Robert Bales.

types of group member behaviour

Bales' third finding was that in the many face-to-face groups that he observed, individual members' behaviour could be classified into four general categories, and that the behaviour in each of the categories tended to occur with about the same frequency in a wide variety of different groups. For example, in all groups, some individuals performed *socio-emotional–positive acts*. These included giving help to others, praising, joking to release tension or agreeing with someone. In group after group, 25 per cent of all individual behaviours fell into this category. *Task-relevant acts* were those that moved the group forward towards solving its problem, for example, giving suggestions, asking for information. These accounted for 56 per cent of all behaviours. *Task-relevant acts – asking questions*, which included requests for orientation, and requests for opinions and suggestions, accounted for 7 per cent of acts. While *socio-emotional–negative acts*, such as statements of disagreement, of tension and aggression, and withdrawal, accounted for 11 per cent of the total.

role differentiation

Bales' fourth major finding was that role differentiation was a universal feature of face-to-face interaction. As the group contends with its problems, individual members begin to 'specialize' in certain types of behaviours. For example, Eric, a member of the group, may begin to concern himself primarily with the social and individual problems of the group, and his behaviour consists mainly of socio-emotional positive acts. He may have few ideas about how to get the task done, but is very knowledgeable about how to hold the group together, reduce anxiety and make everyone feel a worthwhile contributor. Diana, another group member, may constantly push to get the task accomplished. She asks for suggestions and gives her opinion, perhaps stepping on a few colleagues' toes. Soon these two individuals find that this is the way that they are 'supposed' to act. Other group members expect these behaviours of them. Each of them now has a role in the group. This pattern of behaviour becomes more or less defined, not only in Eric and Diana's own minds, but also in the expectations of the other group members. This double pressure constrains both of them from suddenly switching into different roles. In this way, role differentiation – the social division of labour within a group – comes about.

Finally, Bales found that as roles become more differentiated, some of these

Bales' categories and summary of psychological events in small groups

The figure below shows the twelve categories that Bales used to classify the behaviours of group members that he observed. They are grouped into his four general categories.

						rate
socio-emotional – positive acts	shows solidarity					3.4
	shows tension release					6.0
	shows agreement					16.5
task-relevant acts	gives suggestion					8.0
	gives opinion					30.1
	gives information					17.9
task-relevant acts – asking questions	asks for information					3.5
	asks for opinion					2.4
	asks for suggestion					1.1
socio-emotional – negative acts	shows disagreement					7.8
	shows tension					2.7
	shows antagonism					.7

0   10   20   30   40
percentage of total

The data are based on 71,838 observations of 24 groups in 96 different sessions. The behaviour profile shown here can be regarded as typical of many small groups. Of all the behaviours of these group members, 30.1 per cent are of the giving opinions type, while less than 1 per cent show overt antagonism.

adapted from R.F. Bales, 1955, 'How people interact in conferences', *Scientific American*, vol. 192, pp. 31–5. Copyright © 1995 by Scientific American, Inc. All rights reserved.

roles contribute to the progress and welfare of the group, whilst others seemed to add little or nothing to either its happiness or success. The former set of roles come to be more highly regarded than the latter, and are generally referred to as leadership roles. The idea of leadership as a set of behavioural acts was adopted by Edwin Fleishman and Ralph Stogdill at about the same period, and will be examined in a later chapter on leadership.

group structure and group process

When discussing groups, it is useful to distinguish between group structure and group process. Process refers to the group activity which occurs over time. Group process concerns itself with the verbal and non-verbal contributions of group members. Examples of a group's process include who communicates most, least and with whom; the way in which decisions are made; and how problems in the group are addressed and solved. The observation of the process of a group provides information about its structure.

STOP!

Here is a simplified version of Bales' verbal behaviour classification scheme. It consists of six behaviour categories, and each has an explanation alongside. Also provided is a chart for coding group member behaviours. Next time you are at a group discussion, listen to what is said and record the behaviours of each group member, using the chart. Put their names along the top of the chart. Every time they speak, decide what their behaviour is, and place a tick or dot under their names, alongside the appropriate behaviour category. After you have watched and analyzed the discussion, add up your ticks or dots horizontally and vertically. You may wish to share this information with the group members.

verbal behaviour category	explanation
proposing	any behaviour which puts forward a new suggestion, idea or course of action
building	any behaviour which develops or extends an idea or suggestion made by someone else
supporting	any behaviour which declares agreement or support with any individual or idea
disagreeing	any behaviour which states a criticism of another person's statement
giving information	any behaviour which gives facts, ideas or opinions or clarifies these
seeking information	any behaviour which asks for facts, ideas or opinions from others.

verbal behaviour category	names							
proposing								
building								
supporting								
disagreeing								
giving information								
seeking information								
total								

After carrying out this exercise, did you have difficulty in knowing what the group was discussing, that is, the content of its conversation? What does this tell you about the difference between the content of a group's discussion and the process of its discussion?

---

definition

Group process *is the sequence of interaction patterns between the members of the group.*

Group structure and group process are therefore clearly related. The structure of a group can affect its process, and vice versa. The formal structure of a committee defines the persons appointed to sit on it, their roles and status within the group, their heterogeneity, etc. This determines, in part, the interaction that takes place. For example, high-status members may be permitted to speak more and will exert more influence on group decisions than more junior staff. Equally, the processes that occur within an initially unstructured group can lead to the formation of a certain group structure. The individual who speaks most may be referred to as the group leader. The valued contributions of some members may give them enhanced status in the eyes of others.

group member roles

Within a group activity, such as a staff meeting or a tutorial discussion, some persons will show a consistent preference for certain behaviours and not for

'communi-gram' – a diagram showing participation at a meeting

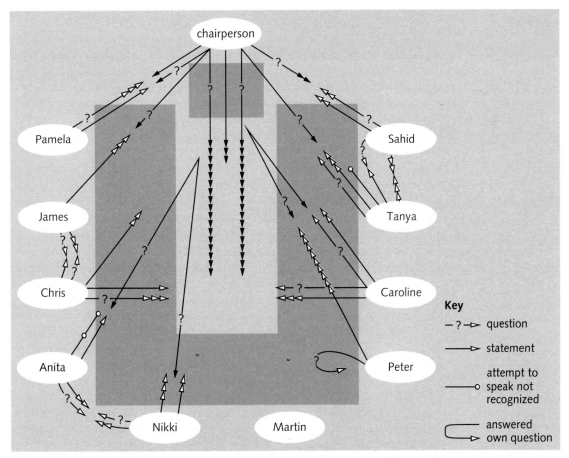

Key

−?−▷ question

——▷ statement

——o attempt to speak not recognized

answered own question

others. The particular behaviour, or set of behaviours, that a person demonstrates in a group can lead them to be seen to be playing a particular role within the group. Bales' work showed that people adopt specific roles in groups. The first major distinction is between leadership and non-leadership roles. The work of Kenneth Benne and Paul Sheats had revealed that there were two types of leader who were responsible for different aspects of the group's functioning and performance. One of them was primarily concerned that the group's task should be completed, while the other's main priority was the social and emotional needs of the group's members. Benne and Sheats's (1948; 1951) list of group member roles were:

Task group roles
- Initiator-contributor
- Information seeker
- Opinion-seeker
- Information-giver
- Opinion-giver
- Elaborator
- Co-ordinator
- Orienter
- Evaluator-critic
- Energizer
- Procedural technician
- Recorder

Building and maintenance group roles
- Encourager
- Harmonizer
- Compromiser
- Gatekeeper and expediter
- Standard-setter or ego ideal
- Group observer and commentator
- Follower

The second distinction within a group was between two classes of roles performed by the group's members. One class of role behaviours was directed towards achieving the group task, while the other was concerned with maintaining the group as a functioning unit by dealing with the social and emotional tensions within it. These distinctions, originally revealed in the 1940s and 1950s research by Benne, Sheats and Bales, have become the foundation for many team-work theories and training. They also laid the foundation for many theories of leadership (see Chapter 20), where leaders are assessed in terms of the 'concern for task "versus" concern for people'.

Belbin and team role theory

Meredith Belbin

Meredith Belbin's (1981; 1996) work linked individuals' personality traits (obtained through psychometric tests) with group role behaviour, and he related both to output performance. His work was rooted in the studies of Bales' attempts to distinguish group member behaviours and to relate these to distinguishable group roles. Belbin studied the performance of specially designed management teams playing a business game at a British management college, as well as that of managers in industry who met frequently to achieve certain agreed objectives.

The research showed that it was possible to identify and distinguish nine distinct management styles which the researchers labelled 'team roles'. A person's team role was separate from their functional role in an organization. People are generally appointed to a job to perform a functional role on the basis of their ability or experience in a particular functional area such as marketing, production, sales or accounting. They are rarely selected for personal characteristics

Belbin's nine team roles

roles and descriptions — team-role contribution	allowable weaknesses
Plant Creative, imaginative, unorthodox. Solves difficult problems.	Ignores details. Too preoccupied to communicate effectively.
Resource investigator Extravert, enthusiastic, communicative. Explores opportunities. Develops contacts.	Overoptimistic. Loses interest once initial enthusiasm has passed.
Co-ordinator Mature, confident, a good chairperson. Clarifies goals, promotes decision-making, delegates well.	Can be seen as manipulative. Delegates personal work.
Shaper Challenging, dynamic, thrives on pressure. Has the drive and courage to over-come obstacles.	Can provoke others. Hurts people's feelings.
Monitor evaluator Sober, strategic and discerning. Sees all options. Judges accurately.	Lacks drive and ability to inspire others. Overly critical.
Teamworker Co-operative, mild, perceptive and diplomatic. Listens, builds, averts friction, calms the waters.	Indecisive in crunch situations. Can be easily influenced.
Implementer Disciplined, reliable, conservative and efficient. Turns ideas into practical actions.	Somewhat inflexible. Slow to respond to new possibilities.
Completer Painstaking, conscientious, anxious. Searches out errors and omissions. Delivers on time.	Inclined to worry unduly. Reluctant to delegate. Can be a nit-picker.
Specialist Single-minded, self-starting, dedicated. Provides knowledge and skills in rare supply.	Contributes on only a narrow front. Dwells on technicalities. Overlooks the 'big picture'.

Strength of contribution in any one of the roles is commonly associated with particular weaknesses. These are called allowable weaknesses. Executives are seldom strong in all nine team roles.

from R. Meredith Belbin, 1996, *The Coming Shape of Organization*, Butterworth Heinemann, London, p. 122.

or aptitudes that fit them to perform additional tasks within the team. In an ideal world, a person's functional role, and their team role that complements that of other team members, would coincide. In practice this rarely happens.

---
definition

Team role *is an individual's tendency to behave, contribute and interrelate ,with other members within a team.*

The research revealed:
1 The managers studied tended to adopt one or two of these team roles fairly consistently.
2 Which role they became associated with was capable of prediction through the use of psychometric tests.
3 When team roles were combined in certain ways, they helped to produce more effective teams.
4 Such team roles were not necessarily associated with a person's functional role (e.g. accountant, production), but the way in which they were combined seemed to affect job success.
5 Factors which seemed to contribute to effective management by individuals included correct recognition of own best role; self-awareness of the best contribution they could make to their team or situation and their ability and preparedness to work out their strengths rather than permitting weaknesses to interfere with their performance.

These roles are related to the personality and mental ability of individuals and reflect managerial behaviour in connection with the aims and demands of the. Since each role contributes to team success, a successfully balanced team will contain all roles. However, it does not mean that all teams need to consist of nine people. A single member can play several roles and thus reduce the overall team size.

---

teamwork: a problem of team role ambiguity

▶ There were four team members named Everybody, Somebody, Anybody and Nobody.
▶ There was an important job to do and Everybody was asked to do it.
▶ Everybody was sure Somebody would do it.
▶ Anybody could have done it, but Nobody did.
▶ Everybody was angry about that, because it was Somebody's job.
▶ Everybody thought Anybody could do it, but Nobody realized that Everybody wouldn't.
▶ In the end, Everybody blamed Somebody when Nobody did what Anybody could have done.

Anon.

---

leadership structure

There are many jobs to be done in a group if it is to be both productive and satisfying for its members. The emergence of a leader in a group is a function of group structure. Usually, a group makes a leader of the person who has some special capacity for coping with the group's particular problem. They may possess physical strength, shrewdness or some other relevant attribute. These functions can be performed by the formal group leader or by the members. The leader and the members all have a role to play in the group. Through them a group atmosphere is created which enables communication, influence, decision-making and similar processes to be performed. It has been found that group performance and satisfaction are affected by the type of leadership exercised within a group. In much of the management literature, leadership is considered exclusively as a management prerogative. Authors write about 'management style' rather than 'leadership style'. This material will be dealt with in chapter 20.

The concept of leadership also suggests a process of goal attainment, follower satisfaction and group support. Actions and activities are performed for and by the leader. There has been an increasing interest in group leadership opposed to the individual leadership research which in the past has sought to identify the characteristics of effective leaders. The group leadership approach aims to study the characteristics of small groups and tries to understand the social context in which they work. It seems, therefore, more useful to view leadership as an activity floating between members rather than a static status associated with a single individual.

Leadership is thus seen as a dynamic and innovative approach to problems commonly perceived by an individual or by a group of people. In helping to understand behaviour in organizations, it can be useful not necessarily to view the manager as the leader, although he could of course be. Not all formally designated supervisors or managers are leaders. By taking the group rather than the individual as the primary focus of study, an attempt is made to identify the way in which the group as a whole attempts to achieve its goals, and link it to the actions which may be required of the group members to achieve this end. From this standpoint, one discusses the roles that group members perform. It is now possible to offer a definition of leadership from a group, rather than from an individual perspective.

definition

Leadership in a group *is the performance of those acts which help the group achieve its preferred outcomes. Cartwright and Zander (1968, p. 304).*

The acts or 'jobs-to-be-done' include defining group goals, promoting good relations between members of the group, and so on. Some acts are task-focused, whilst others are maintenance-focused. These leadership functions can be performed by different group members at different times. The group will differentiate along the leader–follower continuum and will continue to redifferentiate as it progresses, with the leadership structure continually redefining itself.

The relationship between the leader-at-a-point-in-time and the followers may be thought of as one of social exchange. The leader provides rewards for the group by helping its members to achieve their own and the group's goals. They in turn reward the leader by giving her heightened status and increased influence. However, members can rescind that influence at any time if they feel that the leader is no longer worthy of their respect. Viewed as a social exchange process, the leader has power in terms of her ability to influence the behaviour of the group. Nevertheless, it is the group members who give her the power to influence them.

---

collective leadership in groups

Thrasher studied boys' gangs in the Chicago slums during the 1920s. He reported that whilst there was a natural leader in the group, the tasks of leadership often became spread amongst different group members.

> In some cases leadership is actually diffused among a number of strong 'personalities' in the group who share the honours and responsibilities. The gang leader had a number of strong lieutenants which led to the central command being diffused. Another way of viewing it was that supplementary strengths of members were integrated. In addition to this collective leadership, a rotation of leadership relative to the aims or tasks of the group took place.

from Frederick Thrasher, 1927, *The Gang*, University of Chicago Press, Chicago, pp. 345–52.

---

one group, two leaders

When people think of leadership, they usually imagine a single person. Robert Bales and Philip Slater used a laboratory research design with which to study the patterns of leadership that emerged in small, unstructured groups. The subjects of the study were fourteen groups of Harvard University undergraduates, each consisting of between three and six men. They were selected so that they were strangers to each other, and were paid to spend one hour a day solving an administrative case study problem which they were supplied with. Their interactions were recorded and analyzed in terms of Bales' twelve categories.

Photograph by Robert F. Bales.

The researchers found that at the end of the first day, the group member

*Kurt Lewin
(1890–1947)*
Photo source for Kurt Lewin:
Archives of the History of
American Psychology, The
University of Akron, Ohio, USA.

*Ronald O. Lippitt
(1914–86)*

It is therefore useful to distinguish between a leader and acts of leadership. If we accept Cattell's (1951) view that the leader is any group member who is capable of modifying the properties of the group by his presence, then we can acknowledge that any member of the group can, in theory, perform acts of leadership, and not merely the individual occupying some formal position.

group atmosphere and leadership style

Task leaders in groups did not all perform their roles in exactly the same way. They used different approaches which had different effects on group members' performance and satisfaction. Among the most famous of leadership studies were carried

whom the others rated as having the best ideas, that is, who was most helpful in moving the group towards a solution, was also rated as the most liked. However, after the first day, this person's equally high rating for best ideas *and* most liked, dropped sharply.

From then on, two leaders seemed to emerge. One was the *task leader*, who specialized in making suggestions, giving information, expressing opinions and generally contributing most to helping the group achieve its objective. The second to emerge was the *socio-emotional leader*, who helped other group members to state their ideas, expressed positive feelings towards them, made jokes and released tensions in the group. The socio-emotional leader generally acted to maintain the group as a functioning entity.

Bales and Slater thus discovered that leadership in a group split into two. Although there was some rivalry, the two group leaders, *task* and *socio-emotional*, typically co-operated and worked together well. Beyond the laboratory situation, such division of leadership can be seen in families when one parent assumes task leadership while the other deals with socio-emotive issues.

The researchers discovered that a split in leadership only occurred after the task leader had been identified and agreed upon. They argued that it was only after the group knew who would lead it to achieve its external goals that it could afford the luxury of a socio-emotional leader. Thus, the researchers did not view leadership as a single role, but as applying to several roles within the group. A well-organized group, in which the leadership functions were being satisfactorily performed, would have both a task leader and a social leader.

based on Robert F. Bales and Philip E. Slater, 1956, 'Role differentiation in small group decision-making groups', in T. Parsons and R.F. Bales (eds.), *Family, Socialization and Interaction*, Routledge, London, pp. 259–306.

out by Kurt Lewin, Ralph White and Ronald Lippitt. Beginning in 1938, a series of studies designed to investigate group functioning under experimentally induced group atmospheres or social climates were carried out under the general direction of Lewin, and continued throughout the 1950s.

One major study in the series was conducted at the Iowa Child Welfare Research Station by White and Lippitt. It involved four groups of 10-year-old boys operating in a natural setting. Each group was a genuine hobby club which met after school and comprised five members. Each group's members had been matched on characteristics such as age, personality, IQ, physical and socio-economic status, to be as similar as possible. Four adult leaders were trained to proficiency in the three leadership treatments (see table on p. 233), and shifted from club to club every six weeks. The clubs met in the same place and engaged in similar activities (arts-and-crafts, primarily the making of masks) with similar materials. The characteristics of each leadership style are summarized in the table. The accompanying photographs are from the actual experiment, and were taken by one of the researchers, Ronald Lippitt.

Above left: **authoritarian**
Above: **democratic**
Left: **laissez-faire**

White and Lippitt's (1960) research findings supported the following generalizations:

1 Laissez-faire *climates are not the same as democracy.*

(a) There was less work done in it, and poorer work.

authoritarian	democratic	laissez-faire
1 All determination of policy by the leader.	1 All policies a matter of group discussion and decision, encouraged and assisted by the leader.	1 Complete freedom for group or individual decision, with a minimum of leader participation.
2 Techniques and activity steps dictated by the authority, one at a time, so that future steps were always uncertain to a large degree.	2 Activity perspective gained during discussion period. General steps to group goal sketched, and when technical advice was needed, the leader suggested two or more alternative procedures from which choice could be made.	2 Various materials supplied by the leader, who made it clear that he would supply information when asked. He took no other part in work discussion.
3 The leader usually dictated the particular work task and work companion of each member.	3 The members were free to work with whomever they chose, and the division of tasks was left up to the group.	3 Complete non-participation of the leader.
4 The dominator tended to be 'personal' in his praise and criticism of the work of each member; remained aloof from active group participation except when demonstrating.	4 The leader was 'objective' or 'fact-minded' in his praise and criticism, and tried to be a regular group member in spirit without doing too much of the work.	4 Infrequent spontaneous comments on member activities unless questioned, and no attempt to appraise or regulate the course of events.

   (b) It was more characterized by play.

   (c) In interviews, the boys expressed preference for the democratic leader.

2 *Democracy can be efficient.*

   (a) The quantity of work done in autocracy was somewhat greater.

   (b) Work motivation was stronger in democracy as shown, for instance, when the leader left the room.

   (c) Originality was greater in democracy.

3 *Autocracy can create much hostility and aggression, as well as submissive behaviour.*

   (a) In one study, the autocratic group showed more dominant ascendence (individual taking-over behaviour); much more hostility (in a ratio of 30 to 1); more demands for attention; more destruction of own property; and more scapegoat behaviour (aggression towards 'innocent' and helpless members).

   (b) In another study, the typical reaction pattern to the autocratic leader was one of submissiveness.

4 *Autocracy can create discontent that does not appear on the surface.*

   (a) Four boys dropped out, and all of them did so during autocratic club periods in which overt rebellion did not occur.

   (b) Nineteen out of 20 boys preferred their democratic leader.

   (c) There was more discontent expressed in autocracy – even when the general reaction was submissive – than in democracy.

(d) 'Release' behaviour on the day of transition to a freer atmosphere suggested the presence of previous frustration.

5 *There was more dependence and less individuality in autocracy.*

(a) There was more 'submissive' or 'dependent' behaviour.

(b) Conversation was less varied – more confined to the immediate situation.

(c) In the submission reaction to autocracy, there was an absolute (though not relative) reduction in statistical measures of individual differences.

(d) The observers' impression was that in autocracy there is some loss of individuality.

6 *There was more group-mindedness and more friendliness in democracy.*

(a) The pronoun 'I' was used relatively less frequently in the democratic group.

(b) Spontaneous sub-groups were larger.

(c) Group-minded remarks were more frequent.

(d) Friendly remarks were more frequent.

(e) Mutual praise was more frequent.

(f) Friendly playfulness was more frequent.

(g) Readiness to share group property was more frequent.

STOP!

What generalizations can you make about White and Lippitt's findings on leadership styles to organizational situations? Why might you be guarded in your generalizations?

---

communication structure

Group structure was defined as the relationships between different positions in the group. An important relationship between positions is in terms of the nature and frequency of interaction. A consideration of the communication structure of a group represents the final dimension to be considered. The members of a group depend on information provided by others. Solving a problem, making a decision and reaching agreement all require information exchange between members. Usually, that information comes down a chain of people. A tells B, B tells C, and so on. William Foote Whyte (1948) described how a cook in a restaurant may receive an order from a customer via a runner, a pantry worker and a waitress. Such a communication link can produce a distortion in the message. When information arrives in this form, the cook is unable to check it, has no opportunity to negotiate with the message-sender and cannot discuss any problems.

To discover which communication structure is most effective, Shaw (1978) conducted a laboratory experiment to test if certain communication patterns in a group had structural characteristics which limited the performance of the group in its task. While all the communication patterns studied were, in theory, adequate for the group to do the task, he wanted to know if any of them were significantly better. Were certain communication patterns superior in standing up to group disruption? Did some effect the emergence of leadership? Shaw studied the effects of five communication networks on task performance and member satisfaction. These were:

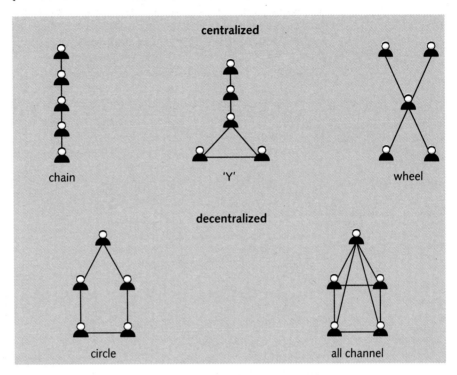

These networks can be compared with the three communication styles identified earlier from White, Lippitt and Lewin's research. It can be seen that autocratic leadership was accompanied by a wheel communication net, and the democratic style with an all channel net. The *laissez-faire* leadership style generated a somewhat fragmented communication pattern. Shaw noted that in centralized networks (chain, wheel and 'Y'), group members had to go through a central person located at the centre of the network in order to communicate with others. This led to unequal access to information in the group, because the persons at the centre had more access to information than did persons at the periphery. In decentralized networks (circle and all channel), information could flow freely between members without having to go through a central person, thus equalizing access to information. A classic study by Bavelas and Barrett (1951) compared five common group communication networks which were different on four important group criteria, to reveal the following differences:

criteria	communication network				
	chain	'Y'	wheel	circle	all channel
speed	moderate	moderate	fast	slow	fast
accuracy	high	high	high	low	moderate
leader emergence	moderate	moderate	high	none	none
satisfaction	moderate	moderate	low	high	high

The way in which different communication patterns affect group functioning in terms of group performance, structure and member satisfaction continues to be a subject of interest. Baron and Greenberg (1990) studied the relationship between the performance of centralized and decentralized communication networks when dealing with simple and complex tasks. They noted that centralized networks are superior on *simple* tasks (top), and decentralized networks are superior on *complex* tasks (bottom).

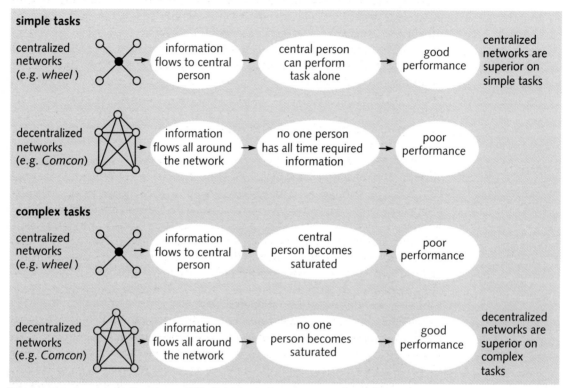

based on R.A. Baron and J. Greenberg, 1990, *Behavior in Organizations*, Allyn and Bacon, New York, 3rd edition, p. 348. Adapted by permission of Prentice-Hall, Inc., Upper Saddle River, NJ.

assessment

The original theoretical developments in the area of group structure and process occurred between the 1930s and 1950s. Many studies were conducted in non-organizational contexts and frequently involved children. Their findings were then applied to companies. The more recent developments have been practical rather than theoretical. Whilst Western companies may have been reluctant formally to structure their organizations around groups, they have been prepared to train their managerial and technical staff to work more effectively in teams. Thus, team-building or team development activities have established themselves as a major element in both management training and in organizational development (OD) activities. Some of these will be discussed in Chapter 17.

The idea underpinning team-building is that the performance of a group (as measured by the number of problems solved, tasks accomplished, decisions successfully implemented) is as much a function of its structure and process as it is of the personalities of the members. If a group or team is not performing well, then one must examine its status, power, liking, role and communication structures. It needs to consider which roles are performed and not performed, and how decisions are typically made. In order to improve the group, one must first diagnose its operation in terms of the processes just described. Only then can it move to implement changes in its own working.

The process of team-building involves intact company teams working with a consultant to diagnose and rectify their functioning. The diagnosis stage may include the use of drawings or questionnaires to elicit members' perceptions of how the team is currently operating. Such an analysis can lead to the identification of the important group problems which prevent it performing more effectively. The second stage of the process then involves exercises and other training activities to help group members change individual behaviours in order to improve team performance. A work team may attend an outward bound course as part of its training in order to explore its functioning.

The concept of the much hyped 'virtual organization' has been operationalized in the formation of globally distributed teams (GDTs) by multinational companies The management of these does pose a challenge to the organization. GDTs consist of members who are located in different countries and who have specific, short-duration project objectives to achieve. Moreover, they are prevented from travelling to meet face-to-face owing to time and other resource pressures. Instead, they work separately and use electronic technology, including video-conferencing, to hold meetings. Miller *et al.* (1996) considered four main issues with respect of GDT performance. These were objectives, technology, motivation and power.

On the question of objectives, the authors stressed the importance of carefully balancing the content and process issues. These concepts were introduced and described at the start of this chapter. On the group content (task) side, they stressed the importance of negotiating and agreeing what is to be achieved by the team at the outset, since the process (interaction) issues, in this case technological ones, created unexpected problems. Distributed teams appeared to need to restate their unifying purpose at every opportunity, in order to avoid losing direction. This is a common problem in all teams, but which is exacerbated in GDTs.

With respect to technology, meeting through video-conferencing rather than face-to-face, changes the way in which group members interact. It emphasizes just how crucial the process dimension is for any form of successful team functioning. On the technological side, voice-activated cameras in video-conferences focus on the person speaking the loudest. This causes problems when more than one person is speaking at a time. Interrupting the speaker, a common and easily managed feature of face-to-face interactions, causes a serious problem during such GDT meetings, as does passing data around, such as spreadsheets. Whilst much effort was devoted to running the technological process of video-conferencing, the researchers found little value-added output, and suggested that e-mail, fax or telephone would achieve as much at less cost.

Turning next to the question of motivation and performance, Miller *et al.* found that, as expected, managers had difficulty motivating people at a distance. Moreover, the chairperson found it difficult to assess the contribution of individual members at remote sites, who could more easily hide their limited input. This stresses the importance, stated at the beginning, of establishing objectives, standards and deadlines early on.

Finally, and perhaps most importantly, the authors reported that the technology had an important impact on organization structure. Specifically, it hid the commonly observed sources of individual power within an organization, and created a more organic and egalitarian form of company structure which appeared to change shape in response to the issues discussed, rather than being fixed by top management. This in turn had three consequences.

First, it made the transfer of responsibility between group members more of a problem. Second, it led to group members considering themselves as more equal. This could either encourage them to contribute more, unencumbered by group pressure, or it could reduce their need to participate and allow them to remain silent more easily. Third, as far as the group's leadership structure was concerned, it had the effect of constantly changing the leadership role within it. Moreover, it moved not only from one group member to another, but also from one geographic site to another. The reason for this was the absence of organizational indicators of individual group member power, which within face-to-face teams constrains such changes in leader role-taking. The authors felt that such leadership switching could be dysfunctional for achieving the group task since it wasted time and encouraged 'power-posturing'. Physically dispersed and technologically integrated, GDTs are likely to increase in number in the future. As yet, multinational companies have not discovered an effective way of managing them.

sources

Bales, R.F., 1950a, *Interaction Process Analysis*, Addison-Wesley, Reading, MA.

Bales, R.F., 1950b, 'A set of categories for the analysis of small group interaction', *American Sociological Review*, vol. 15, no. 2, pp. 257–63.

Baron, R.A. and Greenberg, J., 1990, *Behavior in Organizations*, Allyn and Bacon, New York, 3rd edition.

Bavelas, A., 1967, 'Communication patterns in task-orientated groups', in D. Cartwright and A. Zander (eds.), *Group Dynamics: Research and Theory*, Tavistock, London, 3rd edition.

Bavelas, A. and Barrett, D., 1951, 'An experimental approach to organizational communication', *Personnel*, March.

Belbin, R.M., 1981, *Management Teams: Why They Succeed or Fail*, Heinemann, London.

Belbin, R.M., 1996, *The Coming Shape of Organization*, Butterworth Heinemann, London.

Benne, K.D. and Sheats, P., 1948, 'Functional roles of group members', *Journal of Social Issues*, vol. 4, pp. 41–9.

Benne, K.D. and Sheats, P., 1951, 'Functional roles of group members', *Human Relations and Curriculum Change*, pp. 98–104.

Cartwright, D. and Zander, A. (eds.), 1968, *Group Dynamics: Research and Theory*, Tavistock, London, 3rd edition.

Cattell, R., 1951, 'New concepts for measuring leadership in terms of group syntality', *Human Relations*, vol. 4, pp. 161–8.

Forsyth, D.R., 1983, *An Introduction to Group Dynamics*, Brookes/Cole, Monterey, CA.

French, J.R.P. and Raven, B.H., 1958, 'The bases of social power', in D. Cartwright (ed.), *Studies in Social Power*, Institute of Social Research, University of Michigan Press, Ann Arbor, MI.

Homans, G.C., 1961, *Social Behavior: Forms*, Harcourt Brace, New York.

Jacobs, J.H., 1945, 'The application of sociometry to industry', *Sociometry*, vol. 8, pp. 181–98.

Miller, D.C. and Form, W.H., 1969, *Industrial Sociology*, Harper, New York, 3rd edition.

Miller, P., Pons, J.M. and Naude, P., 1996, 'Global teams', *Financial Times*, 14 June, p. 12.

Olmstead, M., 1959, *The Small Group*, Random House, New York.

Shaw, M.E., 1978, 'Communication networks fourteen years later', in Berkowitz, L. (ed.), *Group Processes*, Academic Press, New York, pp. 351–61.

Thrasher, F.M., 1927, *The Gang: A Study of 1,313 Gangs in Chicago*, University of Chicago Press, Chicago.

Tuckman, B. and Jensen, N., 1977, 'Stages of small group development revisited', *Group and Organizational Studies*, vol. 2., pp. 419–27.

White, R. and Lippitt, R., 1960, *Autocracy and Democracy*, Harper & Row, New York.

Whyte, W.F., 1937, *Street Corner Society*, University of Chicago Press, Chicago.

Whyte, W.F., 1948, *Human Relations in the Restaurant Industry*, McGraw-Hill, New York.

Zeleny, L.D., 1947, 'Selection of compatible flying partners', *American Journal of Sociology*, vol. 5, pp. 424–31.

chapter 9 group control

"Mother, I get enough pressure from my peer group without getting it from you."

from *The New Yorker*, 9 June 1980. Drawing by Weber, © 1980, The New Yorker Magazine, Inc.

concepts and learning objectives
group influences on individuals' motivation
group influences on individuals' perceptions
group socialization of members
group influences on individuals' attitudes and behaviours
conformity to and rebellion against authority
assessment
sources

concepts and learning objectives

Jones (1977) wrote that being a member of a group can make an individual susceptible to social influences that encourage irrational or destructive behaviour. He said that the group pressure that causes us to 'love our neighbour' is closely related to that which leads us to reject those who are different from us.

A problem of choice faces us when we seek to study conformity and control in groups. From what we know already about the nature of psychological groups, it is clear that our interactions with other people can be studied from several different perspectives. Our behaviour is shaped by various influences. These include the *intra-individuals variables* considered in the previous part of the book – our perceptual set, motivation, learning style and personality. The strength of our attitudes and values, how they fit in with those of other people in the group, and our need to feel accepted by other group members, will all play a part in how we behave in groups.

Another set of influences relate not to the individual, but to the structure and process of the group itself. Earlier chapters examined *group variables* such as the hierarchy that exists within a group, the roles people play in it and whether the group is a formal or an informal one. Finally, we can note that the *group dynamics* variable considers the way in which the process of interaction between group members affects them in terms of their attitudes and behaviour. This chapter considers how the attitude and behaviour of an individual is changed or modified when that person joins and becomes a member of a group.

---

key concepts

▸ social influence	▸ social norm
▸ social facilitation	▸ group sanction
▸ shared frame of reference	▸ group socialization

---

learning objectives

When you have read this chapter, you should be able to define those key concepts in your own words, and you should also be able to:
1 Understand why groups are capable of exerting an influence on the behaviour and attitudes of their members.
2 Understand how groups develop 'rules of behaviour' to regulate the conduct of their members, and enforce such rules.
3 Understand why, as individuals, we conform to the dictates of society in general, and to that of our own group in particular.
4 Relate aspects of group control to the groups of which you are a member.
5 Appreciate the organizational consequences of group influence and control.

group influences on individuals' motivation

For the individual, group membership has benefits in the form of satisfaction of some psychological needs. However, there are costs in the form of modifications to behaviour that the individual invariably must make in order to retain membership. The attraction that group members have for one another, that is, group cohesiveness, is influenced by various factors such as the homogeneity of members, amount of communication, isolation from distraction, group size, outside pressure or threat, group status and degree of past success. William F. Whyte (1955, p. 331) wrote:

> The group is a jealous master. It encourages participation, indeed it demands it, but it demands one kind of participation – its own kind and the better integrated with it a member becomes the less free he is to express himself in other ways.

Cohesiveness affects the degree of dedication to group activities. Groups invariably establish rules of conduct in order to maintain consistency of behaviour among group members. These rules are generally referred to as norms and groups develop means by which they enforce such norms. Punishments such as practical jokes, social ostracism or even violence may be used against deviants. There is now impressive research evidence which demonstrates the power of groups to exert profound social influence on individual behaviour. The mere presence of other people can affect what we do. The concept of social influence refers to this phenomenon. It has been found that a person's behaviour is affected by merely knowing that other people are present, or that they soon will be present to observe what he or she is doing.

STOP!

Think of five things that you do alone that you would not do if someone else was with you. Why would you not do these things in the presence of others? What would be the consequences in each case if you did?

---

definition

Social influence *refers to the phenomenon that the mere presence of other people affects, and thereby alters, the behaviour of an individual from what it would otherwise have been.*

The process of social influence can either inhibit or facilitate behaviour. What type of student behaviour does the presence of a university invigilator in an examination hall seek to inhibit? The term social facilitation was coined by the psychologist Floyd Allport. For familiar, well-learned activities such as assembly-line work and similar repetitive tasks, the presence of co-workers is likely to improve performance, and the presence of an observer such as a manager, unlikely to hinder it, unless it carries a message of distrust or punishment. In contrast, a person who is attempting to perform a complex, unfamiliar task will find that observation by others will cause them to make more mistakes.

---

definition

Social facilitation *refers to the observation that whatever the person is doing alone, when he is joined by others, he frequently does it better, faster or more frequently.*

Three different explanations have been offered to explain the arousing effect of the presence of others:
1 The co-presence explanation says that arousal is a natural reaction to the presence of other people (Zajonc, 1980).
2 The evaluation explanation holds that fear of being evaluated by others increases our arousal.
3 The distraction–conflict explanation states that arousal is due to a conflict between paying attention to the task and to the distraction of others (Baron, 1986).

At other times, the effect of the presence of others may be inhibitive, with performance reducing in the presence of others or else certain behaviours being totally eliminated. We all know how sportsmen can achieve an improved performance when they compete at a major international meeting attended by many spectators. Sports commentators frequently refer to the benefit a football team can derive by playing at home in front of its own crowd. In contrast, the presence of others can inhibit or eliminate certain behaviours. We may stop picking our nose in the company of others, or a group of men may stop swearing when they are joined by a female. Frequently it may be a mixture of both. When I join my daughter at the table for a meal, she stops wriggling around in her seat, uses her knife and fork more carefully, and stops hitting her brother.

Research has also shown that the presence of others may, in certain circumstances, have an inhibiting effect. It depends on the task being performed and on how the individual sees the group. If we accept that the individual's perception of his social environment (including other people) influences his behaviour, then this moves the explanation beyond the 'general excitability' thesis and accepts that different overt behaviour can result from the same internal stimulation.

As was shown, while the presence of others (especially the opposite sex) can arouse us, the way we behave as a result of that arousal is not direct. Each individual has acquired during his life many ways of interpreting and reacting (his personality), and individuals differ too much to allow any simple laws to be stated. Man has found in the struggle for survival that a strategy of co-operation is frequently useful, but that the advantage of group membership which that co-operation entails brings with it obligations.

The need to be able to relate to and identify with a group is deep-seated within us. Many different psychologists have identified social or affiliation needs. Moreover, many of the tasks in which we engage cannot be completed alone, but require the assistance of others. Thus for social and practical reasons, we work in and through groups. By virtue of that need and desire for membership of a group, we open ourselves up to the influences that the group can exert on our individual perceptions, values and behaviours. Thus, from the viewpoint of individual freedom, group membership carries with it both costs and benefits.

Some agreement on perception and meaning is essential among the members of a group in order for them to interact, communicate, agree on goals and generally to allow members to act in concert on a common task. Such a shared framework is essential for the group if it is to continue and develop. Moreover, as we work in groups we find that our frame of reference becomes similar to that of the group.

definition

Shared frame of reference *is the assumption that we make about the kind of situation we are confronting. It is the context within which we view it. A frame of reference which is shared by the members of a group means that through their interaction and mutual education the members of this group will tend to perceive a large range of phenomena in broadly the same way.*

---

how the negotiators see it

A negotiating situation is therefore not merely one where two or more people discuss an issue. The people involved belong to groups (unions or management) and a conflict between individuals is always in addition a conflict between groups. Mr A does not just perceive himself as Mr A and perceive Mr B as Mr B, he perceives himself also as a union member and Mr B as a member of management – these groups as well as the individuals are in conflict. The ethos or culture of a management group is in many ways opposed to that of a shopfloor group. Management norms emphasize efficiency, rational efforts to increase productivity and profitability, the orderly conduct of affairs, and a general stress on individual self-advancement through promotion, social progress and approval from others. As people adopt the management reference group and spend their lives with other managers, they come to take this so much for granted that they often hardly notice the existence of the norms and the accompanying social pressures.

Similarly the manual worker may be unlikely to recognize how far his actions and feelings are socially determined and he will probably have only a limited conception of norms different from his own. The typical shopfloor culture is one which is also based upon approval from others (for we have seen that self-esteem through group membership is a basic ingredient of mental health), but here the approval goes to other kinds of behaviour than efficiency and striving for promotion. Efficiency can of course be valued as an individual sign of skill, and promotion can be desired, but prospects are in many cases severely limited. The norms of the manual worker's group are often likely to emphasize an interest in horse-racing or football, an ability to mend cars or television sets, skill at extracting loose piecework rates from management, being one of the lads who sticks up for his mates, and (in some areas) a concern for improving the lot of the working class. The worker, like the manager, aims for group respect or status, but his status is an informal one in the group whereas the manager's is more a formal placement in a hierarchy of positions. In both cases their status comes largely from conformity, but the norms to which they may conform are different ones.

from Peter Warr, 1973, *Psychology and Collective Bargaining*, Hutchinson, London, pp. 15–16.

Why is a frame of reference important? Mainly because it determines the meaning which we attach to events and other people's behaviour. In the annual pay negotiations, for example, the frames of reference of the management representative and the union negotiator about the kind of situation they see themselves as being involved in will probably be radically different. The manager may be concerned with resisting the perceived excessive demands for increased wages by the workers and thereby defending the future of the company and the interests of the shareholders.

The union representative, in contrast, may see herself as representing the just demands of the workforce in a period when they have dramatically improved productivity, and feels that the situation could be settled if the other side chose to act reasonably, but such reasonable behaviour involves their accepting her position. During any major strike, the radio and television interviews between the union and management representatives illustrate this point. They highlight the differences in values and meanings accorded to key notions such as 'fair offer' and 'co-operation'.

group influences on individuals' perceptions

In a study which has now become a classic in experimental social psychology, Muzafer Sherif (1936) showed how group norms emerged. He demonstrated the way in which a person's view can be affected by what others present claim to see. Few of the subjects who took part in Sherif's experiments felt conscious that their judgements had been influenced by others. This reinforces the point that the process of social influence is covert and that its effects last a long time. Sherif's work showed that in a situation where doubt and uncertainty exist, and where first-hand information is lacking, a person's viewpoint will shift to come into line with those of other group members. In essence this situation leads to the creation of a group norm. This occurs quickly amongst group members who have had little previous experience of the group's work, but it also occurs amongst those who have had experience, although somewhat more slowly.

Sherif's work suggested that in order to organize and manage itself, every group developed a system of norms. What are norms and what is their purpose? Norms are behavioural expectations and they serve to define the nature of the group. They express the values of the members of the group and provide guidelines to help the group achieve its goals. They may be developed consciously or unconsciously by a group.

---

definition

Social norms *are the 'expected modes of behaviour and beliefs that are established either formally or informally by the group . . .. Norms guide behaviour and facilitate interaction by specifying the kinds of reactions expected or acceptable in a particular situation'.*

from *Jones and Gerrard (1967).*

Norms develop in a group around those subjects and topics in the life of the group which are important to its functioning as defined by the group members themselves. Group norms develop around the work itself, about how it should be accomplished, how quickly and in what way; around non-work activities as to what clothes should be worn and the appropriate way to pass non-working time; around communication concerning how individuals should interact with each other, what language they should use; and around attitudes and opinions that should be held by group members regarding work, management policies, and so on.

Norms may apply to all group members or only to specific individuals. Norms may also vary in the degree to which they are accepted by the group, and can vary in the range of permissible deviation. In a workgroup, norms might exist regarding what is a fair day's work, how to interact with the foreman, and so on. Topics which are not central to a group's functioning will not have norms associated with them. There may thus be no norms about how one should dress or what is the appropriate length of time for a teabreak. It is certain that a number of norms will develop in any group. However, around which topics these norms emerge, and what behaviour or attitude they specify, will vary from group to group. Similarly, a norm within a single group can change over time.

informal workplace norms: hanging beef tongues

Over a nine-week period, William Thompson used the observational data collection method to study the day-to-day activities of assembly-line workers in a beef-processing plant in the American Midwest. He reported that, 'working in the beef plant is "dirty" work, not only in the literal sense of being drenched with perspiration and beef blood, but also in the figurative sense of performing a low status, routine and demeaning job'. Thompson and his fellow workers had to hang, brand and bag between 1350 and 1500 beef tongues during an eight-hour shift. The work was both monotonous and routine.

Thompson described the camaraderie that existed among the 'beefers' as they called themselves. Because of the noise, the need for earplugs and the isolation of certain work areas, it was virtually impossible for the men on the assembly-line to speak to each other. Instead, they communicated using an elaborate system of non- and para-verbal symbols. These included exaggerated gestures, shrill whistles, 'thumbs up' and 'thumbs down', and the clanging of knives against stainless steel tables and tubs. Thompson observed that, 'in a setting which apparently eliminated it, the workers' desire for social interaction won out and interaction flourished'.

To reduce the feeling of alienation and retain a sense of humanity, the beefers developed certain coping mechanisms. They replaced the formal, managerially imposed norms of the workplace with their own informal ones. At certain times, instead of working at a steady speed which matched the line speed, they would work at a frantic pace, and get ahead of the line. While such behaviour added a few precious minutes to their scheduled break time, its importance was primarily symbolic in that it challenged the company's dictates concerning the speed of the line, and it gave them a small measure of control over the work process.

The informal group norms also encouraged certain types of rule breaking. Indeed, Thompson noted that the 'workers practically made a game out of doing forbidden things simply to see if they could get away with it'. For example, at Thompson's workstation, despite strict rules to the contrary, workers covered in beef blood washed their hands, arms and knives in a tub of water which was reserved for cleaning tongues. In addition, workers often cut out pieces of meat and threw them at other employees. If not noticed by the supervisor or inspector, the thrown meat chunks might be picked up off the floor, and put back on the line – a blatant violation of hygiene rules. Thompson concluded that such 'artful sabotage served as a symbolic way in which workers could express a sense of individuality, and hence self-worth'.

based on William E. Thompson, 1983, 'Hanging tongues; A sociological encounter with the assembly line', *Qualitative Sociology*, vol. 6, Fall, pp. 215–37.

STOP!

We would like you to do some social psychology research by studying your fellow students. You belong to a group of students following a broadly similar course of study and you probably belong to a close sub-group within this larger class. What modes of behaviour are expected of you within that sub-group? What beliefs do you share? How do these norms facilitate your interaction? How are they enforced?

group socialization of members

Once an existing group has established a set of norms and accompanying sanctions with which to enforce those norms, it has to communicate its norms to newcomers who join the group. The name given to this process is socialization and this occurs in families, schools and entire societies. The interest here is upon the group.

The new group member 'learns the ropes' and is shown how to get things done, how to interact with others and how to achieve a high social status within the group. An important aspect of achieving such status is to adhere to the group's rules or norms. Initial transgressions will be gently pointed out. However, the continued violation of norms by a group member puts at risk the cohesion of the group. When there is disagreement on a matter of importance to the group, the preservation of group effectiveness, harmony and cohesion requires a resolution of the conflict. Hence pressure is exerted on the deviating individual through persuasive communication to conform.

---

discovering the norm

Donald Roy, a researcher who acted as a participant observer in a factory, described the pressures that were placed on an individual to adhere to the group norm. Roy's earnings, and those of others, were based on a piece-rate system. The more he produced the more he earned.

From my first to my last day at the plant I was subject to warnings and predictions concerning price cuts. Pressure was the heaviest from Joe Mucha, who shared my job repertoire and kept a close eye on my production. On November 14, the day after my first attained quota, Joe Mucha advised: Don't let it go over $1.25 an hour, or the time-study man will be right down here! And they don't waste time, either! They watch the records like a hawk! I got ahead, so I took it easy for a couple of hours. Joe told me that I had made $10.01 yesterday and warned me not to go over $1.25 an hour . . . . Jack Starkey spoke to me after Joe left. 'What's the matter? Are you trying to upset the applecart?' Jack explained in a friendly manner that $10.50 was too much to turn in, even on an old job. 'The turret-lathe men can turn in $1.35', said Jack, 'but their rate is 90 cents and ours is 85 cents.' Jack warned me that the Methods Department could lower their prices on any job, old or new, by changing the fixture slightly or changing the size of the drill. According to Jack, a couple of operators . . . got to competing with each other to see how much they could turn in. They got up to $1.65 an hour, and the price was cut in half. And from then on they had to run that job themselves, as none of the other operators would accept that job. According to Jack, it would be all right for us to turn in $1.28 or $1.29 an hour, when it figured out that way, but it was not all right to turn in $1.30 an hour.

Well now I know where the maximum is – $1.29 an hour.

from Donald Roy, 1960, 'Banana time: job satisfaction and informal interaction', *Human Organization*, vol. 18, pp. 156–68.

Sherif's study of the emergence of group norms

If you place yourself in a room which is in complete darkness and look fixedly at a small point of light, the light will appear to move in an erratic manner, even though it is in fact stationary. You can test this out yourself if you have a completely dark room and one small pin-point of light. It is not that anything is actually moving, but the effect of fixing your eyes on such a small point of light in the darkness makes the light seem to move. The apparent movement is an optical illusion known as the 'autokinetic effect'. A person in the room who observes the light will be able to report estimates of the distances covered.

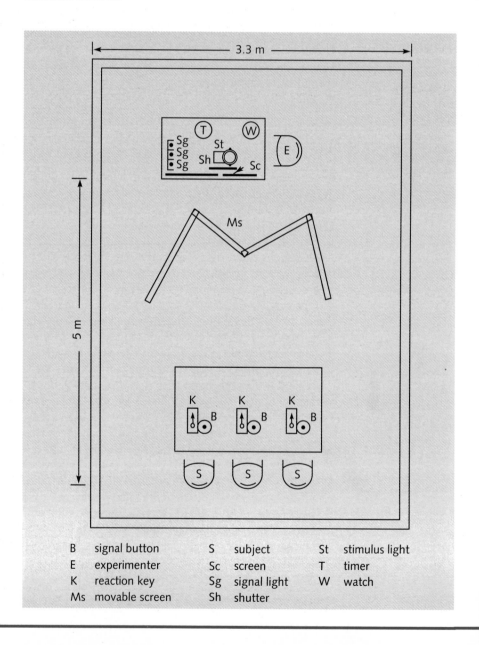

B	signal button	S	subject	St	stimulus light
E	experimenter	Sc	screen	T	timer
K	reaction key	Sg	signal light	W	watch
Ms	movable screen	Sh	shutter		

Muzafer Sherif placed a group of subjects in such a darkened room and presented them with such a small spot of light. Three series of 100 estimates were undertaken by his subjects on successive days. He then asked them to track the apparent movement of the spot, and to say, aloud, each in turn, the direction in which they thought the light was moving. The figure on p. 248 shows the plan of the experimental room used by Sherif.

Initially, each group member differed. There were quite wide individual differences in the response to this situation. Some subjects saw little movement, whilst others saw a lot. However, Sherif discovered that they started to agree quite quickly. Having exchanged information on judgements, their behaviour changed. They began seeing the light moving in the same direction as those who had spoken earlier.

**mean estimates
for a group of
three subjects**

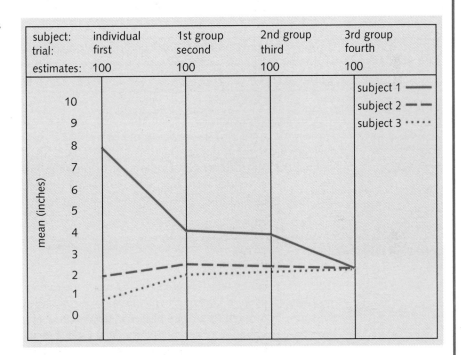

Gradually, all the members came to see the light as moving in the same direction at the same time. There was of course no 'real' movement of the light. Each individual began to see the light in the same way as the group saw it. The results Sherif obtained with two-person and three-person groups are shown in the figure above. When a group norm emerged it was found that it became the basis for subsequent judgement when subjects were re-tested independently. The group norm therefore became a relatively permanent frame of reference for behaviour.

based on Muzafer Sherif, 1936, *The Psychology of Group Norms*, Harper & Row, New York.

---

definition

Group socialization *is the process of inculcation whereby an individual learns the principal values and symbols of the group in which he participates and how these values are expressed in the norms which compose the roles that he and others interact.*

While such pressure towards group cohesion (going along with the other members of the group) may be beneficial in many respects for the group, it also carries costs. If conformity is allowed to dominate, with individuals having little opportunity to present alternative and different views, this can lead to errors of judgement and the taking of unwise actions. The next chapter will consider the phenomenon of groupthink. Such pressure to conform on the individual is applied through the use of sanctions imposed by the group.

---

definition

Group sanction *refers to both punishments and rewards given by group members to others in the process of enforcing group norms. Rewards are a positive sanction and punishments are a negative sanction.*

The earliest examples of sanctions exercised in groups came from the Hawthorne studies. The researchers observed that persons producing either over or under the group norm were binged. This involved a group member flicking the ear of the norm transgressor or tapping him on the upper part of the arm. Both actions were intended to indicate physically that his behaviour was unacceptable. Other sanctions were also used by the group.

---

controlling the deviants

The mechanisms by which internal control was exercised varied. Perhaps the most important were sarcasm, 'bingeing' and ridicule. Through such devices pressure was brought to bear upon those individuals who deviated too much from the group's norm of acceptable conduct. From this point of view, it will be seen that the great variety of activities normally labelled 'restriction of output' represent attempts at social control and discipline and as such are important integrating processes. In addition to overt methods, clique membership itself may be looked upon as an instrument of control. Those persons whose behaviour was most reprehensible to clique A were excluded from it. They were in a sense, socially ostracized. This is one of the universal social processes by means of which a group chastizes and brings pressure to bear upon those who transgress its codes . . . It can be seen, therefore, that nearly all the activities of this group may be looked upon as methods of controlling the behaviour of its members. The men had elaborated, spontaneously and quite unconsciously, an intricate social organization around their collective beliefs and sentiments.

from Fritz J. Roethlisberger and William J. Dickson, 1964, *Management and the Worker*, John Wiley and Sons, New York, pp. 523–4.

A group member deviating from an important group norm has several options. She can try to persuade others to join her position and thus alter the group norm. Alternatively, she may be persuaded to conform to the original norm. The higher her status (and thus power) in the group, the more likely she is to change the attitudes of others and the less likely she is to change her own. If neither of these alternatives takes place, then something else will happen. If she is free to leave the group, and the group is of little importance to her, she may withdraw from it.

Conversely, if she is of little importance to the group, she may be faced with the choice of conforming or else being rejected by the group. She may even be rejected by the act of deviance whether or not she is willing to recant. However, if she is of great importance to the group, that is, if she is a high-status member in terms of power, popularity or special skills, the group may tolerate the deviation in order to avoid the greater threat of a loss of a valued member.

The power which a group has to influence its members towards conformity to shared beliefs and actions depends on three main factors:

▶ The positive and negative sanctions (rewards and punishments) the group has at its disposal.
▶ The degree to which individual members value their membership of the group and its accompanying rewards (e.g. recognition, status, prestige, financial inducements).
▶ The member's desire to avoid negative sanctions such as social and physical punishments or expulsion from the group.

from *The New Yorker*, 6 December 1976. Drawing by Lorenz, © 1976, The New Yorker Magazine, Inc.

group influences on individuals' attitudes and behaviours

Why is it that members do actually conform to group pressure? Part of the answer can be found in what has just been said. However, there is a little more to it. There is a tacit agreement between people that, for life to go on

Asch's study of conformity to group norms

the experimenter and his study

In the early 1950s, Solomon E. Asch (b. 1907) conducted a laboratory experiment into individual conformity in groups.

the situation

Seven men sat around a table supposedly to participate in a study on visual perception.

the subject

Only No. 6 was a real subject (second from the right in the group photograph). The remainder were Asch's paid confederates.

the task

8"
standard
card

6¼" 8" 6¾"
comparison
card

The task was an easy one. To judge which of three lines was equal in length to one they had seen earlier

the problem

In the experimental conditions, the confederates had been instructed to lie about which line was correct. Under pressure, the subject (No. 6) shows signs of conflict of whether to conform to the group judgement or give the response he judges to be correct.

the results

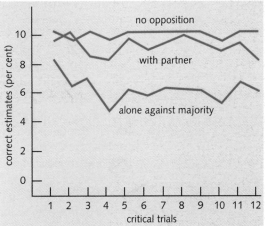

Number 6's correct responses are shown under three conditions: when the group did not lie (no opposition); when they all lied together (alone against opposition); and when only one confederate agreed.

the conclusion

Overall in twelve trials, involving 123 subjects, a total of 75 per cent of experimental subjects accepted the incorrect majority judgement to some degree. Asch found that the level of conformity tended to increase when the group members had a higher status than the 'deviant' individual, and when the group had to continue working together in the future. The subjects in the experiments, both volunteers and stooges, were students who had met only during the experiment itself. They dispersed after it had been concluded. However, as the results show, it only takes one other person to agree with the subject for the conformity effect to be counteracted.

The research indicates how difficult it can be for individuals to express their opinions when these are not in line with those of other team members. It is interesting to consider the pressure that a group can exert on an individual if it can influence something as unambiguous and familiar as judging the length of lines. How much more powerful the influence if individuals have to make subjective and unfamiliar judgements. This may explain why groups are ineffective. The best decisions are not made because group members seek to fit in with the views of others, rather than working for the best solution to the problem.

based on Solomon E. Asch, 1951, 'Effects of group pressure upon the modification and distortion of judgements', in H. Guetzkow (ed.), *Groups, Leadership and Men*, Carnegie Press, New York, pp. 177–90.

without producing continual problems, some general principles and rules need to be observed. For example, in the UK we drive on the left-hand side of the road, we wear clothes, and so on. Observation of such rules is of such personal benefit to us that we are prepared to suppress any personal desires and are thus willing to limit our individual freedom and abide by the rules. Moreover, the benefits which accrue, and the fear of the loss of these, encourages people to punish those who violate the rules. Thus we may report to the police a car driver who crosses a traffic light when it was at red, accusing him of dangerous driving. The more important of these norms have, over time, become backed by the rule of law. The earliest experimental studies into conformity to group norms were carried out by Solomon Asch.

Asch found that those who did yield to group pressure did so for different reasons. He distinguished three types of yielding:

1 *Distortion of perception (under the stress of group pressure)*: In this category belong a very few subjects who yield completely, but are not aware that their estimates have been displaced or distorted by the majority. These subjects report that they came to perceive the majority of estimates as correct. Yielding at this perceptual level was rare and occurred primarily among those subjects who displayed a lack of trust in themselves.

2 *Distortion of judgement*: Most submitting subjects belong to this category. The factor of greatest importance in this group is a decision the subjects reach that their perceptions are inaccurate, and that those of the majority are correct (akin to independence without confidence). These subjects suffer from primary doubt and lack of confidence. Because of this, they felt a strong tendency to join the majority.

3 *Distortion of action*: The subjects in this group do not suffer a modification of perception, nor do they conclude that they are wrong. They yield because of an overwhelming need not to appear different from, or inferior to, others because of an inability to tolerate the appearance of defectiveness in the eyes of the group. These subjects suppress their observations and voice the majority position with awareness of what they are doing.

STOP!

Do you behave differently in different situations or with different sets of people? Why?

A second reason why we conform to norms is that, at an individual level, we each have a desire for order and meaning in our lives. Numerous psychologists have demonstrated how people attempt to 'make sense' of seemingly unconnected facts or events. For the individual, uncertainty is disturbing and is reduced to the absolute minimum. We like to know 'what's going on' and we like to be in command of the situations in which we find ourselves. Norms, and the adherence to norms, provides the sense and predictability which most human beings desire.

Finally, norm conformity can be explained at the intersubjective level. Evidence suggests that individuals learn to adopt the attitudes and behaviour current in society. This is either because they have an innate need for a response from others, or because they acquire such a need very early on in life

---

organizational control through group pressure

in Soviet forced-labour camps during the Stalin era

Why, you may wonder, should prisoners wear themselves out, working hard, ten years on end, in the camps? You'd think they'd say: No thank you, and that's that. We'll shuffle through the day till evening, and then the night is ours. But that didn't work. To outsmart you they thought up work teams – but not teams like the ones in freedom, where every man is paid his separate wage. Everything was so arranged in the camp that the prisoners egged one another on. It was like this: either you got a bit extra or you all croaked. You're slacking, you rat – d'you think I'm willing to go hungry just because of you? Put your guts into it, scum. And if a situation like this one turned up there was all the more reason for resisting any temptation to slack. Willy-nilly you put your back into the work. For unless you manage to provide yourself with the means of warming up, you and everyone else would peg out on the stop.

from Alexander Solzhenitsyn, 1963, *One Day in the Life of Ivan Denisovich*, Penguin Books, Harmondsworth, pp. 51–2.

in a US–Japanese joint venture auto company in the 1980s

By eliminating buffer stocks with just-in-time delivery, parts are made or supplied when needed by the next operation. This puts pressure on production workers, team leaders and junior management to solve assembly-line problems and to catch up. For the system to succeed, management has introduced penalties for failure. These include pressure from management; reduced perks; undesirable new assignments; and disciplinary action. Both personal and system stress are used to keep the operation running smoothly. A key element of this is the peer pressure of the group or team. A worker who is having trouble can 'work into the hole', that is, move further down the line from his assigned position into order to try to catch up. However, this is difficult and frowned upon by fellow workers. He can signal for the team leader to help him, but this makes the leader unavailable to other team members who might need help. The temptation is just to work harder.

The researchers reported that NUMMI workers came in early or used their break times to build up stock, thereby working overtime without payment. Another aspect of peer pressure is the non-reallocation of workers as absentee replacements. Each team consists of 4–8 workers and a leader, and has no built-in slack. The leader deals with equipment distribution, training and parts supply. He does not usually involve himself in production. An absence means that the leader has to do the missing person's production job. If other team members then need help or relief, a team member from another group has to be called in. The system does not push problems upwards, and no department's budget is hurt by absenteeism. The system makes only the absent worker's team members suffer. Critics have argued that management-by-stress plants manipulate workers' human qualities so that peer pressure works to achieve management's ends. The system multiplies stress by continually increasing the demands on the individual while reducing the control he has over his daily work life.

based on *Choosing Sides: Unions and the Team Concept*, 1988, Labor Education and Research Project, Labor Notes, Detroit.

through their interaction with their mothers. Both explanations assume that one receives a satisfying response from others if they see you as like themselves, and if one behaves in accordance with their expectations. It seems that we need meaningful interaction and meaningful status from those we are with or with whom we compare ourselves.

A great number of different circumstances influence conformity to norms. The personality characteristics of individuals play a part in predisposing them to conform to group norms. The kind of stimuli eliciting conformity behaviour is also important. That people conform to norms when they are uncertain about a situation was demonstrated by the Sherif experiments. He also discovered that a person with a high degree of self-confidence could affect the opinions and estimates of other group members.

---

is Japanese teamworking in companies conditioned through the school system?

You are the boss of a company looking for assembly workers for a new factory. What would your model worker be? Probably something like this: highly literate and numerate, hardworking, fastidious, conformist, obedient. In short, Japanese . . . Discipline is strict . . . [in Japanese schools] . . . 'The nail that sticks up', runs a Japanese proverb, 'will be banged down'. It is fiercely applied in schools. Japanese school rules make English public schools of forty years [sic] look like hippie communes . . . Yet discipline is applied more by peer pressure than by the teachers. Since schools are differentiated by ability, classes are not. Everyone in the class does everything together. Lunch is eaten in the schoolroom; pupils take turns to bring in the food. Tidying up the classroom at the end of the day is [sic] collective activity. The effect of the system is to tame a child's natural exuberance and individuality to the point where he or she is most comfortable in a group . . . [when a child] one of *The Economist*'s office assistants in Tokyo was sent to a special kindergarten, 'to teach me how to play with other children'.

from 'Japan's schools: Why can't little Taro think?', 1990, *The Economist*, 21 April, pp. 23 and 25–6.

Upbringing also plays an important part. A value which is particularly salient in Jordan, for example, is the subordination of one's personal interests and goals to the welfare and needs of one's family or group. Group-centredness can be seen in Arab cultures where the individual is regarded as subservient to the group. Berger (1964) alluded to this trait when he wrote that, 'Through most of their history, despite the recent introduction of Western political forms, Arab communities have been collections of groups rather than individuals. The family and the tribe have been the social units through which the individual has related himself to others and to governments' (p. 33). The formal education can be considered as part of the process of upbringing and child socialization. In this context, Japan is particularly noted for the group orientation of its youngsters.

The amount of conformity to a group standard generally corresponds strongly to the degree of ambiguity of the stimulus being responded to. Situational factors are also involved, the size of the group, the unanimity of the majority and its structure all have an effect. It has been found that conformity increased as the group size increased. It is also affected by a person's position in the communication structure of a group, with conformity being greater in a decentralized network than in a centralized one. Finally, there are the intra-group relationships referred to earlier. The kind of pressure exerted, the composition of the group, how successful it has been in the past and the degree to which the member identifies with the group are all examples of this.

---

influencing perceptions – the Dutch Admiral Paradigm

Terrence Deal and Allen Kennedy defined a cabal as a group of two or more people who secretly joined together for mutual advantage, often to progress their careers within a company. The Dutch Admiral Paradigm holds that a cabal which establishes itself within a group can influence the perception of these people as to which members of the group members are high-fliers. The name comes from a story about two young officers from the Dutch Navy. They made a pact with each other that whenever one attended a naval social function, he would make a point of speaking in glowing terms about the merits of the other, and vice-versa. This pact was revealed by them on the day they were both promoted to the rank of admiral, and were the youngest naval personnel to achieve that position. Deal and Kennedy argued that their cabal had influenced the perceptions of senior naval and civil personnel who were influential in decisions concerning promotions. Thus, this was a case of 'believing was seeing' rather than of 'seeing was believing'. The message of the authors was that as long as one could positively influence the way that others perceived you (in relation to those around you), you would be able to rise in the organization hierarchy. The cabal played a crucial element in raising the estimation in which its members were held. This paradigm contradicts the well known 'Peter Principle' proposed by the late Laurence Peter that people get promoted to their level of incompetence.

based on Terrence E. Deal and Allen A. Kennedy, 1988, *Corporate Cultures*, Penguin Books, Harmondsworth, pp. 95–6.

---

conformity to and rebellion against authority

The Asch experiments demonstrated how group pressure affected individual internal standards by enforcing conformity within the group. Other research, this time by Stanley Milgram (1974), showed, amongst other things, that a group can aid the individual to defy authority. When we conform, we are responding to pressures which are implicit. We consider our behaviour to be voluntary. If questioned about our actions we may have difficulty explaining why we went along with the group view. The subjects in Asch's experiments had this trouble and in fact many denied that this is what they did. They preferred to think they were acting independently. Even when their errors were pointed out, they preferred to attribute these to their personal error of judgement. The Milgram experiment presented a situation of conflict in which a group supported an individual member who rebelled against the authority of a superior.

Milgram's 'electric shock' experiments

*Stanley Milgram
(1933–84)*
Photo source:
Archives of the History of American
Psychology, The University of Akron,
Ohio, USA.

Would you torture another person simply because you were told to do so by someone in authority? Of course not, you would probably reply with little hesitation. In a series of now famous and highly controversial experiments, Stanley Milgram examined people's level of obedience to authority. The research involved ordinary people of different ages, sexes, races and occupations. A group of psychiatrists, post-graduate students and social science lecturers were asked by Milgram to predict how many of the research subjects would actually obey the experimenter's order. There was a high agreement that virtually all subjects would refuse to obey. Only 1 in a 100 would do it, said the psychiatrists, and that person would be a psychopath.

Milgram's experiment involved volunteers participating in a learning experiment. They were to act as teachers of people who were trying to learn a series of simple word-pairs. As teachers they were told to punish the student when he failed to learn by giving him an electric shock. At the start the shocks were small in intensity but every time the learner made a mistake, the teacher was told to increase the size of the shock. In carrying out the experiments Milgram found that two out of every three subjects tested administered the electric shocks up to a level which was clearly marked 'fatal' simply because an authority figure told them to do so. In fact, no electric shocks were ever actually given although the volunteer 'teachers' believed that the learners were really receiving the shocks they administered. The photographs from the Milgram experiment show:

(a) The shock generator with 15 of the 30 switches already depressed.
(b) The learner being strapped into the chair and electrodes attached to his wrist. Electrode paste is applied by the experimenter. The learner provides answers by depressing switches that light up numbers on an answer board.
(c) The volunteer 'teacher' (experimental subject) receives a sample shock from the generator.
(d) Milgram's 'learner' pretending to receive a shock.

The main focus of this chapter is on the processes of group influence. Asch's earlier experiment had shown that it only needed one other person to agree with a deviant for the conformity effect to be counteracted. In one variation of his experiment, Milgram placed two of the experimenter's confederates alongside the real subject, so that the testing of the wired-out learner would be done by a group and not by the single subject. This experimental situation is thus similar to Asch's.

The experiment began with one of the confederates administering the shocks. He then refused to continue, argued with the experimenter and withdrew sitting in the corner of the room. The second confederate took over, continued for a bit and then refused just as the previous one had done. The real subject now remained to administer the shocks himself. Milgram repeated this procedure 40 times, each with a different subject. In 30 of these 40 cases, Milgram found that once the subjects had seen their group colleagues defy the experimenter, they also defied him. When group pressure (or support) for such defiance was lacking, only 14 subjects defied the authority figure. Milgram concluded that peer rebellion is a very powerful force in undercutting the experimenter's authority.

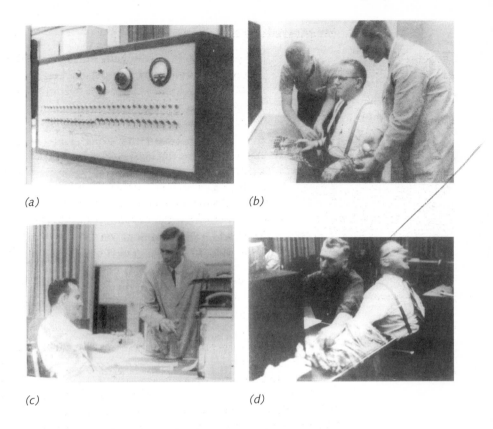

(a)

(b)

(c)

(d)

Milgram offered seven explanations of why the group was effective in helping the individual to do this. The reasons are the same as those which explain the power the group has over the individual:

1 Peers instil in the subject the idea of defying the experimenter.
2 The lone subject has no way of knowing if defiance is a bizarre or common occurrence. Two examples confirm that it is a natural reaction.
3 The act of defiance by the confederate defines the act of shocking as improper. It provides social confirmation for the subject's suspicion that it is wrong to punish a person against his will, even in a psychological experiment.
4 By remaining in the room, the confederates' presence carries with it a measure of social disapproval from the two confederates.
5 As long as the confederates participated in the experiment, there was dispersion of responsibility amongst group members for administering the shocks. As they withdrew, the responsibility focused on the subject.
6 The naive subject witnessed two instances of disobedience and observed that the consequences of defying the experimenter are minimal.
7 The experimenter's power is diminished by failing to keep the confederates in line.

Others have also suggested the effect of 'safety in numbers'. The Milgram experiments have provoked a great deal of controversy and discussion on subjects such as the ethics of research, problems of experimental design and application of findings. Along with the research conducted by Philip Zimbardo (to be discussed in Chapter 13), they have been used to explain the behaviour of Nazi SS guards

diagram showing the room layout of this experiment

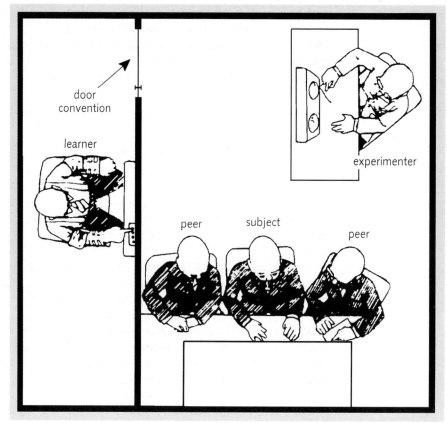

door convention

learner

experimenter

peer subject peer

from Milgram, S., 1979, *Obedience to authority*.

---

the power of the group in 1962

Lewis Yablonsky made a study of violent groups in New York City. Part of his study related to the structure of gangs. The following quotation from this study comes from a member of a group involved in the murder of Michael Farmer in 1959. Farmer was a partially crippled polio victim and, whilst walking home one evening through a park in central Manhattan, New York, he was set on by a gang of youths. They claimed membership of a gang called the Egyptian Kings. Some members felt that allegiance to the gang was such an overwhelming force that it superseded other, more normal values. From the transcript of the interview with these boys, the following extract is taken: 'I was watchin' him. I didn't wanna hit him at first. Then I kicked him twice. He was layin' on the ground lookin' up at us. I kicked him in the stomach. That was the least I could do, was kick 'im.' Another gang member questioned said he attacked the victim because he was afraid that the other members would 'get him later' if he did not swing out.

from Lewis Yablonsky, 1962, 'The violent gang as a near-group', in *The Violent Gang*, Macmillan, New York, p. 37.

in the concentration camps during the Second World War. When a person joins an existing group, he has an existing predisposition to accept the norms of the group. The group 'educates' him into its frame of reference and he is generally keen to learn. The new member's view on key matters are 'corrected' by the group members when these differ from those of the group.

---

the power of the group in 1989

Wilding – 'roaming in a gang looking for trouble'. New Yorkers were shocked by the mass rape of a 28-year-old, white, female investment banker who worked for Saloman Brothers. The woman left her Upper East Side apartment after 9.00 p.m. to jog through Central Park in the centre of Manhattan. At around 10.00 p.m., she was attacked by at least eight youths who were part of a larger gang that had been rampaging through the park. The youths beat the woman with their fists, a brick, a knife and a 12-inch lead pipe. Despite screaming and fighting, she was dragged 200 feet into a thicket where she was stripped, gagged and raped repeatedly. Caked in mud and bleeding profusely she was left for dead. Although used to violence, what shocked New Yorkers was the age of the attackers (between 14 and 17 years) and their casual attitude and lack of remorse after they had been arrested. The eight youths did not come from the Harlem ghetto. Most came from respectable homes, and half lived in a tower block complex which overlooked Central Park and where rents reached $500 per month. Analyzing the reasons for the attack, a newspaper concluded that their motives seem to have been linked more to the psychology of the mob and fear of backing down in front of their peers than to racism or hardship.

based on John Cassidy, 1989, 'New York reels from "Wilders" ', The Sunday Times, 30 April, p. 16.

---

assessment

It has been argued that the studies which have been carried out on the effects of the group on the individual have dealt inadequately with the internal group organization and have focused on the traits of individuals rather than on their personalities. Studying the effects that a group has on an individual is relatively straightforward. One places the person in a group and sees what happens. Do they behave differently compared with when they are alone? However, such research activity needs to be distinguished from that which considers the effect of group life on the individual's personality.

Personality is a dynamic entity with an internal structure. Only psychotherapy has addressed this problem adequately. To study the effects of a group upon an individual, we would have to make an analysis of all influences on that person which can result in their reacting in a vast number of different ways. Moreover, since personality is deemed to be a system, what happens in one part of it has consequences for other parts. Thus this is more complex than a mere stimulus–response sequence. When we seek to understand the interrelatedness of group and personality, we take on a much bigger job than merely noting the reactions of individuals. This perspective requires us to have a theory of personality on which to base our investigations.

The key role of the group resurfaced during the early 1990s within the context of the West's response to the Japanese industrial challenge. Many informed observers argued that among the critical success factors in Japan's superior economic performance was its group approach to work organization as compared to the individualistic approach of the countries of Western Europe. By the late 1990s, America and Europe had made up some of the ground it had lost, and was using teams much more effectively.

---

the Japanese group approach

Because performance is valued less for its own sake than for the sake of the group, it is easier for each member to accede to the will of the majority. Even Japanese industrialists, while possibly as strongly motivated by profit and self-interest as any others, pursue self-interest in the name of the collective interest. Japanese organizational charts show only collective units, not individual positions or titles or names. In identifying himself, a Japanese manager stresses his group identification rather than his personal job title or responsibilities. Loyalty to one's group is a most respected personal attribute – comparable to personal integrity in the West. The reality of everyday life is embodied in group routines and is reaffirmed through interactions with others. Individuals whose advancement is blocked, who have low aspirations or work commitments, often respond to group social recognition and sanctions and thus remain bound to the group norms. Work groups provide social bonds of great importance; Japanese don't want to be left out. When workers retire, they rarely miss their work, but invariably they miss their group.

from Richard T. Pascale and Anthony G. Athos, 1982, *The Art of Japanese Management*, Penguin Books, Harmondsworth, p. 127.

---

sources

Asch, S.E., 1951, 'Effects of group pressure upon the modification and distortion of judgements', in H. Guetzkow (ed.), *Groups, Leadership and Men*, Carnegie Press, New York, pp. 177–90.

Asch, S.E., 1952, *Social Psychology*, Prentice Hall, Englewood Cliffs, NJ.

Baron, R.S., 1986, 'Distinction-conflict theory: Progress and problems', in L. Berkowitz (ed.), *Advances in Experimental Social Psychology*, vol. 9, Academic Press, New York, pp. 1–40.

Berger, M., 1964, *The Arab World Today*, Doubleday & Co., Garden City, NY.

Cassidy, J., 1989, 'New York reels from "Wilders"', *The Sunday Times*, 30 April.

Deal, T.E. and Kennedy, A.A., 1988, *Corporate Cultures*, Penguin Books, Harmondsworth.

Economist, The, 1990, 'Japan's schools: Why can't little Taro think?', 21 April, pp. 23–4 and 26.

Ferris, G. and Rowland, K., 1983, 'Social facilitation effects on behavioural and perceptual task performance measures', *Group and Organizational Studies*, vol. 8, pp. 421–38.

Jones, E.E. and Gerrard, H.B., 1967, *Foundations of Social Psychology*, John Wiley, New York.

Jones, R., 1977, *No Substitute for Madness*, Zephyres, San Francisco.

Kapferer, B., 1970, 'Norms and the manipulation of relationships in a work context', in P. Worsley (ed.), *Modern Sociology*, Penguin Books, Harmondsworth.

Labor Education and Research Project, 1988, *Choosing Sides: Unions and the Team Concept*, Labor Notes, Detroit.

Lewin, K., 1958, 'Group decision and social change', in E.E. Maccoby, T. Newcomb and E.L. Hartley (eds.), *Readings in Social Psychology*, Holt, Rinehart and Winston, New York, 3rd edition.

Milgram, S., 1974, *Obedience to Authority*, Tavistock, London.

Pascale, R.T., 1985, 'The paradox of corporate culture: Reconciling ourselves to socialization', *California Management Review*, vol. 27, no. 2, pp. 26–7.

Pascale, R.T. and Athos, A.G., 1982, *The Art of Japanese Management*, Penguin Books, Harmondsworth.

Roethlisberger, F.J. and Dickson, W.J., 1964, *Management and the Worker*, John Wiley, New York.

Roy, D., 1952, 'Quota restriction and goldbricking in a machine ship', *American Journal of Sociology*, vol. 57, no. 5, pp. 427–42.

Roy, D., 1960, 'Banana time: job satisfaction and informal interaction', *Human Organization*, vol. 18, pp. 156–68.

Sherif, M., 1936, *The Psychology of Group Norms*, Harper & Row, New York.

Warr, P., 1973, *Psychology and Collective Bargaining*, Hutchinson, London.

Whyte, W.F., 1955, *The Organization Man*, Penguin Books, Harmondsworth.

Yablonsky, L., 1962, 'The violent gang as a near-group' in *The Violent Gang*, Macmillan, New York.

Zajonc, R.B., 1980, 'Compresence', in P.B. Paulus (ed.), *Psychology of Group Influence*, Erlbaum, Hillsdale, NJ, pp. 35–60.

Zimbardo, P.G. *et al.*, 1973, 'A pirandellian prison: The mind is a formidable jailor', *New York Times Magazine*, 8 April, pp. 38–60.

chapter 10 group effectiveness

illustration by Steven Appleby

concepts and learning objectives

In Chapter 1, organizations were defined as 'social arrangements for achieving controlled performance in pursuit of collective goals'. Organizations were seen as being concerned with performance in the pursuit of their goals and individuals and groups were tied to standards which were used to judge what was considered good, satisfactory or adequate. If we think of an organization as being a big group consisting of small groups, then organizational performance is the combination of the diverse group performances.

For this reason, a great deal of attention has been paid in the research and management training to increasing group effectiveness or 'teamwork'. Indeed, the earliest British and American studies on group behaviour which began in the 1920s addressed this very problem. The issue of group effectiveness centres on two fundamental questions. First, are groups more effective than individuals, and secondly, in what ways can groups be helped to be made more effective? The individual versus the group issue does not appear to have a single universal answer. The research indicates that to obtain an answer one needs to specify the task to be performed and the circumstances involved.

key concepts

- group effectiveness
- member satisfaction
- group cohesion
- synergy
- brainstorming
- risky-shift phenomenon
- groupthink
- group polarization
- quality circles

learning objectives

When you have read this chapter, you should be able to define those concepts in your own words, and you should also be able to:

1 Distinguish between the concept of group productivity and group satisfaction and relate them to group effectiveness.
2 Describe the elements of the Kretch, Crutchfield and Ballachey model of group functioning.
3 Evaluate critically the research literature on the relative superiority of group performance over individual performance.
4 Identify the positive and negative consequences of group cohesion.

The example of the pit team exemplifies Bowey and Connelly's (1977) suggestions about the type of situations which are most suitable for group working. These are:

1 When co-operative working is likely to produce a better end result (either in terms of speed, efficiency or quality according to which is most important) than working separately.

STOP!

Consider the following situation:

Two groups of workmen set out to build two comparable office blocks. One group takes two years to complete their block, but do so relatively uneventfully and then move on, as an experienced and cohesive workforce to tackle more demanding projects. The second group complete their block in only 15 months, but have to work under such pressure, that two are killed in accidents, five more are seriously injured, and the remainder are so exhausted and disgusted that to a man they subsequently take up market gardening.

Which of the two groups described is the more effective?

from Henri Tajfel and Colin Fraser, 1978, *Introduction to Social Psychology*, Penguin Books, Harmondsworth, pp. 218–19.

---

the 4.81-second tyre change

When the Grand Prix car flicks into the pits to collect fresh tyres, usually just before the half-way distance, it is time for the pit crew to take their brief place in the sun under the eyes of the packed grandstands and the TV cameras. These are the glamorous moments that compensate for the endless hard graft that goes into making a winning racing team. The dream tyre change is the result of constant practice. Every pit team has to work hard in order to achieve it. The rehearsals go on throughout the year. On one occasion, the Benneton Ford pit crew managed to change Michael Schumacher's tyres in 4.81 seconds. Other racing teams aim for under 6 seconds, and some teams achieve 4.3 seconds, although in non-race conditions. Allan Challis, the chief mechanic of Cannon Williams, said, 'Pit stops are a critical time for the lads. The pressure is really on.' The crew know well that a good tyre change can make all the difference between victory and defeat.

The quickness of the mechanics practically defeats the eye. Have you seen a tyre change on a Formula I car? How many mechanics were involved ? You're in for a surprise. The answer is 15. There are three men at each corner of the car; one with the wheel gun, another to remove the wheel and a third to put on the replacement. One mechanic operates the front jack, one the rear jack and the last man holds the crash hoop steady behind the driver's head to steady the car while it is on the jacks. In fact 16 people are needed for a successful tyre change, since the driver, streaking down the pit lane, has to stop no more than 6 to 12 inches in front of where the mechanics are positioned. Moving equipment wastes valuable tenths of seconds.

Curiously it is not a situation the pit crew really relish. It is fraught with the possibilities of a slip up; just one sticking wheel nut; just one man unable to fling arms up in the all-clear signal, and the race can be lost. To achieve systematically such a level of team performance requires a military operation with movement programmes carefully worked out well in advance. It is often not realized just how much effort and how many people are needed to get the top international racing drivers on to a Grand Prix grid.

---

2   When the amalgamation of work into joint task or area of responsibility would appear meaningful to those involved.

3   Where the joint task requires a mixture of different skills or specialisms.

4   Where the system requires fairly frequent adjustments in activities and in the co-ordination of activities.

5   Where competition between individuals leads to less effectiveness rather than more.

6   Where stress levels on individuals are too high for effective activity.

effectiveness, productivity and satisfaction

The concept of group effectiveness within the context of the organization presents a number of problems which need to be addressed at the outset of this discussion.

---

definition

Group effectiveness *refers to the adequacy of a group in performing its functions as an organized system and achieving its task-related objectives.*

Referring to the two groups of builders described in the STOP! box on p. 265, you may have decided that 'it all depends' which is the most effective. Clearly, one group was more productive and if you take a short-term perspective, then as far as their employer was concerned they were the more effective. However, if you look at the situation from the workers' point of view and take a longer-term perspective, the answer is different. From their point of view, and judging it in terms of the continuity of the group, the former group now appears to be the more effective. What this analysis shows is that when we talk about the effectiveness of the group, we need always to consider both group productivity, which refers to the external task achievement (e.g. building a house, solving a problem, making a decision), and group satisfaction, which refers to the internal aspects of the group. The criteria against which productivity and group satisfaction will be measured will be different in each case.

The individual will judge the performance of the group in terms of fulfilling his needs for friendship, developing or confirming his sense of identity, establishing and testing reality and increasing his security and sense of purpose. These are the goals that groups and individuals have. We can use the label *member satisfaction* to refer to the extent to which such internal group goals are achieved.

workers and management have different goals

from Ingram Pinn/TUC Education.

---
definition

Group satisfaction *refers to the extent to which a group satisfies the needs of its members and is successful in maintaining itself as a working unit.*

One can ask if group productivity and group satisfaction are correlated with each other. Is not a happy group also a productive one? This was certainly one of the conclusions drawn by managers from the studies at the Hawthorne plant. Observation of the women workers in the Relay Assembly Test Room led to the conclusion that the factor contributing most to the increases in output was not the change in the physical conditions at work, but the continually increasing cohesiveness and *esprit de corps* of the women workers. Mayo wrote that the satisfaction of social needs in face-to-face co-operative relationships with fellow workers should become a prime goal of enlightened management. Not only was it good for the soul in his view, but it was also good business sense since the policy was both humane and likely to increase productivity.

---

characteristics of effective groups

In his classic book *The Human Side of Enterprise*, Douglas McGregor, a professor of management at the Massachusetts Institute of Technology (MIT), listed eleven features which distinguished an effective task group from an ineffective one. These were:

1 An informal, relaxed atmosphere in the group which shows that members are involved and interested.
2 Full participation by all members in the discussion which remains focused upon the task.
3 Acceptance by all of the group objective.
4 Members listen to each other and are not afraid to make creative suggestions.
5 Disagreements are not swept under the carpet but fully discussed and either resolved or lived with.
6 Most decisions are reached by consensus.
7 Criticism is frank and frequent without degenerating into personal attacks.
8 People are free to express their feelings about both the task and the group's mode of operation in achieving that task.
9 Actions are clearly assigned to group members and are carried out by them.
10 Leadership within the group shifts from time to time and tends to be based on expert knowledge rather than on formal status or position.
11 The group is self-conscious about its own operation and regularly reviews the way it goes about its business.

It is unlikely that any one group would ever possess all of these characteristics. Most commonly, McGregor's list is used as either an audit of current group performance, or to set team-building objectives when newly-formed groups are being developed.

from Douglas McGregor, 1960, *The Human Side of Enterprise*, McGraw-Hill, New York, pp. 232–5.

The Hawthorne studies signalled the birth of the Human Relations school of management. In the eyes of some managers, this in essence involved, 'being nice to workers', and supervisors were sent on training courses which taught them leadership styles which would encourage this. It was not until some time had passed that people started to question this relationship between productivity and satisfaction. Perhaps it had been a fortuitous coincidence rather than some iron law. Sociologists who reviewed the findings and compared them with other data swung to the former explanation.

> ## STOP!
> Think about a group or team of which you are a member. Give it a 1 (= excellent) to 5 (= awful) rating on each of the eleven dimensions proposed by McGregor.

A great deal of research has been conducted into the working arrangements and conditions of employees, their attitudes to work, individual and group member satisfaction and group effectiveness or productivity. One way of looking at this work is to view it as an attempt to discover how one might seek to establish and maintain both high member satisfaction and group productivity. Research of this type has been done into work arrangements for the manufacture of motor cars, the composition and organization of coal mining teams and the introduction of new technology. It is no longer seen as simply a question of providing adequate financial incentives and specifying working methods (as Frederick Taylor would have argued) or of supervisors using a particular leadership style (as Elton Mayo might have seen it). Increasingly, economic, technological, social, psychological and organizational issues are being considered in parallel.

factors affecting group behaviour

A useful way of thinking about the influences on group productivity and satisfaction is provided by Kretch, Crutchfield and Ballachey (1962) and is set out in the following figure. These authors distinguish between three sets of variables which they label independent, intermediate and dependent. Some writers have also given them the title of givens, emergent processes and outcomes respectively. Whatever the label, the idea in each case is the same.

Science attempts to discover relationships between such things as smoking and cancer. Social science has tried to do the same by investigating the relationships between, for example, job satisfaction and productivity, The term used to describe job satisfaction and productivity in this context is variable. When a social scientist studies productivity, job satisfaction, group size, physical setting or the nature of the task to be performed by the group, he is studying variables. Such a study involves manipulating one variable to see what effect it has on other variables. For example, the researchers conducting the Relay Assembly Test Room experiments manipulated the strength of the illumination in the room to see what effect it had on the productivity of the women. In this example, they were studying the relationship between two variables: illumination and productivity. Because it

the Kretch, Crutchfield and Ballachey model of group functioning

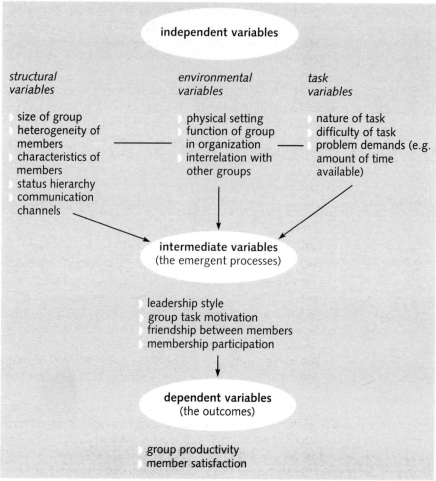

based on D. Kretch *et al.*, 1962, *The Individual in Society*, McGraw-Hill, New York. Reproduced with permission of The McGraw-Hill Companies.

was the illumination level which was changed or manipulated, illumination was the independent variable in the experiment. Since interest was focused upon what effect this had on productivity, this became the dependent variable.

It is possible for there to be a direct causal relationship between an independent variable, such as group size, and a dependent variable, such as member satisfaction. For example, it may be found that as group size increases, the members' satisfaction decreases. However, it is equally possible for an independent variable to cause a change in the dependent variable through an intermediate variable such as leadership style. Thus member satisfaction may be found to decrease (dependent variable) when group size increases (independent variable) and when the leadership style of the appointed leader is autocratic (intermediate variable). Such intermediate variables are also called 'emergent processes'. Let us now examine the Kretch, Crutchfield and Ballachey model. The given features of a group situation interact and lead to variations in emergent processes which in turn result in differences in outcomes. How might this work in practice? Take the example of a company which decides to establish a formal hierarchy in a plant with job titles which have a specific status position. Such a definition is intended to create a particular leadership style for those who occupy the positions.

However, once people begin to interact, differentiation will occur along the influence and leadership dimensions, irrespective of the pattern of communication prescribed by management. In reality, workers will organize their own communication pattern which is likely to be different from the formal one. The emergent processes will involve variations in group norms, task motivation and cohesiveness. All of these act to produce differences in the outcomes.

satisfaction → productivity?

The Kretch, Crutchfield and Ballachey model considers group productivity and member satisfaction as outcomes. A common conclusion drawn from the Hawthorne Studies was that a happy or satisfied worker was a productive one. Following these studies, many American companies adopted a paternalistic management strategy which emphasized a 'human relations approach'. In the three decades following 1930, there was a growth in training courses which taught supervisors about the needs of their workers; provisions were made for employee counselling; and company bowling teams and company picnics were organized. How valid were the findings upon which these actions were based?

During the 1950s and 1960s, many studies sought to discover a consistent relationship between worker satisfaction and productivity, but failed to do so. The research findings show a positive, albeit consistently low relationship between satisfaction and productivity. Other intervening variables have an effect when the employee's behaviour is not externally controlled (e.g. by a machine). It appears, therefore, that the company practices just described were based more on wishful thinking than upon any conclusive evidence.

Studies that have tried to establish this causal relationship have suggested that increased productivity may actually *lead* to increased worker job satisfaction (rather than the other way round!). If an employee is performing her work well, she will feel good about it. If the company then acknowledges her higher performance through verbal recognition, increased pay or promotion, then the rewards act to raise the level of job satisfaction.

making groups perform

Frequently in organizations there is no choice as to whether an individual or a group will perform a task. Legal, political, social and economic factors may dictate that a committee, a task force or some other group will carry out certain activities. The decisions and plans which guide large organizations are made by committees and groups. Organizations implicitly believe that the group is the best means by which to get managerial work done. Millions of pounds rest on the assumption that group decisions are in some way better than individual decisions. In such cases the key question to ask is, do groups perform better than individuals?

---

designing effective work teams

Richard Hackman argued that instead of just throwing people together and hoping that they will form a team, managers can take four conscious steps in order to increase the likelihood of effective team performance.

Step 1: pre-work
The manager identifies the task to be done and establishes the objective accordingly. Is this objective likely to be best achieved by a group, or by the individuals working separately on their own? Is creativity and commitment required, and in which of the two settings are these most likely to be achieved? If the answer is that a group is preferred, then the manager decides on the level of authority it should be given.

Step 2: creating performance conditions
The manager creates the appropriate performance conditions for the team. This involves ensuring that it has the necessary resources to allow it to do its job. These resources may be human (the appropriate people) and non-human (money, accommodation, information).

Step 3: forming and building a team
The three key steps here are: forming boundaries, that is, clarifying group membership; getting members to commit themselves to the task (a problem if they have different expectations); and clarifying expected behaviours, that is, management clarifying which team members will be responsible for which tasks.

Step 4: providing on-going help
In this phase, the manager helps the group to overcome its problems and achieve a high level of functioning. This may mean replacing certain 'non-contributing' members with others who are more productive, and by replenishing non-human resources.

Our knowledge of how a group develops through the forming, storming, norming and performing phases which were described earlier in Chapter 7, plus Belbin's research on group member roles introduced in Chapter 8, can together form the basis for the interventions. While managers may have to learn how to use work teams, Hackman noted that such an investment in learning would pay dividends in terms of improved team performance and team member satisfaction.

based on J. Richard Hackman, 1987, 'The design of work teams' in J.W. Lorsch (ed.), *Handbook of Organizational Behavior*, Prentice Hall, Englewood Cliffs, NJ, pp. 315–42.

The measurement of the performance of a group is the basis for the assessment of how well the group performs. In circumstances where there is some physical or countable task, such measurement is relatively straightforward. For example, the Hawthorne studies sought to relate changes in illumination and teabreaks to the number of relays completed by the women workers. With management teams such assessment is rare because the output of management-level groups has to use a much longer time-scale for evaluation. Moreover, their decisions are likely to be affected by numerous uncontrollable factors. For example, an investment decision made by a group in 1997 might only be judgeable in 2015, by which time it might have been affected by dramatic social, political or environmental factors. Social psychologists have in the main concentrated on laboratory studies of group behaviour, which they hoped would produce findings which could be generalized to the organizational context.

Research into the size of group, the heterogeneity of its members and their characteristics has been carried out, but it has not represented a major force in group studies. The identification of individual characteristics (especially aptitudes and abilities) for staff selection purposes has been more prevalent. Even in studies of leadership style, the attempt to focus on individual features through the identification of personality traits has now been superseded by more context specific approaches. So too with studies of group effectiveness. Individual characteristics have not been forgotten, but they are now incorporated into a broader context. Various approaches and techniques have been developed to enable groups to become more effective. Research has also identified the pitfalls which a group can experience and which reduces its performance.

group cohesion

Group cohesion is an important factor in keeping a group together and thus merits study when one considers group performance and member satisfaction. However, overall, does cohesion help or hinder group effectiveness? Group cohesion is sometimes more colloquially defined as the sum of all the factors influencing members to stay in the group. It is the result of the forces of attraction towards the group outweighing the forces of repulsion away from the group. How cohesive a group is can be judged by indicators such as whether members arrive on time, the degree of trust and support between them, and the amount of satisfaction they gain from their group membership. Various theories of group behaviour emphasize the social exchange idea whereby individuals make an evaluative judgement comparing what they contribute to the group with what they receive back from it in terms of satisfying their personal needs.

definition
Group cohesion *is that property which is inferred from the number and strength of mutual positive attitudes among members of the group.*
Lott and Lott (1965).

The model in the following figure shows a framework for understanding group cohesiveness in a little more detail. Box 1 lists the factors which contribute to a group becoming cohesive. Box 2 defines the state or level of cohesiveness, while box 3 details the possible positive and negative consequences on a group's effectiveness of a high level of cohesiveness.

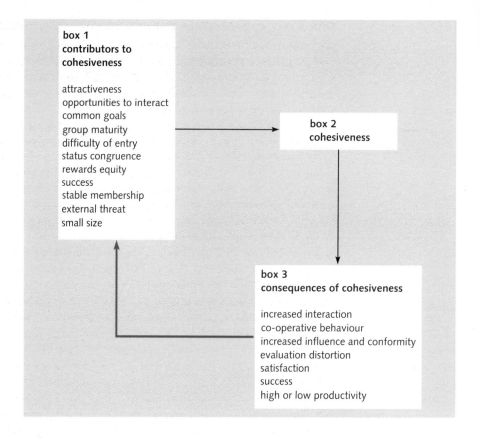

box 1: factors contributing to cohesiveness

> ▶ *Attractiveness of group*: such attraction may be due to meeting your social needs (joining with others like yourself), esteem needs (membership of an exclusive club) or some other need.

> ▶ *Opportunity to interact with all other members*: regular interaction with others leads to the development of strong emotional and social ties.

> ▶ *Members sharing common goals*: these draw the members together by encouraging them to work for one another.

> ▶ *Difficulty of entry to group*: the more difficult to enter, the higher the status the group will have for aspiring members who will gain an elitist feeling on joining.

> ▶ *Status congruence*: consensus among group members about the appropriate status hierarchy and group members behaving according to their status.

> ▶ *Equity of reward for members*: allocation of rewards on a basis that is perceived as fair by all.

> ▶ *Success of group*: the achievement of a meaningful shared goal.

> ▶ *Stable membership of group*: avoidance of change of membership which can disrupt interaction patterns and norms and lead to struggles over status.

> ▶ *External threat to group*: to its goals or interests can lead to members' forgetting their individual differences.

> ▶ *Small size*: permits more informality, interaction and participation, whilst discouraging sub-grouping.

box 3: consequences of group cohesion – positive aspects

As a group becomes more cohesive, its functioning is affected in a number of ways. First, the interaction and communication between members increases. Common goals, interests and small size all contribute to this. In addition, group member satisfaction increases as the group provides friendship and support against outside threats.

But what about management's need for a group to be productive? The relationship between cohesiveness and productivity is more complex than just saying a highly cohesive group is also highly productive. On the basis of the research evidence, Seashore (1954) concluded that when a cohesive group had goals and norms which were consistent with management expectations, productivity was high. In contrast, when its goals and norms were not consistent with management expectations, productivity was low.

This difference closely echoes the findings of Hawthorne studies. The women in the Relay Assembly Test Room had goals consistent with management's (high productivity); whilst the men in the Bank Wiring Observation Room had goals and norms which did not match the company's (restricted productivity). Moreover, Seashore also found that, as you would expect, highly cohesive groups influenced their individual members more (regardless of their productivity level) than low cohesive groups.

While acknowledging these problems, companies appear to consider high group cohesion to be a good thing. Members of cohesive groups appear to experience fewer work-related anxieties than those in non-cohesive work groups, and tend to be better 'adjusted' in the organization. They have higher rates of job satisfaction, lower rates of tension, absenteeism and labour turnover. This better adjustment comes partly from the psychological support provided by the group.

The evidence favouring group cohesion is so great that both at shopfloor and management levels, attempts continue to be made to design and maintain cohesive work teams. At the shopfloor level this may take the form of work redesign which produces new forms of team-based work organization, while at senior levels the same trend is manifested in the use of multi-function project teams and team-building approaches. Companies also frequently take care to ensure that the introduction of new technology does not result in the unanticipated destruction of existing cohesive groups.

productivity between and within high and low cohesive groups

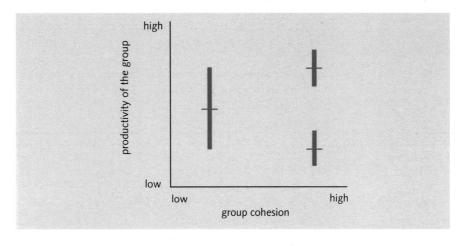

Over the years, and despite some expressions of doubt and caution, there has been an acceptance of the superiority of a cohesive group working over individual activity in organizations. This has been reflected in the promulgation of a number of concepts which are supported by their own training practices. Amongst the most popular of these have been synergy and brainstorming.

synergy

This is the view that a cohesive group is more than the sum of its parts. Jay Hall (1971) conducted a number of laboratory-based group ranking and prediction tasks to which there existed correct answers. The tasks included achieving a correct answer to a task called 'Lost on the Moon' where participants had to pretend they were stranded on the moon and had to choose from a set of supplies in order to survive. He studied the typical behaviours of the effective groups and the strategies of the groups which did poorly. The answers he found and the conclusions he came to related to the processes apparent in the group. He found that the effective groups actively looked for the points on which they disagreed, and in consequence encouraged conflicts among participants in the early stages of the discussion. In contrast, the ineffective groups felt a need to establish a common view quickly, used simple decision-making methods such as averaging, and focused on completing the task rather than on finding a solution they could agree on.

definition
Synergy *is the ability of the group to outperform even its best individual member.*

brainstorming

A second technique which asserts the superiority of a group's performance over that of an individual is that of brainstorming. Its effectiveness is partly attributed to the existence of a cohesive group working well together. Brainstorming was invented in 1939 by Alexander F. Osborn, a principal of the New York advertising agency Batten, Barton, Durstine and Osborn. Osborn coined the term to mean using the *brain* to *storm* a problem creatively. It is based on the belief that, under given conditions, a group of people working together will solve a problem more creatively than if the same people worked separately as individuals. The presence of a group is said to permit members to 'bounce ideas off each other', or gives individuals the chance to throw out half-baked ideas which other group members might turn into more practical suggestions.

definition
Brainstorming *is a technique in which all group members are encouraged to propose ideas spontaneously, without critiquing or censoring others' ideas. The alternative ideas so generated are not evaluated until all have been listed.*

Hall's group decision instructions

Jay Hall (1971) defined consensus as a decision process which made full use of the available resources, and which resolved conflicts creatively. On the basis of his studies, he identified the behaviours which characterized the effective teams, and presented these in the form of group-decision guidelines which could be used to achieve that consensus:

▶ Avoid arguing for your own rankings. Present your position as lucidly and logically as possible, but listen to other members' reactions and consider them carefully before you press your point.

▶ Do not assume that someone must win and someone must lose when discussion reaches a stalemate. Instead, look for the next most acceptable alternative for all parties.

▶ Do not change your mind simply to avoid conflict and to reach agreement and harmony. When agreement comes too quickly and easily, be suspicious. Explore the reasons and be sure everyone accepts the solution for basically similar or complementary reasons. Yield only to positions that have objective and logically sound foundations.

▶ Avoid conflict-reducing techniques such as majority voting, averages, coin-flips and bargaining. When a dissenting member finally agrees, don't feel that he must be rewarded by having his own way on some later point.

▶ Differences of opinion are natural and expected. Seek them out and try to involve everyone in the decision process. Disagreements can help the group's decision because with a wide range of information and opinions, there is a greater chance that the group will hit upon more adequate solutions.

from Jay Hall, 1971, 'Decisions, decisions, decisions', *Psychology Today*, November.

Alexander F. Osborn

Brainstorming contains four rules of procedure. First, the ideas generated by individuals must not be criticized. Second, no suggested ideas are to be rejected, irrespective of how fanciful or bizarre they may be. Third, the group seeks to produce as many ideas as possible. The stress is placed on the quantity of suggestions and not on their quality. The discussion of the ideas takes place at a later stage and thus the more ideas there are, the greater is the chance of finding a winner. Finally, participants are encouraged to 'hitch-hike', that is, to combine the ideas of others with their own to develop new ideas. The proponents of brainstorming argue that the flow of ideas in a group will trigger further ideas whereas the usual evaluative framework will tend to stifle the imagination.

A brainstorming group may often perform better than an individual who applies these rules to his own thought processes. However, if one has four individuals working alone, they can generally greatly outperform a group of four in terms of the number of ideas generated. Research has consistently shown that group brainstorming inhibits creative thinking. Taylor, Berry and Bloch (1958) carried out one of the earliest studies and compared the performance of brainstorming groups with 'pseudo-groups' (constructed by the experimenter from individual scores). The authors found that the brainstorming groups produced more ideas than individuals, that they produced more unique ideas and that the ideas were of better quality as judged by various criteria. However, when the brainstorming groups' performance was compared with that of the pseudo-groups, the pattern was reversed. The pseudo-groups were superior to the brainstorming groups on all criteria. The research demonstrated that the superiority of groups over individuals is simply the product of the greater number of man-hours they take up. Even under brainstorming instructions, the presence of others seems to inhibit rather than enhance the creativity of these *ad hoc* groups. It may be that brainstorming is most effective with established or specially trained groups.

In nine of the twelve studies that compared brainstorming groups with individuals working together independently under brainstorming instructions, the individuals produced more ideas (Lamm and Trommsdorf, 1973). Perhaps listening to others' ideas distracts group members, who fall into one-track thinking. Time limits have also been found to affect productivity. Groups that are allowed longer work periods usually produce more ideas under brainstorming instructions, continuing to produce up to the deadline, whereas individuals working for the equivalent time taper off towards the end (Shaw, 1971).

Brainstorming is based on two assumptions, both of which can be questioned. First, it assumes that people think most creatively when there are no obstacles to the stream of consciousness and that among this torrent of ideas (actually associations) there are bound to be some good ideas. Brainstorming presumes that solving problems is a matter of letting one's natural inclinations run free. Second, it associates the quantity of ideas with the quality of ideas.

---

how effective are brainstorming groups?

The inferiority of group brainstorming over individual thinking may be the result of group members being shy about offering unconventional ideas in the belief that, despite the rules, they will be evaluated anyway. Maginn and Harris conducted an experiment in which they studied 152 psychology students who were split into groups of four and were asked to brainstorm answers to two problems. The first problem concerned 'the benefits and difficulties that would arise if people had found that they had suddenly grown extra thumbs'. The second asked for 'ideas that if put into practice would reduce people's consumption of gasoline'. Some groups were told that their ideas would be assessed for quality and originality by the judges either observing from behind a one-way mirror, or listening to a tape recording. The other group were told that, although fellow students would be listening, their ideas would not be evaluated. The authors predicted that the groups facing evaluation would produce fewer ideas. The findings showed that the output of both sets of groups was similar. If groups brainstorm badly, therefore, it is not due to diffidence. Maginn and Harris concluded with the suggestion that individuals put less effort into a task when they share responsibility for the outcome with others. Unless this diminished responsibility effect can be overcome, individual brainstorming is best, if lonelier.

based on Barbara K. Maginn and Richard J. Harris, 1980, 'Effects of anticipated evaluation on individual brainstorming performance', *Journal of Applied Psychology*, vol. 65, no. 2, pp. 219–25.

creative group problem-solving: Le Meeting du Board

Chairman: Messieurs, welcome à ce board meeting de Flexi-Souvenirs et Cie Ltd.

Wilkins: Merci, Chairman.

Chairman: Shut up, Wilkins. Eh bien, comme vous êtes aware, nous avons un problème ginorme. Nous avons un stockroom qui contient (a) 2,000,000 mugs de Charles et Di. (b) 2,000,000 boîtes de thé Earl Gris, avec les likenesses de Charles et Di. (c) 2,000,000 boîtes de biscuits avec la couple heureuse ditto. Les souvenirs de mariage sont un drug sur le market. Nous sommes ruinés, si on ne peut pas les shifter.

Wilkins: Chairman, j'ai une idée brillante. Pourquoi pas incorporer le thé, les mugs et les biscuits en un *tea-time faites-le-vous-même kit!*

Chairman:Wilkins, vous êtes un idiot. Quelqu'un d'else?

Exécutif: Peut-on faire un dumping des souvenirs sur le 3ème Monde? Faire un deal avec Oxfam, peut-être?

Chairman: Hmm … possible.

2eme Exécutif: On peut les vendre comme props de théâtre pour les films, drames, etc.? Avec un setting de 1980, natch.

Chairman: Hmm … possible.

Wilkins: Est-ce que vous avez une suggestion, vous, Chairman?

Chairman: Wilkins, vous êtes un impudent. Regardez-le. Oui, en effet, j'ai une idée.

Tous: Mon Dieu! Terrif!

Chairman: Si nous faisons une extra inscription sur les souvenirs: SOUVENIR DE BÉBÉ ROYAL.

Tous: (silence).

Chairman: Vous n'approuvez pas?

1er Exécutif: Oh oui, Chairman, c'est une conception cosmique, mais c'est un peu … un peu … cheapo-cheapo.

Chairman: Oh, c'est comme, ça, eh? C'est un coup d'état? Un take-over bid?

1er Exécutif: Non, Chairman, mais …

Chairman: Regardez la compétition. Wedgwood a annoncé un pot de chambre royal. Hamleys ont annoncé une range de corgis qui disent Maman. Heinz va produire des boîtes de bébé food royal – venison, grouse, fillet de swan, etc. Et nous – QU'EST-CE QUE NOUS FAISONS?

Wilkins: Chairman, c'est un shot dans le noir, une idée du top de ma tête, mais – si nous vendions les mugs, biscuits et thé comme un tea-set de kiddy?

Chairman: Wilkins, Vous êtes un génie. C'est une idée de simplicité breathtaking. Avec un portrait de Papa et Maman sur le lid. Je l'aime!

Wilkins: Merci, Chairman.

Chairman: Shut up, Wilkins. C'est mon idée maintenant.

from Miles Kington, 1984, *Let's Parler Franglais One More Temps*, Penguin Books, Harmondsworth. © Robson Books Ltd.

The superiority of individual performance over group brainstorming is an example of how a taken-for-granted assumption can be disproved by social science research. Other studies have revealed that whilst groups are usually able to solve problems more effectively than individuals, they rarely do as well as their best member could do alone. This failure to achieve synergy has led to the devotion of much effort, especially in the area of applied social science.

consequences of group cohesion – negative aspects

Let us now turn to those aspects of group cohesion which can have a negative effect on group decision-making, and hence on group effectiveness. The two that will be considered are the phenomena of risky shift and groupthink.

risky shift

Social psychologists have documented the situation in which individuals in a group begin by taking a moderate stance on an issue related to a common value and then, after having discussed it, end up taking a more extreme stance. This tendency can lead to irrational and hence ineffective group performance. The groups involved may take a biased look at the problems they face and ignore important issues that conflict with its values. This phenomenon is referred to as the risky shift.

---

definitions

The **risky-shift phenomenon** *is the tendency of a group to make decisions that are riskier than those that the members of the group would have recommended individually.*

Group polarization *is when individuals in a group begin by taking a moderate stance on an issue related to a common value and, after having discussed it, end up taking a more extreme stance.*

In the 1950s, the conventional wisdom was that the decisions that groups made were typically cautious and conservative. Jokes about management by committee abounded. James Stoner, at that time a graduate business student at Massachusetts Institute of Technology, decided to test this assumption (Stoner, 1961). He carried out experiments to compare individual with group decisions which involved risk. The research questionnaire which Stoner used was devised by Wallach, Kogan and Bem (1962) and described twelve hypothetical risk situations. Two of these were:

- A man with a severe heart ailment must seriously curtail his customary way of life if he does not wish to undergo a delicate medical operation which might cure him completely or might prove fatal.
- An engaged couple must decide, in the face of recent arguments suggesting some sharp differences of opinions, whether or not to get married. Discussions with a marriage counsellor indicate that a happy marriage, while possible, would not be assured.

Stoner's findings revealed that groups of management students were willing to make decisions involving greater risks than their individual preferences. This counter-intuitive finding was supported by researchers using populations other than management students. This tendency for individuals in groups to take greater risks than the average of the pre-discussion decisions became known as the risky-shift phenomenon. A number of hypotheses have been put forward to account for this shift towards risk by the group.

Diffusion of responsibility hypothesis was the earliest explanation given. When a person makes a decision in a group situation, the responsibility for any failure which might result is assumed to be shared amongst the group members. Since each individual feels less of a personal responsibility for failure, the group consensus moves towards greater risk-taking.

Risk-lovers dominate hypothesis holds that risk-preferring individuals are dominant in any group and lead the other members to greater risk-taking.

Cultural value hypothesis states that in some cultures risk is valued and thus people in those cultures may hold boldness, courage and daring as things to be striven for. During a discussion in a risk-valuing culture, more arguments for risk-taking are likely to be produced.

Social comparison hypothesis. The questionnaire used is ambiguous and whilst a respondent may consider himself too cautious in some situations he is not used to thinking in terms of numerical probabilities (3 in 10). Being uncertain of the choice he makes individually he is pleased to have the chance to compare it with others. Seeing himself as average, he compares his score with another group member whom he also considers to be average. However, the group contains scores all along the range. On some items he argues for risk, on others for caution. The high risk-takers and the low risk-takers will also seek out suitable comparisons.

Even the earliest studies revealed that group decisions tended to shift slightly, but consistently, in the cautious direction on one or two of the hypothetical dilemmas (Wallach, Kogan and Bem, 1962). It has now become clear that group discussion leads to decisions that are not necessarily more risky, but that are more extreme than individual ones. So if group members are initially inclined to be risky on a particular issue, then the group as a whole will become more risky. If, in contrast, the group members are inclined to caution, the group as a whole will become more cautious. In consequence, the risky shift is now called *group polarization*, and over 300 studies of this effect exist (Myers and Lamm, 1976; Myers, 1990).

There are two explanations for group polarization. The first is called *informational influence* and relates to the group members learning new information and hearing novel arguments that relate to a decision. The more arguments that are produced that favour a position, the more likely that the group will move to that position. The bias enters because group members will present points which support the action they initially favour, and the group will discuss these. Discussion will thus be biased in the direction of the group's initial position, counter-arguments will be absent, and the group will polarize as more of its members become convinced (Stasser and Titus, 1985).

The second explanation is labelled *normative influence* and takes place when group members compare their own views with the norms of their group. They learn that others have similar or more extreme views than their own. If they want to be seen positively by the group, they conform to the group's position, or even take a more extreme view. Normative influence goes beyond the group pressure discussed in the previous chapter. The group provides its members with a frame of reference within which they can re-evaluate their initial positions. Both types of influence occur simultaneously in group discussions, with the informational effect being stronger than the normative (Isenberg, 1986).

STOP!

the risky-shift phenomenon: evaluating the evidence

Below is an item from the Choice Dilemma Questionnaire. Tick your own response, and then discuss it with three or four of your colleagues and agree a single group choice.

Mr E is president of a light metals corporation in the United States. The corporation is quite prosperous, and has strongly considered possibilities of business expansion by building an additional plant in a new location. The choice is between building a new plant in the United States where there would be a moderate return on the initial investment, or building a plant in a foreign country. Lower labour costs and easy access to raw materials in that country mean a much higher return on initial investment. On the other hand there is a history of political instability and revolution in the foreign country under consideration. In fact, the leader of a small minority party is committed to nationalization, that is, taking over all foreign investments.

Imagine you are advising Mr E. Listed below are several probabilities or odds of continued political stability in the foreign country under consideration. Please tick the lowest probability that you would consider acceptable for Mr E's corporation to build in that country. The chances that the foreign country will remain politically stable are:

            (✓)

1 in 10   ___
3 in 10   ___
5 in 10   ___
7 in 10   ___
9 in 10   ___

Please tick here if you think Mr E's corporation should not build a plant in the foreign country, no matter what the probabilities.

from N. Kogan and M. A. Wallach, 1967, 'Risk taking as a function of the situation, person and the group', in *New Directions in Psychology*, vol. III, Holt, Rinehart and Winston, New York, pp. 111–278.

Up until now the existence of the risky-shift phenomenon has been discussed as if we had accepted it unequivocally and only needed to understand its causes and effects. In fact, serious doubts have been cast on the findings. With two colleagues, read each of the seven objections that critics have made of this research and which are stated below. For each one in turn, decide whether it threatens the internal (I) or the external (E) validity of these research findings? Refer back to Chapter 2 if necessary.

▶ Risky-shift experiments are conducted on artificial leaderless   I   E
groups, the members of which have never met before.

▶ These artificial groups consist usually of five people and are asked   I   E
to decide on entirely hypothetical risk situations.

> Real organizational committees are longer-lasting, have an   I   E
> established leadership structure and deal with real decisions, which
> have real consequences for their members.

> In the risky-shift experiments, the magnitude of the shift to risk is   I   E
> small and by no means shown by all subjects.

> Researchers who have studied individual and group risk-taking,   I   E
> and who have used different research methods, have obtained
> less consistent findings.

> Studies which use Stoner's questionnaire reveal that on the same   I   E
> question there is sometimes a shift to risk and at other times a
> shift to caution.

> On two of the twelve risk situations presented, participants in   I   E
> groups regularly demonstrate a shift to caution. The overall
> risky-shift effect rests on the shifts shown on the other ten items.

groupthink

A second, potential negative consequence of group cohesion is groupthink. Irving Janis studied a number of American foreign policy 'disasters' such as the failure to anticipate the Japanese attack on Pearl Harbor (1941); the Bay of Pigs fiasco (1961) when the US administration sought to overthrow the Cuban government of Fidel Castro; and the prosecution of the Vietnam War (1964–67) by President Lyndon Johnson.

Studying these events, Janis argued that it was the cohesive nature of these important committees which made these decisions, and which prevented contradictory views being expressed. Janis listed the antecedent conditions and symptoms of groupthink, as well as the symptoms of defective decision-making that resulted from it. These are outlined in the figure on p. 284.

*Irving L. Janis
(1918–70)*

---
definition

Groupthink *is a mode of thinking that people engage in when they are deeply involved in a cohesive in-group, when the members' strivings for unanimity override their motivation to appraise realistically the alternative courses of action.*

based on Janis (1982, p. 8).

A number of symptoms of groupthink were identified. Amongst these were the illusion of invulnerability, there was excessive optimism and risk-taking. Rationalizations by the members of the group were used to discount warnings. Those who opposed the group were stereotyped as evil, weak or stupid. Janis found self-censorship by members of any deviation from the apparent group consensus. There was an illusion of unanimity in the group, with silence being interpreted as consent. Groupthink led to a failure by the group to solve its problems effectively. The group discussed a minimum number of alternatives; the courses of action favoured by the majority of the group were not re-examined from the view of hidden risks or other alternatives considered. The group failed to use the expert opinion that it had, and when expert opinion was evaluated, it was done with a selective bias which ignored any facts and opinions that did not support the group view. The findings of Solomon Asch's experiments into group pressure and conformity, which were described in the previous chapter, are obviously relevant here. In the groups studied by Janis, whilst individual doubt may have been suppressed and the illusion of group unanimity and cohesiveness maintained, the group paid a high price in terms of its effectiveness.

group cohesion and groupthink

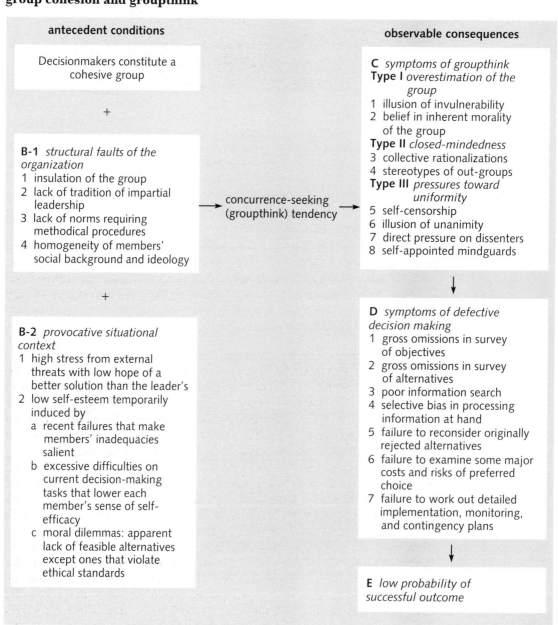

antecedent conditions

Decisionmakers constitute a cohesive group

+

B-1 *structural faults of the organization*
1 insulation of the group
2 lack of tradition of impartial leadership
3 lack of norms requiring methodical procedures
4 homogeneity of members' social background and ideology

+

B-2 *provocative situational context*
1 high stress from external threats with low hope of a better solution than the leader's
2 low self-esteem temporarily induced by
a recent failures that make members' inadequacies salient
b excessive difficulties on current decision-making tasks that lower each member's sense of self-efficacy
c moral dilemmas: apparent lack of feasible alternatives except ones that violate ethical standards

→ concurrence-seeking (groupthink) tendency →

observable consequences

C *symptoms of groupthink*
Type I *overestimation of the group*
1 illusion of invulnerability
2 belief in inherent morality of the group
Type II *closed-mindedness*
3 collective rationalizations
4 stereotypes of out-groups
Type III *pressures toward uniformity*
5 self-censorship
6 illusion of unanimity
7 direct pressure on dissenters
8 self-appointed mindguards

↓

D *symptoms of defective decision making*
1 gross omissions in survey of objectives
2 gross omissions in survey of alternatives
3 poor information search
4 selective bias in processing information at hand
5 failure to reconsider originally rejected alternatives
6 failure to examine some major costs and risks of preferred choice
7 failure to work out detailed implementation, monitoring, and contingency plans

↓

E *low probability of successful outcome*

from Janis, Irving, L. *Groupthink: Psychological Studies of Policy Decisions and Fiascos*, second edition. Copyright © 1982 by Houghton Mifflin Company. Adapted with permission.

"All those in favor say 'Aye.'"

    "Aye."   *"Aye."*   *"Aye."*

               "Aye."   *"Aye."*

Thus, while group cohesion can make a positive contribution to group productivity and satisfaction, it may also have negative consequences. The group loyalty instilled through cohesion can act to stifle the raising and questioning of controversial issues and thus lead to the making of bad decisions.

countering groupthink

At the heart of groupthink is the tendency for groups to seek concurrence and the illusion of unanimity. To prevent groupthink occurring, individuals who disagree with the group's evolving consensus must be willing to make their voices heard. In certain circumstances, a single individual can affect and even change a group's decision. In the film *Twelve Angry Men*, the character of the lone juror is played by Henry Fonda, and he manages to change the guilty votes of the other eleven jurors and persuades them to acquit the young defendant. The film is fictional, and its screenplay was written by Reginald Rose in 1957. However, in his portrayal, Fonda performs a number of actions which research in the 1980s has identified as being important for any minority take when seeking to influence a majority.

In the early part of the film, Fonda makes his objection clearly seen and heard by raising his hand to vote 'Not Guilty' and explaining his doubts to the other jurors, thereby forcing them to take notice of him. In so doing, he destroys the group's illusion of unanimity. Research has shown that a minority must create tension that will motivate the majority to deal with the former's ideas. Fonda creates tension by continuing to press his arguments and by being consistent in his stand, the latter being a persuasion prerequisite. Consistency means ensuring that one's statements and views match up with

---

groupthink and the space shuttle *Challenger* disaster

On 28 January 1986, 73 seconds after its launch from Cape Canaveral, Florida, the space shuttle *Challenger* exploded, killing all seven members of its crew, including a civilian schoolteacher, Christa MacAuliffe. The evidence suggested that the physical cause of the explosion was an O-ring rubber seal that failed to do its job, owing to the freezing overnight temperatures at the launchpad.

Photo credit: NASA

A presidential commission established to investigate the causes of the accident cited flawed decision-making as one of the causes of the disaster. The subsequent analysis of documents and testimony by researchers has led some of them to argue that the negative symptoms of groupthink increased in the 24 hours prior to the launch in the group, which consisted of Morton Thiokol, the builders of the rocket boosters, and NASA management personnel. Thiokol engineers argued for the cancellation of the launch because the O-rings would not withstand the pressure at the launch-time temperatures. The engineers were pressured by their bosses to stifle their dissent, and their opinions were devalued. The past record of success led to overconfidence, and various pieces of information were withheld from key individuals.

In consequence, the group failed to consider fully the alternatives; failed to evaluate the risks associated with their preferred course of action; used information that was biased when making their decision; and failed to work out a contingency plan. Although the physical cause of the disaster was an O-ring seal, many researchers claim that the actual cause was a flawed decision-making process which had been infected by groupthink.

based on J.K. Esser and J.S. Lindoerfer, 1989, 'Groupthink and the space shuttle *Challenger* accident', *Journal of Behavioural Decision Making*, vol. 2, pp. 167–77; and G. Moorhead, *et al.*, 'Group decision fiascos continue: space shuttle *Challenger*', *Human Relations*, vol. 44, no. 6, pp. 539–50.

---

one another. Finally, a minority needs to be firm and unyielding, implying that it is unwilling to back down in the face of group pressure.

When a minority makes itself noticed, creates tension and takes an uncompromising and consistent position, it can have a strong impact on a group, stopping the typical pattern of groupthink conformity. Throughout the remainder of the film, Fonda's character uses a variety of majority-influencing techniques which have been identified by social psychological research. The seven most popular ones will be described in Chapter 22 on power and politics (Mugby, 1982; Moscovici, 1983; Nemeth, 1986, and Huczynski, 1996).

from *Twelve Angry Men*, MGM/UA Communications Company, 1957.

assessment

At the factory floor level, there has been an implicit, if reluctant, acceptance that people working as members of a group or a team perform more effectively than if they are organized as individuals. In the 70-year period since the conclusion of the Hawthorne studies, the question of *team-working*, in its different guises, has never been off the organizational agenda. The labels have changed with the times: autonomous work groups, self-managing groups, self-regulating teams, quality-of-working-life teams, continuous improvement councils, quality circles, intrapreneurial groups, networking and empowered groups.

On the one hand, what makes team-working more attractive to employees than individual-working is the chance to co-operate with others, task variety, choice of work task or problem, responsibility to complete an operation and opportunity for diagnosis and problem-solving. These same features provide a motivational boost, and from management's perspective, produce higher productivity and more efficient problem-solving. On the other hand, teams require nurturing and developing if they are to perform, and there are numerous obstacles to their achieving such effectiveness. These include ingrained individualism and competitiveness; inappropriate team design for the set task; scapegoating of members; team isolation; too many teams; radical changes in a team's work environment; inadequate team communications; lack of inter-team integration; and traditional resistance to change. During 1996, for example, attempts by the management of the Royal Mail to introduce a form of team-working were resisted by the postal workers and their union, and resulted in a series of stoppages. Management's objective was to set up teams of ten, which would organize and approve matters such as annual leave arrangements and absences for bereavement, for their team members. Any one of these obstacles can derail an organization's attempt to establish team-based initiatives (*Bulletpoint*, 1995).

However, the main problem that managers face with respect to team- or group-working has always remained the same. When any work task is organized on a group rather than an individual basis, some part of the requirement to manage its completion transfers from the manager of the group to its members. This same process can be seen to occur at university where student coursework assessment can take the form of either an individual or a group project. In the case of the latter, students organize the task, divide up the job, allocate roles, and so on. In both cases, the manager or instructor loses a degree of control over the process, while the group and its members gain it. It is therefore not surprising that much of the discussion about team-working has taken place in the context of industrial democracy and worker participation or involvement literature.

The history of team-working experiments is one of a series of enthusiastic launches, widespread publicity, limited application in companies, followed by rapid decline. The last such endeavour was the quality circle (QC) movement (Collard and Dale, 1985; Russell and Dale, 1989) in which shopfloor workers joined together to solve work-related problems. QCs consist of a group of volunteer workers (usually between 8 and 12) who meet regularly (weekly or fortnightly) to identify and solve work problems. The problems addressed included obstacles to quality improvement, reduction of costs, improving working conditions and reducing accidents. Companies typically had a number of such QCs meeting on a regular basis, each in its own sphere of responsibility. In order to develop their problem-solving skills, circle members were trained in problem definition, brainstorming techniques, statistical process control and presentation and group working skills.

---

definition

Quality circles *are groups of workers who meet regularly to discuss the way work is performed in order to find new ways to increase performance.*

The first major application of QCs occurred at Rolls-Royce in Derby in 1978, and reached its peak in the mid-1980s, when at least 400 British companies were using circles (Legge, 1995). They went into decline thereafter, and by the start of the 1990s most companies had wound them up. The demise of the quality control groups, despite senior management's interest and support, suggests that there are some fundamental obstacles to the permanent and long-term establishment of team-working. Hill (1991a; 1991b) and Marchington (1994) suggested some of the causes of the collapse of quality circles, and these can be extended to explain why similar team-working experiments may also be doomed to ultimate failure. These authors emphasize the recalcitrance of junior and middle managers to these experiments, whose concerns can be listed under the four headings of control, redundancy, time and culture.

First, managers feared a loss of *control*. The quality circles and similar group working arrangements often created a second and parallel reporting structure to the traditional line of command, which managers felt was not in their interest. In the case of QCs, while being responsible for them, the managers had no authority over who joined them or what they discussed. Moreover, quality circle experiments exposed them to outside scrutiny.

The trouble with teams

Togetherness has its perils

PETER COOK, a British satirist who died on January 9th, loved to poke fun at British private schools and their cult of team spirit. But if you listened to management theorists, you would think that these schools had unwittingly stumbled upon the magic secret of business success. With teams all the rage, management theorists are earning fat fees by proffering advice on how to build them and how to inculcate team spirit.

At first sight, the virtues of teamwork look obvious. Teams make workers happier, by giving them the feeling that they are shaping their own jobs. They increase efficiency by eliminating layers of managers whose job was once to pass orders downwards. And, in principle, they enable a company to draw on the skills and imagination of a whole workforce, instead of relying on specialists to watch out for mistakes and suggest improvements.

Having started with corporate giants such as Toyota, Motorola, and General Electric, the fashion for teams has spread rapidly. A recent survey suggested that "cell manufacturing"—in which small groups of workers make entire products— is being experimented with at more than half of America's manufacturing plants. And teams are growing more powerful as well as more numerous. Their task was at first to execute decisions under the supervision of managers, not to make decisions. The current fashion, however, is for self-management.

Companies as different as Xerox (office equipment) and Johnsville Sausage (you guessed) are allowing teams to decide on everything from hiring and firing to organising the flow of work. At New United Motor Manufacturing, a joint venture run in Fremont, California, by General Motors and Toyota, teams of workers elect their own leaders and invent ways of improving quality and efficiency.

Hewlett-Packard, a computer maker, has gone even further in mixing the specialisms represented in single teams. Its teams bring together engineers, technical writers, marketing managers, lawyers, purchasing professionals and shop-floor workers. At Corning's ceramics plant in Erwin, New York, teams are fed business information so that they can understand how their plant is faring in the market. Informed workers, it is assumed, are less likely to make unreasonable wage demands.

Still, it would not surprise every in-

---

mate of a British private school to learn that teams are not always flawless ways to motivate and inspire people. Like many management fads, the one for teams is beginning to produce its trickle of disappointments. A.T. Kearney, a consultancy that continues to favour teams, found in a survey that nearly seven out of ten teams fail to produce the desired results.

A common error, says A.T. Kearney, is to create teams instead of taking more radical decisions. In many businesses it is

still more effective to automate work than to reorganise the workforce. A few years ago Sweden's Volvo was praised for introducing self-governing teams in its car factories in Kalmar and Uddevalla, in order to make the work more interesting. More interesting it duly became, but also so expensive that the company was forced to close the experimental plants and concentrate production at Gothenburg, on a traditional assembly line.

Even when creating teams really is the appropriate solution to a firm's problem, managers often make a hash of running them. A typical mistake is the failure to set clear objectives. Another is to introduce teams without changing the firm's pattern of appraisal and reward from an individual to a collective system. That can send the workforce fatally mixed signals: employees are expected on the one hand to pull together, on the other to compete for individual rewards.

Teamwork, moreover, costs money, the biggest additional expense being

---

training. Not unreasonably, members of supposedly "self-managing" teams start wondering how to manage. This gives birth to an epidemic of woolly courses on "conflict management" and "stress resolution". Meetings swallow time as "empowered" workers break off from the tedium of making things and chat endlessly instead about "process improvement" or "product imperfections".

Although many such courses are superfluous, advocates of team-based production concede that the best teams are made up of people with broad enough skills to step easily into each other's shoes. Providing such "cross-training", as the theorists call it, is arduous. In some of the more complicated team structures, such as those in chemical plants, it can take team members six to ten years to learn all the jobs they might be called upon to do.

The iron law of oligarchy

However, the chief problem with teams is political. Almost invariably, their creation undermines some existing distribution of power in a firm. Middle managers often see shop-floor teams as a threat to their authority, and perhaps to their livelihoods; many workers see teams as a source of division and a goad to overwork. On at least two occasions American unions have used the National Labour Relations Act of 1935 (which makes it unlawful for an employer to dominate or interfere with the formation or administration of a labour organisation) to foil attempts to introduce teamwork.

Besides, although the cheery vocabulary of teamwork makes excitable use of words such as "empowerment", teams usually replace top-down managerial control with peer pressure, a force that is sometimes no less coercive. "People try to meet the team's expectations," says one worker at New United Motor in Fremont, "and under peer pressure they end up pushing themselves too hard."

Some workers may prefer being told what to do to shouldering the burden of decisions themselves. Those who welcome responsibility sometimes find it hard to discipline their wayward colleagues. And there is always a danger that teams will impose a deadly uniformity and stifle the special qualities of individuals. As many a graduate of Britain's private schools will tell you, such places made little use of the brainy wimp who hated rugby and spent a childhood shivering on the sidelines. That, in a way, was Peter Cook's point, and one that management theorists have been slow to notice.

Second, among the managerial tasks transferred from supervisors to group members were scheduling, controlling and prioritizing. Such changes could have freed up managers' time to deal with higher-level issues. For example, the Rover Group attempted to shift responsibilities previously held by supervisors onto 'self-managing teams', but encountered difficulties. These included not only line managers' concerns about the loss of control already mentioned, but also fear about their own job security, and inexperience in supporting, coaching, and communicating with team members. Personnel staff were also concerned. Not having been trained in team-working, they too feared losing their power. When such experiments coincide with other changes, such as reductions in the number of levels in the company hierarchy ('de-layering'), many managers come to associate team-working with *redundancy*.

Third, almost by definition, team-working increases the *time* needed for decision-making. For example, the QCs had elaborate, inflexible and time-consuming procedures. Another team-working experiment, the matrix team structure, was attempted by the Digital Equipment Company (DEC). Here, workers in functions (e.g. marketing) simultaneously operated in product line teams, e.g. mini-computers. This was abandoned in 1994. The problem was the time required for the functional boss and the product boss to reach consensus. Lacking co-operation, 'turf-wars' ensued, and issues which should have been dealt with by team members were pushed up the organizational hierarchy and took a long time to resolve.

Finally, *culturally*, few middle managers were committed to the principle of participative management of their subordinates. Moreover, they did not see why participation should be extended downwards when they themselves did not have the same rights upwards. As Jaques (1994) pointed out, that culture was underpinned by existing legal and organizational practices. The introduction of team-working experiments has never done away with existing managerial hierarchies. Whatever the group-focused changes introduced, individual managers continued to be held responsible by their superiors for their subordinates' performance, irrespective of the work arrangements in operation. Hill (1991b) summarized the problem by saying that, 'In essence, circles disrupted managers' lives for small returns and created an organizational complexity that confused existing [organizational] structures, and middle management had no reason to make them work.'

Perhaps the most accurate assessment about the use of teams in organizations today is that the only thing more difficult than moving to and operating in teams is operating without them. Given the points made earlier, it is likely that the future will reflect the past. That is, we shall see a continuing series of group-working experiments which seek to release the motivational and creative contributions of their members, whilst at the same time retaining management's traditional form of authority and control over the group members as individuals. This inherent contradiction carries the seeds of its own destruction, and for this reason each experiment is likely to be short-lived.

sources

Bowey, A.M. and Connelly, R., 1977, *Application of the Concept of Group Working*, University of Strathclyde Business School, Glasgow, mimeo.

Buchanan, D.A., 1979, *The Development of Job Design Theories and Techniques*, Saxon House, Farnborough.

Buchanan, D.A. and Boddy, D., 1983, *Organizations in the Computer Age*, Gower, Aldershot.

Bulletpoint, 1995, 'The trouble with teams', August, pp. 1–3.

Cartwright, D., 1968, 'The nature of group cohesiveness' in D. Cartwright and D.A. Zander (eds.), *Group Dynamics: Research and Theory*, Harper & Row, New York, pp. 91–109.

Cohen, A.R., Fink, S.L., Gadon, H. and Willits, R.D., 1988, *Effective Behavior in Organizations*, Irwin, Homewood, IL, 4th edition.

Collard, R. and Dale, B., 1985, 'Quality circles: Why they break down and why they hold up', *Personnel Management*, February, pp. 28–31.

Collard, R. and Dale, B., 1989, 'Quality Circles' in K. Sisson (ed.), *Personnel Management in Britain*, Blackwell, Oxford, pp. 356–77.

Coon, A.M., 1957, 'Brainstorming: A creative problem-solving technique', *Journal of Communication*, vol. 7, pp. 111–18.

Hackman, J.R., 1987, 'The design of work teams', in J.W. Lorsch (ed.), *Handbook of Organizational Behavior*, Prentice Hall, Englewood Cliffs, NJ, pp. 315–42.

Hall, J., 1971, 'Decisions, decisions, decisions', *Psychology Today*, November.

Hill, S., 1991a, 'How do you manage a flexible firm? The total quality model', *Work, Employment and Society*, vol. 5, no. 3, pp. 397–415.

Hill, S. 1991b, 'Why quality circles failed but total quality management might succeed', *British Journal of Industrial Relations*, vol. 29, no. 4, pp. 541–68.

Huczynski, A.A., 1996, *Influencing within Organizations: Getting in, Rising up, Moving*, Prentice Hall, Hemel Hempstead.

Huczynski, A.A. and Fitzpatrick, M.J., 1989, *Managing Employee Absence for a Competitive Edge*, Pitman Publishing, London.

Isenberg, D.J., 1986, 'Group polarization: A critical review and meta-analysis', *Journal of Personality and Social Psychology*, vol. 50, pp. 1141–51.

Janis, I.L., 1982, *Victims of Group Think: A Psychological Study of Foreign Policy Decisions and Fiascos*, Houghton Mifflin, Boston, MA, 2nd edition.

Jaques, E., 1994, 'Managerial leadership: The key to good organization' in C. Mabey and P. Iles (eds.), *Managers Learning*, Routledge/Open University, London, pp. 181–7.

Kogan, N. and Wallach, M.A., 1967, 'Risk taking as a function of the situation, person and the group', in *New Directions in Psychology:* volume III, Holt, Rinehart and Winston, New York, pp. 111–278.

Kretch, D., Crutchfield, R.S. and Ballachey, E.L., 1962, *The Individual in Society*, McGraw-Hill, New York.

Lamm, H. and Trommsdorf, G., 1973, 'Group versus individual performance on tasks requiring ideational proficiency (brainstorming): A review', *European Journal of Social Psychology*, vol. 3, pp. 361–88.

Legge, K., 1995, *Human Resource Management: Rhetorics and Realities*, Macmillan, London.

Lott, A.J. and Lott, B.E., 1965, 'Group cohesiveness as interpersonal attraction: A review of relationships with antecedent and consequent variables', *Psychological Bulletin*, vol. 64, pp. 259–309.

Maginn, B.K. and Harris, R.J., 1980, 'Effects of anticipated evaluation on individual brainstorming performance', *Journal of Applied Psychology*, vol. 65, no. 2, pp. 219–25.

Marchington, M. , 1994, 'Job redesign', in C. Mabey and P. Iles (eds.), *Managers Learning*, Routledge/Open University, London, pp. 188–96.

McGregor, D., 1960, *The Human Side of Enterprise*, McGraw-Hill, New York.

Moscovici, S., 1983, 'Minority influence', in P.B. Paulus (ed.), *Basic Group Processes*, Springer-Verlag, New York, pp. 41–64.

Mugby, G. 1982, *The Power of Minorities*, Academic Press, London.

Myers, D.G.,1990, *Social Psychology*, McGraw-Hill, New York, 3rd edition.

Myers, D.G. and Lamm, H., 1976, 'The group polarization phenomenon', *Psychological Bulletin*, vol. 83, pp. 602–27.

Nemeth, C., 1986, 'Differential contributions of majority and minority influences', *Psychological Review*, vol. 93, pp. 23–32.

Russell, S. and Dale, B., 1989, *Quality Circles – A Broader Perspective*, Work Research Unit Occasional Paper no. 43, May.

Seashore, S.E., 1954, *Group Cohesiveness in the Industrial Work Group*, Survey Research Center, University of Michigan, Ann Arbor.

Shaw, M.E., 1971, *Group Dynamics*, McGraw-Hill, New York, pp. 72–3.

Stasser, G., Taylor, L.A. and Hanna, C., 1989, 'Information sampling in structured and unstructured discussion of three- and six-person groups', *Journal of Personality and Social Psychology*, vol. 57, pp. 67–78.

Stasser, G. and Titus, W., 1985, 'Pooling of unshared information in group decision-making; biased information sampling during discussion', *Journal of Personality and Social Psychology*, vol. 48, pp. 1467–78.

Stogdill, R.M., 1972, 'Group productivity, drive and cohesiveness', *Organizational Behaviour and Human Performance*, vol. 8, pp. 26–43.

Stoner, J.A.F., 1961, 'A comparison of group and individual decisions involving risk', quoted in R. Brown, 1965, *Social Psychology*, Free Press, New York.

Tajfel, H. and Fraser, C., 1978, *Introducing Social Psychology*, Penguin Books, Harmondsworth, 2nd edition.

Taylor, D., Berry, P.C. and Bloch, C.H., 1958, 'Does group participation when using brainstorming techniques facilitate or inhibit creative thinking?', *Administrative Science Quarterly*, vol. 3, pp. 23–47.

Wallach, M.A, Kogan, N. and Bem, D.J., 1962, 'Group influences on individual risk taking', *Journal of Abnormal and Social Psychology*, vol. 65, pp. 75–86.

Wallach, M.A., Kogan, N. and Bem, D.J., 1964, 'Diffusion of responsibility and level of risk-taking in groups', *Journal of Abnormal and Social Psychology*, vol. 68, pp. 263–74.

chapter 11 organization structure

source: New Library World (NLW), vol. 89, no. 1052, February, p. 39, 1988

concepts and learning objectives

At the start of the book, organizations were defined as social arrangements for achieving controlled performance in pursuit of collective goals. Moreover, organizational behaviour itself was defined as partly concerned with the study of an organization's structure. Derek Pugh and David Hickson (1968) noted that:

> All organizations have to make provision for continuing activities directed towards the achievement of aims. Regularities in activities such

295

as task allocation, supervision and coordination are developed. Such regularities constitute the organization's structure, and the fact that these activities can be arranged in various ways means that organizations can have differing structures.

key concepts

- organizational structure
- job definition
- job description
- organizational chart
- hierarchy
- span-of-control
- authority
- responsibility
- accountability

- line employees
- staff employees
- functional relationship
- formal organization
- informal organization
- departmentalization
- centralization
- decentralization
- matrix structure

learning objectives

Once you have read this chapter, you should be able to define those key concepts in your own words, and you also should be able to:

1 Explain how organizational structure affects human behaviour in organizations.
2 List the main elements of organizational structure.
3 Distinguish between job specialization and job definition.
4 Relate the concept of span-of-control to the shape of the organizational hierarchy.
5 Identify line, staff and functional relationships on an organizational chart.
6 Describe five different criteria on which jobs might be departmentalized.
7 Distinguish between the formal and informal organizations.
8 Evaluate the strengths and weaknesses of a matrix structure.

organization structure

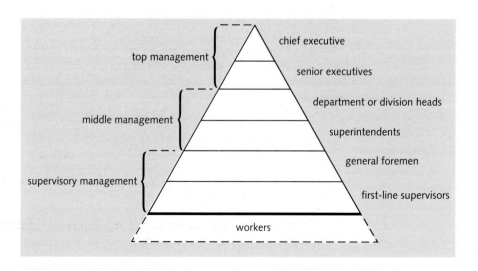

The structure of most large organizations in the twentieth century can be represented by a pyramid, as in the figure opposite. It shows that an organization has both a vertical and a horizontal dimension. Its broad base indicates that the vast majority of employees are located at the bottom, and are responsible for manufacturing the product or providing the service (e.g. making refrigerators, selling insurance). The formal system of task and reporting relationships co-ordinates, motivates and controls employees so that they work together to achieve organizational goals.

---

definition

Organization structure *is the system of arrangements, the pattern or network of relations, between the various positions and their holders.*

Each of the six successive levels above the workers represents a layer of management. On the left-hand side of the figure, the managerial ranks are divided into three groupings: supervisory or first-line management, middle management and senior or top management. The figure's right-hand side lists the commonly used job titles of managers who are members of each grouping. The layers also represent differences in status. While most people will recognize an organization structure, they are less clear about its purpose. Duncan (1979, p. 59) said that,

> Organization structure is more than boxes on a chart; it is a pattern of interactions and co-ordination that links the technology, tasks and human components of the organization to ensure that the organization accomplishes its purpose.

STOP!

The objective of organizational structure appears to differ depending on whether one is designing and managing it, or being managed within it. Compare Peter Drucker's definition of structure (view 1) with that of the Open University (view 2) that follows it:

view 1
'Structure is a means for attaining the objectives and goals of an organization.'

from Peter Drucker, 1974, 'New templates for today's organizations', in *Harvard Business Review*, January–February, p. 52.

view 2
Organization structure is 'the extent to which, and the ways in which, organization members are constrained and controlled by the organization and the distribution of activities and responsibilities and the organizational procedures and regulations'.

from D.T. 352, 1974, *People in Organizations*, Course Book, Open University Press, Milton Keynes, p. 61.

These two views refer to the perceived purpose of organizational structure. In what ways do they differ?

For Duncan, the purpose of a structure was twofold. First, it *facilitated the flow of information* within the company in order to reduce the uncertainty in decision-making, which was caused by information deficiency. Second, a structure *achieved effective co-ordination – integration* of the diverse activities occurring within the firm, integrating the actions of individuals, groups and departments, especially those which were interdependent, so that all became co-ordinated.

structural perspective

Sociologists claim that people's attitudes are shaped as much by the organizations in which they work as by their pre-existing personality variables. The constraints and demands of the job can dictate their behaviour. For this reason, it is impossible to explain the behaviour of people in organizations solely in terms of individual or group characteristics. Alan Fox (1966) has argued that, in seeking to make such explanations, 'the structural determinants of behaviour be included'.

It is not just a question of changing people's attitudes and behaviour by changing the structure of the organization in which they work. Transferring people from one part of the company to another involves moving them from one structural situation to another. Transferring a lecturer from the business studies department of a college to the management studies department, or a sales manager from headquarters to the regional office, can change their behaviour. The changes will be the result of the organizational setting in which these people now operate, for example in the work methods used, the types of communication system operated, the way that performance is judged, and so on. These are separate from any particular characteristic of the individual.

Fox's description stresses an important element in the structural view of organizations. He argued that attention should be paid to the roles that people play and not just to the personalities in these roles. Seeking to understand people's behaviour through their personality or motivation, and changing it with the use of social skills, tends to de-emphasize the structures within which organizational roles are played. Fox criticized analyses which did not take this dimension into account.

Cartoon by H. Martin

structural determinants of behaviour at work

The failure lies in the popular tendency amongst managers and the general public to exaggerate the importance of personalities, personal relationships, and personal leadership as determinants of behaviour. This often results in the wrong kinds of questions being asked and the wrong kinds of remedies being proposed. The so-called 'Human Relations' movement, in its more naive and simplified forms, could be taken to imply that the 'social skills' – or lack of them – of managers and supervisors were the main determinants of how subordinates behaved at work. Such views were highly acceptable to common sense, which is ever ready in this field to seek explanations in terms of personalities and personal relationships . . . The presumption thus created is that in any situation of difficulty, the way out lies through those involved choosing or being compelled to 'change their attitudes', or making a resolve to ensure that the situation works better in future, or exercising more 'inspired leadership' of a personal kind . . . the industrial behaviour of individuals and the relations between them are shaped not only by their being the son of people they are, but also by the technology with which they work, the structure of authority, communication and status within which they are located, the system of punishments, rewards and other management controls to which they are subjected, and the various other aspects of 'the structure of the situation'.

from Alan Fox, 1966, *Industrial Sociology and Industrial Relations*, Royal Commission on Trade Unions and Employers Associations, Research Papers 3, HMSO, London, p. 15.

STOP!

Test Fox's theory yourself by doing some personal research. When there is next a major conflict in the government, a management–union dispute, a boardroom row or something similar, read the newspapers and cut out examples of the journalistic explanations offered.

Analyze your cuttings and distinguish 'individualistic' explanations from 'structural' ones. Provide an interpretation of your findings.

There is a danger of taking the structural perspective to the extreme and ignoring the human element altogether. Some social scientists see individuals as playing only a minor role. Whilst acknowledging that it is people who do the work in companies, they consider their behaviour is determined by the organizational structure within which they operate. Other writers, especially those coming from a management background, tend to ignore the structural aspects of organizations altogether and prefer instead to focus on individual and group characteristics.

The structural approach, therefore, stresses the logical and rational elements of organizations and de-emphasizes people's preferences or feelings. It holds that if efficiency and effectiveness are to be achieved, then people need to adopt organizational plans as their own, and adapt to them as necessary. In contrast, the psychologistic approach argues that it is the internal (individual) factors that are the main determinants of human behaviour in organizations rather than external (structural) ones. Here, effectiveness is achieved if the employees are trained and motivated.

> **STOP!**
> Consider the behaviour of the lecturer teaching this course. Identify aspects of their behaviour which you like and do not like. Decide if these positive and negative behaviours are influenced by that person's personality or by the organizational structure within which they work.

elements of organizational structure

the structure of an organization signals the behaviour expected of its members

concerned with	involves	exemplified in
how the work of the organization is divided and assigned to individuals, groups and departments	▶ allocating tasks and responsibilities to individuals (e.g. how much choice they have about how they work)	▶ organization chart ▶ job descriptions ▶ establishing boards, committees and working parties
how the required co-ordination is achieved	▶ specifying and defining jobs ▶ designing the formal reporting relationships ▶ deciding on the number of levels in the hierarchy ▶ deciding on the span-of-control of each supervisor and manager	▶ rules, policies, procedures ▶ hierarchy ▶ goal clarification ▶ temporary task forces ▶ permanent project teams ▶ liaison roles ▶ integrator roles

Harold Leavitt has suggested that organizations can be viewed as complex systems which consist of four mutually interacting independent classes of variables: organizational objectives, company structure, technology used and people employed. All of these were affected by the firm's environment such as the economic, political or social situation. The differences in organization structure can be accounted for by the interactions of these elements.

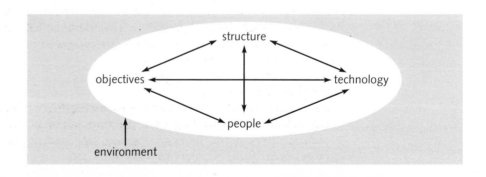

types of job

job specialization

An important series of decisions on organizational design relate to what types of job should be created. How narrow and specialized should these be? How should the work be divided and what should be the appropriate content of each person's job? The detailed answer will, of course, depend on the type of job considered. Is it the job of a nurse, engineer, car assembly worker, teacher or politician that is being designed? Certain general principles need to guide the design. Decisions here relate to the issue of *specialization*, by which is meant the narrowness of the work to be done by the individual.

Specialization is a feature of knowledge, clerical and manual jobs. After their general training doctors become paediatricians, whilst on the assembly-line some workers fit car tyres whilst others fix on the doors. The choice concerning the extent and type of specialization depends on criteria used by the organizational designer. These in turn will be affected by their values, beliefs and preferences. It may be a case of trading off efficiency of production against job satisfaction. A value position might be to seek to maximize both elements. Too rigid specialization can lead to demarcation disputes.

job definition

How well-defined ought a job to be? There is a school of management thought which argues that newly appointed staff ought to know exactly what their duties are in detail. They suggest that this high degree of definition (or specification) helps to motivate employees by letting them know exactly what is expected of them. Such detail can also assist in the appraising of their past performance.

---

definition

Job definition *is determining the task requirements of each job in the organization. It is the first decision in the process of organizing.*

Other commentators believe that, far from being motivating, a high level of job definition acts to control people's behaviour and sets minimum performance standards. What is needed, they argue, is for the employee to create their own job. In practice, a detailed job definition is provided to those doing low-level manual and clerical jobs, while at more senior levels there is a greater degree of own job-making. The physical manifestation of the choice about how much to define the job is the piece of paper on which is written the *job description*. A job description will usually contain the following information:

- job title and the department in which it is located
- job holder's position in the hierarchy
- to whom the job holder is responsible
- the objectives of the job
- duties required of the job holder (regular, periodical and optional)
- liaison with other workers, staff, supervisors and managers
- authority to carry out the task – the degree of freedom permitted to exercise own judgement in carrying out the job

---

definition

Job description *is a summary statement of what an individual should do, or actually does, on the job.*

The specialization of work activities and the consequent division of labour is a feature of all large complex organizations. Once tasks have been broken down (or 'differentiated') into sub-tasks, these are allocated to individuals in the form of jobs. Persons carrying out the jobs occupy positions in the organization's hierarchy. Particular levels of responsibility and authority are allocated to these positions. The division of labour and the relationship of one position to another is reflected in the organizational chart which can act as a guide to explain how the work of different people in the organization is co-ordinated and integrated.

---

part of a job description for a hospital catering manager

title:	Catering Manager
grade:	10
responsible to:	District Catering Manager
objectives:	To ensure the efficient management of all catering services for patients and staff at the hospital.
duties:	▶ Monitor and issue food to all departments. ▶ Organize and monitor kitchen work. ▶ Recruit and train catering staff. ▶ Menu planning within the framework of district policy.
responsibilities:	Responsible for the supervision of ten cooks.
liaison with:	Hospital Administrator, Senior Nursing Officer and other Heads of Department on day-to-day matters.
	Environmental Health Officer to maintain a high standard of hygiene and to ensure standards in accordance with the Health and Safety at Work Act.

The Job Description by Bertie Ramsbottom

I trod, where fools alone may tread,
To speak what's better left unsaid,
The day I asked my boss his view
On what I was supposed to do;

For, after two years in the task,
I thought it only right to ask,
In case I'd got it badly wrong,
Ad-hoc'ing as I went along.

He raised his desultory eyes,
And made no effort to disguise
That, what had caused my sudden whim,
Had equally occurred to him;

And thus did we embark upon
Our classic corporate contretemps,
To separate the fact from fiction,
Bedevilling my job description.

For first he asked me to construe
A list of things I really do;
While he – he promised – would prepare
A note of what he thought they were;
And, with the two, we'd take as well
The expert view from Personnel,
And thus eliminate the doubt
On what my job was all about.

But when the boss and I conflated
The tasks we'd separately stated,
The evidence became abundant
That one of us must be redundant;
For what I stated I was doing
He claimed himself to be pursuing,
While my role, on his definition,
Was way outside my recognition.

He called in Personnel to give,
A somewhat more definitive
Reply, but they, by way of answer,
Produced some vague extravaganza,
Depicting in a web of charts,
Descriptive and prescriptive parts,
Of tasks, the boss and I agree,
Can't possibly refer to me.

So, hanging limply as I am,
In limbo on the diagram,
Suspended by a dotted line
From functions that I thought were mine,
I feel it's maybe for the best
I made my innocent request;
I hopefully await their view
On which job of the three I do!

from *The Bottom Line: A Book of Business Ballads*, by Bertie Ramsbottom, Century Hutchinson Ltd, London.

Once specified and defined, the jobs and the authority and responsibility relations between them are represented on an organizational chart. Organizational charts graphically depict an organization's formal structure and are a universal feature of organizational life. Only their form and contents differ in line with the company being represented. Chandler (1988) wrote that the first modern chart was constructed in 1854 when Daniel McCallum became the general superintendent of the New York and Erie railway. At the time, it had 500 miles of track and was the world's largest. In order to co-ordinate the ever-increasing number of employees and equipment, McCallum needed a guide to indicate who reported to whom. The organizational chart provided this information and became a common feature of American companies by 1910. Possibly the earliest British chart was drawn up by Nobel Industries, and was based on the DuPont model.

---

definition

Organizational chart *is a pictorial record, which shows the formal relations which the company intends should prevail within it.*

Let us consider two organizational charts, since an examination of them can help to clarify some of the basic concepts associated with organization structure. Hierarchy refers to the number of levels of authority to be found in an organization. In a company with a *flat* organizational structure, only one level of hierarchy separates the managing director at the top from the employees at the bottom. In contrast, a company with a *tall* organizational structure has four levels in between the top and the employees at the bottom.

---

definition

Hierarchy *refers to the number of levels of authority to be found in an organization.*

---

flat organization structure

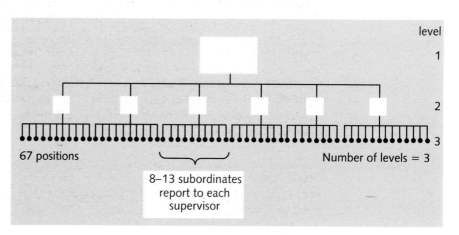

It is useful to distinguish between organizations which have many levels in their hierarchy, such as the armed forces, the police and the civil service (referred to as having a 'tall' hierarchy), and organizations which manage to operate with relatively few levels of hierarchy such as small businesses and universities (referred to as possessing a 'flat' hierarchy). The Catholic Church with its 800 million members, which has been in existence for over 1500 years, operates with five hierarchical layers – parish priest, bishop, archbishop, cardinal and pope.

tall organization structure

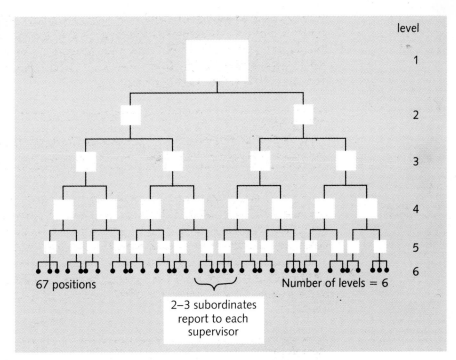

level

1

2

3

4

5

6

67 positions

Number of levels = 6

2–3 subordinates
report to each
supervisor

span-of-control

Span-of-control refers to the number of subordinates who report to a single supervisor or manager and for whose work that person is responsible. Comparing the two organizational charts, it can be seen that in the one with a flat hierarchy, there are many employees reporting to each supervisor. Hence, that person has a *broad* span-of-control. In a tall organizational structure, fewer employees report to each manager and hence the span-of-control of each of the managers is *narrow*. The larger the number of subordinates reporting to one manager, the more difficult it is for her to supervise and coordinate them effectively.

---
definition

Span-of-control *is the number of subordinates who report directly to a single manager/supervisor.*

Harold Koontz wrote that if an organization with 4000 employees broadened its span-of-control from 4-to-1 to 8-to-1, it could eliminate two hierarchical layers of management, which translates into nearly 800 managers. Robbins (1990) explained the simple arithmetic involved. The figure on page 307 shows an organization with 4096 workers at level 7 – the shopfloor. All the levels above this represent managerial positions. With a narrow span-of-control of 4-to-1, 1365 managers are needed (levels 1–6). However, with a broader 8-to-1 span-of-control, only 585 would be required (levels 1–4).

variations in organizational charting

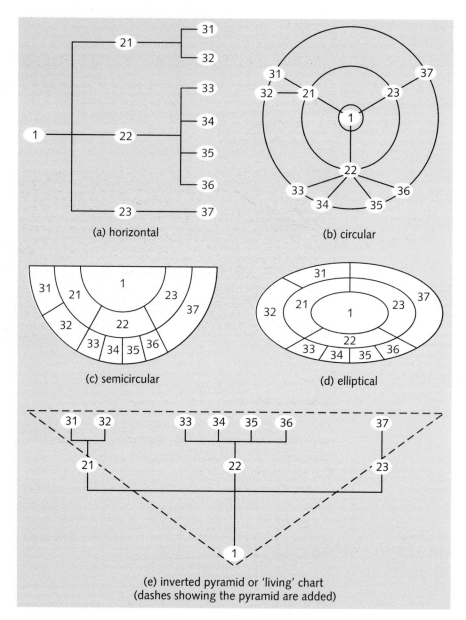

(a) horizontal

(b) circular

(c) semicircular

(d) elliptical

(e) inverted pyramid or 'living' chart
(dashes showing the pyramid are added)

The same organization is charted in five different ways. The functional departments (production, marketing, personnel, etc.) are numbered to permit an easier comparison between charts.

The concepts of span-of-control and hierarchy are closely related. The broader the span-of-control, the fewer the number of levels in the hierarchy. At each level, the contact between the manager and each of those reporting to him will be reduced. A supervisor responsible for eight operatives will have less contact with each operative than if she was responsible for only four. This broad span-of-control with few levels of hierarchy produces a flatter organization structure with fewer promotion

STOP!

telephone exchange in the 1930s, Perth, Scotland

The supervisor of the telephonists is shown standing in the middle of the photograph below. What is her span-of-control?

from Perth Museum, Scotland. Used with permission.

steps for employees to climb. However, it is likely that the communication between the levels will be improved as there are fewer of them for any message to pass through.

With a narrow span-of-control of one supervisor to four workers, the daily contact between the boss and her staff will be closer. This narrower span

**contrasting
spans-of-control**

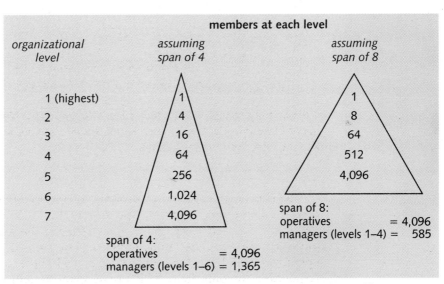

from Robbins, Stephen P., *Organizational Theory*, third edition, 1990. Reprinted by permission of Prentice-Hall, Inc., Upper Saddle River, NJ.

creates vertical differentiation and a taller hierarchy. Although it provides more steps in a career ladder for employees to rise through, communication tends to deteriorate as the message has to go through an ever-increasing number of layers both upwards and downwards. Because resources are always limited, they restrict the decision-making process.

Although flat hierarchies imply a broader span-of-control and fewer promotion opportunities, they also force managers to delegate their work effectively if they are not to be faced with an intolerable workload. Evidence suggests that individuals with high self-actualization needs prefer flat hierarchies, whilst those who emphasize security needs tend to gravitate towards organizations with tall hierarchies. Hierarchy is a co-ordinating and integrating device intended to bring together the activities of individuals, groups and departments, which were previously separated by the division of labour and function.

---

span-of-control in history

The span-of-control is an ancient concept. At the end of the second century BC, Caius Marius reorganized the Roman legions so that ultimately 28–30 legions reported to him. In the Old Testament, the Book of Exodus gives an account of the reorganization of the tribes of Israel using the principles of delegation and span-of-control.

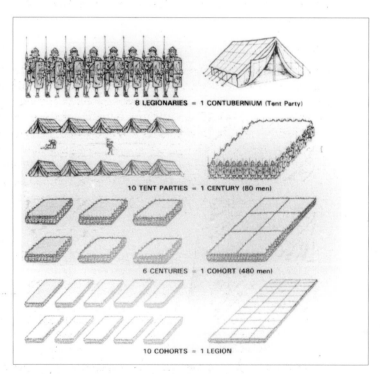

8 LEGIONARIES = 1 CONTUBERNIUM (Tent Party)

10 TENT PARTIES = 1 CENTURY (80 men)

6 CENTURIES = 1 COHORT (480 men)

10 COHORTS = 1 LEGION

based on D.D. Van Fleet and A.G. Bedeian, 1977, 'A history of the span of management', *Academy of Management Review*, July, pp. 356–72. Graphic with permission of The Grosvenor Museum, Chester.

line, staff and functional structures

Organization structures can be classified into three main types: *line*, *staff* and *functional*. The basic one, however, is the line structure, and this is a feature of every organization, irrespective of its size or simplicity. The staff and functional types are modifications of the line structure, which have been made necessary because of increased complexity of operation. These two other forms usually exist in combination with the line structure.

Before elaborating on the differences between these types of relationships, it is important to define the concepts of authority, responsibility and accountability, which will be used in this section. You cannot be held accountable for an action unless you are first given the authority to do it. In a situation where your boss delegates that authority to you, he or she remains responsible to senior management for your actions.

---

definitions

Authority *is the right to guide or direct the actions of others and extract from them responses which are appropriate to the attainment of an organization's goals.*

Responsibility *is an obligation placed on a person who occupies a certain position in an organization structure to perform a task, function or assignment.*

Accountability *is obligation of a subordinate to report back on their discharge of the responsibilities, which they have undertaken.*

---

line structure

A company's line structure consists of the direct vertical relationships which connect the positions at each level with those above and below. It is the series of superior–subordinate relationships which are collectively referred to as the organization's *chain-of-command*. Using the analogy of a river, the line relationships are the designated channels through which authority from its source at the top of the organizational pyramid flow, through the middle management ranks, passes down via the supervisors, to employees at the desk or on the factory floor. Every non-managerial employee has some authority within his job, which may be based on custom-and-practice or formally defined in their job description.

line structure

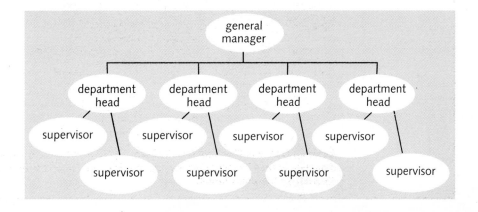

A line structure is possessed by every organization which has differentiated a leader and a follower group. Every individual in an organization reports to a 'superior' from whom he receives orders, instructions, help, approval and, not least, commands. That same superior has the authority to direct the activities of those in positions below on the same line. Thus in the organizational chart shown, the departmental manager has the authority to direct the activities of her supervisors. She in turn can be directed by the general

---

the nuclear button and the chain-of-command

After the end of the Second World War, and particularly at the height of the Cold War between NATO and the now defunct Soviet Union and its Warsaw Pact allies, there was always a debate about the circumstances under which the American president would 'push the nuclear button'. Of course, there is no physical button to push. The order for a nuclear attack is issued by the President and goes down the chain of command shown on the organizational chart below. If there is a button to be pushed, it will be by the commanding officer of the individual ballistic missile submarine.

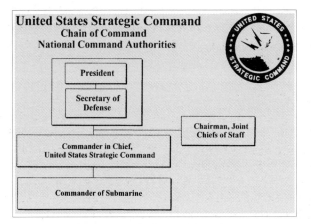

Among the responsibilities of the US Strategic Command (STRATCOM) under the direction of its field commander, is the preparation of forces for use should deterrence fail. STRATCOM's forces for fulfilling its deterrence mission include Minuteman III and Peacekeeper inter-continental ballistic missiles; C-4 and D-5 sea-launched ballistic missiles based on submarines; B-52H and B-1B bombers and other aircraft for battle management and electronic warfare.

STRATCOM's headquarters are located at Offutt Air Force Base in Nebraska, from where its Combat Operations Staff provides continuous manning of its underground command centre and airborne command posts. The Commander-in-Chief, United States Strategic Command (USSTRATCOM) is located in Omaha, Nebraska, and provides command and control for all US strategic nuclear forces for the Commander-in-Chief of the US military – the President of the United States.

from US Strategic Command (STRATCOM), 1993, Factfile, The United States Department of Defense, Department of the Navy, Pentagon, Washington, DC.

manager above her. All these people are in a line relationship with each other. Line relationships in a company are found within departments and functions. Line managers are responsible for everything that happens within their particular department.

---

definition

Line employees *are workers who are directly responsible for manufacturing goods or providing a service.*

Given the pyramidal nature of companies, the managers located towards the top of an organization are given authority to control more resources than those lower down. For this reason, the latter are forced to integrate their actions with those above them by having to ask their bosses to approve some of their actions. In this way, managerial control is exercised down through the organization.

The line structure is the oldest and most basic framework for an organization, and all other forms are modifications of it. It is indispensable if the efforts of employees are to be co-ordinated, since it provides channels for upward and downward communication, and links different parts of the company together with the ultimate source of authority. For this reason, organization designers have to ensure that its integrity and effectiveness are not impaired.

staff structure

As long as an organization is small and simple, and its leaders can exercise effective direction and control, then a line structure will be adequate. A line structure deals with a company's core task, which involves producing the basic good or service – manufacturing refrigerators or selling insurance. However, once a company becomes large and more complex, requiring perhaps an expert on personnel management, advertising or buying, then some modifications to its existing line structure will be required. These new activities support, but do not directly progress, the company's core task. In the way that an old man may lean on his walking stick or staff pole for support, so line managers can lean on their staff specialists for advice and guidance on technical matters.

---

definition

Staff employees *are workers who are in advisory positions and who use specialized expertise to support the production efforts of line employees.*

A firm creates a staff structure in one of two ways. A staff structure can be created by appointing an 'assistant to' an existing line manager. The manager delegates tasks and projects in the assistant's specialist area. The assistant has no authority of her own, but acts in the name of the line manager and with the line manager's authority. Because she is not in a line relationship, she does not constitute a level in the hierarchy.

organization structure showing a staff assistant

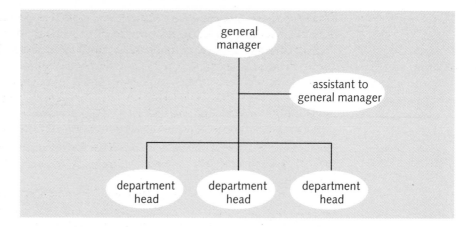

A second approach is to establish separate departments headed by staff specialists This is a modification of the basic line structure, and is referred to as a *line-and-staff-structure*. A staff department, such as market research, personnel, accounting, training, and so on, exists to aid the line structure managers in the areas or functions assigned to it. As with the 'assistant-to' example, the staff department performs its tasks through the line structure, and not independently of it. It does not have command authority over the other departments in the organization. Thus the personnel department cannot

---

line and staff in Frederick the Great's 'mechanized' army

Gareth Morgan (1986) wrote that Frederick the Great who ruled Prussia between 1740 and 1786 inherited an army which was more akin to an unruly mob. He modelled his forces upon the Roman legions and introduced mechanistic principles. Morgan wrote:

> In particular Frederick was fascinated by the workings of automated toys such as mechanical men, and in his quest to shape the army into a reliable and efficient instrument he introduced many reforms that actually served to reduce his soldiers to automata. Among these reforms was the introduction of ranks and uniforms, the extension and standardization of regulations, increased specialization of tasks, the use of standardized equipment, the creation of a command language, and systematic training which involved army drill. Frederick's aim was to shape the army into an efficient mechanism through means of standardized parts. Training procedures allowed these parts to be forged from almost any raw material, thus allowing the parts to be easily replaced when necessary, an essential characteristic of wartime operation. To ensure that his military machine operated on command, Frederick fostered the principle that men must be taught to fear their officers more than the enemy. And to ensure that the military machine was used as wisely as possible, he developed the distinction between advisory and command functions, freeing specialist advisors (staff) from the line of command to plan activities. In time, further refinements were introduced, including the idea of decentralized controls to create greater autonomy of parts in different combat situations.

from Gareth Morgan, 1986, *Images of Organization*, Sage, London, pp. 23–4.

direct shopfloor workers, even when dealing with a personnel problem. It has to work with the line manager of the shopfloor workers concerned.

Staff specialists, such as those in computing or industrial relations, are accountable to managers in the line structure. Within a staff structure, the members who constitute the staff departments can only plan for, recommend to, advise or assist other departments and their line managers, but they lack the authority to insist that their advice is taken.

Staff authority is always subordinate to line authority in a staff structure, and its purpose is to facilitate the activities being directed and controlled by the line structure. Of course, each staff department will have its own internal line structure.

Frederick Taylor's concept of functional foremanship included the idea of separating out from the work of foremen or supervisors all the planning and similar specialist activities, and assigning them to other supervisors who would specialize in this type of work. Although functional foremanship never caught on, the principle of such separation has resulted in the recruitment of staff specialists and establishment of departments from which they operate.

functional structure

A functional relationship exists when a specialist is designated to provide a service which the line manager is *compelled* to accept. This is the third type of organizational arrangement and is called a functional structure. The staff specialist's authority comes by delegation from a common superior. The general manager in the chart may decide that rather than have each piece of advice from the personnel or accounting staff cleared through her for onward transmission down to her departmental heads, it is more efficient for the personnel specialist to issue an instruction directly to the department head.

---
definition

A **functional relationship** *exists where a staff department has the authority to insist that the line manager implement its instructions concerning a particular issue.*

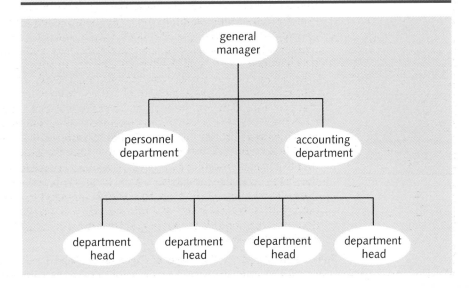

The functional specialist in their function, in this case personnel or accounting, remains accountable to the boss in whose name he issues the instructions. If the general manager requires functional assistance to be given to her subordinates in some area such as accounting, she has to delegate some of her own authority to the functional specialist concerned, and the organizational chart will look like that shown on page 313.

---

functional structure, Frederick Taylor and the Russian Revolution

It was noted earlier that the basic concept of functional structure was suggested by Frederick W. Taylor as a method of organizing the work of foremen. As the figure below shows, each operator thus reported to eight different bosses, each responsible for a different function or aspect of their work. The functional structure had two main problems. First, it meant that each employee reported to several superiors. Second, it became difficult to co-ordinate the eight separate functions. Thus functional structures, in the extreme form advocated by Taylor, were not generally adopted in the West.

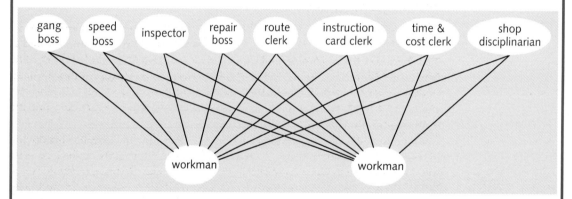

However, one place in which functional structures did catch on was in the newly formed Soviet Union just after the revolution in 1917. Lenin encouraged the study and application of Taylorism and numerous institutes were formed. In 1918 he approved the formation of the League for the Scientific Organization of Work (*Nauchnaya Organizatsiya Truda*) whose aim was to educate workers in the value of time-and-motion study and the notion of 'time thrift'.

However, it was the concept of functional foremanship which made the greatest impact. Since there were few ideologically trustworthy qualified engineers in the 1920s, a system of technical supervision was adopted that put authority in the hands of technical specialists, each of whom was responsible for a particular aspect of factory production. This functional system was admirably suited to a situation where management skills were scarce, and it enabled loyal specialists, who were untrained in management, to meet pressing production needs. Functional foremanship continued well into the 1930s. At that time it was found that it usurped the plant manager's authority and they changed to a line and staff structure.

from Daniel A. Wren, 1980, 'Scientific management in the USSR, with particular reference to the contribution of Walter N. Polakov', *Academy of Management Review*, vol. 5, no. 1, pp. 1–11.

STOP!

In Example 1, does the assistant have authority over and responsibility for the work of B and C? In Example 2, is it the manager or their assistant who exercises authority over B and C?

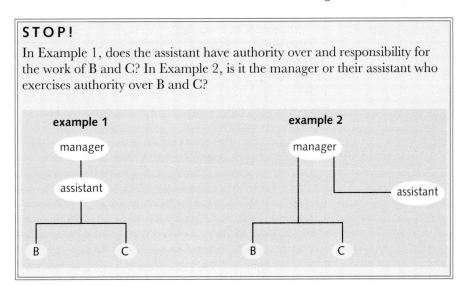

authority and position

The organizational chart shows the formal relationships which exist between positions or offices in an organization. The chart thus indicates positional authority, i.e. the authority to direct the activities of persons below in the line relationship based on the position which one occupies. Formal authority in an organization is assigned to positions and not to people. Formally, the private soldier in the army salutes the 'office' or position of the lieutenant, not the man or woman who happens to occupy it.

Position authority is distributed hierarchically in that persons occupying positions at upper levels in the organization have more power, and exercise more control, than those at successively lower levels. One of the functions of hierarchical authority is to provide predictability. The exercise of authority increases the probability of orderly, regularized behaviour. Authority relationships can be traced on an organizational chart by following the lines downwards. Responsibility relationships can be traced by following those same lines upwards.

STOP!

Explain the differences and relationships between the concepts of responsibility, authority and accountability.

Difficulties can arise when an individual has responsibility for some work, but lacks the concomitant authority. For example, the supervisor may be held responsible for the punctuality of his workers, but is not given the authority to discipline them over latecoming. The converse of this situation may also cause difficulties when a person is empowered to take decisions, but is not held responsible for what results. For example, decisions to appoint employees to a line job may be taken by personnel specialists rather than by the line manager.

---

wot no hierarchy?

The story goes that one morning a letter arrived at the Church of Scotland offices addressed to 'The Second Person of the Trinity', causing no small confusion . . .

There is no hierarchy in the kirk; all ministers are equal in rank. What there is is a Moderator, not of the Church of Scotland, but of the kirk's General Assembly, its supreme court . . . One great advantage of this is the absence of anti-kirk slogans; the aerosol tends to run out before you've completed 'the Moderator of the General Assembly of the Church of Scotland'.

This non-hierarchical structure in a non-established church means that ministers tend not to be intimidated by the Establishment . . . [The Moderator's role] is not to act as a spokesman but a chairman. There is a built-in control against the cult of personality, since he is in post for only a year. Indeed, virtually his sole distinguishing feature is that he gets dolled up in the most bizarre outfit. Kirk ministers are noted for the soberness of their uniform; black cassock and academic hood. The Moderator, however, wears 18th century court dress, complete with knee breeches and lace jabot. His duties involve wide-ranging visits at home and overseas, and the gear means he can be instantly identified in any transit lounge. People can then avoid him like the plague, or immediately latch on to him, as happens to doctors at parties.

from Olga Wojtas, 1989, *Times Higher Educational Supplement*, 2 June, p. 12.

STOP!
Starting with your own position in the organization, institution or college, indicate the different levels of hierarchy above and below you. Add in any other relationships (staff or functional) which clarify your position.

---

formal and informal organizations

Decisions about job descriptions, organizational charts, types of authority, and so on, all relate to designing the formal organization. However, to understand and explain the behaviour of people in an organization, it is necessary to become familiar with the informal organization. There are two main problems with organizational charts. First, they are static and do not show the ever-changing aspects of organizational life. Second, being depictions of how formal relations should prevail, they do not show the informal, social relations that actually do exist between company employees.

---

definitions

Formal organization *refers to the collection of work groups that have been consciously designed by senior management to maximize efficiency and achieve organizational goals.*

Informal organization *refers to the network of relationships that spontaneously establish themselves between members of the organization on the basis of their common interests and friendships.*

understanding and managing the informal organization

Informal organizations are the networks of relationships that employees form across functions and divisions. Using a case study approach, Krackhardt and Hanson studied how these operated in the banking industry. From a managerial viewpoint, such networks can be positive, cutting through reporting procedures, restarting stalled initiatives and meeting ambitious deadlines; or negative, sabotaging their goals by blocking communications and fermenting opposition to change.

The authors carried out a network analysis which consisted of a questionnaire which asked employees about who interacted with whom, about what. The results obtained were cross-checked to ensure a consensus of the group and then drawn onto a network map. This activity revealed three types of relationships: *advice* networks (who depends on whom to solve problems and provide information); *trust* networks (which employees share potential information and back each other in a crisis); and *communication* networks (which employees regularly talk to each other on work-related matters).

Such analyses can reveal the influence of the central figures in informal networks, who wields the power and how various coalitions function. For example, one bank's 80 per cent turnover of its tellers was not due to problems in its formal organization. Instead, the tellers had key informal relationships with others in the trust network, and when these people left the company, so did the tellers.

Krackhardt and Hanson recommend not only revealing the hidden aspects of the informal organization to address company problems, but also using it to implement solutions. For example, they analyzed the functioning of a bank's task force group which was failing to reveal progress. They found that whilst its leader held a central position in the advice network (many employees relying on him for technical advice), he had only one trust link with a colleague. Having understood the cause of the problem, senior management wanted to avoid labelling the group a failure or embarrassing a valued employee by dismissing him as team leader. Instead, it redesigned this task force in line with the natural grain of the informal organization. It added a person in the trust network to share responsibility for the group leadership role.

In a second example, the analysis of the informal communication structure of a bank branch showed that it had divided itself into two distinct cliques, with the tellers, loan officers and administrative staff distributing themselves between the two. Because of their different working times, the two clique cultures never clashed because they rarely interacted. In the end, it was customer complaints which stimulated the branch manager to unify the two groups and their cultures. He did this not by revamping the branch's formal structure, but by expanding the informal organization to integrate both groups. He intentionally mixed members of the two cliques on training courses; temporarily changed their work schedules so that members of one would interact with the other; substituted a member from the other clique where there was a staff absence; and scheduled meetings so that all staff could attend. The level of customer satisfaction rose.

Krackhardt and Hanson recommend that managers should revamp their formal organizational structures to allow the informal one to thrive. By letting the formal organization complement the informal, the latter can be made to help solve problems, improve performance and generally support the achievement of company goals.

based on David Krackhardt and Jeffrey R. Hanson, 1993, 'Informal networks: The company behind the chart', *Harvard Business Review*, July–August, pp. 104–11.

formal and informal organizations

The two figures below show the *same* set of workers and managers. The first depicts their formal relationships, as specified by senior management, and as depicted in the organizational chart. The second shows how these same people actually interact on a day-to-day basis. To obtain these data, the researcher would either have to observe the interactions of these people over a period of time, or ask them to complete a sociometric questionnaire which asks who they prefer working and socializing with.

formal organization

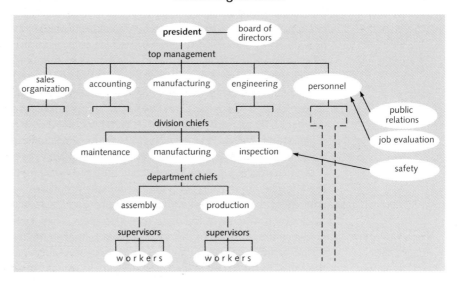

informal organization

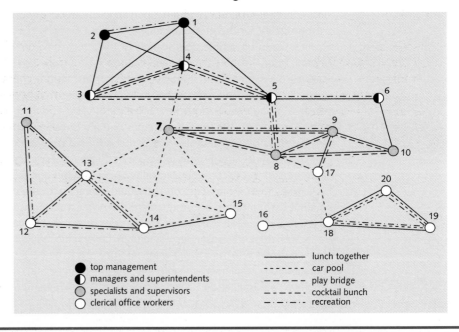

The key differences between the informal and the formal organization are shown in Gray and Starke's table.

formal and informal organizations

	formal organization	informal organization
A structure		
(a) origin	planned	spontaneous
(b) rationale	rational	emotional
(c) characteristics	stable	dynamic
B position terminology	job	role
C goals	profitability or service to society	member satisfaction
D influence		
(a) base	position	personality
(b) type	authority	power
(c) flow	top-down	bottom-up
E control mechanism	threat of firing or demotion	physical or social sanction (norms)
F communication		
(a) channels	formal channels	grapevine
(b) networks	well-defined, follow formal lines	poorly defined, cut across regular channels
G charting	organizational chart	sociogram
H miscellaneous		
(a) individuals included	▶ all individuals in work group	▶ only those 'acceptable'
(b) interpersonal relations	▶ prescribed by job description	▶ arise spontaneously
(c) leadership role	▶ assigned by organization	▶ result of membership
(d) basis for interaction	▶ functional duties or position	▶ personal characteristics status
(e) basis for attachment	▶ loyalty	▶ cohesiveness

adapted from *Organizational Behavior: Concepts and Applications*, fourth edition, by Gray, Jerry L. and Starke, Frederick A., © 1988. Adapted by permission of Prentice-Hall, Inc., Upper Saddle River, NJ.

designing organizational structure

There are many different types of organizations. They include businesses, hospital trusts, schools, local authorities, football clubs and trade unions. All of these have a purpose and hence a policy. Those who design them, or change their design, can be seen as attempting to translate that policy into practices, duties and functions which are allocated as specific tasks to individuals and groups. Different organizations will have different structures. These differences partly represent divergences between goals and policies of the enterprises concerned. The organizational structure that emerges results from the choices made about the division and grouping of tasks into functions, departments, sections and units.

departmentalization

Having decided on the degree of job specialization and job definition, there is the need to group the jobs into sections, place the sections into units, locate the units within departments and co-ordinate the departments. Thus job grouping or the 'departmentalization of jobs' constitutes a second major area of organizational design. Jobs can be grouped on several criteria, and usually an organization will use a mixture of such grouping criteria.

definition

Departmentalization *refers to the process of grouping together employees who share a common supervisor and resources, who are jointly responsible for performance and who tend to identify and collaborate with each other.*

function (e.g. marketing, engineering, production, finance)

Grouping of jobs based on the function which they perform. For example, the jobs in a manufacturing organization will be grouped according to production, marketing, sales, finance, and so on. In a hospital grouping will be physiotherapy, nursing, medical physics.

product or service (e.g. car insurance)

Traditionally, educational institutions are structured on the basis of the service. Thus the lecturers teaching management subjects in a university or college are all located in its business school. Within that school, they are further divided into subject specialisms (corporate strategy, quantitative methods, accounting).

customer (e.g. retail, wholesale)

Separate groups organized for different types of customers. Sales departments that sell in different markets.

geography or territory (e.g. Northern England, Scotland)

Such a grouping is used where the service is most economically provided by a limited distance.

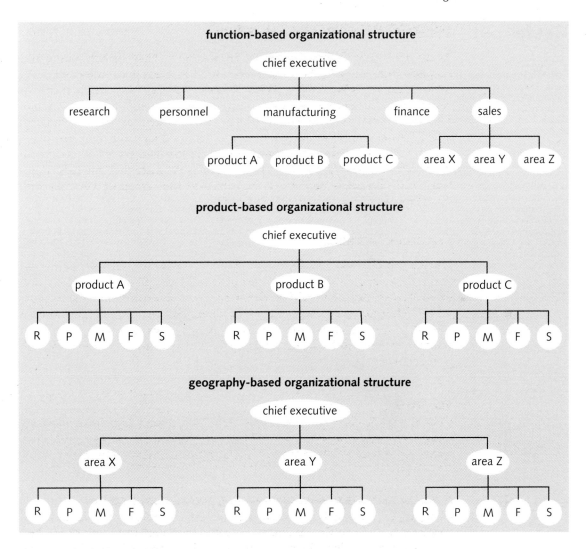

function-based organizational structure

chief executive

research | personnel | manufacturing | finance | sales

product A | product B | product C

area X | area Y | area Z

product-based organizational structure

chief executive

product A | product B | product C

R P M F S | R P M F S | R P M F S

geography-based organizational structure

chief executive

area X | area Y | area Z

R P M F S | R P M F S | R P M F S

time (e.g. shift, non-shift)
Hospitals and factories offering a 24-hour service or producing round the clock will have different groups for different shifts.

technology or equipment used (e.g. small batch, mass production, process)
The type of technology employed can be a criterion especially when several different types are used in a single plant. An organizational chart shows which type of grouping has been adopted.

matrix structure

The distinguishing feature of a matrix structure is that the employees within it report to two bosses rather than the traditional one. There is thus a dual rather than a single chain of command. This occurs because in a matrix, one type of structure has been superimposed upon another one. The matrix structure was developed in the late 1950s to cope with increasingly complex

Get fell out

GREAT moments of history usually wind up as bureaucratic reorganisations. The end of communism meant, among other things, that the North Atlantic Treaty Organisation (NATO) had to redesign itself. Once the Soviet threat had gone, it needed smaller armies, fewer weapons—and a slimmer organisation. Easier said than done.

NATO has always been a compromise between the militarily desirable and the politically possible. One consequence has been too many headquarters and too many staff officers. In the past this did not matter much. Most of the start-up costs were incurred during the hurried move in 1966-67, after de Gaulle had turfed the organisation out of France. Until recently running costs were only a tiny proportion of the alliance's European spending. But, now the armies are being cut, a big command organisation becomes a burden.

The alliance has now got most of its new organisation in place. Although smaller than the old one, it will still be much larger than it needs to be for the number of men under its command. For example, the alliance will still have two levels of authority below the overall European command; one would be plenty.

Perhaps the worst bit of the new organisation is the command known as Baltic Approaches. It is to be transferred from the old Northern region (which also included Norway and Denmark and was commanded, from Kolsas in Norway, by a Briton) to the Central region (the biggest command, run from Brunssum in Holland, by a German), but it will be dependent on a new North-Western region for naval operations. In short, it will have two superiors.

The old Northern region is replaced by the new North-Western region (encompassing Britain, Norway and the seas thereabouts), and the command is being moved from Kolsas to High Wycombe, in Britain. Kolsas will still be used by a subordinate command, but an entirely new headquarters is planned for High Wycombe, mainly because the Norwegians believe that using the existing buildings and equipment at High Wycombe would be a slur on the military importance of their country.

The expense and awkwardness of the present plan make it look, at best, a temporary arrangement. A second try would make more military sense, and could sharply reduce over-staffing.

One proposal being discussed by senior officers at NATO's headquarters would cut the number of large stationary headquarters to a bare minimum. The overall European command, plus the new North-Western command and the Central and Southern commands, ought to be enough. Their appendages could be disbanded or converted into mobile commands and put in appropriately portable (and, ideally, uncomfortable) quarters, with about half the present number of staff officers. That would be a reorganisation worth spending money on. Knock the bottom row off the chart.

Was complicated...

...still is

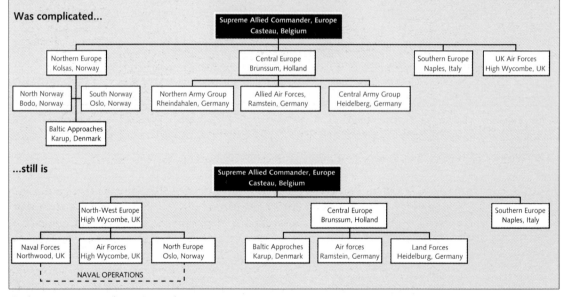

© *The Economist*, London (5 September 1992, p. 49).

technological problems and rates of change. Some writers discuss the matrix structure alongside line, staff and functional ones, while others treat it as yet another form of departmentalization.

Simon Ramo, the co-founder of TRW Inc. is credited with introducing the first matrix structure in 1957. As an aerospace company, TRW found that joint military–industrial projects, such as the manufacture of Minuteman, Atlas and Titan missile systems, could not be co-ordinated through the use of traditional functional or product departmental groupings. These projects were so complex that it was not possible to make a single manager responsible for their entire execution.

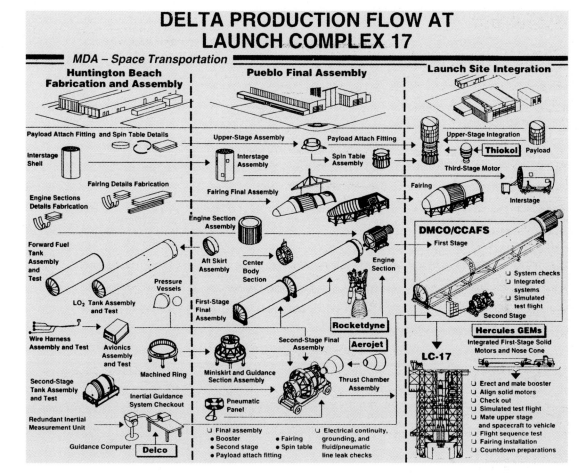

from Boeing/McDonnell Douglas Aerospace, Space Transportation Division, Huntington Beach, California.

The Delta Production flow graphically shows the elements that go into the manufacture of a McDonnell Douglas *Delta* rocket. It highlights the fact that, within the company, many different departments, facilities and people are involved. In addition, numerous outside subcontractors, such as Morton Thiokol, Rocketdyne, Aerojet and Delco, also play a part. Moreover, developments in technology affect those in different functions within the company. To build a rocket, a structural form is needed which blends together the technical expertise of people in different functions and organizations, working at different locations. The matrix form of structure has come to be adopted for the management of complex projects.

The most common type of matrix combination is departmentalization by product and by function simultaneously. Maybe your course is organized using such a structure. The following table shows a matrix structure within a university. The programmes or courses to be taught are listed along the top, whilst the academic departments in which the instructors are based are on the left-hand side. In the case of the aerospace example quoted earlier, the different projects or rockets to be manufactured (*Titan*, *Delta*) would be listed horizontally, while the company functions (engineering, marketing, research, testing) would be shown vertically.

example of a matrix structure for university course teaching

	products (educational programme)		
	director undergraduate programme	director masters programme	director doctoral programme
functions (academic)			
head: accounting department	A	B	C
head: economics department	D	E	
head: psychological department	F		

Notes:
A Department of Accounting lecturer teaching undergraduates.
B Professor of accounting teaching on a postgraduate programme.
C Senior lecturer from Economics Department teaching doctoral students.
D Economics lecturer teaching undergraduate students.
E Professor of economics teaching Masters degree students.
F Psychology lecturer teaching undergraduates.

---

definition

Matrix structure *is a type of organizational design that combines two different, traditional types of structure, usually a functional structure and a project structure, which results in an employee being part of both a functional department and a project team, and in consequence, having two reporting relationships.*

The matrix structure chart shows that the individual instructors report to two different bosses. One of these is responsible for the function, in this case the university academic department of accounting, economic or psychology. Their other 'boss' is the director of the product, in this example, the educational programme being provided – undergraduate, masters or doctoral. Both the heads of departments and the programme directors may in turn report to a common boss, who co-ordinates the activities of the academic functions and the educational programmes. This may be the dean of the faculty.

One consequence of having a matrix structure is that employees simultaneously belong to two different groups. Instructor D is both a member of the Economics Department group (with colleague E and others), whilst at the same time, she is a member of the undergraduate programme teaching group (with colleagues A and F). Instructor D reports to two superiors. Her permanent functional boss is the head of the Economics Department, and her temporary boss, as long as she contributes to undergraduate courses, is the director of the undergraduate programme. In industry, the latter is commonly referred to as the *project manager*.

Thus in every matrix there are three sets of unique relationships: (1) the top manager who balances the dual chains of command; (2) the directors of programmes and heads of functions, who share subordinates; (3) the specialist instructors who report simultaneously to their department head and programme director. Although the integration of product and function structures is the most common form of matrix organization, any two forms of departmentalization are capable of being combined, for example, product and geography.

Companies use matrix structures when they have to be responsive to two sectors simultaneously (e.g. technology and markets), when they face uncertainties that require information to be quickly exchanged between all those involved, and when they are strongly constrained by financial or human resources. The aim of the matrix structure is to gain the benefits of the two, previously separate structures.

There are at least three advantages of the matrix structural arrangement in the university example. First, it avoids the duplication of overhead costs, since existing academic departments provide the teaching input for the different programmes. Second, being a member of a teaching team, instructors from different academic departments and with different backgrounds can focus more directly on the course being delivered. Finally it leaves heads of department free to develop and deploy their academic staff members, whilst programme directors become responsible for delivering the teaching service to students.

STOP!

Can you think of any other advantages of the matrix structure for the university or the individual instructor concerned? What disadvantages might there be for those involved?

Douglas McGregor's Theory X and Theory Y

Douglas McGregor (1906–64)

McGregor (1960) argued that managers made assumptions about the people who worked for them, and that these could, collectively, be considered as two distinct, personal theories. He gave the label 'Theory X' to a set of assumptions which held that people were lazy, had goals that ran counter to the organization's, were not to be trusted, and needed to be closely supervised. In contrast, 'Theory Y' assumed that employees were mature, self-motivated, self-controlled, and needed little in the way of rigid interpersonal or organizational controls.

The assumptions that managers make about their employees – Theory X or Theory Y – will be reflected in the choices that they make about the aspects of organizational structure: how tightly to define jobs, to whom employees will report, how much authority they are given, the number of rules and procedures used, and so on. In this sense, it is possible to distinguish a Theory X from a Theory Y company structure, each of which embodies the values and beliefs of senior management about its workforce.

centralization and decentralization

Some senior company executives like to retain decision-making power in their own hands, and thus run highly centralized organizations. Others prefer to delegate their power and give more junior managers greater responsibility to make decisions. Their organizations are more decentralized in their structure. The question of whether and how much to centralize has been one of the major topics discussed in organizational structuring.

definitions

Centralization *refers to the concentration of authority and responsibility for decision-making power in the hands of managers at the top of an organization's hierarchy.*

Decentralization *refers to authority and responsibility for decision-making being dispersed more widely downwards and given to the operating units, branches and lower-level managers.*

centralization – pros and cons

The advantages and disadvantages of each approach have been widely considered, and are listed by Bedeian and Zammuto (1991, p. 139).

centralization
1 A greater uniformity in decisions is possible.
2 Top-level managers are more aware of an organization's future plans and are more likely to make decisions in its best interests.
3 Fewer skilled (and highly paid) managers are required.
4 Less extensive planning and reporting procedures are required.

decentralization
1 Lower-level decisions can be made more easily.
2 Lower-level management problems can be dealt with on the spot.
3 Lower-level managers have an opportunity to develop their decision-making skills.
4 The motivation of lower-level managers is greater when they are entrusted to make decisions rather than always following orders issued at higher level.
5 An organization's workload is spread so as to allow top-level managers more time for strategic planning.

Bedeian and Zammuto go on to argue that the balance between centralization and decentralization changes on an ongoing basis. It does so, in their view, in response to changes in company size, market opportunities, developments in new technology, and not least, the quality of existing decision-making. On the one hand, it is possible to observe decentralization increasing as companies in new and developing markets, such as Central and Eastern Europe and China, leave decisions for their managers. On the other hand, developments in new technology have meant that banks and building societies make increasingly centralized decisions, shedding thousands of staff

© United Feature Syndicate, Inc.

in the process. Somewhat more cynically, Jay (1970) argued that whichever of the two is currently the fashionable idea, it will be superseded by the other in due course. This may occur for no other reason than the incoming chief executive wishes to make a highly visible impact on his managers, employees, shareholders and City analysts.

assessment

This chapter began with a statement of the function that any structure fulfilled for a company. It then went on to describe its constituent elements and different forms. In predicting the likely shape that structures might take in the future, it is useful to consider two observations. The first of these is Duncan's view that the purpose of any structure is to provide an information flow that aids decision-making and integrates company activities. The second is Zuboff's (1995) contention that the information revolution will blur the distinctions between managers and non-managers, and will have a dramatic impact on an organization in terms of the role and status of its managers. Andreu *et al.* (1996) agree that:

> Any organizational structure answers the need to capture, record, process, structure, store, transform and access the information needed for a company to carry out its activities in the most competitive way possible.

They argue that the potential offered by new technology not only allows management to increase efficiency and accuracy, but more dramatically, to 'transform and reinvent' an organization, permitting it to meet competitive challenges with a more flexible structure. An organization structure contributes to company efficiency by making available whatever information is needed by any decision-maker. In the past, paper and people were used to do this. Lower-level employees were employed to collect information about sales, costs, staff, and so on, and to summarize and transmit them up the hierarchy for the decision-makers.

Andreu *et al.* point out that there have always been problems and significant costs associated with the sharing and the vertical transmission of such information along the hierarchy. One problem is ensuring that all employees gain a common and up-to-date understanding of any topic, for example, the company's competitive position. A cost is incurred when information from 'field activities' such as weekly sales is gathered and summarized, before being transmitted up. It is often incomplete and costly to collect.

Developments in computer hardware, distributed systems, telecommunications and software now allow any authorized person in a company to view the organization as if it had just one hierarchical level, and can provide that individual instantly with a comprehensive view of the whole business, or infinite details on any of its aspects, which they can then use to make a decision. Supermarket scanners at the checkout till provide a real-time update of shopping behaviour; while voice-mail, e-mail and document scanning allow data to be captured and made available in new ways to many different people. Some years ago, Drucker (1989) predicted that the 1990s would experience radical restructuring as information-based organizations required fewer levels as their control-and-command structures became unnecessary. This decade has seen Drucker's predictions come true as major companies in the telecommunications and financial sectors have shed jobs in their thousands. Many of the people made redundant used to collect, summarize and transmit information. Indeed, the very core business of banks is under attack by chain stores, supermarkets and software companies who see a bank as a 'computer network with a bit of confidentiality stuck on at the end'.

The technological developments open the possibility of moves in two directions. The greater *decentralization* scenario considers the case of the head office of a company with many plants or retail outlets, which previously had to collect information from these units, before making a decision based on their expertise and accumulated data. Now, technology allows such centralized data to be accessed at local level. Additionally, expert advice is available through e-mail and video-conferencing. In this scenario, the effect of new technology on organization structure is that decisions are made locally quickly.

Decentralization, currently referred to as *empowerment*, involves delegating decision-making to the lowest possible level of employees; providing them with the training to fulfil their new responsibilities; and providing them with incentives to communicate horizontally. In a decentralized organization, it is essential that one plant or department knows what another is doing, especially if they are interdependent.

The *centralization* scenario, in contrast, holds that new technology no longer makes it cost-effective for tasks to be performed or decisions made at local level. Thus, scanners at supermarket checkouts record which products are being sold and communicate that information to headquarters. The responsibility for reordering is thus taken away from the local manager, and made centrally on the basis of information provided. Requests for certain services from banks, such as standing orders, can be made at dedicated locations miles away from the customer's branch office. For the price of a local telephone call, advice or information from a central government agency can be given by someone located at the other end of the country, where wage costs and rents are lower. As Andreu *et al.* explain, 'IT enables [companies to adopt] organizational forms that would have been almost impossible some years ago. As new competitive challenges force organizations to be more creative with their organizational structures, IT will make their implementation possible'.

The link between technology, structure and control is important. IT can help to control organizational units that are geographically dispersed, whilst at the same time allowing them to be more autonomous and adaptable than in the past. This can be done without the need for traditional hierarchy or supervision, which in turn suggests flatter, leaner and more flexible organizational forms.

Despite the departure of armies of middle managers, co-ordination within the company is achieved by an information centre which detects problems, and alerts the remaining managers to matters requiring their attention. By linking monitoring to performance standards, a non-intrusive form of control is exercised. The typing speeds of secretaries can be monitored remotely, as can the number of 'closes' made by the supervisor of a telesales team. Some argue that recent technological developments have facilitated new, insidious forms of employee control. Andreu *et al.* (1996) conclude that, 'Who, when, and how to use IT [information technology] remain basic decisions that have to do with business strategy implementation.' One can add that managers always have such a strategic choice.

Zuboff (1995) takes the point further: 'the manager's role evolved as the guardian of the organization's centralized knowledge base. His legitimate authority derived from being credited as someone fit to receive, interpret and communicate orders based on the command of information'. Unlike automation of the past which hid operations from workers, the new technology illuminates them. Zuboff uses the term *informate* to highlight the fact that company knowledge can be surrendered to anyone with the skills to access and understand it.

In the context of employees, whereas earlier technology, such as Fordism, decreased the complexity of tasks, the new technology increases the intellectual content of work for employees at all levels. For Zuboff, the workplace comes to depend on workers' ability to understand, respond to, manage and create value from information. The implication is that to be an efficient, 'informated workplace', knowledge and authority have to be distributed more equitably than in the past, with more people knowing and doing more. For example, 'intranets' from within web browsers are being used to retrieve information from all sorts of databases including customer records and inventories. Some companies allow their staff to monitor their own pensions via the internet. Extending the same idea, Federal Express has hitched its database software to a website, and now provides its customers with the tools to track their packages in real time. New customers use whichever web browser reaches the website, and have guaranteed access to it. An average of 13,000 direct checks a day are now being made by customers themselves (*The Economist*, 1996). A major implication of these developments is that the managerial hierarchy that was so successful in the past will have to be dismantled and replaced with a form of information democracy. This in turn will have a major impact on management status and power.

What will the transformed and reinvented company structure of the future, stimulated by competitive forces and technological opportunities, look like? Buzz words like virtual corporation and the network organization abound. The most common prediction is a centre, linked by technology and involved in a multitude of partnerships and alliances at the individual, group and company levels. Handy (1996) suggested that the human resource formula for this type of organization would be $0.5 \times 2 \times 3$. That is, if a company wanted to be productive in the coming years, it should halve the number of its full-time employees at its core; pay them twice as much to retain the best staff; and expect them to produce three times as much added value. Moreover, it had to keep doing that. Already half the British workforce exists outside the organization, working in different forms of permanent, part-time work. For Handy, the future choice about structure is not about centralization or decentralization, but about a form of business federalism in which 'you can combine small and big, be centralised when it matters and yet be decentralised and different when it counts' (Handy, 1996, p. 17). The centre is small, but the power and excitement are in the bits.

sources

Andreu, R., Ricart, J.E. and Valor, J., 1996, 'IT and organization structure', *Financial Times*, 17 May, p. 16.

Bedeian, A.G. and Zammuto, R.F., 1991, *Organizations: Theory and Design*, Dryden Press, London.

Burns, T. and Stalker, G.M., 1966, *The Management of Innovation*, Tavistock, London.

Chandler, A.D., Jr, 1988, 'Origins of the organization chart', *Harvard Business Review*, vol. 66, no. 2, pp. 156–7.

Child, J., 1984, *Organization. A Guide to Problems and Practice*, Harper & Row, London, 2nd edition.

Davis, S.M. and Lawrence, P.R., 1978, 'Problems of matrix organizations', *Harvard Business Review*, May–June, vol. 56, no. 3, pp. 131–42.

Drucker, P.F., 1974, 'New templates for today's organizations', *Harvard Business Review*, January–February, pp. 45–65.

Drucker, P.F., 1989, 'The futures that have already happened', *The Economist*, 21 October, pp. 27–30.

Duncan, R., 1979, 'What is the right organizational structure?', *Organizational Dynamics*, Winter, pp. 59–80.

Economist, 1989, 'Reorganizing the organization', 29 July, p. 82.

Economist, 1996, 'Back to the garage: The software industry survey', 25 May, pp. 5–10.

Fox, A., 1966, *Industrial Sociology and Industrial Relations*, Royal Commission on Trade Unions and Employers Associations, Research Papers 3, HMSO, London.

Handy, C., 1996, 'The white stone: six choices: part 1', *Financial Times*, 17 May.

Jay, A., 1970, *Management and Machiavelli*, Penguin Books, Harmondsworth.

Koontz, H., 1966, 'Making theory situational: The span of management', *Journal of Management Studies*, October, p. 229.

McGregor, D., 1960, *The Human Side of Enterprise*, McGraw-Hill, New York.

Pugh, D.S. and Hickson, D.J., 1968, 'The comparative study of organizations', in D. Pym (ed.), *Industrial Society*, Penguin Books, Harmondsworth.

Robbins, S.P., 1990, *Organization Theory*, Prentice Hall, Englewood Cliffs, NJ.

Van Fleet, D.D. and Bedeian, A.G., 1977, 'A history of the span of management', *Academy of Management Review*, July, pp. 356–72.

Wojtas, O., 1989, Untitled, *Times Higher Educational Supplement*, 2 June, p. 12.

Zuboff, S., 1995, 'The emperor's new workplace', *Scientific American*, vol. 273, no. 3, pp. 162, 164.

chapter 12 scientific management

concepts and learning objectives

Only a handful of theories in the history of management thought can truly claim both to be revolutionary and to have had an enduring and world-wide impact on organizational practice. Scientific management is one of these. This chapter introduces Frederick Winslow Taylor and the principles that he developed, which came to be known as scientific management. It then goes on to describe developments of Taylor's original work, first by the Gilbreths and Henry Gantt, and then more dramatically by Henry Ford.

While acknowledging the importance of techniques and principles, the consideration of Taylorism is set within a broader context of rationalism, a philosophy which transcended political ideology and which was equally espoused by capitalist and communist societies. Rather than treating scientific management as an historical anachronism of a bygone era, the chapter shows how, as we approach the new millennium, scientific management is alive and well, and can be found in factories, offices and restaurants. This chapter is located within the section on organizational structures because scientific management had a dominating effect on the job content of workers, the pattern of their interactions with the technology, and their roles and relationships with one another and with management.

key concepts

- rationalism
- scientific management
- systematic soldiering
- functional foremanship
- mental revolution
- job simplification

- job specialization
- time and motion studies
- Fordism
- systems
- control

learning objectives

Once you have fully understood this chapter you should be able to define those concepts in your own words and be able to:

1 Describe the main characteristics of the scientific approach to management as expounded by Taylor, the Gilbreths, Gantt and Ford.
2 Understand how Fordism developed out of Taylorism.
3 Identify the model of man which underpins the scientific approach to management.
4 Evaluate the strengths and weaknesses of the scientific approach to management.
5 Recognize contemporary applications of scientific management principles and practices.

birth of scientific management

The scientific management movement arose during the first two decades of the twentieth century in the United States, and is remembered to this day, in terms of the 'time-and-motion study man'. It had a tremendous and lasting impact on organizational practices for the rest of the century, not only in America, but around the world. Its chief exponent was Frederick Winslow Taylor, whose methods were refined and extended by Frank and Lillian Gilbreth, and by Henry Gantt. Later, the original scientific management ideas were spectacularly developed by Henry Ford, who used them to build his system of mass production which still bears his name.

All these individuals shared a common belief in rationalism. This is the philosophy which holds that if one understands something, one should be able to state it explicitly and to write a law or rule for it. The consequence of developing and applying rules, laws and procedures is to replace uncertainty with predictability, both in the human and non-human spheres. The rational view of organization is one that will be revisited in Chapter 22 on power and politics.

Frederick Taylor's focus of attention was on the shopfloor worker, the design of the manual tasks that he performed and his motivation. As an approach to prescribing the appropriate organization structure, Taylorism focused on the concept of *task*. Taylor wrote that:

> The most prominent single element in modern scientific management is the task idea. The work of every workman is fully planned out by the management at least one day in advance, and each man receives in most cases complete written instructions, describing in detail the task which he is to accomplish, as well as the means to be used in doing the work. And

the work planned in advance in this way constitutes the task which is to be solved . . . This task specifies not only what is to be done but how it is to be done and the exact time allowed for doing it. (Taylor, 1911, p. 39)

As a designer of organization structures, Taylor's approach was 'bottom-up'. Having established principles for shopfloor workers, he went on to consider the question of appropriate supervision (functional foremanship) and the implications for senior management (Mental Revolution). In contrast, the perspective of other organization structure designers such as Max Weber and Henri Fayol was 'top-down'. They began by looking at an organization as a whole, from the perspective of top management. Their contributions will be considered in the chapters that follow.

---

definition

Rationalism *is the belief that the human mind can discover innate laws which govern the workings of the universe.*

The United States was undergoing a major and rapid industrialization at the turn of the century, and the creation, for the first time, of the large organization. Complex forms of organization were emerging, with new technologies of production and large workforces. Many of the large and well-known organizations of today, such as the Standard Oil Trust (Esso), United States Steel, General Motors and Ford were founded at this time.

The workers who were employed in these new factories came from agricultural regions of America, or were immigrants from Europe, who came seeking security and wealth in the new world. Directing the effort of workers with little knowledge of the English language, few job skills, and no experience of the disciplined work of a factory was a key organizational problem. Scientific management offered companies a way of meeting their technical, economic and social objectives in the early years of the twentieth century. Thus the first solutions to America's production problems came from engineers who recorded their experiences and their successes, and not from university professors or researchers. Taylor's writings are among the first attempts to introduce organizational practices which could be applied to companies in general.

The term *scientific management* was used during the hearings held by the US Interstate Commerce Commission. The railway companies had wanted to increase their charges for carrying freight, but their opponents argued that such increases would be unnecessary if they managed their railways more scientifically. Greater efficiency would save costs and obviate the need to raise charges. Taylor used the phrase in his book *The Principles of Scientific Management*, which was published in 1911 (Baird, Post and Mahon, 1990). Since Taylor and his followers were in broad agreement that the physical movements of workers could be regarded as akin to those of a machine, scientific management is also often referred to as *modern machine theory*.

---

definition

Scientific management *is a systematic method of determining the best way to do a job and specifying the skills needed to perform it.*

Frederick Winslow Taylor

*Frederick Winslow Taylor
(1856–1915)*

Taylor was born into a wealthy Quaker Philadelphia family in 1856 and became an apprentice machinist in a firm of engineers before joining the Midvale Steel Company in 1878, a company which manufactured locomotive wheels and axles. The ideas which were to form the basis of his 'scientific approach to management' were developed in this company in which he rose to the position of shop superintendent.

Taylor managed to increase production by reducing the variety of methods that were used by different workers. He was appalled by what he regarded as the inefficiency of industrial practice and set out to show how management and the workforce could mutually benefit by adopting his approach. His objectives were to achieve:

▶ *efficiency*, by increasing the output per worker and reducing deliberate 'underworking' by employees
▶ *standardization* of job performance, by dividing tasks up into small and closely specified sub-tasks
▶ *discipline*, by establishing hierarchical authority and introducing a system whereby all management's policy decisions could be implemented

In his role of supervisor, Taylor observed that few machinists ever worked at the speed of which they were capable. He labelled this practice *systematic soldiering*, and attributed it to a number of factors:

▶ The view amongst workmen that a material increase in the output of each man in the trade would have the end result of throwing a large number of men out of work.
▶ Poor management controls, which made it easy for each workman to work slowly, in order to protect his own best interests.
▶ The choice of methods of work was left entirely to the discretion of the workmen who wasted a large part of their efforts using inefficient and untested rules of thumb.

---

definition
Systematic soldiering *is the conscious and deliberate restriction of output by operators.*

To overcome these problems, Taylor made several proposals:

1 The task of planning a job should be given to management, and the task of doing it should be left to the workers.
2 Although Taylor was not clear in his use of the term 'scientific', he seemed to have meant the detailed and careful analysis of tasks and functions. Taylor aimed to standardize and simplify the job so that, where possible, a job was broken down into its elements, which were then distributed between several workers, each of whom performed one set of actions.
3 He recommended the scientific selection of the person to perform each task. This meant the selection of workers on the basis of their fitness for the job rather than on the basis of friendship or personal influence. We would nowadays take Taylor's suggestions on employee selection for

granted, but they were considered new and even revolutionary at that time.

4 Training the selected worker to carry out the carefully analyzed task in exactly the manner prescribed by management.

5 Monitoring of the worker to ensure that the work was carried out as specified. Taylor's motivational device was the piecework incentive system of pay. The more pieces the worker produced, the higher the pay that he received. Management's responsibility was to decide how much extra pay was needed.

Taylor's five principles of scientific management

1 a clear division of tasks and responsibilities between management and workers
2 use of scientific methods to determine the best way of doing a job
3 scientific selection of the person to do the newly designed job
4 the training of the selected worker to perform the job in the way specified
5 enthusiastic co-operation with the workers to ensure that the work was performed in accordance with scientific management principles and this was secured by use of economic incentives

---

Taylor's approach involved a detailed analysis of each work task. He chose routine, repetitive tasks performed by numerous operatives where study could save time and increase production. A wide range of variables was measured, such as size of tools, height of workers and type of material worked. Through his studies he tried to answer the question, 'How long should it take to do any particular job in the machine shop?' He wanted to replace rules of thumb with scientifically designed methods. Taylor experimented with different combinations of movement and method to reveal the one best way of performing any task.

the two stages of time study

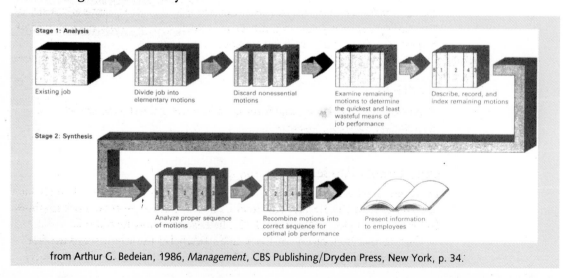

Stage 1: Analysis

Existing job → Divide job into elementary motions → Discard nonessential motions → Examine remaining motions to determine the quickest and least wasteful means of job performance → Describe, record, and index remaining motions

Stage 2: Synthesis

Analyze proper sequence of motions → Recombine motions into correct sequence for optimal job performance → Present information to employees

from Arthur G. Bedeian, 1986, *Management*, CBS Publishing/Dryden Press, New York, p. 34.

---

scientific approach to shovelling

1 Select suitable job for study, which has sufficient variety without being complex, which employs enough men to be worthwhile and would provide an object lesson to all when installed.
2 Select two good steady workers.
3 Time their actions.
4 Get them to use large shovels on heavy material. Total amount within a set time period is weighed and recorded.
5 Shovel size reduced so that weight of shovel-load is decreased, but total amount shovelled per day rises.
6 Determine best weight per shovel-load; identify correct size of shovel for all other materials handled.
7 Study actual movements of arms and legs.
8 Produce 'science of shovelling' which shows correct method for each material and amount which should be shovelled per day by a first class man.

---

functional foremanship

It is not only shopfloor workers who had their jobs fragmented. Taylor felt that every employee in an organization should be confined to a single function. He proposed a system called functional foremanship, which never became popular. The job of the general foreman was to be divided and distributed amongst eight separate individuals. Each of these would oversee a separate function of the work, and would be called:

1 inspector
2 order of work and route clerk
3 time and cost clerk
4 shop disciplinarian
5 gang boss
6 speed boss
7 repair boss
8 instruction card clerk

---

definition

Functional foremanship *was an approach devised by Frederick Taylor in which the job of the general foreman was divided into its constituent parts. Each of the main parts was given to a different individual who would oversee and be responsible for that aspect of a worker's job.*

STOP!

Why do you think functional foremanship never gained widespread popularity? List your reasons.

---

experiments in scientific management

In 1898, Taylor was hired by the Bethlehem Steel Company (which later became part of the Bethlehem Steel Corporation) to improve work methods. In his book (Taylor, 1911, pp. 41–7), he describes how he did this:

> One of the first pieces of work undertaken by us, when we started to introduce scientific management into the Bethlehem Steel Company,

from Bethlehem Steel Corporation, Pennsylvania.

was to handle pig iron on task work. The opening of the Spanish War found some 80,000 tons of pig iron placed in small piles in an open field adjoining the works. Prices for pig iron had been so low that it could not be sold at profit. With the opening of the Spanish War, the price of pig iron rose, and this large accumulation of iron was sold. This gave us a good opportunity to show the workmen, as well as the owners and managers of the works, on a fairly large scale, the advantages of task work over the old fashioned day work and piece work, in doing a very elementary class of work.

The Bethlehem Steel Company had five blast furnaces, the product of which had been handled by a pig iron gang for many years. This gang, at this time, consisted of about 75 men. They were good, average pig iron handlers, were under an excellent foreman who himself had been a pig iron handler, and the work was done on the whole, about as fast and as cheaply as it was anywhere else at the time. A railroad switch was run out into the field, right along the edge of the piles of pig iron. An inclined plank was placed against the side of a car, and each man picked up from his pile a pig of iron weighing about 92 pounds, walked up the inclined plank, and dropped it on the end of the car.

We found that this gang was loading on average, about twelve and a half tons per man per day. We were surprised to find, after studying the matter, that a first class pig iron handler ought to handle between 47 and 48 tons per day instead of twelve and a half tons. . . It was our duty that 80,000 tons of pig iron was loaded onto the cars at the rate of 47 tons per man per day. And it was further our duty to see it was done without bringing on a strike among the men, without any quarrel with the men, and to see that the men were happier and better contented when loading at the new rate of 47 tons than they were when loading at the old rate of twelve and a half tons. (Taylor, 1911, pp. 41–4).

Henry Knolle (alias 'Schmidt')

Taylor first tested out his ideas on a 'little Pennsylvania Dutch-man', to whom he gave the fictitious name of 'Schmidt'. His real name was Henry Knolle. He was 27 years old, 5 feet and 7 inches in height, and weighed 9 stone and 9 pounds. Taylor believed that Schmidt would be receptive to his approach, and challenged him to be a 'high priced man' who could earn $1.85 per day. Taylor (1911, pp. 45–6) explained the method to Schmidt in the following terms:

The task before us, then, narrowed itself down to getting Schmidt to handle 47 tons of pig iron per day and making him glad to do it. This was done as follows. Schmidt was called out from among the gang of pig-iron handlers and talked to somewhat in this way:

'Schmidt, are you a high-priced man?'

'Vell, I don't know vat you mean.'

'Oh come now, you answer my question. What I want to find out is whether you are a high priced man or one of these cheap fellows here. What I want to find out is whether you want to earn $1.85 a day or whether you are satisfied with $1.15, just the same as all those cheap fellows are getting.'

'Did I vant $1.85 a day? Vas dot a high-priced man? Vell yes, I vas a high-priced man.'

'Now come over here. You see that pile of pig iron?'

'Yes.'

'You see that car?'

'Yes.'

'Well, if you are a high-priced man, you will load that pig iron on that car tomorrow for $1.85. Now do wake up and answer my question. Tell me whether you are a high-priced man or not.'

'Vell – did I got $1.85 for loading dot pig iron on dot car tomorrow?'

'Certainly you do – certainly you do.'

'Vell den, I vas a high priced man.'

'Now hold on, hold on. You know just as well as I do that a high-priced man has to do exactly as he's told from morning till night. You have seen this man here before, haven't you?'

'No, I never saw him.'

'Well, if you are a high-priced man you will do exactly as this man tells you tomorrow, from morning till night. When he tells you to pick up a pig and walk, you pick it up and you walk, and when he tells you to sit down and rest, you sit down. You do that right straight through the day. And what's more, no back talk. Do you understand that? When this man tells you to walk, you walk, and when he tells you to sit down, you sit down, and you don't talk back at him. Now you come on to work here tomorrow and I'll know before night whether you are really a high-priced man or not.'

Schmidt loaded the car as instructed, and earned his $1.85 a day. As Taylor did not have access to the modern technology of tape recording, we may assume that he invented that conversation with Schmidt. This probably tells us more about Taylor than about Schmidt.

The effect of the experimental changes that Taylor introduced was to raise productivity by a factor of 4, and to raise wages by 60 per cent. The savings achieved with Taylor's new work plan were between $75,000 and $80,000 per annum at 1911 prices. The cost of handling pig iron dropped substantially, and the employed men did the work previously done by many more. By the third year of working under his plan, the following results had been obtained at Bethlehem Steel (Taylor, 1911, p. 71):

	old plan	new plan
yard labourers	500	140
tons per man per day (average)	16	59
earnings per man per day (average)	$1.15	$1.88
cost of handling a ton (average)	$0.072	$0.033

Taylor's scientific management was a powerful and largely successful attempt to wrest the organization of production from the workers and place it under the control of management. Before Taylor, the *initiative and incentive system*, such as the one that had operated in the Bethlehem Steel Company, meant that management specified production requirements and provided an incentive to workers in the form of a piece rate bonus. It was the workers who decided how these requirements should be achieved. Not only did this result in wasted effort, but more importantly, workers kept their craft secrets to themselves, and worked at a collectively agreed rate that was below their ability. Taylor argued that responsibility for the planning, co-ordinating and controlling of work should be exercised by management, thus leaving the worker to concentrate on performing the actual task.

Taylor's view of workers, unions and management

Taylor's focus on individuals as part of a larger manufacturing system dictated that he 'isolate' them, as far as possible, from their workmates. He had a very negative view of shopfloor culture, believing workers were affected in all the wrong ways by their co-workers. In his book *The Principles of Scientific Management*, he wrote, 'it is an inflexible rule to talk to and deal with only one workman at a time, since the workman has his own special abilities and limitations, and since we are not dealing with men in masses, but trying to develop each individual man to his highest state or rate of efficiency and prosperity' (Taylor, 1911).

To Taylor, this individual was an economic animal who responded directly to financial incentives. Taylor regarded the worker as a machine fuelled only by money; shovel in more money and, given the right methods and working environment, the machine goes faster. The worker was guided in his actions by a pleasure–pain calculation, which would lead him to exert effort in proportion to the rewards. He said:

> Now one of the very first requirements for a man who is fit to handle pig iron as a regular occupation is that he shall be so stupid and phlegmatic that he more nearly resembles in his mental makeup the ox than any other type. The man who is mentally alert and intelligent is for this very reason entirely unsuited to what would, for him, be the grinding monotony of work of this character. (Taylor, 1911, p. 53)

The problem of the restriction of output was to be overcome, first, by eliminating collusion, and then by introducing best practice. Taylor's technical innovations also subdivided the skill base of workers. This rendered their knowledge obsolete and heightened their exposure to demands for change in working practices. This was done independently of changes in job design and specialization. Taylor saw workers and managers as co-operating partners, not adversaries, who pulled together to produce as much product as possible for their mutual benefit. His techniques were meant to improve the efficiency and social harmony of industrial life, and they required a 'mental revolution' on the part of both sides.

---

definition

Mental revolution *refers to Frederick Taylor's belief in the application of the principles of science to determine the best way to perform any given task, and the acceptance of the results by both workers and management.*

Taylor believed that by their mutual submission to the scientific method, the relationship between management and workers would be transformed for the better by the ending of arbitrary decisions. Management would plan and organize the work, and labour would carry it out, all in accordance with the dictates of science. In such a situation, trade unions and collective bargaining would become redundant. Thus, Taylor was not anti-union as is often stated. It is just that under his individually-oriented approach, he saw no place for them. By their nature, unions emphasized group solidarity, common rules, standardization of wages and conditions. This went against his belief in individual assessment of workers, matching workers' abilities to job requirements, fulfilling their personal desires and their 'bettering themselves' in accordance with the Protestant work ethic.

Workers were concerned that scientific management just meant 'work speed-up', that is, getting more work for less pay. Taylor was adamant that after the implementation of his methods, workers would be rewarded by large pay increases and managers would secure higher productivity and profits. Sometimes workers complained about the inequality of pay increases, as when a 300 per cent productivity increase resulted in a 30 per cent pay increase. Taylor argued that his approach enabled people to do more work in less time, using less effort, because of the more efficient physical movements. Because they were expending less effort, this had to be taken into account when calculating their wage increases.

All theories of organization are based on an implicit or explicit model of human behaviour – on a conception of how people behave in organizations. The Taylor model is a machine model. In analyzing the individual at work and by building up a standard set of procedures, Taylor concentrated on the instrumental aspects of human behaviour. He saw workers as units of production. Provided that one knew the laws of scientific management, people could be handled as easily as other tools. He thus neglected the psychological and social variables which affect organizational behaviour. Taylor was aware that workers had feelings and that they associated with others in the factory, but he assumed that these aspects were irrelevant to the problems of productivity.

Taylor's approach is striking in its dismissive interest in people. In his technical research on belting power systems and in developing and discovering high-speed drills, Taylor was a model user of the scientific method. Very thorough and comprehensive, he conducted longitudinal studies which investigated and controlled every relevant factor or variable. However, when his methodology came to people, his studies, by comparison, became very off-hand, suggesting that he did not really believe that they were very important after all.

---

definitions

Job simplification *is the breaking up of the work to be performed into the smallest identifiable tasks.*

Job specialization *is the assignment of workers to perform small, simple tasks.*

---

symphonic engineering

Here is the way in which a literal-minded industrial engineer reported on a symphony concert:

For considerable periods the four oboe players had nothing to do. The number should be reduced and the work spread more evenly over the whole concert, thus eliminating peaks and valleys of activity.

All the twelve violins were playing identical notes; this seems unnecessary duplication. The staff of this section should be drastically cut. If a larger volume of sound is required, it could be obtained by means of electronic apparatus.

Much effort was absorbed in the playing of demi-semi-quavers; this seems to be an unnecessary refinement. It is recommended that all notes be rounded up to the nearest semi-quaver. If this were done, it would be possible to use trainees and lower-grade operatives more extensively.

There seems to be too much repetition of some musical passages. Scores should be drastically pruned. No useful purpose is served by repeating on the horns something which has already been handled by the strings. It is estimated that if all redundant passages were eliminated the whole concert time of 2 hours could be reduced to 20 minutes and there would be no need for an intermission.

In many cases the operators were using one hand for holding the instrument, whereas the introduction of a fixture would have tendered the idle hand available for other work. Also, it was noted that excessive effort was being used occasionally by the players of wind instruments, whereas one compressor could supply adequate air for all instruments under more accurately controlled conditions.

Finally, obsolescence of equipment is another matter into which it is suggested further investigation could be made, as it was reported in the programme that the leading violinist's instrument was already several hundred years old. If normal depreciation schedules had been applied, the value of this instrument would have been reduced to zero and purchase of more modern equipment could then have been considered.

from R.M. Fulmer and T.T. Herbert, 1974, *Exploring the New Management*, Macmillan, New York, p. 27.

Taylorism in action

Exceptional results were achieved by some of Taylor's followers. They redesigned individual tasks and the relationships between production tasks. Materials were systematically scheduled and routed through a plant. Inspection took place between operations. Standardization and simplification of work methods and more systematic ways of distributing tools and materials became commonplace. The savings achieved with Taylor's new plan at the Bethlehem Steel Corporation were between $75,000 and $80,000 (per annum at 1911 prices). It is no surprise that many other companies were eager to apply his ideas.

However, the dramatic improvements in productivity were matched by the negative and often violent reactions to Taylor's techniques among workers, technicians, managers and government. The fragmented tasks designed by Taylor were boring, for the worker required a much lower level of skill. Companies adopted scientific management selectively and many took the opportunity to cut wages. Taylor's methods were disliked by those who had to work under them.

Following Taylor's success with Schmidt, local newspapers calculated that his methods would lead to mass redundancies at the Bethlehem Steel Corporation. Since this did not improve the company's industrial relations, and since it benefited from the houses and shops that it owned near the works, the management of the company asked Taylor to moderate his efforts. Taylor could not tolerate such interference. Eventually he got a one line letter which read, 'I beg to advise you that your services will not be required by this company after 1st May 1901'.

A popular account exists of the application of Taylorism at the Watertown Arsenal in 1911. It is cited as the venue for the first strike under Taylor's system. The often told story concerns General William Crozier, Controller of Ordnance at the Arsenal, who was interested in scientific management methods, but was hesitant to implement them. He was not convinced that bonuses should be paid for methods which reduced job times, and he thought that time studies themselves might lead to a strike. When the approach was adopted, it led almost immediately to a strike by moulding workers in the foundry. However, a closer investigation of the circumstances reveals that Taylor's methods had been successfully applied in the Arsenal's machine shop for about two years prior to the strike by experts, and without any significant staff resistance. It was only when the approach was extended to the foundry area that resistance arose. The analyst who implemented the techniques was not an expert in foundry work, and it is believed that he chose a 'rate buster' as the subject for measurement. The foundry workers were also more interdependent and had greater group cohesion than their colleagues in the machine shop. The strike, therefore, seems to be more a result of managerial ineptitude than an example of worker resistance to scientific management methods.

Nevertheless, the strike, together with the reaction of the American Federation of Labor to Taylor, which was both vocal and stringent, resulted in the establishment of a House of Representatives Committee to investigate Taylor's methods. Explaining his philosophy to this Committee, Taylor (1911, pp. 27–30) said:

> The great revolution that takes place in the mental attitude of the two parties under scientific management is that both parties take their eyes off the division of the surplus as the important matter, and together turn

scientific management and eye surgery

The photograph below shows one of twelve eye surgeries built in Russia in the late 1980s using assembly-line principles. On an automated conveyor belt, eye surgery is carried out using a controversial five-stage assembly-line operation. Up to 15 patients an hour can pass through the specially designed operating theatre at the Moscow Research Institute of Eye Microsurgery. Each step of the operation is performed by a different surgeon, and each operation takes a maximum of 10 minutes. First, the patient receives a local anaesthetic outside the theatre. Then, lying on one of the special tables shown in the photograph, they pass through the automatic doors into the operating room.

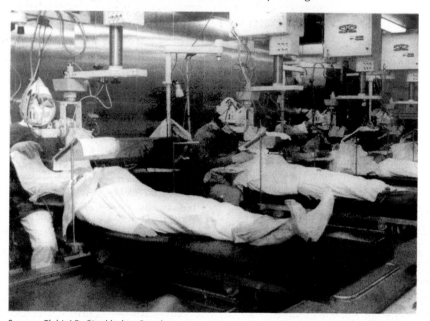

Source: Flakt AB, Stockholm, Sweden

station 1: The first surgeon marks exactly the depth and length of cuts to be made to the cornea which have been calculated in advance by a computer.

station 2: The second surgeon makes between 8 and 16 cuts with a diamond scalpel.

station 3: The third surgeon adjusts the cuts to a micro degree to ensure maximum eyesight gain.

station 4: The fourth surgeon cleans and dresses all the wounds.

station 5: A doctor administers the necessary antibiotics in case of infection. The patient then passes through another automatic door.

Run by Professor Sviatoslav Fiodorov, his 50-strong team can process 200 patients a day, and treat 220,000 annually. His institute has become a $75 million a year business that is growing at 30 per cent per annum. Foreigners can buy an operation package holiday (operation included) for $2000 for a two-week stay. Professor Fiodorov is planning to replace the surgeons on his assembly-line with robots.

based on: Maggie Innes, 1987, 'Eye, eye comrade!', *News of the World Sunday Magazine*, 7 November, pp. 24–5, and Peter Pean, 1989, 'How to get rich off perestroika', *Fortune*, 8 May, pp. 95–6.

their attention towards increasing the size of the surplus until the surplus becomes so large . . . that there is ample room for a large increase in wages for the workman and an equally large increase in profits for the manufacturer.

The Committee reported in 1912, and concluded that scientific management did provide useful techniques. However, in 1914, an attitude survey of Arsenal workers was conducted, revealing the hostility and resentment of the workers to the system. Concerned about industrial unrest in government arms factories in wartime, the American Congress banned Taylor's time study methods in its defence industry.

Scientific management was adopted in other countries. In Britain, it was first applied in the J. Hopkinson works at Huddersfield in 1905. The Iron and Steel Institute evaluated the techniques and criticized them. In Germany, the Director of the Borsig Works noted the hostility of his workmen to the methods. In 1912, Renault introduced scientific management principles at Billancourt which led to violent conflict and strikes. The zealous application of time study in Renault had the following result:

> The workman . . . had to adapt his human machine to the rate of the mechanical one; and workmen incapable of making all the necessary movements with their hands within the measured time aided themselves by using their heads as a third arm. (Friedmann, 1955, p. 42)

Lillian and Frank Gilbreth – the development of Taylorism

Lillian Evelyn Gilbreth (1878–1972) and Frank Bunker Gilbreth (1868–1924)

Frank Bunker Gilbreth's background resembled Taylor's in that both were practising engineers and managers. Gilbreth's experience was in the construction industry, and his most famous experiments involved bricklayers. His main contribution was to refine and develop the techniques for measuring work to a higher level of precision. His wife Lillian was a trained psychologist and her contribution was in the area that came to be known as fatigue study. Gilbreth's first important book, *Motion Study*, was published in 1911, whilst his wife's *The Psychology of Management*, which highlighted the importance of human factors in organizations, was published in 1916.

Taylor's original work had concentrated on the counting and timing of tasks. One of the improvements introduced by Gilbreth was adding the still camera to the stopwatch. He attached lights to workers' hands, and photographed their motions at slow shutter speeds. This 'chronocyclographic method' left paths of light showing on the photographic plate. The pictures produced were then made into wire models. On the basis of these, the work task could be analyzed in detail and redesigned to be done more efficiently. His method was introduced into all sections of industry, particularly mass production. Later, Gilbreth became the first person to use motion picture cameras to analyze a worker's movements. Time-and-motion studies are conducted by experts to this day.

---

definition

Time and motion studies *attempt to make operations more efficient by finding exactly how long it takes to perform a task, and the best way in which to do it.*

Gilbreth's contributions

cyclographic photograph

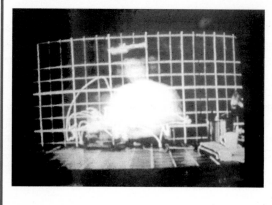

Therblig symbols and colours

symbol	name	colour
search	search	black
find	find	grey
select	select	light grey
group	group	red
hold	hold	gold ochre
transport loaded	transport loaded	green
position	position	blue
assemble	assemble	violet
use	use	purple
disassemble	disassemble	light violet
inspect	inspect	burnt ochre
pre-position	pre-position	pale blue
release load	release load	carmine red
transport empty	transport empty	olive green
rest for overcoming fatigue	rest for overcoming fatigue	orange
unavoidable delay	unavoidable delay	yellow
avoidable delay	avoidable delay	lemon yellow
plan	plan	brown

Another of Gilbreth's contributions to the development of scientific management was the introduction of a comprehensive system of noting actions. There are eighteen different notation symbols which are shown in the box. They are called 'therbligs' – a variation of his name spelt backwards. As with a dance, all the movements of a worker doing a particular job could be choreographed using the therbligs notation. In addition, Gilbreth developed a standard time for each job element, thereby combining time study with motion study. This was used for designing wage payment systems whose universal application Gilbreth advocated.

Like Taylor, Gilbreth set detailed rules on how to find out the best way of doing any job. He discovered that eighteen separate movements were made in laying each brick. By reorganizing the work pattern, he was able to reduce the movements to five and increase the bricklayers' productivity from 120 to 350 bricks an hour.

The nature of the building industry meant that there was a need to develop a way of controlling work carried out at a distance from head office. He set down for his workers, supervisors and managers what he called his 'Field System'. This was a set of written rules and procedures which were designed to establish uniform practice on all worksites. Apart from the Field System, there were the 'Concrete and Bricklaying Systems' which detailed such matters as mixing concrete, transportation, training of apprentices, methods of scaffolding, and so on.

While Gilbreth developed Taylor's ideas and produced a system of time and motion study, the major advances from the social science perspective came from his association with his wife, Lillian. The study of motions, and the elimination of unnecessary and wasteful actions, was intended to reduce the level of fatigue experienced by workers. Since all work produced fatigue for which the remedy was rest, the aim was to find the best mix of work and rest to maximize productivity.

The Gilbreths addressed the problem of fatigue reduction in several ways. One approach was to shorten the working day and introduce rest periods and chairs. Another was the scientific study of jobs to eliminate the fatigue-

---

Gilbreth in action

All Gilbreth's work had one objective – to discover the best method of doing a job. Once at an exhibition in London he gave a devastating display of his ability to do this. This example was quoted by Henry L. Gantt in his introduction to Gilbreth's book on Motion Study.

While in London with the American Society of Mechanical Engineers, Mr. Gilbreth cornered an old friend of his and explained to him the wonderful results that could be accompanied by motion study. He declared that he did not care what the work was, he would be able to shorten the time usually required, provided that nobody had previously applied the principles of motion study to the work.

A few days before, his friend had been at the Japanese–British Exposition and had seen there a girl putting papers on boxes of shoe polish at a wonderful speed. Without saying what he had in mind, Mr Gilbreth's friend invited him to visit the Exposition, and in a most casual way led him to the stand where the girl was doing this remarkable work, with the feeling that here at least was an operation which could not be improved upon.

No sooner had Mr. Gilbreth spied this phenomenal work than out came his stopwatch and he timed accurately how long it took the girl to do twenty-four boxes. The time was forty seconds. When he had obtained this information he told the girl that she was not working right. She, of course, was greatly incensed that a man from the audience should presume to criticize what she was doing, when she was acknowledged to be the most skilled girl that had ever done that work.

He had observed that while all her motions were made with great rapidity about half of them would be unnecessary if she arranged her work a little differently. He had a very persuasive way, and although the girl was quite irritated by his remark, she consented to listen to his suggestion that he could show her how to do the work more rapidly. Inasmuch as she was on piece work the prospect of larger earnings induced her to try his suggestion The first time she tried to do as he directed she did twenty-four boxes in twenty-six seconds; the second time she tried she did it in twenty seconds. She was not working any harder, only making fewer motions.

This account the writer heard in Manchester, England from the man himself who had put up the job on Mr. Gilbreth, and it is safe to say that this man is now about as firm a believer in motion study as Mr Gilbreth.

from A. Tillett, T. Kempner and G. Wills (eds.), 1970, *Management Thinkers*, Penguin Books, Harmondsworth, pp. 102–3.

producing elements. Changes were also made to heating, lighting and ventilation. The final ingredient was termed the 'betterment of work'. It included introducing rest rooms, canteens, entertainment and music into the factory. In the work of the Gilbreths we see the first realization that workers may have a variety of different needs. The Gilbreths thought that individual work performance depended on attitudes, needs and the physical environment as well as correct work methods and suitable equipment. The breadth of Gilbreth's work is succinctly described by Bedeian (1986, p. 42):

> In 1915, he put roller skates on messengers in a Montgomery Ward's office to reduce their fatigue and increase their delivery times. In another experiment, he observed 150 appendectomies to find the 'One Best Way'. In conjunction with Lillian, he authored papers such as 'The Application of Scientific Management to the Work of the Nurse', 'Motion Study in Surgery' and 'Scientific Management in the Hospital'. At one point, he even prepared a study of the motions of epileptics.

Henry Laurence Gantt – the humanization of Taylorism

Henry Laurence Gantt (1861–1924)

Henry Gantt worked for Taylor at the Bethlehem Steel Works. He supported Taylor's approach, but he did much to humanize scientific management to make it more acceptable. He believed in consideration for and fair dealings with workers. He felt that scientific management was being used as an oppressive instrument by the unscrupulous. His system was based on detailed instruction cards in the best scientific management tradition. These showed the time allowed for a job, the operations to be carried out and the methods to be used. However, he replaced the 'one best way' of Taylor with his own 'best known way at present'. This involved a much less detailed analysis of jobs than Taylor suggested.

Gantt also substantially modified the pay system which had caused such bad feelings between management and workers in the past. The piecerate system was replaced by a set day rate plus a 20–50 per cent bonus. The time for the job was set by Gantt, and if it was met, the worker would get the day rate plus the bonus. There existed detailed times for each part of the job, and if the worker could not meet these, the foreman had to demonstrate that it could be done. At the same time the initiative and responsibility was given to the supervisor to ensure that his men performed satisfactorily. There was no functional foremanship here. The supervisor received a bonus for every man who achieved his target and a further payment if all his team achieved it. Gantt's view of the worker was different in some ways from that of Taylor and Gilbreth. He wrote:

> The general policy of the past has been to drive. The era of force must give way to that of knowledge; the policy of the future will be to teach and to lead . . . Time is needed to overcome prejudice and change habits. This is a psychological law. Its violation produces failure just as surely as the violation of the laws of physics or chemistry. (Rathe, 1961, p. 9)

More than the other two scientific management writers, he realized that the worker was a human being with needs and dignity which deserved consideration by management. Nevertheless, he believed that the opportunity to earn money was all the motivation the workers needed to accept the improved methods. Management's job was to create the conditions in which this could happen.

A key element in scientific management was planning. The whole purpose of work study was to improve efficiency and consistency, and these were necessary for effective planning. The most significant development in planning under scientific management was the Gantt Chart, a visual display to show the sequencing of activities over time. It bears Gantt's name, and is still in use today.

Gantt chart for new product-development plan, beginning of 1998

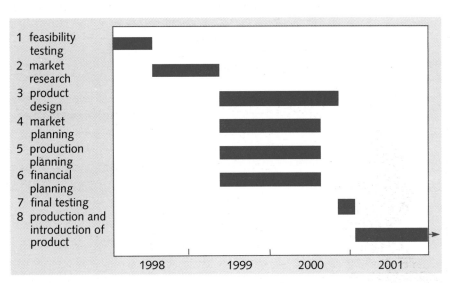

Fordism

Henry Ford (1863–1947)

By 1920, the name of Henry Ford had became synonymous not only with his Model T motor car, but also with revolutionary techniques of mass production. Ford had founded his company in 1903, and his approach to production had three key elements. Ford's work developed quite independently of Taylor's, and preceded Gilbreth's. In history, Ford is known for the analysis of workers' jobs using time-and-motion techniques; the installation of single-purpose machine tools, and the introduction of the assembly-line. All had the objective of increasing control by reducing or eliminating uncertainty.

Until the start of the twentieth century, most products were hand-made by skilled operators who hand-crafted the parts that they required using general-purpose machine tools such as lathes. It took craftsmen years of training to acquire the necessary skill and experience. These men could read a blueprint and visualize the final product and possessed a level of hand–eye co-ordination and deftness of touch that allowed them to manufacture the required item. In the process, they made numerous specific decisions about production. In the 1890s, such craftsmen made motor cars, but Ford realized that there were not enough of them to meet the level of car production that the manufacturers required.

analysis of workers' jobs

Ford's first innovation was to apply the principles of scientific management to his workers' jobs in order to remove waste and inefficiency. The ideas of Frederick Taylor were in the air, and the Studebaker car company in Detroit had earlier implemented some of them. Taylor himself had been invited to present his ideas to automobile company executives. The Ford organization established a Motion Picture Department which used film to study the work methods in different industries.

Applying Taylor's principles of work rationalization, Ford employees were allocated simple tasks, all of which had been carefully designed to ensure maximum efficiency. Ford's approach was entirely experimental, very pragmatic and always open to improvements – try it, modify it, try it again, keep on until it's right. The effects on workers were dramatic. The Ford mechanic, originally a skilled craftsman, became an assembler who tended his machine, only performing low-grade tasks. For example, the wheelwright's job was divided into almost 100 operations, each of which was performed by a different man using different equipment.

installation of single-purpose machine tools

One of Ford's revolutions was to introduce single-purpose machines into his factory. He called these 'Farmer machines' because farm boys, coming off the land, could be quickly trained to use them. Being single-purpose machines, the operator no longer had to be skilled, just quick. The skill was now incorporated within the machine. Moreover, these machines produced exactly the same standard part each time. Creating such uniformity was one way to exert control. Once the parts for the Model T were specified, the production system could be specified, and identical, interchangeable parts produced.

creation of the assembly-line

Despite these two innovations, the worker could still work at his own speed. In 1913, it still took 90 minutes to assemble a car. To overcome this problem, instead of moving the men past the car, the car was moved past the workmen. The assembly-line imposed on the employee the working speed that Ford wanted. By 1914, the plant had installed a continuous automatic conveyer, which met Ford's technical and philosophical objectives. The engineers had arranged work in a logical order. The materials and semi-completed parts made their way through the plant when needed. The conveyor belt took radiator parts to assemblers, and then carried their work to solderers who finished off the product.

After integrating other production processes, the engineers had produced a continuously moving line fed by overhead conveyors. Each worker was feeding, and being fed by, the assembly-line. In 1908, when the Model T was introduced, production ran at 27 cars per day. By 1923, when the River Rouge plant had been completed, daily production had reached 2000 cars.

Collier and Horowitz (1987, p. 63) wrote that, 'More than quantity of production, the assembly line involved, in Ford's words, "the focusing upon a manufacturing process of the principles of power, accuracy, economy, system, continuity, speed and repetition."'.

The credit for the introduction of the assembly line concept has been disputed. Some stories tell of Henry Ford getting the idea at an abattoir where beef carcasses, suspended from moving hooks, were being butchered. Other accounts have him visiting a watch plant, and seeing the staged assembly process of time-pieces (Collier and Horowitz, 1987). Although Henry Ford claimed the authorship of the assembly line in the new manufacturing plant at the Highland Park near Detroit, there is strong evidence to suggest that credit for it should be given to two people. First, Charles E. Sorensen, a Dane whom Ford had hired in 1905. In 1908, Sorensen in his capacity as plant superinten-

---

early Ford assembly-line

The photograph below shows the chassis being pulled manually along the line. Workers located on a ramp above the line manoeuvre the seats into position.

Many songs were written about Ford's assembly-lines. One was sung to the tune of the *Battle Hymn of the Republic*. Its first verse and chorus ran:

Mine eyes hath seen the glories of the making of a Ford,
It's made under conditions that would offend the Almighty Lord,
With a most ungodly hurry, and amidst wild uproar,
The production rushes on.

Hurry, hurry, hurry, hurry.
Hurry, hurry, hurry.
Hurry, hurry, hurry.
Production rushes on.

dent, and some fellow workers in the Piquette plant, had the idea of pulling a car chassis by rope past labourers at their work stations. In his memoirs, Sorensen wrote:

> It was there that the idea occurred to me that assembly would be easier, simpler and faster, if we could make the chassis move along, beginning at one end of the plant with a frame, and adding the axles and wheels: thus moving it past the stockroom to the chassis. (Sorensen, 1956, p. 18)

What we do know is that the setting up of a manually paced assembly-line happened in April 1913, and was followed a few months later by the moving line. The manual's line's 'inventor' is unknown, but the moving line may also be credibly attributed to Clarence W. Avery who, oddly enough, never publicly claimed credit for it. Avery worked until the early 1920s, and then left in a Sorensen-engineered purge.

---

definition

Fordism *refers to the application of scientific management principles to workers' jobs; the installation of single-purpose machine tools, and the introduction of the assembly-line.*

Frederick Taylor's ambition had all along been to wrest control of the production process from the workers and place it into the hands of management. Under Fordism, this was broadly achieved. Ford's objective was to allow unsophisticated workers to make a sophisticated product in volume. He sought to make his workforce as uniform and interchangeable as the parts they handled.

Fordism, workers and the Ford Sociology Department

The speed of the assembly-line was increased, and older workers, often men in their forties, who were unable to keep up were fired. At hiring time, sales of black hair dye rocketed. Some of these men were re-hired at lower wages. This led Henry Ford to be called the 'Speed-up King'. This, plus the monotonous work, meant that in 1913 the company had an astronomical turnover rate. Newly hired workers stayed an average of three months. Indeed, over 70 per cent of the men who left Ford were categorized as '5 day men', i.e. they walked off the job without any formal notification and were simply presumed to have quit after missing five days' work. Since it cost $100 to train each worker, this rate of turnover was costing the company $3 million a year (Wilson, 1995).

Partly in response to this, Ford agreed to cut the working day from 9 to 8 hours, and to double the minimum wage from $2.50 to $5.00 a day, which was twice that offered by any other motor car company. He believed that higher wages would lead to higher production and higher profits. As a result, turnover reduced, absenteeism plummeted from 10 per cent to 0.5 per cent and Henry Ford became a hero overnight. The workers who had cursed him now wore their company identification badges as tie-pins on Sundays with pride. Ford also knew that they could use the extra money to buy his cars. However, he was concerned that this wage increase could lead some workers to depravity. Hence, this increase was dependent on the workers' showing sobriety and industry. But who was to judge this?

The Ford Sociology Department (FSD) was established in 1914 as an early employment or personnel section. It was headed by Samuel Marquis, a former Dean of St Paul's Church in Detroit, and employed 100 investigators. The department met Henry Ford's interest in self-improvement. Ford often stopped in the street to give tramps a lift and offered them jobs at his plant. He was keen on giving ex-convicts a 'second chance'. One of these was Norval Hawkins who, as his future sales manager, built one of the greatest sales forces in the motor car industry. Ford believed that he could apply his car-building techniques to people, turning out better men in the same way that the assembly-line allowed him to turn out better cars.

FSD social workers or investigators visited workers in their homes, with translators, to check on how they lived. They monitored workers' drinking habits, cleanliness, debts and sexual relations. Employees had to produce their bank cheque books and marriage licences at the interviews. Where a Ford investigator considered a worker to be living in a dissolute manner, the latter could receive a pay-cut or suspension. The investigators encouraged single men to enrol in evening correspondence courses.

They also left them a leaflet entitled 'Rules of Living'. This encouraged employees to use plenty of soap and water, not to spit on the floor, avoid hire purchase, and to go to Ford-operated schools if they needed to learn English. The wives of employees were counselled not to take in boarders, in case a sexual relationship developed while the husband was at work. Following Marquis's departure, the interest in worker improvement gave way to spying and bureaucratic interference. The Ford Sociology Department was closed in 1917.

In the 1930s, under the direction of the notorious Harry Bennett, the Plant Protection Service Department at Ford's became the company's secret police force. It was the threat of the United Auto Unions that turned his Rouge plant into an industrial camp. Service Department spies planted microphones, followed men into the toilets to ensure that they did not discuss union matters, ran 9000 informers among the employees, treated a meeting of any two workers as a *prima facie* evidence of conspiracy, required workers walking from one place to another to say where they were going and why, and searched their belongings for union literature while they were on the factory floor.

In addition, workers were banned from smoking in the toilets, with 'Sniffers' standing by the air gauges to monitor any infringements. While on the job, sitting, squatting, singing and whistling were banned, while smiling was frowned upon. Talking on the job and during lunch breaks was prohibited. The workers tried to fight back. They communicated with each other without moving their lips using the 'Ford whisper or whistle', their frozen features being called the 'Fordization of the face'. Outside work, company spies visited local bars and markets frequented by employees listening out for incriminating gossip. The combination of the effects of such on- and off-the-job monitoring, and the speed of the assembly-line, led some employees to develop the 'Ford stomach', a nervous condition based on stress and exhaustion (Sward, 1948). Other workers simply collapsed from exhaustion, a condition which Detroit doctors termed 'Forditis'.

Brave New Management

Aldous Huxley's book *Brave New World* is one of the world's best-known prophetic novels. Huxley describes a chillingly rationalistic society. The publication of the novel in 1932 followed the resurgence of Ford in 1927 as a motor manufacturer with his highly successful Model A. It is therefore not surprising that Huxley used explicit references to Henry Ford and his production system in his novel:

- The World State's years are designated AF – 'After Ford'. The year AF 1 in the new calendar is equivalent to 1908 AD, the year in which the Model T was introduced.
- Henry Ford is deified as a kind of secular god. This underscores the centrality of Taylorism in a society where biology has become an instrument of economic policy. The phrase in the novel 'Our Ford' rhymes with 'Our Lord'.
- At the start of the novel, human birth begins in the fertilization room, proceeds to the bottling room, through the embryo store and on to the decanting room. The science laboratory has merged with the industrial assembly-line. In the Hatcheries, the bottled embryos travel along a continuous conveyor belt.
- Following Taylorist principles, workers are physically and intellectually manufactured to requirements, to carry out predefined tasks effectively in society.
- The economics of the World State are underpinned by controlled, and carefully accelerated rates of production and the enforced consumption of commodities.
- One of the World Controllers, Mustapha Mond, makes an ideological statement which reaffirms Henry Ford's revulsion for the past. Mond refers to 'that beautiful and inspiring saying of Our Ford's: History is bunk!'

based on Aldous Huxley, 1932, *Brave New World*, Penguin Books, Harmondsworth.

Ford's legacy

The debate about Henry Ford has continued to this day. On the positive side, there is agreement about his contribution to productivity. In 1913, before the assembly-line, it took 12.5 hours to put together a car. In 1914, Ford's 13,000 workers produced 267,720 cars, whilst the other motor companies with a workforce of 66,000 employees made 287,770 cars. Further improvements were to occur. By 1920, one Ford car rolled off the line every minute, and by 1925, the figure was one every 10 seconds.

Ford's contribution to raising people's standard of living is also acknowledged. Having shown that something as complicated as a motor car could be built using the techniques of mass production, it was recognized that the manufacture of other, simpler products was also possible. Mass production has led to mass consumption, and has given more people more access to more goods than ever in history. In the fifty years to 1970, the standard of living of Americans sky-rocketed. Other countries adopting Ford's system of manufacturing production also benefited.

Critics argue that Ford destroyed craftsmanship and deskilled jobs. Others argue that, as mentioned at the start, there were insufficient skilled workers available for the jobs to be done, and that Ford basically redesigned work so that the available labour force could cope with it. In their view, it was less a question of forcing a highly skilled, high-priced employee to accept a cheapened, dead-end job, and more an issue of identifying tasks appropriate for unskilled people to do, who would otherwise have performed even less enjoyable, back-breaking work. The same critics also assert that short-cycle repetitive jobs have caused worker alienation and stress, and have subjugated human beings to the machine. The assembly-line is vilified for exerting an invidious, invisible control over the workers. The debate over the balance of costs and benefits of Fordism is likely to continue.

concepts of systems and control

Ford's legacy continues to dominate twentieth-century organization. He showed his successors how the world could be organized to solve problems using the closely related concepts of *systems* and *control*. What Ford built was not just a factory, but an entire production system. This system included the factory, but went beyond its walls. What made that system so effective was the nature and the degree of control that he exerted upon it.

---

definitions

The **systems concept** *is a management perspective which emphasizes interdependence between the various parts of an organization, and also between the organization and its environment.*

The **control concept** *refers to the process of imposing a pattern on previously haphazard activities. Such a pattern may be imposed on the operation of machinery, on the interaction of machinery with people, or on people's actions or words.*

It has been said that 'Ford was determined to gain complete control of all aspects of the manufacture and sale of his car. That he nearly succeeded, testified to his genius' (Zaleznik and Kets de Vries, 1975). Control over the manufacturing process was achieved through the use of single-purpose machine tools and their logical ordering through the plant. The output of one group of workers became the input of others. The production system was like a giant river fed by tributaries which constantly flowed into it.

Control over the worker was exerted through task specialization and assembly-line working. Such control was both invisible and non-confrontational. It was the system and not the supervisor that told the employee to work faster. It depersonalized the authority relationship to such a degree that workers were no longer aware that they were being directed.

Control over the environment was achieved through purchase of vital raw materials. Ford experienced production hold-outs when his suppliers had strikes. To ensure his control over the entire production process, he carved out rubber plantations in the Brazilian rain forest the size of Connecticut which were called *Fordlandia*. He bought coalmines in Kentucky, iron mines in Michigan, as well as shipping lines and railways. He was determined to control every element of the manufacturing process, both inside and outside his company.

STOP!

In the 1930s, the Mexican artist Diego Rivera (1886–1957) was commissioned by the Detroit Institute of Art to paint frescoes devoted to the city's motor car industry. His panels feature Ford's River Rouge plant outside Detroit. In 1935, that plant spread over 1096 acres, had 7.25 million square feet of floor space, 235 acres of glass windows and 90 miles of railway track, employed over 80,000 men, and built 2 million cars each year. Little wonder that it was called the *Cathedral of Industry*. Look at the panels below carefully. What do you see and what does it tell you about Fordism?

Rivera was an independent artist with a Marxist perspective. He painted the factory workers and the machines that they used. The panels show various stages in the production of the car. The men in the murals are depicted as sullen and angry, working amidst the clamour and din of the machinery around them. The strength shown in their faces was perceived as intimidating by some observers, who accused Rivera of producing left-wing propaganda.

Diego Rivera, Detroit Industry (north wall), 1932–3

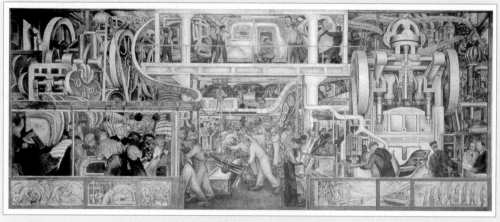

Diego Rivera, Detroit Industry (south wall), 1932–3

The machines themselves are shown as perfect designs, as part of a system that is so complicated and so intimidating that it dwarfs ordinary human beings. The murals exalt the sophistication of the production system, saying to the onlooker, 'Look at this incredible achievement'. They depict the triumph of rationality over nature's apparent disorganization; of new forms of manufacturing over old; and of the new order over the old. However, one obvious thing is missing from the pictures.

Look at the pictures again carefully: can you see a completed car? The panels convey the awe-inspiring nature of Ford's technology – as something that helps human beings, but which simultaneously dominates them.

source of paintings: Detroit Institute of Art, Illinois. © 1995 The Detroit Institute of Arts Founders Society.

scientific management in today's organizations

Popular wisdom holds that scientific management was appropriate in its day but that it has now been superseded by more 'enlightened' approaches to the organization of work and the management of employees. In some cases this may be true, but there are vast tracts of industry, all around the world, where the principles and practices of Taylorism, and its development in Fordism, continue to hold sway. Fordist principles can be found on the shopfloors of modern car assembly plants, and on the kitchen floors of hamburger restaurants which are found in every high street.

Frederick Taylor and fast-food restaurants

George Ritzer saw scientific management as a non-human technology which exerted great control over employees who, when they were required to follow Taylor's methods, worked much more efficiently, all performed the same steps (their work exhibited predictability), and produced a great deal more while their pay increased only slightly (calculability). Ritzer considered how the fast-food restaurant industry has, at least implicitly, used scientific management to organize the way in which their employees work. The industry is highly rationalized, and the objective is constantly to discover the most efficient way of grilling a hamburger, frying the potatoes, or serving a meal. He noted that:

> much of the work in the fast-food restaurant is performed in assembly-line fashion with the tasks broken down into, for example, grilling the burgers, putting them on the rolls, smearing on the 'special paste', laying on the lettuce and tomato, and wrapping the fully dressed burgers. Even the customers are placed on a kind of assembly-line; the drive-thru window is the most obvious example of this. As one observer notes, 'The basic elements of the factory have obviously been introduced to the fast-food phenomenon . . . [with] the advent of the feeding machine.'

based on George Ritzer, 1993, *The McDonaldization of Society*, Pine Forge Press/Sage, CA, pp. 24–6.

Less obviously, scientific management principles permeate service-focused office jobs, such as those of the airline reservation clerks who sell passengers aeroplane seats over the telephone. Here you will find the same Taylorist procedures in operation. First, a study is made of what the good reservation clerk does, and this is then broken down into its constituent steps. Those steps are turned into a procedure which is taught to the other clerks. Those clerks are monitored to ensure that procedure is being followed. One American airline aims to respond to 75 per cent of incoming calls within 20 seconds. There is a central control room where a supervisor listens in on the calls and monitors the performance of all the clerks through a computer. Each clerk knows she is being monitored, but not when. Their procedure includes the requirement to make a number of what salespeople call *closes* ('Do you want the 9 o'clock or the 3 o'clock plane?'). Taylor standardized the working method, Ford standardized the motor car part, now we are standardizing the *conversation*.

Scientific management has now permeated even higher up the organizational hierarchy. While expensive robots can replace cheap shopfloor manual labours, organizations prefer cheap expert systems to replace expensive professionals and senior managers. Both Taylor and Ford sought to extract the knowledge and judgement that was in the craftsman's head and put it into the machine, which could then be operated by less skilled, lower grade and hence cheaper labour. With the development of computer expert systems have come the knowledge engineers. Working with professionals such as doctors, quantity surveyors and loss adjusters, these engineers run knowledge elicitation sessions. The objective is to extract each professional's experience, which they have acquired over the years. Repeated interviews with hundreds of members of the same professional group produce a set of judgement rules which can be stored in an expert system. This expertise can be accessed by less experienced or non-qualified personnel. Having built the manual worker's skill and knowledge into machines, Taylor's successors are doing the same with intellectual work.

STOP!

If Taylorism is as outdated and inhuman as so many people hold, why do you think it is still commonly used in organizations today?

---

assessment

It should be noted that during the nineteenth century, many people before Taylor had sought to bring order and consistency to work operations. Taylor's major contribution was to bring all these developments together and promote them as a 'package' or system. The prominence and success that he achieved was due partly to parallel technical developments. His management changes supported technical changes of the time in process technology and materials like high speed steel. This allowed machine shops to process several times the volume of materials relative to existing methods, and this increased throughput revealed the many shortcomings of unsystematic management (Wilson, 1995).

The objective of the scientific management movement was to increase efficiency by carefully planning workers' movements in the most efficient way. Taylor's ideas and those of his followers led to time-and-motion experts with their stopwatches and clipboards observing workers, and seeking to discover the 'one best way' in which every job could be performed. Much of this is viewed negatively today.

However, after the First World War, many disabled American ex-soldiers returned to civilian life and sought employment. Ford's response was to look at the work within his operations and identify those tasks for which people with various disabilities may be suitable, and then employ them if the opportunity presented itself. He analyzed the work to be done, suggesting that up to 7000 different categories could be identified, each requiring different sets of motions (Ford and Crowther, 1924). Gilbreth went beyond this and suggested that such a passive approach could be augmented by a more proactive one in which analysis of the job movements would help in two ways. First, by designing or redesigning work, it could be made suitable for disabled people. For example,

some tasks could be performed while the person was lying in bed. S⟨
improving the physical efficiency of work, disabled people could avo⟨
and make better use of their more limited strengths or capabilities (Gil⟨
Gilbreth, 1918). Both Ford and the Gilbreths saw this as an exam⟨
humanistic side of scientific management.

In its cold rationality, scientific management resembles the bureaucratic and classical management theories of organization. The conception of the human being is that of an automaton whose performance can be improved by the application of logical engineering principles and simple economic incentives, and whose behaviour can be made predictable. It is easy to criticize Taylor's work today for its deficiencies. Since it was published, academics have been critical of Taylor and his 'scientific' approach to management. They accused him of being naive, of contradicting himself and of calling his personal ideas 'principles'. He claimed that these principles could be applied to any organization, but they have been found to have fairly limited application.

What these writers fail to credit Taylor with is the enormous influence on management practice that his ideas have had. In many organizations today, work is organized in the ways that Taylor suggested. Moreover, it has been shown that having Taylorized manual work, computers are allowing companies to Taylorize intellectual work.

---

common criticisms of Taylorism

1 Assumed that the motivation of the employee was to secure the maximum earnings for the effort expended. It neglected the importance of other rewards from work (achievement, job satisfaction, recognition) which later research has found to be important.

2 Neglected the subjective side of work – the personal and interactional aspects of performance, the meanings that employees give to work and the significance to them of their social relationships at work.

3 Failed to appreciate the meanings that workers would put on new procedures and their reactions to being timed and closely supervised.

4 Had an inadequate understanding of the relation of the individual incentive to interaction with, and dependence on, the immediate work group. Taylor did attribute 'underworking' to group pressures, but misunderstood the way in which these worked. He failed to see that these might just as easily keep production and morale up.

5 Ignored the psychological needs and capabilities of workers. The one best way of doing a job was chosen with the mechanistic criteria of speed and output. The imposition of a uniform manner of work can both destroy individuality and cause other psychological disturbances.

6 Had too simple an approach to the question of productivity and morale. It sought to keep up both of these exclusively by economic rewards and punishments. However, the fatigue studies of the Gilbreths during the 1920s did signal the beginnings of a wider appreciation of the relevant factors than had initially been recognized by Taylor. Incentive approaches under the scientific approach tended to focus on the worker as an individual and ignored his social context.

The period between 1910 and 1939 saw first Taylorism and then Fordism come to prominence in the United States. At the same time, the leaders of the Russian Revolution and their successors also adopted many of the same ideas to their own organizations as the box on functional foremanship showed. At the heart of scientific management was rationality achieved through the application of science. This was an idea which could be adopted by capitalist

---

human engineering

Following the Russian Revolution, Lenin ordered the establishment of the Central Institute of Labour. It was run by Alexei Gastev who photographed and studied workers as if they were parts in a machine. But this was more than time-and-motion study, because Gastev believed that one could teach people to think and behave in a rational way. He wanted to manufacture standardized people.

At the institute he built what he called a *social engineering machine*. It is shown below with its giant structure of pulleys, cogs and weights. How it worked, no one knows. Gastev was executed after a Stalin-orchestrated show trial in 1938. However, the machine's objective was clear. These machines were to be installed all over the Soviet Union. They were to make the entire society function in a totally rational manner. Each Soviet citizen would become a rational component of the machine that was Soviet society.

Alexei Gastev   *social engineering machine*

After Stalin's purges in the 1930s, the bourgeois engineers who had been allowed to run the factories since the revolution were replaced by Bolshevik engineers, who had been trained to do the job. To these new ideologically pure professionals, society was a machine. Indeed, Stalin himself once referred to human beings as tiny cogs. These new engineers believed that a machine-like society could be created through purely technical means.

and communist political systems alike. If the principles of scientific management could be applied to make factories so efficient, why could they not be applied to entire societies?

For a time in the United States the ideas of scientific management spread from the factory into the community in the form of *scientific living*. Many Americans began to run their whole lives on scientific principles. A Technocracy Movement emerged, which called for a production and distribution system based on scientific, national management of the entire population by engineers. At the height of its popularity in the late 1930s, some 400,000 grey-suited technocrats with their grey cars had become members. Some of these attended the Technocratic Conference where *rational dancing* proved particularly popular.

Meanwhile, in the Soviet Union, Henry Ford's concept of the factory system as an enormous machine, which consisted of identical and exchangeable human and non-human parts, all of which functioned in concert, was adopted by Lenin and his successors. For them, Soviet society would become one gigantic machine, provided of course that its citizens could be modified. Thus, for a period of time, two diametrically opposed political systems shared the same organizational principles.

sources

Baird, L.S., Post, J.E. and Mahon, J.F., 1990, *Management: Functions and Responsibilities*, HarperCollins, New York.

Bedeian, A.G., 1986, *Management*, CBS/Dryden Press, New York.

Collier, P. and Horowitz, D., 1987, *The Fords: An American Epic*, Futura/Collins, London.

Cooley, M. 1987, *Architect or Bee?*, Chatto and Windus, London.

Ford, H. and Crowther, S., 1924, *My Life and Work*, William Heinemann, London.

Friedmann, G., 1955, *Industrial Society: The Emergence of the Human Problems of Automation*, Free Press, Glencoe, IL.

Fulmer, R.M. and Herbert, T.T., 1974, *Exploring the New Management*, Macmillan, New York.

Gantt, H., 1919, *Organizing for Work*, Harcourt, Brace and Hove, New York.

Garson, B. 1989, *The Electronic Sweatshop*, Viking Penguin, New York.

Gilbreth, F.B., 1908, *Field System*, The Myron C. Clark Publishing Company, New York and Chicago.

Gilbreth, F.B. and Gilbreth, L., 1916, *Fatigue Study*, Sturgis and Walton, New York.

Gilbreth, F.B. and Gilbreth, L.M., 1918, 'Motion study for the crippled soldier with comments by conference attendees', in *Applied Motion Study*, George Routledge and Sons Ltd, London, pp. 131–57.

Rathe, A.W. (ed.), 1961, *Gantt on Management*, American Management Association, New York.

Rose, M., 1975, *Industrial Behaviour: Theoretical Development Since Taylor*, Penguin Books, Harmondsworth.

Sorensen, C.E., 1956, *My Forty Years With Ford*, W.W. Norton, New York.

Sward, K., 1948, *The Legend of Henry Ford*, Rinehart & Co., Inc., New York.

Taylor, F.W., 1911, *The Principles of Scientific Management*, Harper, New York.

Wilson, J.M., 1995, 'Henry Ford: A just-in-time pioneer', *Production and Inventory Management Journal*, vol. 37, no. 2.

Wren, D.A., 1980, 'Scientific management in the USSR, with particular reference to the contribution of Walter N. Polakov', *Academy of Management Review*, vol. 5, no. 1, pp. 1–11.

Zaleznik, A. and Kets de Vries, M., 1975, *Power and the Corporate Mind*, Houghton Mifflin, Boston, MA.

chapter 13 bureaucracy and roles

"Maxwell! Get the hell back in line!"

concepts and learning objectives

This chapter examines the development and characteristics of a form of organizational design called bureaucracy. Although bureaucracy is not the only form of organizational structure that is possible, it has tended to dominate large, modern organizations. Since bureaucracy stresses the definition of roles and their relationships between one another, this chapter will also consider the concept of role in organizations.

Currently, there is an increasing questioning of the appropriateness of bureaucratic forms of organization to the objectives of companies and the needs of the individuals within them. These concerns are not just academic discussions conducted in textbooks. We are seeing experiments in new forms of organizational designs taking place all around the world.

363

learning objectives

When you have read this chapter, you should be able to define those key concepts in your own words, and you should also be able to:

1 List the main questions which those designing organizational structures need to answer.

2 Distinguish between charismatic, traditional and legal–rational forms of authority.

3 State the main characteristics of a bureaucratic organization as specified by Max Weber.

4 Explain the different ways in which the concept of role is presented in the social science literature.

5 Following Argyris, give an example from your own experience of the way in which organizational structures affect personality development.

organizational structuring

Anyone designing an appropriate structure for an organization needs to ask certain questions. Child (1984) identified the five main ones:

1 Should jobs be broken down into narrow areas of work and responsibility so as to secure the benefits of specialization? Or should the degree of specialization be kept to a minimum in order to simplify communication and to offer members of the organization greater scope and responsibility in their work? Another choice arising in the design of jobs concerns the extent to which the responsibilities and methods attaching to them should be precisely defined.

2 Should the overall structure of an organization be 'tall' rather than 'flat' in terms of its levels of management and spans-of-control? What are the implications for communication, motivation and overhead costs of moving towards one of these alternatives rather than the other?

3 Should jobs and departments be grouped together in a 'functional' way according to the specialist expertise and interests that they share? Or should they be grouped according to the different services and products which are being offered, or the different geographical areas being served, or according to yet another criterion?

4 Is it appropriate to aim for an intensive form of integration between the different segments of an organization or not? What kind of integrative mechanisms are there to choose from?

5 What approach should management take towards maintaining adequate control over work done? Should it centralise or delegate decisions, and all or only some of the decisions? Should a policy of extensive formalization be adopted in which standing orders and written records are used for control purposes? Should work be subject to close supervision? (Child, 1984, p. 8).

STOP!

Select one of the five issues raised above. With one or two fellow students, think about an organization which you are all familiar with. Discuss your views on the chosen issue with each other.

Amongst the first writers to offer answers to these questions was the German sociologist, Max Weber. Weber did not invent the term bureaucracy; that distinction is accorded to a Frenchman, de Gournay (1712–59). The literal meaning of bureaucracy is, 'rule by office or by officials'. It is to Weber that most commentators turn when considering modern developments of the concept. His work, which was carried out at the turn of the century, stemmed from his study of power and authority.

definitions

Power *was the ability to get things done by threats of force sanction; while*

Authority *was managing to get things done because one's orders were seen by others as justified or legitimate.*

Max Weber (1864–1920)
Reproduced by permission of Leif Geiges.

Weber studied societies in history and distinguished three different types of authority.

definitions

Traditional authority, *based on the belief that the ruler had a natural right to rule. This right was either God-given or by descent. The authority enjoyed by kings would be of this type.*

Charismatic authority, *based on the belief that the ruler had some special, unique virtue, either religious or heroic. Hitler and the prophets had this.*

Legal–rational authority *based on formal written rules which had the force of law. The authority of present-day prime ministers and college principals is of this type.*

Because of the process of rationalization in modern society, the authority which predominates is legal–rational. We obey and do what managers and civil servants tell us, not because we think they have a natural right to do so or possess any divine powers, but because we acknowledge that they have a legal right.

---

definition

Bureaucracy *corresponds to the legal–rational type of authority. It is an organizational design characterized by a specialization of labour, a specific authority hierarchy, a formal set of rules and rigid promotion and selection criteria.*

Weber's 'ideal type' bureaucracy

According to Weber, bureaucracy was the most efficient way of running large organizations. He wrote: 'The fully developed bureaucratic mechanism compares with other organizations exactly as does the machine with the non-mechanical modes of production'. The bureaucratic form of organization as Weber saw it had the following characteristics:

1 **job specialization** Jobs are broken down into simple, routine and well-defined tasks. People should specialize and thus learn to do one set of activities well. Work is divided so that authority and responsibility are clearly defined.

2 **authority hierarchy** Offices or positions are organized in a clear chain-of-command hierarchy. Each lower position is controlled and supervised by a higher one, so that workers clearly know to whom they are responsible.

3 **formal rules and regulations** To ensure uniformity and to guide the actions of employees, managers must depend heavily on formal organizational rules. These are set down to monitor employee behaviour.

4 **impersonality** Rules and controls are applied uniformly, avoiding involvement of personalities or the personal preferences of employees.

5 **formal selection** All organization members are to be selected on the basis of technical qualifications demonstrated by training, education or formal examination.

6 **career orientation** Managers are professional officials rather than owners of the units they manage. They work for fixed salaries and pursue their careers within the organization.

Weber used the term bureaucracy to describe a type of formal organization, which was both impersonal and rational. Whereas in the past authority had been based on nepotism, whim or fancy, in bureaucratic organizations it was based on rational principles. For this reason, it offered the possibility of being the most efficient ever, in comparison with what had preceded it. Bureaucracy for him was a form of organization, which emphasized speed, precision, regulation, clarity, reliability and efficiency. This was achieved through creating a fixed division of tasks, imposing detailed rules, regulations and procedures and monitoring through hierarchical supervision.

The strength of bureaucracy lay in its standardization. Employee behaviour was controlled and made predictable. This was achieved not through time-and-motion study, but through the application of rules, regulations and procedures. Bureaucratic organizations have a reasonably consistent set of goals and preferences. They devote few resources to time-consuming information searches or the analysis of current activities to check if they are meeting stated goals. Instead, they rely on rules, tradition, precedent and standard operating procedures. Little time is spent on decision-making since decisions follow from the established routines and few action alternatives are considered. The ideological emphasis is on stability, fairness and predictability (Pfeffer, 1981). Weber was struck by how the bureaucratic structure of a company routinized the processes of its administration, in a way similar to how a machine routinized production. For this reason, Weber's original model is often referred to as a *machine bureaucracy*.

definition

Machine bureaucracy *possesses all the characteristics of a bureaucracy listed earlier. The important decisions are made at the strategic apex of the organizational pyramid; whilst at the bottom, standardized procedures are used which have been developed by specialists at headquarters. There are many support staff, and many layers of hierarchy between the apex and the bottom operating levels.*

Brave New Bureaucracy

In his novel *Brave New World* (1932), Aldous Huxley dramatized Weber's fears about bureaucracy, especially its static nature, inherent conservatism and its opposition to change, innovation or risk-taking. The bureaucratic principles Weber had proposed for the structuring of organizations, Huxley applied to an imaginary society which he called the World State.

The World State was hierarchical, rule-governed and conformist. Authority was derived from expertise. It was rigidly stratified, possessing a vertical, hierarchical structure based on intellectual competency (Alphas, Betas, Deltas). It offered its citizens permanent security within an elaborate social structure and culture. It was replete with rules and norms of behaviour which encouraged conformity. It was impersonal, denying its members personal identity and insisting on conformity. It was a technocracy of experts, a vast social pyramid ruled by scientific specialists who worshipped Weber's ideal of order and regimentation, and who channelled their efforts towards the creation of a world of stable, routine and economic efficiency. Beetham felt that 'The central question is what we can oppose to this machinery, in order to keep a portion of humanity free from this pigeon-holing of the spirit, from this total domination of the bureaucratic ideal'.

based on Aldous Huxley, 1932, *Brave New World*, Penguin Books, Harmondsworth; and D. Beetham, 1987, *Bureaucracy*, University of Minnesota Press, Minneapolis.

In modern usage, bureaucracy is used as a pejorative term by the public and the media when they come up against red tape and obstructiveness in any aspect of organizational life. Weber's view was in direct opposition to this. For him, bureaucracy was the most efficient form of social organization precisely because it was so coldly logical and did not allow personal relations and feelings to get in the way of achieving goals. The change in meaning has

**modern negative
connotations of
bureaucracy**

from *Personnel*, September 1988, p. 87.

That's the Way the Wheels Turn

Fill in this application form in triplicate and do
    Supply the information, what and where and how and who,
We want your registration number, age and height and weight,
    So that we can keep the nation in a law and ordered state.

Chorus   Cause that's the way the wheels turn,
        Round and round the wheels turn,
        That's the way the wheels turn round

The forms are fumigated, then they're filed into files,
    The files are stamped and dated, then they're piled into piles,
The piles are tabulated, then they're sorted into rows,
    The rows are consecrated, so the paper kingdom grows.

I am the man in uniform, the man without a name,
    I'm the man who sees the rules are kept, the rules that others frame,
And if you want a question answered, there may be some delay,
    Because it isn't my department, I'm not authorised to say.

I am a servant of the people, doing what I have to do,
    I'm the man who turns the handles, and I'm turning them for you,
If you want to come and see me, join the queue and while you wait,
    Fill in this form PC three-zero-FX-double eight.

from 'That's the Way the Wheels Turn', Leon Rosselson, *Bringing the News from Nowhere*, Leon Rosselson. © Leon Rosselson/Fuse Records, 28 Park Chase, Wembley Park, Middlesex.

occurred because the principles of bureaucracy, designed to maximize efficiency, also resulted in inefficiencies. During the 1950s, many sociologists devoted themselves to the study of the 'dysfunctions of bureaucracy'.

Weber was a sociologist, not a manager or a management consultant. As such he did not advocate bureaucracy as the answer to the questions posed at the start of this chapter. He did believe that, historically, bureaucracy was the most efficient form of organization available. He feared that its success would produce a deadening effect on people. It was the unintended consequences of bureaucratic forms of organization that have now given the word such negative connotations.

Nevertheless, Weber's outline of bureaucracy, of rationally ordered activity, based on a set pattern of behaviour and distribution of work, did offer guidelines for the design and structuring of organizations. Moreover, while his main focus was on organizations such as the army, government and the Church, bureaucratic forms of organization have been adopted by many other organizations such as hospitals, schools and industrial and commercial companies. Some writers believe that this is the only suitable structural form for a large organization.

rules

Crucial to the success of the bureaucratic organization structure were formal rules. Rules and set-down procedures are used to direct and control the behaviour of its employees. In a bureaucratic form of organization they are a defining feature of it. Weber laid great stress on the organized patterning of relationships between people through the use of rules. He felt that rules, based on rational and logical needs, contributed significantly to the efficient operation of his bureaucratic form of organization. Hood (1986, pp. 21–2) listed the features of rules that, in Weber's terms, would contribute to organizational efficiency and rationality:

- The rules had to be known by all.
- The purpose of the rules had to be clear and based on a valid theory of cause and effect.
- Rules had to be consistent with each other.
- It should be clear where rules applied.
- The scope for subjective interpretation was limited.

---

definition

Rules *are procedures or obligations explicitly stated and written down in company manuals.*

STOP!

Think of some of the rules that you have encountered in organizations to which you currently belong, or used to belong. Give an example of rules which broke one or more of Hood's conditions.

"I was just going to say "Well, I don't make the rules." But, of course, I do make the rules."

Drawing by Leo Cullum. © 1986 The New Yorker Magazine, Inc.

All large organizations have formal rules and train their staff to follow them. Being able to 'follow procedures and take direction' are traits used by recruiters to select new company staff. Companies tend to be reluctant to admit this or make it public, believing perhaps that customers like to feel that staff behave in this way naturally. Internally, management believe that, far from being discouraging, rules enhance performance and encourage staff. They see such rules and guidelines as essential for the successful co-ordination of large numbers of employees. They argue that it makes it easier for individuals within the firm to work towards the same ends; and that a knowledge of the same disciplines establishes the same standards of behaviour and performance in a group. Such rules, of course, also place limits to the creative behaviour of staff.

Research studies on rules suggest that the behaviour of people in organizations cannot be explained in terms of their conforming to rules. In many instances, it is only by ignoring company rules that work can get done. This is what, during the heyday of trade union action in the 1960s and 1970s, made 'working-to-rule' such an effective weapon during the time of an industrial dispute. Individuals all have their own personal views as to what constitutes right and proper behaviour. They often will not accept other people's views which may be represented in certain organizational rules and procedures.

The formal rules and procedures of most organizations are a means of encouraging co-ordination and conformity among employees. However, well-qualified professionals such as doctors, engineers and college lecturers usually want to be free to do their own thing and to develop themselves and their personalities through work. A study of this contradiction was carried out by Dennis Organ and Charles Greene (1981), who tried to find out whether

rules in a supermarket

Here is a list of rules about interacting with customers that is given to newly appointed checkout operators. Next time you visit your local supermarket, tick off how many of them are followed by the person who deals with you.

1 Make eye contact and greet the customer with a smile.
2 Start a conversation, e.g. check whether the customer would like coupons or vouchers.
3 Check there are bags available and open ready for use.
4 Pack frozen goods, meat, bleach and firelighters separately.
5 Do not chat to anyone else during the transaction or complain in front of the customer.
6 Explain any delay to the customer and apologize.
7 Inform the customer of the total amount payable, saying 'Please'.
8 Confirm the method of payment and repeat the cash amount tendered by the customer if applicable.
9 Make eye contact, giving the customer the receipt, explaining any multisaves, voids, etc., and count the change into the customer's hand if applicable.
10 Make a parting comment, with 'Thank You' as a minimum.

The supermarkets are experimenting with a system where customers are given a hand-held scanner which they use to scan the bar codes of the products that they have selected from the shelves. The machine totals up the items as they go. They then receive a total bill for their shopping from their machine and pay at the specially designated express checkout. The need for checkout interaction rules such as those above will become redundant since there will not be enough time for them to have an interaction with the customer.

STOP!
In practice, once taught, few of the checkout operator rules are obeyed by the staff or enforced by the supervisors. Why should this be so?

a question of clarity and certainty

The parable of BT's dress code deserves to be more widely told. After privatization, the company decided it was time to shake off the sloppy dress habits of the public sector. A directive went round telling senior employees that they should adopt suitable business dress. The directive caused some resentment. Those who opposed it demanded greater clarity and certainty. When they went to the wardrobe in the morning, how could they know what would represent suitable business dress? After advice from its legal and regulatory affairs department, the company agreed to promulgate a dress code. Senior male employees were expected to wear smart suits, shirts with collar, and ties. It was not long before someone came to the office in a red suit. When criticized, he pointed to the terms of the dress code. The suit was undeniably smart; but it was the smartness of a night-club rather than a boardroom.

So the dress code had to specify a colour. Red was out, grey was in. But what of blue? Some blues were clearly acceptable. The chairman's favourite suit, in fact, was a fetching shade of navy. But bright blues could not be admitted. So how bright was bright? BT research came up with the answer. Brightness is determined by how much light a fabric reflects. A machine could measure this, and one was soon constructed and installed in the reception areas. But ties posed a more intractable problem. It was simply impossible to define which colours and motifs were acceptable. A clearance procedure seemed the best answer. Anyone who bought a new tie could submit it to the dress code department, which had 42 days to rule on whether or not it was suitable business dress. This was difficult, since the appropriateness of a tie might depend on its context – the suit and the shirt that went with it. So decisions were rather conservative. This raised the issue of an appeals mechanism.

Delegating discretion over approval of ties to the dress code department made it judge and jury in implementing regulations it had devised. But this violated natural justice. The company agreed that a small group of senior directors, with an independent fashion adviser, would hear complaints from employees who felt

bureaucracy cramped the style of this category of company employee. Two hundred and forty research scientists and engineers completed a questionnaire which aimed to measure six different aspects of the respondents' work experience. As expected, organizations with an engineering orientation were found to be more formalized than those engaged in basic research.

Formalization, that is bureaucracy, was associated with role-conflict and self-estrangement, but it was also linked to low role ambiguity, high organizational identification and low self-estrangement. The authors drew the conclusion that bureaucracy can be beneficial in managing professional employees. Formalization avoids the frustrations of uncertainty about job requirements and gives the professional 'a gestalt within which he can define the nature of his own contribution'. To avoid the drawbacks, administrators have to make rules that are consistent with professional standards and avoid rules that create job conflict. Thus bureaucratic forms have successfully adapted to deal with knowledge workers. They are called *professional bureaucracies*, to contrast them with Weber's original conception which is termed machine bureaucracy.

their ties had been unreasonably rejected. But there was the more general problem of changing fashion. After all, it was not so long ago since every gentleman had gone to work in a wing collar and frock coat. Not only were other forms of dress now acceptable, but wing collars had probably ceased to be acceptable. Not the image of a modern information company. A well-known fashion designer agreed to chair a standing working party to advise the company on fashion trends.

By this time, the dress code extended to 50 pages, largely impenetrable. No sensible employee read it, and when they were given a copy they were told that if they only behaved sensibly they would probably be all right. Knowledge of its contents was confined to the dress department, which by this time consisted of 20 people, mostly lawyers, the union representative who negotiated over it, and a few cranks who enjoyed pointing out inconsistencies and anomalies in the code.

Eventually a new management came in, determined to sweep the dress code department away. They quickly realized there were two alternatives. One was to supply a uniform to all employees. This was obviously an intolerable interference in personal affairs. The other was to sweep away the dress code and renew the instruction to everyone to wear suitable business dress. If anyone was in genuine doubt as to what constituted suitable dress – and not many people were – they were advised to have a word with the dress regulator. He had been given this role precisely because of his sound judgement and range of business experience. What the regulator said bound no one, but to ignore his advice was injudicious and might prejudice advancement in the company.

The demand for clarity and certainty in regulation has great superficial plausibility, and it is because it is difficult to argue against clarity and certainty that it is best to resort to parable. The world is rarely clear and certain, and if it seems so today, it will have ceased to be so tomorrow.

abridged from John Kay, 1996, *Financial Times*, 12 January, p. 10.

Professional bureaucracies modify the principle of centralized control and thus allow their staff a greater degree of autonomy. This is appropriate for working in relatively stable conditions in which tasks are relatively complicated. Universities and hospitals are examples of professional bureaucracies, since their staff possess key skills and abilities, and need a large amount of freedom and discretion in their work to get their job done effectively.

definition

Professional bureaucracy *possesses all the characteristics of a bureaucracy listed earlier. Decision-making is decentralized, and there are few levels between the strategic apex and the operating staff (professors, doctors, nurses). Being a flat structure, control of staff is achieved by the professional indoctrination of its members.*

Sailors beat computer

IF ANYBODY can use computers to make a bureaucracy more responsive to central command, it should be a navy. Its hierarchy is rigidly defined; ships are discrete units; the "proper" way of doing things is thoroughly codified. Yet when an American navy captain tried to embody the official rules and hierarchy in an automated command system for his ship, the system flopped. Similar systems have also been tried in the messier world of business with, for the most part, similar lack of success. Managers as well as admirals can learn from the navy's experience.

With help from researchers at Carnegie-Mellon University, the captain created a sort of automated manual-cum-communications system called ZOG for one of the navy's new aircraft-carriers. In theory, ZOG could not only remind a sailor what the proper procedures were, it could also help him to carry them out. The fate of the system is described in the spring issue of *AI Magazine*, the journal of the American Association for Artificial Intelligence.

Although ZOG seems to have done almost everything it was designed to do, few sailors used it be-

cause few of them follow navy procedures in anything like the detail laid down in the rulebook. For example, the rules specify exactly how far apart the ship's air-traffic-control officers should keep aeroplanes coming in to land on a carrier. In practice, however, those controlling the aircraft rely more on their own judgment: if they need to bunch aircraft more closely together to bring in one that is short of fuel, they will (sensibly) do so. ZOG was not nearly flexible enough to cope with that sort of thing.

Similar problems cropped up with

The computer says turn around

ZOG's communicating skills. Navy rules specify who should be consulted on what, and who has the authority to take various decisions, and the ship's communication software incorporated the official rules. In practice, however, real problems were solved by ad hoc working groups that sprang up and dissolved too fast for ZOG to follow.

Lastly, some old navy hands argued that ZOG's emphasis on helping sailors to make the "right" decision missed the point: often there was no absolutely correct decision, and speed was essential. One officer cited the case of an aircraft suddenly discovering a problem with its landing gear.

The trick, say veterans, is to decide quickly whether to land the aircraft on the carrier or on shore, and then stay on top of developments by keeping in communication with the pilot. Again, ZOG's emphasis on maintaining "business as usual" made it too inflexible.

Though dismissing ZOG's abilities as an adviser, sailors seemed happier using it as an intelligent assistant: providing up-to-the-second advice on weather or the condition of on-board systems. In such jobs it helped them do what they needed to do, rather than telling them what they should do.

roles

Organizational structuring also occurs through the specification of the roles members are expected to play. It follows that if individuals at different points in the hierarchy have mutual and complementary expectations, then the patterning and predictability of their behaviour is increased. Following Weber, the formal positions (identified on an organizational chart) in a company can be considered as 'offices' or bureaux. The behaviour expected of any person occupying an office then becomes his or her 'role'. Roles are thus associated with positions in the organization and are involved in interactions.

definition
Role *is the pattern of behaviour expected by others from a person occupying a certain position in an organizational hierarchy.*

A single office-holder, such as an engineer, will have regular interactions with a limited number of other office-holders such as workers, the department manager, trade union officials, and so on. Each individual in an organization, therefore, has his or her own particular role set. This can be drawn on a role set diagram in which the organizational member being considered (focal person) is placed at the centre. It is important not to confuse this concept with the notion of a single person playing a number of different roles in their life (e.g. mother, wife, counsellor). The concept of role is one which has been used extensively to understand the behaviour of people in organizations. A person may be observed in a single role, e.g. nurse, engineer, trade union official, but he may play many different roles at the same time in his normal working life.

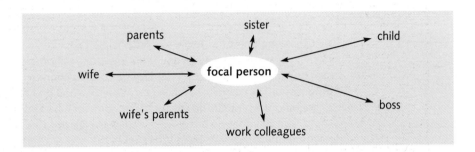

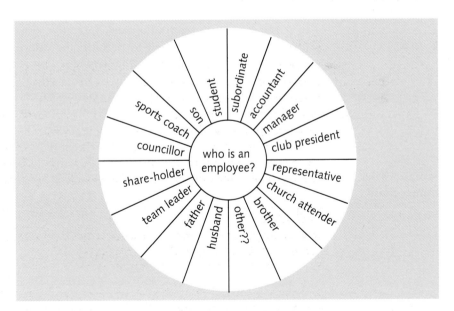

People's roles in organizations are ranked by status. Individuals occupying the role of managers are generally accorded more status that those occupying that of cleaner. In other companies, the ranking of roles is less obvious. Van Maanen (1991) described the rank ordering of occupations at Disneyland. At the top were the Disneyland Ambassadors and Tour Guides. These were the upper-class, prestigious, bilingual women in charge of ushering tourists through the park. Second came those ride operators who either performed skilled work such as live narration, or who drove costly vehicles such as antique trains, horse drawn carriages or the Monorail. Third were all the other ride operators. Fourth were the sweepers who kept the concrete grounds clean. Although designated as *proles*, there was a lower, fifth category of *sub-prole* or peasant status. The 'lowest of the low' included food and concession workers, pancake ladies, peanut pushers, coke blokes, suds drivers and soda jerks.

---

the priest's story

The officiating priest has two roles. He has the task of managing the act of worship, through instructions and more elaborate exhortations. He also has the traditional priestly role of representing the congregation to God and God to the congregation. On certain occasions he addresses God on behalf of the congregation. On others he speaks in the name of God and with His authority. On no occasion does he unequivocally take the part of God, although in the Holy Communion service he in effect takes the part of Christ at the Last Supper. His role is a subtle one, in that it constitutes both a series of acts by which God confronts, instructs, feeds, absolves and blesses the congregation, and also a screen between God and the congregation, in that God's initiatives are always mediated through the priest.

from Bruce Reed and Barry Palmer, 1978, 'The local church in its environment', in E.J. Miller (ed.), *Task and Organization*, John Wiley, Chichester, p. 266.

In a bureaucratic organization structure that emphasizes impersonality, company officials are expected to perform the duties of their role without personal consideration of people as individuals. This is intended to guarantee equal treatment of people as individuals. Internally, it can lead to employees of modern bureaucratic organizations relating to one another primarily in terms of their roles, for example, doctors to nurses in hospitals, rather than through their individual backgrounds. Externally, this may result in their being perceived as cold and uncaring by clients, customers or patients.

bureaucratic impersonality

"I'd like to think of you as a person, David, but it's my job to think of you as personnel."

Drawing by Vietor. © 1986 The New Yorker Magazine, Inc.

defining roles

A role may be viewed in different ways. There is disagreement among social scientists on this issue. Definitions of role depend on how they are to be used. We shall consider prescriptive, evaluative, descriptive and action definitions of the concept of role.

A *prescriptive* definition is concerned with what a person should do when he plays a specific role. Job descriptions which are sent with job application forms represent examples of prescriptive role definitions.

An *evaluative* definition, in contrast, assesses how well or badly a role is being performed. To do this it is necessary to establish criteria or standards against which to make assessments. A role prescription can supply such standards.

STOP!

With the person next to you list the behaviours of someone who occupies the role of a student. Then, individually, rank yourself and the other person on a 1–5 scale (1 = always does this, 5 = never does this). Now compare your rankings.

In organizations, staff appraisal schemes aim to set criteria in order to monitor and evaluate individual role performance. Staff appraisals could be considered to be part of the procedure intended to pattern, and make predictable, the behaviours of organization members.

A *descriptive* definition of a role is based on the actual duties performed by the person being studied. Such a descriptive role statement can be developed by observing and noting in minute detail what a person does. Such forms of analysis have been carried out by researchers who have studied how managers spend their time. These analyses contain the content of the work done alone, as well as the nature of the interactions engaged in.

STOP!

List the main activities you have engaged in today in your role as a student. Rank them in order of importance.

Finally, there is an *action* definition of a role. While a job description may give an account of the duties that should be undertaken by someone playing a specific role (e.g. a teacher should motivate students to learn), in pursuing these duties many actions may be performed. Lecturers establish rapport, joke with students, ask them questions, and so on. A role can, therefore, be specified in terms of actions involved in its performance. Any role may thus be considered under the four aspects of prescription, evaluation, description and action. All four are interrelated and interdependent.

role relationship and socialization

This is the relationship that one has with an individual occupying another position or 'office' in the organization by virtue of their being a member of your role set.

---

definition

Role relationship *is that intangible mixture of feelings and emotions which exist between two or more people occupying different roles.*

A relationship can be considered as the way in which one uses oneself in a disciplined and responsible way when dealing with a group or individual. In achieving his goals and fulfilling his duties, the organization member can use his 'good' relationships with colleagues, bosses, clients and customers to help him to achieve his aims at work: for example, getting support for some new plan of action. The individual needs, however, to be aware that the other people also have needs and feelings, and should show concern for these and be aware of others' responses. Failure to do this can lead to a breakdown in relationships.

Individuals have role relationships with each other, and organizations can be thought of as a set of overlapping and interlocking role sets. In the

---

role modelling in the USA and the former Soviet Union

One aspect of the socialization process involves highlighting to citizens or employees examples of the types of behaviour that the country or company would like them to emulate. The achievements of an individual are publicly recognized and are brought to the attention of others. This form of teaching is called *role modelling*.

The Great Performers programme is run by TRS, an American Express Company. Employees below the level of director can be nominated for the award who have 'gone above and beyond the call of duty in a dramatic and exemplary way'. The nominees, through their actions should have provided 'superior service to a member of one of several customer groups'. The winners receive an inscribed certificate, a cheque for a monetary reward, a gold GP logo pin and a letter of commendation from the chairman of the regional selection committee. Their names, photographs and descriptions of the achievements that won them their awards are all contained in a special edition of the company's in-house newsletter, *TRS Express*, which is circulated to all employees.

based on *TRS Express*, 1988, Special Edition, Great Performers.

Propaganda aimed at encouraging workers to increase output and raise productivity was a key element of Stalin's five-year plans. The feats of individual workers were glorified. The hero of the campaign for 'overfulfilment' in the Stalin years was Alexei Stakhanov, a coal miner in the Donbass, who was said to have hewn 102 tons of coal in a single shift instead of the seven tons demanded. The exercise was an unreal one. The feat was achieved only by halting all other work in his sector of the mine and by using a gang of miners to help him. But the opportunity was used to raise work norms. Workers who emulated Stakhanov were called Stakhanovites, and they were given the best houses and pay rises. Some Stakhanovite workers were lynched by their fellow-workers.

from H. Hamman and S. Parrott, 1987, *Mayday at Chernobyl*, New English Library, London, p. 62.

chapter on groups, the concept of norm was introduced and defined. Here, norms can be seen as the general expectations of how people ought to behave in a given organizational role. Roles are thus more restricted expectations about what behaviour is appropriate in which specific situations.

A role influences the behaviour of an individual by setting limits within which he is expected to act. Roles in organizations are learned through socialization. Pascale (1985) reported how new MBAs joining the consulting company of Bain & Co. were taught the norms of the company's collegial style, which included attending meetings, not competing with peers, making conceptual contributions without being a prima donna, building on the ideas of others, avoiding overt political battles and resolving conflict directly, but not disagreeably. To succeed in this company, reported Pascale, one had to do it through the team.

Many of the tasks involved in the job have been learned and assimilated so well that they become accepted as being part of the person. This raises the question of whether, in behaving in a certain way, we are ourselves or just conforming to what the organization (and society) expects of us. Role relationships therefore are the field within which behaviour occurs. People's behaviour at any given moment is the result of:

- their personalities
- their perception and understanding of each other
- their attitudes to the behavioural constraints imposed by the role relationship
- the degree of their socialization with respect to constraints
- their ability to inhibit and control their behaviours

An important function of role relationships is to reduce the areas of possible uncertainty to manageable proportions. Michael Argyle (1964) has argued that occupants of similar positions, for example firemen, tend to behave in similar ways in certain situations and share various attitudes and beliefs. In many standardized situations, the behaviour which takes place can be accurately predicted from knowledge of the organization and its rules, whilst knowledge of the personality characteristics may be of little use. A person's behaviour is thus not necessarily the result of personality factors, but the consequence of the various influences which mould people to the standard role behaviour for that position.

Such sharing of behaviour, attitudes and personalities can come about in an organization through the staff selection process (self-selection and company selection); through training (role behaviour results from carefully created training courses and spontaneously created initiation ceremonies); and not least through the job itself (new organization members are exposed to job demands and are pressured to perform in certain ways).

In practice, it is a mixture of all three. The way in which individuals behave and the attitudes which they develop are strongly influenced by the roles which are assigned to them in a set of structured relationships, e.g. tutor–student, boss–subordinate. The expectations of other people in related roles, and an individual's own beliefs learned through the process of socialization inside and outside the organization, will affect their decisions as to what is and is not appropriate behaviour in a specified role.

prison experiment

To what extent do our attitudes, values and self-image affect the way we play roles in organizations such as student, lecturer, doctor, nurse or doorman? To what extent are our attitudes, values and self-image determined by the organizational roles we play?

Philip Zimbardo and two graduate student colleagues from the Department of Psychology at Stanford University in California created their own prison to examine the roles of prisoner and guard. Advertising in the Palo Alto city newspaper, they selected 21 young men from the 75 that they interviewed. These individuals were screened to ensure that each was a mature, emotionally stable, normal, intelligent North American male student from a middle-class home with no criminal record. Each volunteer was paid $15 a day to participate in a two-week study of prison life. A toss of a coin arbitrarily designated these recruits as either prisoners or guards. Hence, at the start of the study, there were no measurable differences between the two groups assigned to play the two roles (10 prisoners and 11 guards).

Those taking the role of guards had their individuality minimized by being required to wear uniforms, including silver reflector glasses which prevented eye-contact. They were to be referred to as Mr Correction Officer by the prisoners, and they were given symbols of their power which included clubs, whistles, handcuffs and keys. They were given minimal instructions by the researchers, being required only to 'maintain law and order'. Whilst physical violence was forbidden, they were told to make up and improvize their own formal rules to achieve the stated objective during their 8-hour, 3-man shifts.

Those who were assigned the role of prisoners were unexpectedly picked up at their homes by a city policeman in a squad car. Each was searched, handcuffed, fingerprinted, booked in at the Palo Alto police station, blindfolded and then transferred to Zimbardo's 'Stanford County Prison', which was located in the basement of the university psychology building. Each prisoner's sense of uniqueness and prior identity was minimized. They were given smocks to wear and had nylon stocking caps on their heads to simulate baldness. Their personal effects were removed, they had to use their ID numbers; and they were housed in stark cells. All this made them appear similar to each other and indistinguishable to observers. Six days into the planned 14-day study the researchers had to abandon the experiment. Why?

In a matter of days, even hours, a strange relationship began to develop between the prisoners and their guards. Some of the guards began to treat the prisoners as if they were despicable animals, and began to take pleasure in psychological cruelty. The prisoners in turn became servile, dehumanized robots, who thought only of their individual survival, escape and mounting hatred of the guards. About a third of the guards became tyrannical in their arbitrary use of power, and became quite inventive in developing techniques to break the spirit of the prisoners and to make them feel worthless. Having crushed a prison rebellion, the guards escalated their aggression, and this increased the prisoners' sense of dependence, depression and helplessness.

Within 36 hours, the first 'prisoner' had to be released because of uncontrolled crying, fits of rage, disorganized thinking and severe depression. He was Doug Korpi (Prisoner No. 8612) who suffered a mental breakdown. 'I've never screamed so loud in my life. I've never been so upset,' he said. Three more prisoners were released on consecutive days with the same symptoms. A fifth left with a psychosomatic rash. Others begged to be paroled and nearly all were willing to forfeit their money if the guards agreed to release them.

Zimbardo and his colleagues were surprised by the changes in the behaviour and attitudes of their experimental subjects. The researchers attributed these changes to a number of causes. First, the creation of a new environment within which both groups were separated from the outside world. New attitudes were developed about this new 'mini-world', as well as what constituted appropriate behaviour within it.

A second explanation was that within this new 'mini-world' of the prison, the participants were unable to differentiate clearly between the role they were asked to play (prisoner or guard) and their real self. A week's experience of imprisonment (temporarily) appeared to undo a lifetime of learning. Human values and self-concepts were challenged, and the pathological side of human nature was allowed to surface. The prisoners became so programmed to think of themselves as prisoners, that when their requests for parole were refused, they returned docilely to their cells, instead of feeling capable of just withdrawing from an unpleasant psychological research experiment.

This study raises many different issues. Of particular interest is Zimbardo's conclusion that individual behaviour is largely under the control of social and environmental forces, rather than being the result of personality traits, character or willpower. In an organizational context such as a prison, the mere fact of assigning labels to people and putting them in situations where such labels acquire validity and meaning is sufficient to elicit a certain type of behaviour. The power of the prison environment was stronger than each individual's will to resist falling into his role. In the light of these research findings, what undesirable behaviours might be elicited by assigning the labels of student, lecturer, doctor, nurse or doorman to individuals?

based on Craig Haney, Curtis Banks and Philip Zimbardo, 1973, 'A study of prisoners and guards in a simulated prison', *Naval Research Reviews*, Office of Naval Research, Department of the Navy, Washington, DC, September; and P.G. Zimbardo *et al.*, 1973, 'A Pirandellian prison', *The New York Times Magazine*, 8 April.

roles, self-concept and the self-fulfilling prophecy

Philip Zimbardo

The roles that we play are part of our self-concept. Chapter 6 explained the personality theory which held that we each come to know ourselves through our interactions with others. We play different roles throughout our lives, and these require us to use different abilities, thereby adding more aspects to our self-image. Which roles we play, and how successfully we play them during our adulthood, affects our level of self-esteem. Thus the roles that we play both inside and outside the organization, affect our self-image and self-esteem. Research shows that people possess mental concepts of different roles, and conform to them when asked or required to do so (Zimbardo *et al.*, 1973). It also demonstrates the power of roles, not only to influence behaviour, but also to affect a person's self-image. Zimbardo's study also demonstrates the concept known as the self-fulfilling prophecy. This is the observation that if you have certain expectations of people, and treat them in a way that relates to these expectations, the people concerned will in turn respond in the way that you treat them. Their behaviour comes to fit your expectation of them – they behave as you thought they would.

---

definition

Self-fulfilling prophecy *is an expectation that leads to a certain pattern of behaviour whose consequences confirm the expectation.*

For example, a rumour (prophecy) that a bank is about to collapse leads people to withdraw their money from it all at the same time, and the bank then does indeed collapse. If a teacher expects children to work hard and do well at school, they will do so (Rosenthal and Jacobson, 1968). Interest in this study relates to whether supervisor behaviour may improve employee performance. Rosenthal (1973) identified four factors which produced the effect:

climate The supervisors' expectations lead them to treat workers differently. Such differences are manifested in their eye-contact, smiling, nodding, posture, tone of voice. Their expectation is transmitted in this way.

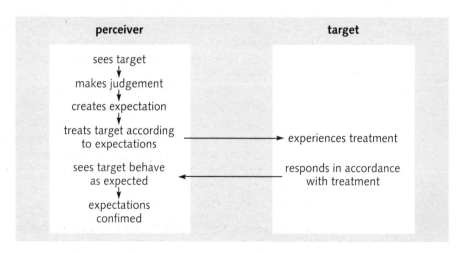

feedback More detailed and accurate information is given to workers about their performance. The supervisor can say how they can improve, rather than just a general 'well done'.

input The supervisor gives workers more demanding tasks to perform that stretch them.

output The supervisor gives the developing worker cues to respond to, for example, asking questions.

Psychologists have explained what must happen before the self-fulfilling prophecy can occur.

Pooh-Bah's role conflict in *The Mikado*

Ko-Ko: Pooh-Bah, it seems that the festivities in connection with my approaching marriage must last a week. I should like to do it handsomely, and I want to consult you as to the amount I ought to spend upon them.

Pooh-Bah: Certainly. In which of my capacities? As First Lord of the Treasury, Lord Chamberlain, Attorney-General, Chancellor of the Exchequer, Privy Purse, or Private Secretary?

Ko-Ko: Suppose we say as Private Secretary.

Pooh-Bah: Speaking as your Private Secretary, I should say that as the city will have to pay for it, don't stint yourself, do it well.

Ko-Ko: Exactly – as the city will have to pay for it. That is your advice.

Pooh-Bah: As Private Secretary. Of course, you will understand that, as Chancellor of the Exchequer, I am bound to see that due economy is observed.

Ko-Ko: Oh! But you said just now 'Don't stint yourself, do it well'.

Pooh-Bah: As Private Secretary.

Ko-Ko: And now you say that due economy must be observed.

Pooh-Bah: As Chancellor of the Exchequer.

Ko-Ko: I see. Come over here, where the Chancellor can't hear us. [They cross the stage.] Now, as my Solicitor, how do you advise me to deal with this difficulty?

Pooh-Bah: Oh, as your Solicitor, I should have no hesitation in saying, 'Chance it'.

Ko-Ko: Thank you. [Shaking his hand.] I will.

Pooh-Bah: If it were not that, as Lord Chief Justice, I am bound to see that the law isn't violated.

Ko-Ko: I see. Come over here where the Chief Justice can't hear us. [They cross the stage.] Now, then, as First Lord of the Treasury?

Pooh-Bah: Of course, as First Lord of the Treasury, I could propose a special vote that would cover all expenses, if it were not that, as Leader of the Opposition, it would be my duty to resist it, tooth and nail. Or, as Paymaster-General, I could so cook the accounts that as Lord High Auditor, I should never discover the fraud. But then, as Archbishop of Titipu, it would be my duty to denounce my dishonesty and give myself into my own custody as First Commissioner of Police.

Ko-Ko: That's extremely awkward.

from Sir W.S. Gilbert, 1983, *The Savoy Operas*, Papermac, London, pp. 325–6.

role conflict

The woman who is both a manager and a mother may experience role conflict when the expectations in these two important roles pull her in opposite directions.

---

definition

Role conflict *is the simultaneous existence of two or more sets of role expectations on a focal person in such a way that compliance with one makes it difficult to comply with the others.*

STOP!

Identify any three roles that you currently occupy simultaneously in three different social contexts, e.g. work, home, leisure. Identify any two conflicts that you regularly experience as a result of such multiple role occupancy.

---

the future: bureaucracy or adhocracy?

In introducing the concept of bureaucracy, Weber stressed its positive aspects. Since the time that he developed his thesis at the start of the century, social scientists have described its negative consequences (or dysfunctions), both for the individual in the organization and for the organization itself. With the increasing speed of environmental change, managers have also questioned Weber's views about the beneficial aspects of bureaucratic forms of organization. Warren Bennis referred to bureaucracy as 'a lifeless crutch that is no longer useful', whilst Michel Crozier felt that as an organization it could not learn from its errors. Hence, one of the major debates within organizational behaviour has been about the advantages and disadvantages of bureaucracy and its suitability as an organizational form for the future. For Weber, of course, bureaucracy was the most efficient form of social organization ever developed. It promised to maximize scientifically correct decision-making. However, many writers have highlighted the negative aspects of bureaucracies, not least those who work in them.

Chris Argyris (1957; 1973) offered a theory of personality development which argued that as an individual's personality matured, the bureaucratic organization was an unsuitable place within which to work. Argyris identified seven dimensions along which he claimed that the personality of an individual developed towards psychological maturity. These were:

1 An individual moves from a passive state as an infant to a state of increasing activity as an adult.
2 An individual develops from a state of dependency on others as an infant to a state of relative independence as an adult.
3 An individual behaves in only a few ways as an infant, but as an adult is capable of behaving in many ways.
4 An individual has erratic, casual and shallow interests as an infant, but develops deeper and stronger interests as an adult.

Chris Argyris
(b. 1923)

problems of bureaucracy

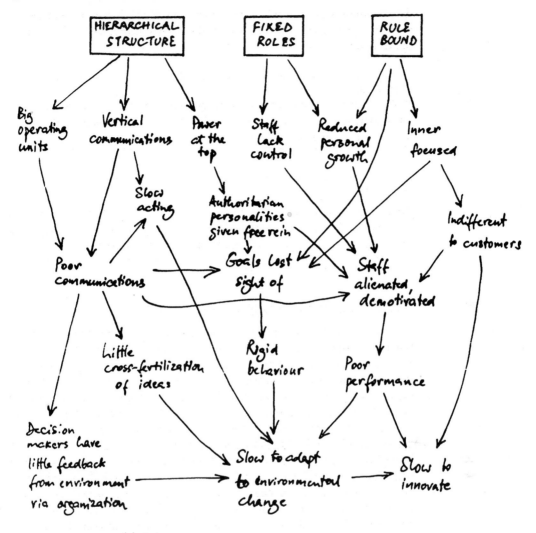

HIERARCHICAL STRUCTURE

FIXED ROLES

RULE BOUND

Big operating units

Vertical communications

Power at the top

Staff lack control

Reduced personal growth

Inner focused

Slow acting

Authoritarian personalities given free rein

Indifferent to customers

Poor communications

Goals lost sight of

Staff alienated, demotivated

Little cross-fertilization of ideas

Rigid behaviour

Poor performance

Decision makers have little feedback from environment via organization

Slow to adapt to environmental change

Slow to innovate

prepared by David Webster.

5 An infant's time perspective is very short, involving only the present, but with maturity this perspective widens into the past and future.

6 An infant is subordinate to others, moving as an adult to equal or superior positions in relation to others.

7 Infants lack self-awareness, but adults are self-aware and capable of self-control.

Argyris argued that the healthy personality developed naturally along the continuum from immaturity to maturity. However, he also said that managerial practices within formal organizations could inhibit this natural maturation process. There was a lack of congruence between the formal demands of the organization and the needs of individuals. Such incongruity led first to frustration and then to conflict. The frustration, said Argyris, increased as one went down to the lower levels of the organization. It was here that directive leadership and managerial control were greatest and jobs most specialized. Here employees in particular are given minimal control over their work environment. With management encouragement, the workers adapted to their situation.

The coping behaviours that these workers developed included daydreaming, aggression, regression and projection; restricting production quotas, making errors, slowing down, stealing and sabotage; formalizing their informal groups which then sanctioned their defence reactions, reinforcing their feelings of apathy, disinterest and lack of self-involvement. Widespread worker apathy and lack of effort was, in Argyris's view, not the result of individual laziness. Employees behaved immaturely, he believed, because they were expected to by the organization. The bureaucratic design of formal organizations frequently incorporates features such as:

- task specification
- rigid chain of command
- principle of unity of direction
- limited span-of-control

Other writers, equally critical of bureaucracy, have argued that bureaucracies, since they display the problems depicted in the figure on page 385, cannot survive in today's fast-changing world, but have to be replaced by more flexible organizational structures. First Bennis (1970) and then Henry Mintzberg (1979) described one such structural form called *adhocracy*. Unlike bureaucracy, it was a loose, flexible, self-renewing organic form, which was tied together by lateral rather than horizontal communication. Adhocracies dispense with traditional hierarchies, job titles and rules. Instead of coming from the top, strategy 'bubbles up', emerging from the decisions made by different units at different levels.

---

definition

Adhocracy *is a form of sophisticated organization structure that typically uses teams and is designed to survive in a complex, dynamic environment.*

Actual examples of adhocracies are rare. In its early days, Apple Computer, under the leadership of Steve Jobs, liked to consider itself as nearly an anarchic organization. However, following an increase in size, revenue and shareholder concern, the rational bureaucratic principles were established. The informal, structureless organizational forms can cause staff anxiety. It can result in conflict and chaos as separately begun projects overlap and bump into each other. It requires a great deal of staff training. Adhocracies are claimed to work best in conditions of turbulence and rapid change, and have been used by advertising agencies, management consulting firms and software development companies.

STOP!

If you had the choice of working in a bureaucracy or an adhocracy, which would you choose and why? What would be the positive and negative aspects of working within your preferred form of organization structure?

Beyond the adhocracy lie the *flexible working* arrangements which include part-time and temporary staff, as well as those who work annual hours and 'zero-hours' contracts. Some organizations have adopted this approach to gain more flexibility and employ staff who can be called in to work 'just-in-time'. The uptake of flexible working has not been as extensive as the business press would suggest. This is despite the government's deregulation of the employment market. Business Strategies (1996), a consultancy which studied labour market flexibility, predicted that the current number of 1.5 million temporary staff will take a decade to reach 2.5 million. Having staff who work from home or who are 'hoteling' or 'hot-desking' with no dedicated office staff, has attracted criticism of its own.

Hoteling

The only drawback to the cubicle-oriented office is that some employees develop a sense of "home" in their little patch of real estate. Soon pride of ownership sets in, then self-esteem, and poof—good-bye productivity. But thanks to the new concept of "hoteling," this risk can be eliminated. Hoteling is a system by which cubicles are assigned to the employees as they show up each day. Nobody gets a permanent workspace, and therefore no unproductive homey feelings develop.

Another advantage: Hoteling eliminates all physical evidence of the employee's association with the company. This takes the fuss out of downsizing; the employee doesn't even have to clean out a desk. With hoteling, every employee has "one foot out the door" at all times. Hoteling sends an important message to the employee: "Your employment is temporary. Keep your photos of your ugly family in the trunk of your car so we don't have to look at them."

© United Feature Syndicate, Inc.

assessment

The anti-bureaucracy school argues that the challenge for management is to create work environments in which everyone has the opportunity to grow and to mature as individuals. This, in essence, means moving away from bureaucratic organizational forms and towards some other type of organizational design. They say that as we approach the millennium, the bureaucratic organization is too expensive to maintain, incapable of responding sufficiently fast to change and does not utilize the innovative resources of its members. Failure to achieve profit targets results in large-scale redundancies. Now that the slimming down has been completed in many companies, runs the argument, the new-look, leaner organizations are experimenting with radically different forms of structures which overcome the dysfunctions of bureaucracy.

Examples of new and different forms of organizational structure have been widely written about include: the *matrix structure*, in which specialists from different functional departments (marketing, research, production) join an interdisciplinary team led by a project leader; *collateral structures*, which are loose, have an organic form and are designed to coexist alongside the bureaucracy on a permanent basis; *network structures* which consist of a small central directing core group of people, and which subcontract their major business functions such as advertising and distribution to others. There are also *intrapreneurial structures*, where groups of employees, within an organization, operate as little businesses. These examples do not include experiments with task forces, committee forms or the collegial models.

*Elliot Jaques
(b. 1917)*

In contrast, pro-bureaucracy writers such as Robert Miewald (1970) and Elliot Jaques (1990) question the need for adhocracies and flexible working, and argue that the bureaucratic structures have either been written off too prematurely or else they have not been properly implemented. Jaques defines bureaucracy more narrowly than Weber, as a hierarchically stratified employment system in which employees are accountable to their bosses for the work that they do. He agrees with the need for companies to release employee energy and improve morale, so as to increase productivity. However, he rejects the fashionable group-based, organizational designs (autonomous work groups, work teams, matrix overlap groups) as neither feasible nor necessary. He contends that bureaucratic hierarchy is the only viable structural form for a large company.

Jaques's argument requires careful attention. Essentially, he says bureaucracy has not worked so far, because it has not been properly tried! For him, the managerial hierarchy is 'the most efficient, hardiest, and in fact the most natural structure ever devised for large organizations' (Jaques, 1990, p. 127). He contends that the admitted deficiencies of hierarchy, and the 'flight to groups', are not due to any inherent deficiency in the model, but to a failure of proper application. That failure stems from a misunderstanding of how a managerial hierarchy functions; how it relates to the complexities of work; and how it can be used to encourage employee talent and stimulate their energy.

Let us consider Jaques's position step-by-step. At the core of this argument about hierarchy is the concept of *accountability*. For him, what was most important about being employed was having a contract that held you accountable for doing so much work in a given period of time in return for payment. You were given just enough authority to allow you to complete the task that you were accountable for, and the boss, who assigned you your tasks, was responsible for their completion to their own boss in turn. The impossibility of having a group-based structure stems from the legal fact that employees are contracted as individuals and not as groups. Even after successful group task completion, they seek individual recognition and individual career progress.

Bureaucratic hierarchy recognizes that both physical and mental work in an organization varies in its complexity. Thus the complexity of a Chief Executive's work differs from that of the cleaners. Jaques held that there are distinct and identifiable classes of complexity, which change in steps and which can be objectively assessed by measuring the target completion time of anyone's 'long task'. This measure he calls the *responsibility time span of the role*. Illustrated simply, the first line supervisor plans the production schedule for the next day or week, but not beyond three months. In contrast, the Chief Executive plans for the next twenty years. For Jaques, the key to making hierarchy work is ensuring that the responsibility–time spans for each position in the hierarchy complement each other.

Jaques found that efficient bureaucracies operated with increasing time spans, and that seven basic steps or strata of timespan were required. These corresponded with levels of thinking capability from concrete thinking at the bottom to abstract thinking and envisioning at the top. The well-documented inefficiencies of bureaucracy, for example over-layering, stemmed from the lack of this complementarity between the strata, or was caused by the insertion of additional levels for other reasons, for example to accommodate extra pay brackets or provide career ladder steps. Jaques's seven layers with their associated time spans are shown in the following figure.

Elliot Jaques's responsibility time span of a role

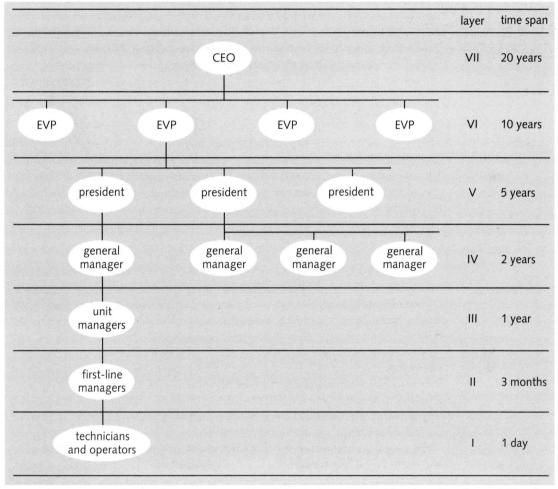

Jaques extended his seven-strata idea in two directions. First, he introduced the concept of the *time span of discretion*. The importance of a job in his view could be evaluated by the length of time taken before an individual's decisions are reviewed or evaluated. At the lower level it may be hourly or daily; at the top, it would be years (Jaques, 1956). Secondly, he linked these seven strata to pay, arguing that the higher the discretion exercised in the seven ascending steps, the more the pay. The creative, motivation aspect was the idea that an individual functioned best when working at a level which corresponded to his current time span capacity, but which allowed him to progress to his maximum time span capacity. Equitable payment would be determined by the time span of the work performed. He concluded that 'Managerial hierarchy or layering is the only effective organizational form for deploying people and tasks at complementary levels, where people can do the tasks assigned to them, where the people in any given layer can add value to the work of those in the layer below them, and finally, where this stratification of management strikes everyone as necessary and welcome' (Jaques, 1990, p. 133).

Irrespective of their strengths and weaknesses, bureaucracies continue to be omnipresent, with the majority of large companies having this structural form. For most of them, it is the most efficient way to organize. Robbins (1990) offers seven reasons to account for the continued existence of bureaucracy:

1   *Success*: For the most part, over the last 100 years, irrespective of technology, environment and people, and irrespective of whether it has been a manufacturing, medical, educational, commercial or military organization, it has worked.

2   *Large size*: Successful organizations survive and grow large, and the bureaucratic form is most efficient with large size.

3   *Natural selection favours bureaucracy*: Bureaucracy's natural features, the six identified at the start of this chapter, are inherently more efficient than any others and thus allow the organization to compete more effectively.

4   *Static social values*: The argument is that Western values favour order and regimentation and bureaucracy is consistent with such values. People are goal-oriented and comfortable with authoritarian structures. For example, workers prefer clearly defined job responsibilities.

5   *Environmental turbulence is exaggerated*: The changes currently being experienced may be no more dynamic than those at other times in history. Management strategies can also reduce uncertainty in the environment.

6   *Emergence of professional bureaucracy*: Bureaucracy has shown its ability to adjust to the knowledge revolution by modifying itself. The goal of standardization has been achieved in a different way among professional employees.

7   *Bureaucracy maintains control*: Bureaucracy provides a high level of standardization, coupled with centralized power, which is desired by those in command. For this reason senior managers who control large organizations favour this organizational design.

In modern organizations, power and authority continue to lie with those at the top. Robbins' seventh reason to explain the appeal of bureaucratic structures among senior management is that it centralizes power in their hands which appeals to them. Those people at the bottom of the hierarchy are strictly controlled by those above them. In the end, the decision to replace bureaucracy may be a political one.

sources

Argyle, M., 1964, *Psychology and Social Problems*, Methuen, London.

Argyris, C., 1957, *Personality and Organizations*, Harper & Row, London.

Argyris, C., 1973, 'Personality and organization theory revisited',
    Administrative Science Quarterly, vol. 18, no. 2, pp. 141–67.

Bennis, W.G., 1970, 'A funny thing happened on the way to the future',
    American Psychologist, July, pp. 595–608.

Blau, P. M., 1966, *The Dynamics of Bureaucracy*, University of Chicago Press, Chicago, 2nd edition.

Buckley, W., 1968, 'Society as a complex adaptive system', in W. Buckley (ed.), *Modern Systems Research for the Behavioural Scientist*, Aldine Publishing Company, Chicago, pp. 490–513.

Business Strategies, 1996, *Labour Market Flexibility and Financial Services*, March.

Child, J., 1984, *Organization: A Guide to Problems and Practice*, Harper & Row, London, 2nd edition.

Economist, 1990, 'Now spend it', 19 May, p. 74.

Edmonds, M., 1990, 'This is your captain speaking . . .', *Weekend Telegraph*, 7 April.

Gouldner, A. W., 1954, *Patterns of Industrial Bureaucracy*, Free Press, New York.

Hamman, H. and Parrott, S., 1987, *Mayday at Chernobyl*, New English Library, London, p. 62.

Haney, C., Banks, C. and Zimbardo, P., 1973, *A Study of Prisoners and Guards in a Simulated Prison*, Naval Research Reviews, Office of Naval Research, Department of the Navy, Washington, DC, September, pp. 1–17.

Hood, C., 1986, *Administrative Analysis: An Introduction to Rules, Enforcement and Organization*, Brighton: Wheatsheaf Books.

Jaques, E., 1956, *The Measurement of Responsibility*, Tavistock, London.

Jaques, E., 1976, *A General Theory of Bureaucracy*, Heinemann, London.

Jaques, E., 1990, 'In praise of hierarchy', *Harvard Business Review*, January–February, pp. 127–33.

Katz, D. and Kahn, R. L., 1966, *The Social Psychology of Organizations*, John Wiley, New York.

Lupton, T., 1971, *Management and the Social Sciences*, Penguin Books, Harmondsworth, 2nd edition.

Miewald, R.D., 1970, 'The greatly exaggerated death of bureaucracy', *California Management Review*, Winter, pp. 65–9.

Mintzberg, H., 1979, *The Structuring of Organizations*, Prentice Hall, Englewood Cliffs, NJ.

Mouzelis, N. P., 1969, *Organization and Bureaucracy*, Routledge & Kegan Paul, London.

Organ, D. W. and Greene, C. N., 1981, 'The effects of formalization on professional involvement: A compensatory approach', *Administrative Science Quarterly*, vol. 26, no. 2, pp. 237–52.

Pascale, R.T., 1985, 'The paradox of corporate culture: Reconciling ourselves to socialization,' *California Management Review*, vol. 27, no. 2, pp. 26–37.

Peters, T.J., 1987, *Thriving on Chaos*, Heinemann, London.

Pfeffer, J., 1981, *Power in Organizations*, HarperCollins, London.

Reed, B. and Palmer, B., 1978, 'The local church in its environment', in E.J. Miller (ed.), *Task and Organization*, John Wiley and Sons, Chichester.

Robbins, S.P., 1996, *Organization Theory*, Prentice Hall, Englewood Cliffs, NJ.

Rosenthal, R., 1973, *On the Social Psychology of the Self-Fulfilling Prophecy; Further evidence for Pygmalion effects and their mediating mechanism*. MSS Modular Publication, vol. 53, pp. 1–28.

Rosenthal, R. and Jacobson, L., 1968, *Pygmalion in the Classroom*, Holt, Rinehart and Winston, New York.

Stewart, R., 1967, *Managers and Their Jobs*, Macmillan, London.

Van Maanen, J., 1991, 'The smile factory: work at Disneyland', in P. Frost,

L. Moore, M. Louis, C. Lundeberg and J. Martin (eds.), *Reframing Organizational Culture*, Sage, Newbury Park, CA, pp. 58–76.

Warr, P., 1973, *Psychology and Collective Bargaining*, Hutchinson, London.

Weber, M., 1947, *The Theory of Social and Economic Organization*, translated by A.M. Henderson and T. Parsons, Oxford University Press, Oxford.

Zimbardo, P.G. *et al.*, 1973, 'A Pirandellian prison', *The New York Times Magazine*, 8 April.

classical management theory

concepts and learning objectives
Henri Fayol's functions, activities and principles
applicability of classical management theory
modern classical management theory
assessment
sources

concepts and learning objectives

A second source of ideas about how to structure an organization has come from practising managers. In the early years of this century, various writers made suggestions about the principles which should guide managers in designing the formal structure of their organizations and administering them. It is thus oriented to the values and interests of management, seeking to create a structure which most efficiently achieves management goals. The theory is called *classical*, said Baker (1972), because it attempted to offer simple principles which claimed a general application. It was also classical in the sense that it followed architectural and literary styles which emphasized formality, symmetry and rigidity.

As with scientific management and bureaucracy, rationality plays an important part in classical management. The theory considers employees as inert instruments who carry out assigned tasks. Their motivations are considered important only to the extent that they lead them to behave properly on the job. All other types of motivations and behaviour are considered non-rational and deviant, and are not discussed by the theory at all.

Classical management theory was based primarily on the work experience of certain key individuals, rather than on empirical research. The publications of ideas which later, collectively, came to be known as the classical management school began in 1914 with the contribution of Henri Fayol, a French mining engineer. Fayol's work complemented and built upon many of the ideas of Frederick Winslow Taylor. However, he took a broader, organization-wide approach with James Mooney, Edward Tregaskiss Elbourne, Mary Parker Follett, Luther Gulick and E.F.L. Brech. These writers together constitute what is referred to as the classical management school. Their views have exerted a lasting impression right up to the present day. Despite the criticisms of their ideas, most major companies are organized in a way which incorporates at least some of their thinking.

learning objectives

When you have read this chapter, you should be able to define those key concepts in your own words, and you should also be able to:

1 Summarize the approach and main principles of the classical management school.

2 Identify the writers who comprise the school and state their main individual contributions.

3 Discuss the strengths and weaknesses of classical management theory in relation to the design of organizational structure and the practice of management.

4 Identify the influence of classical management principles in the design of contemporary organizations.

5 Compare Henri Fayol's managerial activities with Henry Mintzberg's roles of managers.

*Lyndall F. Urwick
(1891–1983)*

The underlying philosophy of classical management theory was summarized by Lyndall Urwick, one of its main proponents (Urwick, 1947, p. 49):

It is the general thesis of this paper that there are principles which can be arrived at inductively from the study of human experience of organization, which should govern arrangements for human association of any kind. These principles can be studied as a technical question, irrespective of the purpose of the enterprise, the personnel composing it, or any constitutional, political or social theory underlying its creation. They are concerned with the method of subdividing and allocating to individuals all the various activities, duties and responsibilities essential to the purpose contemplated, and the correlation of these activities and the continuous control of the work of individuals so as to secure the most economical and most effective realization of the purpose.

This quotation puts in a nutshell the essential features of the classical management theory. In response to the question 'How does one structure an organization?', the writers in this school offered a remarkably similar set of principles and concepts to guide the organizational-designer. They believed these were applicable to all organizations irrespective of their size, technology, environment or employees. For this reason, it is often written that these writers preached the doctrine of 'structural universalism' as a way of achieving organizational efficiency. These principles concerned the issue of how to allocate tasks, control the work being done, and motivate and reward those doing it. The answers which they offered were underlain by the 'logic of efficiency'. This logic stressed:

❱ bureaucratic forms of control
❱ narrow supervisory span
❱ closely prescribed roles
❱ clear and formal definition of procedures, areas of specialization and hierarchical relationships

Moreover, the values which underpinned it held that for a technically efficient organization, one needed to achieve a unity of effort. This meant limiting the freedom and discretion of organizational members. In this sense, the classical writers had a direct similarity with those in the scientific management school – Frederick Winslow Taylor, Frank Gilbreth and Henry Gantt. However, the latter focused on shopfloor arrangement while the former considered the company as a whole.

Henri Fayol's functions, activities and principles

*Henri Fayol
(1841–1925)*

Classical management theory is generally held to have originated in France in the early twentieth century with the work of Henri Fayol. Fayol qualified as a mining engineer in 1860 after which he joined the Commentary-Fourchambault combine, a company in which he was to spend his entire working life. In 1866, Fayol became manager of the Commentary collieries and in 1888 at the age of 47, he was appointed to the General Manager position at a time when the financial position of the company was critical. By the time he retired in 1918, he had managed to establish financial stability in the organization. Fayol's legacy to the practice of management was a list of organizational functions, managerial activities and management principles.

Fayol's organizational functions

It was in the year that Frederick Winslow Taylor died that Fayol's book, *General and Industrial Administration*, was published. Fayol had tried to put down, in as systematic a form as possible, the experience he had gained while managing a large-scale company. In his writings, he stressed not personalities, but methods. He tried to present the latter in a coherent and relevant scheme. This formed the basis of his theory of organization. While Taylor focused on the worker on the shopfloor – a bottom-up approach – Fayol began from the top of the hierarchy and moved downwards. However, like Taylor, he too believed that a manager's work could be reviewed objectively, analyzed and treated as a technical process which was subject to certain definite principles which could be taught. Fayol's book had two parts: (a) Theory of Administration; (b) Training for Administration.

Fayol analyzed the operations which occurred in business and government. He said that, 'To govern an undertaking is to conduct it towards its objective by trying to make the best possible use of the resources at its disposal; it is in fact, to ensure the smooth working of the six essential functions'. In the first part of the book, Fayol identified the six main functions that are performed in any organization – technical, commercial, financial, security, accounting and administrative. The administrative function he further subdivided into six managerial activities which are shown in the following figures.

Henri Fayol's organizational functions and managerial activities

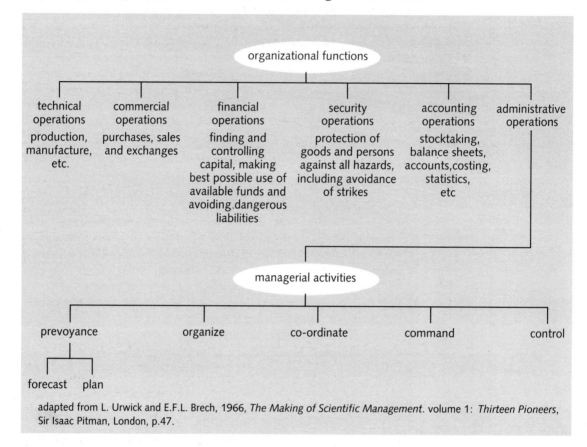

adapted from L. Urwick and E.F.L. Brech, 1966, *The Making of Scientific Management*. volume 1: *Thirteen Pioneers*, Sir Isaac Pitman, London, p.47.

Fayol's managerial activities

Fayol's list of managerial activities, originally developed some 80 years ago, remain broadly intact to this day. Only minor modifications have been made to the labels that he used. His six activities are:

forecasting predicting what will happen in the future.

planning devising a course of action to meet that expected demand.

organizing mobilizing materials and resources by allocating separate tasks to different departments, units and individuals.

commanding providing direction to employees, now more commonly referred to as *directing* or *motivating*.

co-ordinating making sure that activities and resources are working well together towards the common goal.

controlling monitoring progress to ensure that plans are being carried out properly.

The six managerial activities are interrelated. For example, a company management team begins by *forecasting* the demand for its product, for example, steel wire. It requires a sales forecast and will use market research to

---

the plan

In the beginning was the plan, and then came the assumptions.

And the assumptions were without form and completely without substance.

And darkness was upon the face of the workers, and they spoke among themselves saying, 'It is a crock of shit and it stinketh'.

And the workers went to the planners and sayeth, 'It is a pile of dung and none may abide the odour thereof'.

And the planners went to the supervisors and sayeth unto them, 'It is a container of excrement and it is very strong, such that none may abide its strength'.

And the supervisors went to the managers and sayeth unto them, 'It is a vessel of fertilizer and none may abide its strength'.

And the managers went to the Director and sayeth, 'It contains that which aids growth and is very strong'.

The Director went to the Vice-President and sayeth, 'It promoteth growth and is very powerful'.

The Vice-President went to the President and sayeth unto him, 'This powerful new plan will actively promote the growth and efficiency of the department'.

And the President looked upon the plan and saw that it was good.

And the plan became policy.

(Anon.)

---

develop one. Once it is clear that there is a market for the product, the next activity, *planning*, will take place. For Fayol, planning involved 'making a programme of action to achieve an objective'. These two activities, forecasting and planning, are collectively referred to by him as *prevoyance*. Because they are so closely related, some authors and books treat them as a single managerial activity.

Having made the plan, the third activity to be performed is *organizing*. This involves bringing together the money, materials and people needed to achieve the objective. It also involves breaking down the main task into smaller pieces and distributing them to different people. In a company structured along functional lines (accounting, production, marketing), the organizing of people may involve creating a special, temporary project team, consisting of members from the different functions. This is the matrix structure that was introduced in an earlier chapter.

Fayol used the word *commanding* to describe his fourth management activity. It has been defined as 'influencing others towards the accomplishment of organizational goals'. We would now refer to it as either *directing* or *motivating*. Whichever term is chosen, performing this activity involves the manager ensuring that employees give of their best. To do this, managers must possess a knowledge both of the tasks to be done and of the people who are to do them. This management activity is mainly, although not exclusively, performed face-to-face.

Earlier, organizing involved distributing task elements to various individuals. Now those separate elements have to be brought together. This represents the *co-ordinating* activity. Co-ordination can be achieved through

"And so you just threw everything together? . . . Mathews, a posse is something you have to organize."

memos, meetings and personal contacts between the people carrying out their unique activities. The sixth and final activity of managers is *controlling*. This involves monitoring how the objectives set out in the plan are being achieved with respect to the limitations of time and budget that were imposed. Any deviations are identified and action taken to rectify them. It may be that the original plan will have to be amended. Although the six managerial activities have been presented as a sequence, in reality they occur simultaneously in a company. However, forecasting and planning tend to be primary. There are also loops when original plans have to be changed because certain resources are found to be unavailable (when organizing) or when cost overruns are discovered (through controlling).

Fayol's principles of management

It is said that Fayol, in a sense, 'invented' management, by distinguishing it as a separate activity and defining its constituent elements. Interestingly, the word *management* is not translatable into all languages, nor does the concept exist in all cultures. Managing, of course, occurs, but is not always treated as anything special or separate. Fayol's second major contribution was to identify fourteen principles of management. He said that, 'Without principles one is in darkness and chaos', and that these were some that he had to apply frequently. He added that, 'it seems at the moment especially useful to endow management theory with a dozen or so well-established principles, on which it is appropriate to concentrate general discussion'.

Fayol's fourteen principles of management

1 **division of work** efficiency would be maximized if employees specialized in certain tasks.
2 **authority** authority is the right of managers to command and to be obeyed and should match responsibility.
3 **discipline** discipline is necessary to develop obedience, diligence, energy and respect within the limits fixed by an organization.
4 **unity of command** each subordinate should report to only one boss.
5 **scalar principle** the line of authority (scalar chain) in an organization runs from the top of the hierarchy to the bottom, because of the unity of command. Communications usually go up and down this path, but employees at the same level should be able to communicate laterally.
6 **unity of direction** each group of organized activities that have the same objective should have one manager using one plan to ensure consistency and responsibility.
7 **interest subordination** organizational goals and interests should take precedence over individual ones.
8 **remuneration** pay should be fair, sufficient to motivate to perform well, but not unreasonably high.
9 **centralization** refers to the degree that workers are involved in decision-making. The over-centralization of authority and responsibility should be avoided. Delegation of decision-making to encourage subordinates to work well is recommended, but with sufficient centralization to ensure accountability within the organization.
10 **order** people and materials should be in the right place at the right time.
11 **equity of treatment** managers should be fair and kind to their subordinates.
12 **stability of employment** as employee turnover is inefficient, management should provide orderly personnel employment planning and ensure that replacements are available to fill vacancies.
13 **opportunity for initiative** employees should be given the opportunity and freedom to use and execute a plan, even if it sometimes fails.
14 *esprit de corps* promoting team spirit will build harmony and unity within the organization.

based on Henri Fayol, 1916, *General and Industrial Management*, translated by C. Storrs, 1949, Sir Isaac Pitman and Sons, London.

Classical management theory is the collective term for a set of ideas which were propounded by individuals, including Fayol, who came from different backgrounds and different countries. Over a period of some thirty years, between 1920 and 1950, these people expounded a set of remarkably similar ideas in their writings and talks. The main ideas of classical management theory, therefore, do not represent a coherent body of thought. The breadth of contribution can be illustrated by a brief description of the backgrounds of some of the early pioneers of classical management theory.

James Mooney and Alan Reilly had been senior managers in General Motors Company in the United States. Luther Gulick, born in 1892, had both practical public administration experience and was a director of the

New York Institute for Public Administration. He was interested in how to bring together into a single area, amounts of work to affect the best division of labour and specialization while at the same time maximizing machinery and mass production. Oliver Sheldon worked under B. Seebohm Rowntree at the Cocoa Works in York during the 1920s. Lyndall Urwick was the main propagandist in Britain for classical management thought. Colonel Urwick's thoughts and writings had a heavily militaristic flavour. He had had many of his formative experiences in management in the British Army. In 1943, he published 29 principles of administration which reflected his belief that far from being contradictory and inappropriate, all the management principles could be related to one another and had a universal application.

These people did not work together. Their experience of management was based on both commercial, industrial and governmental organizations. Some were managers, others were consultants, but none were academics. In their writings they sought to make sense of their experience, rationalize it, explain it and set it down as a set of principles which appeared to be consistent with their observed practice. They then went on to promote their ideas more widely. Following Fayol, many writers, including Urwick, offered additional principles. Let us consider some of these principles listed earlier in a little more detail.

definition

Scalar principle *asserts that an organization is a group of grades arranged in a chain-of-command. Superior grades carry authority which can be delegated to the grade immediately below. The lower grades carry no authority.*

From this scalar concept stemmed the principle of hierarchy. It held that authority descended from the top to the bottom along a well-defined scale of posts in a continuously clear line.

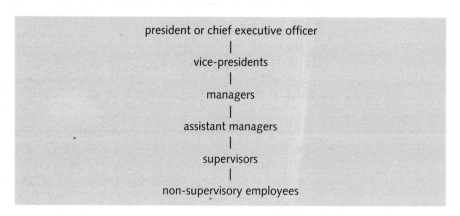

definition

Unity of command principle *holds that an individual must receive orders from only one hierarchical superior.*

Often, after a cutback, several managers may be required to share the same secretary. Such a structural arrangement would break the unity-of-command principle. A solution would be to identify one of those as her reporting link upwards.

---

definition

Span-of-control *refers to the optimal number of subordinates to be put under the authority of one hierarchical chief.*

General Sir Iain Hamilton once said that, 'No one brain can effectively control more than 6 or 7 other brains'.

---

definition

Exception principle *asserts that delegation should be maximized with decisions being taken at the lowest level possible.*

Also known as the centralization principle, this holds that exceptional tasks should be entrusted to the hierarchical superior (centralized), while routine and ordinary (programmed) tasks should be delegated to, and be performed by, subordinates. Nevertheless, the superior remains responsible for the successful completion of these delegated tasks.

---

definition

Unity of direction principle *holds that there can only be one head of the organization, whose job it is to see that all efforts are directed towards the same overall goals.*

Essentially this says that there should be one head and one plan for a group of activities which contribute to the same objective.

---

definition

Principle of the objective *states that every organization, and every part of every organization, must be an expression of the purpose of the undertaking concerned, or it is meaningless and therefore redundant.*

Put somewhat crudely, this means that everybody has to contribute to the bottom-line or they are out! The Business Process Re-engineering (BPR) approach considers whether existing organizational procedures make a contribution to the organizational objective, whether this is profitability, efficiency or service provision. If they do not, it recommends their adaption or elimination.

---

definition

Principle of correspondence *states that in every position, the responsibility and the authority should correspond.*

For example, a person occupying the position of a supervisor, who is held responsible for the work of eight workers, must be given the authority to decide on their appointment, discipline them when required, fire them if necessary; but not necessarily have the final say in their promotion. Her authority should match her responsibilities, being neither too little to prevent her carrying out those responsibilities, nor too much, going beyond what her position requires her to do and achieve.

---

definition

Organizational specialization *states that managerial activities should be differentiated according to their objectives, processes, clientele, materials or geographical location.*

The basis of such departmentalization should be rational and systematic, so as to avoid confusion.

Classical management theory is characterized by a plethora of principles, rules, hints, hunches and tips. These are descriptive, prescriptive or exhortative. This literature can be distinguished by the use of words such as *must* or *should*. Some of Fayol's writings contain recommendations for managerial practice that were based on his personal opinion, whilst others are too abstract for application to practical situations.

---

organizational structure as a function of divine intervention

Another way in which classical principles have appeared in the church has been by attributing to a divine source the nature of the church's structure. The structure of the Roman Catholic church has been understood in this way: there is the typical organizational pyramid with the Pope at the apex and the hierarchies ranged below on ever widening levels. The organization is believed to derive not from human initiative but from a divine source and sanction. That is, a theological foundation is provided for a church organized on classical lines; but the question remains whether this foundation is adequate and whether the classical model is appropriate – the extremes of ultramontanism, the mechanistic view of infallibility and the exercise of authority, the 'pipe-line' theory of apostolic succession are grounds for doubt. The new currents of thought in the papacies of John XXIII and his successor in the second Vatican Council may be evidence of the reshaping of the structure (and perhaps also the doctrine) of the church on lines other than the classical theory of organization.

from Peter F. Rudge, 1968, *Ministry and Management: The Study of Ecclesiastical Management*, Tavistock, London, p. 40.

STOP!

Consider Fayol's list of fourteen principles of management. Can you give examples of their application or non-application in organizations with which you are familiar?

the army's span-of-control

The principle is to have a chain of command, so that each man knows to whom he is responsible and there can be units of different managerial sizes for different purposes. For example, according to Xenophon counting on the fingers of two hands, the divisions of Cyrus's army were:

	form	under	
5 men	1 squad	corporal	5
2 squads	1 sergeant's squad	sergeant	10
5 sergeant's squads	1 platoon	lieutenant	50
2 platoons	1 company	captain	100
10 companies	1 regiment	colonel	1,000
10 regiments	1 brigade	general	10,000

With modifications in the numbers in different units, this is the principle on which armies have been organized. The general does not have to control 10,000 men directly, he controls the ten regimental colonels, and so on. In modern armies this would be considered an excessive span-of-control and two or three armies would form an army group, but the principle remains. Split the task up into manageable proportions and do not have an excessive span-of-control so that real control is lost.

from F. R. Jervis, 1974, *Bosses in British Business*, Routledge & Kegan Paul, London, p. 87.

When considering classical management theories, it is important to locate it in its proper historical context. The managers of the period were dealing with larger, more complex organizations than had existed hitherto. At the beginning of the twentieth century many new companies developed. They employed vast numbers of people, had numerous plants and employed new technologies. All of this needed co-ordinating. With no model or experience to fall back on, those who managed these organizations had no choice but to develop their own principles and theories as to what to do to run them well. Inevitably these principles were grounded in their day-to-day experience of managing and owed much to the models offered by military and religious organizations.

applicability of classical management theory

Given the lack of any universally valid management prescriptions, those concerned with structuring and designing organizations have had to look elsewhere. Having acknowledged the complexity of the task, they have reluctantly admitted that there is no single set of laws or principles which can be successfully applied in all companies. General theories are no longer adequate (if they ever were) to meet the demands of changing organizational environments. The theoretical work in this area has shifted away from the search for rules and towards an analysis of managerial judgement

STOP!

Rudyard Kipling's Guide to Management

How many tips for managers can you find in Kipling's poem, *If*? Rewrite those that you discover beginning with the words 'Managers should . . .'.

IF

If you can keep your head when all about you
Are losing theirs and blaming it on you;
If you can trust yourself when all doubt you,
But make allowance for their doubting too;
If you can wait and not be tired by waiting,
Or being lied about, don't deal in lies,
Or being hated, don't give way to hating,
And yet don't look too good, nor talk too wise;

If you can dream – and not make dreams your master;
If you can think – and not make thoughts your aim;
If you can meet with Triumph and Disaster
And treat those two impostors just the same;
If you can bear to hear the truth you've spoken
Twisted by knaves to make a trap for fools,
Or watch the things you gave your life to, broken,
And stoop and build 'em up with worn-out tools;

If you can make a heap of all your winnings
And risk it on one turn of pitch-and-toss,
And lose, and start again at your beginnings
And never breathe a word about your loss;
If you can force your heart and nerve and sinew
To serve your turn long after they are gone,
And so hold on when there is nothing in you
Except the Will which says to them 'Hold on!'

If you can walk with crowds – and keep your virtue,
Or walk with kings – nor lose the common touch,
If neither foes nor loving friends can hurt you,
If all men count with you, but none too much;
If you can fill the unforgiving minute
With sixty seconds worth of distance run,
Yours is the Earth and everything that's in it,
And – which is more – You'll be a man, my son!

In what ways do Kipling's principles differ from those of the modern classical management writers? In which ways are they similar ?

from *The Definitive Edition of Rudyard Kipling's Verse*, 1989, Hodder & Stoughton, London, pp. 576–7. Reprinted with the permission of A.P. Watt Ltd on behalf of The National Trust.

in specific situational contexts. The research has sought to identify the heuristics used by managers as they make decisions in their job. These studies have tended to use a phenomenological rather than a positivist research approach.

recipes for managing

Since everyday life is dominated by pragmatic motive, recipe knowledge, that is, knowledge limited to pragmatic competence in routine performances, occupies a prominent place in the social stock of knowledge . . . I have recipe knowledge of the workings of human relationships. For example, I must know what I must do to apply for a passport. All I am interested in is getting the passport at the end of a certain waiting period. I do not care, and do not know, how my application is processed in government offices, by whom and after what steps approval is given, who puts which stamp in the document. I am not making a study of government bureaucracy – I just want to go on vacation abroad. My interest in the hidden workings of the passport getting procedure will be aroused only if I fail to get my passport in the end. At that point, very much as I call on a telephone repair expert after my telephone has broken down, I call on an expert in passport-getting – a lawyer, say, or my Congressman, or the American Civil Liberties Union. *Mutatis mutandis*, a large part of the social stock of knowledge consists of recipes for the mastery of routine problems. Typically, I have little interest in going beyond this pragmatically necessary knowledge as long as the problems can indeed be mastered thereby.

from Peter L. Berger and Thomas Luckmann, 1972, *The Social Construction of Reality*, Heinemann, London, pp. 56–7.

Jason Spender (1989) argued that the problem with classical management theory was that it ignored uncertainty, and this fact prevented its prescriptions being implemented. He argued that lacking specific information, managers, like scientists, constructed and relied upon theories, which not only helped them to make sense of the organizational world around them, but also provided them with a basis for their actions. Where did such managerial theories come from?

Spender saw organizations as bodies of knowledge, and managers as creators and users of that knowledge. These bodies of knowledge were specific to industries and represented shared patterns of beliefs and shared judgements. They consisted of what everyone in that industry took for granted and the criteria for success within it. He used the term *industry recipe* to refer to the inherited wisdom of each industry. For example, in the case of managers in the dairy industry:

it is a simple matter of understanding how the market is segmented, how the business must relate to its market, the reciprocal patterns of influence and obligation, how these are sustained and protected from internal disorder and external competition. Once trading relations are established and the inputs and outputs defined, the management focuses on the financial and structural determinants of organizational efficiency. (Spender, 1989, p. 157)

Spender's work empirically demonstrates that there can be no universally valid prescriptions about how to organize and manage since each industry is different. However, it does more than just restate this often made point. By studying a number of different industries, he was able to distil the recipe for each one.

Recipes give managers an understanding of what they must do to sustain their organizational forms and activities. However, it is not just a case of there being different recipes for different industries. An industry recipe was a guide to action, a set of heuristics and a framework which was constructed out of the cumulative judgements of the industry's managers. There were no industry-specific prescriptions either. Spender argued that each manager took the general prescriptions of his industry's recipe and applied these to the specific situation of his firm within that industry. The recipe was useful in offering a partial and ambiguous set of guidelines which were capable of being adapted to fit every company's circumstances. These assisted managers to search for an appropriate response to the uncertainties that they faced. The application of the industry recipe necessitated creative adaptation on the part of management.

Peter Drucker warned against modern challenges in the modern turbulent business environment being handled using yesterday's logic. Every organization encourages, then institutionalizes, its culture and routines. These company-specific ways of thinking, or mindsets, represent the organization's success recipes, their formulas for continued success. When required to decide, the manager will turn subconsciously to these 'one best ways' which have proved successful in the past. They will fail to question their appropriateness and relevance. Drucker believes that, eventually, these success recipes will become failure recipes.

modern classical management theory

A contradiction in terms? While classical management theory refers to the ideas developed by Fayol and his followers at the start of this century, it has also come to represent a distinctive tradition in management knowledge, which continues through to the present day. This tradition emphasizes the experience and knowledge of the most senior and most successful practising managers and consultants; is communicated in the form of principles, rules, tips, hints, anecdotes and 'war stories'; and claims a universal application.

As such, it stands in contrast to management knowledge based on the theories and research conducted by academics at university schools, which is distributed in the form of research findings and abstract models; and which emphasizes the specific and limited applicability of conclusions. Defined thus, classical management theory is not an historical fossil of academic interest, but a way of knowing about management, which both regularly updates itself and continues to have an impact on organizational practice in general, and on company structuring in particular.

The first inheritors of Henri Fayol's tradition have been the manager-authors, the earliest of whom was Alfred Sloan of General Motors. He wrote about the company in the 1930s. Other GM executives, James Mooney and Alan Reilly (1939) established the convention of the successful manager sharing his 'secrets of success'. In the 1980s, Michael Edwardes (1985), then chief executive of Rover (formerly British Leyland), described how he turned the companies around, whilst Akio Morita, the head of Sony, shared his views on management. Indeed, the 1980s saw an explosion in this sort of writing as managers around the world became hungry to learn from the successes of others.

above:
Alfred Pritchard Sloan
(1875–1966)

right:
David Packard
(1912–96)

America's top executives and entrepreneurs, together with their European counterparts, wrote down their own prescriptions (assisted by journalists) about how to manage. Amongst the best known managers in this period were Lee Iacocca (Chrysler), Mark McCormack (ITG), Harold Geneen (ITT), John Sculley (Pepsico and Apple Computer), John Harvey-Jones (ICI) and Jan Carlzon (Scandinavian Airlines). This trend continues in the 1990s with contributions by Bill Gates (Microsoft) and Richardo Semler (Semco). Shortly before his death, David Packard of the Hewlett-Packard Corporation described the principles and practices which underpinned the management of the company that he had co-founded with Bill Hewlett (Packard, 1996).

Some of these books were primarily histories of companies written from the perspective of their founder or long-serving chief executive. Others used the company as the backcloth before providing hints, tips and rules for success. These modern prescriptions seek to offer general guidance to the aspiring manager. For example, Iacocca attributed his success to his effective use of time which he achieved by organizing, setting priorities and timetables, delegating and acting decisively. Mark McCormack, a top-selling entrepreneur-author, encouraged his readers to use their instincts, insights and perceptions. He recommended listening aggressively, 'taking a second look at first impressions' and taking time to use what had been learned. He entreated his readers to be discreet and to remain detached.

The second inheritors of Fayol's tradition have been the consultant-authors. These writers have often had some management experience, but their approach has been to collect the prescriptions and advice offered by top executives; to collate and distil what they believe to be common features of different top managers' successes; and then to re-present these in the form of management principles. Among the earliest examples were Oliver Sheldon (1923) who wrote *The Philosophy of Management*, and Lyndall Urwick (1943) who produced *The Elements of Administration*. More recent collections have been prepared by de Bono (1986), Robinson (1985), Carlisle (1985), Kay (1985) and Ritchie and Goldsmith (1987).

STOP!

Select a business book by a successful manager or consultant which is in the current bestseller lists. This book may be recommended to you by your instructor. Also, review the points in Chapter 2 concerning research design and research method, as well as internal and external validity. Critically evaluate your chosen best-selling author's recommendations and 'principles for success'. What are the strengths and weaknesses of the book?

---

intellectual wallpaper or business pornography?

Judging the merits of bestsellers is a difficult task . . . Some critics have taken the extreme position of calling these books 'intellectual wallpaper' and 'business pornography'. Certainly labels like this, justified or not, should encourage readers to be cautious. A better perspective is provided by an assessment of the *sources* of many of the books, which are often anecdotal in nature. In other words, much of the information in these bestsellers stems from the experiences and observations of a single individual and is often infused with the subjective opinions of that writer. Unlike the more traditional academic literature, these books do not all share a sound scientific foundation. Requirements pertaining to objectivity, reproducibility of observations, and tests of reliability and validity have not guided the creation of much of the material that is being communicated in these books. As a consequence, these authors are at liberty to say whatever they want (and often with as much passion as they desire!).

Unlike authors who publish research-based knowledge, authors of bestsellers do not need to submit their work to a panel of reviewers who then critically evaluate their ideas, logic and data being presented. The authors of these popular management books are able to proclaim as sound management principles virtually anything that is intuitively acceptable to their publisher and readers. Therefore, readers need to be cautious consumers. The ideas presented in these books need to be critically compared with the well-established thoughts from more traditional sources of managerial wisdom.

from Jon L. Pierce and John W. Newstrom, 1990, *The Manager's Bookshelf*, Harper & Row, London, pp. 5–6.

It can be argued that the consultant-authors who have had the greatest impact on decisions on management structure and processes have been Tom Peters and Robert Waterman (1982). Their book, *In Search of Excellence*, reported a study of 62 American companies which, at the time, had been outstandingly successful. From these findings, the authors offered managers guidance as to how they should manage their companies. They translated their recommendations into eight 'new' principles of management.

The logical structure of the Peters and Waterman management system is shown in the figure on page 410. As a body of knowledge about how to manage, their recommendations mirror those Fayol produced nearly seventy years earlier. As such, it can be said to represent *modern classical management theory*.

assessment

In assessing the current status of classical management theory, we need to distinguish between, on the one hand, the body of Fayol's writings – his six organizational functions, six managerial activities and fourteen principles of management – and on the other, the classical management approach, which generates management knowledge that is based on the experiences of practising managers and consultants. It is also necessary to contrast two

---

Peters and Waterman's new management principles

1 A bias for action
   - Project teams that tend to be small, fluid, *ad hoc* and problem/action-focused.
   - Communications are of the essence, and there is an important commitment to learning and experimentation.
   - Complex problems are tackled through a willingness to shift resources.
2 Close to the customer
   - The market-driven principle of commitment to service, reliability and quality, based on an appreciation of 'nichemanship' and the ability to tailor a product or service to a client's needs.
3 Autonomy and entrepreneurship
   - A principle which champions innovation, decentralization, the delegation of power and action to the level where they are needed, and a healthy tolerance of failure.
4 Productivity through people
   - The principle that employees are people and a major resource, and should be trusted, respected, inspired and made 'winners'.
   - Organizational units should be small-scale to preserve and develop people-oriented quality.
5 Hands-on, value-driven
   - Organization guided by a clear sense of shared values, mission and identity, relying on inspirational leadership rather than bureaucratic control.
6 Stick to the knitting
   - The principle of building on strengths and knowledge of one's niche.
7 Simple form, lean staff
   - Avoid bureaucracy; build main commitments to projects or product division rather than to the dual lines of responsibility found in formal matrix organizations; use small organizational units.
8 Simultaneous tight–loose properties
   - The principle that reconciles the need for overall control with a commitment to autonomy and entrepreneurship.

from Gareth Morgan, 1986, *Images of Organization*, Sage, London, p. 61; Peters and Waterman, 1982. © 1986 by Sage Publications, Inc. Reprinted by permission of Sage Publications, Inc.

---

different audiences for his work, university business school academics and practising managers like Fayol himself. We shall deal with these two issues in turn.

Fayol has had a considerable influence on the practice of managerial and the design of organizational structures during this century. The six management activities that he listed continue to be used as an organizing framework around which many management textbooks are written and management training courses are organized. If these have received widespread acceptance, then his principles of management have been criticized. Thomas (1993) summarized the academic debate. He reported that the original attack on management principles was made by James March and Herbert Simon (1958). Their complaint was that management principles, whether Fayol's or anyone else's,

the logical structure of Peters and Waterman's management system

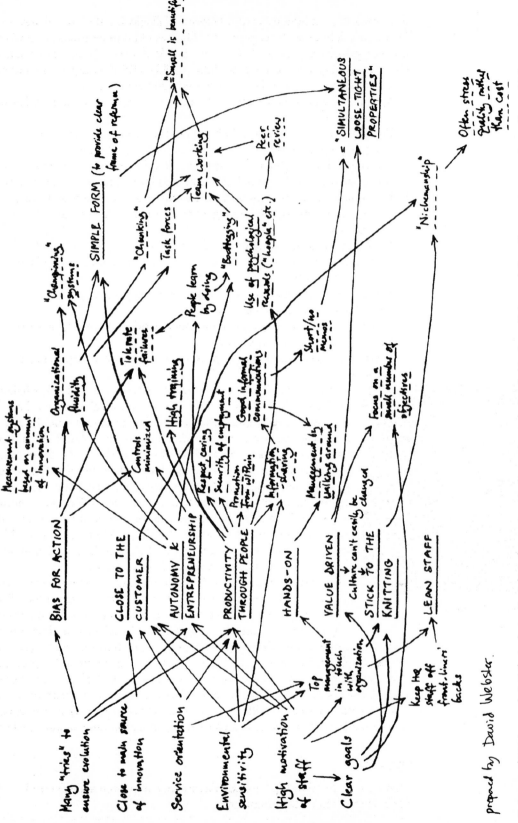

proposed by David Webster.

Peters and Waterman's 'attributes' or principles of success are shown in underlined, block capitals, and the other management practices which they recommend are shown in lower case, with broken underlining.

were vacuous, ambiguous, contradictory and illogical, rather than demonstrably false in the light of evidence provided. They would thus be equally critical of the modern principles produced by Peters and Waterman. Unlike this critique of classical management principles, John Child's (1969) critique was based on empirical research. He and others believed that the principles:

» Misleadingly proposed a single, standardized organizational model as the optimum one.
» Promoted a militaristic, mechanistic organization, which stressed discipline, command, order, subordinates and *esprit de corps*.
» Overlooked the negative consequences of tight control and narrow task specialization which could demotivate employees and hinder efficiency.
» Overemphasized an organization's formal structure, while neglecting processes such as conflict management, decision-making and communication.
» Underestimated the complexity of organizations.
» Were based on unreliable personal knowledge, rather than systematic research evidence.
» Lacked a concern with the interaction between people.
» Underestimated the effects of conflict.
» Underestimated the capacity of individual workers to process information.
» Misunderstood how people thought.
» Were overrated, and that there was no one best way of organizing a company.

Henry Mintzberg (b. 1939)

It took sixty years before his framework was seriously challenged by Henry Mintzberg (1977) whose empirical research into how managers actually spend their time led to a reassessment of the nature of managerial work, and a redefinition of the roles of the manager. Mintzberg's studies revealed a substantial difference between what managers did and what they said they did. It revealed that a manager's job was characterized by pace, interruptions, brevity and fragmentation of tasks. In addition, managers preferred to communicate verbally, and spent a great deal of time in meetings or making contacts with others outside meetings. Mintzberg was able to distinguish ten distinct managerial roles which he classified under the headings of *interpersonal*, *informational* and *decisional*.

Mintzberg argued that the ten roles that he identified can describe the nature of managerial work more accurately than other frameworks or models. The concept of role was introduced in the previous chapter. One aspect of it is that any role-holder can choose how to carry it out. In the case of managers, they can decide how they wish to blend the ten listed roles, taking into account organizational constraints and opportunities. A consequence of this is that management becomes more of an art, rather than a teachable science which can be reduced to a set of prescriptions which can be easily taught. Despite the difference between Mintzberg's work and Fayol's, the former tends to be viewed as complementing rather than supplanting the latter's.

STOP!

Explain the relationship between Fayol's six managerial activities and Mintzberg's ten roles of managers.

Henry Mintzberg's ten management roles

role	description
interpersonal	
figurehead	Symbolic head; obliged to perform routine duties of a legal or social nature.
leader	Responsible for the motivation and activation of subordinates; responsible for staffing, training and associated duties.
liaison	Maintains self-developed networks of outside contacts and informers who provide favours and information.
informational	
monitor	Seeks and receives wide variety of special information (much of it current) to develop thorough understanding of organization and environment; emerges as nerve centre of internal and external information of the organization.
disseminator	Transmits information received from outsiders or from other subordinates to members of the organization; some information factual, some involving interpretation and integration of diverse value positions of organizational influences.
spokesperson	Transmits information to outsiders on organization's plans, policies, actions, results, etc.; serves as expert on organization's industry.
decisional	
entrepreneur	Searches organization and its environment for opportunities and initiates 'improvement projects' to bring about change; supervises design of certain projects as well.
disturbance handler	Responsible for corrective action when organization faces important, unexpected disturbances.
resource allocator	Responsible for the allocation of organizational resources of all kinds – in effect the making or approval of all significant organizational decisions.
negotiator	Responsible for representing the organization at major negotiations.

It is not known what practising managers felt about the principles, but one might speculate that their reaction was more positive than that of the academics. Thomas (1993) reported that the American National Industrial Conference Board, an association for managers, was publishing lists of principles for its members in the 1950s. He also cited Koontz (1961) who defended the principles saying that although they are not based on rigorous research, they were still developed out of long, practical experience of what worked. While they may be called platitudes, platitudes were still true and a truth does not become worthless because it is familiar. Those who criticized them used the example of the non-application of a single principle to reject the entire framework. Management principles continue to be an essential part of management, and need to be developed and tested.

What is the status of classical management theory today? It is fashionable, especially in academic circles, to relegate it to a place in history. A belief in the existence of general principles or rules which can be applied to the management of organizations tends to come in and out of fashion. It is certain that most of the organizations of which you are a member – company, college, church – will be organized using Fayol's classical management principles. At the same time the serious weaknesses of the classical school have been pointed out. Environmental change in the economic and political spheres, together with a revolution in technology based on the microprocessor, have all forced large organizations to re-examine their structures with a view to adapting them so that they best fit the circumstances in which they now find themselves.

Currently, the research focus has shifted towards identifying and relating important variables. How does one combine organizational goals, human needs, technological opportunities and the need for some form of organizational control? How can these variables be related to each other to produce a best fit for the circumstances of the particular organization at the time? How long will that fit last? New and innovative forms of organization are now emerging. What characterizes this new thinking is the recognition that whilst there are no universal prescriptions, there may be specific solutions which are valid for specific industries for a given period of time. Nevertheless, Huczynski (1993) argued that, historically, practising managers have also sought and valued principles which offered them guidance and direction. Whether these principles were classical management ones produced by Fayol in 1916, or principles of excellent management such as those presented by Peters and Waterman in 1982, is less important. In both cases, the principles were implemented and affected what managers did; and in so doing they affected the behaviour of people in organizations.

sources

Baker, R.J.S., 1972, *Administrative Theory and Public Administration*, Hutchinson, London.

de Bono, E., 1986, *Tactics: The Art and Science of Success*, Fontana, London.

Brech, E.F.L., 1965, *Organization: The Framework of Management*, Longman, London, 2nd edition.

Carlisle, E., 1985, *Mac-Managers Talk About Managing People*, Pan, London.

Carlzon, J., 1987, *Moments of Truth*, Harper & Row, New York.

Child, J., 1969, *British Management Thought*, George Allen and Unwin, London.

Edwardes, M., 1985, *Back from the Brink*, Pan, London.

Fayol, H., 1916, *General and Industrial Management*, trans. C. Storrs, 1949, Sir Isaac Pitman and Sons, London.

Gates, B., 1995, *Hard Drive*, John Wiley, Chichester.

Geneen, H., 1986, *Managers*, Grafton, London.

Harvey-Jones, J., 1988, *Making it Happen*, Collins, Glasgow.

Huczynski, A.A., 1993, *Management Gurus*, Routledge, London.

Iacocca, L., 1985, *Iacocca: An Autobiography*, Sidgwick and Jackson, London.

Kay, W., 1985, *Tycoons: Where They Came From and How They Made It*, Pan, London.

Koontz, H., 1961, 'The management theory jungle', *Academy of Management Journal*, vol. 3, no. 3, pp. 174–88.

March, J. and Simon, H.A., 1958, *Organizations*, John Wiley, New York.

McCormack, M.H., 1984, *What They Don't Teach You at the Harvard Business School*, Collins, Glasgow.

Mintzberg, H., 1977, 'The manager's job: Folklore and fact', *Harvard Business Review*, vol. 53, July–August, pp. 49–61.

Mooney, J.D. and Reilly, A.C., 1939, *Onward Industry*, Harper, New York.

Morgan, G., 1986, *Images of Organization*, Sage, London.

Morita, A., 1987, *Made in Japan*, Collins, Glasgow.

Packard, D. 1996, *The HP Way: How Bill Hewlett and I Built Our Company*, Harper Business, New York.

Peters, T.J. and Waterman, R.H., Jr, 1982, *In Search of Excellence*, Harper & Row, New York.

Pierce, J.L. and Newstrom, J.W., 1990, *The Manager's Bookshelf*, Harper & Row, London, 2nd edition.

Ritchie, B. and Goldsmith, W., 1987, *The New Elite*, Weidenfeld and Nicolson, London.

Robinson, J., 1985, *The Risk-Takers: Portraits of Money, Ego and Power*, Allen and Unwin, London.

Sculley, J., *Odyssey: Pepsi to Apple*, HarperCollins, New York.

Semler, R., 1994, *Maverick*, Random/Century Hutchinson, London.

Sheldon, O., 1923, *The Philosophy of Management*, Pitman, London. (Reprinted with an introduction by A. W. Rathe, 1965.)

Simon, H.A., 1947, *Administrative Behaviour*, Macmillan, New York.

Sloan, A.P., 1963, *My Years with General Motors*, Doubleday, New York.

Spender, J-C., 1989, *Industry Recipes*, Blackwell, Oxford.

Thomas, A.B., 1993, *Controversies in Management*, Routledge, London.

Trump, D., 1987, *The Art of the Deal*, Arrow Books, London.

Urwick, L., 1933, 'Organization as a technical problem', reprinted in L. Gulick and L. Urwick (eds.), *Papers on the Science of Administration*, Columbia University Press, New York.

Urwick, L., 1943, *The Functions of Administration*, Harper, New York.

Urwick, L., 1947, *The Elements of Administration*, Pitman, London, 2nd edition.

Urwick, L. and Brech, E.F.L., 1966, *The Making of Scientific Management*. vol. 1: *Thirteen Pioneers*, Sir Isaac Pitman, London.

concepts and learning objectives

The history of organizational design has, during the last seventy years, been one of a progressive shift away from the single, universally applicable model towards the view that different organizational structures are relevant to different situations. The last ten years have taught Western companies that if they are successfully to match their international competitors, they will have to rewrite the book of organizational design. This means creating and adapting their organizational structures to meet new and changing demands. This chapter will begin by introducing the concept of contingency, which has an application in several areas of organizational behaviour. Taking an historical perspective, it will describe the development of the application of the contingency approach to the design of organizational structures.

key concepts

contingency approach	intensive technology
determinism	task variety
strategic choice	task analyzability
technical complexity	differentiation
pooled task interdependence	integration
sequential task interdependence	environmental complexity
reciprocal task interdependence	environmental dynamism
technological interdependence	enacted environment
mediating technology	managerial enactment
long-linked technology	organizational enactment

learning objectives

When you have read this chapter, you should be able to define those key concepts in your own words, and you should also be able to:

1 Explain in what sense the classical management and the human relations approaches claim to be universal in their applicability.
2 Give reasons for the shift away from the classical management approach towards the contingency approach.
3 Distinguish between different types of organizational activities and suggest the most appropriate structure for each.
4 Distinguish between the determinist and the strategic choice perspectives towards organizational design.
5 Understand and be able to contrast different determinist and strategic choice sub-schools.
6 Describe recent trends in organizational design.

contingency approach

The contingency approach in organizational behaviour refers to the view that holds that the appropriate solution in any specific case depends, is *contingent* upon, the circumstances prevailing at the time. Some writers refer to contingency 'theory', but it is nothing of the sort. It is more correct to consider it as a way of thinking rather than as a set of interrelated causal elements which might be said to constitute a theory. For this reason, this chapter refers to it as an approach.

---

definition

Contingency approach *seeks to analyze a problem, and then develop the best managerial or organizational solution to meet it.*

Mary Parker Follett (1863–1933)

Management thinking in the first third of this century was dominated by the search for the 'one best way'. Despite their differing perspectives, Taylor, Weber, Mayo and Fayol all recommended single, universal solutions to management problems, often in the form of laws or principles. For this reason, Mary Parker Follett, writing in the 1920s, stands out as perhaps the earliest of the contingency thinkers. Follett, a management consultant, wrote about the *law of the situation* saying that,

> If any situation is looked at by those concerned, carefully and clear-sightedly, it is found that it has a logic of its own and its own law. It is the situation itself which is dictating the orders of what needs to be done and both managers and managed, in essence, have to take orders from it. (Graham, 1987, p. 17)

Subsequent contributions to the contingency school came from many different researchers who studied diverse topics such as wage payment systems, leadership styles and job design. They sought to identify the kinds of situation in which particular organizational arrangements and management practices appeared to be the most effective.

Despite their differences, what distinguished these writers from their predecessors was their opposition to those theories and principles which held that there was one right way to organize or to manage, which could be applied everywhere. They felt that it was necessary to identify the crucial factors in a company's situation, for example, its labour market, technology, product market, environment, before making recommendations that best fitted the prevailing circumstances.

---

universal prescriptions versus specific choices

It is of great practical significance whether one kind of managerial 'style' or procedure for arriving at decisions, or one kind of organizational structure, is suitable for all organizations, or whether the managers in each organization have to find that expedient that will best meet the particular circumstances of size, technology, product, competitive situation and so on. In practice, managers do, indeed must, attempt to define the particular circumstances of the unit they manage, and to devise ways of dealing with these circumstances. I have often observed that their success in doing so is limited by their belief that there must be a universal prescription. This belief can obscure some of the alternatives that are open. To act in this way could also cause failure to develop criteria for choosing the alternative amongst those that are available and visible, which is best suited to the particular circumstances.

from Tom Lupton, 1971, *Management and the Social Sciences*, Penguin Books, Harmondsworth, 2nd edition, p. 121.

---

contingency and organizational structure

Historically, the contingency approach was first developed in relation to organizational structure. Paradoxically, it is Henri Fayol, the father of classical management theory and of universal principles, who made one of the earliest contributions to the organizational structure contingency approach. He demonstrated a greater degree of sensitivity to and awareness of the complexity of organizational design than he is generally given credit for. He wrote that,

> For preference I shall adopt the term principles whilst dissociating it from any suggestion of rigidity, for there is nothing rigid and absolute in management affairs, it is all a question of proportion. Seldom do we have to apply the same principle twice in identical conditions; allowances must be made for different changing circumstances, for men are just as different and changing, and for many other variable elements. (Fayol, 1949, p. 19)

Following the elaboration of classical management theory during the 1930s and 1940s, concern began to be expressed about the universal application of the principles being expounded. Herbert Simon, for example, noted the steady shift of emphasis from 'principles of administration' themselves, to a study of the conditions under which competing principles are respectively applicable' (Simon, 1948).

By the 1950s, American writers were considering alternative organizational forms. William Foote Whyte (1959) used a scheme based on the work of George Homans to depict the 'it all depends' idea of structural design. He argued that each interaction, activity and sentiment was part of the 'environment of the organization'. By environment, Whyte meant the factory or company environment. It was as if he had drawn a circle around the company and examined what happened to individuals and groups inside that boundary. His perspective is sometimes labelled 'closed systems theory', because it does not take into account factors beyond that boundary. Nevertheless, Whyte stressed that the appropriate structure and management behaviour, for example, the 'good' foreman, were context-specific:

> If we take seriously the statements presented here regarding the impact
> of the environment upon the social system, then we must recognise that
> there is no such thing as the good foreman and the good executive.
> (Whyte, 1959, p. 181)

By this time, various studies raised questions about the validity of the organizational principles preached by the classical management theorists. For example, Blain's (1964) research showed that there was no necessary correlation between organizational performance and the organizational principles advanced by classical theorists, like strict limitation of span-of-control. Moreover, it was found that very different forms of organizational structure could be equally successful. This contradiction forced researchers to look more closely at the relationship between organizational structure, management practice and organizational performance.

It was in Britain in the 1950s that the original research was carried out that established the basis for the contingency approach in general, and for its application to organizational structure in particular. A leading figure here was Joan Woodward, who contributed to our understanding of the effect of technology on organization structure, a variable which was further studied by American researchers like James Thompson and Charles Perrow. Other researchers, Tom Burns and G.M. Stalker (Edinburgh University), and Paul Lawrence and Jay Lorsch (Harvard Business School), examined the effect of a company's environment on its organization structure. Finally, the socio-technical systems work of Rice, Trist, Emery and Miller of the Tavistock Institute of Human Relations is part of this tradition and is discussed in Chapter 19.

With the coming of the contingency approach, organizational design solutions ceased to be single, universal, 'off-the-shelf' ones, and came to be tailored to the specific needs of the organizations. Indeed, a single structure for an entire company, whatever that may have been, was considered as unnecessarily restrictive by some writers. Different parts of the same organization could have their own structural arrangements which fitted their particular situation. Within the same organization, therefore, there could be units of bureaucracy, units operating in a matrix structure and units which were divisionalized. Single design types, neatness, symmetry and permanence advocated in the past, were no longer held to be indicative of 'good' design. The only criteria for good design were task achievement, individual and group satisfaction and organizational performance.

different structures for different activities

An example of this would be the 4077th MASH where to meet the demands of treating emergencies in battle they need to react quickly. But to treat complex injuries with complex technology and maintain records, etc. for the future treatment and other associated administration, a certain level of routine is necessary. Similarly when the unit is overloaded and necessary medical supplies are not available, considerable 'negotiation' and 'dealing' with other units, etc. is undertaken. The organization that has evolved is a sort of a task culture where everyone works as a team to process the work with easy working relationships, etc. but it does have role elements in the efficiency with which paperwork is processed. It has power culture elements for Radar to negotiate and bargain with other units and the unit commander has to use personal intervention to keep the unit going and protect it from the rest of the organization in which it exists.

The problem of imposing an inappropriate organizational design exists in the shape of Major Burns, Hoolahan and the occasional CIA agent. These represent the dominant role organization in which the unit exists. Their attempts to impose military rules and procedures and impose the formal rank in the unit are seen as highly inappropriate, often farcical.

from John Parris, 1979, 'Designing your organization', *Management Services*, October, p. 14.

determinism versus strategic choice

The main debate within the contingency approach to organization structure is between two of its sub-schools – the determinists and the strategic choice thinkers. The determinists assert that a single variable such as technology, environment or company mission determines the form of a company's organization structure. Meanwhile, strategic writers contend that a company's structure is always the outcome of a choice made by those in positions of power within organizations. Linked to the question of the shape of the organization's structure, is that of its performance and efficiency. Both sub-schools are interested in discovering if certain structural arrangements are more conducive to organizational success than others.

definitions

Determinism *is the belief that some variables such as technology or environment determine, that is, are the direct cause of, changes in other variables such as the degree of specialization, standardization, formalization and centralization, that are to be found in an organization.*

Strategic choice *is the view that holds that organizational structure is wholly a company management decision. It is senior management which decides which technology to adopt, how it is introduced and used, what products are to be manufactured and in which markets they are to be sold. Thus decisions about the number of levels of hierarchy, the span-of-control, and so on, are ultimately based on the personal values and beliefs of those who make them.*

technological determinism

*Joan Woodward
(1916–71)*

Joan Woodward, James Thompson and Charles Perrow are the leading figures in the technological determinist school. They share a belief that technology determines an organization's structure, and that different technologies necessitate different structures. However, these authors differ in the way that they classify technologies and in how they conceive of the relationship been technology and structure.

Joan Woodward and technological complexity

It was Woodward (1965) who first introduced the notion of the technological imperative – the view that technology determines an organization's structure. Specifically, she held that it was the complexity of the technology used that determined the structure. Her conclusion was based on the study of 100 firms in south-east England which used different technologies. She classified their technologies according to the first date of introduction; the interrelationship between the equipment used for these processes; and the amount of repetition of operations between one production cycle and the next. This produced a three-fold differentiation of systems of production based on increasing *technical complexity* (9 = most predictable and controllable) as shown in the following figure.

---

definition

Technical complexity *is defined as the degree of predictability about, and control over, the final product permitted by the technology used.*

Joan Woodward's classification of 100 British manufacturing firms according to their systems of production

system of production

unit production

1 production of simple units to customers' orders

2 production of technically complex units

3 fabrication of large equipment in stages

4 production of small batches

mass production

5 production of components in large batches subsequently assembled diversely

6 production of large batches, assembly line type

7 mass production

process production

8 process production combined with the preparation of a product for sale by large-batch or mass production methods

9 process production of chemicals in batches

10 continuous flow production of liquids, gases and solid shapes

In unit production, one person works on a product from beginning to end, for example, a cabinet maker producing a piece of hand built furniture. In mass production, the technology requires each worker to make an individual contribution to a larger whole, for example, fitting a bumper on a car assembly line. In process production, workers do not touch the product, but monitor machinery and the automated production processes, for example, chemical plants and oil refineries.

based on Joan Woodward, 1958, *Management and Technology*, HMSO, London, p. 11. Crown copyright is adapted with the permission of the Controller of Her Majesty's Stationery Office.

Woodward identified differences in the technical complexity of the process of production and examined the companies' organizational structures. Following a statistical analysis, she related their technology to its structure. She found that as the technology became more complex (going from type 1 through to type 10), two main things occurred. First, the length of the chain-of-command increased, with the number of management levels rising from an average of 3 to 6 (see the following figure). The proportion of managers to the total employed workforce rose, as did the proportion of indirect to direct labour.

number of levels of hierarchy in relation to the production system

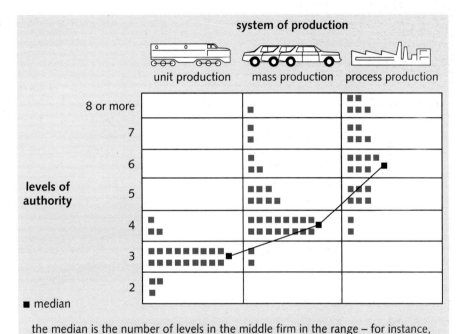

the median is the number of levels in the middle firm in the range – for instance, the sixteenth of the 31 mass production firms.

based on Joan Woodward, 1958, *Management and Technology*, HMSO, London p. 14. Crown copyright is adapted with the permission of the Controller of Her Majesty's Stationery Office.

Her second major finding was that the increasing complexity of technology meant that the chief executives' span-of-control increased, as well as that of the supervisors. The span-of-control of first-line supervisors was highest in mass production and lowest in process production (see the following figure). Span-of-control refers to the number of subordinates supervised by one manager and represents one of the ways of co-ordinating the activities of different employees.

Woodward argued that a relationship existed between a company's economic performance (e.g. profitability) and its organizational structure. Having identified these statistical relationships, she went on to make observations about the effectiveness of performance of the companies. In her view, the companies which had an organizational structure close to the norm for that category would be more commercially successful than those whose structures deviated from the pattern. Her conclusion was that, 'there was a particular form of organization most appropriate to each technical situation' (Woodward, 1965, p. 72).

span-of-control of first-line supervision in relation to production system

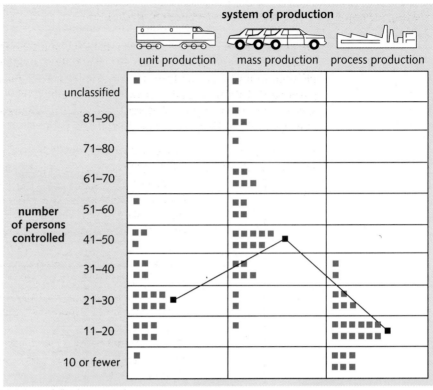

based on Joan Woodward, 1958, *Management and Technology*, HMSO, London, p. 15. Crown copyright is adapted with the permission of the Controller of Her Majesty's Stationery Office.

The reasoning underlying this conclusion is that the technology used to manufacture the product, or make available the service, places specific requirements on those who operate it. Such demands, for example, in the need for controlling work, or motivating staff, are likely to be reflected in the organization structure. The technology–structure link is complemented by the notion of effective performance which held that each type of production system called for its own characteristic organizational structure.

James D. Thompson (1920–73)

James Thompson, technology and interdependence

The second member of the technological determinist school was a sociologist, James D. Thompson. He believed that differences in technology were responsible for differences between organizations at the technical, managerial and institutional levels. He was particularly interested in how technology affected the interdependence between individuals and departments, and what the need to co-ordinate different types of interdependent activities meant for the choice of the most appropriate organization structure. Thompson argued that the appropriate type of co-ordination would depend on how interdependent departments and individuals were dependent on each other's resources or outputs in order to accomplish their own work.

Thompson's three-fold categories of technology (which will be described shortly) appear at first sight to be both more general than

---

contingency approach and types of co-ordination mechanisms

To appreciate the differences between the structural contingency writers, it is necessary to understand the managerial activity of *co-ordination*, and the different forms that it can take. The previous chapter defined co-ordination as ensuring that different 'activities and resources are working well together towards the common goal'. Different co-ordination mechanisms tend to be used in mechanistic and organic organizational structures.

used mainly in mechanistic structures ↑

Rules and procedures: Rules and procedures identify what actions are appropriate in various situations. They are standards to guide managers and employees.

Hierarchical referral: When rules and procedures are inadequate to co-ordinate actions of separate units, co-ordination problems are referred upward to the common supervisor. The hierarchy acts as the integrator.

Planning: Objectives are set to guide people's actions. How units within the organization relate to each other is determined by what needs to be accomplished. Plans define each unit's responsibilities and identify their relationships.

Direct contact among managers: Managers from separate units work together to co-ordinate the work of their units.

Liaisons: Specific people can be made responsible for providing communication and co-ordination among units.

Task forces: Members of the separate units are combined in a task force to work together for a particular task or period of time.

Teams: Teams are permanent task forces responsible for co-ordinating the work of separate units over a long time period and numerous projects.

used mainly in organic structures ↓

Matrix organization: Matrix organizations give employees status in two or more groups simultaneously; co-ordination is done through the formal matrix organization.

from L.S. Baird, J.E. Post, and J.F. Mahon, 1990, *Management*, HarperCollins, London, p. 237.

Woodward's ten-type listing and also incomplete. However, his classification was not based on the differences between the technologies themselves, which had been Woodward's first concern, but on the characteristic types of *relationships of interdependence* that they created. We shall examine these interdependences before considering their associated technologies.

interdependences: pooled, sequential and reciprocal

In a university, a single lecturer teaches her course alone, with colleagues running their own courses in parallel. This is an example of *pooled task interdependence*. Each course has a standard format agreed by the university.

Rules and procedures describe how it should be taught and examined. The combined quality of these individual courses would be measured by the Higher Education Funding Council's Teaching Assessment team, and an overall grade given for the department concerned. Other examples of pooled interdependence based on mediating technology include secretaries in a typing pool, sales representatives on the road, insurance claims units and waiters in a restaurant. In each case, the individual contributor's performance can be easily identified and evaluated; and hence the potential for conflict between departments or individuals is low.

Sequential task interdependence requires specific work tasks to be performed in a predetermined order. For example, in an organizational behaviour course taught by three lecturers, sequential task interdependence means that the first one has to complete his sessions on individual psychology, before the second can teach social psychology, who is then followed by the third, who presents the material on organization structure. In a car factory, a car has to be assembled before it can be painted. Sequential task interdependence means that a department's or group member's performance cannot be easily identified or evaluated, as several make a contribution to a single product.

With *reciprocal interdependence*, all the activities of all the different company departments or all of the team members, are fully dependent on one another. The work output of each entity serves as the input for another. For example, in an organizational behaviour course using the group project method, a group of students can call upon different lecturers to provide them with knowledge or skill inputs to enable them to solve the project problems. Not only would lecturer A's actions affect lecturer B's, as with sequential task interdependence, but they would also impact on lecturer C's, and so on. At the departmental level, reciprocal interdependence can be witnessed at an airport between the aircraft flight crew, the control tower, ground operations and the maintenance section. At the team level, groups which are reciprocally interdependent include operating theatre staff in a hospital.

In each case, the separate departments or team members work together flexibly to produce the good or service required. The selection, mix and sequence of the techniques and skills actually performed is determined in part by feedback from the product itself – the project, the needs of the landing aeroplane or the ill patient, and in part by feedback from earlier stages of production. For these reasons, the sequence of required operations cannot be predetermined.

---

definitions

Pooled task interdependence *results when each department or group member makes a separate and independent contribution to the company or team performance.*

Sequential task interdependence *results when one department or individual group member must perform their task before the next can complete theirs.*

Reciprocal task interdependence *results when all the activities of all company departments or all team members are fully dependent on one another.*

technologies: mediating, long-linked and intensive

Thompson introduced the concept of *technological interdependence* and argued that a company's technology created a particular form of interdependence between its separate departments and between the different individuals within a group. Different technologies created different forms of interdependence and each required its own way of co-ordinating the work activities within it. This led companies with different technologies to make distinct choices about which was the most appropriate organizational structure for them (Thompson, 1967).

---

definition

Technological interdependence *refers to the extent to which the work tasks performed in an organization by one department or team member, affect the task performance of other departments or team members. It can be high or low.*

His view of technological determinism was:

$$\text{technology} \rightarrow \begin{matrix} \text{type of} \\ \text{interdependence} \\ \text{created} \end{matrix} \rightarrow \begin{matrix} \text{type of} \\ \text{co-ordination} \\ \text{required} \end{matrix} \rightarrow \begin{matrix} \text{type of} \\ \text{organization} \\ \text{structure needed} \end{matrix}$$

Thompson distinguished three technology categories which he labelled *mediating*, *long-linked* and *intensive*. These differed in terms of their organization flow patterns; the different degrees of discretion or problem-solving behaviour demanded of their human operators; and also in terms of the mechanisms used by the firm to co-ordinate each type of workflow interdependence. Thompson's idea can be explained by consulting the figure on page 426 while reading the following sections on mediating, long-linked and intensive technologies, and their associated forms of task interdependence.

---

definitions

Mediating technology *links independent but standardized tasks.*

Long-linked technology *is applied to a series of programmed tasks performed in a predetermined order.*

Intensive technology *is applied to tasks that are performed in no predetermined order.*

---

mediating technology and pooled task interdependence

In a situation of pooled task interdependence, the individual department or group member is on his or her own, as inputs are converted into outputs. They perform their tasks independently and do not interact with others. The mediating technology on which this is based categorizes and standardizes the work activities between the different functions to eliminate the need for one department or person to have to adjust to another. Each bank branch classifies its customers into depositors or borrowers, and then treats them according to standardized procedures.

Thus, predetermined rules, common forms and written procedures all act to co-ordinate the independent contributions of different units and separate employees, whilst clearly defined task and role relationships integrate the functions. This produces a bureaucratic organizational form in which the cost of co-ordination is relatively low. It is the collective or 'pooled' performance of the individual departments or of the individual team members which determines how successful the company or the team is. Mediating technology within a building society links savers to borrowers; in an employment agency it links prospective employers to potential employees; and in an estate agency it links house sellers to house buyers.

long-linked technology and sequential task interdependence

Sequential task interdependence requires specific work tasks to be performed in a predetermined order, and the associated *long-linked technology* allows such a series of programmed tasks to be done. Mass-production technology in general, and the assembly line in particular, are good examples. Here, the rules and operating procedures are highly specified; there is a detailed description of how co-ordination is to be effected; and the hierarchy of authority is used to monitor and closely supervise the performance of the interdependent departments or team workers.

At the departmental level, co-ordination is achieved through planning and scheduling which integrates the work of different departments. At the group level, co-ordination is achieved by close supervision of workers, forming workgroups with employees of similar levels of skill; and motivating by rewarding group rather than individual performance. The relative cost of co-ordination with this type of technology is medium.

James Thompson's typology of technology, interdependence and co-ordination

type of technology	form and degree of task interdependence	main types of co-ordination used	cost of co-ordination	example
mediating	'pooled' A B C D low interdependence	*categorization* *standardization* rules and procedures	low	bank and branches university departments baseball teams
long-linked	'sequential' A → B → C → D medium interdependence	*planning* scheduled meetings, committees	medium	assembly-line fast food restaurants American football teams
intensive	'reciprocal' B A D C high interdependence	*mutual adjustment* unscheduled meetings, face-to-face discussions, physical proximity, inter-departmental teams	high	hospitals airports basketball teams

An additional point is that with this technology and form of interdependence, the overall performance of the company or team is determined by the least capable or poorest performer. Moreover, an early mistake made at the start of a process sequence, for example a poorly explained concept by the first lecturer, or a wrongly inserted chassis frame in the car factory, can impede those who follow. The potential for conflict is thus high. Additional examples are fast-food hamburger chains, beer producers (brewing, bottling, distribution), car washes and sprint relay teams in athletics.

intensive technology and reciprocal task interdependence

Because the workflow required for producing the specific good or service cannot be determined, this type of technology and interdependence is co-ordinated by departments and team members adjusting to one another as required by circumstances. The main requirement is for frequent horizontal communication between units and individuals. Thus, the mechanisms of co-ordination include unscheduled meetings, face-to-face contacts, project groups, task forces and cross-departmental teams. This in turn necessitates a close physical grouping of reciprocally interdependent units, so that mutual adjustment can be accomplished quickly. Where this is impossible, then mechanisms like daily meetings, e-mail and teleconferencing are needed to facilitate communication. The degree of co-ordination required through mutual adjustment goes far beyond what is necessary for the other technologies discussed, and is thus the most expensive of the three.

implications for the design of an organization's structure

What are the organizational design implications of Thompson's model? Most organizations experience various levels of interdependence, all of which have to be co-ordinated. Whatever form that co-ordination takes, it will involve some sort of communication and decision-making, and hence costs for the company.

Chapter 11 described the process of departmentalization and the different bases that are used for grouping tasks into departments (e.g. product, customer, geography). In reality, each department performs several functions, so it is impossible to structure a company on one criterion alone. Thus, the average company will have a certain amount of pooled interdependence, less sequential interdependence and even less reciprocal interdependence. Understanding the types of interdependences experienced, and having the aim of minimizing the cost of co-ordinating each one, provides additional criteria for the choice of an organizational structure.

The Thompson model argues for using the cheapest form of co-ordination that is effective for the given interdependence relationship and associated technology. Since co-ordination, communication and decision-making are most problematic between departments or individuals which are in a reciprocally interdependent relationship, the company should give those in that relationship priority when the structure is being designed or revised. Reciprocal departments or individuals should be grouped physically close together, so that access is permitted to assist their mutual adjustment. Numerically, they should remain small and, within prescribed limits, be permitted to be autonomous. They should be placed in the hierarchy under the same superior, as shown on an organizational chart. Their common boss

A comparison of baseball, American football and basketball teams reveals how much they differ from one another. Despite all being popular team sports in the United States, the nature and rules of the three sports means that each creates a different type of interdependency between the players within the team, and this is reflected in the structures of the teams themselves. To be successful, therefore, each type of team must co-ordinate the activities of its members in a different way.

baseball

Baseball is an example of Thompson's 'pooled interdependence'. It is a team game in which the individual player's contribution to the final result is largely independent of the others. Team success depends on the skill of the individual players who take their turn to bat or field in their own position. At the end of the game, the individual performances of all the team's players are pooled, and if these are good enough, the team triumphs over its opponents. When interaction takes place on the field, it rarely involves more than three players at a time. All the nine players on the field are widely dispersed physically, some by significant distances. Players develop their skills through individual training and practice, and management's job is to select the best players for any team.

Because of their independent contributions within the game, little co-ordination is needed between the different players who make up a baseball team. The co-ordination that is needed is achieved through the game's rules with which all players are familiar. The pitcher and catcher (equivalent to the bowler and wicket-keeper in cricket) will need to know what each will do, as will some of the in-fielders. Such interdependence is the exception rather than the rule. In baseball, managers can substitute players during the game; they themselves can be replaced by a new manager during the season; and players are bought and sold, leaving their old team and joining a new one without needing to make any significant adjustment. Baseball has been described as a 'lonely team game'.

American football

American football illustrates sequential interdependence. The American version of football is a rugby-like sport which is increasingly being seen in Europe on satellite and cable television. To the uninitiated, the game looks mystifying. The first-time viewer will notice a medium level of physical dispersion among the players. The linemen and the offensive backs are near enough to hear and touch each other. Each football team consists of a defending and an attacking section. The first line of players blocks the opponents to enable the backs to run or pass.

A match consists of teams performing a number of 'plays'. A play is a specific set of choreographed movements, and each team will have developed their own. The plays are numbered; team members are required to memorize these from a 'playbook'; and on the pitch, the captain will shout a number which indicates to the players what they are to do next. To the spectator, the game consists of a series of starts and stops followed by pauses – somewhat like playing chess with human pieces.

Close inspection reveals that the efforts of each team's players are closely linked together. What the lineman does is prepare the way for the backs. The outcome of the defensive section's members represents the starting point for its attacking section. The aforementioned play is a standardized component. Just as a car part has to be correctly inserted before the next one can be added, so a play has to be successfully executed before the following one can be performed. Plays are performed sequentially from first down to fourth down, and when one occurs, it involves all twenty-two players on the pitch.

Since the efforts of football players are tightly coupled, a higher degree of co-ordination between them is required than in baseball. This is achieved through planning and hierarchical control. The game plan is worked out in advance and based on information about the opposing team, whilst the game rules define what players can do. Additionally, each player is assigned a specific role during the game which complements that of the other team members. However, the primary level of co-ordination is the team. During the game itself, the head coach makes the strategic decisions, whilst his assistants make tactical ones.

Because integration and co-ordination are such important ingredients of high performance, neither players nor coaches are easily changed. Success comes by creating a well co-ordinated team from the players that are available and successfully executing a good strategy. One coach observed that a football team was like a machine. It was made up of parts, and if one of these did not function properly by the player not doing his job, the whole machine failed.

basketball

Basketball provides an illustration of reciprocal interdependence. Each player interacts with the others on the field, and depends on their efforts to succeed. The division of labour is less precise than in the previous two sports described, and there is a rapid movement from attack to defence and back again. Everybody handles the ball, and everybody tries to score. The players move spontaneously in the direction determined by the flow of the game, and act in response to the decisions of their opponents. They are in very close physical contact with the others.

In a successful basketball team, the members will read and anticipate the moves of their colleagues. As with any relationship, this comes from playing together for a long time. New members have to adjust to the particular habits of existing ones. For this reason, a few individual stars cannot turn the team performance. Reciprocal interdependence means that co-ordination is crucial. Whilst coaches may seek to integrate and create cohesion amongst the team members, it is through mutual adjustment that players adapt to the flow of the game and to one another.

continued overleaf

sports and interdependence (*continued*)

America's three most popular sports provide a vivid illustration of Thompson's three types of interdependence. Baseball is organized around autonomous individuals; football around sequentially interdependent sub-groups; and basketball around the free flow of reciprocal players.

	baseball team	American football team	basketball team
nature of interdependence between players (and degree)	pooled (low)	sequential (medium)	reciprocal (high)
geographical dispersion of players	high (widely dispersed)	medium (clustered)	low (high concentration)
autonomy to achieve own and team objectives lies with	individual team member	team manager	shared amongst team members
co-ordination achieved by	rules that govern sport	game plan, complex protocols and role responsibilities	shared responsibility, continuous self-regulation and mutual adjustment by all players
key management job	select players and develop their skills	prepare and carry out the game plan	develop team stability and cohesion
sport organized around	autonomous individuals	sequentially interdependent groups	free flow of reciprocal players

based on R.W. Keidel, 1984, 'Baseball, football and basketball: models for business', *Organizational Dynamics*, Winter, pp. 12–14; W. Passmore, C. Francis and J. Haldeman, 1982, 'Sociotechnical systems: A North American reflection on the empirical studies of the 70s', *Human Relations*, vol. 35, pp. 1179–204; and 'Why don't eggheads love football?', *Newsweek*, 19 December 1994, p. 49.

can ensure that they co-operate, and this reporting arrangement also reduces the time and effort needed for co-ordination.

Once reciprocal relationships (if any) are accommodated in a firm, the next priority is for those in sequential relationships. Here again, the recommendation is for a common group, localized physically and with limited autonomy. The high-performance teams or autonomous work groups which have been used by some companies to build motor cars and personal computers would be examples of this recommendation. Finally, and only after the previous two relationships have been structured for cost-effective co-ordination, should pooled relationships be addressed. As mentioned earlier, these are cheap and easy to integrate through the use of rules and regulations.

For Thompson, differences in technology caused differences in organizations at the technical, institutional and managerial levels. Technical phenomena relate to internal organization aspects such as its task, technology and co-operation of people. Institutional phenomena concern the organization as a whole and its relationship to the environment. Managerial phenomena relate to managers reconciling the internal needs of an organization with the environment in which it exists.

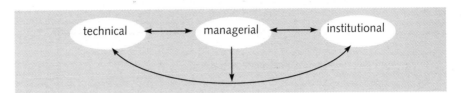

This model stresses co-ordination of interdependent work activities performed by individuals, groups and departments in a firm. First-level co-ordination occurs within each group between its members. Second-level co-ordination involves the co-ordination of different groups within a department. The third level is the co-ordination of several departments within a division, and so on. Thompson's model shows a hierarchy or multi-level structure of an organization, with each overarching unit only linking those sub-groups which are interrelated (on the principle of smallest possible, localized physically, conditional autonomy). For Thompson, the hierarchy of an organization is a steadily, ever more inclusive clustering of sub-units to deal with the problems of co-ordination that they cannot sort out themselves.

Charles Perrow, technology and predictability

Charles Perrow

Charles Perrow is the third leading contributor to the technological determinist school. He saw technology's effect on structure as working through its impact on the predictability of providing the service or manufacturing a product. He considered two dimensions. The first he labelled *task variety*. This was the frequency with which unexpected events occurred in the transformation (inputs to outputs) process. Task variety would be high if many unexpected events occurred during a technological process. The second dimension he termed *task analyzability*. This term referred to the degree to which the unexpected problems could be solved using readily available, off-the-shelf solutions. Task analyzability would be low if individuals or departments had to search around for a solution, and rely on experience, judgement, intuition and problem-solving skills.

---

definitions

Task variety *is the number of new and different demands that a task places on an individual or a department.*

Task analyzability *is the degree to which standardized solutions are available to solve the problems that arise.*

---

types of technology
On the basis of these two dimensions, Perrow categorized technologies into four types and discussed the effects of each one upon an organization's structure. He

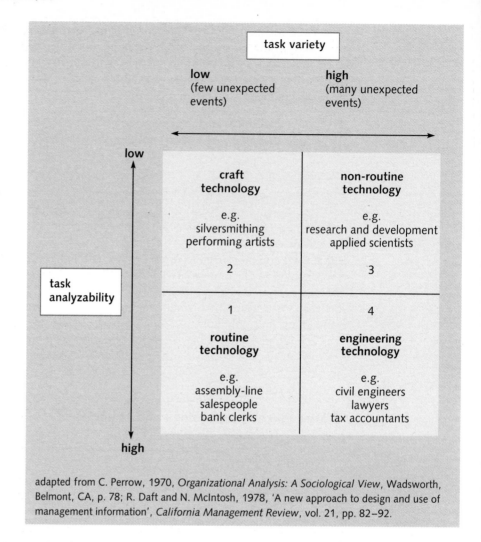

task variety

low
(few unexpected events)

high
(many unexpected events)

task analyzability

low

craft technology

e.g.
silversmithing
performing artists

2

non-routine technology

e.g.
research and development
applied scientists

3

1

routine technology

e.g.
assembly-line
salespeople
bank clerks

4

engineering technology

e.g.
civil engineers
lawyers
tax accountants

high

adapted from C. Perrow, 1970, *Organizational Analysis: A Sociological View*, Wadsworth, Belmont, CA, p. 78; R. Daft and N. McIntosh, 1978, 'A new approach to design and use of management information', *California Management Review*, vol. 21, pp. 82–92.

was particularly interested in co-ordination mechanisms, discretion, the relative power of supervisors and the middle managers who supervise them.

routine technology

The mass production assembly line is an example of routine technology. It has *low task variety* and *high task analyzability*. Tasks are simple, repetitive and make few exceptional or unusual demands on the individuals or departments responsible for their completion. When there is a problem, policies, rules and procedures exist to solve it. It is clear what type of wheel should be fitted to a car, and if a difficulty occurs, it is clear what it is and how it should resolved. This is the type of technology used by Burger King to produce hamburgers or by supermarkets to check out customers.

non-routine technology

The tasks performed by research chemists, advertising agencies and top management teams are all examples of non-routine technology. It has *high task variety* and *low task analyzability*. By definition, researching ideas or products will bring scientists up against new problems (high task variety) that will require new types of solution (low task analyzability). For example, computer designers are already encountering the physical limits imposed by the materials that they are working on. Speed of data transfer and heat production mean that this problem will have to be overcome using creative ideas such as new materials or light as a transmission medium. Problem-solving in non-routine technology requires both creative and analytical skills.

craft technology

The making of jewellery to order by a silversmith exemplifies craft technology. The range of new problems encountered is low (*low task variety*), but when there is a problem, effort is required to find a solution (*low task analyzability*). An accountant preparing a tax return is unlikely to be surprised by the problems he will encounter, but each client's particular problem is unique and will require a different solution, which has to be worked out.

engineering technology

Civil engineering companies which build roads and bridges exemplify this type of technology. Many new problems are thrown up as the project proceeds (*high task variety*), but these can be solved with well-established, off-the-shelf solutions (*high task analyzability*).

How do Perrow's task variety and task analyzability combinations affect the choice of an organizational structure? Routine technology integrates the activities of different individuals, departments and functions through established hierarchical channels of authority using formal rules, operating procedures and policies. This means that managers and supervisors have little discretion, and this leads them to adopt a mechanistic form of organizational structure. Non-routine technology has to encourage creativity, and different individuals and departments have to adjust to one other at the supervisory and middle management levels. Cross-functional teams and matrix organizations can be found here. This leads to a more organic form of organizational structure.

   With engineering technology, since the exceptions and problems encountered are not readily analyzable, the co-ordination of supervisory level personnel is achieved through mutual adjustment. Finally, craft technology organizations co-ordinate at middle management levels because of the high number of exceptions. Middle managers mutually adjust to each other, and gain power and discretion at the expense of first-line supervisors. This is because the exceptions encountered are analyzable through rules, policies and procedures.

   Perrow made two additional points. First, he said that companies could move cells, for example changing from non-routine (3 to 2) to craft by increasing production-runs or clients served, thereby gaining more experience and reducing the number of perceived exceptions. Similarly, a move from non-routine to engineering (3 to 4) could be facilitated by an increase in technical knowledge and accuracy of problem-solving. A move from non-routine to routine (3 to 1) would require a significant increase in experience and technical knowledge. Second, a single large and complex organization was likely to have several different technologies. For example, a university would have a non-routine one in units dedicated to full-time research, but a simple routine technology for its introductory lecturing. The different work-unit technologies would require different types of structures.

summary of technology and structure

As technological determinists, Woodward, Thompson and Perrow all focused upon the way in which they believed that technology determined a company's structure. Following up on Woodward's original work, both Thompson and Perrow sought to explain some, although not all, of the relationships that she had discovered between the type of technology and the most appropriate organizational structure for a company seeking to maximize its performance. Both their explanations focused on how different types of technology created uncertainties within organizations, and these needed to be managed by using co-ordination mechanisms. These, in their turn, produced the company's characteristic structural design.

James Thompson's explanation of the technology–structure relationship was in terms of the type of interdependency (pooled, sequential or reciprocal) which was created by the type of technology used (mediating, long-linked or intensive). As uncertainty increased, so did the need for individual and departmental activities to be co-ordinated flexibly.

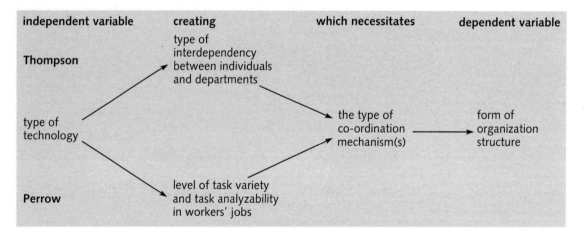

Charles Perrow's explanation of technology's effect on organizational structure was similar, but he emphasized its effect on the jobs of the workers, rather than the interdependences created. He argued that a decline in the certainty with which a company could manufacture a product or provide a service (as measured by the number of unexpected problems it encountered and the degree of their analyzabilty) meant that organizational co-ordination mechanisms such as rules, policies and procedures, which were designed to anticipate problems and suggest solutions in a prescriptive and inflexible manner, became less useful. In their place, more flexible ones, which addressed the unexpected outcomes in a problem-solving manner were needed. For this reason, a prescriptive, rule-based organization structure would be very different from a flexible, problem-solving one.

environmental determinism

Since the late 1950s, writers have had an interest in the relationship between a company's environment and its structure. Some of them argue that success depends on securing a proper 'fit' or alignment between itself and its environment. For these environmental determinists, environment determines organizational structure. One prominent environmental determinist, Peter Lawrence, even said, 'Tell me what your environment is and I shall tell you what your organization ought to be' (Argyris, 1972, p. 88).

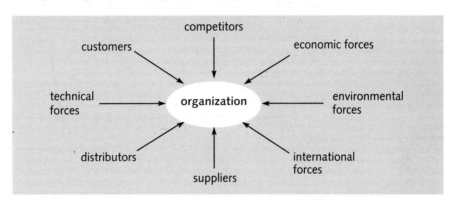

The environmental determinists see the organization as being in constant interaction with the environment within which it exists. It includes the general economic situation, the market, the competitive scene, and so on. They argue that because a company is dependent on its environment for its sales, labour, raw materials and so on, that environment constrains the kinds of choice an organization can make about how it structures itself. As the environmental situation changes, the organization–environment relationship also changes. Hence, to be effective, a company has to structure and restructure constantly to maintain alignment. The environmental determinists use the key concepts of environmental uncertainty and environmental complexity in their explanations. These will be considered later.

Tom Burns, G.M. Stalker, mechanistic and organic organizational structures

In the late 1950s in Britain, Tom Burns and G.M. Stalker studied the behaviour of people working in a rayon mill. They found that this contented, economically successful company was run with a management style which, according to contemporary wisdom about 'best' management practice, should have led to worker discontent and inefficiency. Some time later, the same authors studied an electronics company. Again it was highly successful, but used a management style completely different from that of the rayon mill studied earlier. This contradiction gave the authors the impetus to begin a large-scale investigation to examine the relationship between the management systems and the organizational tasks. They were particularly interested in the way management systems changed in response to changes in the commercial and technical tasks of the firm.

The rayon mill had a highly stable, highly structured character, which would have fitted well into Weber's bureaucratic organizational model. In contrast, the electronics firm violated many of the principles of classical management. It discouraged written communications, defined jobs as little as possible, and the interaction between employees was on a face-to-face basis. Indeed, staff even complained about this uncertainty. The authors gave the label *mechanistic* to the first form of organization structure and *organic* to the second. These represented ideal-types at opposite ends of a continuum. Most firms would be located somewhere in between.

characteristics of mechanistic and organic organizational structures

rayon mill (mechanistic)	characteristic	electronics company (organic)
high, many and sharp differentiations	*specialization*	low, no hard boundaries, relatively few different jobs
high, methods spelled out	*standardization*	low, individuals decide own methods
means	*orientation of members*	goals
by superior	*conflict resolution*	interaction
hierarchical based on implied contractual relation	*pattern of authority control and communication*	wide net based upon common commitment
at top of organization	*locus of superior competence*	wherever there is skill and competence
vertical	*interaction*	lateral
directions, orders	*communication content*	advice, information
to organization	*loyalty*	to project and group
from organizational position	*prestige*	from personal contribution

from J.A. Litterer, 1973, *The Analysis of Organizations*, John Wiley, Chichester, p. 339.

Burns and Stalker argued that neither form of organization structure was intrinsically efficient or inefficient, but rather that it all depended on the nature of the environment in which a firm operated. In their view, the key variables to be considered were the product market and the technology of the manufacturing process. These needed to be studied when the structure of a firm's management system was being designed. Thus, a mechanistic structure may be appropriate for an organization which uses an unchanging technology and operates in relatively stable markets. An organic structure can be more suitable for a firm which has to cope with unpredictable new tasks.

Paul Lawrence, Jay Lorsch, organization design and environmental needs

above:
Paul Lawrence

right:
Jay Lorsch

During the 1960s, Paul Lawrence and Jay Lorsch built on the work of Burns and Stalker, using the concepts of *differentiation* and *integration*. Differentiation refers to the process of a firm breaking itself up into sub-units, each of which concentrates on a particular part of the firm's environment. A university differentiates itself in terms of different faculties and departments. Such differentiation inevitably leads to the sub-units developing their own goals, values, norms, structures, time frames and interpersonal relations, which reflect the job that they have to do and the uncertainties with which they have to cope.

---

definitions

Differentiation *is the degree to which the tasks and the work of individuals, groups and units are divided up within an organization.*

Integration *is the required level to which units in an organization are linked together, and their respective degree of independence. Integrative mechanisms include rules and procedures and direct managerial control.*

Considering *differentiation* first, Lawrence and Lorsch found that effective organizations increased their level of differentiation as their environment became more uncertain. This was because it allowed staff to respond more effectively to their specific sub-environment for which they were responsible. On the other hand, the more differentiated the sub-units became, the more their goals would diverge, the more they would perceive the same things differently, and hence the more conflict there would be between them.

Turning next to *integration*, Lawrence and Lorsch use this term to refer to the process of achieving unity of effort among the previously differentiated sub-systems in order to accomplish the organization task. It is thus equivalent to co-ordination. Thus, having divided the university into faculties and departments, there is the need to ensure that all contribute to the goals of high quality research, excellent teaching and income generation. The authors found that as environmental uncertainty increased, and thus the degree of differentiation increased, so organizations had to increase the level of their integration (co-ordination) between people in different departments, if they were to work together effectively towards a common goal.

When environmental uncertainty is low, differentiation too is correspondingly low. Because the units share common goals and ways of achieving them, the hierarchy of authority in a company and standard procedures are sufficient to

---

organization design and environmental needs

Paul Lawrence and Jay Lorsch studied ten firms in three industries – plastics, packaged foods and standardized containers. These firms differed in terms of their operating environments. Firms in the plastics industry were confronted with a constant necessity for technological innovation, and hence the managers in them were faced with environments that had a high degree of uncertainty and unpredictability. In contrast, the environment for the container industry firms was highly stable, and competition centred on service and product quality rather than on product innovation. The packaged foods firms operated in an intermediate type environment, located somewhere between the first two.

Using standardized questionnaires and interviews with managers, the researchers focused their attention on the nature of the environment and its relation to the degree of differentiation among departments within the same firm, and on the degree and type of integration required across departments within each of the firms. The research revealed that dynamic and complex environments required considerably more differentiation amongst their departments than did relatively stable and simple environments. The firms in the plastics industry were more differentiated than those in the food industry, which in turn were more differentiated than those in the container company.

average differentiation and integration across three environments (higher differentiation scores mean greater differences; higher integration scores mean better integration)

industry	organization	average differentiation	average integration
plastics	high performer	10.7	5.6
	low performer	9.0	5.1
foods	high performer	8.0	5.3
	low performer	6.5	5.0
containers	high performer	5.7	5.7
	low performer	5.7	4.8

Of particular interest was the finding that the environment of the plastics firms appeared to place a larger premium on the proper degree of differentiation than did the environment for container firms. As the table shows, the degree of

---

integrate the activities of different units and individuals. However, as uncertainty increases, so too does the need for integration, and so too do the number of integrative devices used. The table on page 440 lists the number and type of these, depending on the level of the firm's degree of differentiation. Lawrence and Lorsch argue that the level of uncertainty in the environment that a firm has to cope with will determine the organizational structure that is most appropriate for it.

differentiation between the high- and low-performing plastics firms was greater than that between high- and low-performing container companies. The fast-changing environment in plastics required the achievement of a necessary amount of differentiation for organizational success, whereas the relatively stable environment of the container firms did not force this kind of requirement in organizational design in order for a firm to be highly effective.

The environment also seemed to necessitate organizational designs that achieved integration across departments, thus enabling the form to function as a total system. Such an integration requirement was needed for all environments (whether stable or changing). What was most important was that such integration should be of sufficient quantity and of an appropriate kind. Integration could take many forms – for example, structural integration (using committees, appointing co-ordinators), cultural integration (encouraging core values, attitudes, corporate philosophies) and political integration (managing conflicts and differences effectively).

In each of the three environments studied, the more effective organization achieved a greater degree of integration. However, the structural methods of integration used by the three effective organizations differed. In the dynamic environment of the plastics industry, the better performing organizations used a formal integrating department. The environment appeared to demand such an explicit integrating device in order to prevent the highly differentiated departments from working at cross-purposes.

The high-performing food products company used individuals as integrators, whilst the effective but not highly differentiated container firm used the least complex device, namely, direct managerial contact through the chain of command. In these latter cases, the more predictable environments did not appear to force effective organizations to develop elaborate and expensive mechanisms for integrating different units. In fact, the researchers found that the low-performing container firm had designed a special integrating department into its structure, but 'there was no evidence that the integrating unit was serving a useful purpose'. This would indicate that this organization's design was not completely compatible with the fundamental nature of its operating environment.

Lawrence and Lorsch therefore argued that high organizational effectiveness came from high differentiation and high integration in conditions of high uncertainty; and from low differentiation and low integration in conditions of low uncertainty.

based on Paul R. Lawrence and Jay W. Lorsch, 1967, *Organization and Environment*, Addison-Wesley, Boston, MA.

STOP!
How is your educational institution differentiated and integrated? On what evidence do you base your answer? What problems does such differentiation/integration give to you as a client-student?

comparison of Lawrence and Lorsch's integrating mechanisms in three high-performing organizations

degree of differentiation	high	medium	low
major co-ordination devices	1 paper system	1 paper system	1 paper system
	2 managerial hierarchy	2 managerial hierarchy	2 managerial hierarchy
	3 direct managerial contact	3 direct managerial contact	3 direct managerial contact
	4 permanent cross-functional teams at three levels of management	4 temporary cross-functional teams	
	5 integrative department	5 individual integrators	

from Arthur G. Bedeian and Raymond F. Zammuto, 1991, *Organizations: Theory and Design*, Dryden Press, Orlando, FL, p. 327.

summary of environment and structure

As contingency writers, Burns and Stalker and Lawrence and Lorsch argued that a company's structure had to 'fit' its environment and contain the correct balance between differentiation and integration. Thus all four disagreed with universal theorists such as Max Weber and Henri Fayol, who held that one type of structure was suitable for all organizations. Moreover, as *environmental* contingency theorists, they also disagreed with fellow contingency theorists like Woodward, Thompson and Perrow, who believed that it was technology which was the key factor determining the choice of appropriate organizational structure.

Robert Duncan (1972; 1973; 1974; 1979) integrated the work of these environmental contingency theorists by classifying organizational environments into four types according to how complex they were and how fast they changed. His framework is shown in the following figure, and is based on the dimensions of *environmental complexity* and *environmental dynamism*, which act together to place every organization into one of four cells which indicate the degree of environmental uncertainty that they experience.

---

definitions

Environmental complexity *refers to the range of environmental activities which are relevant to what an organization does, e.g. different customer groups, different supplier companies. The greater the number of these, the greater its environmental complexity.*

Environmental dynamism *is the degree to which the environments of a company change. It is measured by the speed of customer demands and responses. The greater the speed, the more dynamic the environment.*

Robert Duncan's characteristics of environmental states

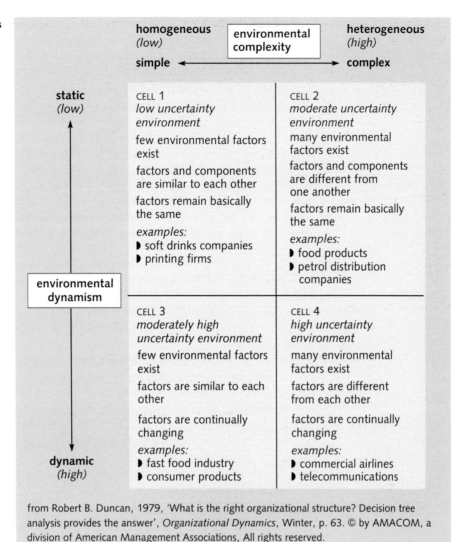

homogeneous
(low)

environmental complexity

heterogeneous
(high)

simple ←——————————→ complex

static
(low)

CELL 1
low uncertainty environment

few environmental factors exist

factors and components are similar to each other

factors remain basically the same

examples:
▶ soft drinks companies
▶ printing firms

CELL 2
moderate uncertainty environment

many environmental factors exist

factors and components are different from one another

factors remain basically the same

examples:
▶ food products
▶ petrol distribution companies

environmental dynamism

CELL 3
moderately high uncertainty environment

few environmental factors exist

factors are similar to each other

factors are continually changing

examples:
▶ fast food industry
▶ consumer products

CELL 4
high uncertainty environment

many environmental factors exist

factors are different from each other

factors are continually changing

examples:
▶ commercial airlines
▶ telecommunications

dynamic
(high)

simple–complex dimension (environmental complexity)

The horizontal dimension of the figure refers to the range of environmental activities that are relevant to what the organization does: for example, the number of customer groups dealt with, different supplier companies, central and local government contacts, the labour market, the number of competitors. Organizations which deal with just a few of these, such as a photo-shop, were held to have a *simple environment*. Those which deal with a lot of these, such as universities, had a *complex environment*. Typically, environmental complexity increased as an organization increased in size.

static–dynamic dimension (environmental dynamism)

The vertical dimension refers to the degree to which the environment of an organization changes. It is measured by the speed of customer demands and responses. When a company produces the same product for similar clients it is said to have a *static environment*. For example, demand for water and electricity tends to be predictable from one year to the next. In contrast, when different customer groups suddenly start demanding new or different products, and there is a high rate of change, that company is said to have a *dynamic environment*. The electronics sector, defined broadly to include microchips, personal computer and telephony manufacturers and service providers, currently represents a dynamic environment.

Duncan's four-cell model differentiates environments on the basis of the different degrees of *uncertainty* that they present to organizations. Every organization experiences uncertainty because it lacks information (what will our customers want next year?); does not know how the environment will affect its performance (will more teenagers mean larger sales and profits?); and does not know the costs of a wrong decision (what if we don't enter this market?).

Cell 1: Low uncertainty (simple–static environments): These are the most certain and most predictable of environments and contain firms such as Burns and Stalker's rayon mill and Lawrence and Lorsch's container companies. All these organizations are structured mechanistically, have a functional structure (marketing, accounting, etc.) and use policies, procedures and rules to control and co-ordinate activities.

Cell 2: Moderate uncertainty (complex–static environments): Although the demands of those in the environment may not change much, there are still many of them to deal with. Thus, such complexity is dealt with by structuring the organization into divisions which have decision-making powers delegated to them. Co-ordination is thus achieved through decentralization and the training of staff to implement it. Public sector organizations such as hospitals and universities fall into this cell.

Cell 3: Moderately high uncertainty (simple–dynamic environments): The number of contacts in the environment to be dealt with may be small, but their demands are highly changeable. Entrepreneurs running small businesses or computer software consultants working for clients on a project basis are examples of these. Their structures are simple, usually functional with medium centralization. Personal supervision is used to control and co-ordinate activities.

Cell 4: High uncertainty (complex–dynamic environments): The organizations in this cell experience the highest level of uncertainty. Many contacts make greatly changing demands and expectations. Such changes may be driven by technology, politics or consumer tastes. The companies here include Burns and Stalker's electronics company and Lawrence and Lorsch's plastics firms. The companies are structured organically, with an emphasis on decentralized matrix forms. Co-ordination and control is achieved using socialization (including training) and the mutual adjustment of one individual, team or department to another.

The following table relates types of environments to aspects of organizational structure. The environmental contingency theorists argue that, given the conditions pertaining in their companies' environments, managers have a relatively restricted range of organizational structures from which to choose.

environmental uncertainty and organizational structure

environment				
	simple–static	*complex–static*	*simple–dynamic*	*complex–dynamic*
	(cell 1)	(cell 2)	(cell 3)	(cell 4)

perceived uncertainty				
	low	low-moderate	moderate-high	high

design characteristics				
unit grouping	*functional (bureaucracy)*	*market-based (divisional)*	*functional (simple)*	*market-based (matrix)*
centralization	high	medium	high	low
job specialization (horizontal) (vertical)	high high	medium low	low high	low low
co-ordination	rules, policies, procedures	training	direct supervision	training, socialization, mutual adjustment

figure from *Organizations: Theory and Design* by Arthur G. Bedeian and Raymond F. Zammuto, copyright © 1991 by The Dryden Press, reproduced by permission of the publisher.

strategic choice

The early contingency researchers of the 1950s and 1960s took a determinist view on the effect of technology and the environment on organizational structure. By the 1970s, later contingency researchers said that more attention should be given to choices being made by those who had the power to direct organizations. This came to be known as the *strategic choice* perspective and stands in contrast to determinism, although both branches are within the contingency approach. Strategic choice writers assert that the relationship between an organization's structure and its technology or environment is not automatically determined by these variables, but is a reflection of the choices made by management, based on their perceptions and interests. The perspective has been summarized by John Child who sees the design of organizations' structures as being: 'an essentially political process in which constraints and opportunities are functions of the power exercised by decision makers in the light of ideological values' (Child, 1972, p. 2).

Strategic choice theorists hold that technology or environment does not determine organizational structure independently of the aims, beliefs and expectations of those who make the decisions. It is not the technology itself but rather how it is used, and it is not the environment but how it is responded to, that are the crucial factors. To understand the impact of technology or the environment on organizational structure, one needs to study the nature of the managerial decision-making process itself, including its political aspects, since it is managers who design an organization structure.

---

some organizations seek to adjust to their environment

Companies now respond to changes in the demand for their product or service in months or weeks. However, there is one organization that has to respond on a minute-by-minute basis – The National Grid. Demand for electricity by companies and households is broadly predictable on the basis of past records. What causes problems are unexpected surges of demand. One of these is associated with television viewing. This problem is so important, that Grid staff regularly review the forthcoming week's programmes in TV listings magazines in order to identify the spikes in demand in the middle and at the end of programmes. These spikes are referred to as the 'mega-watt pick-up', and occur when millions of viewers simultaneously visit the kitchen or bathroom, or switch on the living room lights. There is usually a 2–3 minute pause between the time viewers leave the TV and when they arrive in the kitchen to put on the kettle.

The *Panorama* interview with the Princess of Wales on 20 November 1996 was watched by 22.8 million viewers and created a 1000 MW spike. The *Coronation Street* episode on 5 April 1995 when Tracy Barlow was hospitalized after an ecstasy overdose created a 1600 MW surge. However, the record is still held by the England *v* West Germany World Cup semi-final of 4 July 1990, which was watched by 25.2 million people, and created a pick-up of 2800 MW.

How does the National Grid cope? A special £450 million storage plant was built in Dinorwig in the heart of Snowdonia, largely because of *Coronation Street*. Dinorwig is the largest hydroelectric pumped storage scheme in Europe. There is a similar plant at Ffestiniog in North Wales. Cheap night-time power is used to pump water from a reservoir to a lake at the top of a mountain. When power is needed urgently, water is released from the lake, dropping through pipes, and driving turbines to generate power before ending up at the lower reservoir. This can pick up load within 10 seconds. The four Dinorwig turbines can provide 12,000 MW in all.

from Lawson (1986); Highfield (1993); *The Herald* (1996); and *Radio Times* (1996).

environmental strategic choice

This perspective holds that managers' perceptions of their organizations' environments are the basis for their decisions. Perception theory tells us that whilst some environmental factors will be included, others will be filtered out and ignored. The latter will thus not be considered in their deliberations and choices. Hence exactly the same environment may be perceived differently by two organizations. Managers' perceptions will be important in their decisions, about not only the most appropriate organizational structure, but also the firm's strategy and process. Managers thus *enact*, rather than *react* to their environments. That is, they change them, rather than are changed by them (Weick, 1979). This is different from the view held by the environmental determinist school.

---

definitions

Enacted environment *is that part of the environment that an organization's managers perceive.*

Managerial enactment *is the active modification of the perceived and selected part of the organization's environment.*

Organizational enactment *is the selection and development of a particular domain within its larger environment.*

---

summary of environmental strategic choice

In essence, this approach holds that managers selectively perceive (enact) their organization's environment, making it easier to understand and modify. Selective perception means that different companies in the same environment will perceive different opportunities and threats, and hence choose different strategic options, which will result in the creation of different organizational structures.

By actively choosing which goods to make, which markets to sell them in and which customers to serve, companies define their environment. In addition to defining it, they modify it, using takeover, mergers, joint ventures and political actions. These actions also impact upon and change the environment, and have a knock-on effect on the company's structure. Miles and Snow (1978) showed that some strategies are better pursued using certain structural designs than others. An existing structure may limit the strategy that a company pursues.

The environmental determinist school (Burns and Stalker, Lawrence and Lorsch) and the environmental strategic choice school (Pfeiffer and Salancik, Miles and Snow) are branches of the same contingency approach, since both agree that there is a relationship between environmental conditions on the one hand, and an organization's structure and performance on the other. Where they differ is that the former holds that organization structures *react* to changing environmental conditions, whilst the latter believe that managers create and shape the environments to which their organizations adapt. The company's structure results from the choices that they make about that adaptation. Both branches agree that a company's structure has to be matched with the environmental conditions, irrespective of whether they are imposed from outside or managed from within.

assessment

Among the strengths of the bureaucratic and classical management schools of organizational structuring was the fact that they offered managers prescriptions for action. It told them what they should do and how to do it. In contrast, contingency approaches appear either wishy-washy or incredibly complex. Whilst contingency writers do not offer ready-made answers, they do have a set of questions and do provide a way of thinking which can help managers analyze their organizations within their particular situation to enable them to make an informed choice about the

McDonald's adapts its environment, 1990

In January 1990, shortly before the demise of the Soviet Union, the 'Big Mac' went on sale in the world's largest McDonald's, a 900-seater restaurant in Moscow's Pushkin Square. It was designed to serve 15,000 people a day. The Moscow McDonald's is operated by the Canadian subsidiary of the American parent firm. Mr George Cohon, the head of the Canadian operation, devoted half of his time in 1987–88 to securing this relatively small $50 million deal. The company saw it as an investment for the future.

Luda is a 21-year-old Moscow computer student. She is one of 600 staff selected from among the 25,000 who applied for a job at McDonald's. A task force of McDonald's trainers from Canada was imported to teach Luda and her colleagues the job. Each counter service team is trained to meet the company's target requirement of 60 seconds to serve the customer, thank them for their custom, and ask them to call again.

Since McDonald's policy is that customers in Moscow will be served exactly the same food and drink as they would get in any other McDonald's outlet in the world, the company went to extraordinary lengths to ensure that this happened. Essentially, the company had to build itself an entire food chain from scratch to supply its restaurant. Over a two-year period it contracted with Russian farmers to produce beef and potatoes. It indirectly manages cattle ranches and vegetable plots. It imported its own beef semen to ensure the quality of the beef cattle and taught Russian beef farmers how to extend the cattle's feed cycle. It imported and planted Russet Burbank potatoes (the kind used in its French fries) and instructed the farmers how to maximize their harvests.

To manufacture from this raw material, the world's largest food processing plant was built outside Moscow for $4 million by a Finnish construction firm. At 100,000 square feet, it is the size of five football pitches and cost the company $40 million (the restaurant cost $4.5 million). This plant moulds its beef patties, chips its French fries and bakes its rolls. The plant also includes its own dairy. This processing plant will supply the twenty McDonald's outlets planned for the Moscow area.

The company sent four of its Russian management trainees to its Hamburger University in North America. Vladimir Zukarowski is one of those four. He is a graduate of the Moscow Steel and Iron Institute, and he spent eight months in Montreal and Chicago learning the McDonald's way of doing things.

Source: *Financial Times,* used with permission.

based on 'Pushkin, coke and fries', *The Economist*, 18 November 1989, p. 62; 'Slow food', *The Economist*, 3 February 1990, pp. 84–5; and BBC2, '40 Minutes: Mac to the USSR', 12 April 1990.

McDonald's enacts its environment – 1996

20 March 1996 is known as Mad Cow Wednesday in Britain. It was the day that the Secretary of State for Health informed Parliament that there could be a link between the cattle disease, Bovine Spongiform Encephalopathy (BSE) and its human equivalent, Creutzfeldt-Jakob Disease (CJD). The impact of this announcement was most immediately felt by those companies which used processed cattle meat as a main ingredient in their products – the hamburger restaurants.

McDonald's is one of these, and serves nearly 2 million people each day in its 660 restaurants in Britain. It buys 12 per cent of all British beef. On Saturday, 23 March it made a decision to stop using British beef in its hamburgers. The decision was publicly announced the following day. On Monday, 25 March, it a took full-page advertisment in newspapers headed, 'A message from McDonald's to all our customers'. It contained information from its President and Chief Executive Officer, Paul Preston, that the company would no longer be offering products made from British beef in its restaurants in Great Britain. Hamburgers would begin being sold once again from Thursday, 28 March, and these would be made from non-British beef. When Thursday arrived, McDonald's announced that it was using non-British beef. Within seven days, a major food manufacturer had responded to an environmental challenge that had threatened its business.

---

organizational structure that is most appropriate for their specific enterprise.

During the last 40 years, contingency researchers have studied the effects of production technology, the environment and corporate strategy on the design of organizational structures. More recently, attention has shifted to how the availability of information impacts on structure. Amongst the first of the commentators who raised this question was Peter Drucker. In 1989 he predicted that as we move towards the new millennium, organizations of all kinds will undergo a greater amount of restructuring, and of a more radical nature than hitherto. Managerial levels have already been reduced by a third and many more such reductions will follow. The reason he gave for these reductions was that information-based organizations required fewer hierarchical levels than those based on the traditional classical model of command-and-control.

Drucker argued that in the future, work would go to the people rather than people being brought to the work. Secondly, organizational activities which did not provide opportunities for advancement into senior managerial and professional positions would be subcontracted out – for example, clerical and maintenance work. Finally, Drucker forecast that, by the end of the century, company size would become a strategic decision. Neither of the two axioms, 'Big is Better' nor 'Small is Beautiful' would necessarily apply. Instead, size would follow function (Drucker, 1989).

is your German good enough to distinguish modern from traditional forms of organization?

Revolution in den Betrieben

TRADITIONELLE UNTERNEHMEN   **MODERNE UNTERNEHMEN**

Starke Hierarchie	**HIERARCHIE**	Kleine Managementebenen, flache Führungspyramiden
Entscheidungen werden in zentralen Einheiten gefällt. Sehr bürokratisch	**DELEGATION**	Entscheidungen werden weitgehend auf die Ebene delegiert, wo sie anfallen. Jede Tätigkeit wird in Eigenverantwortung durchgeführt.
Klar abgegrenzte Aufgabengebiete. Extrem: Fließbandfertigung mit einfachen Handgriffen	**ARBEITSTEILUNG**	Aufgaben werden von Teams interdisziplinär und über Hierarchieebenen hinweg gelöst. Fertigung durch Arbeitsgruppen, die auch für früher zentralisierte Aufgaben, zum Beispiel Einkauf, verantwortlich sind.
Schwerfällig, keine unmittelbare Rückkopplung	**FLEXIBILIÄT**	Unternehmen reagiert auf jede Änderung, zum Beispiel des Kundenverhaltens. Ziel: das lernende Unternehmen
Technikorientiert. Beschränkt auf die dafür zuständige Abteilung	**ENTWICKLUNG**	Kundenorientiert. Alle betroffenen Abteilungen einschließlich der Zulieferer sind von vornherein und simultan in den Entwicklungsprozeß eingebunden.
In großen Sprüngen, zum Beispiel durch Einführung neuer Techniken	**VERBESSERUNG**	Ständig fortlaufender Prozeß unter Beteiligung aller Mitarbeiter (Kaizen)
Systemimmanent durch starke Bürokratie und geringe Verantwortung der Beteiligten	**VERSCHWENDUNG**	Wird kontinuierlich vermindert
Hoch, weil viele Puffer notwendig sind und weil auf Vorrat gefertigt wird. Viele unnötige Transportwege	**LAGERHALTUNG**	Gering. Geliefert wird nur, was sofort gebraucht wird (just in time). Gefertigt wird nur, was schon bestellt ist.
Endkontrolle: Fehler werden zu spät entdeckt. Die Beseitigung der Mängel kostet viel Geld.	**QUALITÄT**	Permanente Kontrolle während des gesamten Produktionsprozesses
Starr. Feste Arbeitszeiten	**ARBEITSZEIT**	Flexibel, im Extrem bestimmen die Mitarbeiter (in Abstimmung mit ihrer Gruppe) selbst, wann sie kommen oder gehen. Mehr- oder Minderarbeit wird über ein Zeitkonto ausgeglichen.

from 'Ihr seid weider wer', *Der Spiegel*, 11, 1994, p. 97.

Technological opportunities, together with environmental turbulence, are likely to bring changes in the design of organizations. Coulson-Thomas (1991) commented that, 'Organizations face an unprecedented range of challenges and opportunities in the social, economic, political and business environment. The external environment is characterised by uncertainty, surprise, turbulence and discontinuity'. He then went on to identify some of the structural implications:

- greater flexibility and responsiveness to customer needs
- delegation of work to multifunctional, multilocational teams, with assessment changing from input to output
- flatter and more fluid organizational structures, which are developing into networks with computerized links to customers, suppliers and business partners
- a management approach which pushes responsibility down the organizational hierarchy to individuals, who require access to expertise and specialists

Drucker's prediction was that the manager's role would change to that of decision-maker-in-line-with-corporate-strategic-objectives, rather than data-keeper or the transmitter-of-orders. The slimmed down organizational structures of the future were likely to require just two levels of hierarchy. On top would be the selectors of long-term strategies and the finders of people to implement them. Those below would deal with operational matters including the motivation and leading of staff to accomplish the stated objectives. The intervening levels of hierarchy were likely to wither away, thereby creating a lean and flexible business structure which, even though large, would be resilient to market forces.

Drucker's 'ideal organization' scenario has not yet happened, and is unlikely to for a number of reasons. First, organizations seem prone to employee inflation. Left to themselves, staff numbers tend to expand until a crisis occurs, and a new chief executive officer (CEO) is brought in who slashes the payroll numbers. During the last decade, headline-hitting redundancies have taken place at IBM, General Electric, AT&T and Digital. It seems equally certain that those numbers will creep up again before a new cull is effected by a new CEO.

Second, the new demands made on organizations require new skills and knowledge, often not possessed by existing employees. This is separate from, and in addition to, the employee inflation mentioned. For example, the business opportunities offered by the internet mean that companies need experts to create and maintain websites, as well as respond to website visitors and customers. This specialist work can be subcontracted out or performed in-house. In the case of the former, the subcontracting still has to be managed from within.

sources

Argyris, C., 1972, *The Applicability of Organizational Sociology*, Cambridge University Press, London.

BBC2, 1990, *40 Minutes: Mac to the USSR*, 12 April.

Bedeian, A.G. and Zammuto, R.F., 1990, *Organizations: Theory and Design*, Dryden Press, Orlando, FL.

Bennis, W. G., 1959, 'Leadership theory and administrative behaviour: The problem of authority', *Administrative Science Quarterly*, vol. 4, no. 3, December.

Blain, I., 1964, *Structure in Management*, National Institute for Industrial Psychology, London.

Burns, T. and Stalker, G.M., 1961, *The Management of Innovation*, Tavistock, London.

Child, J., 1972, 'Organizational structure, environment and performance: The role of strategic choice', *Sociology*, vol. 6, pp. 1–22.

Coulson-Thomas, C.J., 1991, 'Developing tomorrow's professional today', *Journal of European Industrial Training*, vol. 15, pp. 3–11.

Drucker, P.F., 1989, 'The futures that have already happened', *The Economist*, 21 October, pp. 27–30.

Duncan, R.B., 1972, 'Characteristics of organizational environments and perceived environmental uncertainty', *Administrative Science Quarterly*, vol. 17, pp. 313–27.

Duncan, R.B., 1973, 'Multiple decision making structures in adapting to environmental uncertainty: The impact of organizational effectiveness', *Human Relations*, vol. 26, pp. 273–91.

Duncan, R.B., 1974, 'Modifications in decision structure in adapting to the environment: Some implications for organizational learning', *Decision Sciences*, vol. 5, pp. 704–25.

Duncan, R.B., 1979, 'What is the right organizational structure?', *Organizational Dynamics*, Winter, pp. 59–80.

Economist, 1989, 'Pushkin, coke and fries', 18 November, p. 62.

Economist, 1990, 'Slow food', 3 February, pp. 84–5.

Emery, F.E. and Trist, E.L., 1965, 'The causal texture of organizational environments', *Human Relations*, vol. 18, no. 1, pp. 21–31.

Fayol, H. [1916] 1949, *General and Industrial Management*, trans. C. Storrs, Sir Isaac Pitman and Sons, London.

Graham, P., 1987, *Dynamic Managing – the Follett Way*, Professional Publishing/British Institute of Management, London.

Herald, The, 1996, 'Power surge following Diana's electrifying performance', 11 January, p. 3.

Hickson, D.J., Pugh, D.S. and Pheysey, D.C., 1969, 'Operations technology and organizational structure: An empirical appraisal', *Administrative Science Quarterly*, vol. 14, no. 3, pp. 378–97.

Highfield, R., 1993, 'How the National Grid will cope when Britain brews up', *Daily Telegraph*, 23 November, p. 18.

Hunt, J., 1992, *Managing People at Work*, Penguin Books, Harmondsworth, 3rd edition.

Lawrence, P.R. and Lorsch, J.W., 1967, *Organization and Environment*, Addison-Wesley, Boston, MA.

Lawson, M., 1986, 'Casual pick-up', *The Sunday Times*, 18 May.

Miles, R.E. and Snow, C., 1978, *Organizational Strategy, Structure and Process*, McGraw-Hill, New York.

Perrow, C., 1967, *Organizational Analysis: A Sociological View*, Tavistock, London.

Pfeffer, J. and Salancik, G.R. 1978, *The External Control of Organizations: A Resource Dependence Perspective*, Harper and Row, New York.

Pugh, D.S., Hickson, D.J., Hinings, C.R. and Turner, C., 1964, 'The context of organizational structures', *Administrative Science Quarterly*, vol. 14, pp. 91–114.

Radio Times, 1996, 30 December, p. 17.

Simon, A.H., 1948, *Administrative Behaviour*, Macmillan, New York.

Thompson, J.D., 1967, *Organizations in Action*, McGraw-Hill, New York.

Weick, K., 1979, *The Social Psychology of Organizing*, Addison-Wesley, Boston, MA.

Whyte, W.F., 1959, 'An interaction approach to the theory of organizations' in M. Haire (ed.), *Modern Organization Theory*, John Wiley, New York, pp. 155–83.

Woodward, J., 1965, *Industrial Organization: Theory and Practice*, Oxford University Press, London.

part 4 organizational change
and development

chapter 16 organizational change

Calvin and Hobbes

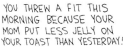

concepts and learning objectives
strategic change: the contemporary imperative
project management and participative management
resistance to change: causes and management techniques
recipe and process: competing views on understanding change
business process re-engineering
the expertise of the change agent
assessment
sources

concepts and learning objectives

is rapid change just a contemporary phenomenon?

That this is an age of change is an expression heard frequently today. Never before in the history of mankind have so many and so frequent changes occurred. These changes that we see taking place all about us are in that great cultural accumulation which is man's social heritage. It has already been shown that these cultural changes were in earlier times rather infrequent, but that in modern times they have been occurring faster and faster until today mankind is almost bewildered in his effort to keep adjusted to these ever increasing social changes. This rapidity of social change may be due to the increase in inventions which in turn is made possible by the accumulative nature of material culture [i.e. technology].

from William Fielding Ogburn, 1922, *Social Change: With Respect to Culture and Original Nature*, B.W. Huebsch, New York, pp. 199–200.

W.F. Ogburn's observations have been repeated often since the 1920s. The rapidity of change – technological and social – has been a central feature of industrialized economies throughout the twentieth century. It was not until the 1950s that the management styles and organization structures appropriate in dealing with stable conditions were shown to be less effective in coping with turbulence and uncertainty. From an organizational behaviour perspective, the management of change has become a central theme. The organizational literature of the second half of the century has thus concentrated on organizational responsiveness, flexibility and adaptability. The literature in this field has mushroomed. These trends are likely to persist, and to intensify, into the twenty-first century.

In this chapter, we first explore perspectives on understanding change, before turning to practical issues. We examine the causes of, and ways of addressing, resistance to change, contemporary methods for process re-engineering, and the skills involved in implementing change effectively. In Chapter 17, the specialized change management methods of organization development are explained. Can corporate culture be changed? Contrasting perspectives on this question are examined in Chapter 18. Chapter 19 concludes this part with an exploration of how technological change affects work and organization design.

key concepts

- adhocracy
- triggers of change
- business process re-engineering
- strategic change
- readiness for change
- future shock
- resistance to change
- change agent
- stakeholders

learning objectives

When you have read this chapter, you should be able to define those key concepts in your own words, and you should also be able to:

1 Understand the main stages in the human response to change.
2 Identify the main external and internal triggers of organizational change.
3 Understand the nature of resistance to change, and the main approaches to avoiding or overcoming resistance.
4 Explain the advantages and limitations of project management and participative approaches to organizational change implementation.
5 Explain the use and limitations of business process re-engineering as an organizational change and development perspective.
6 Outline the skills requirements of the effective change agent.

Rapid change may be 'normal', but it can also have severe psychological consequences. Alvin Toffler (1970) argued that the rate of change was out of control, and that society was 'doomed to a massive adaptational breakdown'. Thirty years on, that massive breakdown does not appear to have happened. However, Toffler also believed that there is a limit to the amount of change that we can handle. He argued that 'the shattering stress and disorientation that we induce in individuals by subjecting them to too much change in too short a time' is unhealthy. He labelled this response *future shock*.

---

definition

Future shock *is the stress and disorientation suffered by people when they are subjected to excessive change. Toffler also called* future shock *'the disease of change'.*

STOP!

Think of the changes – technological, personal, social, organizational, political, economic – that you have observed and experienced over, say, the past two years.

Do you feel that you are suffering from future shock?

Describe your symptoms, and compare your responses to rapid change with friends.

It has been argued that our response to change is neither as simple nor as predictable as Toffler suggested. One particularly influential approach to understanding response to change comes from studies of the ways in which we cope with traumatic personal loss, such as the death of a close relative and also perhaps our own impending death.

Elizabeth Kubler-Ross (1969) argued that we deal with loss, and with impending loss, in moving through a series of stages, each characterized by a particular emotional response. This response cycle has been used to understand resistance and other responses to organizational change, which for some individuals, sometimes, can be particularly traumatic and stressful.

The five typical stages in the Kubler-Ross response cycle are these:

stage	response
denial	unwillingness to confront the reality: 'This is not happening.' 'There is still hope that this will all go away.'
anger	turn accusations on those apparently responsible: 'Why is this happening to me?' 'Why are you doing this to me?'
bargaining	attempts to negotiate, to mitigate loss: 'What if I do it this way?'
depression	the reality of loss or transition is appreciated: 'It's hopeless, there's nothing I can do now.' 'I don't know which way to turn.'
acceptance	coming to terms with and accepting the situation and its full implications: 'What are we going to do about this?' 'How am I going to move forward?'

As with all such models, this 'universal sequence' disguises the fact of individual differences. We may not all experience the same five sets of responses. We may omit particular stages, 'revisit' some stages or pass through them more or less quickly than others. From an organizational perspective, this can be a useful explanatory and diagnostic tool. If one is able to detect where in the response cycle a person may be, in the face of organizational change, one will be better placed to provide appropriate guidance, advice and support.

Change, of different types and on a number of different levels is a central feature of our lives. Organizational change has become a prerequisite for survival and development in a rapidly changing world. We are all likely to experience changes in our employing organizations, in their organization structures and in our job specifications, at various stages in our personal careers. The effective management of change and how we cope with change thus affect our experience of disorganization and frustration.

Change is a main and recurring theme throughout this text.

In Part 1, we explored the possibilities of changing human perception, motivation, learning and personality. In Part 2, we examined how individual behaviour changes in group settings, and how group functioning can be changed to improve performance. In Part 3, we explored changes in organization structure and the concept of adhocracy – which is revisited briefly here. In Part 5, we explore how leaders can change employee behaviour, and also consider whether leaders themselves can and should change their styles.

Change can be studied on many different levels: individual, group, organizational, social, global. Organizational change influences conditions of work, occupational identities and divisions, the training and experience of employees, and hierarchical relationships. These developments in turn shape the structure of our society as a whole (as, for instance, the patterns of employment across agriculture and other 'primary' industries, manufacturing and services have shifted this century). The different levels on which change can be studied are intimately related and this makes it difficult to disentangle cause and effect clearly. Change, therefore, is difficult to study. It is particularly difficult to stand back from a process in which one is closely involved and examine it objectively.

strategic change: the contemporary imperative

Change can be explored over differing timescales. Here, we are concerned with organizational changes over comparatively short periods of time – weeks, months or years. Most commentators in the latter part of the 1990s accept that organizational change is a *strategic* imperative. This simply means that major or radical shifts in organizational design and functioning are required in order to cope with the many and unpredictable changes happening in the wider social, economic, political and technological environment. The organizational emphasis since the mid-1980s has thus been with *strategic change*.

---

definition

Strategic change *is a label used to describe organizational redesign or refocusing that is major, radical, 'frame-breaking' or 'mould-breaking' in its nature and implications. The term 'strategic' here denotes scale or magnitude. Deciding whether or not a particular change or programme of change is strategic will depend on the circumstances.*

To the extent that external environmental changes are rapid and significant, the internal organizational changes must also be timely and wide-reaching. Organizations that are unable to implement appropriate strategic changes, or that are unable to adjust rapidly, are likely to have difficulty surviving. Their business will be taken by those organizations which are able to respond to threats and opportunities in a timely and appropriate manner.

This strategic imperative is usually expressed in terms of the need for organizations to become more flexible, more adaptable, more 'fluid' and more responsive to change. The American academic Warren Bennis (1969) has for three decades argued that the pace of change has made traditional forms of organization obsolete. This argument was explored in Chapter 13. Bureaucratic structures, he claims, cannot cope with:

Warren Bennis
(b. 1925)

> rapid and unpredictable change
> the increasing complexity of modern organization
> diversity of specialist expertise required in many organizations
> humanistic, participative management styles

For Bennis, and others, bureaucratic structure *may* be appropriate to deal with:

> stability, predictability and routine
> simple and orderly organization structures
> standardized, routinized jobs and skills
> impersonal, autocratic management styles

In 1969 Bennis spoke of 'adaptive structures'. Tom Burns and George Stalker (1961; see Chapter 15) distinguished between rigid, *mechanistic* management systems, and fluid, *organic* systems. In 1970, Alvin Toffler used the term *adhocracy*. In 1983, Rosabeth Moss Kanter contrasted rigid *segmentalist* structures with innovative *integrative* approaches. These commentators appear to have considered broadly the same organizational issues and concepts, and to have adjusted the terminology. We shall consider in Chapter 17 how the field of organization development seeks to address these issues.

Rosabeth Moss Kanter
(b. 1943)

---

definition

Adhocracy *is a type of organization design which is temporary, adaptive, creative, in contrast with bureaucracy which tends to be relatively permanent, rule-driven and inflexible. Adhocracy is similar to the concepts of* **organic** *and* **integrative** *organizational styles;* **bureaucracy** *equates with* **mechanistic** *and* **segmentalist** *approaches.*

Organization and management theorists have thus been remarkably consistent in their criticisms of traditional structures and styles, and in their advocacy of flexible approaches to coping with change, uncertainty and turbulence. Cynics might point out that the main innovations in this research tradition have been in the names given to the 'old' and 'new' types of structure prescribed by theorists and organizational management consultants. One major problem that appears to have been recognized only recently concerns the need to create organizations that are flexible enough to adapt to pressures for change, and that are also stable enough to endure. The fluid, shifting organization may in theory seem to be an appropriate vehicle for dealing with external turbulence. However, this kind of organization can be an extremely uncomfortable and insecure place in which to work.

---

out with the segmentalist and in with the integrative

Rosabeth Moss Kanter, in her book on organizational change, claimed that:
I found that the entrepreneurial spirit producing innovation is associated with a particular way of approaching problems that I call 'integrative': the willingness to move beyond received wisdom, to combine ideas from unconnected sources, to embrace change as an opportunity to test limits. To see problems integratively is to see them as wholes, related to larger wholes, and thus challenging established practices – rather than walling off a piece of experience and preventing it from being touched or affected by any new experiences . . .

Such organizations reduce rancorous conflict and isolation between organizational units; create mechanisms for exchange of information and new ideas across organizational boundaries; ensure that multiple perspectives will be taken into account in decisions; and provide coherence and direction to the organization. In these team-oriented co-operative environments, innovation flourishes . . .

The contrasting style of thought is anti-change-oriented and prevents innovation. I call it 'segmentalism' because it is concerned with compartmentalizing actions, events, and problems and keeping each piece isolated from the others . . . Companies where segmentalist approaches dominate find it difficult to innovate or to handle change.

from Rosabeth Moss Kanter, 1983, *The Change Masters: Corporate Entrepreneurs at Work*, George Allen & Unwin, London, pp. 27–8.

In summary, the conventional wisdom of the late twentieth century states that organizations must be able to respond rapidly to external changes if they are to survive, and that the necessary internal restructuring is likely to be strategic, radical or 'mould-breaking'. The mould that needs to be broken appears to be that of rigid, bureaucratic, autocratic approaches to organization and management. The organizational framework required in its place appears to be one that emphasizes flexibility, creativity and participation.

STOP!

Think of the features of your current educational institution.
- Would you describe this organization as an organic, flexible, responsive adhocracy?
- Would you describe it as a mechanistic, inflexible, rule-driven bureaucracy?
- Given what you know about the factors in the organization's external environment (customers, competition, economic and political trends), what strategic changes – if any – do you think the organization needs to consider?

Organizational change can, of course, be prompted or initiated by many different factors or *triggers*.

---

definition

A **trigger of change** is any *'disorganizing pressure'*, arising outside or inside the organization, indicating that current arrangements, systems, procedures, rules and other aspects of organization structure and process are no longer appropriate or effective.

External triggers for organizational change can include:
- developments in technology
- developments in new materials
- changes in customers' requirements and tastes
- the activities and innovations of competitors
- new legislation and government policies
- changing national and global economic and trading conditions
- shifts in local, national and international politics
- changes in social and cultural values

Internal triggers for organizational change can include:
- new product and service design innovations
- low performance and morale, triggering job redesign
- appointment of a new senior manager or top management team
- inadequate skills and knowledge base, triggering training programmes
- office and factory relocation, closer to suppliers and markets
- recognition of problems triggering reallocation of responsibilities
- innovations in the manufacturing process
- new ideas about how to deliver services to customers

This approach to identifying and listing triggers makes organizational change appear to be a reactive process. Clearly this cannot always be the case. In at least some instances, it will be appropriate to anticipate events and trends, and to be *proactive* in introducing appropriate organizational changes. The triggers will not always initiate strategic change. However, strategic changes are the most significant, and the most difficult to manage effectively.

project management and participative management

---

the six phases of a project

1 enthusiasm
2 disillusionment
3 panic
4 search for the guilty
5 punishment of the innocent
6 praise and rewards for the non-participants

Anon.

One popular, influential and conventional approach to change implementation draws on the methods of *project management*. This approach revolves around the concept of the phased project 'life cycle'. The typical life cycle for a new computerized management information system, for example, from Niv Ahituv and Seev Neumann (1986), covers ten activities:

1	preliminary analysis	Do we have a problem here?
2	feasibility study	Can we fix it?
3	information analysis	What do we know already?
4	system design	What's the new specification going to be ?
5	programming	Here's the new software.
6	procedure development	What new rules and processes do we need?
7	conversion to new system	Out with the old, in with the new.
8	operation and maintenance	Running it and fixing it.
9	post-implementation audit	Well, did it work out?
10	project termination	Keep it, replace it or abandon it?

One major British telecommunications organization advises a similar eight stage 'problem-solving process', for any change implementation, following these steps:

1 Identify problem.
2 Gather data.
3 Analyze data.
4 Generate solutions.
5 Select the solution.
6 Plan for implementation.
7 Implement and test.
8 Continue to improve.

There are many such models in the project management literature. Successful change in this approach depends on the clarity with which project objectives are stated, and on the effectiveness of monitoring and control to ensure that the project stays on target with respect to time and money. Ineffective change in this model is usually blamed on the failure to specify goals, tasks, milestones and budgets clearly, and to poor project control. The change agent in this model needs two areas of expertise: first, with respect to the content of the changes being introduced (a new information system, office building, payment system); second, with respect to project control, defining goals and tasks, monitoring progress and taking remedial action to reduce and avoid deviations from plan.

Project management models of change have one striking feature in common. They rely on the assumption that planned organizational change unfolds in a logical sequence. Solutions are not identified until the problem has been clearly defined. The 'best' solution is not chosen until the options have been compared and evaluated. Implementation does not begin until there is agreement on the solution. The key actors in the implementation process each have their clearly defined roles and responsibilities. Implementation is closely monitored and deviations from plan are detected and corrected. The implementation process is bounded in terms of resources (people, money, space) and time, with a clear project completion date.

This 'logical unfolding' property has earned project management accounts the label of 'rational linear' models of organizational change. As we shall see later in this chapter, these assumptions, concerning both rationality and linearity in organizational change, have attracted significant criticism. In short, organizations seem rarely to operate in such a tidy and predictable manner, particularly with respect to strategic (major, messy, radical) change.

A second conventional approach to change implementation advocates a *participative management* approach. This approach drew initially from the influential experiments of Lester Coch and John French (1948) in an American pyjama factory.

The organization which Coch and French studied was the Harwood Manufacturing Corporation in Marion, Virginia. The company faced complaints from employees about the frequent changes to jobs and work methods arising from developments in the product, and in production methods. The company's employees made their displeasure at these changes known through:

- making lots of complaints about pay rates
- absenteeism, and simply leaving the company
- low standards of efficiency, although pay depended on output
- deliberate restriction of output below what they could achieve
- aggression towards management

Company managers were sensitive to the human relations and welfare needs of their employees, and they had used financial incentives to encourage employees to transfer to new jobs and methods, but the problem persisted. Coch and French set out to discover why.

The company employed about 500 women and 100 men, with an average age of 23, and most of them had no previous industrial experience. The company's time study experts set out standards for all the jobs in the factory. Each employee's output was calculated daily and everyone's performance was made public in a daily list, with the best producers at the top and the poorest at the bottom.

High output thus led to more money and to higher status. Most of the grievances concerned the fact that, as soon as they had learned a new job and had started to earn the bonuses that accompanied high output, they were moved to yet another task – so they lost the money and had to start learning all over again.

Coch and French designed an experiment with three production groups in the factory. The changes that affected these groups were minor ones, but the groups each had different levels of participation in introducing the changes.

the non-participation group

A group of eighteen 'hand pressers' changed the way in which they stacked their finished work. The production department announced the change and the time study department announced the new standard work rate. The changes were explained to the pressers, but they were not allowed to participate in any of the decisions surrounding this change.

The group showed no improvement in their efficiency ratings. There was immediate resistance to the change. They argued with the time study engineer and were hostile and uncooperative with the supervisor. The group deliberately restricted their output level, and some left the company. This group was eventually split up and allocated to various different tasks around the factory.

the representation group

A group of thirteen pyjama folders had to fold trousers and jackets, having only done one of these before. The whole group were given a demonstration of the need to reduce costs. The purpose of the meeting at which the demonstration was given was to win general approval for a plan to improve work methods. Three representatives from the group were then given the appropriate training in the new methods, and they subsequently trained all the other pyjama folders. The representatives, it was reported, were interested and co-operative, and offered several useful suggestions for further improvements.

This group adopted a co-operative, permissive attitude and their efficiency ratings rose rapidly. Nobody argued with the time study engineer or the supervisor, and nobody left the group.

the total participation group

Two groups of fifteen pyjama examiners altered their inspection routine. (One group had eight examiners, the other had seven.) They had a preliminary meeting, like that for the representation group, but everyone took part in the design of the new job and in the calculation of the new time standard. Coch and French remarked that, 'It is interesting to observe that in the meetings with these two groups, suggestions were immediately made in such quantity that the stenographer had great difficulty recording them'.

These groups recovered their efficiency ratings very rapidly, to a level much higher than before the change. Again, there was no conflict and no resignations.

Two and a half months later, the remaining thirteen members of the initial non-participation group were brought together again for a new pressing job. This time, however, they followed the 'total participation' procedure, with the same results as the previous total participation group – rapid increase in efficiency, no aggression and no resignations. This result confirmed for Coch and French that it was not the people involved, but the way in which they were treated that respectively generated resistance and welcomed acceptance of change.

Since this study employee participation in change has been one of the standard prescriptions for managers looking for a technique to overcome resistance, and to encourage a welcoming and creative approach to organizational change. Participative management in the Harwood pyjama factory led to faster learning of new work methods, higher efficiency levels and reduced levels of hostility. The employees in the representation and total participation groups knew what was happening. Indeed, the changes were to some extent within their control – and they did not lose hope, as they previously had done, about regaining their pay levels and status.

Participative management has also been called 'the truth, trust, love and collaboration approach' to change. This implies an open, honest, involving and supportive style of change implementation, particularly where organizational changes are radical and traumatic. These values are central to organization development interventions, explored in the next chapter.

However, truth, trust, love and collaboration techniques have been questioned by the research of two Australian academics, Dexter Dunphy and Doug Stace (1990; and Stace, 1996). They first define the *scale* of change using four main categories:

- *Fine tuning* involves refining methods, policies and procedures, typically at the level of the division or department.
- *Incremental adjustment* involves distinct modifications to strategies, structures and management processes, but not radical enough to be described as strategic.
- *Modular transformation* involves the major realignment or restructuring of departments and divisions – which may be radical, but at the level of parts of the organization and not the whole.
- *Corporate transformation* involves radical shifts in strategy, and revolutionary changes throughout the organization, to structures, systems and procedures, to mission and core values, and to the distribution of power.

Corporate transformation is broadly the same as *strategic change* defined earlier in this chapter.

Dunphy and Stace also identify four categories of *change leadership style*:

- A *collaborative* style involves widespread employee participation in key decisions affecting their and the organization's future.
- A *consultative* style entails limited involvement in setting goals relevant to employees' areas of responsibility.
- A *directive* style involves the use of managerial authority in reaching decisions about change and the future, and about how change will proceed.
- A *coercive* style means senior management forcing or imposing change on the organization.

Now plot scale of change against style of change management to produce this matrix:

style of change management	scale of change			
	fine tuning	*incremental adjustment*	*modular transformation*	*corporate transformation*
collaborative *consultative*		type 1 participative evolution		type 2 charismatic transformation
directive *coercive*		type 3 forced evolution		type 4 dictatorial transformation

This matrix generates four ideal change strategies: participative evolution, charismatic transformation, forced evolution and dictatorial transformation. From their studies of a number of Australian organizations, Dunphy and Stace argue that incremental and collaborative or consultative modes of change implementation can be highly inappropriate. These change strategies are time-consuming and can generate conflicting views and ideas, which generate tension and which are not always readily reconciled. On the other hand, where rapid strategic change is necessary for the survival of the organization, transformative approaches carried out in directive and coercive modes can be effective.

from *The Sunday Times*. © Noel Watson/Times Newspapers Limited 1990.

Dunphy and Stace thus propose a contingency approach to change implementation, which in summary looks like this:

	incremental change strategies	transformative change strategies
	participative evolution	*charismatic transformation*
collaborative–consultative modes	Use when the organization needs minor adjustment to meet environmental conditions, where time is available, and where key interest groups favour change.	Use when the organization needs major adjustments to meet environmental conditions, where there is little time for participation, and where there is support for radical change.
	forced evolution	*dictatorial transformation*
directive–coercive modes	Use when minor adjustments are required, where time is available, but where key interest groups oppose change.	Use when major adjustments are necessary, where there is no time for participation, where there is no internal support for strategic change, but where this is necessary for survival.

This argument, with supporting empirical evidence, represents a significant challenge to the universal and oversimplified prescription of participative change management.

resistance to change: causes and management techniques

If I could change the way I live my life today,
I wouldn't change a single thing . . .

from the album *Real Love*, by Lisa Stansfield, BMG Eurodisc, 1991, track 1, 'Change'.

It is sometimes possible to anticipate responses to organizational change and to use that knowledge to build on support and address potential resistance to change at an early stage.

---
definition
Resistance to change *can be defined as an inability, or an unwillingness, to discuss or to accept organizational changes that are perceived in some way damaging or threatening to the individual.*

One cannot expect everyone in an organization to respond in an identical manner to specific change proposals. Different individuals and groups are likely to be affected in different ways, and are also likely to perceive the implications differently from those proposing to implement the change. Anticipating responses becomes possible when one knows and understands the *stakeholders* concerned with a particular organizational change.

---
definition
A **stakeholder** *is anyone likely to be affected, directly or indirectly, by an organizational change or programme of changes.*

Conducting a stakeholder analysis is often a useful preliminary step, before publicizing change proposals for further discussion and consultation. Stakeholder analysis simply means drawing up a list of stakeholders; identifying their direct and indirect involvement, identifying those most important to the success of the change; and then establishing their interests with respect to the change agenda. This analysis can help to decide what action to take with respect to each stakeholder, to maintain their support or to deal with their resistance.

Change has both positive and negative aspects. On the one hand, change implies experiment and the creation of something new. On the other hand, it means discontinuity and the destruction and replacement of familiar social structures and relationships. Despite the positive attributes, change can be resisted because it involves confrontation with the unknown and loss of the familiar.

It is widely assumed that resistance to change is a common and a natural phenomenon. Change can be threatening. Change presents those involved with new situations, new problems and challenges, and with ambiguity and uncertainty. Many people find change, or the thought of change, painful and frustrating.

Arthur Bedeian (1980) cites four common causes of resistance to organizational change.

parochial self-interest
We understandably seek to protect a *status quo* with which we are content and regard as advantageous to us in some way. Change may threaten to move us out of our 'comfort zone', away from those things which we prefer and enjoy.

---

conducting a stakeholder analysis

Gerard Egan identifies nine groups or types of stakeholder that an analysis should consider:

Partners are those who actively support your agenda; do not alienate them.

Allies will support you, given encouragement; do not take them for granted.

Fellow travellers are passive supporters; ensure that they voice their commitment to the agenda, and not their commitment to you personally.

Fencesitters are players whose allegiances are not clear; do not treat them as either neutral or indifferent.

Loose cannons can cause damage by voting against agendas in which they have no direct interest; and finding strategies for dealing with them can be difficult.

Opponents are players who oppose the agenda, but not the sponsor; exploit your relationships either to convert or to neutralize them.

Adversaries are players who oppose both the sponsor and the agenda; find ways to clean up your relationships, or to discredit and marginalize them.

Bedfellows support the agenda, but may not know or trust the sponsor; attend to the relationship, and keep their attention on the agenda.

The voiceless are stakeholders who will be affected by the agenda, but have little power to promote or oppose and who lack advocates; attend to their concerns nevertheless as they may be used by adversaries.

based on Gerard Egan, 1994, *Working the Shadow Side: A Guide to Positive Behind-the-Scenes Management*, Jossey-Bass Publishers, San Francisco.

We develop vested interests in the perpetuation of organization structures and accompanying technologies. Change can mean loss of power, prestige, respect, approval, status and security. Change can also be personally inconvenient for many reasons. It may disturb relationships and other arrangements that have taken much time and effort to establish. It may force an unwelcome move in location. It may alter social opportunities. Perceived as well as actual threats to interests and values are thus likely to generate resistance.

In an organizational setting, we invest time, effort and commitment in programmes, systems, procedures and technologies to make them work for us. We may identify ourselves more closely with our specific functions and roles than with the organization as a whole. We then have a personal stake in our specialized knowledge and skills and in their creations, and may not be willing readily to see these made redundant or obsolete.

misunderstanding and lack of trust

We are more likely to resist change when we do not understand the reasoning behind it, or its nature and possible consequences. Resistance can thus be reduced through understanding.

If managers have little trust in their employees, information about change may be withheld or distorted. Incomplete and incorrect information creates uncertainty and rumour. This has the unfortunate result of increasing perceptions of threat, of increasing defensiveness, and reducing further effective communication about the change.

The way in which change is introduced can be resisted, rather than the change itself.

contradictory assessments

We each differ in the ways in which we evaluate the costs and benefits of change. The major disruptive threat for me can be a fresh and stimulating challenge for you, and vice versa. Human values ultimately determine which changes are welcomed and promoted, which persist and succeed, and which fail.

We differ in our perceptions of what change will mean for us and for the organization. These contradictory assessments are more likely to arise when information about a change is inadequate, and where those concerned lack the relevant information. Bedeian points out that contradictory analyses of change can lead to constructive criticism and improved proposals. Resistance to change is not necessarily dysfunctional, but can in some circumstances lead to more effective forms of change and change implementation.

low tolerance for change

We differ in our ability to cope with change, to face the unknown, to deal with uncertainty.

Change that requires people to think and behave in different ways can challenge the individual's self-concept. We each have ideas about our abilities and our competences. One response to change may thus be self-doubt and self-questioning – 'Can I handle this?' Some people have a low tolerance for ambiguity and uncertainty. The anxiety and apprehension that they suffer may lead them to oppose even potentially beneficial changes.

Because of the many sources of resistance to change, and the need for organizations to adapt rapidly to changing social, political, economic and technological conditions, the management of change has become a crucial issue. The problem is often defined in terms of overcoming resistance to ensure that change is accepted and implemented rapidly and effectively. The human aspects of change have to be managed as carefully – indeed more carefully – as the technical and organizational structure aspects.

Kotter and Schlesinger (1979) developed the participative prescription of Coch and French in a style that predates and incorporates the recommendations of Dunphy and Stace. They identify six methods for implementing change effectively and overcoming resistance.

1 education and commitment

Managers should share their perceptions, knowledge and objectives with those affected by organizational change. This can involve a major and expensive programme of training, face-to-face counselling, group meetings and the publication of memos and reports.

People may need to be trained to recognize the existence of the organizational problems necessitating change; for example, the Harwood pyjama folders were given information about company costs and about the need to reduce these. Resistance, as noted earlier, may be based on misunderstanding and inaccurate information. It therefore helps to get the facts straight and identify and reconcile opposing views. Managers can only use this approach if they trust their employees, and if in return, management appear credible to the employees.

2 participation and involvement

Those who might resist change should be involved in planning and implementing it. Collaboration can have the effect of reducing opposition and encouraging commitment. This helps to reduce fears that individuals may have about the impact of changes on them, and also makes use of individuals' skills and knowledge. Managers can only use this approach where participants have the knowledge and ability to contribute effectively, and are willing to do so.

3 facilitation and support

Employees may need to be given counselling and therapy to help overcome fears and anxieties about change. It may be necessary to develop individual awareness of the need for change, as well as the self-awareness of feelings towards change and how these can be altered.

4 negotiation and agreement

It may be necessary to reach a mutually agreeable compromise, through trading and exchange. The nature of a particular change may have to be adjusted to meet the needs and interest of potential and powerful resistors. Management may have to negotiate rather than impose change where there are individuals and groups who have enough power effectively to resist. The problem is, this creates a precedent for future changes, which may also have to be negotiated, although the circumstances surrounding them may be quite different.

5 manipulation and co-optation

This involves covert attempts to sidestep potential resistance. Management puts forward proposals that deliberately appeal to the specific interests, sensitivities and emotions of the key groups or stakeholders involved. The information disseminated is selective, emphasizing the benefits to particular stakeholder groups and ignoring or playing down the disadvantages. Co-optation involves giving key resistors direct access to the decision-making process, perhaps giving them well-paid, high-status management positions.

— *funny* Business —

by MORRIS

"Stop worrying Harry, youth and enthusiasm can always be beaten by treachery and cunning."

These techniques may work in the short run, but can create problems. Manipulation when discovered may discredit those responsible. Troublemakers who are co-opted may continue to create problems from their new and continuing positions of power and influence.

Nevertheless, Rosabeth Moss Kanter (1983) argues that 'power skills' in influencing others are necessary attributes of the change agent implementing new ideas and maintaining organizational flexibility. Power skills for blocking interference in change include 'waiting them out', 'wearing them down', 'warning them off' and 'inviting them in', appeals to higher authority, displays of support, the use of emissaries to 'talk them round', and steps to reduce the stakes when change is going to be damaging. The significance of the techniques involved in manipulation find support also in the research of David Buchanan and David Boddy (1992), who emphasize the importance of 'backstage activity' in implementing change. Backstage activity involves manipulating language (to make change more appealing and less threatening), manipulating structures (to signal priorities and institutionalize changes) and manipulating relation-ships (to generate support and the perception of support).

6 *implicit and explicit coercion*

Management here abandons any attempt to achieve consensus. This may be appropriate where there is profound disagreement between those concerned with the change, and where there is little or no chance of anyone shifting their ground. This results in the use of force and threats. This need not involve violence. It may be sufficient to offer to fire, transfer or demote individuals, or to stifle their promotion and career prospects. Once again, there are circumstances in which the 'dictatorial transformation' advocated by Dunphy and Stace may be appropriate.

Kotter and Schlesinger point out that these techniques can be used in combination. The choice in a given situation must depend on the likely reactions of those involved and on the long-term implications of solving the immediate problem in that way. Managers who attempt to impose change unilaterally, without participation in some form, are usually responsible for less effective change implementation. Change can be planned, and not left to chance or introduced carelessly. It is normally possible to anticipate the implications of change, and how these will be perceived, and to begin steps to address resistance before changes start to take effect. Stakeholder analysis, described earlier, is one way to achieve this.

---

power skills: choosing an effective political strategy

Gerard Egan argues that, to be effective in implementing organizational change, the change agent must be politically skilled and use effective political strategies. His advice on choosing a political strategy includes the following pointers:

- Learn the name of the game in your organization; how are politics played here?
- Get to know the playing field, the informal organization, the communication networks.
- Identify the key players (not always obvious) and their main interests.
- Get organized; enlist your supporters at an early stage; form alliances with powerful groups, for coalitions to establish a powerful group voice.
- Use informal communication networks to gather intelligence, and to send unobtrusive messages.
- Develop relations with those who you know will support you.
- Know who owes you favours, and call these in when necessary.
- Balance overt and covert action, know when to go public and when to work behind the scenes.
- Learn how to use trade-offs effectively; maximize flexibility without becoming 'slippery'.
- Use drama and theatre, but sparingly; use stirring gestures that don't cheapen the agenda.
- Remember that, even though you may not be willing to adopt these methods, others are.

based on Gerard Egan, 1994, *Working the Shadow Side: A Guide to Positive Behind-the-Scenes Management*, Jossey-Bass, San Francisco.

We have considered the use of power skills from the point of view of the manager or change agent seeking to encourage and implement change, in the face of resistance. The same techniques, of course, can be used by others in the organization to block, divert and otherwise subvert change efforts. These are useful 'counter-implementation' techniques as well.

---

sources of resistance and anti-resistance techniques

The British academic, Tony Eccles, lists thirteen sources of resistance to change.

ignorance	failure to understand the problem.
comparison	the solution is disliked as an alternative is preferred.
disbelief	feeling that the proposed solution will not work.
loss	change has unacceptable personal costs.
inadequacy	the rewards from change are not sufficient.
anxiety	fear of being unable to cope in the new situation.
demolition	change threatens destruction of existing social networks.
power cut	sources of influence and control will be eroded.
contamination	new values and practices are repellent.
inhibition	willingness to change is low.
mistrust	motives for change are considered suspicious.
alienation	alternative interests valued more highly than new proposals.
frustration	change will reduce power and career opportunities.

Eccles also identifies a hierarchy of five anti-resistance techniques:

1 Convince your critics of the selfless validity of your chosen strategy. If they can be brought on side without having to pay them a price, then that must be the most cost-effective strategy, if it works.
2 Demonstrate that the behaviour you want will have a track to the top and that it is in their interests to climb aboard.
3 Buy their support, or flatter them – as with the British health minister who, when asked how he would get the support of complaining medical consultants for the creation of the National Health Service replied, 'We will stuff their mouths with gold'. That worked.
4 Marginalize your critics and use their skills for the benefit of the rest of the organization. They can be 'exited' later if they remain a nuisance.
5 Neutralize or 'exit' them. Termination may be the only effective way to neutralize.

from Tony Eccles, 1994, *Succeeding with Change: Implementing Action-driven Strategies*, McGraw-Hill, Maidenhead.

---

recipe and process: competing views on understanding change

Change has become a familiar feature of the organizational landscape. This has not made change any easier to implement, particularly strategic change with wide-ranging personal and organizational consequences. Much is known about the factors which contribute to effective organizational change and also about the likely barriers. That knowledge has been codified and elaborated by several authors. The literature now contains many formulations of 'best practice' on how to introduce organizational change.

One of the better known formulas, or 'recipes', for effective organizational change is the one proposed by David Gleicher of the Arthur D. Little consulting organization. Gleicher (first cited in a 1960s organizational development text) argued that:

Organizational change will only occur when $K \times D \times V > C$, where

K represents Knowledge of first practical steps.

D represents Dissatisfaction with the status quo.

V represents the desirable Vision of the future.

C represents the Costs (material and psychological) of doing something.

Note the effect of the multiplication signs in this formula. The formula argues, for example, that where dissatisfaction is high, and where there is a strong vision of a desirable future, but no clear ideas about how to proceed, change is unlikely to take place. In other words, if either **K**, or **D**, or **V** is low or zero, then the left-hand side of the equation multiplies out to a sum close to zero, and change is unlikely. This argument has some intuitive appeal.

Eccles (1994) identifies eight preconditions for successful change. These are:

1 pressure for the change
2 a clear and shared vision of the goal and the direction
3 effective liaison and trust between those concerned
4 the will and the power to act
5 capable people with sufficient resources
6 suitable rewards and accountabilities
7 actionable first steps
8 a capacity to learn and to adapt

Where these factors are present, the organization's *readiness for change* is likely to be high, and resistance is likely to be localized and less significant. Where these factors are absent, readiness is poor, and change is likely to be correspondingly more difficult to implement.

---

definition

Readiness for change *can be defined as either an individual or an organizational predisposition – perhaps even an impatience – to welcome and embrace change.*

The concept of readiness draws attention to two practical issues. The first of these concerns *timing*. Some of the readiness factors may simply improve by waiting. The second concerns *action*, to manipulate readiness factors, to heighten the impatience for change, to strengthen a welcoming predisposition. In other words, these readiness factors do not have to be accepted as given constraints; they are potentially manageable.

> ### STOP!
> Consider your own educational organization and any current proposals for change. How do you rate the organization's readiness for change on Eccles' dimensions? What are the practical implications of your 'readiness analysis', with respect to the timing of change and with respect to actions that would improve readiness?

Assuming that the need for change is broadly accepted, Bernard Taylor (1994) identified eight successful strategies, based on the experiences of a number of organizations, including TSB Group, World Wildlife Fund, BP Oil, The Automobile Association, Hewlett-Packard, Rank Xerox, Allied Irish banks, Lloyds Bank and Granada Television. These strategies are:

1 **stretch goals** Managers must define goals in terms of specific, measurable objectives.
2 **future vision** Employees must be shown a 'promised land' where the company will find a prosperous future.
3 **lean organization** Line managers must be given a structure in which they can take charge and be held accountable.
4 **new culture** This means a more open style of leadership, communicating values, and working through teams.
5 **world class** To succeed, organizations must 'reach for the stars' and measure themselves against the world's best.
6 **performance management** Every employee must be involved in delivering high quality products and services; this also means forming teams and giving them the training, measures and rewards they need.
7 **total innovation** To compete successfully, it is no longer enough to do the same things better than everybody else; the challenge is to harness workforce creativity, to do new things and to do things differently; this means tolerating a certain amount of chaos and disorder, relaxing controls, and letting employees 'take charge'.
8 **partnerships and networks** Managers must learn to trust and to co-operate; partnerships must be formed with suppliers, distributors, competitors.

There are some recurrent themes here. Have a clear sense of purpose and direction. Make sure that people know what is expected of them. Plan the change implementation steps with care. Set interesting and challenging goals. Communicate, communicate . . . and keep communicating. Reward those who are involved and who are effective. Foster a culture of openness, trust, creativity and empowerment. These recommendations are consistent with the participative management style recommendations of Coch and French.

Most commentators in this field, like Taylor, support the 'truth, trust, love and collaboration' model of organizational change. This model is difficult to challenge openly in democratic, Western, developed economies where social and cultural values support this style. This kind of approach makes the practice of change implementation sound rather straight-forward.

Eccles (1994), developing his 'readiness for change' analysis, identifies fourteen factors behind successful organizational change, in four main categories. These are:

1 purpose and initiative	
the *pregnant executive*	There has to be a champion who embodies and lives the new dream.
the *single goal*	There has to be a clear and sustained purpose to which people can commit.
clarity of purpose	There has to be a defensible, unambiguous reason for the change.
2 concordance and trust	
the *illusion of unity*	Don't expect everybody to back the change.
how *open to be?*	Tell people as much as practicable, taking some risks by being candid.
communication	Effective communication is vital, and almost impossible to over-do.
3 leadership, capabilities and structure	
the *rule of proportionate responsibility*	The more senior you are, the more responsibility you must take.
the *limitations of empowerment*	Even enterprising employees need to be led.
teams and leaders	Good teams and leaders support each other.
structure and culture	Use structure to change culture.
4 building on action and success	
creating winners	Personal success is a great motivation.
fast change and initial acts	Early successes create productive momentum.
caring for casualties	Caring for people is both morally and organizationally commendable.
minimizing unintended consequences	You cannot avoid all the errors; but you can organize to anticipate some and to recover from others.

from Eccles, T., 1994, *Succeeding with Change: Implementing Action Driven Strategies*, McGraw-Hill, London.

Whilst advocating 'truth, trust, love and collaboration' in part, Eccles is clearly sensitive to the need for 'impression management' as an aspect of organizational change (see discussion of this concept in Chapter 3) and the manipulation involved in this approach.

Here are two more, typical organizational change recipes from the literature of the 1990s. Bernard Burnes (1992) suggests a nine-element approach: create an ambitious vision, develop a catalogue of change strategies, create the preconditions for change, create a flexible culture, assess the type of change required, plan and implement, involve those concerned, keep up the momentum, and seek continuously to improve. John P. Kotter (1995) outlines 'eight steps to transforming your organization': establish a sense of urgency, form a guiding coalition, create a vision, communicate the vision, empower people to act on the vision, create 'short-term wins', consolidate improvements to produce further change, and institutionalize new approaches.

STOP!

Make a list for yourself of the common themes running through the various recipes for organizational change described so far in this chapter. Write your own recipe.

This 'recipe-based' approach to organizational change has been criticized by a number of commentators. The single main problem with these change recipes is the extent to which they seem to oversimplify a complex issue. In particular, the 'rational-linear' model, which presents change unfolding in a logical sequence, seems to misrepresent organizational realities. One of the main critics has been the English academic Andrew Pettigrew (1985; 1987) who argues that organizational change should be seen instead as a complex and 'untidy cocktail' of rational decision processes, mixed with differences in individual perceptions, stimulated by visionary leadership and spiced with 'power plays' and attempts to recruit support and build coalitions behind particular ideas and lines of action.

Pettigrew emphasizes the importance of the *process* of change, which is messy, combining attempts to solve organizational problems with the games of organizational politics. Pettigrew also emphasizes the importance of the *context* of organizational change. The *inner context* of change concerns the structure and culture of the organization and the events in its history that have shaped current attitudes and behaviours. The *outer context* relates to environmental factors: customer demands, competitor behaviour, economic conditions.

FUNNY BUSINESS

"I see you're honest and have integrity. I'm afraid I have no use for you in my company"

The practical problem for the change agent thus involves the simultaneous management of the *content* or substance of the change, the implementation *process*, and both dimensions of the organizational *context*. The political key to organizational change, in Pettigrew's analysis, is *legitimation*. Change will be accepted if it is perceived to be legitimate in the context. Those who wish to advance change can often point to aspects of the internal and external context of the organization to justify their proposals; internal inefficiencies and external threats, for example. This, of course, is likely to be more effective in recruiting support and overcoming resistance than basing proposals on personal preferences and individual career goals.

The main strength of Pettigrew's processual perspective (and that of supportive colleagues such as Whipp *et al.*, 1988; Wilson, 1992; Dawson, 1994) lies in its theoretical richness, which retains much of the complexity, the interrelatedness, and the interdependencies of organizational change. The main weakness of the processual account is that it does not lend itself to the formulation of convenient organizational change formulae or guidelines. The processual perspective on change has become an influential way of thinking about, understanding and theorizing change; it has had limited impact on the actual practice of implementing organizational change. The processual perspective does not lend itself to the production of simple recipes and checklists and guides for organizational change.

business process re-engineering

One of the most controversial developments in the field of organizational change in the mid- to late 1990s has concerned the fashionable methodology of *business process re-engineering*.

definition
Business process re-engineering *is 'the fundamental rethinking and radical redesign of business processes to achieve dramatic improvements in critical, contemporary measures of performance, such as cost, quality, service, and speed'. Hammer and Champy (1993).*

This perspective has polarized opinion. Some commentators argue that rapid and radical process redesign and improvement is essential to enable organizations to deal with increasing environmental hostility and turbulence. Some organizations have reported significant improvements in performance as a result of applying re-engineering methods. Other commentators dismiss the approach as a futile and irrelevant repackaging of traditional management methods. Re-engineering appears to have a high failure rate, despite some of the reported successes. In America, re-engineering earned a 'slash and burn' reputation for the associated job loss or 'downsizing' which seemed often to accompany the approach.

The 'inventors' of business process re-engineering (BPR) include Michael Hammer and James Champy (1993), whose definition of the term is used here, and Thomas Davenport (1993). Their approach has two principal ingredients. First, they advocate a *fresh start* to organizational redesign. In other words, when considering organizational change, start with a blank sheet of paper and redesign work and the organization from scratch. Second, they advocate a *process orientation* to the analysis and redesign of work.

The *fresh start*, blank sheet approach involves ignoring past history and current practice in favour of considering how best to structure the organization and design work to meet the needs of today's business and today's customers. In stark contrast with the processual understanding of change (and despite the similar terminology), BPR is not a 'context-sensitive' approach, in the wider sense of context suggested by Pettigrew.

The *process orientation* also represents something of a departure from traditional approaches to organizational analysis. A process is simply a set of activities that delivers a product or a service to a customer. The customer may be the eventual user of the product or service, or it could be an 'internal customer' – the person or section responsible for the next set of activities in the overall process. This is potentially radical because it requires a *horizontal* analysis of work along an activity chain. Most organizations are structured *vertically*, around functions such as purchasing, warehousing, production, finance, personnel and marketing.

The first step in BPR thus concerns defining and mapping an existing work process. For example, Buchanan and Wilson (1996a and b) mapped the activity chain, or 'patient trail', in a hospital for patients undergoing elective surgery. The nine main stages on the patient trail are:

process	hospital staff functions involved
1 outpatient appointment	clerical and medical
2 outpatient clinic preparation	clerical, and medical records
3 outpatient clinic consultation and addition of patient to surgical waiting list	medical, nursing and clerical
4 waiting list and pre-clerking arrangements	clerical, medical and medical records
5 pre-clerking clinic attendance	nursing, medical and medical records
6 ward admission (elective and emergency)	medical, nursing, clerical, and porters
7 operating theatre procedure	medical, nursing, operating department assistants, clerical
8 recovery and return to ward	nursing, medical, and porters
9 post-operative care and discharge	nursing, medical, and clerical

Note the number of different staff groups involved in processing a single patient, who may come into contact with anything from 50 to 150 different members of the hospital staff. Many of the problems in this situation arise from the fact that staff are concerned primarily with what happens at their own step on the trail, and are not always aware either of what has gone before or of what will happen to the patient afterwards. This 'process fragmentation' leads to unnecessary duplication of some activities, and the unwitting transmission of problems 'down the trail'. This lack of process orientation is typical for an organization structured vertically, into distinct functions, rather than horizontally around work processes.

re-engineering the cure factory

The Karolinska Hospital in Stockholm was among the first in Europe to use BPR
to cut costs and also to cut patient waiting times. The chief executive was
quoted as claiming that, 'What we have done is to organize ourselves according
to how the patient moves through the system'. This meant reorganizing around
the patient flow:

- Nurse co-ordinators now arrange all tests in a single visit – patients used to
  make up to five visits for different investigations.
- Patients are pre-anaesthetized outside the operating theatre to reduce time
  lost before operations begin.
- Operations of similar length and complexity are carried out in the same
  theatre, instead of a wide mix of predictable and unpredictable operations
  being scheduled together.
- Previously separate medical and surgical departments, and their tests, were
  combined.

These changes had significant results:

- Lost operating theatre time was cut by a half.
- Patient flow bottlenecks were reduced.
- The time between operations was reduced, improving quality of care.
- The number of operations increased by 2000 a year (to 28,000 in 1994).
- Four of the sixteen theatres were closed.
- More efficient use was made of nurses and doctors.
- More anaesthetists were employed.
- Waiting time for hernia operations was cut from 8 months to 3 weeks.
- There was some job loss (the report does not disclose how much), but we
  are told that morale remained high.
- Total annual cost savings were made of 100 million Swedish Kroner – 25 per
  cent of the total costs of the areas affected.

based on Christopher Brown-Humes, 1994, 'Production line treatment for patients',
Financial Times, 7 January.

'...entation' features apply to commercial manufacturing
...o healthcare and educational organizations. What does
...ocate in such situations? Hammer and Champy propose
...eral principles:

...unctional department and create process teams.

...rs deal with a 'case manager' and don't get pushed around the
...re.

...power people, and give them enriched jobs with discretion.

...rovide training and education to allow people to perform expanded
roles.

> Flatten the organization hierarchy.
> Measure people on the results they achieve, not just on activity
  performed.
> Promote people on the basis of ability.
> Turn senior managers into leaders, not scorekeepers.

Flatten the hierarchy? Enrich jobs? Encourage teamwork? Empower
people? Overcome functional barriers? *Radical* recommendations? This
advice is similar to that discussed in Chapter 4, where we explored
approaches to motivation through organization and work redesign. As we
shall see in the following chapter, these recommendations are consistent with
those made by the organization development movement since the 1960s.
One criticism of BPR has concerned its implications for job security.
Another criticism is that it is not such a new technique after all. Many
commentators have suggested that horizontal business process analysis is a
conventional method, known to and applied by production and operations
management specialists, and socio-technical systems analysts, for decades
(Buchanan, 1997). The controversy surrounding the approach is likely to
continue.

the expertise of the change agent

The change agent seems now to require less technical expertise, and more
interpersonal and managerial skill, in communication, presentation,
negotiation, influencing and selling. Change agents are often chosen for their
expertise in the substance or *content* of the change in hand. However, expertise
in managing the change *process* is usually more significant.

---

definition

A **change agent** can be any member of an organization seeking to promote,
further, support, sponsor, initiate, implement or deliver change. Change
agents are not necessarily senior managers, and do not necessarily hold formal
'change management' job titles and positions.

Rosabeth Moss Kanter (1989) identifies seven skills which the change agent
of the 1990s requires, to perform effectively in the flexible, 'integrative'
organization. These are:

1 The ability to work independently, without the power, sanction and
  support of the management hierarchy.

2 The skills of an effective collaborator, able to compete in ways that enhance rather than destroy co-operation.
3 The ability to develop high trust relationships, based on high ethical standards.
4 Self-confidence, tempered with humility.
5 Respect for the process of change, as well as the content.
6 The ability to work across business functions and units, to be 'multifaceted and ambidextrous'.
7 The willingness to stake reward on results and gain satisfaction from success.

This 'person specification' for the change agent seems to be consistent with what is known about flexible, organic organization structures, about participative management methods, and about the practice and implications of process re-engineering. Kanter speaks of this 'superhuman' change agent, in possession of such wide-ranging expertise, in terms of a 'business athlete'. She argues (Kanter, 1989, p. 361):

> Our new heroic model should be the athlete who can manage the amazing feat of doing more with less, who can juggle the need to both conserve resources and pursue growth opportunities. This new kind of business hero avoids the excesses of both the corpocrat and the cowboy. Where the former rigidly conserves and protects, the latter relentlessly speculates and promotes. But the business athlete has the strength to balance somewhere in the middle, taking the best of the corpocrat's discipline and the cowboy's entrepreneurial zeal. Business athletes need to be intense, lean and limber, able to stretch, good at teamwork, and in shape all the time.

Arguing that the effective change agent 'does not have to walk on water', David Hutton (1994) does claim that the change agent should be patient, persistent, honest, trustworthy, reliable, positive, enthusiastic, co-operative, confident (but not arrogant), a good listener, observant (of the feelings and behaviours of others), flexible, resourceful, difficult to intimidate, willing to take risks and accept challenge, and able to handle organizational politics. And they should have a sense of humour, a sense of perspective and be able to admit ignorance and ask for help when appropriate. Hutton accepts that this list 'may seem daunting', but argues that 'it is not Utopian'. Experience, he argues, is an effective teacher.

From their experience of change in a telecommunications company near Manchester, Keith Bott and Jonathan Hill (1994) identified ten personal qualities required for effective organizational change, under four headings.

STOP!

Do you have the personal qualities required to make you an effective change agent? Match your expertise against the Bott and Hill list.

What skills development do you think you may need if you are to be effective in a change implementation role?

So, here is another list, or recipe:

setting an engaging direction	
focus	The capacity for goal-setting and persistence, a determination to stick to targets.
pride	The need to define oneself by association with high standards, and to get recognition.
charisma	Contagious energy and an inclination to work at infecting others with enthusiasm.

fostering independent relationships	
positivity	Optimism and a tendency to notice the positive in others.
peacemaker	Enjoys conflict resolution, but may prompt conflict to achieve a constructive outcome.
team	Satisfaction from blending individual efforts to get results.

providing a systematic support structure and schedules	
gestalt	Tendency towards completeness, timeliness, efficiency.
discipline	Developing effective routines, planning and working to plan.
a 'doer'	Turns ideas into action, initiator rather than responder.

stabilizing beliefs	
values	Centre on loyalty, conservation, the work ethic, family, consistency in value expression, perceived as predictable, seen as basis for stability in relationships particularly in the midst of organizational change.

from Bott, K. and Hill, J., 1994, 'Change agents lead the way', *Personnel Management*, August, pp. 24–7.

assessment

Change has become an organizational preoccupation. The effective change agent seems to be someone with an almost superhuman combination of skills and qualities. The change agent in a large organization can thus be lonely and vulnerable. However, the personal and career rewards can be highly significant. The high-flying, fast-track management career is more readily built on contributions to strategic organizational change. Very few fast-track careers are likely to be made by introducing minor, slow, incremental organizational changes.

There are a number of trends evident in this field. Change is set to remain a central theme. While participative management remains socially and ethically appropriate, there is a willingness to accept the use of directive

'It's all right to do your regular work, Sanders, but haven't you caught on yet? The big money is in breakthroughs.'

methods. There is also increasing recognition of the role of organizational politics. The effective change agent must be sensitive to and skilled in appropriate modes of political intervention. There is also recognition of the need for rapid and continual adjustment to events and trends. In other words, change is no longer something which periodically disturbs the stable fabric; change is a feature of organizational life. The significance of a wide range of context factors, in shaping the opportunities for and directions of organizational change, is better understood and appreciated. And finally, while change may still be relevant to improving effectiveness, the ability to change rapidly is viewed increasingly as a factor contributing to competitive advantage and organizational survival.

In keeping with the style of this chapter, these trends may be summarized in this recipe:

from change in the late twentieth century	to change into the twenty-first century
one organizational theme among many	an organizational preoccupation
importance of participation and involvement	significance of political motives and actions
rational-linear model of project management	messy untidy cocktail of reason and motive
content skills are critical	process skills are critical
change as periodic adjustment	change as continual upheaval
aimed at organizational effectiveness	aimed at competitive advantage and survival

sources

Ahituv, N. and Neumann, S., 1986, *Principles of Information Systems for Management*, W.C. Brown Publishers, Dubuque.

Beckhard, R. and Harris, R., 1977, *Organizational Transitions: Managing Complex Change*, Addison-Wesley, Reading, MA.

Bedeian, A.G., 1980, *Organization Theory and Analysis*, Dryden Press, Chicago.

Bennis, W.G., 1969, *Organization Development: Its Nature, Origins and Prospects*, Addison-Wesley, Reading, MA.

Bott, K. and Hill, J., 1994, 'Change agents lead the way', *Personnel Management*, August, pp. 24–7.

Buchanan, D.A., 1997, 'The limitations and opportunities of business process re-engineering in a politicized organizational climate', *Human Relations*, vol. 50, no. 1, pp. 51–2.

Buchanan, D.A. and Boddy, D., 1992, *The Expertise of the Change Agent: Public Performance and Backstage Activity*, Prentice Hall, Hemel Hempstead.

Buchanan, D. and Wilson, B., 1996a, 'Next patient please: The operating theatres problem at Leicester General Hospital NHS Trust', in J. Storey (ed.), *Cases in Human Resource and Change Management*, Blackwell Business, Oxford, pp. 190–205.

Buchanan, D. and Wilson, B., 1996b, 'Re-engineering operating theatres: The perspective assessed', *Journal of Management in Medicine*, vol. 10, no. 4 (in press).

Burnes, B., 1992, *Managing Change: A Strategic Approach to Organizational Development and Renewal*, Pitman, London.

Coch, L. and French, J.R.P., 1948, 'Overcoming resistance to change', *Human Relations*, vol. 1, pp. 512–32.

Davenport, T.H., 1993, *Process Innovation: Re-engineering Work through Information Technology*, Harvard Business School Press, Boston, MA.

Dawson, P., 1994, *Organizational Change: A Processual Approach*, Paul Chapman Publishing, London.

Dunphy, D.C. and Stace, D.A., 1990, *Under New Management: Australian Organizations in Transition*, McGraw-Hill, Sydney.

Eccles, T., 1994, *Succeeding with Change: Implementing Action-Driven Strategies*, McGraw-Hill, London.

Egan, G., 1994, *Working the Shadow Side: A Guide to Positive Behind-the-Scenes Management*, Jossey-Bass Publishers, San Francisco.

Hammer, M., 1990, 'Re-engineering work: Don't automate, obliterate', *Harvard Business Review*, July–August, pp. 104–12.

Hammer, M., 1994, 'Hammer defends re-engineering', *The Economist*, 5 November, p. 96.

Hammer, M. and Champy, J., 1993, *Re-engineering the Corporation: A Manifesto for Business Revolution*, Nicholas Brealey Publishing, London.

Hammer, M. and Stanton, S.A., 1995, *The Re-engineering Revolution – A Handbook*, HarperCollins, New York.

Hutton, D.W., 1994, *The Change Agent's Handbook: A Survival Guide for Quality Improvement Champions*, ASQC Quality Press, Milwaukee.

Kanter, R.M., 1983, *The Change Masters: Corporate Entrepreneurs at Work*, George Allen & Unwin, London.

Kanter, R.M., 1989, *When Giants Learn to Dance: Mastering the Challenge of Strategy, Management and Careers in the 1990s*, Simon & Schuster, London.

Kotter, J.P., 1995, 'Leading change: Why transformation efforts fail', *Harvard Business Review*, vol. 73, no. 2, pp. 59–67.

Kotter, J.P. and Schlesinger, L.A., 1979, 'Choosing strategies for change', *Harvard Business Review*, vol. 57, no. 2, pp. 106–14.

Kubler-Ross, E., 1969, *On Death and Dying*, Macmillan, Toronto.

Mumford, E. and Hendricks, R., 1996, 'Business process re-engineering RIP', *People Management*, 2 May, pp. 22–7.

Ogburn, W.F., 1922, *Social Change: With Respect to Culture and Original Nature*, B.W. Huebsch, New York.

Pettigrew, A.M., 1985, *The Awakening Giant: Continuity and Change in ICI*, Blackwell, Oxford.

Pettigrew, A.M., 1987, 'Context and action in the transformation of the firm', *Journal of Management Studies*, vol. 24, no. 6, pp. 649–70.

Stace, D.A., 1996, 'Transitions and transformations: Four case studies in business-focused change', in J. Storey (ed.), *Cases in Human Resource and Change Management*, Blackwell Business, Oxford, pp. 43–72.

Taylor, B. (ed.), 1994, *Successful Change Strategies: Chief Executives in Action*, Director Books/Fitzwilliam Publishing, Hemel Hempstead.

Thomas, M., 1994, 'What you need to know about: Business process re-engineering', *Personnel Management*, January, pp. 28–31.

Toffler, A., 1970, *Future Shock*, Pan Books, London.

Whipp, R., Rosenfeld, R. and Pettigrew, A., 1988, 'Understanding strategic change processes; some preliminary British findings', in A. Pettigrew (ed.), *The Management of Strategic Change*, Blackwell, Oxford, pp. 14–55.

Wilson, D.C., 1992, *A Strategy of Change: Concepts and Controversies in the Management of Change*, Routledge, London.

organization development

concepts and learning objectives
the OD agenda: goals and processes
the OD matrix: levels and models of intervention
OD techniques: the toolkit
OD applications: the empirical evidence
to be an OD consultant
assessment
sources

concepts and learning objectives

Chapter 16 explored a range of issues, perspectives and techniques concerning the management of change. One approach not explored was *organization development*, or OD as it is commonly known. The OD approach deserves separate treatment because it has a number of specific characteristics, which in some respects set it apart from the general field of change implementation, with which it shares many concepts and frameworks. OD has also contributed to the corporate culture change issues explored in Chapter 18.

Chapter 1 introduced the concept of the *organizational dilemma* – the problem of meeting individual employee needs and aspirations whilst meeting the performance, survival and growth needs of the organization as a whole. The rapid developments in social science methodology and knowledge after the Second World War led to a growth in confidence in the practical application of that knowledge to organizational problems. During the 1960s, in America, this confidence generated a movement committed to the design and use of social science techniques for the development of organizational effectiveness *and* the development of an organization's members. In other words, the organization development movement can be regarded as a long-running confrontation with the organizational dilemma.

The development of OD dates back to the 1960s, when the term first began to find currency, initially in America. OD practitioners have for half a century believed and argued that the apparently conflicting interests of organizations and their members can be reconciled through appropriately designed OD interventions. We have the social science understanding, and we have the organizational change techniques, through which problems can be diagnosed and resolved. As we shall see, OD also makes claims to the development of the organization's independent capability to address and resolve its own problems, and thus to reduce dependence on OD 'experts' beyond an initial intervention. The field of OD has constructed its own literature, with its own conceptual, theoretical and empirical bases, its own specialized courses and its own specialized higher degrees. It can, therefore, be seen as a social science or organizational studies discipline or sub-discipline in its own right, dealing with a specific set of organizational issues, goals and problems.

OD also has some of the features of a religious movement. The approach, or rather collection of approaches, on which OD practice is based relies heavily on the assumption that conflicts between the individual and the organization, and conflicts between individuals and groups in an organization, can and should be reconciled. The approach also adheres to a broad set of underpinning social values, the pursuit of which may be regarded as valuable in its own right, independent of any implications for organizational productivity or financial performance.

key concepts

▶ organization development	▶ OD intervention
▶ force field analysis	▶ process consultation
▶ action research	▶ survey feedback
▶ sensitivity training	▶ inter-group development
▶ role negotiation	▶ team-building

learning objectives

When you have read this chapter, you should be able to define those key concepts in your own words, and you should also be able to:

1 Explain the goals of OD.
2 Understand the values underpinning the OD movement.
3 Understand the main OD interventions, how they work, and what they aim to achieve.
4 List the main skills and areas of knowledge required by an OD consultant.
5 Assess the difficulties in evaluating the effectiveness of OD interventions.

the OD agenda: goals and processes

Organization development has been defined in a number of different ways. However, most definitions share the same characteristics, and this is not a particularly controversial matter when the topic is considered in general terms. One of the founding figures of the OD movement, Richard Beckhard, defined OD as follows:

definition

Organization development *is an effort (1) planned, (2) organization-wide, and (3) managed from the top, to (4) increase organization development and health through (5) planned interventions in the organization's 'process', using behavioural science knowledge. Beckhard (1969, p. 9).*

© United Feature Syndicate, Inc.

It is not clear who first used and defined the term, but it seems likely that it was coined by Richard Beckhard, while he was looking for a label for a consulting programme in which he was involved with Douglas McGregor in 1960. They did not want to describe their work as 'management development' because the whole organization was involved, and they wanted to avoid the term 'human relations training' because that was too narrow. So the term 'organization development' was used instead. One of the other leading founders of the OD movement was Warren Bennis (1969) who defined OD as:

> a response to change, a complex educational strategy intended to change the beliefs, attitudes, values and structure of organizations so that they can better adapt to new technologies, markets, and challenges, and the dizzying rate of change itself.

More recently, Wendell French and Cecil Bell (1995, p. 1) have defined OD as 'a planned, systematic process in which applied behavioural science principles and practices are introduced into ongoing organizations towards the goal of increasing individual and organizational effectiveness'. The organizational boundaries and focus of an OD intervention are a matter for judgement. The approach can be applied to one or more departments or sections of an organization. However, OD practitioners like to talk about 'getting the whole system in the room'. This implies an attempt to understand and to influence the entire organization, involving everyone about everything.

Although written over three decades, these definitions are similar. The targets include individual development and organizational effectiveness. Interventions to achieve these goals are deliberate, planned and systematic. OD seeks to apply social and behavioural science knowledge and techniques in a manner that will enhance both organizational effectiveness and the quality of work experience for the organization's members. In pursuit of these twin objectives, OD has a clear and prescriptive value orientation. These values relate to the individual's experience of employment, and to the manner in which the organization treats and relates to its members.

Stephen Robbins (1986, p. 461) outlines the values underpinning most OD efforts as follows:

▶ The individual should be treated with respect and dignity.
▶ The organization climate should be characterized by trust, openness and support.
▶ Hierarchical authority and control are not regarded as effective mechanisms.
▶ Problems and conflicts should be confronted, and not disguised or avoided.
▶ People affected by change should be involved in its implementation.

Some practitioners argue that the 'human-centred' agenda is worth pursuing in its own right, independent of attempts directly to enhance organizational functioning. Others argue that an organization cannot be productive, efficient and effective unless it adopts this human-centred agenda. The committed OD practitioner asks – can an organization be effective without mutual trust and confidence, honesty, open communications, sensitivity to the feelings and emotions of others, shared goals, and a commitment to addressing and resolving conflict?

Note that a definition of 'effective' in this context depends on who is using the term. Effectiveness can be considered in terms of profitability, in terms of the pursuit of organizational goals (at whatever cost) or in terms of quality of life for those involved. Some of the general characteristics of the 'effective' organization are set out in the table on p. 491. See how many of these you agree with.

Thomas Cummings and Christopher Worley (1993) claim that early practitioners in this field were more interested in projects which concerned the 'people problems' of interpersonal relationships and group dynamics, and were less concerned with productivity issues. However, as French and Bell (1995) point out, the values and assumptions supported by the OD movement in the 1960s represented a radical departure for most organizations at that time. Managers in that era did not think in terms of involving their employees in decision-making, or of inviting their ideas and contributions. Most managers did not recognize a link between interpersonal relationships, self-awareness and the exchange of emotions and feelings on the one hand, and the performance of their businesses on the other.

Since the 1960s the OD movement has been associated with the argument that 'bureaucracy is bad' and that the caring, sharing, empowering organization is not only a better place to work, but is financially and materially more effective. The 'bureaucracy-busting' agenda of OD relies on the following kind of diagnosis of problems and solutions:

bureaucratic disease	symptoms	OD cures
rigid functional boundaries	conflict between sections, poor communications	team-building, job rotation, change the structure
fixed hierarchies	frustration, boredom, narrow specialist thinking	training, job enrichment, career development
information only flows down	lack of innovation, minor problems escalate	process consultation, management development
routine jobs, tight control	boredom, absenteeism, conflict for supervisors	job enrichment, job rotation, supervisory training

Some of the terminology in this table will be explained later in the chapter. OD practitioners claim that the diseases of bureaucracy can be cured in commercial organizations, but have also been concerned that the large public sector bureaucracies are resistant to such cures. Warner Burke (1980), for example, claimed that the confrontation of OD and large organizations in national and local government or health care resembled the confrontation of 'David and Goliath' except, he argued, 'we are not as skilful as David'. Cummings and Worley (1993, p. 647) claim, from personal experience, that 'OD still has limited application in large health systems', because of the special nature of their managerial and organizational problems. Moving into the twenty-first century, the large public sector bureaucracies are probably more in need of OD support and intervention than ever.

Must OD settle for 'fine tuning' in such settings rather than seek radical change? Government policies and demographic trends in the late twentieth century are pressing public bureaucracies to become more commercial in outlook, and in internal structure. Twenty years on, will Warner Burke's pessimism be overturned by a public sector revival of OD?

the OD matrix: levels and models of intervention

The OD toolkit includes a large and expanding number of intervention techniques or strategies. In fact, many of the approaches to organizational improvement covered in earlier chapters – job enrichment, assessment centres, team building, participative management – can be regarded and have been used as *OD interventions*. The first step in any OD project, however, concerns diagnosis. Until one is clear about the nature of the problem and its roots, it is not possible effectively to select an appropriate strategy.

definition
An organization development or **OD intervention** *is a specific methodology or technique used to effect change in the target organization or section of the organization, to improve organizational effectiveness (however defined).*

characteristics of the effective organization	characteristics of the ineffective organization
clearly defined goals	ill-defined or unknown goals
structure related to goals	no link between goals and structure
flexible forward planning	focus on immediate pressing problems
consistent, clear procedures which evolve purposefully	bureaucratic rigidity, or constant change without rationale
meaningful, varied work with learning opportunity	narrow, repetitive jobs with little learning opportunity
commitment to personal growth (planned skills development)	contempt for individuals and groups (the POPOS: pissed on, passed over)
power recognizing mutual influence	politicking and defensive cliques
flexible, participative decisions	'what the boss says, goes'
information openness	secrecy, gossip, failure to listen
mutual trust, support, respect	the FUJIAR syndrome: 'fuck-you-Jack-I'm-all-right'
accurate, timely performance feedback	unclear signals: 'what did the boss mean by that?'
just and equitable rewards	apparently arbitrary rewards
constant scanning of environment and appropriate adaptation	failure to perceive and act on critical environmental changes
initiative in external relations	reactive, selective responses
well-defined concept of social responsibility	'couldn't care less' attitude to community values

based on Dexter Dunphy, 1981, *Organizational Change by Choice*, McGraw-Hill Book Company, Sydney (reprinted 1993), pp. 26–8.

Problems in organizations can arise at different levels:

▶ organizational level ▶ group level
▶ inter-group level ▶ individual level

Let us briefly examine these levels. One particular *individual* may be having difficulties with the work; too difficult, not challenging enough, no future prospects. A *group* or team may not be functioning effectively; lack of leadership, poor relationships, personality clashes, team lacking cohesion. Two or more groups may find themselves in (*inter-group*) conflict for some reason; unwilling to co-operate or liaise, with differences in outlook, physical distance, conflict of priorities. The whole *organization* may experience low morale, be out of touch with its environment, lack an effective structure, lack a clear strategy.

The first step in problem diagnosis thus concerns identifying the level at which the problem has arisen. In most complex organizations, as one might expect, problems are likely to be caused and reinforced by factors at more than one level. For example, those unhappy individuals may be concerned with their positions in the structure, and with a lack of understanding of the organization's strategic purpose, as well as with fellow section or group members, and the lack of challenge in their own individual repetitive tasks. Problem diagnosis, therefore, is not always a straightforward step. The selection of an appropriate intervention strategy, or more often a solutions package, can thus be a complex choice.

To help with these issues of diagnosis and choice, Derek Pugh produced an OD matrix, which can be found in summary form on p. 493. This matrix first outlines the potential problems that can arise at each of the four levels, with respect to behavioural factors, organization structural factors and wider contextual factors. Each cell in the matrix identifies, in italics, potentially relevant OD interventions. If the problem lies with the individual, and the cause or causes are structural, then a job redesign approach may be relevant. If the problem lies at the organizational level, and the cause or causes are contextual, job enrichment is going to be of limited value and a change of organization strategy or location may be necessary.

Many OD texts offer a similar classification of OD problems and interventions. The Pugh OD matrix is a particularly clear example; some offer more detail and complexity. It is important to recognize, however, that an intervention strategy, or package of strategies cannot simply be 'read' from a matrix like this. The matrix is a useful diagnostic and planning guide, and no more. A sound, first-hand knowledge of organizational context is required. The approach that is both relevant, practical and acceptable is in part systematic diagnosis, part local context knowledge, part judgement. The OD matrix cannot be applied in a straightforward mechanistic manner.

The relationship between OD practitioner or consultant, and the target or host organization, has generated much concern and discussion. Consultants, of course, work for clients. In an OD setting, defining 'the client' is not always a straightforward business. The person who invited the OD consultant into a preliminary discussion (the 'gatekeeper') may not be the person (the 'problem owner') who represents the section with the difficulty to be resolved. Someone else again (the 'paymaster') may eventually settle the consultant's invoice. The problem may actually lie, say, with two groups of relatively low-status employees whose poor interaction and conflict is adversely affecting organizational performance in some manner. Can these groups be regarded as 'clients' of the OD consultant? To make matters more complex, the consultant is also likely to become involved in the organization's political system. The people with the most status influence in the organization (the 'powerbrokers') may not be gate-keepers, problem owners or paymasters at all.

We can examine this issue from a theoretical and from a practical perspective.

From a theoretical point of view, once engaged, the consultant quickly becomes involved in a complex and ongoing series of relationships within the host organization. It is useful, then, to consider the consultant interacting with, and intervening in, a 'client system'. Some parts of the client system will be critical, others less so. Some will collaborate willingly, whilst others will manifest resistance to creative interventions. Action that will affect one part of the client system may create 'knock-on' or 'ripple effects' in other parts of the system. The term client system neatly captures the complexity and variety in the OD consultant's net of relationships in the host organization.

From a practical point of view, however, the term 'client system' neatly obscures and confuses a critical issue for the OD consultant as temporary employee of the host organization. In this respect, identifying clearly and without ambiguity the person or group responsible for paying salaries, settling invoices and writing cheques may be vital. But the simplicity of this mercenary stance has to be set against the need to recognize that the OD consultant may have many different clients, with different needs and expectations, within the one organization. It may be appropriate to identify the client differently for different activities and stages of the OD process.

organizational diagnosis and choosing the appropriate OD intervention: the Pugh OD matrix

	behaviour *what is happening?*	**structure** *what is the system?*	**context** *what is the setting?*
organizational level	poor morale, pressure, anxiety, suspicion, weak response to environmental changes *survey feedback, organizational mirroring*	inappropriate and poorly defined goals, strategy unclear, inappropriate structure, inadequate environmental scanning *structure change*	geography, product market, labour market, technology, physical working conditions *change strategy, change location, change conditions, change culture*
inter-group level	sub-units not co-operating, conflict and competition, failure to confront differences, unresolved feelings *inter-group confrontation, role negotiation*	no common perspective on task, difficult to achieve required interaction *redefine responsibilities, change reporting relations, improve liaison mechanisms*	differences in sub-unit values and lifestyles, physical barriers *reduce psychological and physical distance, exchange roles, arrange cross-functional attachments*
group level	inappropriate working atmosphere, goals disputed, inappropriate leadership style, leader not trusted or respected, leader in conflict with peers and superiors *process consultation, team building*	task poorly defined, role relations not clear, leader overloaded, inappropriate reporting structures *redesign role relations, autonomous groups, socio-technical system redesign*	lack of resources, poor group composition, inadequate physical facilities, personality clashes *change the technology, change the layout, change group membership*
individual level	individual needs not met, frustration, resistance to change, few learning and development opportunities *counselling, role analysis, career planning*	poor job definition, task too easy, task too difficult *job restructuring or redesign, job enrichment, clear objectives*	poor individual-job 'fit', poor selection or promotion, inadequate training, inadequate recognition and reward *improve personnel procedures, improve training, align recognition and reward with objectives*

Kurt Lewin (1951) considered organizational change to have three main elements. These concerned *unfreezing* the current state of affairs (attitudes, beliefs, values), the *transition* to a new state and *refreezing* or stabilizing the changes to make them permanent. OD interventions can be considered in terms of how they help with the unfreezing, transition and refreezing states of the OD process.

Lewin also introduced, in 1947, the interesting and valuable technique of *force field analysis* – a change management technique which is also relevant to the organizational change issues discussed in Chapter 16. Lewin argued that the nature and pace of change depend on the balance of driving and restraining forces in relation to a particular change, or 'target situation'.

---

definition

Force field analysis *is a technique for assessing the factors that encourage and the factors that resist movement towards a desired target situation, thus allowing an assessment of the viability of the change, and suggesting action to alter the balance of forces, if necessary.*

A typical force field analysis could look like this:

target situation: emigrate from UK to Australia

driving forces ⟶ ►◄	⟵ restraining forces
friendly natives	family in Scotland
inexpensive lifestyle	high cost of moving
the wide open spaces	the long journey to anywhere
the beer, the wine	the mosquitoes, the spiders
clear skies, sunshine, beaches	sunburn, skin cancer, sharks

A force field analysis involves identifying the factors or forces supporting and impeding movement towards a given target situation. The forces can be weighted, which usually means giving each factor a score from 1 (weak) to 10 (strong) to provide a rough guide to the balance of forces. If the driving forces are overwhelming, then the change can probably go ahead without any significant problems. If the resisting forces are overwhelming, then the change may have to be abandoned or at least delayed until conditions have improved in some respect.

If the driving and restraining forces are more or less in balance, then the force field analysis can be used to plan appropriate action. How can resisting forces be reduced or eliminated? How can the driving forces be strengthened? Are there any new driving forces that can be introduced? The weighting of forces and the adding of scores gives the technique a spurious air of scientific validity. Clearly, the extent to which the force field is balanced is a matter of judgement. Used in a group setting, the technique provides a valuable way to structure what can often be an untidy discussion covering a range of factors.

> **STOP!**
> Consider a change that your educational institution may be about to introduce.
> Suppose the target situation is student assessment in the subject of organizational behaviour using only objective testing. This will mean multiple-choice tests, one-word answer tests and perhaps short answer tests. Multiple-choice tests, of course, can be scanned and marked electronically avoiding the need for tedious essay marking.
> ◗ Identify the forces driving this change.
> ◗ Identify the forces restraining this change.
> ◗ Assess the relative ease or difficulty of introducing this change.
> ◗ Construct a brief action plan for implementing this change.
> ◗ Construct a brief action plan for blocking this change.

It is necessary first to consider the main models of intervention which OD has adopted to implement planned change. We will consider specific OD tools or intervention techniques in the next section. Thomas Cummings and Christopher Worley (1993) outline two main intervention models, the planning model, and the action learning model.

The planning model assumes that change can be implemented in seven related stages:

1 **scouting** Consultant and client share information and ideas, with respect to problems and the appropriate approach.
2 **entry** A formal consulting or helping relationship is established.
3 **diagnosis** Information gathering to define the problem and identify causes.
4 **planning** Jointly establish the goals of an OD intervention, and the proposed approach.
5 **action** The intervention strategies are implemented.
6 **stabilization and evaluation** The change is stabilized (refreezing takes place) and the outcomes are assessed.
7 **termination** The consultant withdraws or moves on to another OD project.

In practice, change rarely unfolds in such a straightforward manner. The original plan is always subject to modification and refinement. The seven steps are not always followed in precisely this sequence. Some stages may be omitted or passed over quickly, or revisited several times during the change process. This does not invalidate the model, which remains a useful guide or route map for participants in the OD process.

The *action research* model differs from the traditional planning model in two respects.

First, it is a cyclical or iterative process. This simply means that the results from an intervention are fed back in such a way that further changes and improvements can be implemented. Of course, this can happen with a planning model too, but in action research, this intention is designed into the approach from the beginning.

Second, the 'research' in the label signals the aim of generating knowledge that can be applied in other organizational settings. This means that action research is a different kind of consulting model, and also a different kind of organizational research model too.

---

definition

Action research *is a model of OD consulting that involves the feedback of findings from interventions, or actions, to help in the design and implementation of further action and improvements to organizational effectiveness.*

Action research can also be defined as a model of organizational research in which generalizable knowledge is produced from attempts actively to change and improve organizational functioning, rather than from passive observation.

Action research is sometimes seen as a contemporary approach, which gained wider acceptance through the 1980s and 1990s. However, applications date from the mid-1940s.

Consistent with the overarching goals of OD, action research in practice is a collaborative method, involving consultant and organization members in joint planning, diagnosis, implementation, evaluation and further planning. The outline stages of an action research programme are, therefore, likely to include:

1 problem identification
2 preliminary diagnosis
3 data gathering from the client group
4 data feedback to the client group
5 joint evaluation of data
6 joint action planning
7 action, or implementation of proposals for change
8 repeat the cycle – fresh data gathering and feedback of results of change

As with the traditional planning model, action research is unlikely in practice always to unfold in such a tidy manner. Once again, the model is a useful guide. The main differences between the planning and action research models lie with their respective emphasis and goals. Action research emphasizes the cyclical nature of organization development and change, whereas the planning model presumes a 'one off' intervention. The goals of the planning model are improved personal and organizational effectiveness. Action research adds the goal of generating new knowledge and insights for application elsewhere.

OD techniques: the toolkit

Designing a package of OD interventions is a creative assignment. The approach has to be tailored to fit the culture and problems of the client system. In any particular organization, some approaches are likely to be more appropriate, and perhaps more acceptable, than others. An examination of the OD toolkit has to bear this in mind. The main and popular intervention techniques are these.

change the structure

There are numerous ways in which the structure or design of an organization can be changed. Examples include the techniques of *job rotation*, *job enlargement* and *job enrichment* which target individual jobs, and which were described in Chapter 4. Another example is *autonomous teamwork*, which targets groups of employees and which are described in Chapter 19. The techniques of socio-technical systems analysis and organizational design (including autonomous groups) have become part of the OD toolkit too, and are discussed in Chapter 19. *Business process re-engineering*, explored in Chapter 16, also leads to structural changes affecting organizational processes. It is possible to change the degree of centralization or decentralization in an· organization, or to flatten or extend the organization structure, or to change the basis of the organization design from region to product, or vice versa. Rules and procedures can be relaxed, or tightened up. These structural issues were discussed in Part 3.

Apparently simple structural changes can have profound implications. Structure has a significant influence over access to information and other resources, over work experience and career opportunities, and over the degree of discretion or autonomy an individual has. Structure also signifies which departments are marked for growth and which for decline, and structure changes can be used to signal changes in the organization's future direction and priorities.

process consultation

Process consultation engages an external consultant in a flexible advisory capacity, helping specific individuals to improve their understanding of internal organizational problems, and helping them to identify appropriate problem-solving action. One of the main advocates of this approach has been Edgar Schein (1969).

---

definition

Process consultation *is an OD intervention in which an external consultant acts in a facilitating, supporting, advisory and catalytic capacity, to enhance the diagnostic, conceptual and action planning skills of managers in the organization.*

The role of the process consultant is to 'give the client insight', or rather to help the client or clients to develop their own insights. This requires a great deal of skill, sensitivity and tact, and there are no standard procedures to follow. The process consultant may or may not be knowledgeable with respect to the problems or changes facing the organization and its members. The critical skills for a process consultant are in diagnosis and in forming a supportive, helping relationship. The diagnostic and problem-solving activities of the process consultant are, by definition, *joint* activities, carried out *with* the client or clients and not *for* the client. The focus, therefore, is on process, which explains the label. Process consultation contrasts with the conventional view of the consultant working in 'expert' mode. Here, the client is buying the consultant's knowledge and expertise, to cover gaps in the organization, and also perhaps to address and resolve a particular problem.

survey feedback

Survey feedback means just what the term implies. The results of an employee opinion survey are fed back (anonymously, protecting individual responses) to managers and employees, to help in identifying action that will improve organizational effectiveness. A typical opinion survey will include questions on leadership and management style, aspects of organization culture such as communications, motivation and decision-making, and member satisfaction with the organization, their job, their supervisor, their pay and their work group.

---

definition

Survey feedback *is an OD intervention in which the results of an opinion survey are fed back to respondents in the organization in a manner that triggers problem solving with respect to the issues highlighted by the survey findings.*

A survey can cover the whole organization, or just a department or section. Those responding may be invited to contribute to the initial design of the questionnaire, suggesting questions, highlighting significant issues. Opinion surveys typically reveal differences in perception around an organization, and usually highlight significant problem areas and issues. These findings are then used to trigger discussion about ways to resolve differences and solve organizational problems. The most popular approach for achieving this is through group discussions, in task forces, working parties or project teams, each working on a particular set of themes or issues or directing their attention to a particular section of the organization.

team-building

Team work, or group work, is fundamental to organizational functioning, and is mentioned several times in this text on organizational behaviour – most notably throughout Part 2. The performance of teams or groups is central to organizational effectiveness. The issue has thus attracted a lot of attention from OD practitioners. The first application of team-building, according to French and Bell (1995), was by Robert Tannenbaum in the early 1950s, at the Naval Ordnance Test Station in California.

---

definition

Team-building *is an OD intervention which seeks to improve team performance by helping members to understand their own team roles more clearly and to improve their interaction and collaboration.*

There are many different approaches to team-building.

One popular team-building technique is based on the work of Meredith Belbin (1981; 1995), and was covered earlier. Belbin argued that teams work most effectively when a number of interdependent roles are covered – co-ordinator, shaper, plant, monitor-evaluator, implementer, teamworker, completer, resource investigator and specialist (see Chapter 8). Belbin developed a questionnaire (now one among several) to help you to identify your personal team role preference or preferences. Once you have identified your preferred role, you can play to that strength. Once the team has identified which roles are present, and which are absent, action can perhaps be taken to compensate for any imbalance. One or more individuals, for example, may be invited to 'hold back' a preferred role if it is over-represented in the group. One or more individuals may be invited to 'cover' roles that are not among their strong preferences, but that are missing from the group's overall profile.

Another popular team-building technique involves the simple process of group effectiveness rating. As with team roles, there are a number of questionnaires that serve this purpose. Team members rate their team on a number of criteria. These criteria may include, for example, clarity of goals, willingness to share ideas, time management, focus on achieving results, willingness to listen to others, ability to allow all team members to contribute, and so on. The rating questionnaire is first completed individually, and these scores are then shared and discussed in a team meeting. The combined data from the rating questionnaires can thus be used to identify and address differences in perception in the team, to highlight problems affecting teamwork and to trigger a discussion of how the team is going to overcome those problems and improve performance.

Some training organizations offer team-building programmes based on 'outward bound' techniques. Participants are typically subjected to a series of outdoor challenges involving, for example, mountain walking (preferably in appalling weather), rock climbing, sailing and orienteering. The activities are designed to require teamwork and to encourage the development of interpersonal trust, group decision-making, communication skills and an awareness of leadership roles.

inter-group development

It is common to find that sections, functions or departments in an organization develop their own unique perspectives and behaviours, which prevent effective interdepartmental communications and collaboration. The functional boundaries that exist between, say, the finance and personnel departments of a

**"We've had a few complaints, Finlay,
that you're not a team player."**

large retailing store, or between the inorganic chemistry and marketing departments in a university, can lead to dysfunctional conflict. Within a single unit or function, groups with different goals, backgrounds and working practices may find it difficult to work together when required. OD has, therefore, tried to find ways to improve intergroup relationships and working arrangements.

---

definition

Intergroup development *is an OD intervention which seeks to change the perceptions and attitudes that different groups in an organization hold with respect to each other, and to improve their interaction and collaboration. Variants of this technique are also known as* **intergroup confrontation** *and* **peacemaking**.

How does one combine, in harmony, within a single organization, two groups (say, cost accountants and mechanical engineers) who have wholly negative stereotypes and perceptions of each other? One technique is the 'mutual expectations' approach. The two groups first meet separately. The members of each group are asked to note:

1 how they see themselves
2 their expectations of the other group
3 what they think the other group expects from them

The groups exchange these lists, then meet together to explore the similarities and differences in their perceptions and expectations. Such an exchange can be confrontational. If the meeting is deliberately designed as confrontational, special facilitation skills are required on the part of the OD consultant to keep the discussion under control and to achieve a positive outcome. Once the differences between conflicting groups are known, their causes can be explored and action can be taken to reduce or remove barriers to effective integration and collaboration.

One variant on the inter-group development technique is known as 'organizational mirroring'. This involves the 'target group' seeking feedback from other groups in the organization on how it is seen and perceived. In this approach, several groups may be involved, and representatives from the other groups are only involved in providing information and ideas, rather than in full negotiation or confrontation with the target group members.

role negotiation

Role negotiation can be a useful way to reconcile differences between two individuals whose working relationship is ineffective. The approach is similar to inter-group development.

---

definition

Role negotiation *is an OD intervention which seeks to change the perceptions and attitudes that different individuals in an organization hold with respect to each other, and to improve their interaction and collaboration.*

The technique assumes that interpersonal friction is caused, at least in part, by a lack of shared awareness and by misunderstanding. The aim in role negotiation, therefore, is to make individual perceptions and mutual expectations explicit, so that differences can be identified and resolved.

sensitivity training

If you join a sensitivity training programme, you will find yourself eventually in a room with other participants, but without an agenda or discussion topic, or other obvious purpose. The aim is to allow participants to discuss themselves, to observe and discuss the ways in which they interact together, and to exchange feedback on their interactions.

---

definition

Sensitivity training *is a technique for enhancing individual self-awareness and self-perceptions, and for changing behaviour, through unstructured group discussion.*

Probably the oldest OD intervention, sensitivity training is also known as laboratory training, T-groups (T stands for training) or encounter groups. Whatever the label, the technique is broadly the same.

The sensitivity training group may have a facilitator, but sometimes participants are brought together initially without anyone being 'in charge' and are left to create their own conversation. When a facilitator is present, he or she denies and rejects any kind of leadership role, pushing any such requests and suggestions back to the group to discuss and resolve. Without an agenda beyond, 'talk about yourselves', the sensitivity training group discussion can quickly turn to feelings and emotions. This may begin with the expression of how participants feel about being in such an unstructured setting. This can then turn into an emotionally charged discussion about how individuals feel about themselves and about other participants. The feelings and emotions exposed in this setting can be personal, confrontational and awkward.

Some participants in sensitivity training claim to develop profound insights about themselves and how they relate to others from the experience. Some participants, however, find the lack of structure and the sharing of emotions uncomfortable, threatening and stressful, and learn little or nothing. Critics have argued that the method can cause psychological damage.

The history of sensitivity training pre-dates the founding of OD, and has had a significant influence in a number of areas. The technique was invented, by chance, in the summer of 1946 when the Connecticut State Inter-Racial Commission asked Kurt Lewin at the Research Center for Group Dynamics at the Massachusetts Institute of Technology to run a training programme for community leaders. Lewin's team designed a programme of lectures, role plays and group discussions. During the evenings, the training team met to share their observations of the course and its participants, to assess how well the programme was progressing. However, some participants were staying in the training centre and asked if they could observe these evening discussions. Lewin gave them permission to do this, although the other trainers were hesitant.

One evening, one participant listening to the training staff discussing her behaviour during the day interrupted to challenge their interpretations, and to describe what had happened from her perspective. Lewin immediately recognized the potential of this exchange, and an increasing number of participants started to join the evening discussions. Soon the evening sessions were proving as valuable in learning terms as the regular daytime sessions were supposed to be. In other words, participants became more sensitive to their own behaviour, to the effects they had on others and to how others saw them and related to them.

The technique of sensitivity training, in unstructured small groups, had been discovered. The method was soon being applied in organizational settings to support change programmes. The first reported use was by the oil company Esso (today Exxon) in their refineries in Louisiana and Texas. Managers were given three-day training laboratories in order to help them develop and to change to a more participative management style.

other approaches: change systems and procedures

Just about any tool, technique or approach for changing attitudes and behaviour and for improving organizational effectiveness can be regarded and used as an OD intervention. Beyond structure change and a number of specific tools, OD uses a range of other methods to change organizational culture, to encourage individual growth, to foster intergroup collaboration and to improve organizational effectiveness. For example, job definitions, work organization and group relationships can be significantly affected by *technological innovation*, in both office and manufacturing settings. Goals, priorities and behaviours can be altered by making appropriate changes to the organization's *payment system*.

There are many other ways in which to encourage the members of an organization to change their attitudes and actions. The organization sends signals about what behaviour is valued through the design of its staff *appraisal system*, where individuals discuss their goals and their performance at least once a year with their manager. The effects of appraisal can be supported by planned *career counselling and development systems* designed to reinforce the same messages. Required changes in skills, knowledge, attitudes and behaviour can be encouraged through specially tailored *training and development programmes*. Communications and working relationships can be improved through a range of mechanisms, such as *conferences, forums, workshops, discussion groups* and *project teams*. These mechanisms can focus on particular groups or can bring together staff from different sections and levels of the organization structure.

the OD package

The OD toolkit thus has two important features. First, it is extremely wide and goes beyond the limited range of special methods outlined here. Second, the design of an OD intervention involves constructing an appropriate package of interventions. This package will be different for each organizational setting. Constructing the package requires knowledge of the organizational context, judgement, and creativity. An appropriate and effective package cannot be designed by reading off a matrix, or pulling mechanically from a toolkit. The box example of OD applied to a local government organization illustrates this point.

---

organization development in local government

Faced with the need to control costs, continue to deliver high quality services and respond in a rapid and flexible way to change, South Somerset District Council embarked on a radical programme of organizational change in 1991. The main changes concerned a reduction in the number of departments and a flatter management structure. Unit managers in the flat structure had more autonomy to make decisions without having constantly to refer to more senior grades as they had to do in the past.

To support and reinforce these changes in behaviours and values, the Council also introduced an organization development programme. The OD programme had the following components, introduced between 1991 and 1993:

- *workshops* for potential unit managers on the theme 'into the future'
- an *attitude survey* to discover the level of public satisfaction with the Council's services and to identify potential further improvements
- a *corporate forum* for elected councillors and senior managers, meeting six times a year informally to discuss strategic issues
- *'service days'* during which teams providing a service meet once a year to explore barriers to improved performance and to plan improvements
- *staff training* to ensure that everyone has the skills, knowledge and attitudes to deliver the Council's services
- a *team leaders' programme* for the 100 managers reporting to unit managers to develop their skills as intermediaries between senior management and the 'front line'
- a *management skills programme*, based on a 'model manager checklist' to provide structured development for unit managers and others requiring similar skills
- a *corporate network* to maintain regular and informal communications between unit managers and others, to share ideas and experience
- *development for elected councillors*, to equip them with appropriate skills and knowledge
- *performance appraisal*, for all staff
- *service reviews*, which regularly explore the need for and delivery of specific services in depth
- *service agreements* to ensure that sections providing internal services work to agreed quality standards
- *upward feedback* otherwise known as 'telling your manager how you think they do something and how you might like them to do it differently'

The aims of this programme were to support a change from a 'command and control' organization culture to one in which staff were empowered to make decisions, and to make the organization more flexible and responsive to the needs of its local population.

based on Bob Darbourne, 1993, *Lessons from Change at South Somerset District Council*, a South Somerset District Council Publication, August.

It is not difficult to see reflected in this toolkit the set of assumptions that underpin OD efforts. These were mentioned earlier in the chapter, but are perhaps now clearer:

- Individual and organizational goals are not incompatible.
- Conflict is caused by misunderstandings.

▶ Conflict is resolved by openly confronting differences in perception.
▶ The open display of emotions and feelings is valuable.
▶ People have a capacity and desire for personal growth.
▶ Working relationships can be improved by enhancing self-awareness.
▶ Collaboration and trust are better than conflict and secrecy.

This is why Warren Bennis described OD as a 'truth, trust, love and collaboration approach' to organizational change and development. OD interventions rely on the free and open sharing of information and emotions. Where these values are compromised, the OD agenda may also be compromised.

OD applications: the empirical evidence

OD practitioners and potential clients are preoccupied with the question, 'Does it work?' However, OD is a package of approaches to improving organizational effectiveness rather than a specific, well-specified technique; 'more of a process than a step-by-step procedure', as Warner Burke (1987, p. 1) notes. The package is configured in quite different ways to suit differing organizational contexts. It is, therefore, difficult or impossible to conduct systematic research that allows comparisons to be made between interventions and organizational settings.

The factors that OD seeks to change include a broad spectrum of attitudes and values, as well as numerous quantitative indicators of organizational performance. The target of a typical OD programme may be the improvement of teamwork, or the enhancement of working relationships between groups or departments, or improvement of the performance of the organization as a whole, or target all of these levels. There may even be disagreement about which measures or indicators are most significant.

In rigorous research methodology terms, the independent variables (OD interventions) are loosely defined and inconsistently applied, and the dependent variables (measures of organizational effectiveness) are similarly difficult to pin down and may be disputed. These problems are compounded when an action research model is used. Here the 'researcher' is both intimately involved with, and actually seeks to influence, the very interventions and consequences which are the focus of study. How can one adequately assess cause and effect when all the research rules about objectivity and rigour appear to be broken?

Nevertheless, advocates of OD have sought to defend the approach with empirical evidence from across a range of applications over a number of decades of experience. Don Warwick (1984), for example, listed ten potentially positive results from OD interventions:

1 improved organizational effectiveness, including better productivity and morale
2 better management throughout the organization
3 commitment to and involvement in making the organization successful
4 improved teamwork
5 better understanding of organizational strengths and weaknesses
6 improved communications, problem-solving and conflict resolution
7 creativity, openness, opportunities for personal development
8 decrease in dysfunctional behaviour – politicking, playing games

9 increased ability to adapt to changing circumstances

10 increased ability to attract and retain quality people

French and Bell (1995) worked through a 'review of reviews', presenting evidence from a broad range of studies and organizational settings. The literature of the field does indeed demonstrate that 'OD programs produce positive changes at the organizational and individual levels' (p. 341). Much of the literature, of course, is produced by OD practitioners who are in turn responsible for publishing the reviews of other reported OD interventions.

It is further interesting to note that French and Bell end their review by noting the *faith* that OD practitioners have in the power of OD intervention. Faith-plus-data would be reassuring, they point out, suggesting that, for many practitioners, faith alone is probably good enough. Is this an unsatisfactory conclusion? We indicated earlier in the chapter that OD has some of the properties of a religious movement. The goals and values of OD concern, in part, the development of individuals through improving conditions of work across a number of dimensions. Improving quality of working life may be seen as a valuable outcome of OD interventions, even where the measurable performance of the organization from an accountant's point of view remains unaffected.

to be an OD consultant

what's it all about?
Wendell French and Cecil Bell (1995, p. 357) conclude their leading text with these words: What is OD all about? OD is really about people helping each other to unleash the human spirit and human capability in the workplace.

What skills and knowledge does it take to be an effective OD practitioner or consultant? Warner Burke (1987, p. 143) opens his discussion of this question as follows:

To be seen as a consultant is to have status, and thus many people aspire to the label and the role. A consultant is one who provides help, counsel, advice, and support, which implies that such a person is wiser than most people.

Burke also lists the personal attributes that the effective OD consultant should possess:

▶ ability to tolerate ambiguity
▶ influencing skill
▶ ability to confront difficult issues
▶ skills in supporting and nurturing others
▶ ability rapidly to recognize one's own feelings and intuitions
▶ conceptual skills
▶ ability to mobilize self and others
▶ ability to teach and to create learning opportunities
▶ a sense of humour, to maintain perspective
▶ self-confidence
▶ a sense of mission about working as an OD consultant

> **STOP!**
>
> Could you be an effective OD consultant?
>
> Assess yourself against Burke's list of personal attributes, and identify your own strengths and weaknesses. Do you want to be a consultant in this field?
>
> To what extent do you think this specification is 'superhuman' and beyond the reach of one individual? Is there a place for humility in the consultant's toolkit?

French and Bell (1995) argue that the OD consultant's role is unique because it is based on a collaborative relationship with the client or client organization. The OD practitioner, in their view, is 'a facilitator, catalyst, problem solver, and educator'. This makes the OD consultant a peculiar kind of expert – expert on process, but not expert on the content or substance of organizational change. The OD consultant who offers the unambiguous diagnosis and prescribes the correct solution is not helping members of the client organization to develop their own diagnostic and problem solving capability. In brief, you do not help someone to learn by simply giving them the right answers all the time.

The traditional approach to management consultancy is based on a medical, or 'doctor–patient' model. In this perspective, the consultant is the expert diagnostician who investigates and prescribes a cure. In contrast, the OD consultant works together with clients, designing interventions that help organization members to diagnose and resolve their own problems more effectively. The medical model is self-perpetuating; next time you get sick, you need to call the expert back in. The OD model, in contrast, is self-developmental; if the intervention worked the last time, then you will be equipped to prescribe your own cure the next time you get sick.

The traditional consultant prescribes cures for the client. The OD consultant develops the client's own diagnostic and problem solving capabilities. In reality, OD consultants in particular, and management consultants in general, use a range of styles, distinguished by their reliance on their own skills and knowledge, or on their clients' skills and knowledge:

consultant knowledge versus client knowledge

use of own expertise   plans the intervention

advocates or prescribes the intervention

proposes criteria for change

identifies options for action

feeds back information and assessments

collects and analyzes data

clarifies and interprets

listens and reflects

use of client expertise   refuses to become involved

Identifying the skills and knowledge of the effective OD practitioner, Cummings and Worley (1993) first identify four critical areas:

intrapersonal skills

These may also be described as self-management capabilities. They include conceptual and analytical skills, integrity and moral judgement, being in touch with your own goals and values, learning skills, and stress management. Cummings and Worley recognize that the role can be extremely pressured and stressful. The OD consultant often faces ambiguity, time pressure, conflict and confrontation, emotional outburst and uncertainty. Handling this kind of environment requires resilience, and an ability to manage one's own emotions and stress responses. The intrapersonal skills are not always visible, but they can be critical.

interpersonal skills

These include general communication skills, listening, establishing trust and rapport, giving and receiving feedback, negotiation, counselling and coaching. This area also includes 'aptitude in speaking the client's language', which is essential in building rapport and credibility, and in maintaining effective helping relationships.

general consultation skills

These include diagnostic capability, and skills in designing and implementing appropriate OD intervention packages. The latter involves action planning, customizing the package to fit the organization and presenting ideas in a style that gains commitment and collaboration. Remember that this also involves understanding when and how effectively to involve the organization's members in collaborative diagnostic and implementation activities. This is a more subtle, complex and difficult skill than individual diagnosis and autocratic implementation would involve. The OD consultant should also be knowledgeable and skilled in the use of process consultation methods.

organization development theory

The OD consultant should be familiar with OD theory and research, and have an understanding of planned change and the action research model. A knowledge of the range of interventions is useful, along with a knowledge of research findings concerning their application. A conceptual understanding of the role of the OD consultant is also valuable.

Cummings and Worley identify a number of other useful skills and areas of knowledge, including:

- entry and contracting
- interviewing
- reward systems
- theories of learning
- personality theory
- cross-cultural theory
- evaluation research
- questionnaire design and use
- participant observation methods
- data collection and data analysis skills
- presentation and training skills
- line management experience
- knowledge of social and industrial psychology, and anthropology

This list of skills and knowledge areas could be applied to many organizational positions. They certainly apply to both internal and external consultants to an organization. Much of this list will, in addition, apply to members of internal project teams, working parties, task forces, or steering groups. Even though we do not carry the job title 'consultant', many of us find ourselves from time to time involved in organizational data gathering, diagnosis, action planning and change implementation. These qualifications should not be seen as belonging exclusively to the 'professional' OD practitioner or consultant.

The OD consultant may not be an 'expert' in a particular organizational area, function, system or problem. However, the range of relevant *process* expertise is extremely wide. It may be difficult to find many individuals skilled and knowledgeable in all of these areas. The role of the OD consultant does seem to be one with plenty of variety and challenge.

assessment

One of the short definitions of OD used at the beginning of the chapter was from French and Bell (1995). Here is their 'full' definition:

> Organization development is a long-term effort, led and supported by top management, to improve an organization's visioning, empowerment, learning and problem-solving processes, through an ongoing, collaborative management of organization culture – with special emphasis on the culture of intact work teams and other team configurations – utilizing the consultant-facilitator role and the theory and technology of applied behavioural science, including action research. (p. 28)

The phrase 'long-term' implies that there is no 'quick fix' for organizational effectiveness. Change is usually difficult and the active support of senior management is essential. OD assumes that people will work more effectively together if they share the same vision of the organization's future, and if they are able to develop skills and understanding through empowerment to make decisions and act on their own initiative. OD also assumes that people are capable of development through appropriate experience, hence the emphasis on problem-solving and learning. As pointed out in earlier chapters, collaborative or participative management is generally believed to be more acceptable and effective than autocratic, directive management. Most commentators in the late 1990s regard the team or group or unit as the basic building block of organizational design. Supporting teams and improving team and intergroup working have been long standing goals of OD.

It is important that the OD consultant is seen as a catalyst and as a facilitator rather than as an expert who is going to carry out the diagnosis single-handed and deliver the prescription based on unique expert knowledge. OD consultants work *with* their clients as well as *for* them. Finally, OD has since its inception retained the goal of applying behavioural or social science knowledge in a more self conscious and deliberate style than most conventional management consultants (who may be excused a more pragmatic approach to the clients and their business). This approach is reinforced by the adoption of the action research model.

As the perceived pace of organizational change increased through the 1990s, many organizations and commentators sought to challenge the 'no quick fix' assumption. Many organizations have found that they need to change more rapidly than OD seems to allow. OD appears to offer the somewhat elusive promise of improved effectiveness, in the long run, probably difficult to measure, following an extended and probably expensive programme of activities, which initially address intangible factors like beliefs, values and attitudes. This is not a particularly compelling promise in a fast-moving, competitive world where even public sector organizations are required to deliver improvements within tight timescales.

Robert Schaffer and Harvey Thomson (1992, p. 80) – harsh critics – argue that:

The performance improvement efforts of many companies have as much impact on operational and financial results as a ceremonial rain dance has on the weather. While some companies constantly improve measurable performance, in many others, managers continue to dance round and round the campfire – exuding faith and dissipating energy.

This 'rain dance' is the ardent pursuit of activities that sound good, look good, and allow managers to feel good – but in fact contribute little or nothing to bottom-line performance. These activities, many of which parade under the banner of 'total quality' or 'continuous improvement', typically advance a managerial philosophy or style such as interfunctional collaboration, middle management empowerment, or employee involvement. ... Companies introduce these programs under the false assumption that if they carry out enough of the 'right' improvement activities actual performance improvements will inevitably materialize. At the heart of these programs, which we call 'activity-centred', is a fundamentally flawed logic that confuses ends with means, processes with outcomes.

Schaffer and Thomson argue the advantages of what they call 'results-driven programs' compared with the 'activity-driven programs' of OD. Results-driven programmes aim to produce significant, short-term, measurable performance improvements, in areas where long-term benefits can also be achieved. In an educational context, a results-driven programme could pursue targets such as: 95 per cent of student assignments will be marked and returned within four working days of submission; all members of staff who are active in research will publish three journal articles in each calendar year.

Results-driven programmes are built on ambition and impatience, on a desire to see tangible results, now. OD in contrast typically requires a sustained commitment to the pursuit of intangible goals such as attitude change and new sets of values.

This does not necessarily mean, however, that results-driven programmes and OD are incompatible. The teams or task forces searching for those rapid performance gains are going to find barriers in their path. As they seek to overcome the barriers in pursuit of their objectives, their actions may well parallel OD interventions and produce culture change. Schaffer and Thomson do not present their approach as 'fast track' OD, but it is not difficult to see how the conventional goals and techniques of OD can be combined with a results-driven emphasis to generate such an approach.

---

the future is flatter

It seems clear that in large part the old organizational paradigm is dying. It doesn't work well in this emerging environment. Top-down, autocratically directed, rigidly hierarchical, fear-generating organizations are giving way to something new. The new paradigm proclaims that the most innovative and successful organizations will be those that derive their strength and vitality from adaptable, committed team players at all levels and from all specialities, not from the omniscience of the hierarchy. Increasingly, organizations will be flatter, with smaller central staffs and with more real delegation to small groups and units. High-performance organizations focusing on the customer and continuous quality improvement and placing high value on human resources, diversity, and high performance teams will be the norm.

from French and Bell, 1995, pp. 349–50.

If French and Bell are correct in their prediction that flatter, organic structures are about to replace those based on the traditional paradigm of hierarchical, bureaucratic control, then OD will continue to play a central role in organizational change and improvement. The values and paradigms that OD advocates appear as relevant in the twenty-first century as they have been since the 1960s. As they also claim, for OD the future is bright, or so it would appear.

sources

Beckhard, R., 1969, *Organization Development: Strategies and Models*, Addison-Wesley, Reading, MA.

Belbin, R.M., 1981, *Management Teams: Why They Succeed or Fail*, Heinemann, London.

Belbin, R.M., 1995, *The Coming Shape of Organizations*, Butterworth Heinemann, London.

Bennis, W.G., 1969, *Organization Development: Its Nature, Origins, and Prospects*, Addison-Wesley, Reading, MA.

Burke, W.W., 1980, Organizational development and bureaucracy in the 1980s', *Journal of Applied Behavioural Science*, vol. 16, pp. 423–37.

Burke, W.W., 1987, *Organization Development: A Normative View*, Addison-Wesley, Reading, MA.

Cummings, T.G. and Worley, C.G., 1993, *Organization Development and Change*, West Publishing Company, Minneapolis/St Paul, fifth edition.

Darbourne, B., 1993, *Lessons from Change at South Somerset District Council*, a South Somerset District Council Publication, August.

Dunphy, D., 1981, *Organizational Change by Choice*, McGraw-Hill, Sydney (reprinted 1993).

French, W.L. and Bell, C.H., 1995, *Organization Development: Behavioral Science Interventions for Organizational Improvement*, Prentice Hall International, Englewood Cliffs, NJ, fifth edition.

Lewin, K., 1951, *Field Theory in Social Science*, Harper & Row, New York.

Robbins, S.P., 1986, *Organizational Behavior: Concepts, Controversies, and Applications*, Prentice Hall International, Englewood Cliffs, NJ, third edition.

Schaffer, R.H. and Thomson, H.A., 1992, 'Successful change programs begin with results', *Harvard Business Review*, January–February, pp. 80–9.

Schein, E.H., 1969, *Process Consultation: Its Role in Organizational Development*, Addison-Wesley, Reading, MA.

Warwick, D.D., 1984, *MODMAN: Managing Organizational Change and Development*, Science Research Associates Inc., New York.

chapter 18 corporate culture

DILBERT — By Scott Adams

© United Feature Syndicate, Inc.

concepts and learning objectives

The topic of corporate, company or organization culture is widely discussed in organizational theory and management practice. Corporate culture can, for the moment, be defined as the collection of relatively uniform and enduring beliefs, values, customs, traditions and practices which are shared by an organization's members and which are transmitted from one generation of employees to the next.

The concept of corporate culture is a controversial topic, with many disagreements. Writers differ not only about fundamental issues, but also question its value as an explanatory tool. The literature is full of theories and models seeking to clarify the concept of corporate culture. Many of them are inconsistent with each other and fail to provide clear guidelines for measurement.

There are two fundamental debates in the field of corporate culture, which cross over each other in places. The first of these can be labelled the *culture-as-a-variable* versus *culture-as-a-metaphor* debate. What is fundamental about it is that the first view holds that culture is an objective reality that can be measured and changed by management. The counter-view asserts that culture is a mental state that has to be tolerated since it is incapable of being changed by management.

The second debate concerns which of three perspectives is the most appropriate for viewing corporate culture. One perspective, called the *integrationist*, holds that corporate cultures consist of people who share one set of common values and basic assumptions. A second one, called the *differentiation perspective*, says that there is no single, common culture, but that sub-cultures form within the corporate culture. The third perspective is called *fragmentation* and asserts that ambiguity within organizations prevents any on-going agreement on values or basic assumptions. Somewhat confusingly, this last perspective on culture denies that a corporate culture can exist at all. Nevertheless, each perspective provides a way of looking at culture in a company. This chapter will begin by presenting the variable *v.* metaphor debate, and will go on to introduce the topic of corporate culture from an integrationist perspective. In the assessment section, the contrasts between the integrationist, differentiationist and fragmentist cultural perspectives will be highlighted.

key concepts
- corporate culture
- organizational value
- organizational belief
- organizational opinion
- organizational attitude
- organizational norm
- organizational socialization

- power distance
- uncertainty avoidance
- individualism–collectivism
- masculinity–femininity
- integrationist cultural perspective
- differentiationist cultural perspective
- fragmentationist cultural perspective

learning objectives

When you have read this chapter, you should be able to define those key concepts in your own words, and you should also be able to:

1 Introduce the concept of corporate culture, highlighting its conceptual problems.
2 Account for the popularity of the concept amongst academics and managers.
3 List and define the elements of corporate culture.
4 Explain how some companies develop and transmit their cultures.
5 Assess the evidence concerning the effect of culture on organizational performance.
6 Consider the role of culture and socialization as a management control tool.
7 Examine the effect of national culture on employee behaviour.
8 Contrast the integrationist, differentiationist and fragmentationist cultural perspectives.

corporate culture: variable or metaphor?

The fundamental debate about corporate culture was summarized by Smirchich (1983), who distinguished between two groups of researchers. The first took a positivistic perspective (see Chapter 2) and saw culture as something that an organization *had*. The second adopted a phenomenological standpoint and conceptualized culture as a 'process of enactment' – not as something that exists 'out there' separate from people, but which was actually 'manufactured' by company employees as they interacted with one another on a daily basis within the workplace.

culture-as-a-variable	culture-as-a-metaphor
positivist	phenomenological
anthropology/biology	social psychology
single, agreed upon culture	several, parallel, sub-cultures
physical reality	mental state
provides an adaptive-regulating mechanism to maintain status quo	cultural conflicts can engender change
directed by actions of senior management changing artefacts and espoused values	reproduced by all culture members in an ongoing way through their negotiation and sharing of symbols and meanings
senior management only manipulate culture for corporate success	managers, as well as other individuals and groups, all seek to influence cultural direction of company

developed from Legge (1995, pp. 185–7).

culture-as-a-variable

Legge (1995) defined the view treating culture as an independent variable (see Chapter 2), 'as when a national culture is imported into an organization via its membership, or as something produced by the organization – its values, language and rituals – as a by-product to the production of goods and services' (pp. 185–6). This view of culture is based on the anthropological and biological approaches. The culture-as-a-variable focus emphasizes consensus and unity. It starts with an assertion about a consensus amongst all managers and employees as to what the culture is, and continues with a description of how all the different elements of a company's culture fit together and support one another. There is considered to be some natural adjustment process to accommodate environmental difficulties.

This dominant perspective holds that corporate culture is 'out there' existing independently of employees and alongside company objectives, technology and structure. It consists of a single set of shared and consistent values and beliefs embedded in stories and symbols, and which are transmitted by company rites and rituals. These act to eliminate ambiguity for members as to how they should think and act. Most importantly, corporate culture is capable of being consciously created and managed by leaders to make it achieve corporate objectives (Scholz, 1987). Changing culture is what top managers do to workers to get them going and working harder in the desired direction. This view of culture is underpinned by the notion of management control and can be found in the writings of managerially-oriented authors (Ouchi, 1981; Pascale and Athos, 1981; Deal and Kennedy, 1982; Peters and Waterman, 1982). It is also known as the *integration* paradigm (Meyerson and Martin, 1987). This perspective sees culture as serving four functions:

1 It provides a sense of identity for employees, increasing their commitment to the company, making their work more intrinsically rewarding and making them identify more closely with fellow workers.
2 It allows them to 'make sense' of what goes on around them, enabling them to interpret the meaning of different organizational events.
3 It helps to reinforce the values of the organization, that is, of senior management.
4 It serves as a control device for management with which to shape employee behaviour.

culture-as-a-metaphor

The contrasting view states that companies *are* cultures. It says that organizations may be 'as a system of shared cognitions, of knowledge and beliefs, or as a system of shared symbols and meanings, cognitions . . . (culture) is both produced and reproduced through the negotiating and sharing of symbols and meanings – it is both the shaper of human action and the outcome of the process of social creation and reproduction' (Legge, 1995, p. 186).

This view of culture sees it as existing in, and through, the social action of cultural members. It acknowledges the possible existence of several competing cultures within a single organization. For example, between different departments or functions such as production and research and development. It also acknowledges a difference between the culture possessed by non-management groups and that espoused by management, and the problems of aligning the two (Anthony, 1994).

For this group of writers, culture is deeper than its symbolic manifestations. Stories, rituals, material symbols and language within organizations are a means of transmitting culture, but are not culture itself. Morgan (1986, p. 133) wrote that, 'the slogans, evocative language, symbols, stories, myths, ceremonies, rituals and patterns of tribal behaviour that decorate the surface of organizational life, merely give clues to the existence of a much deeper and all-pervasive system of meaning'.

This perspective, therefore, offers management fewer levers with which to shape it or use it as a tool of control. Although managers might be able to change the outward manifestations of culture to some degree, the basic assumptions of company employees will remain the same. Several authors subscribe to the culture-as-a-metaphor perspective (Gregory, 1983; Smirchich, 1983; Morgan *et al*, 1983; Anthony, 1994; Meek, 1988). It is also known as the *differentiation* paradigm (Meyerson and Martin, 1992).

The question of defining corporate culture remains problematic (Furnham and Gunter, 1993). Having introduced the two contrasting perspectives on corporate culture, the remainder of this chapter will introduce the concept using the dominant, positivist, culture-as-a-variable, integrationist approach. The assessment section at the end of the chapter elaborates the culture-as-a-metaphor perspective and highlights differences between the three cultural perspectives.

---

definition

Corporate culture *is the pattern of basic assumptions that a given group has invented, discovered or developed in learning to cope with its problems of external adaption and internal integration, and that have worked well enough to be considered valid, and therefore to be taught to new members as the correct way to perceive, think and feel in relations to those problems.*

Schein (1984).

---

rise of the corporate culture concept

Tom Peters
(b. 1942)

Robert Waterman
(b. 1936)

Corporate culture rose to prominence during the 1980s. Two publications can claim to have catapulted the concept of corporate culture to the forefront of management concern. Initially, Tom Peters and Robert Waterman (1982), in their book *In Search of Excellence*, highlighted the potential impact that company values could have on organizational success. In the same year, Terrence Deal and Allan Kennedy's (1982) book *Corporate Cultures* suggested that the culture of any organization could be managed towards achieving greater effectiveness. Given this double stimulus, the concept of corporate culture temporarily attained the status of a management fad. Beaumont (1993) identified three circumstances which facilitated this:

1 The economic success of Japanese organizations which appeared able to establish and maintain co-operative, team-based organizational cultures. Hofstede (1986) noted that the survival of American companies which had withstood the crises of 1974 and 1978 needed an organization-level explanation which took account of their total institutional strength, rather than an explanation by reference to the contribution of individuals, groups, structures or technology alone.

2 There was the growing 'companies of excellence' literature which argued that successful leadership skills were more 'soft' than 'hard', and that it was necessary to motivate and gain the commitment of employees.

3   The belief that there was a correlation between strong corporate cultures and organizational performance, and that a company's culture was capable of being strengthened by managers.

Terrence Deal

Allan Kennedy

Corporate culture is now an established perspective. Academics such as Edgar Schein see culture as a new school of thought within organizational behaviour. There have always been different perspectives or 'levels of explanation' in organizational behaviour. The dominant ones have been individual, group, political and structural. Given a crisis such as a decline in organizational performance, each perspective offers its own explanation. The individual view might emphasize a lack of employee motivation; the group perspective would point to inappropriate norms and sanctions; the political standpoint would highlight ambiguity and differences in objectives; whilst the structural perspective would explain the decline in terms of problems with authority, rules and roles.

Edgar H. Schein

To these four dominant approaches has been added a fifth, that of culture. In explaining organizational success and failure, the cultural perspective considers values and norms. Unlike its structural counterpart which sees decision-making in an organization as based on rational behaviour, the cultural view stresses employees' assumptions and beliefs. Gareth Morgan (1986) offered the cultural metaphor as a way of providing insights about leadership, organization–environment relations and organizational change, and generally emphasizing, 'the truly human nature of organizations and the need to build organization around people rather than techniques' (Morgan, 1986, p. 138). Academics in the field are most interested in how the concept is most appropriately defined, measured and studied. So, corporate culture as a perspective does not stand in opposition to the structural and the other ones, it is merely an alternative to them.

The managerialist literature also accepts the existence of corporate culture, and is interested in how it can be created, institutionalized and changed. It sees it as a tool of management control. Managers have acquired the notion of a 'culture gap'. This refers to the difference between the kind of culture that a company currently possesses and the kind that its senior management would like to have. The belief is that the gap can be filled by the application of techniques that change the culture. Kilmann and Saxton (1983) have even developed a 'culture-gap' survey questionnaire which invites employees to assess their company's culture. It consists of descriptions of what actually happens in the company, and the expectations that others have in the organization. It uses two dimensions to define a culture – the technical versus human dimension, and the short versus long term-time dimension. With its four cells, the instrument attempts to discover the actual and ideal operating norms in the areas of task-support (short-term, technical norms); task innovation (long-term, technical norms); social relationships (short-term, human orientation norms) and personal freedom (long-term, human orientation norms).

models of corporate culture

From the cultural perspective, all organizations are held to possess cultures, but it is only a minority which have 'strong', that is, highly visible ones, which clearly distinguish them from other companies, and which affect the behaviour of their employees. To explain how a strong culture is created, we shall consider it under four headings: core elements, packaging, transmission system and cultural network, using an analogy to clarify.

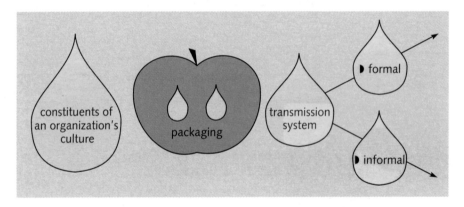

core elements of corporate culture

The definition of culture given earlier states that it is learned and shared by its members, and transmitted, to others. However, what exactly is the 'it' that is learned, shared and transmitted? Trice and Beyer (1984), Schein (1985b) and Anthony (1994) all offer different lists of what constitutes culture. It is these which are packaged and transmitted to employees, and which distinguish the company from others. A horticultural equivalent is the seed of a flower, fruit or vegetable.

In the case of an organization, the elements that constitute its culture are values, beliefs, opinions, attitudes and norms. Of these, values are held to be the most important. In practice, clarifying the distinction between these concepts is not of great use. Most opinions and beliefs are closely linked to attitudes, and can often be rationalizations of attitudes. The most prominent values which have been espoused by management and which have under-pinned the majority of culture change programmes in the last ten years have been: quality of product or service, customer care, cost-effectiveness and cultural network.

definitions

Organizational values *are anything that has personal worth or meaning. Values are typically based on moral, societal or religious precepts that are learned in childhood and modified through life. Shared values produce beliefs.*

Organizational belief *is the acceptance of a proposition. It does not necessarily imply a preference 'for' or 'against' anything. Beliefs are assumptions about the organization and the situation within it.*

Organizational opinion *is a belief that includes an attitude that is for or against something.*

Organizational attitude *is a tendency to respond in a certain way (favourably or unfavourably) to objects, persons or situations.*

Organizational norms *are derived, expected modes of behaviour. They are based on an organization's values and beliefs, and they provide guidelines for individual and group behaviour. These in turn produce outcomes that reinforce shared values and beliefs.*

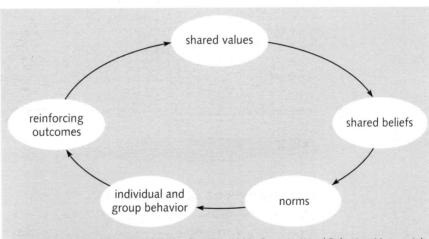

from R. Dennis Middlemist and Michael A. Hitt, 1988, *Organizational Behavior: Managerial Strategies for Performance*, West Publishing, St Paul, MN, p. 462.

For a corporate culture to form – that is, for shared values, beliefs, forms and behaviour to evolve – a fairly stable collection of people need to have shared a significant history, involving problems, in order for a social learning process to occur. Organizations which have such histories, also have resulting cultures that permeate most of their functions (Schein, 1985a). Robbins offers a model to explain how corporate culture develops.

In this model, a company's culture is derived from its founder, and this affects the selection process. Schein (1983) argued that research consistently confirmed the extremely important formative influence of the organizational founder or early senior managers of an organization in creating its culture.

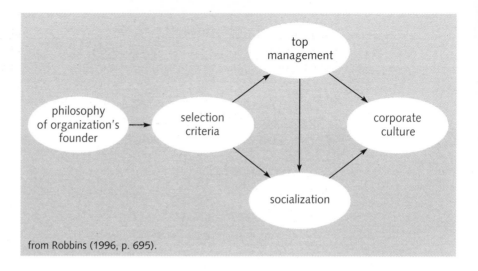

from Robbins (1996, p. 695).

The HP Way: values, objectives, strategies and practices

Established in 1939 by William Hewlett and David Packard, two engineers from Stanford, California, Hewlett-Packard is a maker of high-technology electronic equipment. Headquartered in Palo Alto, California, it is one of the top twenty US companies, employing 102,000 people and earning annual revenues of $31 billion in the mid-1990s. It is often cited as the quintessential strong-culture company. Commentators tend to attribute the company's success to the strength and form of its corporate culture. Its booklet, *The HP Way*, contains information about the three main elements that together constitute its corporate culture – company values, objectives, as well as strategies and practices.

Bill Hewlett and Dave Packard

Photo courtesy of Hewlett-Packard Company

The first element – the *company's values* – is defined as 'a set of deeply held beliefs that govern and guide our behaviour in meeting our objectives and in dealing with each other, our customers, shareholders and others'. It then goes on to define HP's five core values:

▶ We have trust and respect for individuals.

Robbins described a company's current top managers as its 'culture carriers'. These people set the general standards of what was acceptable behaviour, and new employees were socialized into the firm's values, beliefs and norms. The founders of an organization had a vision of what the organization should be like, including its mission, and a view as to how it should be implemented. Since the company was initially small, that vision was capable of being imposed on all its members.

packaging cultural elements

The second requirement for a strong corporate culture to form is for the constituent elements, the values, beliefs and norms, to be effectively packaged. Packaging refers to how these cultural ingredients are encased for their journey. They need to be protected, so that they arrive safely at their destination. The seeds of an apple are packaged by being located deep within the apple and protected by its flesh. The core elements of a company's culture

> - We focus on a high level of achievement and contribution.
> - We conduct our business with uncompromising integrity.
> - We achieve our common objectives through teamwork.
> - We encourage flexibility and innovation.

The second elements of the HP culture are its *corporate objectives*, which provide 'guiding principles for all decision making by HP people'. Following a period of successful production and a rapidly growing organization, the company founders sat down with their key managers in 1957 to formalize a set of corporate objectives. The objectives, underpinned by the corporate values, guide the way the company does business to this day.

There are seven corporate objectives which refer to profit, customers, fields of interest, growth, management, citizenship and Our People. The last of these objectives is to help HP people share in the company's success, which they make possible; to provide employment security based on performance; to ensure them a safe and pleasant working environment; to recognize their individual achievements; to value diversity; and to help them gain a sense of satisfaction and accomplishment from their work.

The third element of the corporate culture described in the booklet are the company's *strategies and practices*. The formation of these is guided by the company's values and objectives described earlier. There are four of these. *Management by Wandering About – MBWA* (using informal communication practices to keep up to date with what is going on); *Management-by-Objectives – MBO* (individuals at each level contributing to company goals by integrating their stated goals with those of their manager, and the goals of the other parts of the company); *Open Door Policy* (assurance that there will be no adverse consequences for responsibly raising issues of concern with management or personnel); and *Open Communication* (belief that people will contribute their best when given the right tools, training and information).

based on *The HP Way*, Hewlett-Packard Company, 1989.

are embedded in stories, myths, sagas, legends, folk tales, symbols and slogans.

Stories: Based on original true events, but can include a mixture of both truth and fiction. They often contain a narrative about the organization's founders, key decisions made by individuals that affect the company's future course. For example, the story of the employee who noticed that the labels on a Procter & Gamble product at his local supermarket were mounted off centre. He bought the whole stock assuming P&G would reimburse him, which they did. Stories anchor the present in the past and provide explanations and legitimacy for current practices.

Myths: These are universal explanations which lack a factual basis and hence are untestable. They often include old-timers stories of things that happened in the past.

Heroes: Individuals, living and dead, who personify the values of the culture and provide role models for emulation. These frequently include company founders, visionary managers and employees whose performance is judged to be outstanding. The thoughts of the late Ray Kroc, who bought the rights to the hamburger restaurants from the McDonald brothers, are captured on audiotape in his own words and are available to staff who attend the company's training courses.

Sagas: Historical narratives describing the unique accomplishments of a group and its leaders. For example, Hewlett-Packard sagas of the accomplishments of Bill (Hewlett) and Dave (Packard) are used to communicate features of the *HP Way*.

Legends: These are accounts of actual events which are irrefutable but which have been embellished with fictional details. The legends frequently concern individuals as heroes and heroines. For example, the 3M legend of the worker who persistently tried to find a way to use rejected sandpaper minerals. He was fired for spending time on this, kept coming back and was ultimately successful, finally becoming the vice-president of the company's Roofing Granules Division, which he helped to create.

Folk tales: Purely fictional stories which nevertheless carry a message for employee behaviour and practice.

Symbols, slogans and mottoes: Symbols are signs that elicit meanings that do not relate to them. Examples of symbols include the Coca Cola and IBM logos. Slogans such as Caterpillar's 'Forty-eight hour parts service anywhere in the world' are well known. The Hard Rock Café's staff motto is 'Love All, Serve All'.

transmitting culture elements

Having packaged the values, beliefs and norms, the third requirement for a strong culture is to distribute them successfully to the employees. An apple tree's seeds are distributed by birds and insects. In a similar way, a company uses rites, ceremonials, rituals, induction and training courses to distribute its core cultural elements amongst its workforce.

The transmission system consists of a formal and an informal part. The formal part refers to the highly visible, consciously designed and regularly occurring events and activities, which provide opportunities for employees to acquire the company values, beliefs and norms. The informal element is as important but less visible. Together, they provide the means whereby the culture of the company is infused into its employees.

formal culture transmission system

This consists of the following events and activities.

Rite: This is a planned and often dramatic activity, which is elaborately staged and which focuses different expressions of culture into a single event. A wedding ceremony or a 'Suggestion Scheme Winner of the Year' award ceremony are examples of rites.

Ceremonial: This involves a linked series of rites within a single event. An occasion which includes the ceremonial unveiling of a product, the honouring of employees' extraordinary work performance and the hearing of visions of the future from an inspirational leader. The annual graduation ceremony with a speech from the vice-chancellor or principal is an example of a ceremonial which is an aspect of every university's culture.

Ritual: A ritual is a repetitive sequence of activities which expresses and reinforces the key ideas, values, beliefs and norms of the company. It is a standardized technique which, while it may manage anxieties, does not produce practical consequences of any importance. American companies arrange regular Friday afternoon 'beer busts' at which workers can get together and relax.

Courses: Induction, orientation and training courses. Companies which

---

Mickey Mouse culture

Marne-la-Vallée is situated 26 kilometres east of Paris and was chosen by the Walt Disney Corporation as the location for its first European theme park. The responsibility for the initial communication of the company's corporate culture lies with the local Disney University (company training centre). This is under the direction of Mary Toedt who has been with the corporation for twenty years. The purpose of the training is to:

1 Familiarize new employees with the Disney tradition and operating philosophy.
2 Teach them Walt Disney's vision by giving them a history of the company from its beginnings through to the death of its founder.
3 Familiarize them with Disneyland language. The operation is a show; the customers are Guests (spelled with a capital G); the collective workforce is the cast; individual employees are hosts; and working with the public involves 'being on stage'.
4 Provide them with an understanding of the Disneyland ethos, teaching them acting and 'atmospherics'.
5 Develop generic skills to be used on guests such as smiling and answering questions.
6 Developing job specific skills such as sweeping up, answering the telephone and attending the car park.

Toedt reported that her French recruits were more reserved than their American counterparts, but had, nevertheless, been transformed. Gillet reported that some of these new entrants had withdrawn from the training complaining that 'Joining the Disney organization is a bit like taking holy orders or, in the opinion of more recalcitrant candidates, joining a sect'.

based on Anne Gillet, 1990, 'Mickey Mouse goes to France', *Tertial*, May 1989, Paris, Groupe Usine Nouvelle. Reprinted in *Best of Business*, vol. 2, no. 1, pp. 28–33.

utilize re-education methods prefer to have their own training facilities. In 1961, McDonald's established its full-time training centre called Hamburger University which offered a 'degree' in hamburgerology (Ritzer, 1993).

informal cultural transmission

This refers to the informal way in which culture is transmitted. For example, the ways in which organization members typically communicate and express themselves, represents elements of their company's culture. Other aspects of the informal transmission system include:

Artefacts: Tools, furniture, appliances and clothes. For example, a great deal of attention has been paid to corporate workwear, especially where employees are in direct contact with customers.

Physical layout: Buildings, open spaces and office layouts. Some companies like Microsoft in Redmond, Washington, have a university campus-type layout, with running tracks. Others have introduced six-seater tables in their canteens to increase the chances of employees from different departments meeting and interacting with each other. Others have replaced offices with cubicles or 'workspaces'.

Language: A number of companies do not have workers. Wal-mart has *associates*; McDonald's has *crew members*; and Disney has *cast members*. British Rail, before privatization, changed from having passengers to *customers*; and the police are still debating whether they are a *force* or a *service*.

STOP!

Choose an organization with which you are familiar – perhaps your own company or university. Read through the elements of culture described and give an example from your chosen organization of any of them. Describe it and draw inferences about the nature of this organization's culture, its values, beliefs and norms of behaviour.

The ultimate strength of a company's culture depends on the homogeneity of group membership, and the length and intensity of their shared experiences in a group. The ongoing transmission of corporate elements that is carried out by the organization into employees is referred to *organizational socialization*. It includes the careful selection of new company members, their instruction in appropriate ways of thinking and behaving; and the reinforcement of the desired behaviours by senior managers.

> **definition**
>
> **Organizational socialization** *refers to the manner in which individuals learn what behaviours are or are not acceptable within a work setting.*
>
> *Van Maanen and Schein (1979).*

Socialization is important because, as Van Maanen and Schein (1979) state, 'New members must be taught to see the organizational world as do their more experienced colleagues if the traditions of the organization are to survive'. Organizational socialization involves the newcomers absorbing the values and behaviours required to survive and prosper in an organization. It reduces the variability of behaviour by imbuing employees with a sense of what is expected of them and how they should do things. By providing an internal sense of how they should behave, plus a shared frame of reference, socialization standardizes employee behaviour. A person undergoing a process of organizational socialization will move through the roles of *outsider*, *new person* and *low person*, before finally becoming a *fully fledged role holder*. This transformation is achieved through the processes of anticipation, initiation and assimilation. The word *process* is particularly apt, as new entrants can be thought of as being *processed* from outsiders into insiders.

organizational socialization

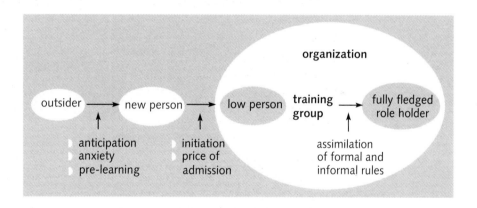

outsider

Individuals present themselves to the organization as outsiders seeking employment. This is the typical job applicant attending their job interview. However, even before applying, the applicant will be influenced by a company's reputation. Pre-information and rumour may depict the organization as a tough one to get into, requiring a certain performance. The promotional literature and presentations by company recruiters at university 'milk rounds' and careers exhibitions are intended to ensure that all prospective applicants will value what lies ahead and will create some anxiety in them.

Some of the applicants will get through to the interview stage. Pascale (1985) described how, at Procter & Gamble, candidates were exhaustively screened by highly trained company interviewers. This had three consequences on corporate culture. First, it ensured that the values and objectives of those recruited meshed with those of the firm, thereby ensuring homogeneity of group membership. Second, it conveyed to the minority ultimately admitted that they had surmounted a rigorous selection procedure, and made them feel that they were members of an elite who had achieved a coveted and distinctive status. Third, it reinforced the image of the company that was projected to future applicants, as the accounts of the experiences of both successful and unsuccessful applicants circulated through the student grapevine. Hence, this part of the socialization process occurs before individuals are admitted to the organization, and is targeted equally at both those who will be accepted and rejected.

---

selecting in and out

Bain and Company, a Boston-based management consulting firm, only hired graduates of the Harvard Business School. In addition to providing talented people, it found that the School's emphasis on competition, verbal dexterity, hard work and ambition were reflected in Bain's core values. Selecting Harvard graduates reduced the time and expense the company would have to invest in socializing their new recruits, and increased the chances that they would fit in with Bain's culture, and actively maintain it.

In contrast, Sony Corporation California wanted to maintain a family-type culture. It therefore recruited those without any previous manufacturing experience, preferring school-leavers and housewives. Since these recruits lacked any preconceptions about how a factory worked, Sony could socialize their new employees into the 'Sony Family' without needing to break down pre-conceived notions and previous assumptions. In both cases, careful selection assisted later socialization.

based on Steven P. Robbins, 1990, *Organization Theory: Structure, Design and Applications*, Prentice Hall, Englewood Cliffs, NJ, 3rd edition, pp. 446–7.

---

new member

The next stage of socialization occurs as the recruit is transformed from an outsider into the organization's new member. There is a price of admission, and the trainees or cadets will be more willing to pay it if they feel that they are lucky to be there. In this stage, members' old reference groups are broken down and replaced with new ones. The old self may be symbolically destroyed by the removal of clothes, previous status symbols and even hair. New names and titles such as cadet and management trainee are conferred. Military and religious organizations are particularly good at this process of purification, which prepares acolytes by altering their previous roles and statuses. Commercial organizations vary in the time and money they invest in socialization. New Disney employees and those of McDonald's spend time at Disney University and Hamburger University respectively, being shown films and listening to lectures about how they are expected to look and behave.

new recruits 'learn the ropes' at Disney

Disney begins tugging on the heart strings of employees even before they are hired. Think about the typical recruiting office in the hospitality industry – a windowless cubby-hole in the sub-basement between the laundry and the boiler room. Then walk into Disney's capacious 'casting centre', and you're in Wonderland. Well, not exactly, but the doorknobs on the entrance do replicate the ones Alice yanked during her adventures . . . Ascend a gentle sloping hallway, whose walls are decorated with whimsical murals, and you're in a vast anteroom where the centrepiece is the original model of Snow White's castle.

Some 50,000 aspiring employees funnel through the Lake Buena Vista casting centre every year seeking jobs that start with pay as low as $5.95 per hour (Disney's other theme parks in California, Japan and France do their own hiring). What are Disney World's 40 interviewers – all of whom started as front line workers – most interested in? . . . Says Duncan Dickson, director of casting: 'We're looking for personality. We can train for skills. We want people who are enthusiastic, who have pride in their work, who can take charge of a situation without supervision.'

. . . Disney has overhauled its approach to orientation, putting less emphasis on policies and procedures, and more on emotion. *Traditions*, the two-day initial training session attended by all new cast members is part inculcation, part encounter group. Guided by two unfailingly upbeat cast members, neatly dressed neophytes seated at round tables in a small classroom discuss their earliest memories of Disney, their visions of great service, their understanding of teamwork.

Next comes the movie, a panegyric to Walt Disney himself. The film depicts the founder as a creative risk taker who overcame setbacks (his first character, destined for obscurity, was named Oswald the Lucky Rabbit), believed in teamwork (he and his brother Roy were partners), and preached the importance of exceeding expectations of his guests. Yes, Walt actually embraced that concept, now being peddled as a new management mantra, way back in 1955.

By encouraging . . . spurts of spontaneity . . . Disney World tries to instil verve in jobs that are otherwise tightly regimented. The 36-page cast members' appearance guide, for example, includes excruciatingly detailed ukases on length and style of hair, colour and quantity of cosmetics, and hues and textures of hosiery. . . Disney World, where the average age of cast members is 37, loses only about 15 per cent of its front line employees to attrition each year, compared with a rate of 60 per cent for the hospitality industry as a whole. Wages are competitive . . . but don't underestimate the power of sentiment. Listen to Rick Anderson, 20, a host in Tomorrowland: 'Sometimes, you get hot in your costume, you get fed up dealing with angry guests who are tired of waiting in line. But then a kid asks you a question, you answer it, and she breaks into a smile. You can make someone happy.'

low person

The cadet next moves from being a new member to a low person when they are placed at the bottom of the company hierarchy. Typically they are assigned to a training or work group within which the process of role assimilation occurs. Typically they are assigned tasks beyond their individual capabilities. This generates feelings of anxiety, fear of failure and possibility of rejection. The bosses, in the form of senior managers, professors, the Mother Superior, become the focus of a love–hate relationship. To survive, the group form informal structures, processes and values, and this peer group takes over the role of indoctrinating the other initiates.

fully fledged role holder

The final transformation in socialization is from low person to fully fledged role holder. It involves the assimilation of the new role, identity and value system. This takes place beyond the training group in the work area, when the neophyte is given their first operational assignment. This stage of socialization diminishes the cosy feeling of being inside the training group with its peer support, and exposes them to the complexities and dilemmas in the real organization.

The low person is introduced to a world of work families, each with their own territories, goals, values and norms. These are all operating, but are somewhat difficult to pick up. The acolyte has to experience the humiliations of initiation, and the learning of new passwords and prayers, until they are eventually absorbed into the apparatus. The structure of the career path slowly reveals itself. Of those initially admitted, a few will be directed to the exits, most will receive relatively routine assignments and be shown the gradual career escalator; while a few will be introduced to the fast escalator with accelerated challenges, status and rewards.

senior management

Socialization is a process that is most intense when the employee enters the organization for the first time, but it continues throughout their stay. For example, senior managers in the company may becomes mentors or coaches to low persons and role holders, to guide and mould them, in line with organizational expectations. Performance-based appraisal systems and formal training programmes may be instituted by senior management to signal visibly which goals they should be striving for and how. Finally, senior management's behaviour, in promoting, censuring and dismissing employees, also sends

information to employees about company expectations about norms, risk-taking, acceptability of delegation, appropriate dress, topics of discussion, and so on.

---

socialization at Salomon Brothers

In his book *Liar's Poker*, Michael Lewis vividly and humorously describes the process of socialization that he and 124 other graduate recruits underwent in preparation for assuming responsibilities as full Salomon Brothers employees.

Salomon Brothers – New York trading floor

How to talk like a trader

▶ **Forward**: A contract obligating one party to buy, and the other to sell, a specific asset for a fixed price at a future date.

▶ **Future**: A forward contract traded on an exchange.

▶ **Swap:** An agreement by two parties to exchange a series of cash flows in the future, as, for example, fixed interest rate payments for floating-rate payments.

▶ **Call**: An option giving the holder the right, but not the obligation, to buy a specific quantity of an asset for a fixed price during a specific period.

▶ **Put**: An option giving the holder the right, but not the obligation, to sell a specific quantity of an asset for a fixed price during a specific period.

▶ **Underlying**: The asset, reference rate, or index whose price movement determines the value of the derivative.

▶ **Cap**: A contract that protects the holder from a rise in interest rates or some other underlying beyond a certain point.

▶ **Floor**: A contract that protects the holder against a decline in prices below a certain point.

▶ **Swaption**: An option giving the holder the right to enter into or cancel a swap at a future date.

photo: John Abbot, 1995, *Fortune*, 12 June, p. 82;
text: Carol J. Loomis, 1994, 'The risk that won't go away', *Fortune*, 7 March, p. 24.

corporate culture and economic performance

Strong culture theory was put forward by Deal and Kennedy (1982) and holds that companies with strong cultures perform better than those with weak ones. In addition, Peters and Waterman's 'excellently managed' companies and Ouchi's Theory Z organization were both seen as using their cultural harmony to outperform their rivals. Strength refers to the degree to which employees share a commitment to a range of goals and values espoused by management, and of having a high level of motivation to achieve these because of an absence of bureaucratic controls. Schein (1984) defined culture strength in terms of the homogeneity and stability of group membership, and the length and intensity of the shared experience of the group. He felt that if a company consisted of stable groups of employees, who had been together for a long time, worked closely together and had been challenged and successfully overcome problems, then it was likely to

---

strong culture – economic performance link

Although managers tend to attest to the benefits of culture on a company, organizational researchers are less convinced. John Kotter and James Heskett (1992) researched the relationship between corporate culture and economic performance. These authors empirically tested this theory by measuring the strength of the culture of 207 large firms from a variety of industries. Of these, Wal-mart, J.P. Morgan and Procter & Gamble scored highest on strength of culture. They used a questionnaire to calculate a culture strength index for each firm, and then correlated it with the firm's economic performance over an eleven year period. The research showed a positive correlation, but it was weaker than most management theorists would have expected. Strong-culture firms seemed almost as likely to perform poorly as their weak-culture rivals. The authors concluded that the popular view that a strong corporate culture led to economic success was 'just plain wrong'.

Another theory holds that only those corporate cultures that help organizations adapt to environmental change are associated with excellent performance. Authors like Kilmann *et al.* (1986) and Kanter (1985) have argued that an adaptive culture can encourage confidence and risk-taking among employees, and possesses a leadership that focuses on the changing needs of customers. To test this theory, Kotter and Heskett studied a sub-sample of 22 firms with adaptive and non-adaptive cultures. They found that what distinguished the successful from the unsuccessful was that the former did not let the short-term interests of the shareholders dominate over others, but they cared equally for all the company's stakeholders – customers, employees and shareholders. The main problem is that the right corporate climate can take decades to evolve. This can be speeded up by either appointing an unconventional boss from inside, or choosing an outsider.

based on John Kotter and James Heskett, 1992, *Corporate Culture and Performance*, Free Press, New York.

have a strong culture. Legge (1995, p. 190) raised three problems with establishing this linkage:

1 The culture-performance link is not monolithic: initially, as more and more employee behaviour is aligned with senior management's values and goals performance may be enhanced. Later, however, resistance may develop and performance can decline (Saffold, 1978).

2 Cultural values may act as obstacles to high performance. Whilst a cultural value may integrate members, it could also act as an obstacle to effectiveness. A strong culture can be a weakness if members cannot break out from old-established, but currently inappropriate ways of seeing or doing things. Equally, a weak corporate culture, which incorporates a wide range of sub-cultures, may be more flexible and thus more capable of adapting quickly to environmental change.

3 There are problems of measurement. Researchers have to show that a highly performing company with a strong culture cannot achieve that same level of performance with a weak culture. Finally, Beaumont (1993) added a fourth difficulty, noting that the corporate culture of a particular multinational company may complement and be appropriate to some of the national cultures of the countries in which it operates, but inappropriate in others. As large organizations with distinct corporate cultures increasingly operate globally, this is likely to be an increasingly important issue for them.

STOP!

How might multinational companies, operating in numerous different countries and cultures, resolve this issue?

---

changing cultures

Newly established companies, and old plants relocating to new greenfield sites, are the places where attempts are often made to establish consciously a distinct culture from the first day and prevent one evolving unconsciously over time. However, the majority of companies do not have this option, so their managers want to know whether an existing corporate culture can be changed. One answer to this question is that if culture is sustained through selection processes, socialization, management action and the absorption of company stories, rites and rituals, then, theoretically at least, all of these should be capable of being unlearned and changed, and a new culture implemented. The counter-view holds that the longer any culture perpetuates itself, the stronger it becomes, because of its self-reinforcing nature. That strength means that beliefs and practices are more widely shared and deeply held, and thus harder to change. It is the very stability of cultural elements that resist change. Being formed over many years, they are not susceptible to be changed or unlearned overnight.

Four constraints to culture change can be identified:

1 Structural and technological ones. Much of a company's culture is embedded in the content and form of written documentation and procedures, physical spaces and buildings, entrenched rituals and its formal

structure. In the very long term, these are probably changeable, but in the short to medium term, corporate culture change is impracticable.

2 Management-initiated culture change is often resisted by company employees. Since a company's culture provides the foundation for their life in it, there is a limit to how much of it they can assimilate. Mergers are a particularly difficult time for staff as familiar symbols, beliefs, values and shared meanings are thrown into the melting pot. It is not surprising that seemingly rational requirements for introducing organizational, procedural and other changes may be resisted or even sabotaged by existing staff, whose identities have been disrupted and who might be seeking to cling on to the pre-change culture they know (Buono *et al.*, 1985).

3 The managers themselves can be an obstacle to culture change. Andrew Pettigrew (1986) considered how difficult it was to change the core beliefs of top management. Amongst the barriers to such change were entrenched power interests, deep historical roots, conflicting sub-cultures and the interdependence of particular corporate philosophies and structures. Culture extends beyond people and their relationships and beliefs. It is manifested in company products, structures, corporate mission and modes of recruitment, socialization and reward. The pervasiveness of corporate culture, and the fact that so much of it is taken for granted, makes it difficult to change that which is implicitly part of people's thinking and behaviour. In Pettigrew's view, this makes culture remarkably difficult to change.

4 Constraints on culture change are imposed by every organization's societal and industrial context. Fombrun (1984, p. 209) saw corporate culture as being the outcome of three independent variables operating at the levels of society, industry and organization. From this perspective, culture was a dependent variable. The culture that a company could develop (or got landed with!), was the result of independent variables such as societal arrangements; the industry in which it operated and what it produced; and the company's corporate strategy. Within these constraints, managers sought to change and adapt their corporate cultures.

corporate culture and competitive strategy

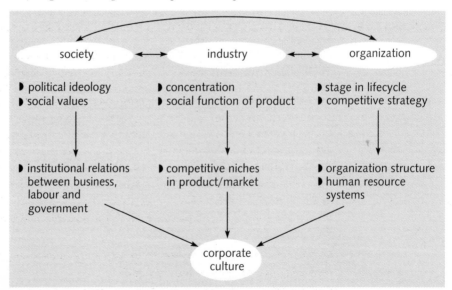

> **STOP!**
>
> Explain why the police force is unlikely to develop a corporate culture which emphasizes customer care, promotes norms of casual dress, rewards risk-takers even if they are unsuccessful, and encourages members to voice radical ideas such as the legalization of soft drugs.

Having said this, societal, industry and organizational obstacles have not prevented many brave attempts by companies to change their cultures. Indeed, corporate culture change programmes are featured regularly in the business press. Legge (1995) offers a listing of some of the recent ones: British Airways' 'Putting People First'; British Rail's 'Customer Care and Total Quality Management' programmes; Lucas's 'TQM and Just-in-Time'; and the use of quality circles in Hardy Spicer, Jaguar, Nissan and Rover. The majority of these are based on the premiss that changing employee attitudes is a prerequisite for changing their behaviour.

corporate culture as a tool of management control

To what extent can corporate culture be considered a tool of management control? Hales (1993, p. 216) wrote that,

> the power of organizational culture resides in the fact that it is not just another management 'technique' which can be applied at will, but is, rather, an influence upon behaviour which is not recognized as overt 'management'. The beliefs and values which shape employee behaviour are internalized, taken for granted and accepted as unobjectionable; therein lies their force. Culture can therefore exercise the most powerful and insidious form of control because it combines *de facto* compulsion with perceived freedom from coercion.

The Society of Jesus and the Hewlett-Packard Corporation: two examples of internal control?

St Augustine once gave, as the only rule for Christian conduct, 'Love God and do what you like'. The implication is that if you truly love God, then you will only ever want to do things which are acceptable to Him. Equally, Jesuit priests are not constantly being rung up, or sent memos, by the head office of the Society. The long, intensive training over many years in Rome, is a guarantee that wherever they go afterwards, and however long it may be before they even see another Jesuit, they will be able to do their work in accordance with the standards of the Society. They may constantly face new situations and unfamiliar problems, but they will handle them exactly as the head of the Society would himself, because they are so efficiently centralized internally.

from Anthony Jay, 1970, *Management and Machiavelli*, Penguin Books, Harmondsworth, p. 70.

Bill Hewlett (1987) said, 'The HP Way, when you really come down to it, is respecting the integrity of the individual.'

from *The HP Way*, Hewlett-Packard Company, 1989.

Ray (1986) distinguished different types of management control in history. She noted the move away from *bureaucratic control* towards *humanistic control*. The former focused on external, overt control of employees through rules, procedures, close supervision, appraisal and reward. Frederick Taylor, Henry Ford, Max Weber and Henri Fayol, all recommended this rationalist approach to direct the behaviour of employees towards organizational goals. It was expensive in terms of supervisory manpower required, frequently caused resentment and elicited grudging compliance from the workers. Humanistic control, in contrast, sought to satisfy employees' needs by providing a satisfying work task, or a pleasant working group life to promote internal control. Promoted by Mayo (1933; 1945), the hope was that individuals would willingly meet organizational goals by meeting their individual ones.

Ray suggested that by the end of the twentieth century, writers such as Deal and Kennedy and Schein suggested the possibility of using a third, more effective control tool – corporate culture. The selective application of rites, ceremonials, myths, stories, symbols and legends by managers to direct the behaviour of employees is termed *symbolic management*. In the long term, this form of control could be cheaper, avoided resentment, and built employee commitment to the company and its goals:

> more than any other forms of control . . . corporate culture elicits sentiment and emotion, and contains possibilities to ensnare workers in a hegemonic system, by providing an integrated set of corporate values and beliefs. (Ray, 1986, p. 287)

---

bureaucratic control (F.W. Taylor)
manipulation of rewards → loyalty → increased productivity

humanistic control (Elton Mayo)
'satisfying' task or work group → loyalty → increased productivity

culture control (Deal and Kennedy, Schein)
manipulation of culture including myth, ritual → love of firm and its goals → increased productivity

from Ray (1986, p. 362).

Although it is associated with 1980s management thinking, symbolic management has its roots in both bureaucratic and humanistic control . Their proponents allowed for the possibility of internal control. Thus, Frederick Taylor and his successors viewed workers as rational, economic, competitive, future-oriented individuals, who needed 'carrots and sticks' to direct their behaviour. Nevertheless, the idea that shared values could replace the stick was voiced as early as the 1930s when Chester Barnard, one of the classical management writers, stated that, 'the inculcation of belief in the real existence of a common purpose is an essential executive function . . . [the manager] is primarily an expert in the promotion and protection of values' (Barnard, 1938, pp. 28, 87–8).

Humanistic control is associated with Elton Mayo (1933; 1945) whose writings are contemporaneous with those of the famous sociologist, Emile

Durkheim (1933). Durkheim considered morality to be social in nature, beginning with a disinterest in the self and an attachment to something larger than the self. He concluded that people sought meaning in institutions, as the ties to their community and the Church were weakened. Mayo, too, emphasized the need for co-operative, integrative organizations, which provided employees with a sense of stability and identity in all aspects of their lives. For him, the workplace was the employee's new psychological home.

The 1950s saw a continuation of this theme. In his book *The Organization Man*, William H. Whyte (1956) argued that people needed a faith to give meaning to what they did, and the *social ethic*, emerged to fill this need. The ethic stressed that the individual was meaningless by himself, but when absorbed into a group with others, the whole was greater than the sum of its parts. Man needed togetherness in belongingness. It was insufficient merely to be part of the company. You had to immerse yourself with other people in small groups. Whyte described the career progress of these middle-class managers who not only worked for, but also belonged to, The Organization. Whilst few of them ever became senior managers, they had all committed themselves to it, having 'taken the vows of organizational life'.

William H. Whyte

Whyte's description of the 1950s contains many of the elements to be found in contemporary corporate culture writings. He described how The Organization recruited for itself those who would fit in, who would get along with others, who did not have any disturbingly exceptional characteristics and who both competed and co-operated with co-workers. Whyte's critique was on the loss of individuality in group and organizational life. He warned that the social ethic might delude the individual into believing that their interests were being looked after, when all the time The Organization was out to achieve its own goals.

national cultures

Culture researchers have studied individual company cultures in their wider national settings. They have been interested to see how attempts to establish a common corporate culture in a multinational firm can be undermined by the strength of national cultures. Fombrun (1984) saw corporate culture being partly the outcome of societal factors, whilst Laurent (1989) argued that the cultures of individual countries were more powerful and stable than those of individual organizations.

Geert Hofstede (1984) carried out a cross-cultural study to identify the similarities and differences among 116,000 employees of the same multinational company located in forty countries. His aim was to identify the basic dimensions of differences between national cultures. He discovered four such dimensions – power distance, uncertainty avoidance, individualism–collectivism and masculinity–femininity. Each of the forty countries could be rated from high to low on each of these four dimensions. The research design sought to control for individual and organizational variables so that any differences in attitudes or values revealed could be attributed to

Geert Hofstede

cultural differences. The following summary draws heavily on the work of the Open University (1985) and begins by defining each of the four dimensions.

---

definitions

Power distance *(PD) is the extent to which an unequal distribution of power is accepted by members of a society.*

Uncertainty avoidance *(UA) is how much members of a society are threatened by uncertain and ambiguous situations.*

Individualism–collectivism *(I) is the tendency to take care of oneself and one's family versus the tendency to work together for the collective good.*

Masculinity–femininity *(M) is the extent to which highly assertive masculine values predominate (acquisition of money at the expense of others) versus showing sensitivity and concern for others' welfare.*

The *power distance dimension* assessed the degree to which the culture encouraged bosses to exercise their power. In countries that ranked high on power distance, such as Argentina and Spain, inequality was accepted and managers were actually expected to act in a powerful manner. Relationships between superiors and subordinates in this type of culture are characterized by low trust with the latter avoiding disagreement, and preferring to be directed by the boss who both takes the decisions and carries the responsibility. In low power cultures, such as Australia and Canada, the relationships between individuals at different levels in the hierarchy were close. A more collegial relationship existed, with greater mutual trust being possible, and employees expecting to be involved in decision-making.

The *uncertainty-avoidance dimension* identified the degree to which a culture encouraged or discouraged risk-taking. The research revealed differences in people's attitudes to risk in different countries, as well as their ability to tolerate ambiguity. Japan, Iran and Turkey were three of several countries which were high on uncertainty avoidance. People could reduce the high levels of anxiety and stress caused by uncertain situations by working hard, avoiding changing jobs and becoming intolerant of those who did not follow the rules. In contrast, people in low uncertainty-avoidance cultures, such as Pakistan and Taiwan, experienced less stress from ambiguous situations, and did not attach as much importance to rule-following.

The *individualism–collectivism dimension* assessed the extent to which the culture emphasized individualist as opposed to group concerns. In individualist cultures, such as Britain and the United States, the identification was with the individual. Stress was placed on individual performance, achievement, initiative and assessment. An individual's concern only extended to himself and his immediate family. Collectivist cultures in contrast, such as the Philippines and Singapore, emphasized wider loyalties to the extended family and to the tribe. In this close framework, the individual received support and protection in return for giving loyalty.

The *masculinity–femininity dimension* distinguished what kind of achievements were valued. In masculine or 'macho' cultures, such as Italy and South

Africa, stress was placed on money, material possessions and ambitions. The more of each of these you had the better. Hofstede also found a high level of male–female role differentiation. In contrast, in feminine cultures, exemplified by the Netherlands and the Scandinavian countries, the emphasis was placed on the environment, quality of life and caring. There was greater flexibility in gender roles and greater equality between the sexes.

Using these dimensions, Hofstede located forty countries on his cultural map of the world. These are shown in the following figure. Each of the four dimensions represents a continuum so that each country is located somewhere along each one, and not necessarily just at the extremes. The values represent averages, so whilst the data may be valid at the cultural level, they still acknowledge individual differences. Hofstede's work stresses the importance of

classifying cultures by the dimensions

I **more developed Latin**	II **less developed Latin**	
high power distance	high power distance	
high uncertainty avoidance	high uncertainty avoidance	
high individualism	high individualism	
medium masculinity	whole range on masculinity	
Belgium	Columbia	
France	Mexico	
Argentina	Venezuela	
Brazil	Chile	
Spain	Peru	
	Portugal	
	Yugoslavia	

III **more developed Asian**	IV **less developed Asian**	V **near Eastern**
medium power distance	high power distance	high power distance
high uncertainty avoidance	low uncertainty avoidance	high uncertainty avoidance
medium individualism	low individualism	low individualism
high masculinity	medium masculinity	medium masculinity
Japan	Pakistan	Greece
	Taiwan	Iran
	Thailand	Turkey
	Hong Kong	
	India	
	Philippines	
	Singapore	

VI **Germanic**	VII **Anglo**	VIII **Nordic**
lower power distance	low power distance	low power distance
high uncertainty avoidance	low to medium	low to medium
medium individualism	uncertainty avoidance	uncertainty avoidance
high masculinity	high individualism	medium individualism
Austria	high masculinity	low masculinity
Israel	Australia	Denmark
Germany	Canada	Finland
Switzerland	Britain	The Netherlands
South Africa	Ireland	Norway
Italy	New Zealand	Sweden
	USA	

from International Perspectives, T244, Unit 16, Block V, Wider Perspectives, *Managing in Organizations*, Open University, 1985, p. 60.

cultural differences in all aspects of organizational behaviour – motivation, group behaviour, leadership style, conflict management, and many others.

The classification is arranged according to the four dimensions, together with the summary names allocated to them. The forty countries are arranged in eight culture areas according to a statistical technique known as 'cluster analysis'. This forms clusters by placing together countries which are most alike as possible, whilst being as different as possible from other ones. Remember that these clusters were formed entirely on the basis of answers to questions on the four work values, and the scores were calculated from these. The area names were given after the clusters had emerged from the analysis.

STOP!

If your class contains students from different countries, or who have worked in different countries, group yourself according to some of the eight cultural cluster areas shown in the figure on p. 537.

Each group should identify specific examples of practices, norms and rituals, etc., from the work and non-work fields of their country of origin or work experience, which illustrate any of the four dimensions identified by Hofstede.

---

assessment

In order to introduce the concept of corporate culture, this chapter adopted an integrationist paradigm. A paradigm is a point of view used by researchers, managers or employees to understand a situation. A paradigm provides a guide that determines both what we attend to and notice, and equally what we do not attend to, and hence fail to notice. This integrationist paradigm is not the only one available, and in this final section we contrast it with two other perspectives. The *differentionist* and *fragmentationist* paradigms will be offered as alternative ways of viewing and understanding corporate culture.

This section draws heavily on the work of Joanne Martin, conducted in association with her colleague (Meyerson and Martin, 1987; Martin, 1992). Martin explains the failure of corporate culture writers to summarise what has been learned as being due to their vehement disagreements on four fundamental questions:

1 Is culture a source of harmony, an effect of irreducible conflicts of interests, or a reflection of the inescapable ambiguities that pervade contemporary organizational life?
2 Must culture be something internally consistent, integrative and shared? Or can it be inconsistent and expressive of difference? Can it incorporate confusion, ignorance, paradox and fragmentation?
3 What are the boundaries around culture(s) in organizations? Are boundaries essential?
4 How do cultures change?

As a way of moving forward from this controversy, Martin does not synthesize the existing writings, but instead organizes them into three distinct schools or perspectives. Rejecting the idea that one is better or more accurate than another, she sees each as offering a unique and valuable insight into the

multinational firm runs into customs barrier

Cultural differences present a much greater problem than language for companies setting up multinational teams or expanding into foreign countries. Neale and Mindel looked at problems in a new British Petroleum office in Brussels which contained forty staff from thirteen countries. BP asked them to provide training that would make employees of different nationalities appreciate differences in the way they approached their work and to make allowances. Despite a year of training to overcome cultural differences, the misunderstandings still persisted. They ranged from the fundamental to the trivial, and confirmed previously held stereotypes.

They found that while a British member of the team considered working late to be a sign of loyalty and enthusiasm, a Scandinavian thought that it showed inefficiency or incompetence. Another potential area for misunderstanding came with rank. The survey revealed that a French executive would expect authority to come naturally with office, and would be horrified to have his judgement challenged. In contrast, managers from Britain, Scandinavia and the Netherlands expected to have their decisions questioned or at least discussed. Indeed, Dutch managers wanted to discuss more than other nationalities and were most concerned about being able to express their opinions. They were most relaxed about management style and happy for subordinates to go to managers above them for help.

The Germans were most anxious that whatever decisions were arrived at, were put into operation quickly. They insisted on a more hierarchical management structure, and when invited to seek advice or opinions from more senior managers, they suspected that they were being 'set up'. The Americans were surprised to find their French colleagues wanting to shake hands every morning, considering it to be excessively formal for day-to-day greetings. The French, on the other hand, considered it to be 'simple friendliness'. The BP team developed their own set of ground rules for interacting with one another at work. These so-called, 'multi-cultural action points' included:

▶ Do not pre-judge people, functions or cultures.
▶ Create a climate where people are not embarrassed to ask.
▶ Give time to express yourself.
▶ You are talking to a person not a country.
▶ Give and ask for feedback.
▶ Accept the differences.
▶ Avoid clique building.
▶ Try to eliminate stereotyping.

Neale and Mindel concluded that building multi-national teams was a venture that should be undertaken with the utmost thought and planning. Although it could be achieved, given time and encouragement, it usually took longer for a multinational team to become effective than a monocultural one. When they did perform well, they performed exceptionally well. Neale and Mindel's advice to those establishing multi-cultural offices was to encourage staff to accept differences in approaches, prevent cliques developing, and to make more jokes!

based on Rosemary Neale and Richard Mindel, 1992, 'Rigging up multicultural teamworking', *Personnel Management*, January, pp. 36–9.

effect of corporate culture on the behaviour of people in organizations. She labels the perspectives *integration, differentiation* and *fragmentation.*

distinguishing characteristics of three perspectives on corporate cultural

perspective	integration	differentiation	fragmentation
orientation to consensus	organization-wide consensus	subcultural consensus	multiplicity of views (no consensus)
relation among manifestations	consistency	inconsistency	complexity (neither clearly consistent nor inconsistent)
orientation to ambiguity	exclude it	channel it outside subcultures	focus on it
metaphors	clearing in jungle, monolith, hologram	islands of clarity in sea of ambiguity	web, jungle

from Martin (1992, p. 13).

integrationist perspective on culture

The integration perspective or paradigm holds that culture is manifested in a company's values. It ignores evidence of dissent among employees and makes little reference to ambiguity in the workplace. Culture is seen as an integrating mechanism, the social glue that holds a potentially diverse group of organizational employees together. Integration-focused researchers (integrationists) look for anything that is 'shared' by members. They concentrate on common language, shared values and agreed on, appropriate behaviours. There are four essential features of the integration perspective: organization-wide consensus amongst cultural members, consistency across cultural manifestations, clarity of interpretation and meaning, and a focus on leaders as culture creators.

---

definition

Integrationist cultural perspective *sees culture as a monolith, characterized by consistency, organization-wide consensus and clarity. It holds that these integrating features will lead to improved organizational effectiveness through greater employee commitment and employee control, as measured by productivity and profitability.*

based on Martin (1992, p. 61).

---

organization-wide consensus

Integrationists begin with a statement of the values or basic assumptions which they find inside the organization. They tacitly assume, assert or occasionally empirically demonstrate that employees from different departments and hierarchical levels in the company all share a similar viewpoint about the same corporate values. Amongst the values commonly emphasized in integration studies is egalitarianism. This is manifested in employees being involved in a profit-sharing programme; empowerment and delegation downwards; horizontal as well as upward promotion; informal practices like 'Management by Walking About'; and the use of rituals such as training courses and award ceremonies. Related values often include innovation and employee well-being. The emphasis is on a one-culture company world from which doubt, uncertainty and collective dissent have successfully been banished.

consistency

Integrationists give the impression that the dominant cultural values and assumptions which constantly manifest themselves within the company are all consistent with one another. They do this by the simple method of focusing on consistent manifestations only while ignoring inconsistent ones. Three types of consistency are demonstrated. *Action consistency* occurs when a value like innovation encouragement is matched by management behaviour. For example, publicly recognizing those who produce new ideas. *Symbolic consistency* occurs when the symbolic meanings of cultural forms like stories, rituals and language are congruent with content themes – for example, egalitarian values symbolized by a single cafeteria for all employees. Finally, *content consistency*, when corporate values are consistent with each other – for example, encouraging innovation can be consistent with valuing egalitarianism.

clarity and denial of ambiguity

By recognizing only those values that are shared, and cultural manifestations that are consistent with each other, integrationists define culture as that which is clear. They see cultures as 'existing to alleviate anxiety, to control the uncontrollable, to bring predictability to the uncertain, and to clarify the ambiguous' (Martin, 1992, p. 51). Employees are said to understand intuitively what they are to do and why this is important. When different employees all interpret and 'make sense' of things in the same way, and all arrive at common 'correct' solutions to previously ambiguous problems, they increase harmony and predictability of collective behaviour within the organization.

leader's role in culture

Integrationists stress the role of original company founders and later leader-managers, as the creators, transformers and transmitters of a vision that enacts a culture. Often that vision is based on the leader's own value system and charisma. The leader is seen as capable of inspiring intense employee loyalty and commitment, resulting in increased productivity and profits. Those same individuals are seen as playing a dominant role in establishing, maintaining and renewing a stable, unified corporate culture. Their charisma may be institutionalized in the culture as an organizational form of immortality.

Martin (1992) argues that the integrationist perspective has become the dominant view of organizational researchers and practitioners in the United States. The perspective, which sees culture as a variable to be manipulated, offers the possibility of managerial control, worker commitment and organizational effectiveness. Moreover, its leader-centred, activist emphasis has also made it appealing to managers in general, and high-ranking executives in particular. It is so dominant that it is seen by some as being the *only* perspective on corporate culture. Amongst the well-established authors who write from the integration perspective are Schein (1986), Ouchi (1981) and Ouchi and Jaegar (1978).

differentiation perspective on culture

The differentiation approach emphasizes difference and diversity. A company is seen as consisting of sub-cultures which coexist, 'sometimes in harmony, sometimes in conflict, and sometimes in indifference to one another' (Martin, 1992, p. 83). The perspective emphasizes power, conflict and the differences of interests and opinions among different groups. Differentiationists study a lack of consensus, inconsistencies and non-leader-initiated aspects of culture. They acknowledge the elements of a dominant culture and the existence of similarities, consistencies and unities that are highlighted by integrationists. They just choose to focus primarily on inconsistencies and sub-culture differences, where consensus is absent.

---

definition

Differentiationist cultural perspective *sees each company sub-culture as being a fenced-in island of localized consensus, beyond which ambiguity reigns. Attention is paid particularly to cultural manifestations that are not consistent with each other, and this reduces the complexity of understanding culture to a series of dichotomies. In conflict situations things are clear enough for cultural members to know that they disagree on particular issues or interpretations. There is no agreement among differentiationists as to whether a particular cultural arrangement improves organizational effectiveness.*

based on Martin (1992, p. 103).

This differentiation perspective focuses on those things that are dissimilar rather than similar. It sees culture as being formed by influences from both inside and outside of the organization; and views the relations between different sub-culture groups as always being hierarchical and never neutral. That is, one group in relation to another either possesses or lacks power; either enables or prohibits actions; and is either superior or subordinate. This oppositional mode of thinking is a feature of this perspective. Its defining elements are inconsistency, sub-cultural consensus and sub-culture boundary clarity–peripheral ambiguity. It emphasizes disagreements rather than consensus. Three features distinguish the differentiation perspective from the others.

Differentiationists stress inconsistency by emphasising that the cultural practices and forms that exist in companies are interpreted differently by different company employees, and not always in the way intended by top management culture-planners. Inconsistency occurs when a cultural manifestation, such as a profit-sharing programme, is interpreted in different ways by different groups of employees. For example, one group may see it as a sign of egalitarianism, whilst another considers it to be a bribe for compliance.

As mentioned in the previous section, three types of inconsistency may be present. *Action inconsistency*, when a corporate value such as promotion on merit is actually made on the basis of who-you-know. *Symbolic inconsistency*, when the company has a value which emphasizes co-operation and team-work, yet the language of its employees is regularly peppered with metaphors of violent conflict. Finally, there is *ideological inconsistency* when corporate values conflict with each other, for example, when the priority given to a concern with employees' well-being conflicts with that of maximizing shareholder value.

sub-culture boundary consensus

A second feature of the differentiation approach is the stress on consensus, not at the organizational, but at the sub-cultural boundary level. Typically, differentiationists describe the dominant culture as articulated by top management, and then go on to examine the inconsistencies at the organizational level. The sub-culture differences among lower-level employees are studied in detail, and two most dominant, yet contrasting sub-cultures may be compared in some depth.

sub-culture boundary clarity and peripheral ambiguity

The final feature that distinguishes differentiation-based culture research is its orientation to ambiguity. Within each sub-culture, there is a coherent meaning system. This provides clear solutions to the problems that are common to sub-culture group members. Within that sub-culture boundary, clarity operates and ambiguity is relegated to the periphery.

Differentiation research focuses on each sub-culture identified within an organization, as possessing cultural manifestations that either are or are not consistent with each other. Those within the 'fenced-in' sub-cultures share a common perspective, whereas for those outside, chaos reigns, ambiguities abound. Martin argues that the popularity of the differentiation perspective is affected by the tendency of people to value that which unifies and devalue that which differentiates. This approach to culture reflects the views of groups of organizational members who lack either power or status, and hence has not been prominent in the managerial literature, and is more a feature of labour process studies. Contributors to the differentiation perspective include Smirchich and Morgan (1982) and Riley (1983).

fragmentation perspective on culture

Corporate culture studies conducted from a fragmentation perspective stress ambiguity rather than consistency (as do integrationists) or inconsistency (as do differentiationists), and in so doing reject the notion of either a company-wide or sub-cultural set of shared, integrated values. Instead, there is a shared awareness of ambiguity. Ambiguity is an internal state in which a person feels confused. Such confusion occurs when what employees see around them in the company is unclear, inexplicable or capable of several interpretations. This type of ambiguity may be resolved by the provision of information, but other types may be unresolvable, and an employee has to embrace two or more meanings. Fragmentalists hold that the dominant feature of organizational life is ambiguity – not as a temporary state on the way to attaining a new vision of clarity, but as a permanent and continuing situation of 'how things are'.

---

definition

Fragmentation *as a cultural perspective sees culture as a loosely structured and incompletely shared system that emerges dynamically as cultural members experience each other, events and the organization's contextual features.*

based on Martin (1992, p. 152).

Fragmentationists argue that companies lack clear centres owing to decentralization and delegation; and employ temporary and part-time workers who interact with changing contractors and customers. These actions blur the distinctions between company insiders and outsiders. Work arrangements determined by technological developments and commercial considerations leave employees physically separated, and their fleeting and superficial social interactions leave them socially distanced. From the fragmentation perspective, the organizational world is characterized by distance, obscurity, disorder and uncontrollability. It stands in contrast to the integrationist perspective which emphasizes a clear delineation of who belongs where; uses a socialization programme to transform selected outsiders into insiders; and sees work arrangements as continually bonding old and new members within a shared culture. For the integrationists, the organizational world is characterized by closeness, clarity, order and predictability.

Fragmentationists see ambiguity occurring in different forms. *Action ambiguity* occurs when employees are unclear between a company's espoused values, for example, with respect to employee well-being and its benefits policies. The confusion may have been due to their ignorance of the policy instigators or the complexity of the policies themselves. Whatever the reason, the employees reacted with confusion and were unable to act. *Symbolic ambiguity* holds that there are no clearly consistent or inconsistent relationships between cultural themes like employee well-being and cultural forms like jokes, physical arrangements or organizational stories. The relationship may be difficult to decipher because it is obscure or indistinct. *Ideological ambiguity* is expected in this perspective. The relationships between the content themes of culture are unclear and do not provide a clarifying ideology.

The fragmentation perspective portrays culture as neither harmonious nor full of conflict. Employees share some viewpoints, disagree on others and are indifferent to yet others. What occurs is a mixture of consensus, disagreement and indifference. Such confusion makes it difficult to draw cultural or sub-culture boundaries. Fragmentationism offers a new way of understanding cultural phenomena. It is the newest approach in corporate culture research, and so far has attracted the least number of studies. It is a perspective that offers no comfort for either academics or managers who seek clarity (Cohen *et al.*, 1982; Becker, 1982).

Each cultural paradigm emphasizes some aspects of organizational behaviour and de-emphasizes others. The integrationist/organizations-have-cultures paradigm draws attention to what company employees have in common. The differentiationist perspective/metaphor perspective stresses the deviations, adaptations from the dominant culture, and how it is affected by environmental factors. Finally, the fragmentist/metaphor view emphasizes the dynamic, paradoxical and confusion of enacted culture, and how uncontrollable the changes in organizations may be. Martin argued that all three had a role to play in understanding the complex relationship between an organization's culture and the behaviour of people within it. Is this offering a 'no culture' culture perspective? Feldman (1991, p. 54) offers a clarification:

> culture does not necessarily imply a uniformity of values. Indeed quite different values may be displayed by people of the same culture. In such an instance, what is it that holds together the members of the organization? I suggest that we look to the existence of a common frame of reference or a shared recognition of relevant issues . . . [individuals may] array themselves differently with respect to that issue, but whether positively or negatively, they are all oriented to it.

The following figure depicts the extent to which the three perspectives each see the three values of well-being, innovation and egalitarianism as being shared by members within an organization. The integrationist view shows the greatest degree of consensus by function and by hierarchical level. The differentiationist view emphasizes that sub-cultures exist, and that these are organized by function and hierarchical level. Within each sub-culture values are shared, but these are different from the values of other sub-cultures.

contrasting perspectives on corporate culture depicted in terms of how each views three sets of values being viewed by employees in different functions and at different hierarchical levels

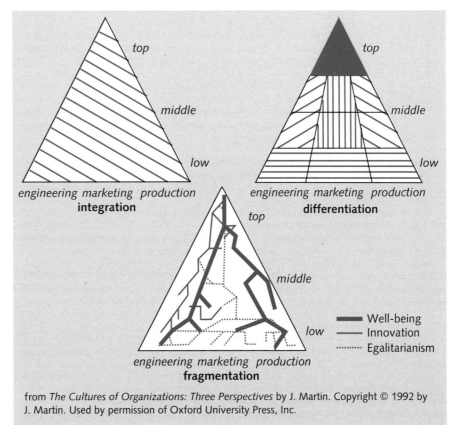

from *The Cultures of Organizations: Three Perspectives* by J. Martin. Copyright © 1992 by J. Martin. Used by permission of Oxford University Press, Inc.

Finally, the fragmentationalist view questions the existence of any shared values.

sources

Anthony, P.D., 1994, *Managing Culture*, Open University Press, Milton Keynes.

Barley, S. 1983, 'Semiotics and the study of occupational and organizational cultures', *Administrative Science Quarterly*, vol. 28, pp. 393–414.

Barnard, C., 1938, *The Functions of the Executive*, Harvard University Press, Cambridge, MA.

Beaumont, P.B., 1993, *Human Resource Management: Key Concepts and Skills*, Sage, London.

Becker, H., 1982, 'Culture: A sociological view', *Yale Review*, vol. 71, pp. 513–27.

Buono, A.F., Bowditch, J.L. and Lewis, J.W., 1985, 'When cultures collide: The anatomy of a merger', *Human Relations*, vol. 38, no. 5, pp. 477–500.

Cohen, M., March, J. and Olsen, J., 1982, 'A garbage can model of organizational choice', *Administrative Science Quarterly*, vol. 17, pp. 1–25.

Deal, T.E. and Kennedy, A.A., 1982, *Corporate Cultures: The Rites and Rituals of Corporate Life*, Addison-Wesley, Reading, MA.

Durheim, E., 1933, *The Division of Labour in Society*, Free Press, New York.

Feldman, M., 1991, 'The meanings of ambiguity: learning from stories and metaphors', in P. Frost, L. Moore, M. Louis, C. Lundberg and J. Martin (eds.), *Reframing Organizational Culture*, Sage, Newbury Park, CA, pp. 145–56.

Fombrun, C.J., 1984, 'Corporate culture and competitive strategy', in C.J. Fombrun, N.M. Tichy and M.A. Devanna (eds.), *Strategic Human Resource Management*, John Wiley, New York.

Furnham, A. and Gunter, B., 1993, 'Corporate culture: Definition, diagnosis and change', in C.L. Cooper and I.T. Robertson (eds.), *International Review of Industrial and Organizational Psychology*, John Wiley and Sons, Chichester.

Gregory, K.L., 1983, 'Native view paradigms: Multiple cultures and culture conflicts in organizations', *Administrative Science Quarterly*, vol. 28, no. 3, pp. 359–76.

Hales, C., 1993, *Managing Through Organization*, Routledge, London.

Hewlett-Packard, 1989, *The HP Way*, Hewlett-Packard Company, USA.

Hofstede, G., 1984, *Culture's Consequences: International Differences in Work-related Values*, Sage, Beverly Hills, CA.

Hofstede, G., 1986, 'Editorial: The usefulness of the concept of organizational culture', *Journal of Management Studies*, vol. 23, no. 3, pp. 253–7.

Hofstede, G., 1991, *Cultures and Organizations*, McGraw-Hill, Maidenhead.

Hofstede, G., 1994, *Uncommon Sense about Organizations*, Sage, Beverly Hills, CA.

Jay, A., 1970, *Management and Machiavelli*, Penguin Books, Harmondsworth.

Kanter, R.M., 1985, *The Change Masters: Corporate Entrepreneurs*, Allen & Unwin, London.

Kilmann, R.H. and Saxton, M.J., 1983, *Kilmann–Saxton Culture Gap Survey*, Organizational Design Consultants, Pittsburgh, PA.

Kilmann, R.H., Saxton, M.J. and Serpa, R., 1986, 'Introduction: Five key issues in understanding and managing culture', in R.H. Kilmann, M.J. Saxton and R. Serpa (eds.), *Gaining Control of the Corporate Culture*, Jossey-Bass, San Francisco, pp. 1–16.

Laurent, A. 1989, 'A cultural view of organizational change', in P. Evans, Y. Doz and A. Laurent (eds.), *Human Resource Management in International Firms*, Macmillan, Basingstoke, pp. 83–94.

Legge, K., 1995, *Human Resource Management: Rhetorics and Realities*, Macmillan, Basingstoke.

Martin, J., 1985, 'Can organizational culture be managed?', in P.J. Frost, L.F. Moore, M.R. Louis *et al.* (eds.), *Organizational Culture*, Sage, Beverly Hills, CA, pp. 95–8.

Martin, J., 1992, *Cultures in Organizations: Three Perspectives*, Oxford University Press, Oxford.

Mayo, E., 1933, *The Human Problems of an Industrial Civilization*, Macmillan, New York.

Mayo, E., 1945, *The Social Problems of an Industrial Civilization*, Harvard University Press, Cambridge, MA.

Meek, V.L., 1988, 'Organizational culture: Origins and weaknesses', *Organizational Studies*, vol. 9, no. 4, pp. 453–73.

Meyerson, D. and Martin, J., 1987, 'Cultural change: An integration of three different views', *Journal of Management Studies*, November, vol. 24, no. 6, pp. 623–47.

Morgan, G., 1986, *Images of Organization*, Sage, London.

Morgan, G., Frost, J. and Pondy, L., 1983, 'Organizational symbolism', in L. Pondy, P. Frost, G. Morgan and T. Dandridge (eds.), *Organizational Symbolism*, JAI Press, Greenwich, CT, pp. 55–65.

Ouchi, W., 1981, *Theory Z*, Addison-Wesley, Reading, MA.

Ouchi, W. and Jaeger, A., 1978, 'Type Z organization: Stability in the midst of mobility', *Academy of Management Review*, vol. 3, p. 305.

Pascale, R.T., 1985, 'The paradox of corporate culture: Reconciling ourselves to socialization', *California Management Review*, vol. 27, pp. 26–41.

Pascale, R.T. and Athos, A.G., 1981, *The Art of Japanese Management*, Penguin Books, Harmondsworth.

Peters, T.J. and Waterman, R.H., 1982, *In Search of Excellence*, Harper & Row, New York.

Pettigrew, A., 1986, *The Awakening Giant*, Basil Blackwell, Oxford.

Ray, C.A., 1986, 'Corporate culture: The last frontier of control?', *Journal of Management Studies*, vol. 23, pp. 287–97.

Riley, P., 1983, 'A structuralist account of political cultures', *Administrative Science Quarterly*, vol.28, pp. 414–37.

Ritzer, G., 1993, *The McDonaldization of Society*, Pine Forge Press, Newbury Park, CA.

Robbins, S.P., 1996, *Organizational Behaviour: Concepts, Controversies, Applications*, Prentice Hall, Englewood Cliffs, NJ, 7th edition.

Saffold, G., 1978, 'Culture traits, strength, and organizational performance; Moving beyond the "strong" culture', *Academy of Management Review*, vol. 13, pp. 546–58.

Schein, E.H., 1983, 'The role of the founder in creating organizational culture', *Organizational Dynamics*, Summer, pp. 13–28.

Schein, E.H., 1984, 'Coming to a new awareness of organizational culture', *Sloan Management Review*, Winter, pp. 3–16.

Schein, E.H., 1985a, 'How culture forms, develops and changes', in R.H. Kilmann, M.J. Saxton and R. Serpa (eds.), *Gaining Control of the Corporate Culture*, Jossey-Bass, San Francisco, pp. 17–43.

Schein, E.H., 1985b, *Organizational Culture and Leadership*, Jossey-Bass, San Francisco.

Schein, E., 1986, 'What you need to know about organizational culture', *Training and Development Journal*, vol. 40, no. 1, pp. 30–3.

Schein, E.H., 1991, 'What is culture', in P. Frost *et al.*, *Reframing Organizational Culture*, Sage, London.

Scholz, C., 1987, 'Corporate culture and strategy – the problem of strategy fit', *Long Range Planning*, vol. 20, no. 4, pp. 78–87.

Smirchich, L., 1983, 'Concepts of culture and organizational analysis', *Administrative Science Quarterly*, vol. 28, no. 3, pp. 339–58.

Smirchich, L. and Morgan, G., 1982, 'Leadership: The management of meaning', *Journal of Applied Behavioural Science*, vol. 18, pp. 257–73.

Trice, H.M. and Beyer, J.M., 1984, 'Studying organizational cultures through rites and rituals', *Academy of Management Review*, vol. 9, pp. 453–69.

Van Maanen, J. and Barley, S., 1984, 'Occupational communities: culture and control in organizations', in B. Staw and L.L. Cummings (eds.), *Research in Organizational Behaviour*, vol. 6, JAI Press, Greenwich, CT, pp. 287–366.

Van Maanen, J. and Schein, E.H., 1979, 'Toward a theory of organizational socialization', *Research Organization Behaviour*, vol. 1, pp. 209–64.

Weick, K.. 1979, *The Social Psychology of Organizing*, Addison-Wesley, Reading, MA, 2nd edition.

Whyte, W.H., 1956, *The Organization Man*, Simon & Schuster, New York.

technology as a trigger of change

ALL PROGRESS IS BASED ON FAULTY ASSUMPTIONS

© United Feature Syndicate, Inc.

concepts and learning objectives
definitions and predictions
determinism or choice?
the politics of technology
characteristics of mass production
socio-technical systems analysis and design
team versus lean: competing socio-technical paradigms
advanced technology and the changing nature of work
assessment
sources

concepts and learning objectives

Technology in the second half of the twentieth century has come to be seen as a trigger for unemployment, and as a main cause of the deskilling and dehumanization of work. In support of this perception it is not difficult to find people who have been replaced by computers and robots, and not difficult to discover jobs that have been radically deskilled through computerization or automation. Technology has come to be viewed by some with deep scepticism and suspicion, and with apparent good cause.

In this chapter we shall develop two arguments that contradict that negative view. First, we shall argue that the employment effects of technological innovation are indeterminate and can be positive, by triggering demand for new and improved products and services. Second, we shall demonstrate how technology can have a skills upgrading effect rather than a deskilling one, and that the outcomes are dependent on how work is organized around technology.

Summarizing research into robots in manufacturing, Toby Wall concludes that:

> There is no doubt that robots can make a major contribution to manufacturing performance. Nevertheless, it has been recognized for some time that the full potential of robotic systems, as for other forms of advanced computer-based manufacturing technology, is often not realized. . . . Of . . . particular interest is the suggestion that suboptimal performance stems not so much from the inadequacies of the technology itself, but more from deficiencies in the associated work organization. . . . Precisely because [computerized systems] can be so effective when they are up and running, any operating problems, of which there are often many, become correspondingly more important. The key role for humans is to manage that production uncertainty so as to minimize its effects. In this regard, robotic systems reflect one of the '*ironies of automation*' more generally, that '*the more advanced the system, so the more crucial can be the contribution of the operator*'. (Wall, 1996, p. 163; emphasis added)

We shall argue that technology can trigger job creation and improvements in the quality of working life. Technology can trigger positive organizational development and change.

key concepts

apparatus	technique
organization	technological determinism
material technology	social technology
replacement mechanisms	compensatory mechanisms
autonomous work group	characteristics of mass production
system	open system
socio-technical system	human-centred manufacturing

learning objectives

When you have read this chapter, you should be able to define those key concepts in your own words, and you should also be able to:

1 Explain the different and contradictory uses of the term 'technology' and the causes of this confusion.

2 Explain why doom-laden predictions about the effects of technological innovation on jobs are potentially exaggerated.

3 Define the characteristics of mass production and identify organizational approaches for overcoming them.

4 Apply the socio-technical system perspective to organizational analysis and design, and explain why technology does not uniquely determine the organization of work.

5 Contrast what has come to be called the Scandinavian model of work organization, based on teams, with the Japanese model, which combines task fragmentation with group problem-solving.

6 Demonstrate how the consequences of technological innovation depend on the organization of work and not simply on technical capabilities.

definitions and predictions

We live in an age of technology. We live in a technological society. Our organizations are dependent on technology for their daily operation and for their survival. Our lives are shaped and conditioned by technological innovation. Most of the technology that we use today was unknown to and barely imagined by our parents. What will the next century offer us?

© Dave Brown/*The Sunday Times*, 21 June 1996, p. 3 (supplement).

These observations are meaningless unless we are clear what we mean by the term technology. Unfortunately, it is now used with such a wide range of meanings that it has become ambiguous. Alvin Toffler referred in 1970 to 'that great, growling engine of change – technology'. It has been fashionable for the past three decades to pronounce on 'technological implications'. Much of the concern, particularly in an organizational context, has been with developments in information technology. Despite the fact that computing has been with us since the 1940s, the term 'new technology' is still in daily use.

Langdon Winner (1977), an American commentator in this field, has demonstrated how our use of the term technology has changed as concern for 'technological implications' has grown. The term was commonly used in the eighteenth and nineteenth centuries, he argues, simply to refer to machines, tools, factories, industry, craft and engineering. However, the term today 'is now widely used in ordinary and academic speech to talk about an unbelievably diverse collection of phenomena – tools, instruments, machines, organizations, methods, techniques, systems, and the totality of all these things in our experience' (Winner, 1977, p. 8).

How has this confusion arisen? Rapid developments in technology leave the language behind. The word technology is simply a convenient umbrella term. Ambiguity in the use of the term thus reflects the pace of innovation, and the growing influence of and concern with technology and its consequences – individual, organizational and social. Winner also argues that this simplification of the language leads us to oversimplify and polarize the issues and arguments. Technology is either a good thing or a bad thing; you are either for it or against it.

We need a more precise definition. As Winner points out, a term that has come to mean everything and anything threatens to mean nothing. Winner identifies three distinct uses of the term 'technology': as apparatus, as technique and as organization.

---
definition

Apparatus *simply refers to physical, technical devices such as tools, instruments, machines, appliances, gadgets and weapons.*

Apparatus is probably still the most common conception of technology.

---
definition

Technique *refers to technical activities, such as skills, methods, procedures and routines.*

The Greek word *techne* means art, craft or skill. Apparatus is not purposive. Techniques are related to particular human or organizational goals.

---
definition

Organization *refers to social arrangements such as factories, bureaucracies, armies, research and development teams, and so on, created to achieve technical, rational, productive ends.*

When someone uses the term 'technology', they could be speaking about a physical device, a skill, a social arrangement or some combination of these factors. For example, one influential British researcher, Joan Woodward, defined technology in the following way:

> The specific technology of the organization is, then, the collection of plant, machines, tools and recipes available at a given time for the execution of the production task and the rationale underlying their utilization (Reeves, Turner and Woodward, 1970, p. 4).

Note the use of the terms 'recipe' and 'rationale' in this definition, and the way in which Winner's concepts of apparatus, technique and organization are combined here.

The British industrial sociologist Alan Fox (1974) suggested another way of looking at this issue. He makes a distinction between *material technology* and *social technology*.

---

definitions

Material technology *is the technology that can be seen, touched and heard.*

Social technology *is the technology which seeks to order the behaviour and relationships of people in systematic, purposive ways through structures of co-ordination, control, motivation and reward.*

Material technology is what Winner calls apparatus. Social technology is a combination of Winner's technique and organization and includes job definitions, payment systems, authority relationships, communications, control systems, disciplinary codes and 'all the many other rules and decision-making procedures which seek to govern what work is done, how it is done, and the relationships that prevail between those doing it' (Fox, 1974, p. 1).

Why devote so much time to unpicking the language of such a common term? Considerable research effort has been devoted to identifying the effects of technology on organizations, jobs and society at large. Technology has often been regarded as the independent variable – the factor whose effects are to be studied. Organization structures, job skill requirements, and quality of working life become dependent variables in this approach – variables that are expected to be changed in some way by technology. However, many definitions of technology seem to combine and overlap notions of the independent and dependent variables.

Many studies of technological implications in organizational behaviour can, in fact, be seen as attempts to plot the impact of material technologies on aspects of social technology. As the discussion of socio-technical systems design later in the chapter demonstrates, such a perspective may be seriously misguided. The degree of choice with respect to how the social technology is configured is not wholly constrained or determined by the material technology.

Advances in technology, and developments in computing and information technology in particular continue to attract predictions of disaster and doom. Does the evidence support these predictions? What impressions do media accounts offer in this domain?

> **STOP!**
>
> How have the media and academic works influenced your beliefs in the following statements about the implications of technology?
>
> ▹ Computers and robots will replace people in manufacturing; the 'unstaffed factory' is a reality.
> ▹ Office automation does away with clerical and administrative work; the 'paperless office' is here to stay.
> ▹ Robots will soon be able to do most things for us.
> ▹ Where people are still required, work will tend to be simple, routine, dehumanized.
> ▹ The days of craft skill and worker autonomy are gone.
>
> Compare your views with those of colleagues.

These predictions are all correct, in the sense that some jobs have indeed been eliminated by machinery, some work has indeed been dehumanized by technological change, much paperwork has been declared redundant and some traditional crafts have disappeared.

The popular media image claims that technology, particularly in the form of computing and information technology, will increase organizational productivity through what are known as *replacement mechanisms*, leaving many people unemployed as a result.

---

definition

Replacement mechanisms *are processes through which intelligent (or at least clever) machines are used to substitute for people in work organizations.*

Claims about the unemployment consequences of technology rely on the assumption that, as machines do more, people will be required to do less. Job opportunities are thereby reduced through replacement mechanisms; unemployment becomes chronic.

These unemployment fears date from the early nineteenth century, when Luddites destroyed the looms and spinning jennies that they felt were stealing their jobs. Why has technological development since then not dramatically confirmed those concerns?

Technological change and development this century has, broadly, been consistent with employment growth and stability. Despite complaints and concern in developed economies during the last years of the century, unemployment levels are not historically higher than in earlier decades, and there is certainly little proof of a technology-led fall in job opportunities.

The overall effects of technological developments depend on the operation not only of replacement mechanisms, but also of *compensatory mechanisms*.

---

definition

Compensatory mechanisms *are processes that delay or deflect replacement effects, and can also lead to the creation of new products and services, new organizations, new sectors and new jobs through technological innovation.*

"This used to take hours."

There are six main compensatory mechanisms:

1 the development of new products and services

Technological innovation has given us mobile telephones, video recorders, portable multimedia computers, the internet and electronic mail, cyber-cafés, electronic engine management systems in motor cars, remote video-conferencing, compact discs and their players, smart bankcards, and so on. These innovations create and shape patterns of consumer demand. This leads to investment in factories, offices and other infrastructure to provide these goods and services – and to the creation of jobs in their production and delivery.

2 lower costs increase demand

Technical innovation should improve productivity of existing operations. Higher productivity gives the same output for fewer resources, or a higher output with the same resources. The consequent reduction in cost can lead to lower prices and hence to increased demand for those items. This also means that consumers could have more money to spend on other goods and services, increasing demand and job opportunities elsewhere. It is not realistic to assume that consumer tastes and demands are static, although it may be difficult to predict changes.

3 time lags delay the implications

It takes time to build new technology into existing systems or into new products and services. Technical and organizational problems need to be overcome. These take time and other resources to resolve. Organizations rarely adopt technological innovations as soon as they become available, and it is expensive to replace existing facilities quickly. Significant investments in factories and offices cannot be written off overnight. Despite the common complaint about the rapid pace of change, technological and organizational change are in reality often slow.

4 hedging risk can also delay the implications

Most organizations turn to experimental and untested technologies slowly at first. The 'learning curve' with a new technology can be expensive, time-consuming, and painful. One way to carry these risks is to introduce technological innovation gradually and cautiously.

5 expectations of demand

Why should an organization embark on expensive technological innovation, accompanied by disruptive organizational change, unless the market for its goods and services is expected to expand? And if that is the case, then the organization will probably need to retain, if not expand, its existing work-force. Organizations which expect demand for their output to fall or remain stable are unlikely to invest in change, other than in an attempt to reverse those expectations.

6 technical limitations

New technologies do not always live up to the claims of those who sell them. They may, in fact, not be able to do everything that the 'old' technology was capable of doing. Existing jobs, skills and equipment may be found working alongside new devices for some time. It is still common to find 'old' electric typewriters in offices equipped with word processing equipment. It is still common to find 'old' machine tools in machine shops equipped with computer numerically controlled devices and flexible manufacturing systems. The 'old' technology, combined with 'old' human skills, can often perform some tasks more easily, faster and more effectively than new technology can achieve.

---

over-hyped utopia

Tom Forester offers this explanation for why the 'factory of the future' has failed to appear on a widespread scale:

> people got carried away with the utopian visions of automated factories, overlooking the high cost of high tech and the enormous complexity of factory operations. Robots were absurdly over-hyped: it was conveniently ignored that they are both much more expensive and less flexible than humans. As one commentator put it, 'Contrary to the early hype, it rarely makes business sense simply to replace a human worker with a robot and expect the machine to pay for itself in saved labour costs'. Much can be achieved by improving quality and product or inventory flow without resorting to this expensive high-tech 'fix' . . . a total machine take-over in factories no longer seems to be the goal. Rather, it is a common sense *partnership* between machine and man.

from Tom Forester (ed.), 1989, *Computers in the Human Context: Information Technology, Productivity and People*, Basil Blackwell, Oxford, p. 10.

"My own story's much the same, actually. Tired of the sickening materialism and soul-destroying routine of modern existence, I finally decided to give it all up and hit the open road, taking with me only the absolute bare necessities of life . . . "

Reproduced with permission of Punch Ltd.

It is unrealistic to assume that new technology and productivity increases, will simply increase unemployment. One factory run exclusively by robots does not mean that all manufacturing operations can function this way. It is equally plausible to argue that technological innovation could create as many jobs as it eliminates, and could create more. In other words, the effects of technology on employment are indeterminate, depending on the complex interrelationship between replacement and compensatory mechanisms, and their respective timing.

Some of the headlines thus appear to be wrong, and some of them are probably wildly incorrect. However we define 'technology', the implications for work, organizations and employment are complex and are not easy to predict. In this section, we have tried to demonstrate why the implications for employment are indeterminate. Later in the chapter we shall explore the implications for skill requirement and quality of working life. The implications here also turn out to be determined not by technology alone, but by choices concerning how work will be organized around technology.

determinism or choice?

Different technologies make different demands on those who work with them. The technology of an organization appears to determine the nature of work there. When we compare a hospital with a biscuit factory, or a retail store with a coal mine, it seems reasonable to argue that each organization's technology determines:

- the kinds of task that need to be done
- the design of jobs
- the organization of work and the grouping of jobs
- the hierarchy through which work is planned, co-ordinated and controlled
- the knowledge and skills required to perform the work
- the values and attitudes of the organization's employees

Does technology really determine these factors? Can we predict the shape of an organization, and the nature and content of jobs, from a knowledge of technology?

> **definition**
>
> **Technological determinism** *is the name given to the argument that technology can be used to explain the nature of jobs, work groupings, hierarchy, skills, values and attitudes in organizational settings.*

The determinist position assumes that work has to be organized to meet the requirements of the machinery. Different technologies have different 'technological imperatives'.

---

an early expression of technological determinism

This research started with the concept that every industrial job contained certain technologically determined task attributes which would influence the workers' response. By 'task attributes' we meant such characteristics of the job as the amount of variety, autonomy, responsibility, and interaction with others built into the design.

from A.N. Turner and P.R. Lawrence, 1965, *Industrial Jobs and the Worker: An Investigation of Response to Task Attributes*, Division of Research, Harvard Business School, Boston, MA.

The determinist position also presumes that technology is beyond human control, beyond social and cultural influence, and that technological innovation is a self-stimulating, self-perpetuating process with a logic of its own. Innovation encourages further innovation. From this perspective, organization design appears to be locked into an unassailable tyranny of technological demands. Organizations may also be forced into the adoption of new technology to maintain their competitive position against other users.

It is now widely accepted that technological determinism is an oversimplified and flawed perspective. Technology suggests and enables; technology does not merely determine. There are at least three broad areas of choice in the technological change process.

First, there are choices in the design of tools, machinery, equipment and systems. One area of choice appears to be the extent to which control of operations is built into the machine or left to human intervention and discretion. There are many instances of automatic controls being removed from aircraft cockpits, ships' bridges and railway engine cabs following the discovery that pilots and drivers lost touch with the reality of their tasks, surrounded by sophisticated controls which functioned without their understanding or help.

Second, there are choices in the goals that technology is used to achieve. Competitive pressure is one reason for technological innovation, and as David Preece (1995) demonstrates, this can be an overriding pressure. The needs to reduce costs, improve quality and customer service, and improve management information are key needs in many sectors. Managers also promote innovation for personal and political reasons, to enhance power over resources and influence over decisions, to enhance status and prestige, and to exert closer surveillance and control over employees.

Third, there are choices in the way work is organized around technology. Job design depends on management decisions as well as on the machinery in use. As explored later in this chapter, car assembly work can apparently be designed in a number of different ways, and it is not clear which of these approaches may be 'correct' or 'best'.

Technological determinism is weakened by choices over the design of technology, the goals behind its adoption and the organization of work around it. These choices depend more on the assumptions we make about human capabilities and organizational characteristics; they depend less on the capabilities of items of equipment. These are called 'psychosocial assumptions', because they relate to beliefs about the behaviour of individuals and groups in our organizations.

To consider the impact of a technology, therefore, is to consider the wrong question, or at best to consider only one aspect of the matter. Technological innovations trigger an organizational decision-making process which is driven by the assumptions and beliefs and perceptions and goals of those involved. It is the choices that are made in that process that determine the organizational consequences. Technology has a limited impact on people or performance in an organization independent of the purposes of those who would use it and the responses of those who have to work with it. The technological determinist argument seems weak; the organizational choices appear to be crucial.

We can summarize this argument using the terminology of independent and dependent variables introduced earlier. In exploring this causal relationship, we need to take into account the *mediating* factors – a decision-making process concerning the organization of work, and the psychosocial assumptions that underpin those decisions:

independent variables	mediating variables	dependent variables
▶ computing and information technologies, in manufacturing and office settings	▶ decisions about work organization ▶ the goals and psychosocial assumptions of decision makers	▶ job variety ▶ skill demands ▶ discretion, autonomy ▶ quality of work life ▶ individual performance

the politics of technology

The production demands of the Second World War increased awareness of the effects of job design and work organization on morale and productivity. The notion that good human relations alone could build a happy and productive workforce began to lose its appeal.

One critic of the human relations approach, the American sociologist Robert Merton argued in 1947 that technology had several social implications. He noted that technological change increased task specialization, took skill and identity from work, and increased discipline in the workplace. Merton's argument resurfaced in a somewhat different guise in the 1980s, following publication of a highly influential book by Harry Braverman: *Labor and Monopoly Capital: The Degradation of Work in the Twentieth Century*. That work triggered a 'labour process debate', which continues to generate a substantial and controversial literature. As with Merton, the central argument of Braverman and his supporters has been that advances in technology afford managers progressive opportunities to reduce skill and discretion in work, and to tighten management control.

---

humanization of work or work intensification?

The problem as it presents itself to those managing industry, trade, and finance is very different from the problem as it appears in the academic or journalistic worlds. Management is habituated to carrying on labour processes in a setting of social antagonism and, in fact, has never known it to be otherwise. Corporate managers have neither the hope nor the expectation of altering this situation by a single stroke: rather, they are concerned to ameliorate it only when it interferes with the orderly functioning of their plants, offices, warehouses and stores.

For corporate management this is a problem in costs and controls, not in the 'humanization of work'. It compels their attention because it manifests itself in absenteeism, turnover, and productivity levels that do not conform to their calculations and expectations. The solutions they will accept are only those which provide improvements in their labour costs and in their competitive positions domestically and in the world market.

from Harry Braverman, 1974, *Labor and Monopoly Capital: The Degradation of Work in the Twentieth Century*, Monthly Review Press, New York, p. 36.

This argument identifies technology as a political tool – as something that management uses to manipulate employees and conditions of work. This is a significant argument, because the apparatus of manufacturing and office activity is typically discussed as if it were politically neutral. However, if management can increase task specialization and reduce the level of skill required in a job, lower wages can be offered and the organization's dependence on particular groups and individuals is weakened. If management can increase the discipline in work, improve surveillance of work activities (perhaps through remote computer monitoring) and thus gain tighter control of employees, this enhances the potential for work intensification. Reduced skill and increased control mean less discretion for employees over work methods and other conditions.

The organization of work around a given technology can be used to control labour costs, to control decision-making scope and opportunities, to control the relative status of different groups in an organization, and to control promotion and career paths. Managers may be able to manipulate employees in these ways through appeals to the technological determinist argument: we have to do it this way because of the technology. Technological determinism can thus be used to justify unpopular management decisions and protect them from effective challenge. Those who want to argue just don't understand the technology.

Improved control can lead to lower costs and, in turn, to higher profits. Control also maintains the role and status of management – the controllers. Some of the 'implications' of 'technology' may thus be viewed instead as the result of management strategies to improve control through appropriate forms of work organization. The consequences of technical change are not simply the inescapable outcomes of the rigid demands of machinery.

Chapter 11 explored scientific management methods, developed around the turn of the century, but still applied today, and with some apparent success by Japanese motor manufacturing companies. Scientific management offers a rationale for task simplification and fragmentation, and thus for tighter management control. The scientific management method can thus become self-perpetuating. How? The typical response to specialized, repetitive work can simply confirm the management view that tight control of employees is necessary to maintain discipline and to produce goods and services effectively. Scientific management can become self-justifying through a 'vicious circle of control' (Clegg and Dunkerley, 1980), which looks like this:

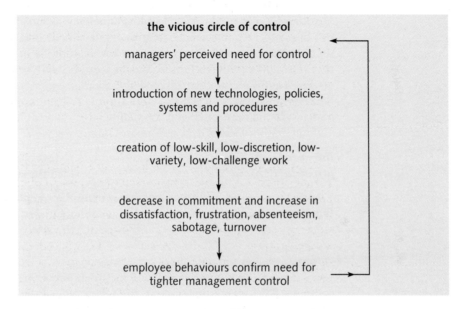

the vicious circle of control

managers' perceived need for control

↓

introduction of new technologies, policies, systems and procedures

↓

creation of low-skill, low-discretion, low-variety, low-challenge work

↓

decrease in commitment and increase in dissatisfaction, frustration, absenteeism, sabotage, turnover

↓

employee behaviours confirm need for tighter management control

This vicious circle can only be broken by a change in management perceptions, with higher trust in and higher discretion for employees. Braverman and his followers argue that such a change is unlikely in a capitalist economy. Technological determinism is thus replaced in this perspective by a gloomy and inevitable economic, political and technological logic.

characteristics of mass production

One of the first classic studies of the relationship between technology and the experience of work was that carried out by Charles Walker and Robert Guest. Their seminal book, *The Man on the Assembly Line*, was published in 1952. In it they argued, in a technological determinist mode, that some production technologies prevent the formation of work groups and frustrate the social needs of factory employees. Their attitude survey of 180 American automobile assembly workers identified six *characteristics of mass production work*:

---

definition

The **characteristics of mass production** *identified by Walker and Guest are:*
- *mechanical pacing of work*
- *no choice of tools or methods*
- *repetitiveness*
- *minute subdivision of product*
- *minimum skill requirement*
- *surface mental attention*

The jobs of the car workers were scored on each of these mass production characteristics. The workers said that they were happy with pay and working conditions. However, those in jobs with a high 'mass production score' disliked those aspects of their work and had a higher rate of absenteeism than those in low-scoring jobs.

Other studies in the 1950s produced similar results, and some managers did begin to recognize that scientific management principles had taken task specialization too far. Morris Viteles, for example, had argued in 1950 that the combination of increased mechanization and scientific management created routine, repetitive tasks. The resultant experience of monotony and boredom can reduce work rate and output, reduce morale, and also lead to high levels of absenteeism and complaints.

The 1950s solutions to boredom and monotony were:

job rotation Workers are switched from task to task at regular intervals.
job enlargement Tasks are recombined to widen the scope of a job.

The aim was to restore the variety that scientific management had eliminated. Job rotation and enlargement are still in use today. These early methods can reduce monotony and boredom and increase job variety, but they do this in a superficial way.

The first reported account of job enlargement was from Charles Walker in 1950. The project was carried out in the Endicott plant of the American company IBM on the initiative of the Chairman of the Board. In 1944, the jobs of the machine operators were enlarged to include machine set-up and inspection of finished product. These two jobs were previously done by other groups of workers. There is nothing in the technology of machining to prevent or discourage machine operators from accepting responsibility for these additional tasks.

The benefits of job enlargement at Endicott included improved product quality and a reduction in losses from scrap, less idle time for men and machines, and a 95 per cent reduction in set-up and inspection costs. This simple change had significant consequences.

Work with mass production characteristics can cause stress and illness, as well as boredom and monotony. Arthur Kornhauser's study of car assembly workers in Detroit, published in 1965, showed that low-grade factory work could lead to job dissatisfaction and poor mental health. The workers that he studied had a long list of grievances, including:

- low pay
- simplicity of job operations
- job insecurity
- repetitiveness and boredom
- poor working conditions
- lack of control over the work

- low status
- restricted promotion opportunities
- the style of the supervisors

- non-use of abilities
- feelings of futility

Workers in jobs with these characteristics had lower mental health, which meant that they:

- were anxious and tense
- had negative self-concepts
- were hostile to others

- were less satisfied with life
- were socially withdrawn
- suffered from isolation and despair

Each of these features alone does not imply much, as most of us have such feelings at some time regardless of the work we do. Kornhauser (1965) argued that work with mass production characteristics produces this *pattern* of psychological reactions. In a subsequent study, Karasek (1979) showed that the most stressful jobs were those which combined high workload with low discretion. Typical examples of such jobs included assembly workers, garment stitchers, goods and materials handlers, nursing aides and orderlies, and telephone operators. The main symptoms found in this study included exhaustion and depression (including nervousness, anxiety and sleeping difficulties).

Swedish carmakers were among the first to show that mass production characteristics can be avoided through other approaches to work organization. The Swedish Employers' Confederation, the Swedish Central Association of Salaried Employees and the Confederation of Manual Workers' Unions established a Union Management Development Council for Collaborative Questions in 1966. The Council's objective was to carry out experiments of various kinds aimed at improving both satisfaction and productivity.

By 1974, it was estimated that over 1000 such experiments had been started in Sweden, although many had failed and some were used for publicity purposes (Valery, 1974). The work organization movement in Sweden relied on the well-publicized projects of three companies in particular: Atlas Copco, Saab-Scania and Volvo. The organizational experiments of those companies remained management tourist attractions into the 1990s. Volvo received the most publicity in the organizational behaviour and management literature.

The Saab-Scania Group's experiments began in 1970. Forty production workers in the chassis shop of a new truck factory were divided into small production groups (Norstedt and Aguren, 1973). Group members were responsible for deciding how they would rotate between the different tasks, and also absorbed maintenance and quality control functions. The company set up 'development groups' which included a supervisor, a work study specialist and a number of operators. These groups met monthly and issued a report on their decisions, stating who was to be responsible for actions they recommended. These changes were designed to reduce labour turnover and absenteeism, and had the following results:

- The new work methods spread to the rest of the chassis works, affecting about 600 manual workers.
- Productivity increased.
- Unplanned stoppages of production were significantly reduced.
- Costs were reduced to 5 per cent below budget.
- Product quality improved.

---

job enlargement: the Linn Products experience

Linn Products Limited was founded in 1973, near Glasgow, to manufacture high quality, specialist hi-fi equipment, including amplifiers, record decks, compact disc players and speakers. The company was nominated in 1990 by the British Institute of Management as one of the country's most advanced manufacturers.

Linn initially used a traditional assembly-line to make its products. However, as the business grew, problems arose over productivity, and delivery promises to customers were being broken too often. The company's founder and managing director, Ivor Tiefenbrun, explains how they changed their methods, following a late-night brainstorming session:

The next day I asked one of our assembly girls to go and get all the parts required to build a record player, build it and bring it into my office. Somewhat mystified, she did just that and returned about 17 minutes later. It took 27 minutes of labour to build the same item on our production line.

So we re-organized our factory. We eliminated 47 different main and buffer storage areas, went to a single store and a single-stage build where one responsible person builds the product from start to finish. To do this, we invested to create surplus capacity, so that we could pursue our objective of real-time manufacturing: to make what our customers want when they want it. Within six weeks we had made remarkable progress and three months later we were despatching the product the day the customer ordered it.

We now employ our home-grown principles of single-stage build and real-time manufacturing throughout our organization. This approach requires a higher skill level but is the route to a superior quality build. The actual output per employee on any specific product is irrelevant compared to the gain through improved labour flexibility.

The single-stage build method gives one person responsibility and control. Within the envelope of total time allocated to any particular task the individual has the freedom to take the time necessary over tasks which are difficult and to perform simpler tasks rapidly. No single component failure, instrument or plant failure or the non-appearance of any individual will necessarily have any impact on our ability to satisfy our customers' requirements. Pressure is removed from the manufacturing process and the person who builds, tests and packs his own product can take pride in his own workmanship and spot the connection between what he does, the way that product works and customer satisfaction.

Each employee on a conventional assembly-line has to work at the same pace as the others, so that the whole line operates in a 'balanced' manner. Single-stage build, or job enlargement, overcomes this problem, and offers more meaningful and varied work at the same time.

from Ivor Tiefenbrun, 1993, 'Manufacturing in the future', *RSA Journal*, July, p. 552.

▶ Labour turnover was cut over four years from 70 to 20 per cent.
▶ Absenteeism was not affected.
▶ Co-operation between management and workforce improved.

The best-known experiment at Saab began in 1972 in their engine factory at Sodertalje. The company decided to design a new factory layout and work organization from scratch. The layout consisted of an oblong conveyor loop which moved the engine blocks to seven assembly groups, each with three members. An island of potted plants enclosing a café with a telephone was placed alongside the assembly-line. Visitors noted the quiet, clean, relaxed and unhurried atmosphere (Thomas, 1974).

Each production group had its own U-shaped guide track in the floor, to the side of the main conveyor loop. Engine blocks were taken from the main track, were completely assembled by the group, and were then returned to the conveyor loop. The engine blocks arrived with their cylinder heads already fitted and the groups handled the final fitting of carburettors, distributors, spark plugs, camshafts and other components.

Each group assembled the complete engine and decided themselves how their work was allocated. The guide track for each group was not mechanically driven. The group simply had half an hour to build each engine, and the group decided how that time would be spent. Individual jobs on the conventional assembly track had cycle times of less than 2 minutes.

This form of organization is referred to as an *autonomous work group*.

---

definition

An **autonomous work group** *is a team of workers allocated to a significant segment of the workflow, with discretion concerning how the work will be carried out, and how tasks and responsibilities will be allocated, shared and rotated.*

Autonomous work groups are also known as self-regulating or self-managing groups or teams. It is useful, however, to remember that these labels apply to a wide range of organizational systems. Autonomous groups vary, in particular, on the dimension of autonomy. In some organizations, groups function in a highly independent manner in the absence of direct traditional supervision; elsewhere, the constraints imposed on group discretion seem to render the term 'autonomous' inappropriate.

This is similar to the *high performance work system* methods of Digital Equipment Corporation, discussed briefly in Chapter 4. This is also the approach adopted by Sweden's other carmaker, Volvo, until the early 1990s. Volvo's plant at Kalmar pioneered the concept of 'dock assembly', in which teams completed whole stages of the final car assembly process in bays to one side of the main moving assembly track, in a specially designed factory layout.

It was estimated in 1974 that Saab-Scania saved around 65,000 Swedish kroner a year on recruitment and training costs alone. Autonomous work groups were during the 1960s and 1970s part of the toolkit of the quality of the working life movement. During the 1980s and 1990s, such methods were increasingly challenged as ways to improve organizational responsiveness and flexibility. The challenge came from Japanese car manufacturers, who used a completely different production paradigm, examined later in this chapter.

socio-technical systems analysis and design

Swedish managers did not invent the idea of the autonomous work group. This was initially a product of the work of British researchers and consultants at the Tavistock Institute of Human Relations in London. It was the Tavistock influence on Norwegian industry in the 1970s that prompted Swedish managers to copy the example, with more publicity.

The Tavistock group developed the concept of the organization as a *system*. This apparently simple notion has a number of valuable implications.

---

definition

A **system** may be defined as something that functions by virtue of the interdependence of its component parts.

above:
Albert Kenneth Rice

right:
Eric Miller

The term *system* can be applied to a vast number of phenomena: solar system, nervous system, traffic management system, telecommunications system, waste disposal system. The problem with such a broad definition is that the term can be applied to almost anything. However, what one defines as a system depends entirely on where one defines the system *boundaries*. This in turn depends on what one wants to study, and why. It makes sense, therefore, to study the human perceptual system, the digestive system or the nervous system. In an organizational context, we may wish to analyze a performance management system, a product distribution system, a raw materials purchasing system or a production system. In other words, we can choose to focus on specific *sub-systems*.

The human organism and the organization share one important property. They are each dependent on their ability to conduct an exchange with their environments. We breathe air, consume food and drink, and absorb sensory information. We convert these imports into energy and action, disposing of waste products and expending energy in chosen behaviours. The organization, like the human body, is also an *open system*.

---

definition

An **open system** is a system that interacts, in a purposive way, with its external environment in order to survive.

Open systems import resources, such as people, materials, equipment, information and money. They transform those inputs in organizations through producing services and goods. They then export those products back into the environment, as goods and satisfied customers. This treatment of organizational behaviour in terms of living organisms is known as the 'organic analogy' (Rice, 1963; Miller and Rice, 1967).

Another interesting property of such open systems is their ability to reach a particular outcome from a variety of starting points and routes. The autonomous work group at Saab, for example, can assemble an engine in many different ways. A chemical reaction, on the other hand, is a closed system in which the end result depends on the concentrations and quantities of the items used to begin with.

This property is known as 'equifinality', and it has an interesting consequence for organizational design. Equifinality suggests that it is not necessary to specify in detail the organization structure and the duties of every member. If the organization as an open system can develop its own unique mode of operating, and change that as required by circumstances, then it will only be necessary to detail the basic and most significant aspects. This approach to organizational design is called 'minimum critical specification'.

above:
Fred Emery

right:
Eric Trist

We should thus expect to find that organizations, as open systems, are self-regulating, flexible and adaptable. Unlike closed systems which maintain or move towards states of homogeneity, organizations become more elaborate and diverse in structure in attempts to cope with their environment (Emery and Trist, 1960). Although almost half a century old, this argument sits comfortably with contemporary demands for organizations to become even more flexible and responsive in an increasingly turbulent world.

The Tavistock researchers developed systems thinking significantly beyond the ideas we have covered so far. One of their number, Eric Trist, introduced the idea that an organization can be considered not just as an open system, but as an open *socio-technical system*.

---

definition

A **socio-technical system** *is a system which possesses both a material technology and a social organization.*

The social system and the technical system in an organization clearly must interact and are interdependent. Trist argued that a social organization has social and psychological properties independent of the demands of technology. The socio-technical system concept can be illustrated like this:

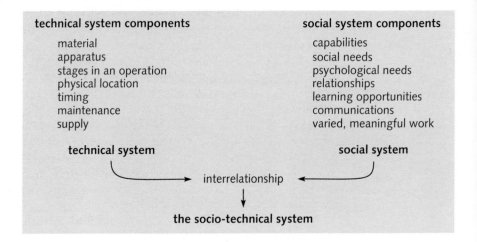

technical system components	social system components
material	capabilities
apparatus	social needs
stages in an operation	psychological needs
physical location	relationships
timing	learning opportunities
maintenance	communications
supply	varied, meaningful work

technical system → interrelationship ← **social system**

↓

the socio-technical system

The socio-technical system design problem lies in finding the 'best fit' between the social and technical components. Trist and his colleagues argued, however, that an effective socio-technical system design could never fully satisfy the needs of either sub-system. This 'sub-optimization' is a necessary feature of good socio-technical design. There are trade-offs which must be accepted. Clearly a system designed with an emphasis on social needs and ignoring technical system needs could quickly run into technical problems. Conversely, a system designed according only to the demands of technology could be expected to generate social and organizational difficulties. What is required is a design approach aimed at 'joint optimization' of the social and technical components and their requirements.

One further point, however, is that the design of each sub-system is not wholly dependent on the design of the other. The final design is a matter of organizational choice, not technological imperative. The socio-technical systems perspective has thus proved to be a valuable and influential way of looking at organizations and their design.

The socio-technical approach was developed through two major studies carried out by Tavistock researchers. The first of these studies took place in the coal mines around Durham. The second was in a textile mill at Ahmedabad (north-west India). Here we shall look at the Durham study. The concepts of the systems approach can appear awkward on first sight. It is useful to know their origins, and to see how they were first applied.

the north-west Durham coal mines

Eric Trist and his colleagues seem to have had problems deciding the title of the book in which they published this research. The full title is *Organizational Choice: Capabilities of Groups at the Coal Face under Changing Technologies: The Loss, Rediscovery and Transformation of a Work Tradition* (Trist *et al.*, 1963). The book deals with a variety of issues, and a brief summary can give little indication of the wealth of detail to be found in the original.

The main argument of that research was that the form of work organization introduced when mechanical coal-getting methods replaced traditional techniques was not determined by the new technology. In other words, technical change is consistent with 'organizational choice'. John Bessant (1983) usefully defined this kind of organizational choice as 'design space'.

Britain's coal mining industry was nationalized by a Labour government in 1946. The predicted improvements in productivity and industrial relations did not occur. Labour turnover and the incidence of stress among coalface workers remained high. Trist felt that these problems arose from the organization of work associated with mechanized mining methods. So an alternative form of work organization, which had developed in some pits (by the miners themselves, and *not* by the researchers), was studied to see if it made any difference. Their research thus compared two different kinds of work organization in coal mines that were comparable in other ways, such as underground conditions and equipment.

The first report from this study, published in 1951, described the social and psychological problems of the 'conventional longwall' method of getting (that is, obtaining) coal. This method had gradually replaced conventional 'hand got' methods since the turn of the century. Trist's colleague at the time, K.W. Bamforth, had been a miner himself for eighteen years.

The coal-getting cycle in the 1950s had three stages:

1 **preparation** the coal was either cut by hand – previously with a pick and now with a pneumatic pick – or it was undercut and blown down into the cleared space with explosive.
2 **getting** the coal was loaded onto tubs or a conveyor for transport to the surface.
3 **advancing** the roof supports, gateway haulage roads and conveyor equipment were moved forward, ready for the next cycle.

Mechanization had replaced 'single place' working, where one or two miners worked with picks at faces (or places) up to 11 metres long. These men had worked in self-selecting groups, shared a common paynote and worked the same place on the same or different shifts. Each miner performed a *composite work role*: this simply meant that each was competent to perform all the necessary facework tasks:

He is a 'complete miner' – the collier – who supervises himself and is the person directly responsible for production. (Trist *et al.*, 1963, p. 33)

The traditional composite miner had several advantages. The production tempo was slow, but was maintained across and throughout shifts. This avoided periodic overloading of the winding gear and ensured the constant use of services such as haulage and the flow of supplies. Very little management effort was required to keep production up, because work on the coal seam was virtually self-regulating. The pit deputy's main responsibilities concerned safety regulations, keeping the colliers supplied and shotfiring when necessary.

The length of coal face that could be worked at any one time was greatly increased by the introduction of belt conveyors. In the Durham pits, straight longwall faces were generally 80–100 metres long, which explains the term 'longwall'. The advantage of the face conveyor was that the amount of stonework involved in advancing the gateways, in relation to the area of coal extracted, was greatly reduced. The coal-to-stone ratio becomes more important to the economics of a pit with thinner seams.

The extension in the length of the coal face led to a novel organization of work at the face. The first longwalls were simply extensions of single place working. Preparation and getting were carried out together for the first two shifts, and advancing was done in the third. These were called 'hewing longwalls'. However, with the introduction of the electrical coal cutter, the cycle was finally separated into its three discrete stages. The 'cutting longwall' was the most widespread longwall method in Britain at the time of the Tavistock research.

On a cutting longwall, the three stages of the cycle, preparation, getting and advancing, were each performed by separate task groups working on separate shifts. This meant that coal was removed on only one of the three shifts each day. The task group on each shift had to finish its stage of the work before the next stage could begin. Balancing the work of the three shifts thus became a significant problem.

The most significant change to the organization of facework with longwall methods was the abolition of the composite autonomous faceworker. Trist compared the conventional longwall technique with the mass production characteristics identified by Charles Walker and Robert Guest. The technique involved extreme job specialization. Miners were each allocated to one task on one shift only. They had no opportunities for job rotation and no means of developing a broad base of skills. The close relationships between miners were retained to some extent in the new single task groups which covered one stage of the mining cycle. On the whole, the new work organization was not as appropriate to work underground as the previous form of organization had been.

The miner has to deal with two kinds of task at the same time – the work of the production cycle and the background task of coping with the difficulties that arise from underground working conditions and hazards. The production skills were physically demanding, but were not complex and could all be learned by one person fairly quickly. However, skill in dealing with under-ground dangers was of a much higher order, and was only developed through experience over several years. The organization of work underground should ideally ensure that this experience can be gained and that this skill can be developed. Trist's team argued that the conventional longwall method prevented the underground worker from developing these skills, making this method both less appropriate and less effective.

The nature of the task breakdown and the resulting new payment system in the conventional longwall pits created new status differences between miners. The cuttermen who worked the length of the face with a large and powerful piece of machinery formed a 'face aristocracy'. The fillers worked on their own, shovelling coal in confined spaces and had comparatively low status. The pay of each task group was calculated on a different basis, and each group conducted separate negotiations with management. The primary concern of each task group was to improve its relative financial position, and not simply to win coal.

The conventional longwall method was not self-regulating. Management became responsible for co-ordinating the production cycle. Because self-regulation was no longer possible, management had to rely on wage negotiations to control the work of the three shifts. This became a key factor in the conventional longwall pits and 'management through the wage system' developed into a highly complex bargaining process. Sub-tasks and ancillary activities, as well as the main production work, were the subject of separate wage agreements. No common factor could be used to establish rates of pay for the different task groups. Several factors were used, such as tonnage, yardage, cubic measure or number of operations completed. Each task group would thus typically ask for special payment for any work not finished by the shift that preceded them – and which had to be completed before they could begin their allocated shift duties. Each shift thus had a vested interest in the previous shift failing to complete its state in the production cycle. The negotiating procedures consumed vast amounts of the time and energy of faceworkers and pit management.

Some pits, however, had developed a form of 'shortwall' working with some features similar to single place methods. These 'composite shortwalls' were worked by multi-skilled groups responsible for the whole coal-getting cycle on any one shift, and they were paid on a common paynote.

In one of the Durham pits, roof conditions had meant a return to shortwalls, as long faces had become impossible to support. Increasing costs, however, forced management to consider a return to longwall working. The miners resisted this move, because they did not want to give up the 'composite' form of work organization, to return to a system which would tie them to specific tasks and shifts. Instead, an agreement was negotiated which preserved the social and psychological features of composite groups, whilst exploiting the economic advantages of longwall mining. The result was the creation of self-selected groups of 41 men who allocated themselves to tasks and to shifts, and who again received their wages on a common paynote. This became known as the 'composite longwall' method.

The composite longwall had four main characteristics.
1 Continuity of production was restored. Each shift simply picked up the production cycle from the point at which the preceding shift stopped, regardless of the stage reached. When the main task of a shift was finished, they went on to the next stage of the cycle.
2 The method required multi-skilled miners. Each man did not have to possess all the necessary skills, as long as the group as a whole contained the skills required on each shift. The groups were *composite* in terms of the range of skills they each contained. They were also *autonomous* as they operated their own shift and job rotations.
3 The work groups were self-selected and not allocated by management.
4 Each group was paid on a common paynote as all the members were regarded as making equivalent contributions to the work.

Composite groups were leaderless. Their 'team captains' acted as representatives, not as first line managers. Team members retained their broad mining skills and were constantly reminded of the conditions under which the other shifts had to work. The whole atmosphere of life and work in the mine was completely transformed by the composite longwall method.

The composite longwalls were more productive, miners preferred them and absenteeism was much lower than on conventional longwalls. The method also affected management. The composite approach, like single place working, was self-regulating. The pit deputies were thus relieved from

---

the whole atmosphere on a composite longwall was different

The astonishing change in the physical appearance of the workplace, which would be the first thing to impress itself on a visitor, has come to be recognized as almost a hallmark of a composite group . . . although the men were not responsible for equipment in the gates, they would use their lunch break to check and, if necessary, do repairs to the mothergate belt which leads to the face, anticipating and preventing possible disturbances of their work. No man was ever out of a job. If he finished hewing or pulling before others he would join and help them, or go on to some other job which was to follow. If work was stopped owing to breakdowns in the transport system on which the group was dependent for its supply of tubs, the men would go on to do maintenance work.

from P.G. Herbst, 1962, *Autonomous Group Functioning*, Tavistock, London, p. 6.

'propping up' the conventional longwall cycle which was always collapsing on itself. Management and miners were no longer involved in the endless wage renegotiations of the conventional approach.

This and other similar studies led the Tavistock researchers to two main conclusions. First, work in groups is more likely to provide meaningful work, develop responsibility, and satisfy human needs than work that is allocated to separately supervised individuals. Second, work can be organized in this way regardless of the technology in use. Social system design is not uniquely determined by technical system characteristics and demands.

Composite autonomous group working can thus be regarded as another kind of job enrichment. However, job enrichment is usually applied to individuals. Autonomous group working applies to teams of people whose work is related or interdependent.

team versus lean: competing socio-technical paradigms

Until the early 1990s, the pioneering, team-based manufacturing plants of the Swedish motor manufacturers Saab and Volvo were popular 'management tourist' attractions. Volvo's charismatic president, Pehr Gyllenhammar, had explained his own and his company's approach to making cars and organizing people in a book published in 1977. The team-based approach remained popular in America into the 1990s, one study suggesting that over half of American manufacturing companies had scrapped their assembly-lines in favour of 'cellular manufacturing' methods (*The Economist*, 1994). Companies like Compaq (computers), W.L. Gore (the makers of Gore-Tex fabric) and Harley-Davidson (motorcycles) reported benefits in terms of productivity, flexibility and quality from their multiskilled autonomous teams.

Extending the team-based assembly idea, developed at Kalmar, Volvo built a new final assembly plant at Uddevalla, on Sweden's west coast, in the late 1980s. Here, autonomous teams of 8–10 car-builders were responsible for the final assembly of the car, on a static 'assembly dock', and not on a paced assembly-line. The plant had a central materials store from which parts and sub-assemblies were delivered to teams by automatically guided vehicles.

STOP!

Here is a summary diagram outlining the approach to work organization developed by the socio-technical system school. Compare this with the job characteristics model described in Chapter 4. What similarities and differences can you identify?

the work organization approach to job design

individual jobs should provide

1 optimum variety
2 meaningful task
3 optimum work cycle
4 control over work standards and feedback of results
5 preparation and auxiliary tasks
6 use of valued skill, knowledge and effort
7 contribution to end product

psychological requirements of job content

1 variety and challenge
2 continous learning
3 decision-making
4 social support and recognition
5 relationship between work and social life
6 desirable future

human needs

1 affiliation
2 achievement and self-esteem
3 control
4 curiosity
5 security

work group organization should provide

1 job rotation or physical proximity where individual tasks:
a are interdependent
b are stressful
c lack perceivable contribution to end product
2 grouping of interdependent jobs to give:
a whole tasks which contribute to end product
b control over work standards and feedback of results
c control over boundary tasks
3 communication channels
4 promotion channels

from David Buchanan, 1979, *The Development of Job Design Theories and Techniques*, Saxon House, Aldershot, p. 112.

Each team was responsible for its own training, maintenance, tooling, task planning and for the selection of new members. Without supervisors, teams elected rotating spokespersons who handled planning for the group, assigned work, led discussions, dealt with individual and work problems, and were responsible also for reporting to management.

Volvo's even cited these developments in its advertising around Europe in 1990: The assembly-line is gone. Instead, cars stand in workshops during assembly, a small team building a complete car.

The teams of workers see themselves as families and that is just what they are. Men and women of all ages work side by side, using special ergonomically designed machines evolved especially for them.

The Uddevalla workers have already demonstrated that their way of making cars is more natural, and often more efficient, than the traditional assembly line. They have confirmed Volvo's belief that responsibility, involvement, comradeship and joy increase work satisfaction and raise product quality.

However, in 1990 Saab was forced to sell its motor car business to the American company, General Motors. In 1991, Saab closed its team-based plant at Malmo. In 1993, Volvo closed its plants at Kalmar and Uddevalla, and concentrated production at its traditionally organized factory at Torslanda, outside Gothenburg.

These developments tarnished the image of team-based, human-centred manufacturing methods. As the Swedish car manufacturers were selling and closing their facilities, Japanese car manufacturers such as Toyota, Honda and Nissan were opening new plants in Europe and America, with much publicity and apparent success. What went wrong?

One explanation comes from the work of James Womack, Dan Jones and Daniel Roos. In their book *The Machine that Changed the World* (1990), they compare the productivity of car manufacturers around the world and explain the wide variations in terms of production methods. One of their key measures was the number of hours of direct labour used to build, paint and finally assemble a car. In summary, the main differences in 1989, between the best and the worst companies, on this measure of labour assembly hours, were as follows:

	best	**worst**
Japan	13.2	25.9
North America	18.6	30.7
Europe	22.8	55.7

These comparisons appear damning, and point to significant advantages in Japanese manufacturing methods. At Uddevalla, the training time for team members was high, and the assembly time for each car was twice the European average. Despite the favourable working conditions, absenteeism and labour turnover also remained high (Wickens, 1993).

Womack, Jones and Roos argued that those productivity differences were due, not to automation, but to the combination of production methods used. The Japanese advantage, they claimed, was due to their use of 'lean organization'. Lean organization, or lean production, combines the following features:

- 'Just in time' delivery of materials to the point of assembly, replacing the need to hold an expensive inventory of component parts, reducing the need to hold buffer stocks in the manufacturing process, and reducing the need for storage space in the plant.
- A conventional machine-paced assembly-line, with specialized task design, using scientific management principles, placing responsibility on workers to find improvements to the 'one best way' of performing each task.
- A rigorous approach to standardizing methods; when the individual worker identifies an improvement, this is first agreed with supervision and engineering staff, and the standard work procedure sheet is rewritten. This is known as continuous improvement, or *kaizen*.

- An aggressive approach to problem-spotting and problem-solving, through at least three mechanisms. One is *kaizen*: keep looking for ways to save time, improve productivity. A second concerns the formation of problem-solving teams which focus on sections of the assembly line. A third is the use of 'quality circles' – another team approach to *kaizen*, for addressing broader quality and manufacturing problems.
- A ruthless approach to reducing equipment adjustment and retooling times, and eliminating defects in manufacturing. In a Japanese manufacturing plant, a single worker can stop the assembly process – can bring the whole plant to a halt – if a problem arises. The plant or line is not restarted until the problem is rectified.
- Powerful first-line supervisors who monitor and encourage continuous improvement.

As various commentators have pointed out, 'teamwork' in Japanese companies is not the same as 'teamwork' in most Scandinavian, European or American companies (MacDuffie, 1988; Buchanan, 1994). The assembler in a Japanese plant carries out a short-cycle repetitive task under conventional supervisory control, and is under constant pressure to improve productivity through adjustments to the individual task or aspects of the manufacturing process. This is quite different from the experience of multi-skilled autonomous team members, who decide how to allocate and rotate tasks, and who solve problems, in collaboration with each other, at their own pace and discretion.

Is it safe to conclude that the Anglo-American–Scandinavian model of team-based manufacturing has been discredited, and that lean production is a more effective and productive socio-technical paradigm? This conclusion must be premature.

There is considerable evidence to suggest that lean production is also 'mean' production. The work pace and intensity, the unlimited demands of *kaizen*, strict supervisory regulation of methods and lack of discretion can be extremely stressful. Parker and Slaughter (1988) studied a plant run jointly by Toyota and General Motors in California – New United Motors Manufacturing Incorporated (NUMMI). This was publicized as a lean 'industry standard' production approach, but Parker and Slaughter called it 'management by stress', with every worker motion and action timed meticulously to remove wasted effort, reduce time and inventory, and streamline production continuously.

Hammarstrom and Lansbury (1991) point out that these workplace pressures are typically offset by high pay and job security, and that Japanese transplants are often located in areas of high unemployment and low trade union membership. They conclude that Japanese methods based on scientific management methods appear 'natural' and 'safe' to many managers. Local labour market conditions can, in addition, make lean methods acceptable to a workforce primarily interested in secure employment and reasonable rates of pay.

Swedish researchers have been forceful in their criticisms of the work of Womack, Jones and Roos on the one hand, and in defence of the Scandinavian socio-technical paradigm on the other. Christian Berggren, at the Swedish Institute for Work Life Research in Stockholm, has been scathing of the narrow range of measures used in the American research, which focused on final assembly hours and paid less attention to the way in which the overall supply chain, from design to customer, was organized (Berggren, Bjorkman and Hollander, 1991; Berggren, 1993; 1995).

Berggren also argues that Volvo's decision to close the plants at Kalmar and Uddevalla was reached despite internal company analyses, which revealed that these plants were at least as productive as the conventional, but much larger and older, plant at Torslanda. The company had excess production capacity in the early 1990s, and internal logistics and politics made it expedient to close the smaller and more experimental plants located some distance from the company's main facilities.

We are therefore faced with a dispute between two socio-technical paradigms, between two quite different ways of organizing people around production. A partial resolution to this debate began to emerge during the second half of the 1990s.

One dimension of this resolution concerns the extent to which it is possible to combine elements of the two approaches, to emphasize both concern for production and also maintain and improve quality of working life. Peter Wickens (ex-Personnel Director, Nissan, Sunderland, UK) argues for the 'ascendant organization' which emphasizes both employee commitment and management control of manufacturing operations.

A second dimension relies on the observation that some cultures and groups more readily accept the 'high pay, high security, high intensity' work package of lean production, which is resisted strongly in some countries, such as Sweden. The collection of papers by Ake Sandberg (1995) supports this view; Volvo has rarely used its Scandinavian model of manufacturing in its plants elsewhere in the world (in Holland, Britain or Canada, for example).

However, the 'team versus lean' debate is far from resolution. The arguments in motor car production are not resolved, and it is not clear how these issues can be applied to other manufacturing and service sector organizations. This debate seems likely to run into the twenty-first century.

advanced technology and the changing nature of work

If technology does not create unemployment, then surely many of those jobs that remain will be deskilled at best, and dehumanized at worst? The evidence once again suggests that 'technological implications' are not as one-dimensional in reality as they tend to be portrayed in the media. Technological innovations can create a combination of deskilling in some contexts, and increase the demands on human skill and understanding in other settings.

As discussed earlier, the consequences of technological change for skill are mediated by the way in which work is organized. It is difficult to make general claims about the impact of technology, on jobs, on skills, on dehumanization, or about a robot takeover. Technological devices – forms of apparatus – are simply components or building blocks for a range of different types of socio-technical systems. As we have seen, social system design is not wholly constrained by technical components. One of the best general claims that has been made about the impact of new technology is perhaps captured in Melvin Kranzberg's First Law, which states that: 'Technology is neither good nor bad, nor is it neutral' (Kranzberg, 1985).

automate or informate?

> Information technology is characterized by a fundamental duality that has not yet been fully appreciated. On the one hand, the technology can be applied to automate operations according to a logic that hardly differs from that of the nineteenth century machine system – replace the human body with a technology that enables the same processes to be performed with more continuity and control. On the other, the same technology simultaneously generates information about the underlying productive and administrative processes through which an organization accomplishes its work. It provides a deeper level of transparency to activities that had been either partially or completely opaque. In this way information technology supersedes the traditional logic of automation. The word that I have coined to describe this unique capacity is *informate*. Activities, events, and objects are translated into and made visible by information when a technology *informates* as well as *automates*.
>
> from Shoshana Zuboff, 1988, *In The Age of The Smart Machine: The Future of Work and Power*, Heinemann Professional Publishing, Oxford, pp. 9–10.

In this section, we shall examine a limited range of studies, exploring applications of new technology in manufacturing and office settings respectively. The broad aim in this approach is to show that technological innovation in the organization can have a spread of implications, from deskilling to significant skills increases.

new technology in manufacturing

Computing devices clearly replace human effort and thought in manufacturing in a number of obvious ways. Machine tool operators have no wheels or levers to move on a computer numerically controlled machine tool, or on a computerized conveyor. Chemical process plant and steel manufacturing process operators control manufacturing activities through electronic displays in a remote control room not through physical intervention. Machined components can be inspected with computerized machines (computer co-ordinate measuring machines, or CCMMs) which check dimensions with an electronic probe, replacing traditional hand-held engineering inspection devices (such as the micrometer). The problem is this:

> . . . at first sight there is little the modern robot cannot do. In shipyards, robots weld, sandblast, paint and scrub. Robots were used to clean up Chernobyl; they hunt for mines. They make cars, shear sheep, repair pipes and mix chemicals. A robo-surgeon is currently operating on prostates at Guy's Hospital in London; a knee surgeon may follow next year. In short, for unthinking and repetitive tasks, or for dangerous but straightforward undertakings, a robot is your man.
>
> The problem is, of course, that it isn't a man. Although all these machines are sophisticated bits of engineering appropriate to their jobs, they are just tools. Their inability to be flexible often limits their applications; each repetitive task requires a tool of a different shape. ('Not clever enough?', *The Economist*, 18 May 1996, p. 105)

© United Feature Syndicate, Inc.

Research has confirmed the view, expressed over two decades ago by Louis Davis and James Taylor (1975; 1976) – that technological innovation opens up new opportunities for work organization and can increase the demands made on cognitive and social skills. As Zuboff concludes, from her influential studies of automated process control applications:

> As information technology restructures the work situation, it abstracts thought from action. Absorption, immediacy, and organic responsiveness are superseded by distance, coolness, and remoteness. Such distance brings an opportunity for reflection. There was little doubt in these workers' minds that the logic of their jobs had been fundamentally altered. As another worker from Tiger Creek summed it up, 'Sitting in this room and just thinking has become part of my job. It's the technology that lets me do these things'.

> The thinking this operator refers to is of a different quality from the thinking that attended the display of action-centred skills. It combines abstraction, explicit inference, and procedural reasoning. Taken together, these elements make possible a new set of competences that I call *intellective skills*. As long as the new technology signals only deskilling – the diminished importance of action-centred skills – there will be little probability of developing critical judgement at the data interface. To rekindle such judgement, though on a new, more abstract footing, a reskilling process is required. Mastery in a computer-mediated environment depends on developing intellective skills. (Zuboff, 1988, pp. 75–6)

Zuboff's conclusion about the growing importance of 'intellective' or problem-solving and cognitive skills is supported by a considerable body of research evidence. For example, Buchanan and Boddy (1983b) compared the consequences of computerization on two occupations – doughmen and ovensmen – in a Glasgow biscuit factory.

The company's first production computer was installed in 1971 to control the mixing process. To change a recipe, a new paper tape had to be prepared. This required computer programming skill, and took about half an hour. In 1982, a new 'recipe desk' was installed, allowing recipe changes to be made simply with small thumb wheels, requiring no special skill. The doughman's job became repetitive, and was reclassified as semi-skilled, with a cycle of around 20 minutes. This job was originally done by time served master bakers, but the computer now controlled the mixing process, doing 60 mixes every 24 hours. Bored doughmen sometimes forgot to add sundry ingredients such as salt, and this was only discovered at the end of the mix, or at the oven test.

---

too complex for mere mortals to comprehend

Instead of manning the bridge with helmet and heavy binoculars, the skipper of a $1 billion Aegis class cruiser exercises command from the hi-tech CIC, or Combat Information Center, a windowless room linked to the outside world through glowing computer and radar screens. Never before has a warship's captain had access to so much instant and accurate information. Even so, the skipper and his crew are not immune to confusion – the 'fog of war'. A horrified world learned precisely that in July [1988], when the US *Vincennes* shot down an Iranian airliner, killing 290 civilians.

The tragedy marked the first time an Aegis cruiser had fired its missiles in combat. And it should rekindle efforts to tame the complexity of weapons systems – especially with programs such as Star Wars looming. Ever since the Aegis was designed in the late 1970s, critics have worried that its systems are too complex for mere mortals to comprehend. In its recently released investigative report, the Navy touched on the issue of breakdowns between man and machine. But the inquiry team found that the highly sophisticated computer and radar systems aboard the *Vincennes* had performed flawlessly.

The real lesson of the *Vincennes* is that electronic systems can produce far too much data for human beings to digest in the heat and strain of battle. Engineers who design such systems often forget this. . . . A review board did recommend some changes in Aegis. One culprit: a hard to read computer display that doesn't show an aircraft's altitude beside its radar track. Investigators called for a redesigned screen and better training . . .

The loss of 290 innocent lives is too high a price for working out a new weapon system's bugs.

from Dave Griffiths, 1988, 'When man can't keep up with the machines of war', *Business Week*, 12 September 1988, p. 28.

Buchanan and Boddy argue that, in replacing the craft skills of the doughman, and in requiring continued human intervention at that stage of the process, computerization created a *distanced* role in which:
1 Operators had little understanding of the process and equipment, and they could not visualize the consequences of their actions.

2 Operators could not identify the causes of equipment faults, there were no backup systems for them to operate, and specialist maintenance staff were needed.
3 Operators became bored, apathetic and careless and rejected responsibility for breakdowns.
4 Operators developed no skills to make them eligible for promotion.

Buchanan and Boddy conclude that these four *distancing* features are typical of many jobs in 'nearly automated' systems, where the operators develop neither the ability nor the motivation to perform residual functions effectively. In Zuboff's terms, the need for action-centred skills has been reduced and the worker has no opportunity to use intellective skills.

In this biscuit factory, the implications of computerization for another occupation, the ovensman, were different. An ovensman was responsible for baking biscuits that had the correct bulk, weight, moisture content, colour, shape and taste. This was complex because action to correct a deviation on one of these features could affect the others. The training time for this job was 12–16 weeks.

A computer-controlled check weigher was installed to replace the old electromechanical system. As each packet passed over the weigh cell, its weight was recorded and displayed on a screen close to the wrapping machine. The computer calculated summary information on packet weights, shown on another display for the ovensman and updated every 2 minutes.

This new system gave the ovensman information on the performance of the line, enabling him to adjust the oven controls and to reduce waste by producing more accurate packet weights. If packet weights were too high and the wrapping machine could not compensate, the ovensman could tell the machine operator to adjust the weight of dough blanks, or he could increase the oven temperature to increase the bulk and reduce the number of biscuits per packet.

The information from the new system showed when something was wrong, but could not indicate what was causing the problem or what corrective action to take. The ovensman had to take into account the properties of the flour being used and the dough that it made. When packet weights wandered, the ovensman decided what to do to correct this. He had become a 'process supervisor'.

Buchanan and Boddy argue that the introduction of computerized weighing technology *complemented* the skill and knowledge of the ovensman, creating a role in which he:
1 Got rapid feedback on performance and had discretion to control the process more effectively.
2 Had a good understanding of the relationships between process stages.
3 Had a visible goal that could be influenced.
4 Felt that the job had more interest and challenge.

Equipment could have been designed to let doughmen see and hear the mixing process. Why not take the recipe desks out of the production office and let the doughman adjust ingredient quantities himself? Autonomous groups could have been organized, each responsible for a whole production line. The work experience of these two occupations was conditioned only in part by technological innovation and was influenced by work organization choices.

Many such studies of manufacturing technology suggest that sophisticated, flexible, expensive equipment needs sophisticated, flexible, expensive people to operate it effectively. Richard Walton and Gerald Susman (1987) argue that advanced technology increases:

- interdependencies between organizational functions
- skill requirements and dependence on skilled people
- capital investment per employee
- the speed, scope and costs of mistakes
- sensitivity of performance to changes in skill and attitudes

---

technology and alienation

One classic study of the impact of technology is that of Robert Blauner, who analyzed working conditions in the early 1960s in

- printing, dominated by craft work
- cotton spinning, dominated by machine minding
- car manufacture, dominated by mass production
- chemicals manufacture, dominated by process production

Blauner identified four components of alienation, concerning feelings of:

1 *Powerlessness*: loss of control over conditions of work, work processes, pace and methods.
2 *Meaninglessness*: loss of significance of work activities.
3 *Isolation*: loss of sense of community membership.
4 *Self-estrangement*: loss of personal identity, of sense of work as a central life interest.

Printing workers set their own pace, were free from management pressure, chose their own techniques and methods, had powerful unions, practised a complex skill, had good social contacts at work, had high status, identified closely with their work and were not alienated.

Textile workers performed simple, rapid and repetitive operations over which they had little control, worked under strict supervision, and had little social contact at work. Alienation among textile workers, however, was low. Blauner argued that this was because they lived in close rural communities whose values and way of life overcame feelings of alienation arising at work.

Car assembly workers had little control over work methods, saw little meaning in the tasks they performed, were socially isolated, and developed no meaningful skills.

Chemicals processing workers operated prosperous, technically advanced plants where manual work had been automated. They controlled their own work pace, and had freedom of movement, social contact and team work. They developed an understanding of the chemical reactions which they monitored, and also developed a sense of belonging, achievement and responsibility. In addition they had close contact with educated, modern management.

Blauner concluded that advanced technology would eliminate alienation.

based on Robert Blauner, 1964, *Alienation and Freedom: The Factory Worker and His Job*, University of Chicago Press, Chicago.

Walton and Susman argue that the appropriate organizational response to these trends should have four ingredients. First is the need to develop a highly skilled, flexible, co-ordinated and committed workforce. Second is the need for a lean, flat, flexible and innovative management structure. Third concerns the ability to retain experienced people. The final ingredient is a strong partnership between management and trade unions.

Effective 'people policies', according to Walton and Susman, include:

- job enrichment
- multi-skilling
- teamwork
- 'pay for knowledge' reward systems
- reconsideration of the organizational level at which decisions are taken
- attention to selection and training, and to management development

These considerations have led to the development of what is now known as *human-centred manufacturing*.

---

definition

Human-centred manufacturing *is an attempt to design production technologies in a way that complements human skills and abilities, rather than distance or replace them.*

Finance from the European Community's Esprit programme enabled researchers in Britain, Denmark and Germany to develop a 'human-centred lathe' project during the 1980s. This machine is programmed by its operator, not by a specialist in an office remote from the factory floor. The human-centred manufacturing project faces at least two major problems, according to Ian McLoughlin and Jon Clark (1994). One concerns persuading organizations preoccupied with improving production control and reducing costs to adopt such systems. A second concerns the problems of involving those who will work with such systems in their design, given the growing complexity of the technology itself, and the location and membership of technical and academic research teams.

new technology in the office

Research has shown how technological advance also encourages skills upgrading and teamwork in office settings. Word processing during the 1980s became the building block of the 'office of the future'. Many office 'typists' today work with a multimedia computer capable of performing a staggering range of tasks in comparison with the humble typewriter, including various data analysis and presentation operations, and national and international communications, through the internet and electronic mail.

In one early study in this area, David Buchanan and David Boddy (1982) analyzed the effects of word processing in one of the largest marine engineering consultancy firms in Europe.

The work of the 'video typists', as they were then known, was affected in several ways by the introduction of word processing. The new technology reduced task variety, the meaning of the work, control over work scheduling, feedback of results, involvement in preparation tasks, contact with authors and the sense of contribution to the company's end product – client reports. The changes had, however, increased the typists' control over typing quality, required knowledge of the computing system in use, and improved pay and promotion prospects. The overall quality of the typing service was felt to have been reduced.

This research demonstrated that the video typists could only use the powerful capabilities of the new technology effectively in an appropriate form of work organization. The Department of Trade and Industry organized a series of office automation 'demonstrator' projects during the 1980s. Among their findings, they concluded that:

> Technology has no imperative of its own – management of technology and of the process of change is more significant. Managers must harness the 'people' resource and enable users to influence the way technology is introduced and exploited, in order to help them, and the organization, to win from office automation. (Pye, Bates and Heath, 1986, p. 36)

Word processing and the other capabilities of personal computers increase the skill demands on its user in visualizing, creating and amending text, in organizing and presenting data, and in conducting effectively a range of electronic communications tasks. Buchanan and Boddy argued that the word processing system which they studied would have been more effectively used if work had been organized in such a way that the technology *complemented* the existing skills, knowledge and capabilities of the typists. Findings such as this have led several commentators to argue for a more human-centred approach to the design of office systems, in parallel with developments in human-centred manufacturing (Smith, 1989).

Rick Long (1987), from Saskatchewan, Canada, argues that failures in office automation systems are due rarely to technical problems. Most of the problems are human and organizational, such as:

- poor planning
- poor technical management skills
- lack of training for users of the technology
- lack of clarity about which technical or organizational problems to address

"It's clear from reading your report, Anderson, that you have emerged unscathed from the information explosion."

Long's conclusions were based on a study of 2000 American organizations with office automation systems. At least 40 per cent of those systems had failed to achieve their intended results, mainly through failure to consider the organizational issues in system design and implementation.

assessment

The worst predictions about the impact of technology on jobs and on quality of working life do not appear to have come true – yet. The way in which work is organized around technology has more influence on the outcomes of innovation than technical capabilities.

This conclusion can be summarized in the following figure. This argues that the consequences of technical change in an organization depend on technical capabilities, on why the technology is being used and on how work is organized.

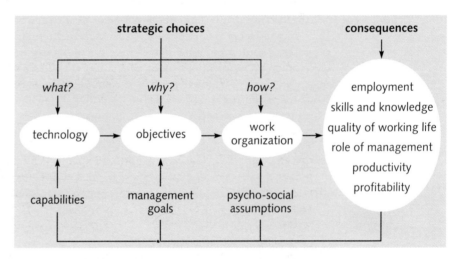

So, we are not looking at 'technological implications' as such. We are instead looking at the implications of organizational choices. Technological innovation simply acts as a trigger for these decision-making processes.

Is this argument oversimplified? Surely technology must have some independent influence on the nature of work and organizations? Two prominent commentators who have challenged the 'organizational choice' argument, Ian McLoughlin and Jon Clark (1994, p. 150) claim that rejection of technological determinism 'results in the technology baby being thrown out with the determinist bathwater'. Instead, they argue that new computing and information technologies *do* create imperatives, and that these include:

- a reduction or elimination of the number of complex tasks that require manual skills
- the creation of complex tasks that require interpretive and problem-solving skills, and an understanding of system interdependencies
- the ability to combine knowledge of new with old technology for the effective performance of some tasks
- a relationship between technology and user that relies on informed intervention, rather than on traditional machine operation capability

In other terms, 'action-centred' skills and abilities become less important, and cognitive or 'intellective' skills become more valued. This is not to deny completely the significance of organizational choice or the role of social shaping and negotiation in affecting the outcomes for work experience that accompany particular technological innovations. Technology appears to have 'enabling' properties: the technology of motor car production enables task fragmentation and rigid supervisory control, but it also enables multi-skilled, autonomous teamwork. The questions that have not found satisfactory answers here include:

▶ Which is more productive – lean or team manufacturing?
▶ Which is more socially desirable?
▶ How can we strike an appropriate and acceptable balance?

Note that the answers to these questions depend in part on the comparative performance statistics for different organizations and their manufacturing plants, and also in part on individual and cultural values and preferences. The assessment of technology must therefore combine economic with social and political considerations.

This chapter is dedicated to the memory of Tom Forester, who was a prolific, widely informed and influential commentator in the field of technology and organizational behaviour, and a good bloke.

sources

Berggren, C., 1993, 'The Volvo Uddevalla plant: Why the decision to close it is mistaken', *Journal of Industry Studies*, vol. 1, no. 1, October, pp. 75–87.

Berggren, C., 1995, 'The fate of the branch plants – performance versus power', in Ake Sandberg (ed.), *Enriching Production: Perspectives on Volvo's Uddevalla Plant as an Alternative to Lean Production*, Avebury, Aldershot, pp. 105–26.

Berggren, C., Bjorkman, T. and Hollander, E., 1991, 'Are they unbeatable?', Centre for Corporate Change paper 012, Australian Graduate School of Management, University of New South Wales, Kensington.

Bessant, J., 1983, 'Management and manufacturing innovation: The case of information technology', in G. Winch (ed.), *Information Technology in Manufacturing Processes*, Rossendale, London, pp. 14–30.

Blauner, R., 1964, *Alienation and Freedom: The Factory Worker and his Industry*, The University of Chicago Press, Chicago.

Braverman, H., 1974, *Labor and Monopoly Capital: The Degradation of Work in the Twentieth Century*, Monthly Review Press, New York.

Buchanan, D.A., 1979, *The Development of Job Design Theories and Techniques*, Saxon House, Aldershot.

Buchanan, D.A., 1994, 'Cellular manufacture and the role of teams', in John Storey (ed.), *New Wave Manufacturing Strategies: Organizational and Human Resource Management Dimensions*, Paul Chapman Publishing, London, pp. 204–25.

Buchanan, D.A. and Boddy, D., 1982, 'Advanced technology and the quality of working life: the effects of word processing on video typists', *Journal of Occupational Psychology*, vol. 55, no. 1, pp. 1–11.

Buchanan, D.A. and Boddy, D., 1983a, *Organizations in the Computer Age: Technological Imperatives and Strategic Choice*, Gower, Aldershot.

Buchanan, D.A. and Boddy, D., 1983b, 'Advanced technology and the quality of working life: The effects of computerized controls on biscuit-making operators', *Journal of Occupational Psychology*, vol. 56, no. 2, pp. 109–19.

Clegg, S. and Dunkerley, D., 1980, *Organization, Class and Control*, Routledge & Kegan Paul, London.

Davis, L.E. and Taylor, J.C., 1975, 'Technology effects on job, work, and organizational structure: a contingency view', in L.E. Davis and A.B. Cherns (eds.), *The Quality of Working Life: Problems, Prospects and the State of the Art*, The Free Press, New York, pp. 220–41.

Davis, L.E. and Taylor, J.C., 1976, 'Technology, organization and job structure', in R. Dubin (ed.), *Handbook of Work, Organization and Society*, Rand-McNally, Chicago, pp. 379–419.

The Economist, 1994, 'The celling out of America', 17 December, pp. 71–2.

The Economist, 1996, 'Not clever enough', 18 May, p. 105.

Emery, R.E. and Trist, E.L., 1960, 'Socio-technical systems', in C.W. Churchman and M. Verhulst (eds), *Management Science, Models and Techniques*, Pergamon Press, London, vol. 2, pp. 83–97.

Forester, T., 1989, *Computers in the Human Context: Information Technology, Productivity and People*, Basil Blackwell, Oxford.

Fox, A., 1974, *Man Mismanagement*, Hutchinson, London.

Griffiths, D., 1988, 'When man can't keep up with the machines of war', *Business Week*, 12 September, p. 28.

Gyllenhammar, P., 1977, *People at Work*, Addison-Wesley, Reading, MA.

Hammarstrom, O. and Lansbury, R.D., 1991, 'The art of building a car: The Swedish experience re-examined', *New Technology, Work and Employment*, vol. 6, no. 2, pp. 85–90.

Herbst, P.G., 1962, *Autonomous Group Functioning*, Tavistock, London.

Karasek, R.A., 1979, 'Job demands, job decision latitudes, and mental strain: implications for job redesign', *Administrative Science Quarterly*, vol. 24, no. 2, pp. 285–308.

Kornhauser, A., 1965, *Mental Health of the Industrial Worker*, John Wiley, New York.

Long, R., 1987, *New Office Information Technology: Human and Managerial Implications*, Croom Helm, London.

MacDuffie, J.P., 1988, 'The Japanese auto transplants: challenges to conventional wisdom', *ILR Report*, vol. xxvi, no. 1, Fall, pp. 12–18.

McLoughlin, I. and Clark, J., 1994, *Technological Change at Work*, Open University Press, Milton Keynes, 2nd edn.

Miller, E.J. and Rice, A.K., 1967, *Systems of Organization: The Control of Task and Sentient Boundaries*, Tavistock Publications, London.

Norstedt, J.P. and Aguren, S., 1973, *Saab-Scania Report*, Swedish Employers' Confederation, Stockholm.

Parker, M. and Slaughter, J., 1988, *Choosing Sides: Unions and the Team Concept*, Labor Notes, Detroit.

Preece, D., 1995, *Organizations and Technical Change: Strategy, Objectives and Involvement*, Routledge, London.

Pye, R., Bates, J. and Heath, L., 1986, *Profiting from Office Automation: Office Automation Pilots*, KPMG Thomson McLintock, London.

Reeves, T.K., Turner, B.A. and Woodward, J., 1970, 'Technology and organizational behaviour', in Joan Woodward (ed.), *Industrial Organization: Behaviour and Control*, Oxford University Press, London, pp. 3–18.

Rice, A.K., 1958, *Productivity and Social Organization*, Tavistock Publications, London.

Rice, A.K., 1963, *The Enterprise and its Environment*, Tavistock Publications, London.

Sandberg, A. (ed.), 1995, *Enriching Production: Perspectives on Volvo's Uddevalla Plant as an Alternative to Lean Production*, Avebury, Aldershot.

Smith, S., 1989, 'Information technology in banks: Taylorization or human-centred systems?', in Forester, *op. cit.*, pp. 377–90; first published in *Science and Public Policy* (1987).

Storey, J. (ed.), 1994, *New Wave Manufacturing Strategies: Organizational and Human Resource Management Dimensions*, Paul Chapman Publishing, London.

Thomas, H., 1974, 'Finding a better way', *Guardian*, 17 January, p. 12.

Tiefenbrun, I., 1993, 'Manufacturing in the future', *RSA Journal*, vol. CLXI, no. 5441, July, pp. 549–57.

Trist, E.L. and Bamforth, K.W., 1951, 'Some social and psychological consequences of the longwall method of coal-getting', *Human Relations*, vol. 4, no. 1, pp. 3–38.

Trist, E.L., Higgin, G.W., Murray, H. and Pollock, A.B., 1963, *Organizational Choice*, Tavistock Publications, London.

Turner, A.N. and Lawrence, P.R., 1965, *Industrial Jobs and the Worker: An Investigation of Response to Task Attributes*, Division of Research, Harvard Business School, Boston, MA.

Valery, N., 1974, 'Importing the lessons of Swedish workers', *New Scientist*, vol. 62, no. 892, pp. 27–8.

Viteles, M.S., 1950, 'Man and machine relationship: the problem of boredom', in R.B. Ross (ed.), *Proceedings of the Annual Fall Conference of the Society for Advancement of Management*, New York, pp. 129–38.

Walker, C.R., 1950, 'The problem of the repetitive job', *Harvard Business Review*, vol. 28, no. 3, pp. 54–8.

Walker, C.R. and Guest, R.H., 1952, *The Man on the Assembly Line*, Harvard University Press, Cambridge, MA.

Wall, T.D., 1996, 'Working with robots', *The Psychologist*, April, pp. 163–6.

Walton, R.E. and Susman, G.I., 1987, 'People policies for the new machines', *Harvard Business Review*, March–April, no. 2, pp. 98–106.

Wibberley, M., 1993, 'Does "lean" necessarily equal "mean" ?', *Personnel Management*, July, pp. 32–5.

Wickens, P., 1993, 'Steering the middle road to car production', *Personnel Management*, June, pp. 34–8.

Wickens, P.D., 1995, *The Ascendent Organization: Combining Commitment and Control for Long-term Sustainable Business Success*, Macmillan, Basingstoke.

Winner, L., 1977, *Autonomous Technology: Technics-out-of-Control as a Theme in Political Thought*, MIT Press, Cambridge, MA.

Womack, J., Jones, D. and Roos, D., 1990, *The Machine That Changed the World*, Rawson Associates, New York.

Zuboff, S., 1988, *In the Age of the Smart Machine: The Future of Work and Power*, Heinemann Professional Publishing, Oxford.

leadership and management style

concepts and learning objectives
the functions of leaders and managers
are leaders special people?
leaders need followers
the importance of context
the importance of culture
can leaders change their style?
assessment
sources

concepts and learning objectives

The manager is the dynamic, life-giving element in every business. Without his leadership 'the resources of production' remain resources and never become production. In a competitive economy, above all, the quality and performance of the managers determine the success of a business, indeed they determine its survival. For the quality and performance of its managers is the only effective advantage an enterprise in a competitive economy can have.

from Peter F. Drucker, 1955, *The Practice of Management*, Heinemann, London, p. 13.

What is the difference between management and leadership? How can we best describe and analyze management and leadership styles? How can we identify and develop 'leadership'? What advice can we offer about different leadership and management styles? These questions reflect some of the main preoccupations about leadership in the twentieth century.

These concerns were heightened significantly in the closing decades of the century. Many of the world's worst, and therefore best publicized, disasters – the *Challenger* shuttle explosion, the Chernobyl reactor failure, the Townsend Thoresen ferry capsize – were attributed at least in part to failures, not in technology, but in management processes. Management was seen, visibly, to matter. During the 1980s and 1990s the world's superpowers seem to have been led by relatively bland politicians, who have been considerably less charismatic than those who preceded them in the immediate post-war decades. Does this matter?

---

the roots of management

manus agere	Latin	to work with the hand
le manège	French	horse training, horsemanship, a riding school
maneggiare	Italian	to train and handle horses
management	English	1 the action or manner of managing
		2 the use of contrivance for effecting some purpose; often in bad sense, implying deceit or trickery
manager	English	1 one who manages
		2 one skilled in managing affairs, money, etc.
		3 one who manages a business, an institution, etc.

From *The Shorter English Dictionary*

The manager's job can, therefore, be broadly defined as deciding what should be done and then getting other people to do it.

from Rosemary Stewart, 1963, *The Reality of Management*, Pan/Heinemann Books, London, p. 74.

---

key concepts

leadership	legitimate power
consideration	expert power
initiating structure	contingency theory
great man theory	least preferred co-worker score
reward power	structured task
coercive power	unstructured task
referent power	situational leadership

learning objectives

When you have read this chapter, you should be able to define these key concepts in your own words, and you should also be able to:

1 Identify the main functions of leaders in organizations.
2 Understand why there is little relationship between personality traits and effective leadership.
3 Understand why there are still relatively few women managers.
4 Understand the bases of a leader's power in organizations.
5 Understand why effective managers typically adopt a democratic leadership style, which takes into account the needs of subordinates as well as the task needs of the organization.
6 Identify the circumstances in which an autocratic leadership style can be effective.
7 Recognize how cultural differences influence leadership and management style and effectiveness.

Research into leadership was initially driven by the assumption that the traits of effective leaders could be identified and measured. When that had been achieved, individuals who possessed those traits could be schooled into leadership positions. Considerable effort was devoted to identifying, defining and measuring the traits of known leaders in an attempt to explain individual success, and to find ways to develop leadership potential.

The failure of that line of research was accepted in the late 1940s. No consistent set of traits was established. Research findings were contradictory and inconclusive. The context in which a leader operates was recognized as a critical influence both on leadership behaviour and on effectiveness. The behaviour that leads to success as a leader in one situation may be wholly inappropriate in a different setting. The search for traits as explanatory variables was largely abandoned.

However, Alan Bryman (1986) has more recently argued that there is evidence supporting some relationships between personality characteristics and leadership success, and he claims that this line of thinking should not be completely ignored. Some contemporary commentary still adopts this basic assumption. The use of assessment centres as employee selection and development tools is based in part in a continuing faith in the popular belief that one can 'see' leadership in a person, in how they behave and how they interact with others. Depending on how personality traits are defined and measured, there is evidence to support the use of psychometric assessments in certain contexts.

the functions of leaders and managers

what is leadership?
Leadership is the lifting of a man's vision to higher sights, the raising of a man's performance to a higher standard, the building of a man's personality beyond its normal limitations. Nothing better prepares the ground for such leadership than a spirit of management that confirms in the day-to-day practices of the organization strict principles of conduct and responsibility, high standards of performance, and respect for the individual and his work. For to leadership, too, the words of the savings bank advertisement apply: 'Wishing won't make it so; doing will.'   from Peter F. Drucker, 1955, *The Practice of Management*, Heinemann, London, p. 195.

Our interest is with leadership in organizations, not with leadership in general. Most managers would probably claim to be able to exercise leadership in some form or another. A manager can be regarded as someone who, by definition, is assigned a position of leadership in an organization. Most definitions of management incorporate some notion of leadership in some respect. The two concepts are thus difficult to disentangle.

It may, therefore, appear reasonable to treat the terms leader and manager as meaning the same thing. Our understanding of these terms, however, suggests that this would be an oversimplification. There are many people who would be reluctant to describe their managers as leaders. And there are many leaders who could not be described as managers. To look at these issues from a negative perspective, to complain that 'we need effective management', is probably quite different from the cry, 'what we need is good leadership'.

Bryman (1986, p.6) offers us the following:

---

definition

Leadership *is 'the creation of a vision about a desired future state which seeks to enmesh all members of an organization in its net'.*

Management, on the other hand, 'tends to involve a preoccupation with the here-and-now of goal attainment' (Bryman, 1986, p.6). Here is the classic contrast between the manager as operator, as technician, as fixer and problem-solver, and the leader as visionary, as prophet, as catalyst and mover-shaker. This way of expressing the contrast seems to capture the ways in which these terms are now used to fix extreme differences between the roles. In reality, of course, the leader and the manager may be the same person.

Interest in organizational leadership was stimulated by the human relations movement in industrial sociology after the Second World War. The Hawthorne studies suggested that, if managers took an interest in their employees and involved them in decisions affecting their work, they would work harder. Those studies claimed to have identified the style of supervision most likely to guarantee a happy, harmonious, motivated workforce. Leadership or management style thus became a major interest and focus for research.

Many commentators have argued or assumed that the performance of an organization depends on the quality of leadership exercised by its managers. But in many organizations, tasks have been designed to be so routine, standardized and controlled that the dynamic, inspirational aspects of the leadership of other people may become redundant. These extreme views are probably incorrect, and it is reasonable to claim that what managers do in their leadership capacity does affect organizational performance – along with many other factors.

The managerial activities include:

1 Establishing overall purpose and policy.
2 Forecasting and planning for the future.
3 Organizing work, allocating duties and responsibilities.
4 Giving instructions or orders.
5 Co-ordinating the work of others.
6 Control – checking that performance is according to plan.

The exercise of those six management activities alone has little directly to do with lifting vision, raising performance and building personality. Leadership is clearly something more than the mere discharge of administrative functions, as Bryman and Drucker suggest, and is related instead to the creative exercise of influence. It is the way in which these functions are discharged – in the style of the manager – that the features of leadership are sought.

Some commentators have argued that communication and motivation are also management activities. But these are not administrative duties like

the Expansive Personality

As a model of executive personality, Bob Kaplan of CCL [Centre for Creative Leadership] has developed what he calls the Expansive Personality. This identifies six crucial characteristics of the leader's personality:

- need for mastery
- active, assertive, persistent
- belief in self
- goal-orientated relationship
- a need for recognition
- ability to accept the need for self-development

The dividing line between the positive and negative aspects of each characteristic is a thin one. It is advantageous to be hard-working and dedicated, but to know when to ease off. To be extremely compulsive and work-absorbed can be unhealthy.

One executive, for example, behaved just the same at home as he did at work. The routines and approaches of work were translated into his personal life with meetings and goal-setting sessions with his daughter instead of a spontaneous relationship.

from Stuart Crainer, 1988, 'Making boss-power positive', *The Sunday Times*, 9 October, p. E20.

people prefer considerate leaders

As psychiatrists are too expensive for most of us, managers at work end up dealing with their employees' personal problems. Factory foremen, for example, do not just give orders to subordinates to organize and co-ordinate their work. They have to deal also with a range of employee queries and difficulties. The style in which they carry out these extra responsibilities may influence their effectiveness as foremen.

Elizabeth Kaplan and Emory Cowen studied how American factory foremen felt about counselling. This is important as psychological well-being and productivity can be related.

They asked 97 foremen in 12 companies in New York about the kinds of problem that their subordinates brought to them, how much of their time this took up, how they went about solving these problems, and how they rated the importance of this part of their job.

The average foreman spent 7 per cent of his working time – about 2½ hours a week – dealing with the personal problems of subordinates. The most difficult problems for the foremen to solve were those which concerned marriage, money and other employees.

The foremen's most popular counselling technique was 'the sympathetic ear'. They usually encouraged subordinates to work out their own solutions, and rarely suggested that they seek professional help.

Most of the foremen were happy to have been approached for this kind of help, felt that this was an important issue and felt satisfied when their advice had been successful.

The authors argue that this informal counselling service is important to subordinates and to productivity, and that supervisors who have to provide the service should be given formal training in listening and advisory skills.

based on Elizabeth M. Kaplan and Emory L. Cowen, 1981, 'Interpersonal helping behaviour of industrial foremen', *Journal of Applied Psychology*, vol. 66, no. 5, pp. 633–8.

planning and organizing. They are concerned with *how* the manager influences others to carry out the plan, to accept instructions and to pursue the vision. They are again concerned with management style. Recall Bryman's definition of leadership, which involves the creation of a vision which will enmesh. Leaders are people who exercise influence over others.

This approach makes leaders out of most managers, because most managers will lay claim to influencing skills and to the need to use them. But managers do not automatically become leaders. The ability to influence also needs the permission of those to be influenced.

The functions of leaders in organizations may include:

- Enabling people and groups to achieve their objectives.
- Setting and communicating objectives.
- Monitoring performance and giving feedback.
- Establishing basic values.
- Clarifying and solving problems for others.
- Organizing resources.
- Administering rewards and punishments.
- Providing information, advice and expertise.
- Providing social and emotional support.
- Making decisions on behalf of others.
- Representing the group to others.
- Arbitrator in disputes.
- Father figure.
- Scapegoat.

This list could easily be extended. The point, however, is that you do not need to have the word 'manager' in your job title to be able to carry out leadership functions. Almost anyone could perform most of these tasks, and it has been suggested that these functions are best distributed depending on who can do each most effectively. There is, therefore, no necessary connection between these functions and a formally appointed manager. Similarly, managers do not become leaders just because they have job titles such as 'team leader' or 'section leader'. Our notions of management and leadership thus overlap, and there is no clear or simple distinction between them.

Edwin Fleishman and Ralf Stogdill's studies at the Bureau of Business Research at Ohio State University in the late 1940s are a classic and influential attempt to make sense of the complexity and diversity of leadership behaviours. They first designed a Leadership Behaviour Description Questionnaire based on how people in leadership roles actually carried out their functions. Foremen in the International Harvester Company, and employees in other organizations, were then asked to rate the frequency with which their own superiors behaved in the ways described in the questionnaire. Demonstrating the potential overlap and confusion in the terminology, Fleishman and colleagues described their work in terms of leadership and chose managers as research subjects.

Analysis of the questionnaire results revealed that the behaviour of leaders was described on two distinct categories – *consideration* and *initiating structure*.

Ralf M. Stogdill
(1904–78)

consideration

This type of leader behaviour is *needs- and relationships-oriented*.

---
definition

Consideration *is the term used to describe leadership behaviours that demonstrate sensitivity to the social needs of employees.*

The considerate leader is interested in and listens to subordinates, allows participation in decision-making, is friendly and approachable, helps subordinates with personal problems and is prepared to support them if necessary. The leader's behaviour indicates genuine trust, respect, warmth and rapport. This enhances subordinates' feelings of self-esteem and encourages the development of communications and relationships in a work group.

This is the emphasis that the human relations school encouraged, except that some of its advocates tended to exaggerate the benefits of superficial 'first name calling' and the 'pat on the back'. The researchers first called this leadership dimension *social sensitivity*.

In the Leadership Behaviour Description Questionnaire, subordinates rated their superiors as needs-oriented if they agreed with the following kinds of statement (the exclusively male-oriented language is from the original):

- He stresses the importance of high morale among those under him.
- He backs up his foremen in their actions.
- He does personal favours for the foremen under him.
- He expresses appreciation when one of us does a good job.
- He is easy to understand.
- He helps his foremen with their personal problems.
- He sees that a foreman is rewarded for a job well done.
- He treats all his foremen as his equal.
- He is willing to make changes.
- He makes those under him feel at ease when talking with him.
- He gets the approval of his foremen on important matters before going ahead.

Subordinates with inconsiderate superiors agreed with statements like:

- He refuses to give in when people disagree with him.
- He criticizes his foremen in front of others.
- He insists that everything be done his way.
- He rejects suggestions for change.
- He changes the duties of people under him without first talking it over with them.
- He refuses to explain his actions.

initiating structure

This type of leader behaviour is *task-oriented*.

---
definition

Initiating structure *is the term used to describe leadership behaviours that emphasize performance of the work in hand and the achievement of product and service goals.*

The leader initiating structure plans ahead, decides how things are going to get done, assigns tasks to subordinates, makes expectations clear, emphasizes deadlines and achievement, and expects subordinates to follow instructions closely. The leader's behaviour stresses production and the achievement of organizational goals. This type of behaviour can stimulate enthusiasm to achieve objectives as well as encouraging and helping subordinates to get the work done.

This is the kind of emphasis that the scientific management school encouraged, except that here it is recognized that task orientation can have a positive motivating aspect. The researchers first called this leadership dimension *production emphasis*.

In the Leadership Behaviour Description Questionnaire, subordinates would rate their superiors as task-oriented if they agreed with the following kinds of statement:

▶ He rules with an iron hand.
▶ He criticizes poor work.
▶ He talks about how much should be done.
▶ He assigns people under him to particular tasks.
▶ He asks for sacrifices for the good of the entire department.
▶ He insists that his foremen follow standard ways of doing things in every detail.
▶ He sees to it that people under him are working up to their limits.
▶ He stresses being ahead of competing work groups.
▶ He 'needles' foremen under him for greater effort.
▶ He decides in detail what shall be done and how it shall be done.
▶ He emphasizes the meeting of deadlines.
▶ He emphasizes the quantity of work.

Subordinates whose superiors lacked task orientation agreed with statements like:

▶ He lets others do the work the way they think best.
▶ He waits for subordinates to suggest new ideas.

The Ohio State University study created a dichotomy that still survives in management and leadership thinking, between employee-centred and job-centred leadership. This is also often expressed as the distinction between *democratic* and *autocratic* leadership. These two dimensions have been found in numerous similar subsequent studies of the way in which leadership behaviour is perceived by others.

These dimensions do not represent opposite poles of a continuum of leader behaviour. The Ohio State studies showed that the two types of behaviour are independent. A leader can emphasize either or both.

The Ohio State studies and subsequent research show that the most effective leaders are those who emphasize both consideration and structure. The leader thus has two main functions: to get the job done and to maintain group relationships. Inconsiderate leaders tend to have subordinates who complain and leave the organization, and tend to have comparatively unproductive work groups. Most of us prefer considerate supervisors and dislike those who are task orientated.

Note that this study and its approach emphasize what leaders or supervisors actually do in an organizational context in the course of their work. In other words, the focus is on their *behaviour* and not on personality traits or characteristics. This has profound significance for the selection and development of organizational leaders. While it may be difficult or impossible to 'train' someone to become a different personality, a combination of awareness and practice is often enough to train someone in the use of 'new' behaviours. The behaviours identified as effective by Fleishman and colleagues are not complex.

---

inconsiderate leaders are bad for your health

Employees who have lost interest in their job, and who just go through the motions, are always tired, or having colds, 'flu and headaches, may be suffering from *burnout*. This phenomenon has been researched by Cary Cherniss who puts the blame on leadership style.

Cherniss argues that the condition begins with a mismatch between the demands of the job and the abilities of the individual. This mismatch causes stress. Stress induces anxiety and exhaustion, which provoke either action to resolve the problem, or burnout which is a form of psychological escape. The burnt-out employee becomes cynical and works mechanically. This seems to be common in social work, healthcare and education, where the demands of the job are high, but where the effects of the individual's efforts are not always clear.

Cherniss analyzed the experiences of two community mental health workers over nine months.

Karen worked with a large and geographically spread case load of mentally retarded patients who had little hope of rehabilitation. The goal was simply to meet their physical needs. Karen could not devote much time to individual cases and had little chance to use her skills. Her department was a medical one and did not appreciate the function of social workers. Staff meetings run by the director were formal and businesslike with no time for informal contact with colleagues to share experiences. The main concern of Karen's boss was that she did not 'rock the boat' by breaking the rules. She got no emotional or technical support. Karen's attempts to overcome bureaucratic obstacles were not supported and she was labelled a troublemaker. After nine months she lost enthusiasm, and felt powerless and frustrated. She was even apathetic about looking for another job.

Diane worked with a small group of alcoholics who initially resisted treatment, but were intelligent and responsive. Opportunities to work with families, employers and other agencies, and to mix individual and group therapies, gave her variety and a chance to use her abilities. Management trusted staff and concentrated on support and development rather than on control. Diane became committed to a career in this field.

Cherniss argues that the outcomes in these cases were determined by the different styles of the managers. Cherniss suggests that to overcome Karen's problems:

▶ Staff have to be allowed to participate in management decisions.
▶ Managers have to understand the adverse effects on their subordinates of mistrust and lack of consideration.

based on Cary Cherniss, 1980, *Staff Burnout*, Sage Studies in Community Mental Health, no. 2.

are leaders special people?

Some of the material used in this chapter so far implies that leaders are *men* with special qualities. The early research into leadership thus concentrated on discovering what these special male qualities might be. There is a widespread and persistent assumption that women are unsuited to positions in which management and leadership qualities are required. Women are thus poorly represented in the ranks of management and have been largely ignored, until recently, in leadership research. Notably successful women in management and leadership roles attract special attention, and are treated to some extent by the media as unrepresentative, e.g. Steve Shirley, Anita Roddick, Margaret Thatcher.

The search for the qualities that made good leaders was influenced by the *great man theory* of history.

---

definition

The **great man theory** *of history states that the fate of societies, and organizations, is in the hands of key, powerful, idiosyncratic individuals, who by force of personality reach positions of influence from which they can direct and dominate the lives of others.*

The great man theory thus claims that our (predominantly male) leaders are simply born great and emerge to take power in any situation, regardless of the social or historical context.

STOP!

List the five most powerful and influential figures that you know about, who are alive today and who you would describe as leaders. They may be political or religious figures, or organizational managers.

Now write down the special qualities which you believe each of these people has.

Compare your list of special qualities with that of your colleagues and see if you can agree on a 'master list' of the attributes of leaders.

You have just worked through one of the first stages of many typical trait-based research projects on leadership. It used to be thought that a good starting point would be to identify the personality traits that make leaders effective. The next stage is to measure the extent to which good and bad leaders possess these personality traits. One would then hope to be in a position to be able to identify the traits which distinguish effective from ineffective leaders.

Rosemary Stewart (1963) cites an American study in which organization executives were asked to identify what they thought were the indispensable qualities of top managers. They came up with the following fifteen attributes:

judgement	initiative	integrity
foresight	energy	drive
human relations skill	decisiveness	dependability

- emotional stability   - fairness   - ambition
- dedication   - objectivity   - co-operation

How many of these attributes did you have in your own list of special leadership qualities? Leaders, of course, may also have undesirable qualities and be stubborn, self-centred, vain and domineering. The problem is that research has been unable to identify a common, agreed set of attributes. Successful leaders seem to defy classification and measurement from this perspective. Remember that leadership seems to be about influence. The chemistry of interpersonal influence is difficult to analyze in terms of one party's personality traits.

---

are leaders men with special qualities?

Discussion of leadership is so often overloaded with vague but emotive ideas that one is hard put to it to nail the concept down. To cut through the panoply of such quasi-moral and unexceptionable associations as 'patriotism', 'play up and play the game', the 'never-asking-your-men-to-do-something-you-wouldn't-do-yourself' formula, 'not giving in (or up)', the 'square-jaw-frank-eyes-steadfast-gaze' formula, and the 'if . . . you'll be a man' recipe, one comes to the simple truth that leadership is no more than exercising such an influence upon others that they tend to act in concert towards achieving a goal which they might not have achieved so readily had they been left to their own devices.

The ingredients which bring about this agreeable state of affairs are many and varied. At the most superficial level they are believed to include such factors as voice, stature and appearance, an impression of omniscience, trustworthiness, sincerity and bravery. At a deeper and rather more important level, leadership depends upon a proper understanding of the needs and opinions of those one hopes to lead, and the context in which the leadership occurs. It also depends on good timing. Hitler, who was neither omniscient, trustworthy nor sincere, whose stature was unremarkable and whose appearance verged on the repellent, understood these rules and exploited them to full advantage. The same may be said of many good comedians.

from Norman F. Dickson, 1976, *On the Psychology of Military Incompetence*, Futura Publications, London, pp. 214–15.

From their wide-ranging study, *Shattering the Glass Ceiling: The Woman Manager*, Marilyn Davidson and Cary Cooper (1992) point out that women are not disqualified from management roles by ability, personality or aspiration. The single, main beneficial change, they argue, to expand opportunities for women in management would be in male attitudes. The evidence suggests that the pace of change in this area is slow.

They also argue, however, that it is not necessarily effective for the ambitious woman to adopt a masculine style of behaviour. In contrast, the solution they suggest is to adopt a flexible combination of masculine and feminine attributes. This combination, known as *androgyny*, means being decisive and emotionally expressive, independent and tender, aggressive and gentle, assertive and yielding. This involves flexible, adaptive behaviour and rejection of traditional, simple stereotypes – 'typical female' or 'one of the boys'.

Davidson and Cooper (1992, p.97) quote one top female executive who told them:

> There seem to be three types of career women stereotype in industry from my experience: the 'army tweed and brogues' type, the 'burning bra' type and the 'easy floozy' type. The answer I have developed over time is to ensure managers get to know me as a person. I deliberately disclose aspects of myself and my life which defy stereotype. I also refuse to be 'miracle woman' and let the men know when I'm not coping. I have experienced an identity crisis at work. There are expectations and temptations to be like men, the 'one of the lads' syndrome. How feminine should I be in dress, behaviour and general appearance? The release of tension when I decided to be 'me' was enormous. I'm my own personality and *that* I will *not* trade for my career.

STOP!

Chapter 6 argues that the relationship between personality traits and job success is inevitably weak. On that evidence, what would you predict has been the outcome of research that has tried to find the personality traits that are associated with effective leadership?

---

do women have the right qualities?

Top managerial jobs still tend to go to men who are rational, efficient, tough-minded and unemotional. Women have to fight the popular stereotype that says they are dependent, sociable, subjective and emotional – traits that disqualify them from positions of managerial responsibility. Is the stereotype correct?

Rhona Steinberg and Stanley Shapiro used a series of questionnaires to test the personalities of 29 female and 42 male students on a university management course. The results showed that there were few personality differences between the sexes. All the students got high scores on the 'managerial' characteristics like dominance, self-assurance and the needs for responsibility and achievement.

The female students in fact had some strong 'masculine' personality traits. They were more tough-minded and suspicious of others than the men. The men were more tender-minded, humble, trusting, imaginative and introspective – traditional 'feminine' traits.

The researchers argue that women may exaggerate the masculine facets of their personalities to help them to compete more effectively for managerial jobs which they can perform just as well as men.

based on Rhona Steinberg and Stanley Shapiro, 1982, 'Sex differences in personality traits of female and male Masters of Business Administration students', *Journal of Applied Psychology*, vol. 67, no. 3, pp. 306–10.

Attempts to identify the personality traits of effective leaders have failed for three main reasons:

1 It is extremely difficult to reach any agreement on how vague concepts such as 'judgement' and 'dedication' are to be defined and measured consistently.
2 Personality traits and job success are not generally associated. Job performance is influenced by many factors other than personality.
3 A leader in an organization is a person in a role. The characteristics of that role will influence leader behaviour and success.

Effective leaders are not necessarily special people with special qualities. Women are not disqualified by personality from leadership positions. The qualities needed in a leader depend to a large extent on the demands of the situation in which he or she has to function. The two main aspects of the situation are the people being led – the 'followers' – and the tasks that they have to perform.

---

can fear of success prevent women becoming managers?

Women could fear success because they get anxious in situations where they are expected to behave in 'masculine' ways. As one has to be aggressive and competitive to be a successful leader, and as these traits are not usually considered 'feminine', this theory might explain why there are so few female managers. Research suggests that this theory is wrong.

Gary Popp and William Muhs gave a questionnaire to 214 American civil servants who gave information about their sex, age, pay, background, work experience and attitudes to success.

The results showed that women were not more afraid of success than men. Fear of success was strongest among young employees in low pay grades. The researchers argue that junior employees are more anxious because they face greater uncertainty over their careers than their older and more affluent and experienced superiors. They conclude that the stereotype of the female frightened by success is false.

based on Gary E. Popp and William F. Muhs, 1982, 'Fear of success and women employees', *Human Relations*, vol. 35, no. 7, pp. 511–19.

The idea that 'leadership qualities' can be identified persists and experienced a revival in the late 1980s as leadership became 'popular' again as a management topic. The Brussels-based business school Management Centre Europe in 1987–88 asked over 1000 senior and middle managers in Europe to describe 'crucial leadership characteristics' and to assess whether their own chief executive officers possessed these (Devine, 1988). The results showed that human resource management skills were given priority in five areas:

1 team-building
2 listening
3 independent decision-making
4 knowing how to retain good people
5 being surrounded by the right top people

---

discrimination prevents women becoming managers

In Northern Ireland, about 40 per cent of the workforce are women but less than 5 per cent of them hold management jobs.

Stanley Cromie got 99 female and 79 male replies to a questionnaire which he posted to professional teachers, managers and secretaries in Belfast. The questions measured the importance of work to the individual, and attitudes to women as managers were assessed.

The results showed that women valued their jobs just as much as the men in the sample. Professional women in fact had higher degrees of commitment to their work than professional men, but the male and female managers had similar commitment scores. The job involvement of the secretaries was low, but Cromie argues that this was due to the low status of their work, and not to their sex alone. The women all felt that women could happily handle management jobs, but the men felt that female managers were incompetent.

Cromie argues that management jobs are closed to women by male bias and discrimination, not because women lack ambition, capability or the 'right' personality traits.

based on Stanley Cromie, 1981, 'Women as managers in Northern Ireland', *Journal of Occupational Psychology*, vol. 54, no. 2, pp. 87–91.

Except for decision-making, fewer than half the managers questioned felt that their chief executives had these key leadership qualities. Characteristics like ruthlessness and paternalism were rated least important, but in this survey these traits were possessed by 25 per cent of top executives. The ideal and the reality were different. The typical chief executive revealed in this survey was a lonely, ambitious, strong-willed autocrat, making his own decisions, motivated by power and money.

The survey also showed that the emphasis on the leader's role as spokesman for the organization, with customers, suppliers, government and investors, was often inappropriate. A Danish chief executive said:

> I spent most of my time as a leader seeing people and acting as a public-relations figure. That is what I regret. My real job was to see to it that the 20 people who reported to me were the best there were.

One possible explanation for the weak people skills of chief executives concerns the assumption that the effectiveness of an organization depends ultimately on one leader. The head of human resources at Motorola is cited as saying:

> It is difficult to imagine what we think of as leadership all residing in one individual in the future. My vision is of two, three or even four people directly involved with operating at the top.

John Adair (1990) has argued that a 'strategic leader' requires three characteristics.

The first of these is what Adair calls *direction*. This is the 'visionary' dimension of leadership identified by Drucker, and is the dimension which Bryman (1986) uses to distinguish leadership from management. The ability to communicate a desirable image of the future and to unite groups of people in a common purpose is intuitively close to our expectations and understanding of leaders and leadership.

"That's an excellent suggestion, Miss Triggs.
Perhaps one of the men here would like to make it."

The second 'core requirement' according to Adair is *team-building* capability, incorporating the notions of common objectives and good communications. The effective leader is someone who creates an effective team extending beyond the senior management group.

The third key characteristic is *creativity*. Given contemporary rates of change, top management innovation, recruiting innovators, and empowering people to innovate have become critical factors.

STOP!

John Adair spoke in 1990 of 'the new emerging leadership culture'. Why did 'leadership' assume such significance as a social, political and organizational issue during the 1990s?

---

leaders need followers

The Cult of Leadership

> And those who hew the wood and hump it
> Are firmly told that they can lump it –
> A system known to learned sages
> To mark the Neolithic ages,
> But now unknown to observation
> Outside the business corporation.
>
> So leadership, as a result,
> Is consecrated as a cult,
> Endowed with charismatic powers
> Light-years from the likes of ours:
> Particularly useful while
> The new machismo is in style.

So might it not be best to say
That leaders, too, have feet of clay,
And any claim to lead is hollow
Unless the troops consent to follow?
If not, I think the special pleaders
Should find another word than 'leaders'!

from *The Bottom Line: A Book of Business Ballads*, by Bertie Ramsbottom, Century Hutchinson Ltd, London.

If we accept the argument that, at least in part, leaders do not need special qualities, then perhaps we should turn to followers to find an explanation of leadership. One cannot be a leader without followers. The one essential attribute of followers is that they must be willing to comply with the instructions of their leader. If followers are for some reason unwilling to comply with those orders, then the leader can do nothing, and may forfeit the title.

The use of physical violence by thugs and bullies to get people to comply is not recognized as the exercise of leadership. It is not just individual qualities that make someone a leader. The willingness of potential followers to comply with instructions or follow directions is equally important.

---

definition

Leadership *is a social process in which one individual influences the behaviour of others without the use or threat of violence.*

Leadership in this definition is a property of the *relationship* between leader and follower. It is not simply some characteristic or feature of the individual leader. This helps to explain why an examination of the characteristics of leaders alone has offered limited insights. To understand leadership we have to understand compliance. We need to know why people are willing to let themselves be influenced by some individuals and not by others. We need to understand the nature of the relationships involved.

We have now defined leadership in terms of 'followership', in terms of the ability of one person to exert influence over others. One problem with this view is that everyone exerts some influence on everyone else. The 'leaders' of strike action and other, more subtle, forms of organizational sabotage and disruption, for example, do not always belong to the ranks of management. The exercise of leadership is by no means a white-collar, managerial, high-status prerogative. An added complication is that followers in many instances clearly influence their leaders. It follows from this observation that one ingredient of leadership success may be the ability to assess what others wish to do, before directing (or leading) them to do it.

Those whom we call leaders, however, seem to be different in at least two respects. First, they appear to have a stronger and more readily effective influence than others. Second, they try to influence others to behave in ways that are beyond mere compliance with the rules and routines of the organization. We give the title 'leader' to those who seem able to motivate us ordinary people to behave in extraordinary ways.

Power is a useful concept with which to explain why different people exert different degrees of influence over others. As with leadership, power is a property of the *relationship* between the more and the less powerful. The exercise of power is a social process. Power is a critical dimension of leadership, and the two terms are often used with the same or similar meanings: a leader is someone with power, powerful individuals are leaders. We can thus define power in the same way that we have defined leadership – as the ability of an individual to control or to influence others, to get someone else to do something that they would perhaps not otherwise do. However, we must distinguish between different types or *bases* of power.

John French and Bertram Raven (1958) identified five main bases of power (see Chapter 8).

reward power

definition
Reward power *is based on the belief of followers that the leader has access to valued rewards which will be dispensed in return for compliance with instructions.*

A leader has reward power if followers believe that the leader is able to control rewards that they value, and that the leader will part with these rewards in return for compliance with the leader's directions and demands. In an organization, rewards may include pay, promotion, allocation to desirable work duties, diversion from undesirable duties, membership of particular (perhaps prestigious or important) groups or teams, responsibility for significant tasks and activities, new equipment, favourable leave and holiday arrangements, and recognition for good performance. Reward power is not dependent on money.

If the leader controls rewards that followers do not value, then the leader may have little or no reward power. If the leader has no control over valued rewards, but followers *believe* that such rewards will be forthcoming, then the leader has reward power.

coercive power

definition
Coercive power *is based on the belief of followers that the leader can administer penalties or sanctions that are considered to be unwelcome.*

A leader has coercive power if followers believe that the leader is able and willing to administer penalties that they dislike. The intensity of the penalties and the probability of them being applied are what really matter. In an organization, these penalties may include humiliation and other forms of oral abuse, withdrawal of friendship and emotional support, loss of favours and privileges such as allocation to desirable work, allocation to disliked activities, the creation of problems with respect to casual absence and holiday requests, curtailment of promotion opportunities, and delayed pay rises. Coercive power is not dependent on threats of job loss.

referent power

---
definition

Referent power *is based on the belief of followers that the leader has desirable abilities and personality traits that can and should be copied.*

A leader has referent power if followers believe that the leader has characteristics that are desirable and that they should copy. Followers thus identify themselves with the leader, regardless of what he or she actually does. Referent power thus depends on the personality and attractiveness of the leader, as these features are perceived by followers. Referent power has also been called *charisma*. Not many people have the charisma of, say, John F. Kennedy or Nelson Mandela. However, organization managers are sometimes able to command respect and admiration from their employees, exercising charisma on a local scale.

legitimate power

---
definition

Legitimate power *is based on the belief of followers that the leader has a position of authority in the organization hierarchy which gives them the right to issue orders, with which followers have an obligation to comply.*

A leader has legitimate power if followers believe that the leader has a right to give them orders which they in turn have an obligation to accept. This is also called 'position power' because it depends on the formal organizational position and title of the individual. The leader's legitimacy can rely on a job title – professor, doctor, matron, director, captain, chairman – which followers see as conferring on the leader the right to give them orders.

expert power

---
definition

Expert power *is based on the belief of followers that the leader has superior knowledge relevant to the situation and the task in hand.*

A leader has expert power if followers believe that the leader has superior knowledge and expertise which is relevant to the particular tasks or activities in hand. Expert power can thus confer leadership on anyone with the requisite knowledge and skills, regardless of their job title or organizational position. The expert power of many organizational managers may be limited to narrow specialisms and functions. The leader must demonstrate relevant ability. The followers' perceptions of the leader's understanding, credibility, trustworthiness, honesty and access to information are fundamental to their perception of the leader as a person with expert power.

These five power bases have a number of significant features.

First, they all depend on the beliefs of followers. These beliefs may be influenced by the abilities and behaviour of the leader, but it is subordinates' beliefs that count. A leader may be able to control rewards and penalties, have superior knowledge and so on, but if subordinates do not believe that the leader has these attributes, then they may not be willing to be easily led. Similarly, leaders may be able to manipulate subordinates into the belief that they possess power which they in fact do not have. From this perspective, power is not just a property of the leader, something that the leader may or may not possess.

Second, these power bases are interrelated. The exercise of one power base may affect a leader's ability to use another. The leader who resorts to coercive power may, for example, lose referent power. The leader may be able to use legitimate power to enhance both referent and expert power. Leadership, power and influence are therefore not static concepts.

Third, a leader can operate from multiple bases of power. The same person may be able to use different bases in different contexts and at different times. Few leaders may be able to rely on a single power base.

STOP!

Which power base, or which combination of power bases, would you expect to be most effective for an organization leader? What is the power base, or what are the power bases, of your organizational behaviour instructor(s)?

A prestigious job title may give a manager in an organization, or an academic in an educational establishment, a certain amount of legitimate power, which he or she can then use to exert leadership over others. A job title creates a shared expectation that the holder gives the orders, whilst others (whether they be employees or students) carry them out.

Legitimate power on its own is not enough. Some employees may have sources of power of their own which they can use to subvert the leader's position. The 'prerogatives' or 'rights' of management are increasingly challenged, and employment does not guarantee loyalty or commitment to the objectives of the organization. Many employees are suspicious of managers and their motives, and react cautiously to what managers say and do. Prestigious job titles no longer automatically confer legitimacy on the bosses' orders.

Leadership style has thus become a central problem for managers. How should leaders or managers handle their followers or subordinates? How can managers overcome suspicion and caution and ensure high work motivation and performance? What is the most effective management style? These questions have generated an enormous quantity of research and commentary. This is an issue in which there are no simple theories or solutions. But the evidence does seem to point in the same broad direction.

The most effective style of management seems to be one in which the manager shares power with subordinates. This style can increase both the satisfaction and effectiveness of those who are led. In other words the most effective managers are those who appear to relinquish power to their subordinates. Many managers, however, are not keen to share power, influence and decision making with people towards whom they feel superior. Many managers feel that they personally must lose the influence that they give to their subordinates. This is in fact not the case. Managers who give discretion to their subordinates can increase their personal influence over those subordinates.

Rensis Likert
(1903–81)

One influential study which demonstrated the effectiveness of this 'power sharing' management style was that carried out by Rensis Likert at the University of Michigan Survey Research Centre. Likert was concerned with the characteristics of effective supervisors. He interviewed twenty-four supervisors and 419 clerks in highly productive and less productive departments in an American insurance company.

He found that the supervisors in the highly productive sections were more likely to:

▷ Get general as opposed to close supervision from their superiors.
▷ Enjoy their job authority and responsibility.
▷ Spend more time on supervision.
▷ Give general as opposed to close supervision of their subordinates.
▷ Be employee rather than production oriented.

The supervisors in the sections where productivity was low had the opposite characteristics. They were close, production-oriented supervisors, who concentrated on keeping their subordinates busy with specified tasks and methods and achieving targets on time.

Likert's effective supervisors were not just concerned with the needs of their employees. They were seen by their subordinates as emphasizing high levels of performance and achievement and had a 'contagious enthusiasm' for the

---

rules for leaders and followers

The job satisfaction and health of subordinates are better when supervisors establish a warm, friendly and supportive relation and look after their welfare; and when supervisors consult them, allow them to take part in decisions, and explain and persuade rather than give orders. Our study showed the most important rules for supervisors to be:

▷ Plan and assign work efficiently.
▷ Keep subordinates informed about decisions affecting them.
▷ Respect the other's privacy.
▷ Keep confidences.
▷ Consult subordinates in matters that affect them.
▷ Advise and encourage subordinates.
▷ Fight for subordinates' interests.
▷ Be considerate about subordinates' personal problems.

There is no corresponding research on the skills of subordinates, and it is not clear what 'success' consists of here. Research by colleagues and myself indicates these rules for subordinates:

▷ Don't hesitate to question when orders are unclear.
▷ Use initiative where possible.
▷ Put forward and defend own ideas.
▷ Complain first to superior before going to others.

importance of achieving these goals. This clearly supports Fleishman's argument that leaders need to stress both consideration and structure. Likert and his research team at Michigan identified four main styles or systems of leadership in organizations, based on their research:

System 1: *Exploitative autocratic*, in which the leader:

⦁ Has no confidence and trust in subordinates.
⦁ Imposes decisions on subordinates; never delegates.
⦁ Motivates by threat.
⦁ Has little communication and teamwork involving subordinates.

System 2: *Benevolent authoritative*, in which the leader:

⦁ Has superficial, condescending confidence and trust in subordinates.
⦁ Imposes decisions on subordinates; never delegates.
⦁ Motivates by reward.
⦁ Sometimes involves subordinates in solving problems; paternalistic.

System 3: *Participative*, in which the leader:

⦁ Has some incomplete confidence and trust in subordinates.
⦁ Listens to subordinates but controls decision making.
⦁ Motivates by reward and some involvement.
⦁ Uses ideas and opinions of subordinates constructively.

System 4: *Democratic*, in which the leader:

⦁ Has complete confidence and trust in subordinates.
⦁ Allows subordinates to make decisions for themselves.
⦁ Motivates by reward for achieving goals set by participation.
⦁ Shares ideas and opinions.

⦁ Respect others' privacy.
⦁ Be willing and cheerful.
⦁ Don't be too submissive.
⦁ Be willing to accept criticism.
⦁ Keep confidences.
⦁ Be willing to take orders.

The rules we found for co-workers were:

⦁ Accept one's fair share of the work load.
⦁ Respect others' privacy.
⦁ Be co-operative over shared physical working conditions (like light, noise).
⦁ Be willing to help when requested.
⦁ Keep confidences.
⦁ Work co-operatively, despite feelings of dislike.
⦁ Don't denigrate another employee to superiors.

If the rules are followed, it is probably easier to sustain these relationships without getting into further trouble. For example, saying nasty things about people very often gets back to them.

from Michael Argyle, 1983, 'Pleasures and pains of working together', *New Society*, 9 June, pp. 382–3.

---

one of Rensis Likert's less effective supervisors

This interest-in-people approach is all right, but it's a luxury. I've got to keep pressure on for production, and when I get production up, then I can afford to take time to show an interest in my employees and their problems.

---

one of Rensis Likert's more effective supervisors

One way in which we accomplish a high level of production is by letting people do the job the way they want to so long as they accomplish the objectives. I believe in letting them take time out from the monotony. Make them feel that they are something special, not just the run of the mill. As a matter of fact, I tell them if you feel that job is getting you down get away from it for a few minutes . . . . If you keep employees from feeling hounded, they are apt to put out the necessary effort to get the work done in the required time.

I never make any decisions myself. Oh, I guess I've made about two since I've been here. If people know their jobs I believe in letting them make decisions. I believe in delegating decision-making. Of course, if there's anything that affects the whole division, then the two assistant managers, the three section heads and sometimes the assistant section heads come in here and we discuss it. I don't believe in saying that this is the way it's going to be. After all, once supervision and management are in agreement there won't be any trouble selling the staff the idea.

My job is dealing with human beings rather than with the work. It doesn't matter if I have anything to do with the work or not. The chances are that people will do a better job if you are really taking an interest in them. Knowing the names is important and helps a lot, but it's not enough. You really have to know each individual well, know what his problems are. Most of the time I discuss matters with employees at their desks rather than in the office. Sometimes I sit on a waste paper basket or lean on the files. It's all very informal. People don't seem to like to come into the office to talk.

from Rensis Likert, 1961, *New Patterns of Management*, McGraw-Hill Book Company, New York, pp. 7–8.

Likert's research shows that effective managers are those who adopt either a System 3 or a System 4 leadership style, which is based on trust and pays attention to the needs of the organization and the employees. This is a difficult conclusion for some managers to accept. The research shows, however, that democratic management means involvement, mutual respect, openness, trust, motivation and commitment. It is an 'alternative organizational life style', which has been found mainly in successful companies.

Democratic leadership seems to erode the influence of managers. Some managers prefer formal, written rules and believe in the necessity of hierarchy to achieve order, discipline and control which they feel are essential to achieve high performance. This view ignores the politics of organizational life in which people at all levels compete for power and influence – the ingredients of leadership.

Democratic leadership may increase a manager's ability to exert influence over subordinates. If a manager allows subordinates to take part in management decisions, the influence of that manager is not necessarily eroded. By demonstrating confidence and trust in subordinates, the manager's ability to exert further influence on them may be significantly increased.

We have defined leadership as a property of the relationship between leaders and followers. This is not a simple relationship in which there is a

---

the changing role of first-level supervision

Tom Peters (1987, p.302), the American management consultant, has argued that improved economic performance is dependent on 'committed, flexible, multi-skilled, constantly retrained people, joined together in self-managing teams'. However, this has implications for the first-line supervisor. Peters further argues that, 'if you do not drastically widen the span of control, and shift the supervisor's job content, the self-managing team concept will not work – period' (p. 300). He sees the role of the first-line supervisor changing like this:

traditional	new
span-of-control of ten	span-of-control of 50 to 75 +
scheduler of work	coach and sounding board for self-managing teams; leader/co-ordinator working on training and skill development
rule enforcer	facilitator, getting experts to help teams as needed
lots of planning	lots of wandering around
focused up and down the organization structure	focused horizontally, working with other functions to speed action
transmitting management needs down	selling team ideas and needs up
providing new ideas for workers	helping teams develop their own ideas and providing ideas for cross-functional systems development

based on Tom Peters, 1987, *Thriving on Chaos: Handbook for a Managerial Revolution*, Macmillan, London.

straightforward division of labour with the leader carrying out all the functions and making all the decisions on the one hand, and the followers passively doing what they are told on the other. Leadership functions are thus dispersed in an organization rather than being concentrated in the hands of formally appointed managers. Leadership functions, as we have identified them here, are best carried out by people who have the interest, knowledge, skills and motivation to perform them effectively. These people are not always formally appointed managers.

The leadership tasks of managers may therefore be:

1 To find ways of handling the inconsistency between organizational objectives and individual needs through a democratic leadership style that concentrates on both consideration and initiating structure.

2 To identify those individuals best able to carry out the various different aspects of the leadership function and to delegate accordingly.

the importance of context

We have discussed how the characteristics of leaders and followers can influence the effectiveness with which a leader operates. But there are other factors that can affect the behaviour and effectiveness of leaders, such as the nature of the task that is to be done, the skills and perceptions of followers, and the wider organizational context.

The context in which the leader has to work complicates the management dilemma. Employees asked to dismantle a machine for repair will probably react differently from those who have to dismantle the machine because their department has been made redundant. People working constantly under severe time pressure, as in many restaurants and hospitals, behave differently from those whose daily routine is more relaxed. The organizational leader's behaviour may thus be affected by features of the task that has to be managed.

Leadership behaviour that is appropriate in one context may not, therefore, be effective in another. People accustomed to impersonal directive leadership may be suspicious of someone with a friendly, democratic style. People who are accustomed to participative management may, on the other hand, accept an autocratic style if they can see that pressure of work makes this necessary to achieve their work objectives.

This suggests that a leader must be able to 'diagnose' the human and organizational context in which he or she is working and be able to decide what behaviour will best 'fit' the situation. As the best style to adopt is thus contingent on the situation, this approach is referred to as a *contingency theory* of leadership. It also follows that leaders who are not able to adjust their style to fit different circumstances are likely to be effective only in those contexts where their inflexible style applies.

---

definition

*The **contingency theory** of leadership states that the leader, to be effective, must adjust his or her style in a manner consistent with critical aspects of the organizational context, such as the nature of the task, and attributes of employees carrying out the work.*

The leadership research and contingency theory of Fred Fiedler (1967; 1974) provides a useful, systematic approach to diagnosing contextual factors. Fiedler worked with groups whose leaders were clearly identified and whose performance was easy to measure – such as basketball teams and bomber crews. Fiedler first developed a new measure of a leader's basic approach to managing people – the leader's *least preferred co-worker* (**LPC**) *score*.

---

definition

The **least preferred co-worker score** *is a rating, across several dimensions, of the kind of person with whom a particular leader feels they could not work effectively.*

Fred E. Fiedler

Fiedler's leaders were asked to think of the person with whom they could work least well. They were then asked to rate that person on sixteen dimensions:

1 pleasant/unpleasant	9 quarrelsome/harmonious
2 gloomy/cheerful	10 rejecting/accepting
3 helpful/frustrating	11 unenthusiastic/enthusiastic
4 tense/relaxed	12 distant/close
5 self-assured/hesitant	13 cold/warm
6 friendly/unfriendly	14 efficient/inefficient
7 co-operative/unco-operative	15 open/guarded
8 supportive/hostile	16 boring/interesting

The leaders who rate their least preferred co-workers negatively get low LPC scores and are task-oriented: they regard anyone whose performance is poor in wholly negative terms. Leaders who rate their least preferred co-workers positively get high LPC scores and are relationships-oriented: they tend to see positive values even in those they dislike.

The high and low LPC scores are similar to consideration and initiating structure – the Ohio study dimensions of leadership behaviour. Fiedler appears to have found with the LPC score another way to uncover an individual manager's orientations, biases, preferences and predispositions. It should not be surprising, however, to find that Fiedler's initial attempts to correlate the LPC scores of leaders with the performance of their groups was not successful. This led Fiedler to the argument that effectiveness is influenced by three main sets of factors:

1 The extent to which the task in hand is structured.
2 The leader's position power.
3 The nature of the relationships between the leader and followers.

---

definitions

A **structured task** *is one with clear goals, few correct or satisfactory solutions or outcomes, few ways of performing it, and clear criteria of success.*

An **unstructured task** *is one with ambiguous goals, many correct solutions or satisfactory outcomes, many ways of achieving acceptable outcomes, and vague criteria of success.*

> **STOP!**
>
> Would you describe the task of writing a term assignment or essay in organizational behaviour as structured or unstructured?
>
> Would you prefer the task to be more or less structured, and how would you advise your tutor to achieve this?

Fiedler identifies three typical or extreme sets of situations under which a leader may have to work.

situation 1:
- The task is highly structured.
- The leader's position power is high.
- Subordinates feel that their relationships with the boss are good.

Task-oriented (low LPC score) leaders get good results in these favourable circumstances. The task-oriented leader in this situation detects that events are potentially under his or her control, sets targets, monitors progress and achieves good performance.

Relationships-oriented (high LPC score) leaders get poor results in these circumstances. They try to get the work done by building and maintaining good relationships with and among subordinates. However, when relationships are already good, and the other conditions are favourable, the leader may take subordinates for granted and start to pursue other, personal objectives.

situation 2:
- The task is unstructured.
- The leader's position power is low.
- Subordinates feel that their relationships with the boss are moderately good.

Relationship-oriented leaders get better results in these moderately favourable circumstances where the maintenance of good relationships is important both to the ability of the leader to exert influence over subordinates and to get the work done. The task-oriented leader ignores deteriorating relationships and as the task lacks structure and the leader lacks position power the results are likely to be poor.

situation 3:
- The task is unstructured.
- The leader's position power is low.
- Subordinates feel that their relationships with the boss are poor.

According to Fiedler, task-oriented leaders get better results in these very unfavourable situations. Why? The relationships-oriented leader is unwilling to exert pressure on subordinates, avoids confrontations that might upset or anger them, gets involved in attempts to repair damaged relationships and ignores the task. The task-oriented leader gets impatient, tries to structure the situation, ignores resistance from subordinates, reduces the ambiguity surrounding the work and achieves good performance.

Fiedler argued that the leader's orientation was a relatively fixed aspect of personality. The leader in the 'wrong' kind of situation should thus try to change key aspects of that situation, or move to a leadership context more favourable to their orientation. Fiedler did not consider it appropriate to change the individual's leadership style.

The research to support this contingency theory is positive but weak, and Edgar Schein argues that it has three main problems. First, the three key variables, task structure, power and relationships, are difficult to assess in practice. The leader who wants to rely on this framework to determine the most effective style for a given situation has to rely more on intuition than on systematic analysis. Second, the framework does not directly take into account the needs of subordinates. Third, the need for a leader to have technical competence relevant to the task is ignored.

This theory has at least two strengths. First, it demonstrates the importance of contextual factors in determining leader behaviour and effectiveness. It reinforces the view that there is no one best style or one ideal personality that a leader must have to be successful. Second, it provides a systematic framework for developing the self-awareness of managers.

Fiedler's framework can be used to increase the sensitivity of organizational leaders to their own personalities, to their relationships with their subordinates and to the nature of the context in which they manage. This increased self-awareness is fundamental to the leader's ability to change style to fit different settings, assuming that such adjustment is possible.

Fiedler's theory ignores technical competence

The popular stereotype of the successful top manager is of a man who enjoys manipulating and controlling other people, who likes to make harsh decisions and who does not worry about what others think of him. David McClelland and Richard Boyatzis argue that this type of management style is effective only in some managerial jobs.

Their research studied 235 male managers who had worked with the American Telephone and Telegraph company for over twenty years. Between 1956 and 1960, the managers were given a series of personality tests. They were asked to write creative stories about ambiguous pictures. The contents of their stories were then assessed for themes and images concerning the managers' needs for power and for friendship. The careers of these managers were followed up to 1978. (The personality tests in this research were similar to the projective Thematic Apperception Tests explained in Chapter 6.)

Some of these managers had 'technical' jobs and worked on the manufacture, installation and repair of telephone equipment. Others had 'non-technical' jobs and were concerned with customer services, accounting, sales, administration and personnel management.

The non-technical managers who had a strong need for power and a weak need for friendship had been promoted faster. But the technical managers had been promoted for their technical, engineering abilities, not because of their personalities.

McClelland later argued that top managers in particular tend to have a high need for power and only a moderate need for affiliation. Excessive need for achievement can be a handicap to reaching high office; high achievers seem to perform well up to middle management levels, but it is those with high power needs who rise further.

based on David C. McClelland and Richard E. Boyatzis, 1982, 'Leadership motive pattern and long-term success in management', *Journal of Applied Psychology*, vol. 67, no. 6, pp. 737–43; and David C. McClelland and David H. Burnham, 1976, 'Power is the great motivator', *Harvard Business Review*, March–April, reprinted in the January–February 1995 edition, pp. 126–39.

Robert J. House

Developing a similar contingent approach, Robert J. House (1971) proposed a 'path-goal' theory of leadership style. The theory's title is based on the proposition that the leader's main function is to 'clear a path' to the achievement of desired goals.

House based his theory on four typical leadership behaviours:

- **directive** The leader concentrates on the performance of the work, clarifies performance expectations, allocates roles to work group members.
- **supportive** The leader demonstrates concern for employee needs, is open, warm, friendly and approachable, treats employees as equals.
- **participative** The leader actively consults with employees, considers suggestions and ideas seriously before making decisions.
- **achievement-oriented** The leader emphasizes excellent performance, sets high goals, shows confidence of ability of employees to excel.

Directive behaviour can be equated with 'initiating structure'. Supportive behaviour is the same as 'consideration'. Those were the two main dimensions of leadership behaviour identified by Edwin Fleishman and his colleagues in the Ohio State leadership studies, described earlier in the chapter.

In addition, House identified two sets of contingent variables that could influence how effective a choice of leader behaviour would be in a given context. These contingent factors concern employee characteristics and the workplace characteristics respectively.

Significant employee characteristics include:

- the perceptions that employees have about their *ability* level
- whether they feel that their *locus of control* is internal (that they are individually self-directing) or external (that they are moulded by other people and events)
- their degree of *authoritarianism* (see Chapter 23), and whether they view those in positions of power favourably or otherwise

Significant workplace characteristics include:

- the nature of the *task*, and whether it is routine (structured) or ambiguous (unstructured)
- the extent to which *formal authority* is well defined, or not
- whether employees identify strongly with each other in their *primary work group*

In path-goal theory, the leader must select the behaviours most relevant and helpful to particular employees in the given context. A directive style will be appropriate where it is necessary to provide clear guidance about tasks, timing and performance standards. Supportive behaviour will be more effective when employee social needs are not being adequately met. Participative behaviour may be more appropriate where problems need to be addressed and solved and employees can contribute knowledge and ideas. An achievement-oriented style may be highly challenging to a skilled, cohesive and self-confident group of employees.

Path-goal theory can be summarized in the following figure:

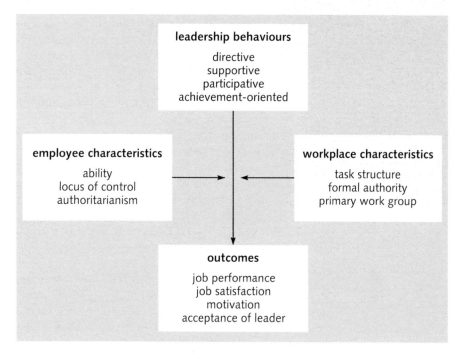

It is clear that some employees are likely to need more order, structure and guidance than others, and that some tasks are more mundane, predictable and routine than others. There is some intuitive appeal in the conclusion that leaders must therefore adjust their behaviours to take these factors into account. As with Fiedler's theory, the evidence is weak. Leaders who do not adjust their styles, however, are likely to have difficulties with some work groups.

Another highly influential contingency theory of leadership effectiveness has been developed by Paul Hersey and Ken Blanchard (1988). With Fiedler and House, they argue that the effective leader 'must be a good diagnostician' and adapt style to meet the demands of the context in which they operate. Hersey and Blanchard call their approach *situational leadership*.

above:
Paul Hersey

right:
Kenneth Blanchard

definition

Situational leadership *is an approach to determining the most effective style of influencing, taking into account the amounts of direction and support the leader gives, and the readiness and maturity of followers to perform a particular task.*

Hersey and Blanchard illustrate and explain situational leadership with the following figure:

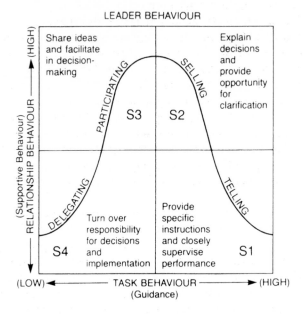

This apparently complex figure first categorizes leader behaviour on two main dimensions.

The first dimension, on the horizontal axis of the top half of the figure, concerns 'task behaviour', or the amount of guidance and direction a leader gives to subordinates. This can vary from total delegation at one extreme, to providing specific instruction at the other. Hersey and Blanchard identify two intermediate positions on this continuum, where leaders either facilitate subordinates' decisions, or take more care to explain and clarify their own.

The second dimension, on the vertical axis, concerns 'supportive behaviour' and the amount of social backup a leader gives to subordinates. This can vary from limited communication with subordinates at one extreme, to considerable communications and listening, facilitating and supportive behaviours at the other.

This model establishes four basic leadership styles, labelled S1–S4. The four styles are:

S1   High amounts of task behaviour, telling subordinates what to do, when to do it, how to do it and so on, but with little relationship behaviour.

S2   High amounts of both task behaviour and relationship behaviour.

S3   Lots of relationship behaviour and support for subordinates, but little direction or task behaviour.

S4   Not much task behaviour or relationship behaviour.

Hersey and Blanchard also argue that the readiness of followers to perform a particular task is a key factor in establishing an effective leadership style. This is explained by the lower half of the figure, in which follower readiness is drawn on a continuum from low to high – with insecure subordinates unwilling to act at one extreme to confident followers able and willing to perform at the other. Superimpose the readiness continuum on the top half of the model and we have a basis for selecting an effective leadership style. It is compelling to suggest that insecure and recalcitrant subordinates need telling, while willing and confident groups can be left to get on with the activity delegated to them. This, after all, is one aspect of the message from House in path-goal theory.

Bryman (1986) points to some of the limitations of this model. For example, there is no clear reason why S2 and S3 should be associated with R2 and R3 respectively. The S3 style could be appropriate with individuals and groups in a high state of 'psychological' readiness, but without the depth of experience in the job that would enable them to perform effectively – that is with an R2 group (Bryman, 1986, p.149). Bryman also points to the lack of convincing evidence to support the model in practice.

As with Fiedler and House, however, the main benefit of the model may be in the emphasis on the need for flexibility in leadership behaviour, and in highlighting the importance of contextual factors.

the importance of culture

One of the key management and leadership issues for the twenty-first century will concern the ability to manage across different countries and cultures. The models of leadership that we have discussed so far deal with the notion of 'context' in a relatively narrow manner. The country and the culture in which an organization operates is another critical aspect of context which creates other demands on an organization's members.

The demand for expertise in working with different country nationals, and with different belief and value systems, grew rapidly during the 1990s, for several reasons, including:

- international recruitment to overcome domestic staff shortages
- cross-border mergers, acquisitions and joint ventures
- the potential opening up of new markets in Eastern Europe, South East Asia and China
- European social policy directives, like the Social Chapter
- continuing developments in communications technology with global reach

What management and leadership styles will be required to deal with this environment?

Sharon Colback and Michael Maconochie (1989) have attempted to profile the typical 'Euromanager' at the turn of the twenty-first century. He – and presumably she – will be a graduate with a second degree in European studies, and will speak fluently at least one European language as well as English, and possibly Japanese. Experienced in working for multinationals, they will have worked around Europe and will understand senior management operations in American, Japanese and European settings. They conclude:

His [or her] most important attribute is the most self-evident. The European executive of the present and future needs to be cosmopolitan in the truest sense of the word, at ease socially, linguistically and culturally in all the countries of the EC.

---

the challenge of culture

Lennie Copeland (1985, p.49) describes the future challenge to management in developing ability to understand, co-operate with, manage and do business with other cultures:

Success or failure depends upon the degree to which people who have different ways of doing things and different priorities can work together. Intercultural relationships are fragile. Countless hazards are created by communication problems, cultural differences in motivational and value systems, diverse codes of conduct, even differences in orientation to fundamentals such as perception of time and space.

He describes the problems of international technology transfer experienced by an American multinational construction company in terms of three lessons they learned from their mistakes.

The first lesson concerned the conflict between efficiency and relationships. The company lost its Venezuelan contract to a French company because, in South America, quality of interpersonal relationships is considered more important than efficiency, costs, timing and deadlines. American managers concentrated on efficiency and thus failed to develop the necessary rapport, trust and mutual understanding. The Venezuelans preferred to work with people who were 'simpatico', and the French understood and concentrated on this. In contrast, Copeland points out that Americans 'are amazed that anyone puts such considerations over price and product'.

The second lesson concerned the conflict between truth and face. The company's American engineers in Japan caused great offence with their communications style whilst helping local engineers with plant construction. They would tell a Japanese directly when they had done something wrong. This hurt Japanese sensibilities, implied loss of face and should have been achieved through indirect communication. The Americans felt that the Japanese were 'beating about the bush' and would actually say 'yes' when they really meant 'no'. Americans attribute achievement and failure to the competitive individual. The Japanese in contrast value teamwork and harmony. So, American-style communication of praise and criticism caused great discomfort.

The third lesson concerned the conflict between work and family. American managers found that work in Saudi Arabia is not considered a central life interest, and that family responsibilities take priority. In the Arab world, what Westerners consider nepotism is obligation to family and relatives who come before the job and the company; the Western concept of the 'self-made' individual is incomprehensible.

based on Lennie Copeland, 1985, 'Cross-cultural training: the competitive edge', *Training*, July, pp. 49–53.

Marion Devine (1988) characterizes the elusive 'Euromanager' as someone 'able to work effectively in different cultures. They understand the languages, the customs and the business and political systems of the countries where their companies operate, and also have a broader, European outlook.' Pointing to the shortage of such skill combinations, she argues that new recruitment and management development strategies are required. One approach is to create multinational boards; these are still, however, rare. One consulting firm is cited as arguing that, as companies have not formulated strategies to deal with these issues effectively, the onus lies with the individual to establish their own career goals and to look for the businesses which will offer appropriate opportunities and experiences.

Michael Finney and Mary Ann von Glinow (1990) argue that the call for 'international experience' is simplistic and inadequate. They claim that we need 'cognitively complex self-monitoring managers who have global perspectives and boundary spanning capabilities' (p. 25), with a geocentric and not an ethnocentric value orientation. They also make a useful distinction between technical competence and contextual competence. Technical competence concerns industry knowledge, functional expertise and knowledge of the role of the subsidiary and the company's global strategy.

Contextual competence, on the other hand, concerns ability to:

- Understand home and host country value orientations.
- Speak the language with conversational fluency.
- Adapt management practice to local conditions.
- Recognize the importance of local customs, religion, history, climate, politics and regional alliances.
- Introduce change at an appropriate pace.
- Focus on global performance, not local results.
- Distinguish technical from social information, and act as a 'boundary-spanning interpreter' for both home and host country personnel and decision-makers.
- Balance need for control with need for flexibility.

From these specific technical and contextual skills and abilities, Finney and von Glinow then identify what they describe as a 'superordinate value orientation and set of managerial strategies' for the international manager. These are:

orientation	description
cognitive complexity	intuitive perceptual sensitivity to different cultures' thought and behaviour patterns
self-monitoring	personal flexibility, adjusting to social demands of different cultures
boundary spanning	acting as interpreter between home and host countries across technical and socio-cultural issues
global orientation	understanding of interrelated and systemic nature of global community, and of role of home and host countries in global economy
geocentric	internalization of multiple world views and value orientations

Cognitive complexity is identified in their analysis as the ability to use 'multiple solution models' rather than 'one best way' approaches to solving management issues. They further point out that the development of such cognitive flexibility and complexity is best achieved by addressing live, 'messy' problems rather than through the typically clinical business school case approach.

Self-monitoring is defined in the following terms:

the high self-monitoring individual is one who, out of a concern for the situational and interpersonal correctness of his or her social behaviour, is sensitive to the expression and self-presentation of those with whom social interaction is occurring and uses these cues as behavioural (verbal and non-verbal) guidelines for his or her own self-presentation. The self-monitoring manager possesses the ability to perceive the behaviour and thinking patterns associated with differing value orientations and match his or her behaviour to the demands of the orientation. (p. 25)

Finney and von Glinow surveyed a 'small but select sample of large multinationals' in America to identify general guidelines for developing the

---

seven rules for doing business in Asia

First	Learn English. The language of Australia and New Zealand is also an official language in Hong Kong, Singapore and the Philippines. Most businessmen in Japan, South Korea and Taiwan also speak it.
Second	Dress conservatively. Traditional business suits for men and plain dresses for women are the business uniform in most of Asia. When you visit someone at home in Japan or dine on tatami mats in a traditional restaurant you must remove your shoes, so make sure you are wearing clean socks with no holes in them.
Third	Offer a simple handshake and a nod when greeting people. Foreigners are not expected to bow from the waist as a Japanese would do, or to fold hands as if in prayer (wai) as in Thailand. Use titles and surnames except in Thailand and Australia where first names are expected.
Fourth	Read business cards carefully, bring a full pack of your own, and both present and receive them with both hands. Close scrutiny of a received card is a sign of respect for the other person.
Fifth	Avoid physical contact. Do not slap your contacts on the back or pat their hands.
Sixth	Monitor body language and coded meanings. Most Asians communicate indirectly and do not offer blunt refusals which could lead to a loss of face. If someone wants to turn down your request, this may be signalled by a sharp intake of breath and a statement like, 'It's difficult', or 'We will consider this in a forward-looking manner'.
Seventh	Practise singing before you go. Be prepared for your business host in Tokyo or Seoul to take you to a karaoke bar where customers take turns to sing along to pre-recorded music. This is where the formal business community in Asia loses its inhibitions.

based on Frederick H. Katayama, 1989, 'How to act once you get there', *Fortune*, vol. 120, no. 3, pp. 69–70.

key success factors. They were not able to do this. They found instead that current practice in international management development in the companies surveyed involved a parochial focus on organization-specific activity in specific countries, emphasized company and task-related knowledge at the expense of cross-cultural understanding, placed importance on 'international experience', and was based in a belief in on-the-job experience and language proficiency.

It seems clear that an ethnocentric approach to management style and competence, which ignores the demands and challenges of contrasting cultural contexts, is inadequate, unrealistic and impractical.

can leaders change their style?

Contemporary theories of leadership are mostly contingency theories which argue that the most effective style for the leader to adopt depends on the context. Organizations, the skills of their managers, the characteristics of their employees, the nature of their tasks and their structures are unique. No one style of leadership appears universally better than another.

There is, however, a good deal of research that indicates that a participative style of leadership in organizations is generally (if not always) more effective. There are two main reasons for this.

First, the development of participative management is part of a wider social and political trend, which has encouraged increased public participation in all spheres of social life. Participation thus reflects evolving democratic social and political values.

Rising levels of affluence and educational standards in Western industrial countries have developed expectations about personal freedom and the quality of working life. Education may also be expected to raise ability to participate effectively. There is a widespread recognition of the rights of the individual to develop intellectual and emotional maturity. These values encourage resistance to manipulation by mindless, impersonal bureaucracies and challenge the legitimacy of management decisions. This trend has affected local and national government as well as private industry, and is well established. The trend appears to be a universal one, and is not restricted to Britain or America. European and Scandinavian countries have legislated on the rights of employees to information about and participation in the activities of their employers.

Second, participative management has been encouraged by research which has demonstrated that this style is generally more effective, although an autocratic style can be more effective in some circumstances.

A participative management style can improve organizational effectiveness by tapping the ideas of people with knowledge and experience, and by involving them in a decision-making process to which they then become committed. This style can thus lead to better quality decisions which are then more effectively implemented.

People who are involved in setting standards or establishing methods are thus more likely to experience 'ownership' of such decision, and are more likely to:

- Accept the legitimacy of decisions reached with their help.
- Accept change based on those decisions.

▶ Trust managers who actually make and implement decisions.
▶ Volunteer new and creative ideas and solutions.

Autocratic management may stifle creativity, not use available expertise, and fail to establish motivation and commitment. Autocratic management can, however, be more effective when time is short, when the leader is the most knowledgeable person, and where those who would participate will never reach a decision with which they all agree.

---

participative management leads to better decisions

Many managers reject the concept of participative management because they do not want to lose control over 'management' decisions. Participation thus depends on the attitudes of managers towards this aspect of their job. There is a lot of research demonstrating the advantages of such attitude change.

William Pasmore and Frank Friedlander were asked to study work injuries which were reducing productivity in an American electronics company. About a third of the company's 335 employees had complained about pains in their wrists, arms and shoulders, some had undergone surgery to relieve their symptoms, and one woman had permanently lost the use of her right hand. A series of medical and technical investigations had failed to find the cause of the injuries.

But the company management had never thought of asking the employees themselves about the possible causes of their injuries. So the researchers suggested that a 'Studies and Communications Group' be set up, drawing workers' representatives from each area of the factory. The group members discussed their own work experiences and injuries, designed a questionnaire, surveyed over 300 other employees, and produced 60 recommendations for solving the injury problem.

Management at first rejected the Group's recommendations because management practices were identified as the main cause of the problem. The Group had found that injuries were related to:
▶ inadequate training
▶ rapid, repetitive arm movements
▶ badly adjusted machines
▶ frustration at machine breakdowns
▶ stress from supervisors' behaviour (such as favouritism)
▶ pressure from management for more output

The first attempts by management to solve the problem had in fact made it worse. When workers were injured, production fell, management increased the pressure for more output, which increased workers' stress, which in turn led to more injuries.

The researchers conclude that a permanent change in the relationships between workers and management is necessary to create a climate of effective participation. The managers in this company felt that they had lost control over the situation. But as the workers' recommendations were gradually implemented, the number of injuries fell and the overall performance of the factory rose.

based on William Pasmore and Frank Friedlander, 1982, 'An action research programme to increase employee involvement in problem solving', *Administrative Science Quarterly*, vol. 27, no. 3, pp. 343–62.

Research and theory thus suggest that organizational leaders should adopt a contingency approach and choose the most appropriate style for each occasion. There are, however, three reasons why an organizational leader may not be able to change style and still be effective.

First, personality may not be flexible enough. One of the theories of personality examined in Chapter 6 argues that personality is inherited and fairly static. This would create problems for the manager who wished to be participative in some circumstances and dictatorial in others. The manager who is motivated by affiliation and who values the friendship of others may find it hard to treat employees in an impersonal and autocratic style.

Second, the demands of the task and of other managers constrain what is acceptable for an individual manager to do. If a manager's own boss believes in the effectiveness of a directive leadership style, then it may be hard for managers to behave in a way that could block their own promotion chances.

---

bastards and bad bastards

On the shop floor it's said, about a couple of Riverside managers in particular, that 'They aren't bad blokes. Given that they're managers, that is. They'd do anything for you personally.' 'Personally' means letting a bloke borrow your car-spraying equipment, or talking to him about what it would be like for his son to do O-level chemistry, or, providing things aren't too tight, helping him to get time off. It also means not driving it home unnecessarily that you are a manager. But 'personally' or not, these men are still managers. The theories of psycho-sociology notwithstanding, they've had to learn the hard way about 'man-management' and how to defend their 'right to manage'. And this means that 'in this game you can either be a bastard or a bad bastard'. ('Bad bastards' are managers who behave like bastards because they are bastards. Common-or-garden 'bastards' are men who find that, as managers, there are unpleasant things they have to do.)

from Theo Nichols and Huw Beynon, 1977, *Living with Capitalism: Class Relations and the Modern Factory*, Routledge & Kegan Paul, London, p. 34.

Third, there may be advantages in honesty and consistency. People may not accept the fickle behaviour of the participative manager who adopts an autocratic style when that appears to be necessary. Employees may see through the act of the autocrat who tries to act in a participative way. The leader who changes style from one situation to another may not inspire confidence and trust.

There are, on the other hand, three reasons why an organizational leader should be able to change style to suit the circumstances in order to be more effective.

First, theorists disagree about the rigidity of human personality. Many theorists have argued that it is possible for individuals to develop and deploy new behaviours as a result of their experiences. So the autocrat who finds that a task orientated style does not always work well could adopt a participative approach at least in some circumstances.

Second, organizations themselves are not rigid social arrangements with fixed tasks and structures. The work of an organization, and the people who carry it out, are constantly changing. Organizational leaders thus need to be able to change as organizational circumstances change. As demands for improved quality of working life and more worker participation develop, managers who fail to respond appropriately will find themselves in difficulty.

Third, the manager who is able to adapt in a flexible way to changes in circumstances may be seen as more competent than one who sticks rigidly to traditional routines, or who fails to adapt to the expectations of another culture.

---

management styles vary around the world

André Laurent, from Insead in France, asked nationals from twelve countries whether they agreed with the statement: 'It is important for a manager to have at hand precise answers to most of the questions that his subordinates may raise about their work.' The percentages agreeing with this were:

Japan	78
Indonesia	73
Italy	66
France	53
Germany	46
Belgium	44
Switzerland	38
Britain	27
Denmark	23
United States	18
Holland	17
Sweden	10

Managers in France and Indonesia, for example, are seen as experts who are expected to have the answers. Managers in America and Holland are regarded as participative problem-solvers. Differences like this explain some of the problems that, for instance, Japanese managers might have when working in Denmark, or that Swedish managers might have in relationships with colleagues and employees in Italy.

based on André Laurent, 1983, 'The cultural diversity of Western conceptions of management', *International Studies of Management and Organization*, vol. 13, nos. 1–2.

Leadership style is not a problem that an organization manager can approach in a mechanical way. The factors that have to be taken into account are many and complex and include:

- the manager's own personality
- the needs of subordinates
- the demands of the task
- organizational constraints
- cultural values and expectations

There is, therefore, no simple recipe for the manager looking for the most effective style. Management style probably can be changed, but only if management values change too. Any attempt to change deep-rooted values is ambitious, but this may be necessary in the interests of organizational effectiveness.

---

participative management saves money

Western executives, jealous of Japanese economic success, are always assessing Oriental management techniques. One Japanese technique that first became popular in the late 1970s is the quality control (QC) circle. QC circles are groups of workers who meet regularly to discuss work problems, and the method has remained popular in Japan and elsewhere. Stephen Bryant and Joseph Kearns evaluated the technique in an American naval dockyard.

The dockyard employed 11,000 people on submarine maintenance and had to compete with similar yards for work. To improve productivity, management set up a QC circle programme, supported by the slogan, 'It makes sense to reap from workers' brains as well as their bodies'.

Volunteers were invited to set up nine circles whose members were trained in group problem-solving and decision-making. Each circle included workers and a supervisor who led their discussions. The circles met during working hours and were responsible for identifying problems, recommending solutions, and for taking the necessary action with management approval. The circles even gave themselves names like 'Wild Bunch', 'Sparkers', 'Red Eye Express' and 'Supply Storm Troopers'.

The researchers calculated that the circles saved the yard over $200,000 a year through their recommendations for:

- better tools and equipment
- more effective waste disposal
- savings in workers' time and effort

The researchers conclude that two main conditions are necessary for success with QC circles – workers who are willing to participate, and managers who are willing to let them.

based on Stephen Bryant and Joseph Kearns, 1982, '"Workers' brains as well as their bodies": quality circles in a federal facility', *Public Administration Review*, vol. 42, no. 2, pp. 144–50.

---

assessment

Graham Prentice (1990), personnel manager at one of Nestlé's manufacturing plants in Britain, argued that a 'soft' or 'nurturing' or participative style of management based on behavioural characteristics such as listening, supporting and empathy had become more critical to organizational effectiveness:

> I believe the successful management style of the future will be one which is strongly focused on behavioural characteristics. This means managers who value quality and prefer openness, who will share goals with subordinates, be concerned about others, supportive, good listeners, receptive to suggestions, and who communicate easily. In managing in a more behavioural way, managers will need to be more 'nurturing', which is perhaps not automatically regarded as a business-oriented characteristic.

Prentice identified three reasons for this. First, organizations now depend more on creating value from knowledge and information, and less on physical effort. Second, organizations increasingly depend on networks of suppliers and contractors for support in various forms, including 'homeworkers', some of whom operate from computer terminals and have become 'teleworkers'. Third, Prentice argues that:

> In the future organizations will not be managed by command, but by persuasion and consent. Management style will need to be open and democratic; shared problem-solving will be key. Managing will be concerned with developing other people's capacity to handle problems. The culture of consent will not have authority bound in the job; rather the style will be based on persuasion and continual encouragement. (p. 61)

In this chapter, we have argued that several factors influence leadership effectiveness and that there can be no 'one best way' in which to influence or indeed lead others. Many writers, however, have argued that changes in the competitive climate and in conditions of work require supportive, participative and achievement-oriented styles of management, to encourage employee commitment and flexibility. A directive style may only be appropriate in a very limited range of circumstances.

STOP!

Graham Prentice claimed to have identified the 'one best way' to manage in future.
- What arguments and evidence would you use to support his view?
- What arguments and evidence would you use to challenge his view?

---

sources

Adair, J., 1990, *Great Leaders*, Talbot Adair Press, Brookwood.

Argyle, M., 1983, 'Pleasures and pains of working together', *New Society*, 9 June, pp. 382–3.

Bryant, S. and Kearns, J., 1982, '"Workers brains as well as their bodies": Quality circles in a federal facility', *Public Administration Review*, vol. 42, no. 2, pp. 144–50.

Bryman, A., 1986, *Leadership and Organizations*, Routledge & Kegan Paul, London.

Cherniss, C., 1980, *Staff Burnout*, Sage Studies in Community Mental Health, no. 2.

Colback, S. and Maconochie, M., 1989, '. . . and the rise of the executive nomad', *Business World*, December, pp. 22–5.

Copeland, L., 1985, 'Cross-cultural training: The competitive edge', *Training*, July, pp. 49–53.

Crainer, S., 1988, 'Making boss-power positive', *The Sunday Times*, 9 October, p. E20.

Cromie, S., 1981, 'Women as managers in Northern Ireland', *Journal of Occupational Psychology*, vol. 54, no. 2, pp. 87–91.

Davidson, M.J. and Cooper, C.L., 1992, *Shattering the Glass Ceiling: The Woman Manager*, Paul Chapman Publishing, London.

Devine, M., 1988, 'Time to create Euromanagers', *The Sunday Times*, 20 November, p. F1.

Dixon, N.F., 1976, *On the Psychology of Military Incompetence*, Futura Publications, London.

Drucker, P., 1955, *The Practice of Management*, Heinemann, London.

Fiedler, F.E., 1967, *A Theory of Leadership Effectiveness*, McGraw-Hill, New York.

Fiedler, F.E. and Chemers, M., 1974, *Leadership and Effective Management*, Scott, Foresman, Glenview, IL.

Finney, M. and von Glinow, M.A., 1990, 'Integrating academic and organizational approaches to developing the international manager', *Journal of Management Development*, vol. 7, no. 2, pp. 16–27.

Fleishman, E.A., 1953a, 'The description of supervisory behaviour', *Journal of Applied Psychology*, vol. 37, no. 1, pp. 1–6.

Fleishman, E.A., 1953b, 'The measurement of leadership attitudes in industry', *Journal of Applied Psychology*, vol. 37, no. 3, pp. 153–8.

Fleishman, E.A. and Harris, E.F., 1962, 'Patterns of leadership behaviour related to employee grievances and turnover', *Personnel Psychology*, vol. 15, pp. 43–56.

French, J. and Raven, B., 1958, 'The bases of social power', in D. Cartwright (ed.), *Studies in Social Power*, Institute for Social Research, Ann Arbor, MI.

Hersey, P. and Blanchard, K.H., 1988, *Management of Organizational Behavior: Utilizing Human Resources*, Prentice Hall International, Englewood Cliffs, NJ.

House, R.J., 1971, 'A path-goal theory of leader effectiveness', *Administrative Science Quarterly*, vol. 16, pp. 321–38.

House, R.J. and Mitchell, T.R., 1974, 'Path-goal theory of leadership', *Journal of Contemporary Business*, vol. 3, pp. 81–97.

Kaplan, E.M. and Cowen, E.L., 1981, 'Interpersonal helping behaviour of industrial foremen', *Journal of Applied Psychology*, vol. 66, no. 5, pp. 633–8.

Katayama, F.H., 1989, 'How to act once you get there', *Fortune*, vol. 120, no. 3, pp. 69–70.

Laurent, A., 1983, 'The cultural diversity of Western conceptions of management', *International Studies of Management and Organization*, vol. 13, nos. 1–2.

Likert, R., 1961, *New Patterns of Management*, McGraw-Hill, New York.

McClelland, D.C. and Boyatzis, R.E., 1982, 'Leadership motive pattern and long-term success in management', *Journal of Applied Psychology*, vol. 67, no. 6, pp. 737–43.

McClelland, D.C. and Burnham, D.H., 1976, 'Power is the great motivator', *Harvard Business Review*, March–April, reprinted in the January–February 1995 issue, pp. 126–39.

Nichols, T. and Beynon, H., 1977, *Living with Capitalism: Class Relations and the Modern Factory*, Routledge & Kegan Paul, London.

Pasmore, W. and Friedlander, F., 1982, 'An action research programme to increase employee involvement in problem solving', *Administrative Science Quarterly*, vol. 27, no. 3, pp. 343–62.

Peters, T., 1987, *Thriving on Chaos: Handbook for a Managerial Revolution*, Macmillan, London.

Popp, G.E. and Muhs, W.F., 1982, 'Fear of success and women employees', *Human Relations*, vol. 35, no. 7, pp. 511–19.

Prentice, G., 1990, 'Adapting management style to the organization of the future', *Personnel Management*, vol. 22, no. 6, June, pp. 58–62.

Robock, S. and Simmonds, K., 1983, *International Business and Multinational Enterprises*, Irwin, Homewood, IL.

Steinberg, R. and Shapiro, S., 1982, 'Sex differences in personality, traits of female and male Masters of Business Administration students', *Journal of Applied Psychology*, vol. 67, no. 3, pp. 306–10.

Stewart, R., 1963, *The Reality of Management*, Pan/Heinemann Books, London.

Stogdill, R.M., 1948, 'Personal factors associated with leadership', *Journal of Psychology*, vol. 25, pp. 35–71.

Stogdill, R.M. and Coons, A.E. (eds.), 1951, *Leader Behavior: Its Description and Measurement*, Research Monograph no. 88, Ohio State University Bureau of Business Research, Columbus, OH.

chapter 21 managing conflict

concepts and learning objectives
perspectives on organizational conflict
functional and dysfunctional conflict
Buchanan–Huczynski co-ordination–conflict model
assessment
sources

concepts and learning objectives

Conflict is a state of mind. It has to be perceived by the parties involved. If two or more parties are not aware of a conflict, then no conflict exists. This broad definition encompasses conflicts at different levels within an organization, as shown in the following table.

level	conflict	between
1 individual	inter-personal	line manager and staff expert
2 group	intra-group	senior managers and middle managers
	inter-group	union and management
3 department	intra-departmental	research unit and development section
	inter-departmental	marketing and production departments

This chapter looks at the common aspects of conflict at all these levels. It will draw on examples and research from these as appropriate. To avoid repeating individual, group, unit or department, the term *parties* will be used to indicate that the conflict can be at any of these three levels. However, personality clashes between individuals are excluded, and instead, the focus will be on structurally derived conflict, that is, conflict that emerges from the formal interactions or job requirements of individuals within an organization.

Conflict in organizations is seen as the outcome of organizational politics, as individuals, groups, units and departments attempt to influence the decisions made towards their own interests, usually at the expense of others' interests. This perspective holds the causes of conflict to be rooted in difficult situations rather than difficult people, and also implies a conflict management strategy that changes the situation rather than the people.

key concepts

- conflict
- traditional (unitary) perspective
- pluralistic perspective
- interactionist perspective
- functional conflict
- dysfunctional conflict
- organizing

- co-ordinating
- conflict resolution
- distributive bargaining
- integrative bargaining
- mediation
- arbitration
- conflict stimulation

learning objectives

When you have read this chapter, you should be able to define those key concepts in your own words, and you should also be able to:

1 Distinguish between the three main perspectives on conflict.
2 Distinguish between functional and dysfunctional conflict.
3 Explain the relationship between co-ordination and conflict.
4 List the main inter-party co-ordination devices.
5 Describe Thomas's five conflict resolution techniques.
6 Distinguish between distributive and integrative bargaining.
7 Explain the need for using conflict stimulation techniques.

perspectives on organizational conflict

Your view about the causes of conflict will depend on the particular perspective you take on the nature of society and of the organizations in it. Three perspectives or frame of references are presented in this section. Whichever is adopted is important because it:

- Determines how people are expected to behave.
- Affects your reactions to others' behaviour.
- Determines the choice of methods used to change that behaviour.

---

definition

Conflict *is a process which begins when one party perceives that another party has frustrated, or is about to frustrate, some concern of his.*

from Thomas (1976).

---

traditional (unitary) perspective

This perspective holds that conflict represents a malfunction within the group, department or organization. Within it, conflict is seen as bad and harmful, and hence should be avoided if possible, and eradicated if it erupts. This perspective is called *traditional* because it has its roots in the Hawthorne studies, which were conducted in the United States in the 1924–32 period. It is also referred to as *unitary*, following the presentation of a research paper by the British academic, Alan Fox, to the Donovan Commission on Trade Unions and Employers' Associations (Fox, 1966).

This view sees organizations as fundamentally harmonious, co-operative structures, where no systematic conflict of interest should exist. Common goals are assumed, and company success or failure is seen as leading to success or failure for employees and managers alike. Everyone is in the same boat! Managers holding the unitary perspective see their companies as analogous to teams, with all the team members – workers and managers – striving towards the achievement of common goals. In their presentations and publications, they use phrases such as workers and management are 'all pulling together', 'striving towards a common good' and showing '*esprit de corps*'.

The perspective stresses *oneness,* and in so doing implies other things. These are that workers must believe that management knows what is best for the organization and, by implication, what is best for them; that they accept managerial decisions unquestioningly; and generally acknowledge management as the leaders of this supposed team. Attempts to emphasize or change the corporate culture typically promote a unitary perspective of an organization. An emphasis is placed on inspirational leadership, developing employee commitment and loyalty, and on promoting the harmony of purpose.

Explaining conflict from this perspective is a problem because, as just stated, all members of the organization – managers, workers and shareholders – are held to share common objectives and values which unite them; while managerial prerogative is accepted with unified authority and there is strong company loyalty. Unions are tolerated, but are no longer seen as serving any useful purpose, other than perhaps as a channel of communication. The organization is seen as team or a family with the 'father-manager' having the right to impose his will for the long-term interest of all.

The unitary perspective sees consensus (non-conflict) as the ideal, natural state. When conflict occurs, its existence tends to be explained in one of three ways. Most commonly, it is attributed to poor communication. Management accepts its responsibility for failing to get its intended message through to its employees, and to meet their needs and aspirations. Conflict is thus seen as being caused by misunderstandings. The instability which led to the conflict breaking out is held to be the result of a lack of trust, openness and adequate communications; which needs to be rectified.

Alternatively, conflict may be seen as a failure by management to design an organizational structure that allows individuals, units or departments to co-operate to achieve corporate objectives. Finally, management may claim that it has shown workers how their proposed course of action is to the benefit of the organization and hence to themselves. However, its proposal has been rejected by a vocal, unrepresentative minority, which managed to mislead the others; or by the stubbornness or inflexibility of the majority. Irrespective of which of the three explanations is adopted, the manager's job remains the same. It is simply to identify the causes of the conflict, eliminate them and re-establish industrial peace.

pluralist perspective

Fox (1966) contrasted his unitary perspective with the *pluralist* one. It is called pluralist because it rejects the view that individual employees have the same interests as the management on the one hand, and that an organization is best seen as one big team on the other. Instead, it holds that individuals have unique and different interests, that they form into cliques on the basis of these, and that an organization is best seen as consisting of many separate but related interest groups, each pursuing their own objectives. Some of the time these interests coincide, whilst at others they will clash, and thus cause conflict. The obvious clashes may be between unions and management, but will also include differences between management functions (production *v.* marketing); levels of management (senior management *v.* middle management), and between individual managers. Moreover, it may be a disagreement between three or more parties, and not just two.

From this perspective, the job of management becomes one of keeping the balance between potentially conflicting goals, and managing the differences between these different interest groups. This involves seeking a compromise between the different constituents such as the workers, managers, shareholders and others, so that all these stakeholders, to varying degrees, can continue to pursue their aspirations. Underlying the pluralist view is the belief that conflict can be resolved through compromise to the benefit of all. However, it requires all parties to limit their claims to a level which is at least tolerable to the others, and which allows further collaboration to continue. A mutual survival strategy is agreed.

Acceptance of the pluralist perspective implies that conflict is inevitable. Indeed, given the nature of social relationships, it will be endemic. However, unlike the traditional perspective, which sees conflict as harmful and something to be eliminated, in the pluralistic view conflict should be accepted since, in certain circumstances, it may even enhance performance. After all, is not our parliamentary democracy based on representing the views of many sectional interests? Lewis Pondy (1967, p. 320) wrote that,

> Conflict is not necessarily good or bad, but must be evaluated in terms of its individual organizational functions and dysfunctions. In general, conflict generates pressure to reduce conflict, but chronic conflict persists and is endured under certain conditions, and consciously created and managed by the politically astute administrator.

The pluralist perspective sees conflict as reinforcing the status quo. Conflict, within limits, is held to assist evolutionary rather than revolutionary change. Discussing societies, Coser wrote that:

> conflict, rather than being disruptive and dissociating, may indeed be a means of balancing and hence maintaining society as a going concern.
> ... A flexible society benefits from conflict because such behaviour, by helping to create and modify norms, assists its continuation under changed conditions. (Coser, 1956, pp. 137 and 154)

The same point may be applied to mini-societies such as organizations. Conflict acts as a safety-valve, and keeps them responsive to internal and external changes, whilst retaining intact their essential elements such as the organizational hierarchy and the power distribution.

For pluralists, then, the company is not one big happy family or a single boat being rowed by all its members in the same direction. Instead, it is a system of interrelationships between the individuals and groups within it, each pursuing their own goals. The inevitable conflict which results has to be managed, so that organizational goals are reconciled with group interests to the benefit of mutual survival and even prosperity. This ongoing internal struggle is seen as generally acting to maintain the vitality, responsiveness and efficiency of the organization.

organizations as conflicting cliques

Melville Dalton described organizational structure as consisting of conflicting cliques which engaged in struggles in order to increase their power and thus obtain a greater share of the rewards which the organization had to offer. He found that individuals and groups were primarily interested in the pursuit of their own narrow interests. They tried to consolidate and improve their own position of power, even if this was at the expense of the organization as a whole. He described how such political activity was skilfully and scrupulously camouflaged. As a result of this, the policies pursued appeared to be in harmony with the official ideology and the organizational handbook. His view of organizational life is one of swiftly changing and conflicting cliques cutting across departmental and other boundaries.

based on Melville Dalton, 1959, *Men Who Manage*, John Wiley, New York.

differences can be fruitful

Conflict can improve rather than impede organizational decision-making. When those who have opposing ideas try to agree, they develop a better understanding of each other's positions, bring their differences to the forefront, and reach a decision with which everyone is satisfied. This conclusion was reached by Dean Tjosvold and Deborah Deemer from the results of an experiment which they designed.

They asked 66 student volunteers to take the roles of foremen and workers at an assembly plant. Conflict had arisen over the workers' job rotation schemes. The 'student workers' were first given information about the benefits of the scheme (it gave more job satisfaction) and were asked to defend it. The 'student foremen' were told about its disadvantages (workers did not remain in their jobs long enough to develop expertise) and were asked to argue for its abolition. A third group of students was told that the company had a good industrial relations record and that the company tried, where possible, to avoid controversy.

Another group was told that the company had a history of open, frank discussion of differences and that the norm was co-operative controversy, and that groups tried to win any arguments that arose. The students were offered lottery tickets for complying with these norms in the experiment. Workers and foremen then met in pairs for 15 minutes to discuss and resolve the issue. They then noted their decision and answered questions about their attitudes to their discussions. It was found that where controversy was avoided, the decisions were dominated by the views of the foremen. Where controversy was competitive, the students were generally not able to reach any agreement and experienced feelings of hostility and suspicion towards their adversary. Under the co-operative controversy conditions, decisions were reached that integrated the views of workers and foremen. Feelings of curiosity, trust and openness were also found to be induced. Co-operative controversy may therefore be good for decision making. But how does one get real foremen and real workers to comply with this apparently useful social or organizational norm?

from Dean Tjosvold and Deborah Deemer, 1980, 'Effects of controversy within a co-operative or competitive context on organizational decision making', *Journal of Applied Psychology*, vol. 65, no. 5, pp. 590–5.

interactionist perspective

The interactionist perspective goes beyond the pluralist school's toleration and management of conflict. It actually encourages both conflict stimulation and conflict resolution. This perspective argues that a group or department that is too peaceful, harmonious and co-operative can become apathetic and unresponsive to changing needs. Such extreme group cohesion can lead to the groupthink phenomenon identified by Irving Janis (1982). The interactionist view encourages leaders to maintain an on-going minimum level of conflict which is just sufficient to keep the group viable, self-critical and creative.

functional and dysfunctional conflict

The three perspectives on conflict just described differ in terms of their evaluation of conflict. The traditional view sees all conflict as bad, whilst the pluralist and interactionist perspectives hold that certain conflicts can be good. This debate is conducted in terms of whether any given conflict is functional or dysfunctional. A conflict is functional if it improves the quality of decisions, stimulates creativity and innovation, encourages interest and curiosity amongst group members, provides a way of airing grievances, releases tensions and encourages self-evaluation and change. It is dysfunctional if it breeds discontent, dissolves common ties, leads to the destruction of the group, retards communication, reduces group cohesion, individual interests supplant group goals, reduces group effectiveness and threatens group survival. Functionality is thus defined at the level of the group as a whole in terms of outcomes, rather than in its effects on its individual members.

---

definitions

Functional conflict *supports the goals of a group or an organization and improves its performance.*

Dysfunctional conflict *hinders group or organizational performance.*

Robbins (1996) depicts functionality on a bell-shaped curve. Insufficient conflict, and the unit or group is not performing at its best; too much, and its performance deteriorates. Performance improvement occurs through conflict exposing weaknesses in organizational decision-making and design, which prompts changes in the company. Adjustments are made by managers and the power structure is realigned, shifting the balance of power to those groups which can best meet organizational goals. Beyond that point, conflict can get out of control; the organization breaks up into competing interest groups, the performances of which decline. However, the Robbins figure does not tell us how much conflict is appropriate and how a given group will respond to it. For example, the same degree of conflict may be functional for one group, but dysfunctional for another. What is most important is how any given level of conflict affects a specific group's performance.

The interactionist perspective recommends that if the level of conflict is located to the left of Robbins' bell-shaped curve, managers should raise it, so

proposed relationship between inter-group conflict and organizational performance

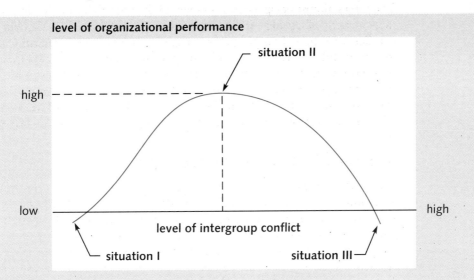

	level of intergroup conflict	probable impact on organization	organization characterized by	level of organizational performance
situation I	low or none	dysfunctional	slow adaptation to environmental changes few changes little stimulation of ideas apathy stagnation	low
situation II	optimal	functional	positive movement toward goals innovation and change search for problem solutions creativity and quick adaptation to environmental changes	high
situation III	high	dysfunctional	disruption interference with activities coordination difficult chaos	low

from James L. Gibson, John M. Ivancevich and James H. Donnelly, 1991, *Organizations: Behaviour, Structure, Process.*, Irwin, Chicago, 7th edition, p. 300.

as to gain its benefits. Van de Vliert (1985) identified three occasions when this might be appropriate:

1 *To bring about change:* Conflict is a vehicle for radically changing organizations. The existing power structures, entrenched attitudes and established behaviour patterns can all be dramatically modified through conflict.

2 *To change group cohesiveness:* Conflict between members in a group (intra-group conflict) can increase hostility between members and overcome complacency. External threats (inter-group conflict) can cause group members to bury their differences and pull together more. The importance of perceived internal differences is reduced and group cohesion increases.

3 *To improve group and organizational effectiveness:* The stimulation of conflict unleashes a new search for goals and methods for their achievement. Successful conflict resolution can create more trust, openness, interpersonal support, and thus more organizational effectiveness.

conflict as a failure of co-ordination

The conflicts considered in this chapter, organizational conflicts, emerge from the formal interactions or job requirements of individuals, groups and departments within an organization. The process of organizing by senior managers acts to differentiate activities, and an outbreak of conflict can thus be seen as a symptom of management's failure to adequately co-ordinate these same activities later on.

STOP!

Restate the two sentences above in your own words, and check with your instructor that you have understood them correctly.

Buchanan–Huczynski's co-ordination–conflict four-stage model organizes the diverse theoretical discussions and research findings into a framework which explains how conflict in organizations arises and is resolved.

Buchanan–Huczynski co-ordination–conflict model

stage 1: organizing

The first stage of the Buchanan–Huczynski model consists of organizing. This concept was encountered in Chapter 14 where it was seen as involving the breaking up of a single task and dividing it among different departments, groups or individuals. For example, a car company allocates the work involved in building a new vehicle to its different sub-divisions (departments, groups and individuals) – personnel, accounting, production, sales and research. Such functional specialization is one of many bases on which to divide the total work involved. Specialization is rational because it concentrates specialists in proper departments, avoids duplication, allows performance goals to be established and specifies practices.

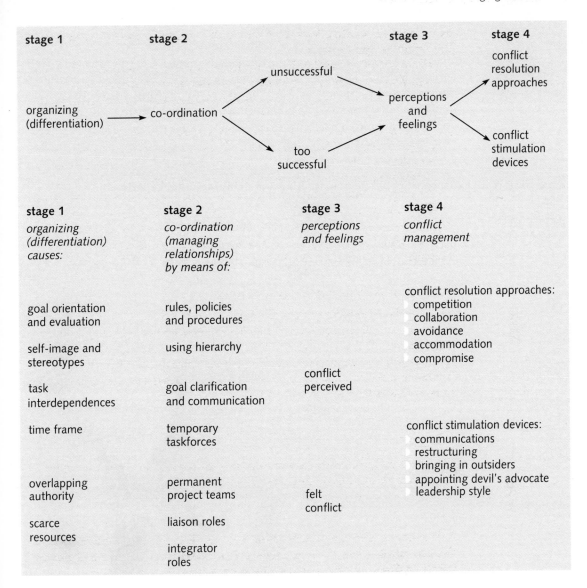

All forms of horizontal specialization result in each sub-unit becoming concerned with its particular part in the total objective and work process. The degree of such separation of tasks can vary, but it creates the conditions in which conflict can potentially arise. It does so because, by definition, each department, group or individual receives a different part of the whole task to perform. This makes it distinct from the other departments on at least six major dimensions.

goal orientation and evaluation

Each department is given its own goal and its members are evaluated on the extent to which they achieve it. Ideally, the goals of different departments, groups and individuals, although different, should be complementary, but in practice this may not be so. Moreover, the measurement process can reinforce differences. Each department's unique goals and evaluation methods lead it to have its own view about company priorities and how these are best achieved.

---

areas of potential goal conflict between marketing and manufacturing departments

goal conflict	*marketing:* versus operative goal is customer satisfaction	*manufacturing:* operative goal is production efficiency
conflict area	*typical comment*	*typical comment*
1 breadth of product line	'Our customers demand variety.'	'The product line is too broad – all we get are short, uneconomical runs.'
2 new product introduction	'New products are our lifeblood.'	'Unnecessary design changes are prohibitively expensive.'
3 production scheduling	'We need faster response. Our lead times are too long.'	'We need realistic customer commitments that don't change like wind direction.'
4 physical distribution	'Why don't we ever have the right merchandise in inventory?'	'We can't afford to keep huge inventories.'
5 quality	'Why can't we have reasonable quality at low cost?'	'Why must we always offer options that are too expensive and offer little customer utility?'

based on Benson S. Shapiro, 1977, 'Can marketing and manufacturing coexist?', *Harvard Business Review*, vol. 55, September–October, pp. 104–14.

---

self-image and stereotypes

Employees in each department become socialized into a particular perception of themselves and the other departments in the company. A group may come to see itself as more vital to a company's operations than others, and come to believe that it has higher status or prestige. Such an evaluation can engender an 'us-and-them' attitude. The higher-status groups may cease to adapt their behaviours to accommodate the goals of other groups, and indeed, may try to achieve their objectives at the cost of others, thus creating conflict. Whenever differences between groups and departments are emphasized, stereotypes are reinforced, relations deteriorate, and conflict develops. Departments will often blame each other for problems and shortcomings.

'Robbers' Cave' studies of inter-group relations

Following his 1949 study of group formation at a boys' summer camp in Connecticut (see Chapter 7, pp. 192–4), Muzafer Sherif investigated inter-group relations in the same location with similar types of subjects. These studies combined the advantages of a planned and controlled experimental design, with a natural, real-life setting. The research design is called a *field experiment* and is particularly useful because the results can be generalized to non-experimental situations. The experiment took place over a three-week period. It was, therefore, a longitudinal study (Sherif and Sherif, 1956).

The boys were told that they were attending a summer camp to study camping methods. The isolation of the camp from outside influences allowed the researchers to manipulate conditions and circumstances of social interaction. The experimental design was arranged sequentially first to maximize the co-ordinated activity within each group around goals of high value in order to achieve in-group cohesiveness. Then, in experiment 1, inter-group conflict was induced by the selection of activities in which success for one group led to frustration for the other. In the second experiment conflict was first induced and then reduced. The data were collected using hidden microphones, candid cameras, direct observation, sociometric tests, interpersonal ratings and laboratory-like manipulated events.

Red Devils' table smeared with food by Bulldogs

one of the posters made by the Red Devils

experiment 1: production of inter-group conflict

Two established groups, the Bulldogs and the Red Devils, took part in a five-day contest of competitive games and contests. The prizes were awarded on the basis of an individual's contribution to their own group, and referees were briefed to favour the Bulldogs. The initial good sportsmanship rapidly degenerated into hostility between the two groups. Following the contest, a party was proposed by the camp staff (research team) to let bygones be bygones. However, at the party, half of the refreshments placed on the table were whole and appealing, while the remainder were crushed and unappealing. The Red Devils were allowed in first and took the good half. From then on, inter-group hostilities reached a pitch. For two days, the boys vented their feelings of aggression through name-calling, threatening posters and food-throwing. Despite the fact that the experiment was stopped at this point, the two groups continued to act with extreme hostility to each other.

continued overleaf

'Robbers' Cave' studies (*continued*)

experiment 2: production of inter-group conflict and its reduction

Bulldogs raiding Red Devil bunkhouse

one of the posters made by the Bulldogs

Building on the previous study, this was conducted at a summer camp at Robbers Cave State Park in Oklahoma. This study used 'matched subjects', that is, a sample of 22 middle-class, 11-year-old, white boys, who did not have previous friendship or group relationships. In the first stage of the study, the boys were randomly divided into two equal groups. In the second stage, a series of contests were announced by staff, in which the winning team would receive a silver cup, and each team member a penknife. In the third phase, tasks were introduced by staff which required the co-operation of boys from both groups.

The researchers found that in the first stage, each group developed its own culture and norms; gave itself a name (Rattlers and Eagles); and that its individual members did not favour their own group members above those of the other group. In the second stage, the competition led to increased inter-group hostility. Members derided and attacked those of the different group; each group became more cohesive, and the most aggressive boys became leaders. Immediately after the contest, discrimination and prejudice remained, which mere contact between both sets of group members was unable to dispel. However, in the third stage, the boys from both groups were forced to co-operate on tasks that used their pooled resources – for example, collectively inspecting pipes and tanks to see why the camp was out of water, and pulling a broken-down truck to get it

task interdependences

The process of organizing that results in differentiation makes individuals, groups and departments dependent on one another to perform their own jobs satisfactorily and achieve their own objectives. The degree of such interdependence varies. In Chapter 15 we considered Thompson's (1967) three types of dependence – *pooled*, *sequential* and *reciprocal*. Groups in sequential interdependence, and even more, in reciprocal interdependence, required a high degree of co-ordination between their activities. If this was achieved, then each group would perform effectively and its members would experience satisfaction. When it was not, the result would be conflict. From this perspective, inter-group conflict is the result of a failure in co-ordination.

In addition, the types of task that individuals, groups and departments are allocated can cause difficulties. Such tasks can be either routine or non-routine. Perrow's (1970) classification based on *task variety* and *task analyzability* was also discussed in Chapter 15. Tasks which had high variety (many unexpected

Rattlers and Eagles co-operate

solving a water tank problem   *preparing a meal*

started so that it could collect food for them. Following these co-operative activities, the inter-group hostility disappeared. Indeed, when the food arrived, the two groups jointly participated in the preparation of a meal for all.

Sherif and his colleagues concluded that groups develop norms; and that conflict between groups increases the cohesiveness of the in-group, whilst leading to prejudice and discrimination towards the out-group. Each group's members develop negative attitudes and stereotypes towards the other. Inter-group conflict can be reduced by introducing urgent, superordinate goals that are desired by both groups, which can only be achieved through the joint efforts and pooled resources of the otherwise conflicting groups.

based on M. Sherif and C.W. Sherif, 1956, *An Outline of Social Psychology*, Harper & Row, New York, Chapter 9, pp. 280–332; and M. Sherif, O. Harvey, B.J. White, W.R. Hood and C. Sherif, 1954, *Experimental Study of Positive and Negative Intergroup Attitudes Between Experimentally Produced Groups: Robbers Cave Study*, University of Oklahoma Press, Norman, OK.

events) and low analyzability (no ready-made solutions) required a lot more information processing. Groups performing such tasks had to interact more with other groups in order to obtain the volume and quality of the information that they needed. This increased the chances of conflict between them.

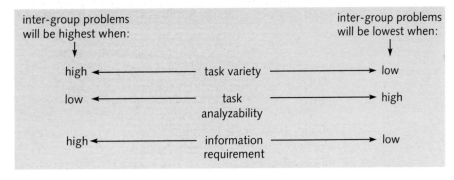

time frame

Lawrence and Lorsch's (1967) study found that people's perceptions of the importance accorded to different items depended on the time frame that governed their work and their goal orientations. Groups with different perceptions would find it difficult to co-ordinate their activities, and this would result in greater inter-group conflict. This is partly because their time frames differ. These different goals are often incompatible, hindering communication, impeding co-ordination and encouraging conflict.

overlapping authority

Demarcation disputes have always caused difficulties, and ambiguity over responsibility or authority is one example of this. Individuals or groups may be uncertain as to who is responsible for performing which tasks or duties, and

who has the authority to direct whom. Each party may claim or reject responsibility and the result can be conflict. This can occur particularly when a growing organization has not yet worked out the relationships between different groups or after a takeover or merger, when new roles and responsibilities have yet to be clarified. Groups may fight for the control of a resource, whilst individual managers may attempt to seize one another's authority.

---

staff–line conflict

In his classic study, Melville Dalton studied the conflict between line managers, those directly responsible for production, and staff managers, those not directly involved, but performing an advisory or staff function, for example, personnel. He attributed the cause to the different roles occupied in the company and their personal characteristics. Conflicts between staff and line continue to this day, and are based on similar concerns.

Authority reduction: Whilst line managers are afraid that staff specialists will intrude on their jobs and reduce their authority and power, staff specialists complain that line managers do not make good use of them or provide them with enough authority.

Social and physical differences: Line and staff personnel differ in terms of age, background and educational level. Dalton found that staff specialists had received more education and training, were appointed to their posts at relatively senior hierarchical levels and tended to be members of professional associations. Line managers were generalists, had less professional training, often had worked their way up from the shopfloor.

Line dependence on staff knowledge: Dalton also found that conflict could result because staff specialists considered their knowledge to be more relevant and up-to-date than the line manager's, whilst the latter felt that his experience was more relevant than 'book-learning'. However, line managers are often dependent on staff personnel for current, specialist knowledge, such as employment legislation. They have to visit staff personnel, who are often lower in the company hierarchy, to fill the gap between their knowledge and authority. This can cause conflict.

Different loyalties: Other sources of conflict included the staff member's loyalty to the company, in that they would pursue their professional career in different organizations, while the line manager was likely to remain with the same firm. When loyalties to a particular function or discipline are greater than to the overall company, conflict is likely.

based on Dalton (1959), Balasco and Alutto (1969) and Sorenson and Sorenson (1974).

---

scarce resources

Once a task is allocated to an individual, group or department, it is also allocated resources to achieve it. Since resources are finite, conflict can arise with respect to how personnel, money, space or equipment are shared out. From a win–lose perspective, one party's gain is another's loss. For this reason, conflicts often arise at times of budget cuts, reduced promotion opportunities and no increases in salaries or wages.

winning and losing: inter-group conflict

Schein (1970) stated that Sherif's original research has been tested with adult groups, and has produced consistent results concerning the outcomes of inter-group conflict. When there is competition between groups:

A. *within* each group
   1 Each group becomes more cohesive and demands more conformity from its members.
   2 Concern for task accomplishment increases, while that for members' psychological needs declines.
   3 Leader's style becomes more autocratic and less democratic, and is tolerated by members.
   4 Each group becomes more highly structured and organized.

B. *between* competing groups
   1 Each group begins to see the other as the enemy.
   2 Each group sees the best in itself and the worst in the other group.
   3 Communication decreases and hostility increases towards the other group.

Turning to what happens if one group wins out over another:

C. the *winner*
   1 Becomes more cohesive.
   2 Releases tension, becomes complacent and confirms their self-image of being better than the other group.
   3 Becomes more concerned with members' psychological needs and less concerned with task accomplishment.

D. the *loser*
   1 Denies the loss if the situation is ambiguous enough, or rationalizes the loss by blaming it on bad luck, unclear rules, and so on.
   2 Tends to splinter and personal conflicts increase.
   3 Tries to find someone or something to blame.
   4 Expresses concern to accomplish task needs, and less concern with members' psychological needs.
   5 Tends to learn more about itself because its preconceived ideas about being the best group are upset. The long term result of the loss can have positive outcomes, if the group realistically accepts its loss.

The net effect of the win–lose situation is that the loser is not convinced that it has lost, and inter-group tension is higher than before the competition took place.

based on Edgar H. Schein, 1969, *Process Consultation: Its Role in Organizational Development*, Addison-Wesley, Reading, MA, pp. 72–4.

STOP!

Think of two organizational conflict situations with which you are familiar. Which of the six causes – goal orientation, self-image, interdependencies, time frame, overlapping authority and scare resources – help to explain them?

prisoner's dilemma

Research into the management of conflict between groups has revealed how fragile the levels of trust are between them; how quickly they can demonstrate interpersonal competition; and how difficult it is to encourage intra- and inter-group competition. The research findings are often demonstrated through an exercise called the *Prisoner's Dilemma*. A blue team competes against a red one for money or tokens. In each round, the blue team chooses between option X or Y, while the red team decides between A or B. As shown in the figure below, the rewards or 'pay-offs' for both teams are determined by their combined choices – AX, AY, BX, BY.

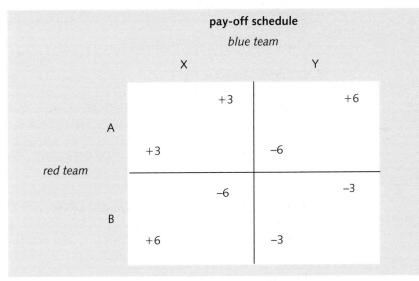

As the pay-off schedule reveals, both teams could win if they co-operated. However, there is a temptation for each one to maximize their own self-interest at the expense of the other team. When both teams opt to do this at the same time, both of them lose. The game simulates processes to be found in companies when individuals, teams and departments pursue their own objectives at the cost of others'.

This exercise takes its name from the police procedure of separating suspects at a police station, and interviewing them separately. The prisoners concerned have to decide whether to co-operate with each other by sticking to their agreed stories, or to welch on one another in the hope of personally getting off with a lighter charge.

stage 2: co-ordinating

If organizing involved breaking up the task into bits, then co-ordinating is bringing the bits together again. Co-ordination involves ensuring that the previously divided tasks which were allocated between different departments, groups and individuals, are brought together in the right way and at the right time. Co-ordination involves synchronizing and making compatible the different aspects of the work process. The process of organizing creates these differences, but does not automatically result in conflict between parties breaking out.

Provided that the relationships between the differentiated departments, units, groups or individuals are successfully co-ordinated, then conflict will not occur. By effectively using inter-party *co-ordination devices*, a company can prevent conflict breaking out in the first place. The devices are designed to manage the relationships between the different individuals, groups, units or departments, so that the reason for conflict to arise is eliminated. It is only if and when these co-ordination devices fail that conflict occurs and that *conflict resolution techniques* will be required.

---

definition

Co-ordination *is making sure that activities and resources are working well together towards the common goal.*

---

inter-party co-ordination devices

1 rules, policies and procedures
All of these specify how one party is to interact with another. Thus, a standardized operating procedure will specify when additional staff can be recruited to a department. The departmental manager fills in a form and sends it to the personnel department, who initiate the recruitment process. Rules and procedures reduce the need for both interaction and information flow between parties. They are most useful when inter-party activities are known in advance; when they occur frequently enough to merit establishing rules and procedures to handle them; and when there is sufficient stability to make them relevant.

2 using hierarchy
Co-ordination of different parties' activities is achieved by referring any problems to a superior located higher in the organizational hierarchy. The superior uses their legitimate authority, based on their position in the hierarchy, to resolve the conflict. For example, the heads of the personnel and accounting department who cannot agree on a schedule can take the problem to the executive vice-president. However, the approach does not encourage them to co-operate, and if every difference had to be resolved in this way, the boss would have little time for anything other than resolving such disputes. Resorting to hierarchy is effective in the short run to provide solutions to specific problems.

devices for co-ordinating relationships in organizations classified by class

class of co-ordination	description	device
formal direction	written guidelines and adjudication by senior staff	▶ rules, policies and procedures ▶ using hierarchy
mutual adjustment	members carrying out the work adjust to each other	▶ goal clarification and communication ▶ temporary task force ▶ permanent project team
special liaison	specially employed co-ordinators use consultation and communication	▶ liaison roles ▶ integrator roles

based on Colin Hales, 1993, *Managing through Organization*, Routledge, London, p. 55.

3 goal clarification and communication

If each party specifies and communicates its specific goals to the others in advance, then each knows what the other is attempting to do. At the individual level this may mean clear job descriptions, whilst at the departmental level, it may mean the clarification of reporting relationships through the production of an organizational chart. Parties can meet to ensure that they do not compete or interfere with the goals of others. Such discussions can have the added benefit of reducing the chances of each party misperceiving the others' abilities, skills or traits. Obviously, if an individual or a group does not have clearly defined goals to discuss then planning and communication will not be effective.

4 temporary task force

Representatives of several different departments can come together on a temporary basis to form a task force. Once the specific problem they were created for is solved, the task force disbands and members return to their usual duties and departments. During their membership, individuals come to understand the goals, values, attitudes and problems of their fellow members. This helps the frank and accurate exchange of views and information, and helps them to resolve their differences more effectively. This is particularly good for co-ordinating activities if more than two parties are involved.

5 permanent project team

If the complexity of a task results in lines of communication being extended and decisions delayed, so requiring senior management to devote time to day-to-day operation, it may choose to establish a permanent team. For example, meeting the specific computer needs of specific client groups like schools, hospitals or local government may mean that dedicated teams consisting of people from engineering, marketing, finance and production may be formed to serve those clients. This creates a matrix structure, since each individual retains a responsibility to the permanent team leader and to their functional department. This solution allows co-ordination to occur at the team level, thus improving communication and decision-making.

6 liaison roles

If higher-level managers do not successfully resolve differences, then a liaison role may be created. It would be used most by departments between whom the potential for conflict is highest, for example, the units that make up the production department (see the following figure). An individual can fill this role, but needs to be well informed about the needs and technology of the units involved, and be seen to be unbiased and acting fairly. By holding meetings and supplying units with information, they keep the employees in different sections in touch with each other.

7 integrator roles

Rather more formally, an individual or an entire department may be dedicated to just integrating the activities of several departments or groups. Again, they would integrate those departments between whom the conflict

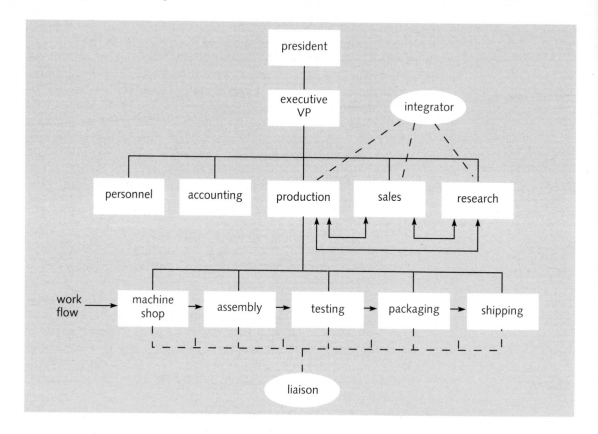

potential is highest, for example, production, sales and research (see figure above). A scientist with financial and sales experience may be recruited to occupy an integrating role. By having a 'foot in a number of camps', this person can assist the departments to co-ordinate their activities, as each strives to achieve their specific goal. The integrator may check the various departments' objectives to ensure they complement each other; assess timetables to ensure that the output of one can become a timely input to the other; and set up and chair meetings over points of contention between groups, to ensure that differences are resolved.

The effectiveness of a person in a integrator role depends on his or her ability to deal with the information flow between the departments, especially if these are large and their interactions frequent. The integrator will seek to achieve co-operation and collaboration between members of different departments, by meeting them and exchanging information. To be effective, the integrator must be able to understand both groups' concerns and be able to develop a mutually acceptable solution. If these co-ordinating devices work, then there will be no conflict potential. If they fail and there is conflict potential, will it result in conflict breaking out?

stage 3: perceptions and emotions

The conditions described in the previous stage can exist without igniting a conflict. It is only if one party, individual, group or department becomes aware of, or is adversely affected by, them and cares about the situation that latent conflict becomes perceived conflict. It realizes that its goals are being thwarted by the other. In this stage, the conflict issue becomes defined, and 'what it is all about' gets decided. Specifically, each party considers the origins of the conflict; why it emerged, and what problems are being experienced with the other party. The way it is defined at this stage determines the type of outcomes that the parties are willing to settle for in the later stages.

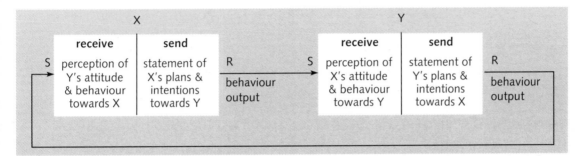

The choice of how you approach a conflict situation depends on your perceptions. One party to the conflict infers the other's intent, before responding with their own behaviour. In the figure above, X's perception of Y's behaviour leads to X's response, which is then interpreted by Y according to her attitudes towards X, and this structures Y's response. X's behaviour acts as a stimulus which, together with Y's attitudes, colour her perceptions (stimulus + attitude = perception). Moreover, X's behaviour acts as a stimulus for Y's response (stimulus→response). This stage is crucial because by wrongly attributing an intention to the other party's behaviour, you can escalate a conflict.

Not only must a party perceive a conflict, but it must also must feel it. That is, it must become emotionally involved in experiencing feelings of anxiety, tenseness, frustration and hostility towards the other party. The emotional dimension of conflict shapes perceptions. For example, negative emotions result in an oversimplification of issues, reductions in trust and negative interpretations of other parties' behaviour. Positive emotions, in contrast, increase the chances of the parties taking a broader view, seeing the issue as a problem to be solved and developing more creative solutions.

Finally, we should note that a manager may both perceive and feel that the co-ordination devices are too successful! That the relations between individuals, groups or departments are too smooth, that they are becoming too complacent and conflict needs to be actively generated to stimulate change and make the group more effective.

stage 4: conflict management

Conflict management techniques can thus be divided into two types: *conflict resolving* and *conflict stimulating* (Robbins, 1996).

---

definition

Conflict resolution *refers to a process which has as its objective the ending of the conflict between the disagreeing parties.*

---

conflict resolution approaches

The process of resolving conflict is dynamic in that, if you do something to me, I react and you respond to my reaction. Kenneth Thomas (1976) identified five conflict-resolution approaches, each of which was based on two dimensions:

▶ How assertive or unassertive each party is in pursuing its own concerns.

▶ How co-operative or uncooperative each is in satisfying the concerns of the other.

The five approaches to conflict resolution he labelled *competition* (assertive and uncooperative); *collaborative* (assertive and co-operative); *avoidance* (unassertive and uncooperative); *accommodation* (unassertive and co-operative); and *compromise* (mid-range on both dimensions). They are summarized in the following table and figure.

comparison of conflict resolution approaches

approach	objective	your posture	supporting rationale	likely outcome
1 forcing	Get your way.	*'I know what's right. Don't question my judgement or authority.'*	It is better to risk causing a few hard feelings than to abandon the issue.	You feel vindicated, but the other party feels defeated and possibly humiliated.
2 avoiding	Avoid having to deal with conflict.	*'I'm neutral on that issue. Let me think about it. That's someone else's problem.'*	Disagreements are inherently bad because they create tension.	Interpersonal problems don't get resolved, causing long-term frustration manifested in a variety of ways.
3 compromising	Reach an agreement quickly.	*'Let's search for a solution we can both live with so we can get on with our work.'*	Prolonged conflicts distract people from their work and cause bitter feelings.	Participants go for the expedient, rather than effective, solutions.
4 accommodating	Don't upset the other person.	*'How can I help you feel good about this? My position isn't so important that it is worth risking bad feelings between us.'*	Maintaining harmonious relationships should be our top priority.	The other person is likely to take advantage.
5 collaborating	Solve the problem together.	*'This is my position, what is yours? I'm committed to finding the best possible solution. What do the facts suggest?'*	Each position is important though not necessarily equally valid. Emphasis should be placed on the quality of the outcome and the fairness of the decision-making process.	The problem is most likely to be resolved. Also, both parties are committed to the solution and satisfied that they have been treated fairly.

from *Developing Management Skills*, second edition, by David A. Whetton and Kim S. Cameron. Copyright © 1991 by HarperCollins Publishers, Inc. Reprinted by permission of Addison-Wesley Educational Publishers Inc.

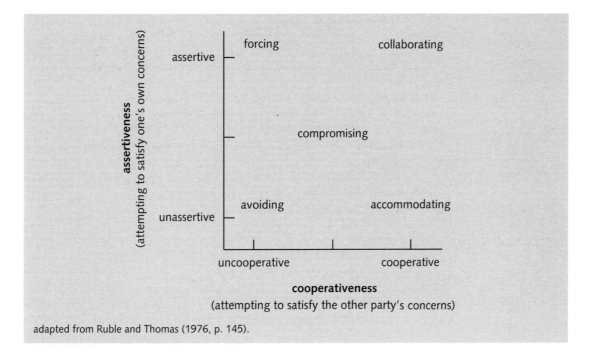

adapted from Ruble and Thomas (1976, p. 145).

Kenneth Thomas

Thomas (1977) also identified the types of situations in which each conflict-resolution orientation was to be preferred over another (see the table on page 656). Unless the manager was flexible and capable of switching between styles, their ability to resolve conflicts effectively would be limited. In practice, all individuals, whether managers or not, habitually use only a limited number of styles (perhaps just one) to resolve all the conflicts in which they are involved. It is not surprising that their success is limited.

> **STOP!**
>
> People appear to handle conflict in one fixed way (Sternberg and Soriano, 1984; Baron, 1989). They will use this in different conflict situations. To resolve conflict effectively, however, it is useful for individuals to become aware of their preferred conflict resolution approach, and gain practice in using the other four approaches.
>
> Think about the conflict situation in which you have been involved in at home or work. Consider:
>
> ▹ When do you avoid conflict?
> ▹ When do you compete with others?
> ▹ When do you collaborate in conflict situations?
> ▹ How do you feel when you accommodate others?
> ▹ How often do you secure compromises?
>
> If you are able to identify your preferred conflict-handling orientation, you will have the basis from which to develop your under-utilized styles.

when to adopt which conflict resolution approach

conflict resolution approach	appropriate situations
competition	1 When quick, decisive action is vital (e.g. in emergencies).
	2 On important issues where unpopular actions need implementing (e.g. in cost-cutting, enforcing unpopular rules, discipline).
	3 On issues vital to an organization's welfare when you known you're right.
	4 Against people who take advantage of non-competitive behaviour.
collaboration	1 To find an integrative solution when both sets of concerns are too important to be compromised.
	2 When your objective is to learn.
	3 To merge insights from people with different perspectives.
	4 To gain commitment by incorporating concerns into a consensus.
	5 To work through feelings that have interfered with a relationship.
avoidance	1 When an issue is trivial, or more important issues are pressing.
	2 When you perceive no chance of satisfying your concerns.
	3 When potential disruption outweighs the benefits of resolution.
	4 To let people cool down and regain perspective.
	5 When gathering information supersedes immediate decision.
	6 When others can resolve the conflict more effectively.
	7 When issues seem tangential or symptomatic of other issues.
accommodation	1 When you find you are wrong – to allow a better position to be heard, to learn, and to show your reasonableness.
	2 When issues are more important to others than yourself – to satisfy others and maintain cooperation.
	3 To build social credits for later issues.
	4 To minimize loss when you are outmatched and losing.
	5 When harmony and stability are especially important.
	6 To allow subordinates to develop by learning from mistakes.
compromise	1 When goals are important, but not worth the effort or potential disruption of more assertive modes.
	2 When opponents with equal power are committed to mutually exclusive goals.
	3 To achieve temporary settlements to complex issues.
	4 To arrive at expedient solutions under time pressure.
	5 As a backup when collaboration or competition is unsuccessful.

from K.W. Thomas, 1977, 'Towards multidimensional values in teaching: the example of conflict behaviours', *Academy of Management Review*, July, p. 487.

bargaining

Thomas's *compromising* conflict resolution intention was defined as a situation in which each party to a conflict is willing to determine the terms of a contractual exchange that is acceptable to both sides. Such an exchange involves giving up something, in return for something else. A compromising approach to resolving conflict disputes uses bargaining as its main tactic; however, competition (in the form of force or threats) and accommodation (hoping that a concession will be reciprocated) may also be employed. Collaboration on some issues is also possible, as both parties seek a mutually acceptable solution.

---

definitions

Distributive bargaining *is a negotiation situation in which a fixed sum of resources is divided up. It leads to a win–lose situation between the parties.*

Integrative bargaining *is a negotiation situation that seeks to increase the total amount of resources. It creates a win–win situation between the parties.*

A *distributive bargaining* situation occurs if one party's gain is at another's expense. For example, if a union bargains with management about pay, each £1 union gain is a £1 management loss. Some work conflicts can only be resolved in this way. Appropriate bargaining tactics in such a situation include asking initially for much more or less than you are finally willing to accept; persuading the opponent that their objective is unattainable or unrealistic; encouraging them to accept a figure nearer yours; and getting the other party to feel emotionally generous towards you.

forms of bargaining

		distributive	
		high	low
integrative	high	conflict moderate 2	conflict low 3
	low	1 conflict great	4 conflict intermediate (little need or desire for interaction)

based on R.E. Walton and R.B. McKersie, 1965, *A Behavioral Theory of Labor Negotiations*, McGraw-Hill, New York.

In contrast, *integrative bargaining* is built on the belief that there exist one or more settlements that can create a winning outcome for both parties. As a strategy, integrative bargaining is preferable to distributive because it builds long-term relationships and facilitates working together in the future. It bonds the parties, allowing each to believe that they have achieved a victory. Distributive bargaining creates animosities, deepens divisions amongst those who have to work together and leaves one party a loser. To operate integrative bargaining, both parties need to be open with their concerns, open in their communication; be sensitive to the others' needs, trust each other, and be willing to be flexible. These conditions are rarely present in an organization, and hence bargaining tends to be win at any cost.

bargaining strategies

win–win strategy	win–lose strategy
1 Define the conflict as a mutual problem.	1 Define the conflict as a win–lose situation.
2 Pursue joint outcomes.	2 Pursue own group's outcomes.
3 Find creative agreements that satisfy both groups.	3 Force the other group into submission.
4 Use open, honest, and accurate communication of group's needs, goals, and proposals.	4 Use deceitful, inaccurate, and misleading communication of group's needs, goals, and proposals.
5 Avoid threats (to reduce the other's defensiveness).	5 Use threats (to force submission)
6 Communicate flexibility of position.	6 Communicate high commitment (rigidity) regarding one's position.

adapted from David W. Johnson and Frank P. Johnson, 1975, *Joining Together: Group Theory and Group Skills*, Prentice Hall, Englewood Cliffs, NJ, pp. 182–3.

mediation

Mediation involves bringing in a third party in order to resolve the issues in the dispute. In a negotiation situation, the behaviour and feelings of the parties can become sharply polarized, and each becomes isolated from the other. When this happens, a mediator can maintain contact and communication between the parties in dispute. In hostage-taking situations and local wars, independent third parties are often brought in to act as mediators. They do not control the agreement, but influence the conflict resolution process. They guide the two parties to discover the solution to their problem.

---

definition

Mediation *is a process in which a neutral third party to the conflict assists in the achievement of a negotiated solution by using reason, persuasion and the presentation of alternatives.*

Mediation techniques include asking each party to state the problem, to state the other's view of the problem, and to ask them to confirm the accuracy of the other's repetition. Once the initial positions have been presented and understood, alternative solutions are generated using brainstorming. The use of recesses in the mediating process is valuable. These can help calm the parties after an emotional encounter, can be used to conduct private enquiries about interests, as well as to de-escalate conflict.

"Gentlemen, instead of trying to mediate this thing, why don't you just slug it out?"

printed by permission of the publisher of *Personnel*, May–June 1968. © 1968 by the American Management Association, Inc.

---

ten ways to fail as a mediator

1 After having listened to the argument for a short time, begin to communicate non-verbally your discomfort with the discussion (e.g. sit back, begin to fidget).
2 Take sides and communicate your agreement with *one* of the parties (e.g. through facial expressions, posture, chair position, reinforcing comments).
3 Say that you shouldn't be talking about this thing at work or where others can hear you.
4 Discourage the expression of emotion. Suggest that the discussion be held later after both parties have cooled off.
5 Suggest that both parties are wrong. Point out the problems with both points of view.
6 Suggest part way through the discussion that possibly you aren't the person who should be helping solve this problem.
7 See if you can get both parties to attack you.
8 Minimize the seriousness of the problem.
9 Change the subject (e.g. ask for advice to help you solve one of your problems).
10 Express displeasure that the two parties are experiencing conflict (e.g. imply that it might undermine the solidarity of the work group).

from David Whetton, Kim Cameron and Mike Woods, 1994, *Developing Management Skills for Europe*, HarperCollins, New York, p. 362. © Addison-Wesley Educational Publishers, Inc. Reproduced by permission of Addison-Wesley Educational Publishers, Inc.

---

arbitration

If mediation fails, disputes often go to arbitration. This may occur if negotiations between unions and management have reached an impasse; a grievance is presented and the arbiter listens to both sides. In this process, the dispute is referred to a third party. In this approach, a third party is given the power to formulate a settlement that is binding on both parties. This is similar to a judge in a courtroom. Arbitration may be voluntary or compulsory. The former occurs when both parties involved have the choice of whether or not to have a decision imposed on them. Compulsory arbitration, perhaps due to government regulations, denies them that choice.

---

definition

Arbitration *is a process in which a third party to a conflict has the authority to impose an agreement that is binding on the parties in conflict.*

---

managers and conflict resolution

So far, it has been assumed that just two parties are involved in a conflict. However, a manager's job also involves resolving conflicts between their subordinates. This task is disliked by managers because they have to choose sides and deal with the loser's frustrations. For this reason, managers avoid dealing with conflicts, smooth them over or force the parties to work it out themselves. They may even punish subordinates who bring them problems by ensuring no one ever wins, creating so-called lose–lose situations.

Managers can, however, use these conciliation techniques with their subordinates-in-conflict by applying the principles of integrative bargaining. It may be possible to convert win–lose situations into win–win ones, and thus allow both parties to achieve their goals. A holiday allocation decision may be of this type. Two employees both want two weeks off in July, but there are not enough staff to cover. If one person gets their fortnight, the other does not (win–lose). Since one cannot have it, the other is similarly prevented from having theirs (lose–lose). If the manager investigates and finds that one of them wants it for a particular reason and the other for another reason, it may be possible to resolve the situation, and create a win–win outcome for all concerned.

Alternatively, managers can choose to mediate between their subordinates. This conflict-resolution strategy is preferred by both subordinates and their supervisor. However, since staff have little experience of their boss guiding the conflict resolution process without making the final decision, they are rarely sure of how to respond. Some managers are more comfortable with arbitration. Playing the role of judge can be a fast and definitive conflict-resolving process, especially if one of the parties has obviously violated a rule or a policy. However, on the negative side, it rarely results in the parties being committed to the settlement that is imposed on them. Finally, the supervisor might use delegation, telling the parties to solve the conflict themselves. This may appeal to those who wish to smooth over conflicts, but is often ineffective, because the parties lack the skills, information and impartiality to work through the conflict on their own.

conflict stimulation devices

There are situations where what is needed is more and not less conflict. At the organizational level, Kotter (1996) discussed the dangers of complacency and the need to drive employees out of their comfort zones. Amongst the complacency-smashing and potentially conflict-stimulating techniques used by senior management were the following:

⫸ Create a crisis by allowing a financial loss to occur or an error to blow up.

⫸ Eliminate obvious examples of excess like corporate jet fleets and gourmet dining rooms.

⫸ Set targets like income, productivity and cycle times so high that they can't be reached by doing business as usual.

⫸ Share more information about customer satisfaction and financial performance with employees.

⫸ Insist that people speak regularly to dissatisfied customers, unhappy suppliers and disgruntled shareholders.

⫸ Put more honest discussions of the firm's problems in company newspapers and management speeches. Stop senior management's 'happy talk'.

STOP!

Suggest how Kotter's ideas might stimulate conflict within a company.

At the level of the group, research into group decision-making by Janis (1972) and Cosier and Stewing (1990) suggests that teams can become too cohesive. Moreover, if a decision to be made is unique, multidisciplinary, ambiguous and important, then some degree of conflict can actually be useful (Rose *et al.*, 1982). Various conflict-stimulation techniques can be adopted when there is insufficient conflict to engender the new thinking or problem-solving mentioned earlier.

1 *Communications*. Managers can regulate the flow of information in the communication system, providing either too much or too little. Alternatively, they can send ambiguous or threatening messages.

2 *Restructuring a company*. Realigning working groups and altering rules and regulations, so as to increase or create interdependence between previously independent units, acts to stimulate conflict, especially if the goals of the newly interdependent departments are incompatible.

3 *Bringing in outsiders*. Adding employees to a group whose backgrounds, values, attitudes or management styles differ from those of existing members.

4 *Appointing a devil's advocate*. Designing a critic intentionally to argue against the majority position held by the group.

5 *Leadership style*. Too much or too little in one direction can create conflict.

assessment

In his review of the past and present trends in the field of conflict theory and research, Beaumont (1996) distinguished the *organization theory* approach to conflict from the *industrial relations* approach, and emphasized the importance of negotiation and networking in non-union contexts. He considered the differing perspectives within each. With respect to organization theory, he argued that before the 1960s, mainstream organizational theory essentially ignored conflict. Classic works such of those of Henri Fayol did not discuss it at all and treated organizations as apolitical systems. The earliest references to conflict are to be found in the work of Louis Pondy (1967). Although he failed to integrate the topic into mainstream organization theory, Pondy did make two substantive points. First, that conflict could be a naturally occurring phenomenon, that is, it was endemic to organizations, and second, that it was not necessarily a bad thing.

Pondy wrote in the 1960s which were also the high-water mark of contingency theory. The main message of this theory was that there was no one best way to manage. However, the theory was still essentially apolitical. It focused on fitting one's strategy to one's particular environment and circumstances. Contingency theory did not talk about conflict. It is only fairly recently that mainstream organization theory has really begun to discuss conflict in an analytical way. The work of Jeffrey Pfeffer (1981) was important because it stressed *intra-managerial conflict*. This is the perspective that holds that an organization is, in essence, a loose grouping of sectional coalition forces, that there is a great deal of variance in sub-unit power within organizations and that decisions have to be negotiated and bargained over.

This same perspective was encountered in Chapter 18, on corporate culture. Martin (1992) distinguished the differentialist and fragmentationist perspectives to the subject as standing alongside the currently popular integrationist-unitary one. In order to explain the nature of negotiation and conflict, Pfeffer and his colleagues drew heavily on Emerson's (1962) perspective of power dependency. That is, that A has power over B because he has control of resources that B cannot obtain from elsewhere. Pfeffer's and Martin's approaches represent a significant move away from the rational, decision-making paradigm of organizations and emphasize the importance of the political model of organizations. This will be dealt with in depth in Chapter 22.

Alongside the traditional organizational theory, which has moved from the apolitical, rationalist perspective to the sectional conflict-negotiating perspective, another conflict perspective has been discerned. This is the unitarist perspective which originated in the 1930s with Elton Mayo and the human relations school of thought. The linear development of that school of research and writing was the organizational change and development (OD) literature of the 1960s. This was discussed in Chapter 17.

The most recent stage of this unitarist school of thinking is represented by William Ouchi's (1981) Theory Z, and the work of Peters and Waterman (1982) and their successors. These authors differ from the mainstream organizational theorists mentioned earlier in that, while they recognize conflict, they regard it as neither legitimate nor desirable. Moreover, they propose that it can be solved through increased trust and open communications. Whilst this perspective on conflict is limited, it does nevertheless recognize that conflict exists. These writers advocate an integrationist perspective on corporate culture, recommending that culture should reflect the values of senior management and be embodied in a company value statement. The human resources policy mix within the firm should be designed so as to encourage employees to buy into these corporate culture values. The assumption made is that *high culture organizations* like Hewlett-Packard, McDonald's and Disney are also high performance organizations, partly at least through being conflict-free.

The second body of knowledge to be considered in relation to conflict theory is *industrial relations*. This literature has conflict at its core. There are two perspectives within it. The first is the Marxist perspective which sees conflict as emanating from outside the organization. It derives from wider ownership control structures within society at large. The second and more mainstream industrial relations literature derives from the pluralist tradition which sees conflict as inevitable and to some extent desirable within an organization. Such inevitability is the result of the differences in interest between management and workers. Management is committed to change as it relates to dynamic organizational performance. The workers, in contrast, are more status quo-oriented, wanting job security.

The pluralist perspective also makes the point that conflict arises from the superior–subordinate relationship. Once there is a hierarchy, some degree of conflict is inevitable – and arguably desirable. A good pluralist will qualify that statement by saying that the conflict, in order to produce positive advantages, must be functional in nature. However, a pluralist cannot operationalize the notion of functional conflict. There is no empirical way of saying what level of conflict is too high or too low. A pluralist talks instead about the need for institutional channels to ensure that conflict does not take an unacceptably destructive form. They traditionally look to collective bargaining and trade unionism to institutionalize and functionalize conflict.

Within the industrial relations paradigm, the pluralists differ from someone like Pfeffer, in trying to operationalize the determinants of conflict. Pfeffer's approach goes back to the sociological perspective of Emerson's power dependency notion of control over resources and the ability to minimize organizational uncertainty. The industrial relations paradigm, in contrast, draws heavily on Neil Chamberlain's (1951) work, which stresses not so much intra-management conflict as employee–management–union conflict. There, the emphasis is on trying to operationalize the notion of bargaining power where the perspective is on the costs of agreement relative to the costs of disagreement. Thus the union will have increased power in relation to management if it can increase the costs of management disagreeing with the union's demand or lower the costs of management agreeing to the union's demand.

As we approach the new millennium, what new themes are emerging within the area of conflict management? Beaumont (1996) argued that developments such as 'The Organization of the Future', globalization, networking and flatter hierarchies were likely to enhance the importance of both negotiation and conflict resolution practices. This was because the more equally that power was distributed in a company, the more likely it was that conflicts of interests and goals would surface as open conflicts. In a sense, organizations were becoming more 'political', as the next chapter will explain. In addition, conflict was likely to become more complex in nature, as negotiations come to involve more parties, and not just the union and management with their clearly defined and fixed identities.

These developments have a number of implications. First, an increase of networking by firms, that is, the use of strategic alliances across national boundaries, has led to an interest in cross-cultural negotiations and conflict resolution, for example, in international joint ventures where the selection of culturally appropriate negotiating is vital. Weiss (1994) argued that, given the diversity of interests in modern organizations, there was a need for flexible, multi-option avenues for resolving differences before they escalated into costly win–lose or lose–lose battles.

Second, the increase in the number of non-union firms and costs of legal cases has led to the emergence of Alternative Dispute Resolution (ADR) systems. These emphasize managerial practices to eliminate the root causes of problems, the use of informal participatory processes to encourage the resolving of problems close to their source and the use of trained mentors, peers, facilitators and ombudsmen to replace expensive, outside legal settlements (Rowe, 1993). It is not surprising that 'how to negotiate' books have grown in popularity. Amongst the earliest of this genre was that by Fisher and Ury (1981). The publication of such books has expanded greatly during the 1990s. All have a strong emphasis on win–win bargaining, as opposed to the traditional adversarial approach.

sources

Argyris, C., 1970, *Intervention Theory and Method: A Behavioral Science View*, Addison-Wesley, Reading, MA.

Balasco, J.A. and Alutto, J.A., 1969, 'Line and staff conflicts: Some empirical insights', *Academy of Management Journal*, March, pp. 69–77.

Barnes, R., 1965, 'Appeals procedure at the Glacier Metal Company', *Industrial and Commercial Training*, vol. 8, no. 10, pp. 383–6.

Baron, R.A., 1989, 'Personality and organizational conflict: Effects of type A behaviour pattern and self-monitoring', *Organizational Behaviour and Human Decision Making Processes*, October, pp. 281–96.

Beaumont, P. B., 1996, Personal communication, Department of Social and Economic Research, University of Glasgow.

Chamberlain, N., 1951, *Collective Bargaining*, McGraw-Hill, New York.

Coser, L.A., 1956, *The Functions of Conflict*, Routledge & Kegan Paul, London.

Cosier, R.A. and Schwenk, C.R., 1990, 'Agreement and thinking alike: Ingredients for poor decisions', *Academy of Management Executive*, February, pp. 69–74.

Dalton, M., 1950, 'Conflict between staff and line managerial officers', *American Sociological Review*, June, pp. 342–51.

Dalton, M., 1959, *Men Who Manage*, John Wiley, New York.

Drucker, P.F., 1968, *The Practice of Management*, Pan Books, London.

Emerson, R.M., 1962, 'Power dependence relations', *American Sociological Review*, vol. 27, pp. 31–40.

Fisher, R. and Ury, W., 1981, *Getting to Yes*, Houghton Mifflin, New York.

Fox, A., 1966, *Industrial Sociology and Industrial Relations*, Research Papers 3, Royal Commission on Trade Unions and Employers' Associations, HMSO, London.

Fox, A., 1971, *A Sociology of Work in Industry*, Collier-Macmillan, London.

Fox, A., 1975, 'Industrial relations: A social critique of pluralist ideology', in B. Barrett, E. Rhodes and J. Beishon (eds.), *Industrial Relations and the Wider Society: Aspects of Interaction*, Collier-Macmillan, London.

Harvard Business Review, 1984, 'Overcoming group warfare', pp. 98–108.

Janis, I.L., 1982, *Victims of Groupthink*, Houghton Mifflin, Boston, MA, 2nd edition.

Kerr, C., 1964, *Labor and Management in Industrial Society*, Doubleday, New York.

Kotter, J.P., 1996, 'Kill complacency', *Fortune*, 5 August, no. 15, pp. 122–4.

Lawrence, P.R. and Lorsch, J.W., 1967, *Organization and Environment*, Harvard University Press, Boston, MA.

Martin, J., 1992, *Culture in Organizations: Three Perspectives*, Oxford University Press, Oxford.

Ouchi, W., 1981, *Theory Z: How American Business Can Meet the Japanese Challenge*, Addison-Wesley, Reading, MA.

Pfeffer, J., 1981, *Power in Organizations*, HarperCollins, New York.

Pondy, L., 1967, 'Organizational conflict: concepts and models', *Administrative Science Quarterly*, June, pp. 296–320.

Robbins, S.P., 1974, *Managing Organizational Conflict: A Non-traditional Approach*, Prentice Hall, Englewood Cliffs, NJ, pp. 59–89.

Robbins, S.P., 1996, *Organizational Behavior: Concepts, Controversies and Applications*, Prentice Hall, Englewood Cliffs, NJ, 7th edition.

Rose, G.L., Menasco, M.B. and Curry, D.J., 1982, 'When disagreement facilitates performance in judgement tasks: Effects of different forms of cognitive conflict, information environments and human information processing characteristics', *Organizational Behaviour and Human Performance*, vol. 29, pp. 287–306.

Rowe, M., 1993, 'Options and choice for conflict resolution in the workplace', in L. Hall (ed.), *Negotiation: Strategies for Mutual Gain*, Sage, New York, pp. 105–19.

Ruble, T. and Thomas, K., 1976, 'Support for a two-dimensional model of conflict behaviour', *Organizational Behaviour and Human Performance*, vol. 6.

Schelling, T.C., 1960, *The Strategy of Conflict*, Harvard University Press, Boston, MA.

Scott, W.G., 1965, *The Management of Conflict: Appeals Systems in Organizations*, Irwin Dorsey, Homewood, IL.

Sherif, M. and Sherif, C.W., 1956, *An Outline of Social Psychology*, Harper & Row, New York.

Sherif, M., Harvey, O., White, B.J., Hood, W.R. and Sherif, C., 1954, *Experimental Study of Positive and Negative Intergroup Attitudes Between Experimentally Produced Groups: Robbers Cave Study*, University of Oklahoma Press, Norman, OK.

Sorenson, J.E. and Sorenson, T.L., 1974, 'The conflict of professionals in bureaucratic organizations', *Administrative Science Quarterly*, March, pp. 98–106.

Sternberg, R.J. and Soriano, L.J., 1984, 'Styles of conflict resolution', *Journal of Personality and Social Psychology*, July, pp. 115–26.

Thomas, K.W., 1976, Conflict and conflict management', in M.D. Dunette (ed.), *Handbook of Industrial and Organizational Psychology*, Rand-McNally, Chicago, pp. 889–935.

Thomas, K.W., 1977, 'Towards multi-dimensional values in teaching: The example of conflict behaviours', *Academy of Management Review*, July, pp. 889–935.

Tjosvold, D. and Deemer, B.K., 1980, 'Effects of controversy within a co-operative or competitive context on organizational decision making', *Journal of Applied Psychology*, vol. 65, no. 5, pp. 590–5.

Van de Vliert, E. 1995, 'Escalative Intervention in Small Group Conflicts', *Journal of Applied Behavioural Science*, Winter, pp. 19–26.

Weick, K., 1969, *The Social Psychology of Organizing*, Addison-Wesley, Reading, MA.

Weiss, S.E., 1994, 'Negotiating with Romans, Part 2', *Sloan Management Review*, Spring, pp. 85–99.

chapter 22 organizational power and politics

"In his mysterious way, God has given each of us different talents, Ridgeway. It just so happens that mine is intimidating people."

concepts and learning objectives

Power and politics have a major influence on the behaviour of people within an organization. It has been argued that among the causes of management failure are political incompetence, political naïveté, and the inability or unwillingness to perform effectively the required political tasks in the organization (Kotter, 1985; Yates, 1985).

Politics is about overcoming the problem of resolving situations where different organization members bring different values to their work, and consequently do not share common goals or views, but yet have to continue to work with one another (Kakabadse, 1983). Politics includes identifying the objectives of different groups and individuals in the company, the use of strategies to maintain an individual's power against others who want to take it away from them, forming coalitions with others, developing and applying influencing skills, and so on. Politics can involve both the long-term manipulation of relationships in order to improve a person's position and also short-term actions to give them a tactical advantage.

Bolman and Deal (1991) summarized this political view of organization, seeing goals and decisions as emerging from bargaining, negotiation and jockeying for position by individuals and coalitions. These coalitions were composed of varied individuals and interest groups which possessed enduring differences of values, preferences, beliefs, information and perceptions of reality. This is very different from the rational model of organizations.

The chapter begins by introducing one of the major debates in organizational behaviour, the question of whether the rational or the political model best explains the actions of individuals and groups in organizations. It then goes on to explain why political behaviour occurs within organizations and indicates the personality traits of individuals who are most likely to engage in political activities.

It is well known that in any company some departments and individuals are more powerful than others. It is less obvious why this should be so. To explain this, the bases of power will be considered separately from the sources of power. The bases of power refer to what power-holders possess that gives them power (e.g. ability to reward, to coerce, having expertise, etc.). In contrast, the sources of power tell you from where power-holders get their power bases (e.g. others' dependency on them, their centrality in a network, the non-substitutability of their knowledge, etc.).

The different bases or types of power that organization members can exert were introduced and defined in the chapter on leadership and management style. These are elaborated and added to in order to provide examples of how the abstract concept of power is exercised in practice. Finally, the chapter relates the concept of influencing to power, and shows how the latter acts as a foundation for the former. The concluding assessment section provides an historical outline to the wide-ranging, and often complex, debate about power and politics. It provides extensive references for those wishing to study this crucial subject in greater depth.

key concepts

rational organizational model	Machiavellianism
political organizational model	locus of control
organizational politics	risk-seeking propensity
personalized power	organizational power
socialised power	strategic contingencies
need for power	influencing

learning objectives

When you have read this chapter you should be able to define those key concepts in your own words, and you should also be able to:

1 Distinguish between the rational and political models of organization.
2 Explain why politics is a feature of organizational life.
3 Identify the type of individuals most likely to engage in political behaviour.
4 Identify the main sources of departmental power in a company.
5 List six bases of power.
6 List seven influencing strategies.
7 Explain the relationship between power and influencing.

organizations: rational or political?

A major debate in organizational behaviour relates to the question as to whether organizations are *rational* or *political*. The popular layperson's view is the rationalist one, and is summarized on the left-hand side of the following table, while the political is described in the right-hand side column. These two different social science views or models have different implications for how people are understood to operate within organizations, and which interests they are held to give priority to.

rational versus political models of organization

rational model	political model
The goals of an organization seem obvious. Commercial organizations seek to make a profit; trade unions to protect their members' interests; schools educate their pupils; hospitals try to cure their patients, and so on.	An organizational goal can get distorted as when technological leadership takes precedence over profitability. Union leaders can lose touch with their members; and schools can acquire latent functions like keeping youngsters off the labour market .
Within the company, the goals and preferences are consistent among different departments, units and members.	The idea of a single, agreed organizational goal is a fiction. Different parties have their own set of interests and priorities which change, and which may be placed ahead of those of the company as a whole.
Even if an organization's goals get distorted, the means for achieving them remain clear and rational. The organization structure provides a rational way of achieving ends. Most firms have an organizational chart showing who is responsible for what.	Max Weber's seemingly rational organization has many dysfunctions (e.g. goals are displaced; cliques develop; units compete with each other). The formal structure (chart and rules) only ever gives a partial guide to factors like leadership style, employee morale or informal group behaviour.
Information available in the company is extensive, systematic and accurate.	Ambiguous information has to be used, and is withheld strategically.
Even if both aims and means get distorted, employees behave rationally when dealing with work tasks and each other.	Corporations have cultures which can distort what goes on. Culture becomes unconsciously and uncritically adopted.
Even if corporate culture can distort reality, communication can overcome this by showing clearly what is really happening.	Good communication involves more than consulting or telling people. It comes from shared goals and values. Where consensus on these is absent, communication cannot fill the gap.
Improved top-down managerial decision-making can overcome the problems listed by making choices that maximize benefits.	Perhaps the real problem is too much management control, producing low levels of employee involvement and commitment. Decisions can be the outcome of bargaining and interplays between competing interests.

table adapted from *Power in Organizations* by Jeffrey Pfeffer (Copyright © 1981 by Jeffrey Pfeffer. Reprinted by permission of HarperCollins Publishers, Inc.) and Joseph (1989, p.109).

We shall return to these two models in the assessment section, where the rational view will be discussed in terms of its managerialist-functionist implications, and the political model will be considered in terms of radical-sociological assumptions.

rational model

This model of organization is founded upon rationalism. Rationalism is a concept that was first encountered and defined in Chapter 12 on scientific management. Rationalism consists of four key elements.

1 *Reason*: A rational action is one undertaken on the basis of reason. If conduct is substantiated by one or more reasons, a person performing that action is judged to be acting rationally.
2 *Consistency*: A person adopts the same actions under the same circumstances, and expresses logically consistent preferences.
3 *Empirical*: Choices are made on valid knowledge rather than on intuition, and is thus knowledge held to provide objectivity.
4 *Means–ends relationship*: Rationality is identified when appropriate means are chosen to attain the stated ends.

In the organizational context, the rational model's beliefs are summarized in the left-hand column of the table. They are contrasted with those held by the political model against eight key organizational characteristics. At the very heart of this perspective is the belief that employees possess goals that conform to and are compatible with those around them. These individuals are considered to share a collective purpose, which can even be called the organizational goal. All the remaining features of the model assume the existence of this goal.

For example, people's behaviour in organizations is not random or accidental, but their actions are held to be directed towards the achievement of this organizational goal. Next, rationalists argue that when making a choice, the decision-maker is guided by the norm of optimization, that is, seeking the most favourable outcome for a particular end. In this process, the various available alternatives are uncovered, their likely consequences assessed and the risks of each considered. Finally, the course of action is selected which best meets the organizational goal which, as mentioned earlier, is held to exist and be shared by all.

---

definition

The **rational model of organizations** *holds that behaviour within a firm is not random, but goals are clear and choices are made in a logical way. In making decisions, the objective is defined, alternatives are identified and the option with the greatest chance of achieving the objective is selected.*

Rationalists hold that this is the best way to make choices on issues such as the introduction of new technology, work organization, distribution of rewards, organization structure, and so on. However, rational writers are not only *prescriptive*, saying how, in their view, things should be done, but also claim to be *descriptive*, that is, they claim to be describing how decisions are actually made in real organizations.

Max Weber (1947) predicted that rationality would become the dominant mode of action in modern industrial society, displacing both affective action, which was based on a person's emotional state at the time, and traditional action, which was founded upon established custom. This trend has been accelerated by three main stimuli:

1 The process of bureaucratization, which dominated the twentieth century, has emphasized clear goals, strict rules and impersonal behaviour towards the achievement of objectives.

2 Management education, first in the United States and then in Europe, which stressed analytical techniques and quantitative decision-making methods.

3 Management consultancy, which, since the time of Frederick Taylor and scientific management, has believed in the application of scientific methods to solve production problems (Merkle, 1980; Wren, 1994).

We can also note that the rationalist model of organizations shares the currently fashionable integrationalist perspective encountered in the chapter on corporate culture, which stresses organization-wide consensus and clarity with respect to organizational goals. For all these reasons, rationality has always been an important concept amongst managers, and in consequence, the view of organizations as rational entities has tended to dominate.

It is perhaps most visibly reflected in practices such as strategic planning and management. Since 1945, companies have been encouraged to set specific and measurable goals, systematically arrange activities in order and commit themselves to implement the conceived plan. Many established dedicated corporate strategy departments do nothing else (Moore, 1992).

Less visibly, rationality manifests itself within organizations in a diverse and on-going way. Staff selection procedures commonly make use of psychometric testing, which claims to assess objectively the suitability of candidates for a job. Most staff appraisal systems are based on a form of Management-by-Objectives (MbO) procedure in which an employee's performance over the past year is evaluated against predefined, written objectives. Payment systems, be they payment-by-results such as sales staff commissions or merit pay, aim to relate financial reward to individual performance. Personnel policies, such as succession and career planning, popular in the past, have recently been superseded by the competencies movement, which involves identifying and developing the work and management competencies needed by employees to achieve the business goals of the company. All the aforementioned practices reflect the rationalist view of organization.

The rationalist view of organizations has dominated discussions about management and organizational behaviour, both in the past and in the present. The majority of the textbooks used by students studying management at college and university are founded on the rationalist assumptions summarized earlier. In addition, the professional literature designed to improve management practice is similarly rationally-oriented. 'How to . . .' books are published which guide managers in the setting of company goals, monitoring their achievement, solving problems, making decisions, and so on.

STOP!

Suggest reasons that might account for the popularity of the rationalist view of organizations amongst managers, management consultants and management academics.

   Select either a management university textbook or a professional management book, and look for examples of the rationalist assumptions that it makes about organizations.

---

political model

Rationalism, however, has not gone unchallenged. James March (1962) was amongst the earliest writers to highlight that the rationalist model failed to take into account the differences of interests and objectives that existed between individuals within organizations. Indeed, March described business firms as *political coalitions*. As mentioned above, the rational model is founded on the belief that an organizational goal exists and is accepted by those in the organization.

Historically, the earliest attempts to engender a commonality-of-interests amongst employees was through the use of bureaucratic control devices such as standardized treatment for all, performance-based pay, career ladders and rules and procedures. These were used in combination with organizational socialization processes, such as careful staff selection, induction programmes and company training courses. Together it was hoped that these would get employees to agree on set of collective goals to which all would subscribe. In the process, the operation of individual self-interest would be eliminated. Writers such as Cyert and March (1963) argued that these attempts had failed.

The political model of organizations holds that normally there is no overarching organizational goal to which all members subscribe; that the behaviour of individuals and cliques within organizations can be explained with reference to their attempts to achieve their own unique goals; and that those who possesses the greatest amounts of power will be the most successful in furthering their interests and achieving their goals. The rational model, in contrast, asserts that individual and departmental goals typically fit into the main organizational objective.

Other researchers investigated how decisions were actually made in organizations. They discovered an absence of the use of reason, consistency, empirical data or means–ends sequencing which was supposed to characterize rational organizational decision-making. In the place of consensus they found conflict and discovered decisions being made on the basis of bargaining and compromise (Allison, 1971). In the place of an organization-wide consensus on the organizational goal, they found individuals, groups, units and departments which had their own objectives, and who were in conflict with each other to attain their own parochial ends through negotiation and the use of power.

---

definition

*The **political model of organization** views it as being made up of groups that have separate interests, goals and values, and in which power and influence are needed to reach decisions.*

These studies have led another group of writers (Baldridge, 1971) to promote the political model of organization. The key characteristics of organizations, as they see them, are summarized in the second column of the table. Their point of departure is the view that this is no overarching organizational goal to which all members subscribe, and even where there is a written, company 'mission statement', decisions are rarely made which further its achievement. This is because people's goals are considered to be inconsistent with each other. For example, the differences between management and workers' goals were examined with the concept of the *organizational dilemma* in Chapter 1.

On the question of rules and norms, the political writers hold that optimization is impossible, because people disagree about goals, and hence about what constitutes the most 'appropriate action', in any given situation. In the absence of rules and norms to guide behaviour, different individuals and groups in the company attempt to achieve their own unique goals, and those who possess the greatest amounts of power will be the most successful in furthering their interests, since power is used to overcome the resistance of others.

STOP!

Suggest reasons that might account for the relative unpopularity of the political view of organizations among managers, management consultants and management academics.

From your experience of organizations (school, club, church, work), does the rationalist or the political model best explain the behaviour of people within it?

Users of the political model focus on who participates in the decision-making process; analyze what determines their position with respect to issues and where their power derives from; consider the process by which decisions are arrived at; and seek to determine how the preferences of different participants in the decision-making process are combined or resolved. Taggert and Silbey (1986) humorously contrasted the difference between the rational and the political model with respect to the implementation of computer systems within organizations. The rational cycle, shown on the left in the table below, stresses the logical, considered, step-by-step approach to decision-making in a company. In contrast, the political cycle, depicted on the right hand side of the table, highlights the irrationality, chaos and power struggles used by those involved to gain advantage.

conventional (rational) system cycle	real (political) development cycle
1 feasibility study	1 wild enthusiasm
2 requirements analysis	2 disillusionment
3 systems analysis	3 total confusion
4 specification	4 search for the guilty
5 design and development	5 punishment of the innocent
6 implementation	6 promotion of non-participants

The rational and the political views of organization represent different sides of the argument about the nature of organizations, and also how the behaviour of people within them can be best explained. Rather like the *nature–nurture* debate on personality encountered in Chapter 6, the rationalists and the politicals each have their own supporters and each can provide theoretical and empirical evidence in their defence. Each view is necessarily partial, not giving the full picture of what is happening. One view is neither better nor more realistic than the other. Perhaps it is best to treat the rational and political models as 'different ways of seeing' what goes on in organizations.

organizational politics

Engaging in political activities, performing political acts or 'politicking', is done to overcome opposition. If there is no opposition within an organization to what a manager wants to do, then it in unnecessary for them to use politics. Organizational politicking involves individuals engaging in activities to acquire, develop, retain and use power, in order to obtain their preferred outcomes in a situation where there is uncertainty or disagreement about choices. Politicking concerns the actions that individuals take to influence the distribution of advantages and disadvantages within their organization (Allen *et al.*, 1979; Farrell and Petersen, 1982). The study of politics, whether inside or outside of organizations, is the study of who gets what, when and how.

---

definition

Politics *in organizations involves those activities taken within the company to acquire, develop and use power and other resources to obtain one's preferred outcomes in a situation in which there is uncertainty or dissension about choices.*

Pfeffer (1981, p. 7).

Jeffrey Pfeffer

The political model of organization holds that organizational life is about differences. It is very rare for an organization to have a single, unambiguous, clearly defined objective, with which all its members agree. Some small religious organizations might be an exception, but historically Churches have been riven apart by political differences. The following table summarizes Pfeffer's (1981) model of the conditions that produce the use of power and politics in organizational decision-making. A step-by-step explanation of his model is provided.

1 differentiation

Our starting point is the observation that in large organizations tasks are divided up amongst a number of departments. Differentiation is the term used to refer to this specialization of both departments and employees' jobs in an organization by task. This division of labour enables an organization to achieve certain economies. However, it also has a number of divisive consequences.

conditions producing the use of power and politics in organizational decision-making

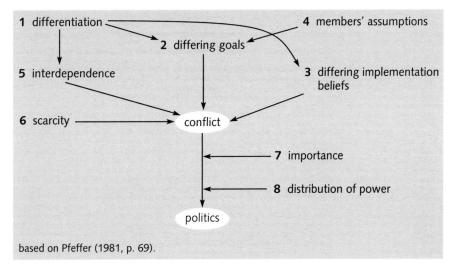

based on Pfeffer (1981, p. 69).

2 differing goals

First, it creates differences in goals and understandings about what the company does, or should do, because each department is assigned its unique goal as part of the differentiation process. Marketing's task may be to maximize sales, whilst production's may be to minimize costs. Such objectives are frequently in conflict. Second, different departments receive different sets of information. Marketing receives data on sales, whilst production receives data on costs. This causes parochialism, with each employee seeing the world through their own department's perspective.

3 differing implementation beliefs

Differentiation also causes the creation of differences in *beliefs* about how something should be done. Individuals can agree on a goal, yet disagree on decisions and their outcomes. They can have different views as to what are the appropriate means to achieve the stated, and perhaps agreed, ends.

4 members' assumptions

People are physically recruited into a department, not a company. For example, the research and development department (R&D) recruits scientists, whilst the human resources department hires personnel specialists. The differing personalities and backgrounds of the staff who compose the different company departments, socialization, background, training and way of addressing business problems, affects not only how they see their department's goals, but also how they believe these should be achieved.

5 interdependence

Differentiation also creates *interdependence* between people and departments, where the actions of one affect the other. It thus ties groups and individuals together, making each concerned with what the other does and gets in terms of resources.

6 scarcity

Resources that are defined as scarce in an organization are perceived as being relatively valuable. Labelling a resource as scarce produces a vigorous action to obtain it and more dissatisfaction with its apparent unavailability. Gandz and Murray (1980) saw scarcity as existing in the following organizational areas: promotions and transfers, hiring, pay, budget allocation, facilities and equipment allocation, delegation of authority, interdepartmental co-ordination, personnel policies, disciplinary penalties, work appraisals and grievances and complaints.

All these areas have two things in common. First, the organizational decision-making procedures and performance measures associated with each are highly uncertain and complex. Weber's bureaucratic rules and procedures cannot easily settle the issues involved. Second, in each case, the competition between individuals and groups for them is strong, managerial discretion is high and decisions have widespread consequences, both on success or failure at work, and on vertical, lateral and inter-unit relationships. The last of these is an aspect of organizational integration and is the most difficult to subject to routinization and techno-economic rationality so beloved by rationalists (Beeman and Sharkey, 1987).

The combined existence of these factors can certainly lead to conflict between departments, groups and individuals, as was shown in the previous chapter. However, will these conditions inevitably result in the use of power and politicking? Pfeffer argues that they will if two further conditions are met.

7 importance

It depends on how critically the resource or issue is perceived. That is, how important it is to those involved. Importance is relative since, as Chapter 3 showed, what one person considers important may be perceived as trivial by another. The use of power and engagement in political behaviour requires time and effort, so will tend to be reserved for important issues.

8 distribution of power

Finally, a wide *distribution of power* needs to exist within the organization for politicking to flourish. Political activity, bargaining and coalition formation only occur when power is dispersed widely, and not when it is centralized at the top.

STOP!

'*Power* is the property of the organization system at rest, while *politics* is the study of power in action.'

What do you understand this statement to mean? How accurate do you believe it is?

---

power in the company political landscape

The division of labour means that some departments are more central and contribute more directly to the primary goals of the organization than others. A company's political landscape, therefore, consists of departments and people who possess differing amounts of power. What are the true indicators of power in an organization, and how powerful are the different departments on this criteria? To assess an individual's power within departments, one has to see if they have the ability to intercede successfully on behalf of someone in trouble, secure a desirable placement for a talented subordinate or gain approval for expenditure beyond the budget. A second consequence of division of labour is the creation of interdependence. In order for one department to achieve its objectives, it requires the co-operative effort of another. While this may cause conflict, it also creates opportunities for coalition as individuals work with and through others to get things done.

To facilitate implementation, a decision will often be delayed in order to get as many different interested parties as possible behind it, whilst seeking to outmanoeuvre the opponents. Internal alliances are founded on common interests among participants who need one another. Once an issue is highlighted on which there are common positions, potential coalitions can form. Hence, political managers will identify individuals, units and departments with whom they share a common view and objective, and take time to talk to these with whom you do not, so as to persuade them over to their viewpoint.

---

change management – chemicals giant sidelines HR department in staff culture change project

The human resources department at the chemicals giant ICI was deliberately sidelined during a major drive to make staff more market-focused. A project team set up by ICI to promote a market-centred culture avoided contact with the personnel function . . . 'We sold direct to management and tried to avoid human resources, training and education departments who might act as "gatekeepers" and restrict our access', the Market Focus leader Same Hay told a conference run by the magazine, *The Economist*.

Instead of using established internal channels to change the organization's culture, ICI set up a bureau in 1990 staffed by three employees and six academics. Hay said that rather than prescribing change, ICI's board relied on the bureau to market the new ethos internally. The bureau, which is now an independent consultancy, compiled a confidential list of key managers in ICI who were for and against the Market Focus programme. 'One very valuable, but non-public aid which we generated was The List. This contained the names of every influential manager in ICI and whether they were supportive of, against or neutral to Market Focus' said Hay. 'We worked with friends, added in neutrals when we could and avoided the "againsts" except where we felt their influence might endanger us'.

The bureau's initial range of services included workshops on performance improvement and a day-long consultancy with an academic. Hay claimed that the bureau's approach has been successful. 'We set out to change ICI staff to operate in a market driven fashion alongside our manufacturing and technology strengths. We did this without prescription.'

from David Pringle, 1996, 'ICI cuts HR function out of culture shift', *Personnel Today*, 16 July, p. 3.

---

political behaviour and personality traits

Having power alone is not enough; in order to make use of power, it has to be exercised. There are several systems of exercising power, and politics is one of them. The fact that politicking is a universal feature of organizations does not mean that all employees engage in it to the same degree. Four individual personality traits have been related to a willingness to engage in political behaviour and to use power (House, 1988).

need for power

In the 1940s, David McClelland (1961) developed a theory that people culturally acquired, that is learned, three types of needs. These were the need for power (nPower), for achievement (nAch) and for affiliation (nAff). In any single individual the strength of these three needs varied. Some individuals had a strong desire or motive to influence and lead others, and thus were more likely to engage in political behaviour within organizations. Since a desire to control others and events, and thus to have an impact on what is going on, is often associated with effective management, it is not surprising that selectors look for this trait in candidates for managerial jobs (McClelland and Burnham, 1976; McClelland and Boyatzis, 1982).

---

definition

Need for power *is the desire to make an impact on others, change people or events, and make a difference in life.*

Presidents' needs for power, achievement and affiliation

| United States' President | needs | | |
	power	achievement	affiliation
Clinton, Bill	moderate	high	high
Bush, George	moderate	moderate	low
Reagan, Ronald	high	moderate	low
Kennedy, John F.	high	low	high
Roosevelt, Frank D.	high	moderate	low
Lincoln, Abraham	moderate	low	moderate
Washington, George	low	low	moderate

based on R.J. House, W.D. Spangler and J. Woycke, 1992, 'Personality and charisma in the U.S. President: A psychological study of leader effectiveness', *Administrative Science Quarterly*, vol. 36, p. 395.

An individual's strong power needs can take two forms – personalized and socialized power. Managers who desire personalized power seek to dominate those around them and want them to be loyal to themselves rather than to the organization. Managers wanting socialized power seek to use it for the common good, on behalf of the organization as a whole. They exercise this form of power to create a good working climate for those around them, help others to perform their tasks and commit them towards organizational goals. Ragins and Sundstrom (1989) found that female managers demonstrated a greater need for socialized than for personalized power.

"I have to take one three times a day to curb my insatiable appetite for power."

from *The New Yorker*, 25 April 1977. Drawing by Dana Fradon: © 1977 the New Yorker Magazine, Inc.

---

definitions

Personalized power *is that which is self-serving and used for personal gain, influence and advancement.*

Socialized power *is that used for the common good on behalf of the whole organization. It is also commonly referred to as authority.*

Authority *is the right to guide or direct the actions of others and extract from them responses which are appropriate to the attainment of organizational goals.*

Machiavellianism

A second trait possessed by those who tend to engage in the use of power and politics in companies is termed *Machiavellianism*. Niccolò Machiavelli was a sixteenth-century Italian philosopher and statesman who wrote a set of guidelines for rulers to use in order to secure and hold power. These were published in a book called *The Prince,* and suggested that the primary method for achieving power was the manipulation of others (Machiavelli, 1961). Since that time, Machiavelli's name has been turned into both an adjective and a noun, and has come to be associated with the use of opportunism and deceit in interpersonal relations. Thus we speak about people's Machiavellian behaviour, or describe them as being Machiavellians.

---

definition

Machiavellianism *is a personality trait or style of behaviour towards others which is characterized by (1) the use of guile and deceit in interpersonal relations; (2) a cynical view of the nature of other people; and (3) a lack of concern with conventional morality.*
from Christie and Geis (1970).

© United Feature Syndicate, Inc.

'High-Machs', those who score highly on pencil-and-paper tests to measure their level of Machivellianism, would agree to statements such as:

) The best way to deal with people is to tell them what they want to hear.

) It is simply asking for trouble to trust someone else completely.

) Never tell anyone the real reason you did something unless it is useful to do so.

In behaving in accordance with Machiavellian principles, they prefer to be feared than be liked, effectively manipulate others using their persuasive skills, especially in face-to-face contacts, initiate and control interactions, use deceit in relationships, engage in ethically questionable behaviour and believe that any means justify the desired ends.

locus of control

The third personality trait affecting the likelihood of an individual engaging in political behaviour is the locus of control. Some people believe that what happens to them in life is under their own control. These are said to have an internal locus of control. Others hold that their life situation is under the control of fate or other people. This group is classed as having an external locus of control (Rotter, 1966). 'Internals', those who believe that they control what happens to them, tend to be more political in their behaviour than 'externals', and are more likely to expect that their political tactics will be effective. Internals are also less likely to be influenced by others.

---

definition

Locus of control *is an individual's generalized belief about internal (self-control) versus external control (control by the situation or by others).*

---

risk-seeking propensity

The final personality trait that is likely to determine whether a person engages in political behaviour is their willingness to take risks. Engaging in political behaviour in companies is not risk-free, and there are negative as well as positive outcomes for those who do it. They could risk being demoted, passed over for promotion, being given low performance assessments, and so on. Some people are natural risk-avoiders, whilst others are risk-seekers (Sitkin and Pablo, 1992; Madison *et al.*, 1980). Generally speaking, risk-seekers are more willing to engage in political behaviour than risk-avoiders. For the latter, the negative consequences of a failed influencing attempt outweigh the possible benefits of a successful outcome.

---

definition

Risk-seeking propensity *refers to the willingness of an individual to choose options which entail risks.*

STOP!

Do you think that those with a high risk-seeking propensity would make better or worse managers?

---

organizational power

Weber (1947) saw power as the ability to get others to do what you want them to do, even if this was against their will. Most writers agree that power is the capability of one person to impose their will on another, in achieving their desired goal or result. As such, power is the basis of influence. At work, each individual has some capacity to influence other people and the daily events in the organization. However, the more power a person has, the more they are able to influence these. The person exercising different types of power, the influencer, need not necessarily always be a manager. All organizational members need to influence others all the time. Thus the person being influenced, the influencee, may be a boss, as when a subordinate is trying to persuade her boss to give her a day off.

---

definition

Power *is a relationship between social actors in which one social actor, A, can get another social actor, B, to do something that B would not otherwise have done.*

based on Dahl (1957, pp. 201–15).

---

sources of departmental power and strategic contingencies

Why do different departments in the same company exert varying degrees of influence? Why is it that in the firms studied by Charles Perrow (1970), sales and production departments were more powerful than the finance and research and development departments? Although it is always individuals who exert power or who have power exercised over them, we are considering this process within an organizational context. Perrow stated that when differentiation occurred in complex organizations, that is when tasks were divided between a number of different departments, it was inevitable that these sub-units would come to differ in terms of the power that each possessed. The consequence of this was that power should be considered as primarily a structural phenomenon. That is, its distribution is predominantly determined by the organizational structure of a company, which is itself created by the choices made by its managers about how work is to be divided and who is to do what.

---

the power of the sales department

All groups – sales, production, R&D, finance and accounting – contribute to satisfying customer demand, of course, or there would be no need for them to exist of course. But sales is the main gate between the organization and the customer. As gatekeeper, it determines how important will be prompt delivery, quality, product improvement or new products, and the costs at which goods can be sold. Sales determines the relative importance of these variables for the other groups and indicates the values which these variables will take. It has the ability, in addition, of changing the values of these variables, since it sets pricing (and in most firms adjusts it temporarily to meet changes in opportunity and competition), determines which markets will be utilized, the services that will be provided, and the changes in products that must be made.

from Perrow (1970, p. 65).

STOP!

The management of departmental differences plays a key part in determining company success or failure. Can these problems ever be solved? How?

The theoretical concept that explains the differences in the relative power of different departments in the same company is called *strategic contingencies*, and research by Jeffrey Pfeffer and Gerald Salancik (1977) has developed the strategic contingency theory of intra-organizational power. Strategic contingencies are events and activities that must occur, either inside or outside an organization, for it to attain its goals. In the short term, a firm must manufacture a product and sell it to a customer at a profit to survive. Developing the next product or counting the money it has received is less important. In this short-term example, the sales department and production department provide greater strategic value to the company than do the R&D or finance departments. Hence, those departments that are responsible for dealing with the key issues and dependencies in the company environment, that solve its pressing problems or that deal with a current crisis, will be more powerful than those that do not.

---

definition

Strategic contingencies *are events and activities, both inside and outside of an organization, that are essential for it to attain its goals.*

The power sources that indicate a department's ability to respond to strategic contingencies include dependency-creation, financial resources, centrality of activities, non-substitutability and ability to decrease uncertainty. These five sources overlap, and the more of them a department possesses the greater the power that it will exert with its organization.

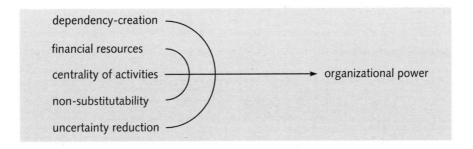

dependency-creation

A department is powerful if other units and departments depend on its products or services. These may include materials, information, resources and services which flow between departments. The receiving department is always in an inferior power position. If the production department is dependent on cost data provided by the finance department, the latter is more powerful than the former. The number and strength of the dependencies are also important. If the great majority of university departments are totally dependent on the Computing Services Centre to acquire and maintain their machines, then the CSC is very powerful. Similarly, if a department depends on many others to achieve its goals, then it is very powerless.

financial resources

A department's ability to control financial resources gives it power. Money can be converted into many different resources that are required and valued by others. Cohen and Bradford (1991) listed some of the currencies into which such conversion could take place. One of the reasons that sales departments possess more than average power in companies is that they ensure the inward flow of money. Within universities, departments of management and business schools are often treated as 'cash-cows' owing to their ability to generate additional, non-traditional income. In the short term, senior administrators are able to use this money to subsidize less popular academic departments and activities, but in the longer term they cede power to the point where the business school runs the university. Because of the power-enhancing value of financial resources, departments in all organizations compete with others to grasp new projects or tasks which have new financial budgets attached to them.

centrality of activities

Centrality refers to the degree to which the department's activities are critical to producing the company's main product or service. It reflects the relative importance of the contribution made by one department in comparison with another, with respect of the organization's goal. The more central, the more powerful. A good indicator of the centrality of different functions is: which ones tend to get subcontracted? The most common ones are training, payroll management, computer management, personnel and advertising. Whilst many companies possess their own ones, they may judge that for cost and other reasons, they are not central to their mission. Centrality is, of course relative and will depend on whether the organization is a bank, a car manufacturer or a cable television company.

---

knowledge is power

During the late 1950s and early 1960s, Michel Crozier investigated a factory in the French nationalized tobacco industry. It was located outside Paris and employed 350–400 workers. At first glance, one would have expected that the production department which manufactured the product would be more powerful than its maintenance department. The cigarette production was automated and consisted of women whose job it was to operate the semi-automatic machines turning out the cigarettes. These production workers' jobs were routine, limited in scope, low skill and remunerated on a piecework basis so as to encourage productivity.

All matters to do with finance, raw material acquisition, distribution and sales were all controlled centrally from Paris. All the factory had to do was to produce cigarettes, without any other distraction. The only problem the factory manager had to deal with were machine stoppages due to equipment breakdowns. These were caused by variations in the tobacco leaf which required the constant adjustment of the machines. When the machines stopped, the work stopped, and the factory stopped producing what it was there for.

The maintenance department consisted of twelve male workers who reported to the factory's technical engineer. Only they knew how to set and to repair the machines, and did not explain what they did to anyone else. Their work was unpredictable, complex and required many years of experience to gain the craft skills needed. Moreover, the vital knowledge needed for machine repair was contained in the maintenance men's heads and not in any manuals.

The maintenance department was so powerful because it possessed three of Salancik and Pfeffer's five characteristics. First, the production department was dependent on the maintenance department because of the unpredictable nature caused by the assembly-line breakdowns. Second, the maintenance department had centrality, that is, it was critical to the final output of the organization. Third, it had non-substitutability. The production department could not effect the repairs themselves and the maintenance staff kept their knowledge to themselves. For these three reasons, the maintenance staff had gained control over a strategic contingency in this factory – the knowledge and ability to prevent or resolve work stoppages.

based on Michel Crozier, 1964, *The Bureaucratic Phenomenon*, University of Chicago Press, Chicago.

non-substitutability

If what a department does cannot easily be done by another department, either inside or outside the organization, then it has great power. The more specialized the work that is done, and the greater the skill and knowledge required to do it, then the more power accrues to it. During industrial disputes, the power of strikers is reduced if management is able to bus in 'strike-breakers' to do the work of the usual staff. Management can reduce the power of professional and staff groups by bringing in consultants.

The nature of the work that needs to be done and the skill needed to do it changes over time. Thus different groups of employees can gain and lose power. Once the technology in the print industry ceased to require physical typesetting, the awesome power exerted by the printers through their trade unions dissipated. When computer programming was a difficult skill possessed by few, programmers controlled the use of computers in companies. Once the hardware and software made computers easier to use, their users regained some of that power for themselves.

---

substitutability and power

After many years of resisting the demands from the Professional Air Traffic Controllers' Organization (PATCO) for the installation of a computerized air traffic control system to replace out-of-date equipment, the US Federal Aviation (FAA) finally introduced a flow control system. The computers in the new system distributed the arrivals and departures which had previously produced dangerous peaks and troughs in air traffic activity.

When in 1981, PATCO's 11,500 members went on strike over pay and working conditions, FAA managers found that the new flow control system enabled 50 per cent of the pre-strike workforce was to deal with 83 per cent of the traffic load. In this case, the new technology undermined PATCO members' expert power, and hence bargaining position. In late 1981, with the support of the newly-elected president, Ronald Reagan, the FAA management de-certified the union. The moral of the story is to check one's substitutability power and assess the accuracy of the old adage that 'No one is indispensable'.

based on A.B. Shostak, 1987, 'Technology, air traffic control, and labour-management relations", in D.B. Cornfield (ed.), *Workers, Managers and Technological Change*, Plenum Press, London.

STOP!

Which company departments are likely to be non-substitutable for at least the next five years?

---

uncertainty reduction

Organizations are uncertain as to how many customers will buy their products and services, and which ones they will choose; they are uncertain as to whether they will receive a regular flow of raw materials from their suppliers; and they are uncertain whether they can maintain full production and not have it disrupted by industrial action. Uncertainties abound for companies, both external and internal ones. A department can increase its power by helping other departments cope with and reduce such uncertainties.

Three main uncertainty-reduction techniques exist. The first is *securing prior information*. Examples of this include the forecasting and market research studies conducted by the sales department; and worker morale and job satisfaction surveys performed by the human resource department. When these different departments make successful predictions, they gain power and prestige by reducing critical uncertainties. A second technique is *prevention*, as when a negative event is predicted and its occurrence forestalled. The final technique is *absorption*, when a department acts after an event to reduce its negative consequences (Hickson *et al.*, 1971).

bases of power

The previous section identified the five major sources of departmental power as proposed by the strategic contingencies theory of intra-organizational power. These provide sub-units, teams and individuals within the company with their power bases. Pfeffer and Salancik's (1974) resource dependency theory of power holds that different phenomena become resources in different contexts, and thus anything can become a base of power under the appropriate circumstances. Acknowledging this point, we briefly defined and illustrated the main bases or types of power in Chapter 20 (pp. 607–9) within the context of leadership. Since each power type forms the base for different influencing tactics, French and Raven's (1958) five power types will be augmented with a sixth, that of information power. All six will be considered in greater depth, with an emphasis on how the influencer uses each type of power to persuade the influencee.

reward power

This is the power to give rewards to those who comply with requests. To do this, an individual must control the resources from which those rewards flow. Power-seekers, therefore, position themselves where they have or can approve budgets. Nothing is as effective in coping with recalcitrant staff as the power to cut off funding for their projects, whilst nothing promotes gratitude and co-operation as successfully as the financial support of others' favourite projects. However, the rewards need not be just financial. Cohen and Bradford (1989) identified a range of rewards which they termed *organizational currencies*, and which could be used to motivate and persuade those within an organization. These are listed and exemplified in the table that follows.

organizational currencies traded in the exchange process

currencies	examples
resources	lending or giving money, personnel or space
assistance	assisting with current projects or performing unpleasant tasks for others
co-operation	helping on a task, responding quickly to requests, approving a project or aiding implementation
information	sharing specific technical or company knowledge
advancement	providing a task that can assist in another's promotion
recognition	acknowledging another's effort or achievement
network/contacts	providing opportunities for linking with others
personal support	giving personal and emotional support

based on A.R. Cohen and D.L. Bradford, 1989, 'Influence without authority: The use of alliances, reciprocity and exchange to accomplish work', *Organizational Dynamics*, Winter, pp. 4–17.

People have different needs, and thus would view different currencies as rewards. Power-seekers, therefore, look to control and dispense required organizational resources, accumulating slack ones and allocating these in exchange for reciprocal favours, obedience or compliance. However, if reward power is used too frequently by a manager, influencees may come to expect special rewards every time something new or unusual is required of them. For this reason, managers tend to reinforce desirable behaviour only after it has already occurred, to show the employee concerned that they are appreciated as a competent and committed person.

coercive power

Martin (1977) explains that coercion arises when employees have to comply unwillingly with the wishes of others out of a direct fear of dismissal. He notes that direct coercion is rarely to be found in organizations, because of its corrosive effects on trust and the high cost of replacing departed personnel. More important in his view is the diffuse atmosphere of fear and unease which is created by competition and uncertainty within the firm. Although he wrote with middle managers in mind, Martin's points have equal relevance to staff at all levels in the company.

Coercive power is the ability to punish. Often it is the threat of coercion that is sufficient. A manager may threaten to prevent a pay rise, fire a subordinate, give an unsatisfactory performance evaluation, deny promotion or withdraw overtime. Coercion encompasses both physical and mental pressure and succeeds by eliminating the influencee's options. Managers who use coercion emphasize to the influencee that there is no alternative and eliminate the possibility that their requirement is in any way negotiable. They inform the person about the rules and penalties, and warn them before punishing them. They check the situation before acting and match the punishment to the infraction.

---

middle managers on the way out?

There is the constant possibility of being planned out of the present job. The management hierarchy is regularly reorganized. A pendulum swings from central control to regional autonomy. New advisors; liaisons with accounts or finance; development teams; executive development programmes are all on the drawing board. Management is always susceptible to rationalization at middle management positions especially. A middle manager is a junior in a big department or the senior of a sprawling department. In either situation, rationalization can make him technically redundant. A new norm may be decided 'on consultant's advice' . . . it involves a 'bit of a shake-up', 'a complete face-lift' or 'an organizational set' for the [future].

"Any more objections?"

from C. Fletcher (1973) 'The end of management' in J. Child (ed.), *Man and Organization*, George Allen & Unwin, London, p. 18. Cartoon by Bill Scott.

---

referent power

Referent power refers to the loyalty of one person to another, based on the desire to please them. It is derived from an individual's personal qualities and the relationship that they have with the influencee. It thus differs from all the previous types of power which are all, in their different ways, related to position within the organization structure. Although Perrow played down its importance, referent power still affects the behaviour of people in organizations.

Referent power comes from an individual's ability to convey feelings of personal acceptance and approval to others. It is increased if they are considerate to others, show concern for their needs and feelings, treat them fairly and defend their interests when dealing with superiors and outsiders. It is diminished when they express hostility, distrust, rejection, or indifference to those around them, or when they fail to defend the interests of their subordinates or others.

Referent power is based on the influencee's attraction to th
which itself is a function of their friendliness, gregariousness, c
honesty, candour and integrity. The power derives from the
possessing valued qualities. Poise, wealth or confidence may lead
identify with the influencer. The influencee wants to be like the infl
Film, pop and sports stars are adored by their fans, and thus exert re
power. Their capacity to influence young consumers is reflected in ule
willingness of companies that sell clothes, shoes and soft drinks to pay them to
advertise their products.

Charisma refers to the nearly magical ability of some individuals to
influence others. Research and folklore have suggested that charismatic
leaders can inspire others to increase their performance, and engender the
respect of others. What are the personal qualities of charismatic leaders?
Research has found that charismatic leaders are perceived as dynamic,
enthusiastic, inspiring, outgoing, sociable and jestful; as insightful, bright,
intellectual, wise and competent; and as confident, secure, unflappable and
not meek (Conger and Kanungo, 1987). From an impression management
perspective, charisma-inspiring behaviours are capable of being taught and
learned. Pfeffer (1981) felt that we tended to over-attribute power to personal
characteristics, believing them to be the sources of power, rather than their
consequences. Nevertheless, they may be important to develop, or at least to
project to others.

legitimate power

Legitimate power is also often referred to as position power. In a sense, all
organizational power is position power, because an individual's position in a
company gains them access to organizational resources. The focus here
however, is on *authority* – the power invested in all organizational positions. A
position holder, like an accountant, can legitimately exercise the power within
the boundaries of that position. Position power is the manager's ability to
make a subordinate feel responsible to them. Position power is most clearly
seen in a military organization where rank is visibly displayed. For this reason,
it is most effective after a clear statement in writing of a person's duties,
responsibilities, reporting relationships and scope of authority has been
obtained. This is to be found in their job description.

Different positions in organizations carry different amounts of power.
Power is accumulated fastest in jobs that allow their incumbents to use their
discretion (non-routinized action), permitting flexible, adaptive and creative
contributions, and that give them recognition (being visible to and noticed by
others) and relevance (being centrally located to address pressing organizational problems).

Managers occupying an organizational position can expand their power by
gaining control of a unit rich in resources, information or formal authority. At
the minimum, they may seek to prevent their opponents from doing the same.
Once they control a unit, they may modify its structure to expand their
territory and sphere of influence. Power is built by controlling as much
territory and activity as possible. Once control is achieved, it is rarely
challenged and eventually becomes converted to legitimate authority. Kanter
identified factors which contributed to legitimate position power and these are
listed in the following table.

factors contributing to power in an organizational position

factor	generates power when factor is
1 rules inherent in job	few
2 predecessors in job	none/few
3 established routines	few
4 task variety	high
5 rewards for reliability/predictability	few
6 rewards for unusual performance/innovation	many
7 flexibility in use of people	high
8 approval needed for non-routine decisions	none/rarely
9 physical location of office	central
10 visibility of job activity to others	high
11 relationship of task to current company problems	central
12 focus of tasks	outside of work unit
13 contact with others through the job	high
14 allows participation in projects, meetings and conferences	high
15 participation in problem-solving teams	high
16 advancement prospects of subordinates	high

expert power

Expert power is based on the fact or impression that an individual has the most relevant experience and expertise, and that they know the best course of action in a given situation. A person's expert power increases when they suggest a course of action that turns out to be highly successful and decreases when their suggestions fail. As the problems under discussion change, so too does the opportunity to be the expert. At a meeting, different managers will emerge as most influential on different topics. Expertise can be consciously acquired through systematically seeking specific experiences or gaining qualifications.

To accumulate expert power, managers foster an image of experience and competence, avoiding careless statements and rash decisions. Drummond (1991) advised preserving your power and mystique and never making anything look easy. Managers should show others their credentials and demonstrate expert knowledge by citing facts and figures, referring to important but not commonly known features, and discussing points from several perspectives. She recommended circulating articles or newspaper clippings which they had written, or to which they referred. Being referred to or quoted in an article or an interview suggested expertise.

The rise in the importance of the expert is partly the consequence of the way that companies have modified the roles of employees who are encouraged to develop expertise in a relatively specialized field. As a result, problems have to be tackled by teams of such experts, each bringing to bear their own specialist capabilities. Managers responsible for such problem-solving groups have to become competent at handling these often loose collections of experts, each of whom has their own professional axe to grind. It is also partly the result of the fact that in certain circumstances, external recommendation and sanction are frequently more powerful than internal arguments.

A consultant-as-expert serves to legitimate the decisions reached and provides an aura of rationality to the decision process. When power is widely dispersed in an organization, individuals holding different positions may be unable to muster enough support for their view to prevail and an impasse results. The person who can get agreement to hire a consultant and participate in his selection can break the deadlock to his advantage by introducing new elements. So outside experts will be used more frequently if power is widely dispersed in a company. If power is concentrated, there will be less need to bring in an outside expert to buttress a position, since internal power will be enough to carry the day. These strategies employ power unobtrusively and legitimate decisions which have to be made, but about which there is a disagreement concerning both the definition of the situation and favoured action. The use of an outside expert results in the less visible use of power in decision-making.

PROMIS and the politics of medical expertise

The Problem Oriented Medical Information System (PROMIS) was developed in the United States during the 1970s. Its objective was to address the problems of medical records organization and the over-reliance on doctors' memory. The system stored medical records in relational data bases, and performed sophisticated automated functions through the use a touch screen terminal.

Despite the advantages it offered in information processing, the adoption of PROMIS in large hospitals was slow. Research revealed that the new system was supported by nursing staff as it gave them access to information which had the effect of increasing their professional discretion, and allowed them to intervene in patient treatments without having to wait for a doctor's approval. Pharmacists approved of the system for similar reasons. The greatest resistance to this new technology, however, came from the medical staff. What PROMIS did was to codify the elements of the doctors' knowledge base, and thus ceded some of their expert power to these other professional groups in the hospital.

This potential threat to the doctors' loss of power and freedom of action was diminished by advances in medical knowledge, which had the effect of preventing their knowledge base from being pinned down sufficiently, to enable systems like PROMIS to capture and codify it. The doctors' expert power in the field of medicine, and their legitimate power from the senior organizational positions that they occupied in the hospital hierarchy, was sufficient to enable them to delay the introduction of PROMIS.

Can you think of other organizational situations in which something similar has, or might happen?

based on L. Willcocks and D. Mason, 1987, *Computerising Work: People, Systems Design and Workplace Relations*, Paradigm Press, London.

information power

Francis Bacon said that 'knowledge is power'. Information is the life-blood of all organizations, and is the main currency of exchange between its members. Information is power if there are those who need it, and who are willing to trade something for it. Information power resembles expert power, except that in this case you are not presenting yourself as an authority on a particular topic, but as the one who has information not possessed by others. There are two dimensions of information power: gaining and using it. Both affect how influential a manager will be. To gain information, a person needs to position themselves in networks through which relevant information flows. Without these, they are isolated.

They also need to become involved in regular meetings with individuals inside and outside the organization, and subscribe to relevant journals. Such actions ensure that the information which they provide is up-to-date, relevant and will be sought by others. Information can also be used as a reward currency as suggested by Cohen and Bradford (1989) earlier. Included is not only technical information about aspects of the work process, but also information about the firm's social system. An employee's access to the latter depends on their level of interaction with others. To gain information power, it is necessary to become well placed in the company's communication net and develop useful social connections with key organizational players. Powerful people have powerful friends. Three aspects are crucial to becoming centrally located so as to gain the greatest power, and these are *betweenness*, *connectedness* and *closeness*. They are summarized in the following figure.

betweenness, connectedness and closeness in a communication network

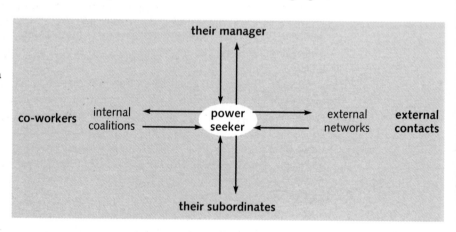

Betweenness refers to the need for an information power-seeker to place himself between others in a communication path. For example, the secretary is between the power-seeker and the boss. The salesperson is between the power-seeker and the customer. *Connectedness* refers to the number of other people with whom the power-seeker has contact, both within and outside the organization. Provided they contribute to power enhancement, the more the better. Finally, *closeness*, which is also called proximity, is the distance between the power-seeker and all the other people in the network. Power-seekers have to ensure that they can reach other people with as few intermediate steps as possible. The closer they are, the more independent they are, since others cannot control their access to the focal person. Andrew Pettigrew (1973)

described how a computer manager exercised power over his mail order company's decision to purchase a particular type of computer. This individual was able to present himself as an expert; to control the flow of information between senior management and the computer vendors; and possessed an insider's knowledge of the company's 'political landscape' and how decisions in the company got made.

Being central in a communication network is most easily achieved through the careful choice of job and office location. A low-visibility job is unlikely to lead to relationship building. In contrast, jobs which straddle departments and units tend to get noticed, allow their incumbents to develop contacts across the organization, and thus help them to become more influential through their central position in the communication structure. Staff or assistant-to positions, whilst they may not carry formal authority, do give power by providing access to key people in the organization. Thus a staff job offers connection power, whilst a line job provides resources with which to exert reward or coercive power. Ambitious employees evaluate job opportunities in terms of the contacts that they provide with other company personnel. Information power depends on knowing and interacting with others.

Office location affects the number of interactions that room occupants have with others, the content of those interactions, who gets to know them, what they get to know, and it determines their relationship with others (Brass, 1984; 1985; Freeman, 1979). Hence, power-seekers check how near their facility is to head office, and how near their office is to senior management's. They avoid out-of-the-way locations in godforsaken postings, unless they are sure that these are necessary stepping stones to the more senior positions.

Information is power because people believe that there are right answers to problems which can be uncovered if illuminated by information and analysis. Rationality can be the Achilles' heel of organizations. All organizations strive to appear rational and to be seen to be using the proper procedures (including information and analysis) to justify their decisions. Companies often construct the appearance of legitimate and sensible decision processes to support their intended courses of action, even when these are based on emotion or intuition. Because of this, information power can be used potently and surreptitiously. By following the prescribed and legitimate procedures, decisions will be perceived to be better, and more readily acceptable. The appearance of bureaucratic rationality is essential in making companies appear legitimate (Kramer, 1975; Meyer and Rowan, 1977). Hence, power-seekers hunt out information, not necessarily to make a decision, but to make it appear that a decision has been made in the correct fashion, that is, on the basis of information and not on uninformed preference or hunch. Decisions made on the latter basis do not produce the same level of comfort or legitimacy as the former.

power and influence

A useful way of understanding the relationship between these two concepts is to consider power as the basis for influencing. Individuals in any organization will possess different amounts of power. The total amount of power each person possesses will be composed of varying amounts of the six power types described in the previous section. This is illustrated in the next figure, which shows the six power bases as underpinning influencing. The more power a manager has, in terms of type and amount, the greater the number of influencing strategies that they can use, and the greater the success with which they can use them Moreover, the amount of power possessed is not fixed. Organizational members both gain and lose power depending on what they do or fail to do, and on the actions of those around them.

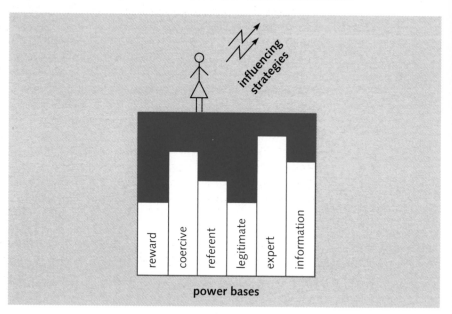

Influencing can be defined as one person's ability to affect another's attitudes, beliefs or behaviours. Its distinguishing feature is that generally it is seen only in its effect, and is done without the use of either coercion or the use of formal position. If performed successfully, the person being influenced, the influencee, will believe that they are acting in their own best interests. Let us examine this definition in a little more detail.

ability to affect another

Ability is defined as a natural or acquired competence in doing. The ability to influence is not a mysterious gift or talent possessed only by those at the top of an organization with power. Anyone can have influence, at any level in the organization.

attitudes, beliefs and behaviours

The focus in this definition is upon *behaviour* and *action*. Changing another's attitudes, values or beliefs is only important to the extent that this affects what other people do and say. Research shows that changing a person's behaviour can lead them to change their original attitudes, values and beliefs. The arrow of causation thus points in both directions. Ultimately, influence is about getting one person to do what another wants.

seen only in its effect

Arthur C. Clarke, the science fiction writer, wrote that, *any sufficiently developed technology is indistinguishable from magic.* In a similar way, influencing is a process that will be unobservable to both the influencee or an observer. The first influencees will know of it is when they have supported the influencer's proposal or suggestion, or agreed to act as requested.

without exertion of force or formal authority

Influence is an alternative to the use of coercion or formal authority. Moreover, it is one which has long-term effects, avoids distrust and hostility and, if well executed, is not noticed. People will do things for others, without knowing exactly why, but feeling good about it. Their positive feelings come from their assessment that they are primarily acting in their own best interests, helping themselves to achieve their own personal goals, rather than for the benefit of the influencer.

---

definition

Influencing *is the ability to affect another's attitudes, beliefs or behaviours – seen only in its effect – without using coercion or formal position, and in a way that influencees believe that they are acting in their own best interests.*

from Huczynski (1996, p. 6).

The ethics of influencing, and indeed the question of whether organizational politicking is manipulative or deceitful, have been extensively discussed, but not surprisingly, remain unresolved (Gandz and Murray, 1980; Farrell and Petersen, 1982; and Drory and Romm, 1990).

influencing strategies

Kipnis *et al.* (1984) studied how managers influenced their own managers, co-workers and subordinates. They identified seven influencing strategies: reason, friendliness, coalition, bargaining, assertiveness, higher authority and sanctions. Each will be dealt with briefly.

reason

Reason describes a strategy of influencing which relies on the presentation of data and information as the basis for a logical argument that supports a request. You are saying to the influencee, 'I shall explain the reasoning behind my idea'. It involves planning and preparation on the part of the influencer, who arranges her facts and arguments in a way that convinces the influencee. The basis of the influencer's power is their own knowledge and ability to communicate the information. Reason is the most widely used strategy in organizations, and is the first choice when influencing bosses and subordinates. If the information and logic presented are challenged or are suspected, then the reason strategy is inevitably weakened.

friendliness

Friendliness is a strategy that depends on the influencee thinking well of the influencer. This can be accomplished by 'acting friendly', showing sensitivity and understanding ('I'll come and see you when you are less busy'), creating goodwill (perhaps by a joke) and using flattery. For example, consciously deciding to compliment someone on a recent achievement before making your own request. As a strategy, friendliness involves a strong emotional component since it plays on the influencee's feelings. Your use of this influencing strategy will be based on your own personality, interpersonal skills and sensitivity to the feelings and attitudes of others. Friendliness is most frequently used with co-workers, but is also popular with subordinates and superiors. It is nearly as widely used as reason. Influencers are most likely to use friendliness when they seek personal favours, help with their work, or when their organizational power base is weak. Overuse of this strategy can lead other people to suspecting your motives and your work competence. Some people, of course, are just naturally friendly!

coalition

Coalition is mobilizing other people in the organization to support you, and thereby strengthening your request. You operate on the premiss that there is power in numbers. If many people make the same request or argue for the same action, the influencee is more likely to grant the request. Your power when using this strategy is based on your alliances with others in the organization. These supporters may be used to show similarity of view, or be brought in as go-betweens. In the latter case, you might ask a colleague to persuade someone on your behalf, because they know them better than you. Coalition is a complex strategy which requires substantial skill and effort. Nevertheless, it is widely used, mainly when influencing co-workers and bosses. Coalitions are used to attain both personal and organizational goals, but usually as a back-up strategy. Its use is not without its dangers, and overuse can create the impression that you and your allies are conspiring against the influencee.

Aesop's fable: The Lion and the Dolphin

The king of beasts was pacing majestically along the shore of the sea one day when he spied a dolphin basking on the surface of the water. 'Hello there, friend dolphin,' roared the lion. 'This is a fortunate meeting indeed. I have long wanted to suggest that you and I form an alliance. As I am king of the beasts and you are king of the fishes, what is more natural than that we should be strong friends and powerful allies?' 'There is much in what you say,' replied the dolphin.

Not long afterwards, the lion again came to the seashore where he was challenged by a wild bull. The fight was not going well for the lion, so he called upon the dolphin for his promised support. The latter, though ready and willing to aid his ally, found himself unable to come out of the sea to join the battle. After the wild bull had been put to flight, the lion upbraided the dolphin. 'You are a fine ally,' said the lion. 'I could have been killed, and you never turned a fin to help me.' 'Do not blame me,' said the dolphin in reply, 'but blame nature, which makes me more powerful in the sea but altogether helpless on land.'

Moral: In choosing allies, look to their power as well as their will to help you.

from *Aesop's Fables*, 1994, Bloomsbury Books, London, p. 35.

bargaining

Bargaining is influencing through negotiation and the exchange of benefits based on the social norms of obligation and reciprocity. It comes down to, 'If you do this for me, I'll do that for you'. The influencer reminds their target of the past favours that they have received from them, or promises future ones. Implied in this strategy are the notions of finding common ground, equity and compromise. In short, the influencer relies on a trade that involves making concessions in exchange for getting what they want. What the influencer has to trade is derived from two sources – their own time, effort and skill, and the organization's resources over which the influencer has control. Bargaining is common, but is used more with co-workers than subordinates or bosses. It is used when the influencer seeks personal benefits. Its weakness is that it creates obligations in the future that the influencer must honour.

assertiveness–insistence

Kipnis *et al.* use the term *assertiveness* to refer to an influencing strategy which involved influencing people through your insistent, forceful manner. In this sense, their use of this term is different from its common usage in management. To emphasize this difference, whilst still retaining the original label, this influencing strategy will be relabelled *assertiveness–insistence*, to emphasize that the behavioural style involved is closer to the aggressive end of the continuum. An assertive–insistence influencing strategy involves overtly making strident verbal statements such as 'I should like you to do this'; repeating your request in an unfaltering tone and regularly reminding the influencee of your request. More covertly, it can involve setting deadlines, deciding who attends certain meetings, deciding which items will be included on an agenda, how the issues will be framed and which alternatives will be considered. Assertiveness–insistence gives the impression that the influencer is 'in charge' and expects compliance with their wishes. At times, visible emotion and displays of temper will also be present. It is used more with subordinates and less with co-workers and superiors.

higher authority

Higher authority is an influencing strategy which uses the chain of command and outside sources of power to influence the target person. Kipnis *et al.* limited themselves to the situation of the influencer appealing for the support of senior people who had power over the influencee. For example, saying to a co-worker, 'If you do not accept this proposal, I'll have to take it to our boss'. However, there are additional applications of this strategy. Higher authority can be used when framing your requests. For example, claiming that you are expressing senior management's preferences as in, 'I know the divisional head would go along with this proposal'. Another application is not appealing to a person with higher authority to gain agreement, but to higher order of ethical or moral values. For example, saying to the influencee, 'I'm asking you because it is the right thing to do'. You might invoke company tradition or its value system if your organization has a strong corporate culture. It is most often used as a backup strategy when the influencer does not expect the influencee to agree to her request, tending to be used slightly more often on co-workers. Overuse of this strategy can undermine your relationship with both your influencee (who may feel that you are threatening them), and the person with the higher authority (who expects you to sort out your own problems and not bother them). Perhaps the threat of higher authority is as far as you can realistically go.

sanctions

Sanctions can be either positive or negative, and involve either desirable benefits or undesirable consequences. 'If you finish this project, you will get a promotion, if not, you will spend another year in this job'. The use of sanctions is a classic approach to influencing people and may seem to be an obvious influencing strategy. However, its use clearly depends on the influencer's ability to provide rewards and administer punishments. Even so, this is the least favoured of all the influencing strategies studied. Kipnis believed that it was primarily managers who used sanctions on their subordinates as a last resort. However, sanctions can also be used by staff on both their bosses and co-workers. They have to be used carefully since a failure to follow through can lead to a loss of credibility. Used in moderation sanctions can be effective, but repeated or excessive use will lead to resentment. The popularity of the seven strategies was found to vary depending on the direction of influence – upwards towards managers, downwards towards subordinates, or laterally towards co-workers. The frequency of use is shown in the figure below.

preferred order of use of influencing strategies

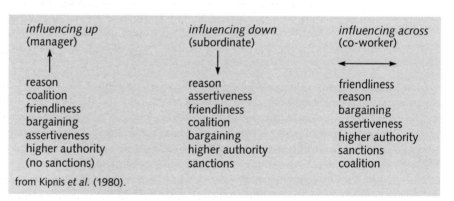

influencing up (manager)	*influencing down* (subordinate)	*influencing across* (co-worker)
reason	reason	friendliness
coalition	assertiveness	reason
friendliness	friendliness	bargaining
bargaining	coalition	assertiveness
assertiveness	bargaining	higher authority
higher authority	higher authority	sanctions
(no sanctions)	sanctions	coalition

from Kipnis *et al.* (1980).

The relationships between the six power bases and the seven influencing strategies are shown in the next figure. The greater the range of power bases available to an organizational member, the greater will be the choice of strategies that they can use, and the more effectively they will be able to use them.

relationship between power bases and influencing strategies

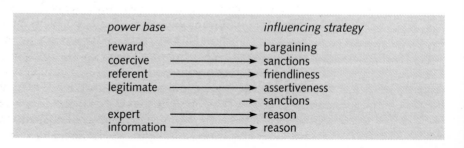

power base	*influencing strategy*
reward	⟶ bargaining
coercive	⟶ sanctions
referent	⟶ friendliness
legitimate	⟶ assertiveness
	⟶ sanctions
expert	⟶ reason
information	⟶ reason

> **STOP!**
>
> Below are three key concepts encountered in this chapter. Explain the relationship between them.
>
> ▷ *Power* is a relationship between social actors in which one social actor, A, can get another social actor, B, to do something that B would not otherwise have done.
>
> ▷ *Authority* is the right to guide or direct the actions of others and extract from them responses which are appropriate to the attainment of organizational goals.
>
> ▷ *Influencing* is the ability to affect another's attitudes, beliefs or behaviours – seen only in its effect – without using coercion or formal position, and in a way that influencees believe that they are acting in their own best interests.

assessment

In assessing power and politics as a topic in organizational behaviour, three points need to be stressed. First, the importance of the subject in providing us with an understanding of why people behave in organizations as they do. Second, the surface simplicity that masks a deeper complexity which can create and put off those seeking to understand the role of power and politics in the organizational context. Third, the existence of two differing approaches to the study of power and politics that are to be found in the writings on organization behaviour and management. A clarification of these three issues can provide a useful foundation for the subsequent study of the subject.

Turning first to the issue of importance, individual explanations of behaviour (personality, motivation) tend to be preferred by students and managers over social ones (groups). Structural and technological explanations are even less popular, whilst the political one tends to be totally neglected, or even considered inappropriate for explaining organizational behaviour by some commentators. In contrast, Henry Mintzberg was unequivocal in asserting that a thorough understanding of power was the basis for controlling the behaviour of organizations, and the people within them. We would agree with him. In response to the question of why one should bother studying power. He wrote:

> although there are many other, more tangible forces out there that affect what organizations do – such as the buying habits of clients, the invention of a new machine, an upturn in the economy – power is a major factor, one that cannot be ignored by anyone interested in understanding how organizations work and end up doing what they do. If we are to improve the functioning of our organizations from within, and to gain control of them from without to ensure that they act in our best interests, then we must understand the power relations that surround and infuse them. (Mintzberg, 1983, p. 1)

Because something is important, it does not automatically mean it is easy to come to grips with. In considering the history and development of the concept of power, Hardy (1995) commented on a contradiction. On the one hand, she noted simplicity. The seemingly simple definitions of power provided by

Weber (1947) and Dahl (1957), which were introduced earlier in this chapter, had proved themselves robust, even withstanding the challenges, critiques, amendments, expansions and rejections of different authors. These definitions have provided generations of students with an entry point into what she called a 'remarkably diverse body of literature'.

On the other hand, she saw complexity. This academic literature was diverse because it included research from sociology, psychology, anthropology, economics and, not least, from political science. A major consequence of this multidisciplinary interest in power and politics was that different aspects of it were studied in different ways, for different reasons, by different people. Whilst such a variety of work was beneficial for the healthy development of the topic itself, it could cause confusion for those studying the subject for the first time. Hardy made her point forcefully when she wrote:

Power has been both the *independent* variable, causing outcomes such as domination, and a *dependent* variable, usually the outcome of dependency or centrality. Power has been viewed as *functional* in the hands of managers who use it in the pursuit of organizational goals, and *dysfunctional* in the hands of those who challenge those goals and seek to promote self interest. It has been viewed as the means by which *legitimacy* is created, and the incarnation of *illegitimate* action. Power has been equated with formal organizational arrangements, and as the *informal* actions that influence outcomes. It has been seen as *conditional on conflict*, and as a means to *prevent conflict*. It has been defined as a resource that is *consciously* and deliberately mobilized in pursuit of self-interest, and as a system of relations that knows no interest, but from which some groups *unconsciously* and inadvertently benefit. It has been seen as an *intentional* act to which causality can be attributed, and as an *unintentional*, unpredictable game of chance. The study of power has created a *behavioural* focus for some researchers, and *attitudinal* and ideological factors for others. Power has been berated for being *repressive* and lauded for being *productive*. Small wonder then that there is little agreement! (Hardy, 1995, pp. xx–xxi)

This complexity and confusion are the result of the way in which the study of power has coalesced around two, unequal approaches. This brings us to the issue of the two, apparently unrelated approaches, to the study of power and politics. The mainstream perspective on power and politics is the rationalist one, and was summarized on the left-hand side column of the table on p. 669. It distinguishes power from authority. Power being the getting someone to do what you want them to do, possibly against their will; and authority being the right to guide or direct the actions of others, and extract from them responses which are appropriate to the attainment of an organization's goals. Authority is held to be legitimate, and both a normal and inevitable aspect of formal design of organizations. Moreover, that managerial authority is seen as being embedded in structural and technological aspects of the formal organization. It is considered to be apolitical, taken-for-granted and functional, in the sense of contributing to the achievement of the organizational goal. The perspective is also called *functionalist or managerialist*.

Having translated power into authority, the functionalist-managerialist perspective excludes it from analysis and research. Instead, it concentrates on what it labels are 'illegitimate' power. This is defined as any power falling outside the legitimate authority that is embedded in organizational structures. Non-authority power and any associated politics are considered illegitimate in this view. Writers such as Gandz and Murray (1980), Mayes and Allen (1977) and Drory and Romm (1990) reflect the managerialist-functionalist perspective, seeing power exercised by any non-managers as illegitimate behaviour, which is designed to promote self-interest rather than the achievement of organizational goals.

The focus of this perspective is placed on those who seek to challenge the smooth operation of the enterprise. Power is seen as a political tool used by non-managers to disrupt operations. When managers use power, it is only in self-defence, to counter such attacks. This perspective sees power as a useful and flexible resource; good when used by managers, and 'bad' when used against them. Historically, studies of managerial power have been conducted from this perspective. They have ignored questions of how power becomes embedded in a company's structure, culture, practices, rules and regulations. Hardy believed that the functionalist perspective concentrates on the surface aspects of power, advocates the status quo, hides the way in which powerful groups on the organization maintain their dominance and generally neglects the way power operates to shape the lives of both employees and managers.

An alternative, albeit much less influential approach views power as a means of domination, and sees resistance to power as an emancipatory tool. This political perspective was summarized in the right-hand column of the table on p. 669. It was also referred to as the critical or sociological perspective, and has passed through four phases. Originally, it examined power from the standpoint of decisions, asking who makes them. Within the context of communities in the United States, critical researchers found that the views of numerous rather than a few groups prevailed, and that America was a pluralist rather than an elite society (Wolfinger, 1971). In the second phase of the critical tradition, researchers asked if perhaps the interests and grievances of particular groups were not being recognized, and were thus being excluded from the decision-making arena. Power was being exercised by excluding them in favour of safe decisions. This process was termed 'non-decision-making', and emphasized the ability of powerful players to determine outcomes behind the scenes (Bachrach and Baritz, 1963).

The third phase of critical writing looked at power and non-observable conflict. The argument was that while the previous phase had assumed that a conflict was necessary to initiate non-decision-making, it was perfectly possible for the powerful to prevent conflict arising in the first place, by shaping perceptions, cognitions and preferences of others. They used their power to get others to accept their positions as natural and unchangeable, and prevented them raising grievances. This phase of research studied how power-holders sustained their dominance by reducing the inclination to use the discretionary power they had (Lukes, 1974).

The fourth and current stage of the critical perspective is labour process theory. The interest of these researchers is upon how seemingly neutral, legitimate working arrangements – the choice of technology, the culture of the company, the shape of its formal structure – mask the means by which workers are dominated in the organization. Labour process writers hold that the legitimacy is neither natural nor inevitable, as managerial functionalists like to claim, but is in fact created (Braverman, 1974; Burawoy, 1979;

Knights and Willmott, 1985).The current interest of the writers of the critical school is on how the creation and manipulation of managerial legitimacy obviates the need for more coercive and visible forms of power. The efficient achievement of goals requires workers to comply willingly with managerial directives towards the achievement of organizational goals.

The managerial functionalists, in contrast, ignore such issues, considering the formal organizational arrangements to be natural, logical and functional. Their chosen technologies, cultures and structures are treated as apolitical tools, and thus are considered as neither power nor domination. To the critical writers, this represents a surface approach which misrepresents the true balance of power. It attributes too much power to subordinate groups who are castigated for using what little power they have, whilst hiding the way in which senior managerial power-holders use the power they have, behind the scenes, to further their own positions by shaping legitimacy, values and technology and information. The functionalist managerialist perspective essentially depoliticizes organizational life.

The overwhelming dominance of the functionalist approach in the managerial literature has indeed been largely successful in eliminating the discussion of power and politics within organizations. As noted earlier, the power embedded in organizational structures and technology is not seen as power. Research studies of the powerless in organizations have ceased to be fashionable, and their academics' chances of receiving funding from government research bodies for such work are low. The emphasis on value-for-money social science research that may contribute to national prosperity means that those interested in studying the organizationally powerless, or questioning organizationally embedded power, are likely to be labelled irresponsible, irrational and perhaps even subversive.

It may not be an exaggeration to say that power and politics have become dirty words in management education. Textbooks addressing the subjects do so from the functionalist perspective. The management literature on power during the 1980s focused almost exclusively on managerial attempts to defeat conflict that arose when individuals and groups sought to preserve their vested interests within the company. Other writers just avoid power and politics altogether. Academics in the field of corporate culture, for example (a topic examined in Chapter 18), have assiduously distanced themselves from any consideration of power balances or the political issues involved. Changes in corporate culture are predominantly considered from an integrationalist-rationalist perspective depicted as neutral and assumed to be to the benefit of all organizational members.

sources

Allen, R.W., Madison, D.L., Porter, L.W., Renwick, P.A. and Mayes, B.T., 1979, 'Organizational politics: Tactics and characteristics of actors', *California Management Review*, vol. 22, no. 1, pp. 77–83.

Allison, G.T., 1971, *Essence of Decision*, Little, Brown and Co., Boston, MA.

Bachrach, P. and Baratz, M.S., 1962, 'The two faces of power', *American Political Science Review*, vol. 56, pp. 641–51.

Baldridge, J.V., 1971, *Power and Conflict in the University*, John Wiley, New York.

Beeman, D.R. and Sharkey, T.W., 1987, 'The use and abuse of corporate politics', *Business Horizons*, March–April, pp. 26–30.

Bolman, L. and Deal, T., 1991, *Re-framing Organizations*, Jossey-Bass, San Francisco.

Brass, D.J., 1984, 'Being in the right place: A structural analysis of individual influence in organizations', *Administrative Science Quarterly*, vol. 29, pp. 518–39.

Braverman, H., 1974, *Labor and Monopoly Capital*, Monthly Review Press, New York.

Burawoy, M., 1979, *Manufacturing Consent*, Chicago University Press, Chicago.

Christie, R. and Geis, F.L., 1970, *Studies in Machiavellianism*, Academic Press, New York.

Cohen, A.A. and Bradford, D.L., 1991, *Influence without Authority*, John Wiley, New York.

Conger, J.A. and Kanungo, R.N., 1987, 'Toward a behavioural theory of charismatic leadership', *Academy of Management Review*, vol. 12, pp. 637–47.

Cyert, R. M. and March, J. G., 1963, *A Behavioral Theory of the Firm*, Prentice Hall, Englewood Cliffs, NJ.

Drory, A. and Romm, T., 1990, 'The definition of organizational politics: A review', *Human Relations*, vol. 43, no. 11, pp. 1134–54.

Drummond, H., 1991, *Power: Creating It, Using It*, Kogan Page, London.

Farrell, D. and Petersen, J.C., 1982, 'Patterns of political behaviour in organizations', *Academy of Management Review*, vol. 7, no. 3, pp. 403–12.

Freeman, L.C., 1979, 'Centrality in social networks: conceptual clarifications', *Social Networks*, vol. 1, pp. 215–39.

Gandz, J. and Murray, V.V., 1980, 'The experience of workplace politics', *Academy of Management Journal*, vol. 23, no. 2, pp. 237–51.

Hardy, C., 1995, *Power and Politics in Organizations*, Dartmouth, Aldershot.

Hickson, D.J., Hidings, CR., Lee, C.A., Schneck, R.E. and Pennings, J.M., 1971, 'A strategic contingencies theory on intraorganizational power', *Administrative Science Quarterly*, vol. 16, pp. 216–29.

House, R.J., 1988, 'Power and personality in complex organizations' in B.M. Staw and L. L. Cummings (eds.), *Research in Organizational Behaviour: Volume 10*, JAI Press, Greenwich, CT, pp. 305–57.

Huczynski, A.A., 1996, *Influencing within Organizations: Getting in, Rising up, Moving on*, Prentice Hall, Hemel Hempstead.

Joseph, M., 1989, *Sociology for Business*, Basil Blackwell, Oxford.

Kakabadese, A., 1983, *The Politics of Management*, Gower, Aldershot.

Kanter, R.M., 1979, 'Power failure in management circuits', *Harvard Business Review*, July–August, pp. 65–75.

Kipnis, D., Schmidt, S.M., Swaffin-Smith, C. and Wilkinson, I., 1984, 'Patterns of managerial influence: Shotgun managers, tacticians and bystanders', *Organizational Dynamics*, Winter, pp. 58–67.

Knights, D. and Willmott, H., 1985, 'Power and identity in theory and practice', *Sociological Review*, vol. 33, pp. 122–46.

Kotter, J., 1985, *Power and Influence*, Free Press, New York.

Lukes, S., 1974, *Power: A Radical View*, Macmillan, London.

Machiavelli, N., 1961, *The Prince*, trans. G. Bull, Penguin Books, Harmondsworth.

Madison, D.L., Allen, R.W., Porter, L.W. and Mayes, B.T., 1980, 'Organizational politics: An exploration of managers' perceptions', *Human Relations*, vol. 33, pp. 79–100.

March, J.G., 1962, 'The business firm as a political coalition', *Journal of Politics*, vol. 24, pp. 434–53.

Martin, R., 1977, *The Sociology of Power*, Routledge, London.

Mayes, B.T. and Allen, R.W., 1972, 'Toward a definition of organizational politics', *Academy of Management Review*, vol. 2, pp. 672–7.

McClelland, D.C., 1961, *The Achieving Society*, Van Nostrand, Princeton, NJ.

McClelland, D.C. and Burnham, D., 1976, 'Power is the great motivator', *Harvard Business Review*, March–April, pp. 100–11.

McClelland, D.C. and Boyatzis, R.E., 1982, 'Leadership motive pattern and long term success in management', *Journal of Applied Psychology*, vol. 67, pp. 744–51.

Merkle, J.A., 1980, *Management and Ideology: The Legacy of the Scientific Management Movement*, University of California Press, CA.

Meyer, J.W. and Rowan, B., 1977, 'Institutional organizations: Formal structures as myth and ceremony', *American Journal of Sociology*, vol. 83, pp. 340–63.

Moore, J.I., 1992, *Writers on Strategy and Management*, Penguin, Harmondsworth.

Perrow, C., 1970, 'Departmental power and perspectives in industrial firms', in M.N. Zald (ed.), *Power in Organizations*, Vanderbilt University Press, Nashville, TN, pp. 59–89.

Pettigrew, A.M., 1973, *The Politics of Organizational Decision Making*, Tavistock, London.

Pfeffer, J., 1981, *Power in Organizations*, HarperCollins, New York.

Ragins, B.R. and Sundstrom, E., 1982, 'Gender and power in organizations: a longitudinal perspective', *Journal of Applied Psychology*, vol. 67, pp. 737–43.

Rotter, J.B., 1966, 'Generalised expectations for internal v external control of reinforcement', *Psychological Monographs*, vol. 80, whole no. 609, pp. 1–28.

Salancik, G.R. and Pfeffer, J., 1974, 'The bases and use of power in organizational decision-making', *Administrative Science Quarterly*, vol. 19, pp. 453–73.

Salancik, G.R. and Pfeffer, J., 1977, 'Who gets power – and how they hold on to it: A strategic contingency model of power', *Organizational Dynamics*, Winter, pp. 3–21.

Sitkin, S.B. and Pablo, A.L., 1992, 'Reconceptualising the determinants of risk behaviour', *Academy of Management Review*, vol. 17, pp. 9–38.

A.M. Henderson and T. Parsons,, Free Press, New York

Taggert, W. M. and. Silbey, V., 1986, *Informational Systems: People and Computers in Organizations*, Allyn and Bacon, Boston, MA.

Weber, M., 1947, *The Theory of Social and Economic Organization*, trans. by A.M. Henderson and T. Parsons, Free Press, New York.

Wolfinger, R.E., 1971, 'Nondecisions and the study of local politics', *American Political Science Review*, vol. 65, pp. 1063–80.

Wren, D., 1994, *The Evolution of Management Thought*, John Wiley, Chichester, 4th edition.

Yates, S., 1985, *The Politics of Management*, Jossey-Bass, San Francisco.

chapter 23 management control

concepts and learning objectives

Harry Braverman (1974, p. 68) writes: 'like a rider who uses reins, bridle, spurs, carrot, whip and training from birth to impose his will, the capitalist strives, through management to control. And control is indeed the central concept of all management systems.'

Richard Pascale and Anthony Athos (1982, p. 105) write: 'The inherent preferences of organizations are clarity, certainty, and perfection. The inherent nature of human relationships involves ambiguity, uncertainty, and imperfection. How one honours, balances, and integrates the needs of both is the real trick of management.'

It is possible to argue that to manage *is* to control. This argument is true in a number of respects. However, this position also appears to have clear moral and ethical dimensions. Individuals and occupational groups who claim rights of control over the activities of others become socially and politically suspect, as Braverman implies. This is a perennial management dilemma, and is one

705

aspect of the organizational dilemma introduced in Chapter 1, concerning the conflict between the collective purpose of the organization and the needs of individuals. Pascale and Athos advocate finding some kind of balance.

Despite the ethical concerns, control in organizations has a number of beneficial properties. We shall seek to develop a balanced view of the benefits, in contrast with the negative dimensions of control.

key concepts
- management control
- rigid bureaucratic behaviour
- social control
- insidious control
- authoritarian personality

learning objectives

When you have read this chapter, you should be able to define those key concepts in your own words, and you should also be able to:

1 Distinguish between the different uses of the concept of control.
2 Appreciate the economic and psychological need for control in organizations.
3 Understand the political nature of management control.
4 Identify the different ways in which control is exercised in organizations.
5 Understand the importance to management of the legitimacy of control.

perspectives on management control

The concept of control has a number of positive meanings. It stands for predictability, order, reliability and stability. The absence of control, from this point of view, suggests anarchy, chaos, disorder and uncertainty.

Control in an organization means that people know what they have to do and when. Suppliers know what they have to deliver and when. Customers know when they are going to get their goods or services. Employees know how much they are going to get paid, and how often. Control from this point of view is a necessary and desirable aspect of organizational life. Most of us appreciate a degree of order, predictability and certainty in our lives. Most of us complain when the goals we are meant to attain and the expectations of our behaviour and performance are not made clear. Control also appears to be psychologically desirable.

However, the concept of control also means coercion, domination, exploitation and manipulation. The absence of control from this point of view suggests freedom, individuality, discretion, responsibility and autonomy.

Control in an organization can mean stifling the personality and intellect of the individual. This notion of control runs counter to our democratic political ideal which suggests that individuals should have a say in matters that concern them. Most of us dislike being told what to do all or most of the time. Managers who attempt to manipulate and dominate their employees invariably meet with resistance, hostility and poor performance. Control from this point of view appears to be an undesirable aspect of organizational life.

The ability to exercise freedom of choice and expression appears to be necessary to the development of the mature personality. Control thus also appears to be psychologically abhorrent.

Organizational control can have three main connotations:

1 Control is an *economically necessary* activity. If control breaks down, then operations get out of hand, resources are wasted, money is spent unnecessarily. Control is therefore a means of securing efficiency by achieving the continuing best use of resources.

2 Control is *psychologically necessary* to create stable and predictable conditions within which people can work effectively. Control is thus a means of establishing predictability as psychological well being and work performance can be disrupted by uncertainty, ambiguity and disorder.

3 Control is a *political process* in which certain powerful individuals and groups dominate others. Decisions in the control process are taken by managers who resist attempts to let others, particularly subordinates, interfere. Control is thus a means of perpetuating inequalities of power and other resources in organizations.

the nature of management control mechanisms

Graeme Salaman (1981, p. 152), presenting a 'politics-free' perspective on control, writes: 'Control, then, is neutral; it is demanded by the task in hand, which in turn is for the benefit of society at large, indeed for the workers themselves as citizens and consumers, and is achieved through the application of science and technology.' Salaman was merely presenting such a view in this quotation; his personal stance is much closer to that of Harry Braverman.

Social science has had difficulty in defining just what constitutes an organization. It is not clear what aspects distinguish organizations from other forms of social arrangements. Most people would agree that Bill Gates' company Microsoft, and Richard Branson's company Virgin, are organizations. But what about the local sports club? The neighbourhood babysitting circle? What criteria should be used to make the distinction?

We suggested in Chapter 1 that it is the preoccupation with controlled performance that sets organizations apart from other forms of social arrangement. If the managers and players of the local football team have such a preoccupation, then perhaps we should think of their team as an organization. The performance of an organization as a whole determines whether or not it survives. The performance of a department or section within an organization determines the amounts of resources allocated to it. The performance of individuals determines their pay and promotion prospects, and their continuing membership.

Organizations are concerned with the adequacy of group and individual performances. Not just any level of performance will do. We live in a world in which the resources available to us are not sufficient to meet all our conceivable needs. We have to make effective use of the resources that we have. The performances of individuals, departments and organizations are therefore tied closely to standards which stipulate what counts as adequate, satisfactory or good performance. Such a specific concern with what constitutes adequacy in terms of performance is not a feature of other social arrangements such as families. So we do not feel happy about putting 'family' into the category of 'organization'.

It is economically necessary, therefore, to control performance in an organization, to ensure that it is good enough, and to ensure that remedial action is taken when it is not good enough. The production of most modern goods and services is a complex process. The varied work activities of large groups of people have to be organized and co-ordinated to achieve the controlled performances required to mass produce toothpaste or build portable computers.

---

definition

Management control *is the process through which plans are implemented and objectives are achieved by setting standards, measuring performance, comparing actual performance with standards and then deciding necessary corrective action and feedback.*

We met this concept in Chapter 5 (learning theory), where we discussed the concept of a feedback control system. Management control can be described in the same terms. The main elements of a feedback control system are:

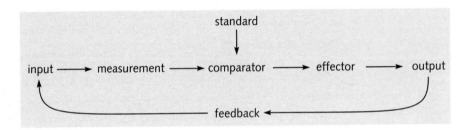

Management control thus involves a recurring sequence of activities. Objectives and standards provide guidelines for performance and set the norms for activities and procedures. They specify what performance levels are required or what levels of performance are going to be regarded as satisfactory, unsatisfactory and superlative. It is sometimes difficult to decide on the level at which standards should be set. If they are set too high, they are usually ignored. If they are set too low, then performance may be artificially lowered. It is also sometimes hard to decide on the number and complexity of standards to set. A large number of potentially conflicting standards that are also difficult to understand may produce a cumbersome and ineffective organization.

The performance objectives for most students are expressed in terms such as, 'Get at least 50 per cent in assignments and exams'. This can in practice be an ambiguous standard as many students are not clear what they have to do to achieve it. Examination answers tend to be assessed on several criteria, such as style, content, structure, quality of critical evaluation, comparison of arguments and theories, synthesis of material, and so on. But it is hard to specify what these criteria mean in practice in clear terms. The performance objectives for a typist, on the other hand, may be expressed as '50 words a minute' and 'no errors', and for a hairdresser in terms of the number of clients per hour or day. These are comparatively unambiguous standards and it is usually quite clear when they have been achieved.

> **STOP!**
>
> Consider the course in organizational behaviour that you are now studying.
> In collaboration with your fellow students, analyze the process through
> which your performance on the course is controlled in the following terms:
>
> ▸ What standards of performance are you expected to achieve?
> ▸ Who sets the standards?
> ▸ Do you know what the standards are?
> ▸ Are the standards clearly defined or ambiguous?
> ▸ Do you think the standards are too high or too low?
> ▸ How is your performance measured?
> ▸ Do you know what the criteria are?
> ▸ How often is your performance measured?
> ▸ Who compares your performance with the standard?
> ▸ Is this done publicly or in secret?
> ▸ Is this done by one person or by several?
> ▸ Are students involved as well as teaching staff?
> ▸ Is the comparison objective or subjective?
> ▸ What happens if your performance is not up to standard?
> ▸ What kind of feedback do you get?
> ▸ Is the feedback useful in telling you how to improve?
> ▸ Is the feedback provided frequently or rarely?
> ▸ Is the feedback accurate?
>
> Now prepare a report based on your analysis and submit it with a series of
> recommendations for improvement of the control process to the teaching
> staff involved with the course. Note their reactions to your proposals.
>
> Finally, how do you feel about your actions being controlled in this way?
> Is this something you resist, or something you welcome? Why?

Actual performance clearly has to be measured in some way to see if it is
consistent with the standards that have been set. Measurement can involve
personal observation by the superior, oral and written reports from subordinates, the collection of statistics and the measurement of performance
indicators by mechanical or electronic mechanisms.

The measurement of student performance is usually achieved through a
combination of written work, contributions in seminars and tutorials, and
sometimes through the tutor's assessment of oral presentations. These forms of
measurement can be very subjective. The measurement of factory work can
be expressed in terms of saleable units of output, say packets of biscuits over
an hour or a day. This is a comparatively objective measurement, which may
be made by personal observation or through reports or by automatic
computer logging.

The timing of measurement is also important. Students' performance is
traditionally measured at the end of each semester or term. The performance
of a biscuit-making line and its operators is measured continuously throughout
each shift. If performance is measured too early or too late, the value of the
feedback in correcting problems will be reduced.

Corrective action or feedback involves a control decision to put things
right, or the provision of information to enable those involved to take

appropriate action. This step is itself sometimes identified as the control task, but it is important to see this as only one stage of a logical process, or system, of control. The control process can be used to identify performance trends that should be either defeated or encouraged, as well as simply to ensure that predefined targets are being achieved.

Lecturers often tell their students whether their understanding of course material is adequate, leaving decisions about corrective action to the student. Tutors vary in their willingness and ability to give feedback. Comments like 'not bad, could do better' may be informative, but this is not a particularly helpful guide to remedial action. A supervisor in a biscuit factory who discovers problems with the baking process can tell operators about the problem and expect them to solve it. The supervisor may, on the other hand, decide to take action and, say, replace a faulty piece of machinery or shut the process down until a repair team arrives.

strategies and problems of management control

The problem is to establish control processes that are effective, in that they lead to the achievement of the desired levels of performance. Control has traditionally been regarded as one of the main functions of management. Fayol, for example, regarded control as one of six main management activities. Some commentators have argued that control is the single most important management function. Others have suggested that management in all its aspects is a control function.

---

design your own control process

You are head of a department of business and management studies, responsible for twenty-five academic staff covering the usual wide range of business disciplines. Your institution managers are concerned with the limited volume and quality of the research output from your department. You have been asked to implement a control system to improve matters. What actions would you now consider under the following headings?

- Setting standards for volume and quality of academic staff research output.
- Measuring the performance of individual staff members.
- Comparing performance with the standards.
- Giving appropriate feedback and taking corrective action.

Will you produce a written statement of the standards, and how they are to be controlled? Will you involve the academic staff in setting and monitoring standards, or is this a management responsibility? Will the standards be the same for all subject disciplines?

What do you see as the main strengths of your approach – and what do you see as the main problems which such a system could create?

The control process has to ensure that the members of the organization are behaving as they are required to behave, as well as ensuring that their activities are achieving the desired results. Performance has to be standardized to some extent to achieve consistent output quantity and quality. Organizations have to reduce waste, theft, sabotage and fraud in the interests of economic survival.

The main mechanism through which management control is achieved is organization structure. Organization members have to carry out the tasks of the control process as well as the operating tasks required to fulfil the organization's objectives. The need for controlled performance leads to a deliberate and ordered allocation of functions, or division of labour, between the organization's members, and to the establishment of hierarchical authority relationships. The activities and interactions of staff and workers are intentionally structured. Admission to membership of organizations is also controlled. The price of failure to perform to standard is invariably loss of membership.

The steps in the management control process are achieved in a number of ways that are less obvious than those we have identified so far. Don Hellriegel and John Slocum (1978) identify six common management control strategies.

control through the organization structure

Most large organizations give their employees written job descriptions which set out the individual's tasks and responsibilities. These job descriptions can be more or less narrow, detailed, specific and unambiguous or broad, general, vague and ill-defined. They also establish communication flows and the location of decision-making responsibility.

Job descriptions constrain the behaviour of the individual by identifying what things can and cannot be done, and by placing the individual in the organization hierarchy. The standards that have to be achieved are thus part of the description of the job that the individual holds.

control through recruitment and training

Organizations preoccupied with controlled performance cannot afford to be staffed with people who behave in unstable, variable, spontaneous, idiosyncratic and random ways. Organizations require stability and predictability in the behaviour of their members – even with people in creative occupations (marketing copywriters, research laboratory staff) who may be expected to display some idiosyncratic traits. Predictability is typically achieved through the selection of stable and reliable individuals, and through an emphasis on consistency and reliability in training.

Managers can exercise a great deal of discretion in the criteria that are used in selection and in the content of training programmes. Managers usually try to select those who will 'fit' the organization in terms of their attitudes and values as well as their skills. (It is possible to discriminate against people on many dimensions other than sex and ethnic origin.) Training can cover attitudes and values relevant to the company culture as well as skill and knowledge training. These processes try to ensure that the standards that have to be achieved are part of (or through training become part of) the individual's personal value system.

---

control through recruitment

Peter Blunt describes how a Kenyan security company used their recruitment strategy as a means of employee control.

The company employed 300 watchmen and more than 90 per cent of these came from the Luo ethnic group. The white company owner had deliberately used the traditional kinship and ethnic solidarity of the Luo as a means of control.

He actively encouraged his existing employees to bring their kinsmen to join the workforce of his company, making clear to them that desertion with company property or damage to it by one of them would involve their collective responsibility. This was not seen as unusual or as a hardship by the workforce because they were accustomed to being held responsible in this way for the actions of their kinsmen. The workforce therefore did not consider this policy exploitative, and preferred this.

M.R. Seth's study of a modern factory in India revealed that new employees were hired on the basis of recommendations from relatives who were already working in the factory. As with the Luo in Kenya, kin were being hired by the factory owners to facilitate co-ordination and control, the training of new employees, and to ensure commitment to the organization. Employees welcomed this system as a way of helping them to meet their wider social obligations.

based on Peter Blunt, 1980, 'Bureaucracy and ethnicity in Kenya: some conjectures for the eighties', *Journal of Applied Behavioural Science*, vol. 16, pp. 336–53; and M.R. Seth, 1968, *The Social Framework of an Indian Factory*, Manchester University Press, Manchester.

---

control through rewards and punishments

Organizations provide their members with a number of extrinsic and intrinsic rewards. Extrinsic rewards are material, monetary incentives and associated fringe benefits such as cheap loans, company car, free meals, and so on. Intrinsic rewards include satisfying work, personal responsibility and autonomy.

The behaviour of employees can be controlled by offers to provide and to withdraw these rewards in return for compliance or defiance with respect to management directions. Although psychology has shown that punishment (or the threat of punishment) is not an effective means for controlling behaviour, the withdrawal of rewards is still a common organizational control mechanism. Individuals whose performance is up to standard are thus rewarded while those who do not comply find that their rewards are diminished or withheld.

control through policies and rules

Written policies and rules guide employees' actions, structure their relationships and try to establish consistency. Some typical organizational rules were examined in Chapter 13. Rules establish acceptable behaviour and levels of performance and are another attempt to lay down standards.

control through budgets

Individuals and sections in an organization can be given financial and other

controllers sometimes give inaccurate feedback

Daniel Ilgen and William Knowlton suggest that supervisors do not always tell their subordinates the truth about how good – or how bad – their performance is.

They asked forty students each to supervise a group of three workers who were coding questionnaires for two hours. The 'workers' were collaborators of the researchers and had been specially trained for the experiment. The student supervisors were first shown the results of a 'personnel test' which they were told had measured the abilities of their subordinates for the coding job. Each work group had one 'discrepant' worker who worked much better, or much worse, than the other two. The discrepant worker behaved enthusiastically in some groups and apathetically in others. The supervisors were thus led to attribute the performance of the discrepant worker to either high or low ability or to high or low motivation.

After the work session, the supervisors rated the ability and motivation of all their subordinates on scales which ranged from 'unsatisfactory' to 'outstanding'. They then completed a separate 'feedback report form' using the same scales, in the belief that they would then have to convey the contents in person to one of their subordinates who would be chosen 'at random'. In fact the discrepant worker was always chosen.

For the purposes of the feedback, the supervisors had to select one of twelve statements that best described their evaluation of the subordinate, such as 'You have done very well. I believe I would try to do even better next time if I were you', or 'Your performance is not good at all. You really need to put more into it'. In addition, the supervisors had to make recommendations for the subordinate, such as 'attend a special training session', 'concentrate more on the task' or 'try harder'. When they had done this, the supervisors were told that there would be no feedback session and the deception was explained to them.

As expected, the ratings of ability and motivation of the subordinates were higher when supervisors believed that they would have to give personal feedback. Where low performance was attributed to motivation, the feedback reflected this accurately. But where low performance was attributed to ability, the supervisors recommended an inappropriate mix of feedback, directed at both motivation and skill.

The researchers argue that if supervisors in organizations systematically distort their assessments in this way, many employees will have inflated views of their abilities.

based on Daniel R. Ilgen and William A. Knowlton, 1980, 'Performance attributional effects on feedback from superiors', *Organizational Behaviour and Human Performance*, vol. 25, no. 3, pp. 441–56.

resource targets to guide their performance. These targets may concern the level of expenditure that the section has, the level of costs incurred or the level of sales volume to be achieved in a month. Production budgets may involve non-financial standards such as labour hours used, machine downtime, materials used, waste material, and so on.

control through machinery

This form of control has been most popular in process industries where chemicals are manufactured automatically with very little human intervention. Computer sensors capture process performance information, compare it with pre-programmed standard performance criteria and decide automatically on corrective action when necessary. Developments in electronics and computing have increased the extent to which machinery takes over all the steps of the control process in manufacturing operations. Machines can even control other machines and so the need for human controllers is reduced.

People subjected to organizational control systems do not always behave in required and expected ways. Edward Lawler (1976) has argued that management control strategies create three major human problems for organizations.

First, management controls lead to what Lawler describes as *rigid bureaucratic behaviour*. Most people want to behave in ways that make them look good. In other words, as soon as you discover that your behaviour is being measured on some factor or dimension or criterion, you are likely to concentrate on that factor. If the consequences of a 'poor' measurement are significant, then you are understandably going to pay less attention to dimensions of your work that are not assessed. The standards in the control process tell people what they have to do to perform well and maybe to get promoted. People then behave in ways required by the control process, and this is not necessarily in the interests of the organization as a whole.

---

definition

Rigid bureaucratic behaviour *is behaviour that follows strictly the organization's rules, regulations and procedures, regardless of whether these rules apply to, or are effective in, the particular circumstances facing the individual at a given time. This can also be described as 'working to rule'.*

Lawler cites research in a department store which used a pay incentive scheme to reward employees according to the volume of sales they achieved. Sales increased when the scheme was introduced. But employees were busy 'tying up the trade' and 'sales grabbing' to sell as much as they could, while other essential tasks such as display work and stock checking were ignored. The control system did not set any standards for stock and display work, only for sales volume.

STOP!

Can you identify examples of rigid bureaucratic behaviour in your education institution? Can you explain those behaviours in terms of the institution's control system?

The control process cannot measure everything. It is therefore difficult to establish just what should be measured. The problem is that controls focus attention on whatever criteria are chosen. Rigidity arises from the desire of individuals to defend their actions by pointing to their satisfactory performance on the measure – such as the level of sales.

Second, inaccurate information can be fed into the control process. Several studies have suggested that the more important the measure, the more likely it becomes that the information in the process will get distorted. Subordinates are prone to provide incorrect information both on what has been done and on what can be done. Lawler (1976, p. 1260) cites the following examples:

> In one case, a group, who worked together in assembling a complicated and large sized steel framework, worked out a system to be used only when the rate setter was present. They found that by tightening certain bolts first, the frame would be slightly sprung and all the other bolts would bind and be very difficult to tighten. When the rate setter was not present, they followed a different sequence and the work went much faster.

> The budget bargaining process managers go through with their superiors is not too dissimilar from the one that goes on between the time study man and the worker who is on a piece rate plan or work standard plan. The time study man and the superior both try to get valid data about what is possible in the future, and the employees who are subject to the control system often give invalid data and try to get as favourable a standard, or budget, as they can.

---

some subordinates give inaccurate information

Do subordinates always tell their bosses the truth about how well they are performing? An experiment conducted by Janet Gaines suggests that some subordinates distort the information they feed into the management control process in systematic ways.

Gaines gave forty employees in an American aluminium company a description of an 'organizational situation'. Half of the subjects were given a story about 'troublesome communications', such as getting bad news through the grapevine or not getting clear instructions. The others were given a story about 'routine communications'. When the employees had finished reading their story they were asked to rate the chance that they would tell their superior about it, compose a memo (assuming that they decided to tell) and to rate their trust in their superior and their own personal ambition.

Their memos were classed as either 'withholding', 'puffing' (exaggerating) or 'sieving' (selecting) information.

Withholding was the most popular form of information distortion. Ambitious subordinates who trusted their bosses were less likely to tell them about routine matters. They perhaps felt competent to deal with these issues themselves and would have shown weakness by asking for the boss's help.

But ambitious and trusting subordinates were more likely to pass on information about problems, perhaps because they felt that their superior needed to know and would find out anyway.

The results suggested that, contrary to popular belief, ambitious people do not exaggerate and do not try to deceive others to achieve their personal aims. Managers have most to worry about where their subordinates are unambitious and do not trust them.

from Janet H. Gaines, 1980, 'Upward communication in industry; an experiment', *Human Relations*, vol. 33, no. 12, pp. 929–41.

Information may be distorted or withheld where employees want to look good and where mistakes and poor performance can be hidden in some way. Information may also be distorted where employees feel that the standards imposed on them are unfair. If standards are felt to be unreasonable, it may be seen as legitimate to cheat. Information that is used for assessment and reward is therefore more likely to get distorted than information supplied for 'neutral' purposes.

---

information used for reward purposes may be distorted

In the United States many so-called commercial blood banks in large cities pay donors for the blood they give. In large cities there is a high incidence of patients coming down with hepatitis after they have received transfusions. The research shows that the incidence of hepatitis is much higher among patients receiving commercial blood than among those receiving free blood. Apparently the blood of paid donors is more likely to contain hepatitis than the blood of voluntary donors. The reason for this is that blood banks have to rely on their donors to give accurate medical histories in order to prevent harmful blood from being collected.

from Edward E. Lawler, 1976, 'Control systems in organizations', in H.D. Dunnette (ed.), *Handbook of Industrial and Organizational Psychology*, Rand-McNally, Chicago, p. 1263.

Third, controls may be resisted when they threaten need satisfaction and create hostility and lack of co-operation. Controls may:

▸ Automate human skill and expertise. Skill is a source of identity and self-esteem and its loss may be hard to bear.
▸ Create new experts with new sources of power and autonomy. Those who used to have the expertise and power may resist this.
▸ Measure performance more accurately and comprehensively. It may be to the advantage of the individual for everyone to know how hard they work. But some people will fear exposure from all-embracing controls on their behaviour.
▸ Change the social structure of an organization and disrupt social groupings and friendship opportunities. This can also mean the creation of competing and conflicting groups.
▸ Reduce opportunities for intrinsic need satisfaction by reducing individual autonomy.

STOP!

▸ Can you identify examples of resistance to controls in your educational institution?
▸ Can you explain that resistance using Lawler's observations?

These three reactions to management controls are sometimes described as dysfunctional because they create human behaviours that run counter to the behaviours that the controls are seeking to establish. This is the dilemma of management control system design.

the psychological need for control

The previous section emphasized the necessity of management control in achieving satisfactory organizational performance. The following section presents a contrasting critical perspective on management control. Before we proceed with that it is useful to consider the positive psychological advantages of control in organizations.

Why would anyone want to be controlled at all? This notion is inconsistent with our social values of democratic decision-making and individual freedom of expression. Lawler suggests that control has three psychological functions.

First, control processes give us feedback on our performance. This feedback constitutes information which we can use to improve our performance. Without feedback, learning is difficult or impossible, and feedback is generally sought for this reason. Feedback can also have a motivating effect by providing recognition for past achievement, which in turn provides incentive to sustain and to improve performance levels. How would you feel, as a student, if academic staff did not release any information about the standards you were expected to achieve, if your assignment and examination work was not assessed or measured, if you were given no feedback to help you improve on future performance?

STOP!

Consider what your reaction would be if your lecturers stopped telling you how well you had performed in term assignments and examinations (with the exception of telling you at the end of the course whether you had got your degree or diploma or not).

Is there evidence in your response, and that of your colleagues, to suggest that you have a psychological need for control?

In other words, people naturally want to know how well they have done on a particular task and welcome the feedback information from a control process which tells them just that. Supervisors in organizations, however, often lack the skill to provide the quantity and quality of feedback that employees require for the development of their skills and motivation.

Second, control processes give us structure, define methods and indicate how our performances will be measured. Most of us require some degree of structure and definition in what we do. Some of us need a lot, and prefer defined, well-specified jobs where the duties, responsibilities, rules and limits are clear. It is reassuring to know precisely what one is required to do and how the outcome will be evaluated.

Third, controls encourage dependency. Some people seem to enjoy submitting themselves to authority. This enjoyment goes beyond the reassurance of knowing the rules of the control process and appears to be part of the *authoritarian personality*. This personality type was first identified by American researchers during and after the Second World War.

---

definition

The **authoritarian personality** *is a personality type which includes a cluster of personality traits concerned with conservative attitudes, submission to and preoccupation with authority, fatalistic and rigid thinking, and hostility to humanistic values.*

---

employees need helpful feedback

It is difficult to maintain or improve work performance in the absence of feedback on how well one is doing. Many organizations have schemes in which supervisors annually appraise the performance of their employees and give them feedback. But these schemes are often ineffective.

Daniel Ilgen, Richard Paterson, Beth Martin and Daniel Boeschen studied the performance appraisal process in an American wood products company with 7000 employees. The supervisors were supposed to meet employees regularly to discuss their performance. At the end of each year the supervisors held special sessions with each employee to rate their performance and to decide standards for next year. The supervisor's rating decided the employee's salary increase.

Sixty separate pairs of supervisors and subordinates were chosen at random for the study. Their attitudes to the company's appraisal procedures were assessed by two questionnaires, issued two weeks before and then one month after the annual review sessions.

Supervisors and employees had different perceptions of the appraisal scheme. The supervisors overestimated their knowledge of their subordinates' jobs and the quality of the feedback they gave them. The subordinates felt that their supervisors' ratings of their performance were too low and that the feedback they got was vague. The subordinates who were most satisfied with the scheme were those who got frequent, detailed and considerate feedback.

The authors conclude that feedback should be regular, not annual, and that supervisors should improve their knowledge of their subordinates' perceptions. Feedback works if it is understood and regarded favourably by the recipient. But supervisors may try to maintain a friendly atmosphere by avoiding criticism and unpleasant feedback.

based on Daniel Ilgen, Richard Paterson, Beth Martin and Daniel Boeschen, 1981, 'Supervisor and subordinate reactions to performance appraisal sessions', *Organizational Behaviour and Human Performance*, vol. 28, no. 3, pp. 311–30.

The *authoritarian personality* is an extreme form of personality type with complex causes related mainly to early socialization. Individuals with authoritarian personalities need and like tight organizational control processes. But Norman Dixon has argued that large bureaucratic organizations like the military attract individuals with this cluster of personality traits, precisely because they offer a structured, ordered, controlled environment, which is consistent with authoritarian needs.

Authoritarian individuals fit the military organization so well that they get promoted to responsible positions. The problem, however, is that the rigid thinking of the authoritarian personality can produce disastrous decisions. Dixon provides numerous illustrations of this phenomenon from military history. The same may be true of large non-military bureaucratic organizations.

---

nine traits of the authoritarian personality

1 *Conventionalism*: rigid adherence to conventional middle-class values.
2 *Authoritarian submission*: a submissive, uncritical attitude towards the idealized moral authorities of the group with which he identifies himself.
3 *Authoritarian aggression*: a tendency to be on the look-out for and to condemn, reject and punish people who violate conventional values.
4 *Anti-intraception*: opposition to the subjective, the imaginative and the tender-minded.
5 *Superstition and stereotypy*: a belief in magical determinants of the individual's fate, and the disposition to think in rigid categories.
6 *Power and 'toughness'*: a preoccupation with the dominance–submission, strong–weak, leader–follower dimension, identification with power-figures, overemphasis on the conventionalized attributes of the ego, exaggerated assertion of strength and toughness.
7 *Destructiveness and cynicism*: generalized hostility, vilification of the human.
8 *Projectivity*: the belief that wild and dangerous things go on in the world; the projection outwards of unconscious emotional impulses.
9 *'Puritanical' prurience*: an exaggerated concern with sexual 'goings-on'.

from Norman F. Dixon, 1976, *On the Psychology of Military Incompetence*, Futura Publications, London, p. 258. Reproduced by permission of Blackwell Science Ltd.

The work of Tom Burns and George Stalker in the Scottish electronics industry in the 1950s is often used to illustrate the effectiveness of flexible 'organismic management systems' in dealing with change and of rigid 'mechanistic management systems' in dealing with routine.

Mechanistic management systems use rigid job descriptions, clear hierarchical lines of authority and responsibility, and rely on position power when decisions have to be taken. Such organizations can also be described as bureaucratic in Max Weber's sense of that term. Organismic management systems, on the other hand, use loose and flexible job descriptions, have vaguely defined lines of authority and responsibility, and rely on expert power to take decisions, regardless of where in the organization the expert happens to be.

At first glance, the organismic management system with its absence of hierarchical controls on behaviour sounds like a more pleasant place in which to work. The individual has considerable autonomy in the absence of oppressive hierarchical authority. However, Burns and Stalker present evidence to suggest that some individuals do not like working within organismic systems because of the insecurity that the apparent freedom can create.

---

lack of control creates insecurity

. . . when individuals are frustrated in their attempts to get their own work successfully completed, when they are worried by the successful rivalry of others, when they feel insecure or under attack – these situations provoke an urge for the clarity, the no-nonsense atmosphere, of a mechanistic organization. It promises so many other dividends too. It is not only quicker to divide tasks into parcels, label them 'responsibilities', and post them to subordinates or other parts of the structure; this kind of procedure has the connotations of visibly controlling others, and the appearance of knowing one's own mind, which are valued aspects of executive authority. Conversely, one has the security of knowing the limits of one's responsibility and of the demands and orders of superiors, which the existence of something like Queen's Regulations can give.

from Tom Burns and George M. Stalker, 1961, *The Management of Innovation*, Tavistock Publications, London, p. 132.

Burns and Stalker argue that what they termed the 'penumbra of indeterminacy' that surrounds roles in an organismic organization has three major implications. First, the lack of job specifications leads to feelings of insecurity because individuals do not know where they stand in relation to others. Second, although anxious about the insecurity, people in these kinds of circumstances do not want their positions clarified – the advantages of freedom of manoeuvre are too great. Third, the uncertainty surrounding individual jobs is a source of flexibility and efficiency in dealing with rapid technical change.

Organizations that have to cope with rapid change benefit from organismic flexibility. But their members have to suffer insecurity and anxiety.

---

insecurity – good for organization, bad for individual

. . . the insecurity attached to ill-defined functions and responsibilities and status, by increasing the emotional charge of anxiety attached to the holding of a position, increases also the feeling of commitment and dependency on others. By this means the detachment and depletion of concern usual when people are at, or closely approaching the top of their occupational ladder, the tendency to develop stable commitments, to become a nine-to-fiver, was counteracted. All this happened at the cost of personal satisfactions and adjustment – the difference in the personal tension of people in the top management positions and those of the same age who had reached a settled position was fairly marked.

from Tom Burns and George M. Stalker, 1961, *The Management of Innovation*, Tavistock Publications, London, p. 135.

Before we argue that control is an undesirable feature of organizational life, therefore, it is necessary to recognize the positive features of the control process and the relationships between control and psychological needs. There

*"Miss Bradley, I have a clean desk and a free afternoon.
Bring me everything we have on somebody."*

are clearly instances where the absence of control will have adverse consequences for the psychological well-being of the individual.

social control

Graeme Salaman argues that organizations can be described as 'structures of control'. Consistent with this perspective, Theo Nicols and Peter Armstrong (1976, pp. 5 and 9) claim:

> if [the worker] chooses not to do what management tells him (which he may be 'told' either directly and personally by managers, or through their impersonal rules and regulations about working practices, or indirectly through the technology which mediates the imperative to produce for profit) – if and when he chooses not to comply with these dictates, he will make explicit what otherwise can lie dormant, namely the question of control. . . .
>
> to manage is to control. When managers lay claim to the 'right to manage' they lay claim to the right to control 'their' workers.

To control in the social sense means to dominate, to give orders, to exercise power, authority or influence over others, and to obtain compliance. Management control is not simply an administrative process designed to achieve economic goals. Control of employee behaviour and attitudes is an essential component of organizational functioning and survival, but clearly has undesirable connotations of domination and exploitation.

The inequality of power in our organizations, and in society as a whole, is not regarded by everyone as legitimate. Management control is a social process with political and moral components. In organizations, some individuals are controlled by others. Managers control the allocation and withdrawal of rewards and penalties such as money, career chances, conditions, status, approval and other benefits of organizational membership. This control can be regarded as a form of exploitation of those in weak subordinate positions. Control is not simply a logical process for the achievement of economic efficiency.

---

definition

Social control *is the process through which obedience, compliance and conformity to predetermined standards of behaviour are achieved through interpersonal and group processes.*

Control is thus a property of the social relationship between controller and controlled. Social control is a pervasive aspect of our social and organizational lives. Our behaviour is influenced in numerous ways, more or less obvious and subtle, through our relationships with others.

STOP!

In what ways is your behaviour controlled through your relationships and interactions with others?

Frederick Winslow Taylor argued that manual and managerial work should be clearly separated in the interests of efficiency. This division of labour relies on the assumption that experts are necessary to handle the complex tasks of achieving effective organizational control. This argument makes the management control function a legitimate one and explains the higher financial rewards that controllers get compared with mere workers.

But Karl Marx and his followers argue that management control is necessary for another reason. Capitalism as an economic system creates two broad classes of people. The capitalist class includes those who own and control the means of production. The working class includes those who do not own and control the means of production and who have to sell their labour-power in order to make a living. However, in this contractual arrangement, the buyers are comparatively powerful, and the sellers of labour are comparatively weak.

The capitalist and working classes need each other – they are interdependent. But their interests are different. The aim of the capitalist is to make profits, which can be used to accumulate more capital and make still more profits. The aim of the workers is to earn higher wages to improve their standards of living. These interests are in direct conflict and cannot be reconciled within the capitalist system. Marx regarded this as one reason why capitalism would eventually be overthrown (a prediction that has so far not come true).

The manager in a capitalist organization, therefore, cannot rely on the willing co-operation, commitment and loyalty of the workforce. The relationship between capitalist and worker is not merely one of interdependence and conflict of interest. It is also an exploitative one due to inequalities of power between the classes. The capitalist controls the resources and can refuse employment to those who question the way in which those resources are used.

The apparent compliance of workers with management directions is thus superficial. Compliance appears to be remunerative, but is in reality coercive. This in part explains the organizational preoccupation with controlled performance. Employees cannot be expected to produce adequate levels of performance if left to their own devices.

---

managers cannot rely on a willing workforce

The political dimension of organization employment is revealed in another obvious feature of organizations: the unequal nature of organizational life and the constant possibility of subordinates resisting or avoiding the efforts of their seniors (however mediated and obscured) to control them.

from Graeme Salaman, 1981, *Class and the Corporation*, Fontana, London, p. 144.

Harry Braverman, an American Marxist sociologist, has stimulated a great deal of interest in contemporary forms of management control and their implications for the experience of work. Braverman was not just an academic. He was a skilled coppersmith who enjoyed the practice of his craft and understood most other crafts in the shipbuilding industry. He practised pipefitting, sheetmetal work, worked in a naval shipyard and a railroad repair shop, sheetmetal shops and in the manufacture of steel plate and structural steel.

Braverman argued that the need for management control to cope with uncommitted workers led to the degradation of work skills and workers. He claimed that although science and technology were demanding more education, training and exercise of mental effort, work was increasingly being subdivided into routine and easy to learn fragments as Taylor had suggested. Braverman (1974, p. 7) did not argue for a return to traditional forms of craft working, or for the rejection of technological development. Instead, he argued that:

> my views about work are governed by nostalgia for an age that has not yet come into being, in which, for the worker, the craft satisfaction that arises from conscious and purposeful mastery of the labour process will be combined with the marvels of science and the ingenuity of engineering, an age in which everyone will be able to benefit, in some degree, from this combination.

Braverman argued that this new age was prevented by the class relationships formed by the capitalist mode of production. The need to maintain a disciplined workforce leads managers into a process in which approaches to control are perpetually refined and intensified.

Control of work and workers is a central theme of scientific management practice. This involves gathering workers together in one place, setting performance standards, dictating work times, using personal supervision to ensure diligence and the enforcement of rules against distractions (such as talking and smoking). Management control is made much easier through the simplification and standardization of work activities into well-defined and simple to measure tasks in which workers have no discretion. In addition, workers who exercise less skill get paid less than skilled craftsmen.

These extensions of management control erode craft skill, reduce the worker's independence and reduce the importance of the worker's knowledge of the craft. Workers are excluded from decisions about methods and the pace of work. Braverman (1974, p. 445) on the other hand wanted to see workers:

> become masters of industry in the true sense, which is to say when the antagonisms in the labour process between controllers and workers, conception and execution, mental and manual labour are overthrown, and when the labour process is united in the collective body which conducts it.

Braverman saw technology being used to reduce skill and discretion, to fragment tasks as Taylor recommended, and to stifle individual development, reduce wages and enhance management status. Note, however, that Braverman was arguing against the way in which technology was being deployed by management in pursuit of control, and was not arguing against technological development in industry as such.

---

control is a central theme of scientific management

Taylor raised the concept of control to an entirely new plane when he asserted as an absolute necessity for adequate management the dictation to the worker of the precise manner in which work is to be performed. Management, he insisted, could be only a limited and frustrated undertaking so long as it left to the worker any decision about the work. His 'system' was simply a means for management to achieve control of the actual mode of performance of every labour activity, from the simplest to the most complicated.

from Harry Braverman, 1974, *Labor and Monopoly Capital: The Degradation of Work in the Twentieth Century*, Monthly Review Press, New York, p. 90.

Braverman regarded the progressive deskilling and degradation of work, clearly, as undesirable, as a logical and natural consequence of the capitalist organization of production. Attempts to improve the quality of working life through job enrichment schemes leave the inequalities of capitalism intact and are thus superficial. They do not alter the exploitative nature of management control in capitalist organizations.

Inequalities of power in organizations lead to inequalities in the distribution of other resources. These inequalities can be seen in the conditions of work of those at the bottom of the organizational hierarchy. Lower-level employees generally have lower wages, poorer working conditions, sometimes have to perform duties that are psychologically and physically damaging, have limited promotion and career opportunities and less job security. Those further up the hierarchy have better working conditions, financial rewards, fringe benefits and opportunities. The obvious inequalities should increase the chances of resistance to management controls.

---

employees cannot be trusted

Capitalism, being based upon the exploitation of those who sell their labour, necessarily sets the capitalist, or his agents, problems of control, direction and legitimacy. Employees cannot be 'trusted' to identify with the goals of management, or to adhere to the spirit – or the letter – of their work instructions, for the goals of their organization, and the procedures and specifications which follow from them, are quite antithetical to their interests. The structure of the organization, and everything within it, reflects the employer's pursuit of profit at the expense of his employees and the constant possibility and occasional reality, of their apprehending this over-riding fact, either as a source of personal withdrawal, 'instrumentality' or bloody-mindedness or as a cause for group, organized resistance.

from Graeme Salaman, 1981, *Class and the Corporation*, Fontana, London, p. 164.

There does, however, appear to be a widespread acceptance or at least tolerance in modern organizations of the need for management control. Why should this be the case when management controls highlight inequalities and adversely affect the quality of working life? The answer lies in the ways in which managers attempt to legitimate their role.

Most managers today are, of course, not capitalists, and few actually own the organizations in which they are employed. Most managers are also employees. The picture that Marx painted, of two principal and conflicting classes, is oversimplified and the modern reality is rather more complex. But the positions that managers hold lead them to behave as 'agents of capitalism'; they are paid to do their work and take their decisions as if they were owners of their employing organizations.

Managers are thus concerned with the legitimacy of their controlling role. In order to fulfil the responsibilities with which they have been charged, they need agreement from those being controlled that the management function is indeed necessary and desirable. Managers thus argue that the complexity of modern technology, the scale of manufacturing and commercial operations and the need for efficiency all make control through hierarchy and rules necessary. These aspects of modern organizational life make the management function, and management control, appear legitimate and socially and individually acceptable.

Managers rely on popular acceptance of the values associated with capitalism and efficiency. The extent of compliance with management directives is a measure of the social acceptance of those values. One way in which legitimacy has been achieved has been through the use of control processes that appear to be neutral – through bureaucratic hierarchy, formality, impersonality and rules. These mechanisms are generally regarded as necessary aspects of a modern efficient organization and not as attempts by a managerial elite to retain a dominant social or organizational position.

Managers want to retain their dominance, but do not wish to be seen as domineering because that could potentially threaten their perceived legitimacy. Managers design control systems that have the appearance of impartiality, that appear to reflect some kind of 'bureaucratic logic', and that are determined by the interplay of markets, technology and administrative necessity.

Peter Blau and Richard Schoenherr (1971) argue that management achieve legitimacy for their controls by designing them in ways that make them unobtrusive as well as apparently neutral. They call these *insidious controls*.

---

definition
Insidious controls *are controls which influence behaviour and attitudes in ways that do not involve the experience of being controlled or manipulated.*

---

management control must appear 'neutral'

Organizational control is required by capitalism and the search for profit through exploitation, not by the task, or technology, except inasmuch as these themselves are designed in terms of the search for profit. It is therefore capitalism, not industrialism, which establishes the need for control. Furthermore, all aspects of the organization reflect, in one way or another, this constant and necessary preoccupation; profit and control. The achievement of control, however, depends as much on extra-organizational factors as on internal ones. It is only in the light of external preparation and experience that internal arrangements can appear 'normal' or rational, or succeed in their purpose of employee control and direction. Finally, the centrality and primacy of control within capitalist employing organizations requires, if it is to succeed, that it appear neutral, a requirement of neutrally-designed tasks, or a reflection of some natural ordering of individual qualities and achievements. Successful organizational control is regarded as legitimate and necessary. Hence the significance attached to such legitimacy.

from Graeme Salaman, 1981, *Class and the Corporation*, Fontana, London, p. 167.

Blau and Schoenherr argue that bureaucratic hierarchy of authority, explicit rules and regulations, traditional incentives and machine pacing are more or less obvious forms of control. The chain of command in an organization enforces discipline through orders and sanctions passed down a fixed hierarchy. Obedience to rules ensures discipline and predictability in behaviour and decisions. Incentives are dependent on compliance with management instructions and adequate performance levels. Machinery constrains the worker's behaviour and determines the pace of work in a variety of ways. These overt forms of control leave their recipients with the clear feeling that they are being controlled.

Blau and Schoenherr argue that three forms of *insidious control* have become more important in modern organizations. These include:

control through expert power
Educated and qualified employees can be controlled by appealing to their professional commitment to their work. Physical force, threats and mere

money are not necessary. They will behave as required and achieve the required performance level because they feel that this is the 'right thing to do', and value competence in their fields.

This form of insidious control creates problems. It is often difficult to identify the real decision-makers in an organization. When decision-makers are found, they resort to expert, technical arguments about efficiency. It is difficult to challenge or blame experts who take decisions on technical or 'efficiency' grounds for the human, social or political consequences of their decisions.

control through selective recruitment

Management can either recruit whoever applies for work and manage them autocratically, or recruit only those individuals with the technical competence and professional interest to perform on their own the necessary tasks to the required performance levels.

This is how universities and research institutes are run. Staff have discretion on how to perform their duties within broad policy constraints. Lecturers are rarely told what to do or how to do it. But control over lecturing activities is achieved in the long run through selective recruitment.

control through the allocation of resources

In universities, administrators cannot significantly interfere in any direct manner with teaching and research activity. Staffing decisions are made by individual departments and faculties. But administrators control the direction of activities in the long run by the way in which resources are allocated which determines which fields can expand and which contract. As Blau and Schoenherr (1971) point out:

> The allocation of personnel and other resources is the ultimate mechanism of organizational control, not only in the sense that it is fundamental and nearly always complements other mechanisms, but also in the sense that reliance primarily on it is the polar opposite of Weberian bureaucratic control through a chain of command backed with coercive sanctions.

They also observed that:

> Slave drivers have gone out of fashion not because they were so cruel but because they were so inefficient. Men can be controlled much more effectively by tying their economic needs and interests to their performances on behalf of employers. . . . The efforts of men can be controlled still far more efficiently than through wages alone by mobilizing their professional commitments to the work they can do best and like to do most and by putting these highly motivated energies and skills at the disposal of the organization.

Blau and Schoenherr argue that insidious controls are:

- **deceptive** because they leave those who are controlled with the feeling that they are simply conforming with the 'logic of the situation', in terms of the requirements of the task in hand, or of conforming with widely agreed social values such as the need for efficiency and competence
- **elusive** because nobody can be held accountable for harmful decisions
- **unresponsive** because they are not recognized as forms of control and are thus immune to democratic constraints

YOU'RE EMPOWERED TO DO WHAT YOU'RE TOLD.

(DAVID AUSTIN)

The experience of insidious control is thus different from the experience of overt manipulation and direction by authority figures. This is not a question of superiors abusing their positions. The problem lies in organization structures which create opportunities which individuals may exploit. Insidious controls *appear* neutral and *appear* also to be consistent with democratic values because they do not rely on direct commands from superiors. So insidious controls attract little resistance and are more effective than overt uses of authority.

Many organizational employees may thus not challenge the management controls which reduce their discretion and erode their skills because the controls are not visible as such. Many facets of organizational life which are regarded as normal, taken for granted, necessary attributes of effective performance can still have a significant influence on members' behaviour. These attributes are unchallenged because they may never be regarded as management controls at all.

assessment

Managers are responsible for the success of the organizations which employ them. The management function incorporates tasks that have to be carried out if the organization is to survive. These functions are, however, carried out mainly by an occupational group – some would say an elite – who have a vested interest in maintaining their status.

Managers are preoccupied with the control of employees for two reasons. First, the goals of individual employees may not be consistent with the goals of the organization as a whole. Second, wider social class conflict creates antagonisms that lead managers to place little trust in the loyalty and commitment of their subordinates.

Managers are thus also preoccupied with the legitimacy of their organizational roles. A lot of management behaviour can be interpreted as an attempt to reaffirm that legitimacy. It is clear from this why some writers emphasize control as the single most important management function – that to manage is to control. Most of the chapters of this book have in fact concerned control in some form or other.

We have suggested, however, that managers do not necessarily lose power by delegating control. By 'empowering' employees to take decisions on matters where they in fact know better – that is where they have more expert power – the manager may strengthen subordinates' beliefs in the manager's own expert power. To delegate in an appropriate manner, and to show warranted trust and confidence in others, are hardly signs of incompetence or weakness, far less signs of lack of managerial skill.

Why do managers seem more concerned with the struggle to legitimate their position power than with developing their expert power? The former is a much more complex and difficult task than the latter.

The problem for most managers here is that they too are controlled in two distinct ways. First, managers also have superiors whose directions they must follow and to whom they must answer for their actions. The range of choices of action for the individual manager may thus be narrowly constrained. Second, managers are constrained in their behaviour by the social and organizational contexts in which they work. In the organizations that we have been discussing here, that context is a capitalist one with inherent conflicts and antagonisms. Position power is more useful than expert power in circumstances where groups are destined perpetually to disagree with each other.

Managers can thus display reluctance to implement participation schemes which potentially represent an erosion of the 'right to manage' and of management control. To lose control is to lose occupational status. Managers as an occupational group defend their controlling role because their legitimacy and social status are perceived to depend on it. Many management techniques for increasing organizational effectiveness appear to erode management control. These techniques include job enrichment, autonomous work groups, organizational development programmes, organismic management systems and democratic leadership style.

Richard Walton (1985) has argued that managers have to choose between a strategy based on imposing control and a strategy based on eliciting commitment. The latter approach involves precisely those techniques which give employees increased discretion over their working life and which fall under the broad heading of 'high-involvement management'. Walton argues that a commitment-based strategy is consistent with the recognition of employees as 'stakeholders' in an organization and leads to higher levels of performance. He concludes that organizations must develop cultures of commitment if they are to remain competitive, to meet customer expectations with respect to quality, delivery and responsiveness to market changes. In contrast, these two strategies look like this:

workforce strategy	control	commitment
job design	deskilled, fragmented, fixed	emphasis on whole task, flexible, use of teams
performance expectations	minimum standards defined	emphasis on 'stretch' goals
management structure	many layers with rules and procedures and status symbols	flat structure with shared goals and values, and minimal status differentials
rewards	individual incentives, linked to job evaluation	group incentives, with gain sharing, linked to skills and competence
employee participation	narrow, with information given on a 'need to know' basis	encouraged, with widely shared business information
industrial relations	adversarial	joint planning and problem-solving

Walton (1985, p. 79) summarizes the commitment strategy in this way:

In this new commitment-based approach to the work force, jobs are designed to be broader than before, to combine planning and implementation, and to include efforts to upgrade operations, not just maintain them. Individual responsibilities are expected to change as conditions change, and teams, not individuals, often are the organizational units accountable for performance. With management hierarchies relatively flat and differences in status minimized, control and lateral co-ordination depend on shared goals, and expertise rather than formal position determines influence.

Ten years later, we find this approach being discussed as a 'new paradigm' of organizational design, by Wendell French and Cecil Bell (1995, pp. 349–50). Their statement of the 'new paradigm' was cited in Chapter 17 on organization development: 'Top-down, autocratically directed, rigidly hierarchical, fear-generating organizations are giving way to something new. The new paradigm proclaims that the most innovative and successful organizations will be those that derive their strength and vitality from adaptable, committed team players at all levels and from all specialities, not from the omniscience of the hierarchy.'

It is tempting to argue that Walton, and French and Bell, have identified a whole new approach to organizational effectiveness for the late twentieth century and beyond. It is, on the other hand, tempting to point out that their arguments merely summarize what the organizational behaviour literature has been saying about effective organization and management for the past fifty years or so. The advice one finds in the literature, of course, may not reflect what one finds in organizational practice.

sources

Blau, P.M. and Schoenherr, R.A., 1971, *The Structure of Organizations*, Basic Books, New York.

Blunt, P., 1980, 'Bureaucracy and ethnicity in Kenya: Some conjectures for the eighties', *Journal of Applied Behavioural Science*, vol. 16, pp. 336–53.

Braverman, H., 1974, *Labor and Monopoly Capital: The Degradation of Work in the Twentieth Century*, Monthly Review Press, New York.

Burns, T. and Stalker, G.M., 1961, *The Management of Innovation*, Tavistock Publications, London.

Dixon, N.F., 1976, *On the Psychology of Military Incompetence*, Futura Publications, London.

French, W.L. and Bell, C.H., 1995, *Organization Development: Behavioral Science Interventions for Organization Improvement*, Prentice Hall International, Englewood Cliffs, NJ, fifth edition.

Gaines, J.H., 1980, 'Upward communication in industry: An experiment', *Human Relations*, vol. 33, no. 12, pp. 929–42.

Hellriegel, D. and Slocum, J.W., 1978, *Management: Contingency Approaches*, Addison-Wesley, Reading, MA.

Ilgen, D.R. and Knowlton, W.A., 1980, 'Performance attributional effects on feedback from superiors', *Organizational Behaviour and Human Performance*, vol. 25, no. 3, pp. 441–56.

Ilgen, D.R., Paterson, R., Martin, B. and Boeschen, D., 1981, 'Supervisor and subordinate reactions to performance appraisal sessions', *Organizational Behaviour and Human Performance*, vol. 28, no. 3, pp. 311–30.

Lawler, E.E. 1976, 'Control systems in organizations', in H.D. Dunnette (ed.), *Handbook of Industrial and Organizational Psychology*, Rand-McNally, Chicago.

Nichols, T. and Armstrong, P., 1976, *Workers Divided*, Fontana, London.

Pascale, R.T. and Athos, A.G., 1982, *The Art of Japanese Management*, Penguin Books, Harmondsworth.

Salaman, G., 1981, *Class and the Corporation*, Fontana, London.

Seth, M.R., 1968, *The Social Framework of an Indian Factory*, Manchester University Press, Manchester.

Walton, R.E., 1985, 'From control to commitment in the workplace', *Harvard Business Review*, March–April, pp. 77–84.

index

Notes: 1. References to *organization* are ubiquitous. This word has therefore been omitted as a qualifier wherever possible e.g. *structure* rather than *structure, organizational*;
2. Emboldened page numbers refer to **definitions**. There are frequently also textual references on these pages;
3. Names or initials in brackets indicate *firms* rather than people e.g. Smith (W.H.);
4. Cross-references in *brackets* refer to sub-entry immediately preceding